ABSTRACTION AND REALITY

The Sculpture of Ivor Roberts-Jones

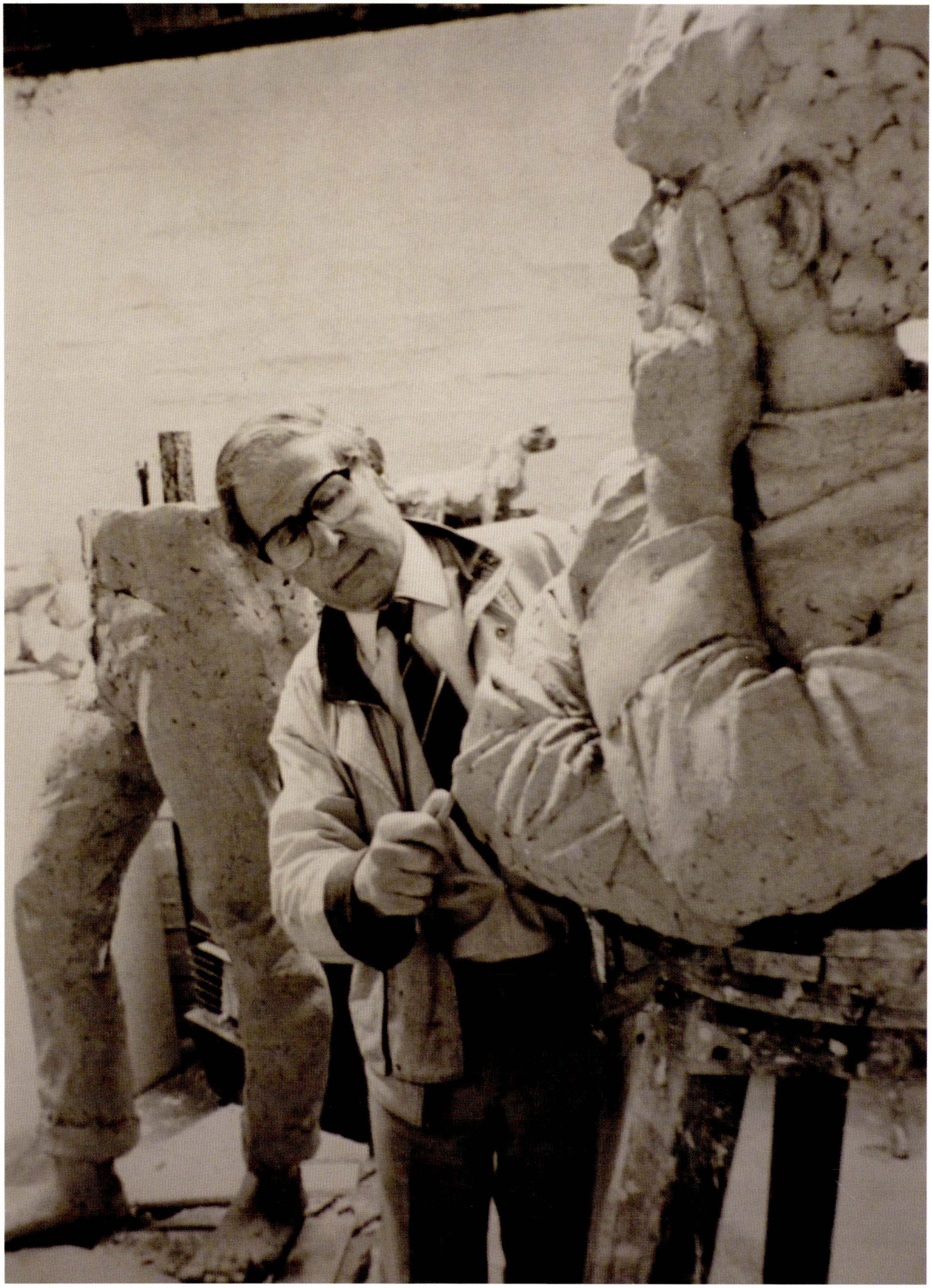

ABSTRACTION AND REALITY

The Sculpture of Ivor Roberts-Jones

Jonathan Black
Sara Ayres

PWP

Published in 2013 by Philip Wilson Publishers
an imprint of I.B.Tauris & Co Ltd
6 Salem Road
London W2 4BU
www.philip-wilson.co.uk

ISBN: 978-1-78130-010-7

Distributed in the United States and Canada
exclusively by Palgrave Macmillan
175 Fifth Avenue, New York NY 10010

Designed by Ian Ross www.ianrossdesigner.com

Printed and bound in China by Everbest

Front cover: *Sir Winston Churchill KG, OM, CH*, 1970–73 (cast in 1999) (Cat. 135)
Back cover: *Augustus John OM, RA*, (1963–67) (Cat. 133)
Frontispiece: Ivor Roberts-Jones working on the full-size plaster model of *Rupert Brooke* in his studio, Shimpling, Norfolk, c. April 1988; Image: Courtesy of the HMI, Leeds

Contents

Acknowledgements

The authors particularly wish to thank the following for their much-appreciated help during the research undertaken for this book: Dame Mary Archer, Jane Bhoyroo (sculpture curator, Arts Council Collection, London), John and Sylvia Black, Nigel Boonham FRBS, Dr Peter Cannon-Brookes, Sophie Bridges (archivist, Churchill Archives Centre, Churchill College, Cambridge), Gay Gore Brown (archivist, Oswestry Grammar School), Jane Callaghan (Grierson Trust), Milan Ćesky, James J. Coleman OBE (honorary consul for Louisiana), Jane Collard (archivist, Worksop College), Ellie Dawkins (documentation officer, Glynn Vivian Art Gallery, Swansea), Kate Denton, Sarah Dick (registrar, Beaverbook Art Gallery, Canada), Philippa Duckworth (Fordingbridge Museum Trust), Professor Brian Falconbridge PPRBS, Oliver Fairclough (keeper of art, National Museum of Wales, Cardiff), Lisa Le Feuvre (head of sculpture studies, Henry Moore Institute for the Study of Sculpture, Leeds), Sir Nicholas Goodison, Odd Grann, David Hawkins (Philip Wilson Publishers, London), Caroline Herbert (Churchill Archive, Churchill College, Cambridge), Isabel Hitchman, Professor Paul Hubbard (Moore University, Philadelphia), His Excellency Milan Jakobec (foreign ministry of the Czech Republic), Professor Kamil Janáček, Brian Jarvis (Goldsmiths College, London), Ruth Jeavons, Martin Jennings FRBS, Ian Jones (Oriel Ynys Môn), Robert Jones (Government Art Collection), Professor Fran Lloyd (Kingston University), Gunn Løwe (archivist, National Archives of Norway), Joan Lyall (documentation officer, Colchester and Ipswich Museum Service), Robin Maggs (National Museum of Wales, Cardiff), Brenda Martin (curator, Dorich House Museum, Kingston University), Etienne Millner FRBS (president of the Society of Portrait Sculptors), John W. Mills FRBS, Tomáš Mikeska, Brian Morley, Clare Mayoh (archivist, Henry Moore Institute for the Study of Sculpture, Leeds), Allen Packwood (director, Churchill Archive Centre, Churchill College, Cambridge), Sir Richard and Lady Jeanie Hyde Parker, Lady Barbara Plastow, Mark Pomeroy (archivist, Royal Academy, London), William Riley (Leathes Prior Solicitors, Norwich and the Estate of Ivor Roberts-Jones), David Robb (headmaster, Oswestry School), Denis and Eirian Short, Clare Smith (National Museum of Wales, Cardiff), Evelyn Smith (administrator, Glynn Vivian Art Gallery, Swansea), Rosemary Smith, Bridget Heriz-Smith, Professor Steven Spier (Kingston University), Mari Takayongi (Parliamentary Archives, Houses of Parliament, London), Megan Crofton-Thomas, Melanie Unwin (deputy curator, Parliamentary Art Collection), Michael D. Uva, Lily Vikki (sculpture curator, Oslo Cultural Affairs), Rebecca Weaver (Wolsey Art Gallery, Ipswich), the late Michael Winner, Dr Jon Wood (Henry Moore Institute for the Study of Sculpture, Leeds) and Victoria Worsley (Henry Moore Institute for the Study of Sculpture, Leeds).

The authors are also indebted to the Arts and Humanities Research Council for its generous financial support.

Kingston University London

Visual and Material Culture Research Centre
Faculty of Art, Design and Architecture

Henry Moore Institute

Arts & Humanities Research Council

List of Figure Illustrations

All dimensions in cm, height before width
HMI: The Henry Moore Institute for the Study of Sculpture

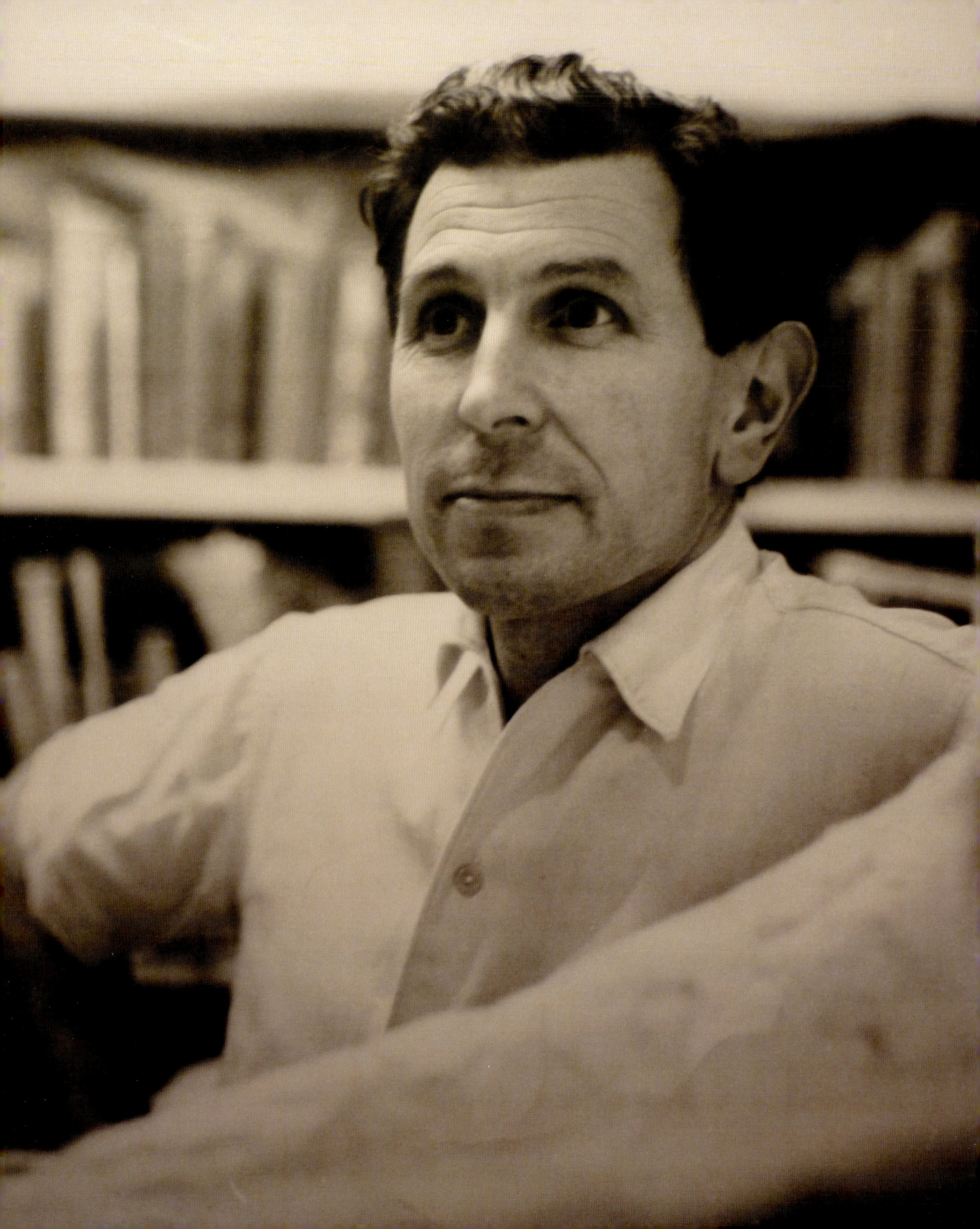

IVOR ROBERTS-JONES

Introduction and Biographical Sketch

Jonathan Black

'Ivor Roberts-Jones was an immaculate, in fact pre-eminent draughtsman, a brilliant sculptor with an uncanny ability to interpret the characters of his sitters, a superb modeller of animals and an artist in everything he did. His reputation can only be enhanced over the years to come.

Sir Kyffin Williams, 2005[1]

'Bobby Jones was one of the best portrait sculptors of his period.'

John W. Mills PPFRBS, 2011[2]

'Ivor was a mesmeric teacher.'

Etienne Millner FRBS, 2012[3]

'[Ivor Roberts-Jones] was out of step with what was acclaimed. The welded and bolted assemblages, so fashionable in the 1960s and 1970s, were just as alien to him as were Carl Andre's bricks and the performance art and installations of more recent years ... He will, however, be seen to have stood in the central tradition of European sculpture. Because he was sensitive to individuals, was ever exploring subtleties and was a devoted and vastly accomplished craftsman, he will not be forgotten.'

Terence Mullaly, 1996[4]

Fig. 1.1 Ivor Roberts-Jones in the early 1960s, Image: Courtesy of the HMI, Leeds

Ivor Roberts-Jones (Fig. 1.1), often known to his friends as 'Bobby' Jones, was a prickly, mercurial and passionate man; above all, he was passionate about sculpture, about working with clay with a view to casting the result in bronze. Throughout his life Rodin was his God, his guiding star, his ultimate exemplar.[5] He also deeply admired many forms of ancient sculpture he repeatedly revisited in the British Museum – from archaic Greece, Sumeria and Egypt.[6]

Ivor held a number of contemporary sculptors in high regard, including Charles Despiau, Henry Moore, Frank Dobson, Eduardo Paolozzi, Alberto Giacometti, Marino Marini, Giacomo Manzu, Elisabeth Frink and Jacob Epstein – as well as some who are less well-known names today, such as Charles Sargeant Jagger, Charles Wheeler, Germaine Richier and Jean Foutrier.[7] However, above all, Rodin remained throughout his life his absolute benchmark for sculptural perfection.[8]

Many years later he was to tell Dr Peter Cannon-Brookes (cat. 64), Keeper of Art at the National Museum of Wales, Cardiff (1978–86), that he owed an immense debt to Rodin, who had provided an exemplar for portraiture and figurative sculpture and compelled him to acknowledge the importance of drawing and memory as the essential underpinning for sculpture: '[Rodin's] sculptures frequently have a sense of perpetually arriving, of their own free will. Memory and immediate impulse appear to have become one thing.'[9]

In his lifetime he was widely regarded by many of his sculptural and critical peers as Britain's leading sculptor of figures for public monuments that remained firmly rooted in a rigorous nineteenth-century figurative tradition while continuing to appear stimulating, challenging and 'modern', as well as one of the country's most accomplished and gifted portrait sculptors, producing some eighty heads of identifiable individuals. His many animal sculptures of the 1970s and '80s – some three dozen survive – were also held in high regard, while lots of his contemporaries continued to acknowledge the superb standard of his draughtsmanship. During his life, admirers and collectors of his work numbered many prominent names within the nation's cultural sphere, ranging from artists such as Henry Moore, Sir Charles Wheeler, George Fullard, Ceri Richards, Carel Weight, Graham Sutherland and Sir William Coldstream, to leading arts administrators and gallery directors like Sir John Rothenstein, Sir Hugh Casson and Sir Kenneth Clark.

For a man who so often gave the impression of complete inner confidence, he nevertheless experienced during his career a number of what he referred to as 'wobbles', when he seriously contemplated giving up sculpture to pursue some other profession. In the early 1950s he wondered whether he should become a full-time poet; later that same decade he considered becoming a full-time scriptwriter, producing plays for television.[10] On each occasion, however, his doubts were overcome by what he referred to as 'an irresistible compulsion to create'; rather in the manner of his hero Rodin, Ivor was always thinking about the next possible commission, the next competition in which he had been asked to participate – work he had beenasked to do, as well as sculptures he wanted to do purely for his own enjoyment and to release in a torrent the ideas that had welled up within his imagination.

To that end he drew and sketched ceaselessly, usually starting on any paper to hand (Fig. 1.2) when the post arrived over tea, toast and marmalade at the breakfast table – on the back of a letter, a bill, a circular. When an idea came to him, it had to find release and expression on paper. He so sought to emulate Rodin that he came to share one of the Frenchman's failings, if it was a failing. Ivor was never satisfied with anything he had created – as some of his friends and admirers have commented, he never knew when to leave well alone and call a halt to the unceasing alteration and modification of his compositions.[11]

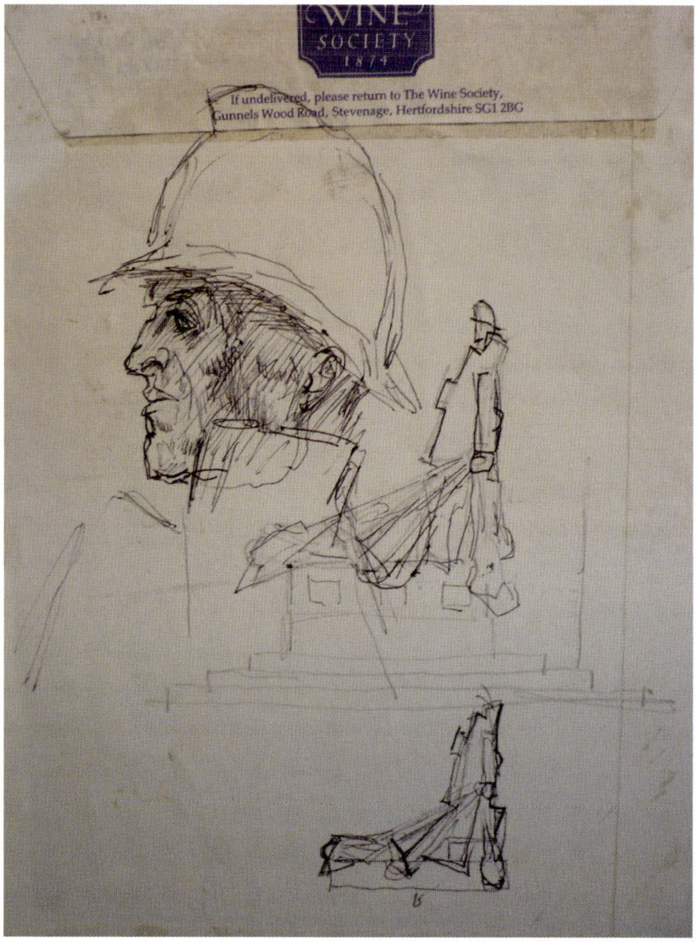

Fig. 1.2 Ivor Roberts-Jones, *Sketch of a Policeman for the National Police Memorial*, c. 1995–96, pen and ink on paper, 23 x 16 cm, Image: Courtesy of the HMI, Leeds

Maquettes and even full-sized models were worked and reworked, tested to the point of destruction, and often beyond to utter dissolution. Clay maquettes would be made and unmade, plaster casts of figures would be sawn in half or into three pieces, with Ivor pursuing the realisation of ever more extreme combinations in which figures were stretched and contorted. Even when one of his major public figures – ranging from *Augustus John* for Fordingbridge, in Hampshire (1967) (cat. 133) to the utterly compelling *Winston Churchill* in Parliament Square (1973) (cat. 135) to the last commission raised in his lifetime, *Field Marshal Alanbrooke* on Whitehall (1993) (cat. 154), quivering with barely suppressed impatient energy – had been erected and unveiled with panoply, Ivor could not stop himself from continuing to sketch on photographs of the figures in situ, to envisage solutions he perceived as better, more fitting, more imaginative. As he was occasionally willing to acknowledge, he did not know when the time had come to extricate himself from the embrace of a project he might already have been working on for three or four years, such as the haunting *Two Kings* outside Harlech Castle (1978–83) (cat. 144), or the powerful yet enigmatic *Lazarus Rider* (1976–80) (cat. 140), the latter made for Sir Richard Hyde-Parker.

He produced a great deal of work during his life – perhaps as many as 300 sculptures. However, the majority were in plaster and often did not survive his frequent attempts to rework or re-create them. Perhaps just over half this number have survived in either bronze or plaster, the materials in which he invariably cast his modelled works. Some 600 drawings in pen and ink, pencil, pastel and charcoal on paper can be found today in the collection of the Henry Moore Institute for the Study of Sculpture, Leeds, or remain in private hands.

Ivor was born on 2 November 1913, at No. 28 Victoria Road, Oswestry, Shropshire, the only child of William Roberts-Jones (1870–1938), a solicitor, and Florence née Owles (d. 1915), who worked in the local telephone exchange as an operator.[12] William came from a Welsh-speaking family of five children which lived in Aberystwyth – the family name was Jones, but William decided there were enough Joneses in Wales and added his mother's maiden name to become 'Roberts-Jones'. A talented rugby player, he represented Aberystwyth and Wales in that sport.[13] Florence was apparently a talented amateur musician and watercolourist who tragically died when her son was only eighteen months old.[14] Many years later Ivor told Sir John Rothenstein that, despite the fact he was only half Welsh, 'I had always thought of myself as a Welshman.'[15]

Ivor would later recount that he started drawing at the tender age of three, and by the age of five was already producing sketches inspired by visits to the busy market in Oswestry.[16] He grew up fascinated by the interior of Oswestry Market Hall and the effect of light falling on women carrying geese. He later recalled that this was one of his first 'artistic memories', when he was aged about ten years old (i.e. around 1923).[17] Years later, he told Peter Cannon-Brookes that, from his earliest days, even before going up to art school, 'I have always drawn – always to develop a response and rarely to develop sculptural ideas ...[18]

Ivor studied first at Oswestry Grammar School, between September 1923 and July 1926 (Fig. 1.3).[19] He then moved, aged twelve, to a minor public school, Worksop College, in Nottinghamshire – then known as 'St Cuthbert's' – where he remained from September 1926 until December 1931.[20] The artist later recalled that he had been happy at both schools – especially St Cuthbert's, where he won prizes for his prowess at the long jump and a Chaplain's Divinity Prize; he would always retain an extensive knowledge of the Bible.[21] It was at St Cuthbert's, around 1930, that Ivor declared to his father that he wanted to become an artist; his father had hoped his son would study Law and one day qualify as a barrister – perhaps even become an eminent judge. Ivor reflected to Sir John Rothenstein in 1978:

> My father made a sort of bargain with me ... if I carried through my studies at Worksop College, I could choose for myself whether I should go on to University to study Law, or go on to an art school. It is a tribute to him that he kept to it absolutely and when the time came, disappointed as he must have been, he allowed me to go to art school without demur.[22]

Having just turned eighteen, in 1932 Ivor went up to Goldsmiths College, London, to study painting. He later recalled that the principal of the college, Clive Gardiner, had 'responded to my rather undeveloped talent for drawing and painting but became less interested when [I] became more drawn to sculpture ' Gardiner was the 'dominant influence at the School', and Ivor found that he

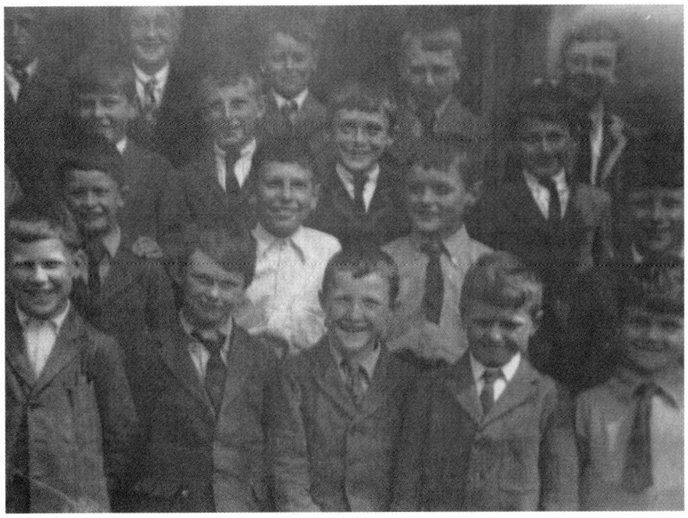

Fig. 1.3 Ivor Roberts-Jones (wearing white shirt) aged 10, 1923, Image: Courtesy of the HMI, Leeds

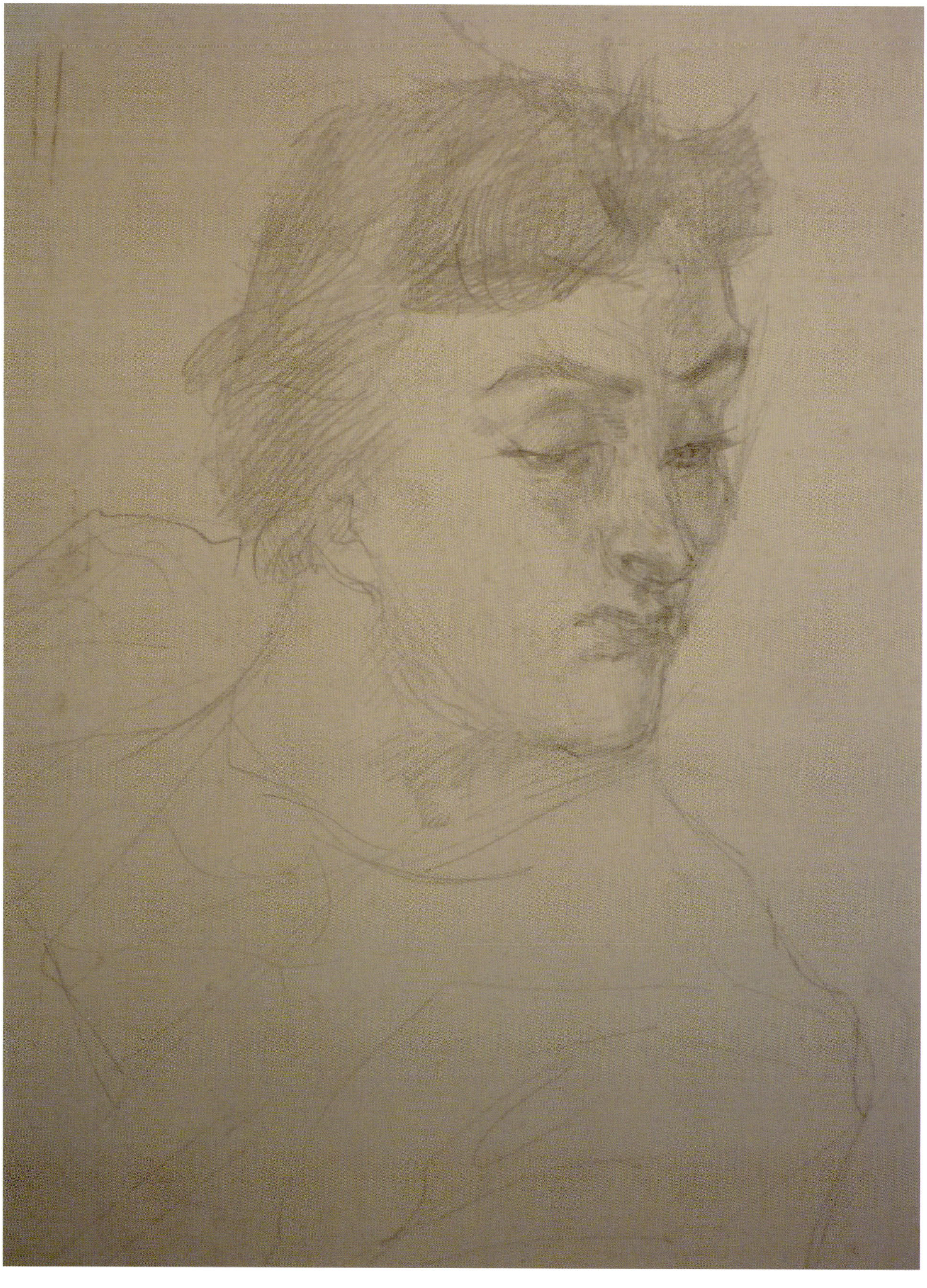

benefited greatly from 'the breadth of his understanding'. He recalled how, one day, 'Gardiner came into the College speaking of how brown the rain in London always seemed to him and the brown, velvety light of London rain' often reminded Ivor fondly of Gardiner.[23] Gardiner would later be the subject of one of Ivor's earliest and finest portrait sculptures (cat. 11).[24]

It was during this time (c. 1933–34) that another tutor at Goldsmiths, John Mansbridge, introduced Ivor to the work of a sculptor he would admire for the rest of his life. He gave Ivor a book illustrating the 'sculptured portraits of Despiau', adding that it was an influence that had lasted for him. Mansbridge also urged him to study Jacob Epstein, whose work had initially greatly impressed Ivor. By the late 1970s, however, he felt that Epstein's influence had 'perhaps, lessened over the years'.[24]

In his early days at Goldsmiths, Ivor befriended a painter with whom he remained close for much of the rest of his life: Carel Weight (1908–1997) – a future Professor of Painting at the Royal College of Art.[25] Thirty years later he would make an affectionate yet compelling portrait head of Weight's partner, *Helen Roeder* (cat. 32) and (Fig. 1.4), whom Weight had met at Goldsmiths in the early 1930s.[26]

In 1934 Ivor decided that, from now on, he really wanted to become a sculptor and to model in clay; this would always remain his preferred medium, and he was contemptuous of the view he encountered in the late 1940s among some commercial gallery owners that 'proper' sculpture meant carving in stone, while modelling in clay was dismissed as somehow effeminate and obsolescent.[27] Though Clive Gardiner was convinced that Ivor possessed the talent to become a first-rate poster designer – another tutor at Goldsmiths, Edward Bawden (1903–1989), also thought Ivor showed great potential as a future graphic artist – he reluctantly approved Ivor's move later that year to focus on sculpture at the Royal Academy Schools.[28] Ivor made this move in the knowledge that he would now have to fund himself by winning prizes and scholarships, as his father could no longer pay for his higher education. It is interesting, and may well have been crucially formative in Ivor's attitudes towards art, that he attended by far the most conservative, even reactionary, sculpture course in the capital – rather than studying at an institution that was more open minded in its view of developments within Continental modernism, such as the Royal College of Art, whose director at the time was Sir John Rothenstein's brother Sir William, or at the Slade School at University College, London.

Fig. 1.4 Ivor Roberts-Jones, Portrait of Helen Roeder, 1950s, pencil on paper, 22 x 19 cm, Image: Courtesy of the HMI, Leeds

At the Royal Academy he initially embraced the course offered to him, and over two consecutive years won prizes and scholarships. In October 1935 he was awarded a two-year British Institution Scholarship in Sculpture, worth £75 per annum. That month he was also awarded a prize for a relief panel depicting three male figures (cat. 103).[29] In December the following year, he was awarded a coveted Landseer Scholarship for two portrait busts (cats. 3, 4) that he had modelled in clay and then cast in plaster.[30]

But he later recalled that, as time passed at the RA Schools, he had begun to bridle at the repetitive and uninspired teaching he was offered and, during 1937–38, began to take a much closer interest in sculptors he found more appealing, such as Jacob Epstein, Henry Moore, Ivan Meštrović, Leon Underwood and the Swede Carl Milles – though they were regarded with pronounced disapproval by his tutors.[31]

One particular friend Ivor does appear to have made while at the Academy was fellow sculptor Daphne Hardy (later Hardy-Henrion, 1917–2003). In 1946 she held a solo show at Helen Lessore's Beaux Arts Gallery, which would represent Ivor for much of the following decade. At the time she was in a relationship with Hungarian-Jewish writer Arthur Koestler, and introduced Ivor to Koestler and a circle of Eastern European Jewish émigré musicians and writers living in London.[32] Hardy and Ivor would remain in intermittent touch well into the 1980s. Also while at the RA Schools, Ivor befriended painter Leonard Rosoman (1913–2012).[33]

Little evidence has survived of the work he produced while a student at the Royal Academy Schools. There are photographs – mostly of heads cast in plaster – that strongly suggest he already possessed a gift for portraiture, if of a conventional type (Fig. 1.5; cat. 1). One can understand why, around 1936, he caught the eye of leading public sculptor Sir William Reid Dick (1879–1961) – at the time President of the Royal British Society of Sculptors (1933–38) and soon to be appointed Sculptor to King George VI in Scotland (1938–52) – who offered Ivor the chance to become his studio assistant. Ivor decided not to accept this offer as he felt he was still finding his path forward as a sculptor.[34]

In the late 1930s he became even more fascinated by the work of Despiau, and visited the Frenchman's major July 1938 retrospective at the Wildenstein Gallery on New Bond Street. According to *The Times*, this exhibition established Despiau and Aristide Maillol as 'the two greatest living sculptors', while 'his only rival in portraiture is Epstein'.[35] Despiau's impact on the development of Ivor's approach to portraiture will be explored in greater detail in Chapter 2.

In May 1940, aged twenty-six, Ivor (Fig. 1.6) married student Monica Booth (1915–2002) (cat. 7) at Kensington Registry Office. At the time she was an art student from St John's Wood, at Goldsmiths College, hoping ultimately to train as a dancer.[37] By all accounts theirs was a loving and successful marriage. They remained together, very much a team, until Ivor's death in December 1996. She provided a secure and stable home environment, emotional support and reassurance – Ivor was prone to often quite violent mood swings, shifting abruptly between optimism and pessimism. She was an excellent cook, and later provided the Elizabeth David–inspired meals that so impressed dinner guests to 31 St James's Gardens in the 1950s and early 1960s. In many ways, she supplied Ivor with a confidence and emotional stability that he otherwise lacked. Ivor proved a generally faithful husband, though there are hints that he had affairs with one or two of his female students in his early days teaching at Goldsmiths College, in the late 1940s and early 1950s.[38]

Just prior to his marriage, Ivor was able to buy a somewhat dilapidated house at 31 St James's Gardens, between Notting Hill and Holland Park. This would be his home until around 1966, when he moved to Woodbridge in Suffolk to pursue a long-held love for sailing small boats. This move also enabled him to find the additional studio space he urgently required to complete his first major piece of life-sized public figurative sculpture – *Augustus John* (1964–67) (cat. 133), for Fordinbridge in Hampshire.[39] Until the move to Suffolk, for the next quarter of a century his main studio was a large, narrow room at the top of 31 St James's Gardens, with a high ceiling and a skylight set into the roof. Many years later, Ivor maintained that the move to Suffolk had been critical in allowing him to tackle large sculptural commissions with confidence, as he now had the physical space in which to work.[40] Working at the top of 31 St James's Gardens largely dictated the size and scope of the sculpture he produced – mostly portrait heads and statuettes – though he did succeed in making large-scale works there for exhibition at the Beaux Arts Gallery in the 1950s.

According to Ivor, the majority of his pre-war sculptures – most were fragile plaster casts – were destroyed when his studio on Lillie Road, Chelsea, was hit by a bomb during the London Blitz of 1940–41 and totally demolished.[41]

At the outbreak of the Second World War, Ivor volunteered to serve in the Royal Artillery. It would appear

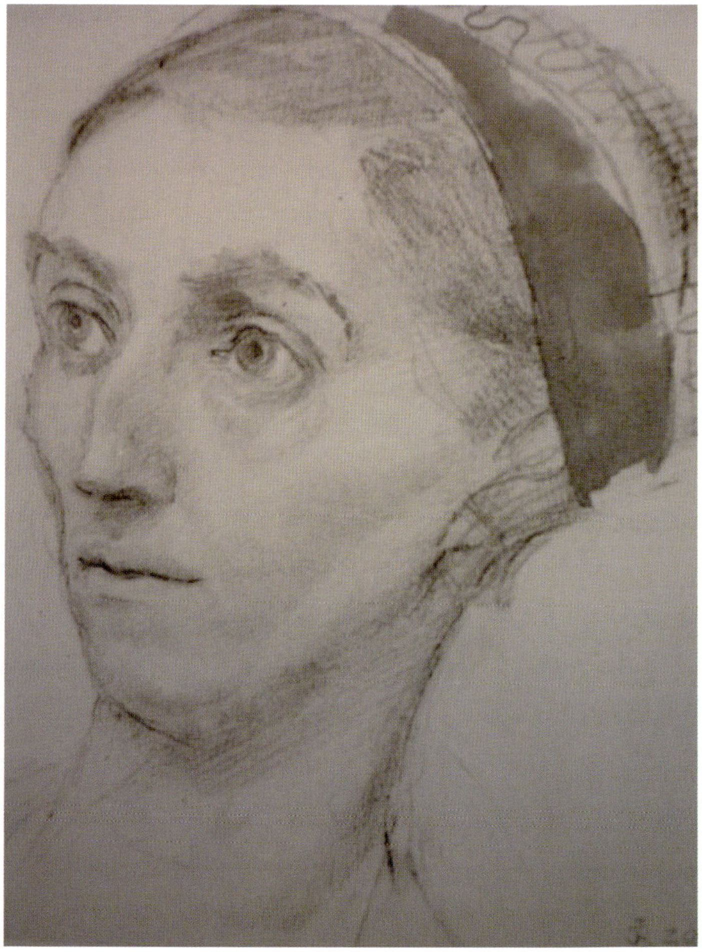

Fig. 1.5 Ivor Roberts-Jones, *Portrait of a Young Woman*, 1938, pencil and watercolour on paper, 11.1 x 11 cm, Private Collection
Image: J. Black

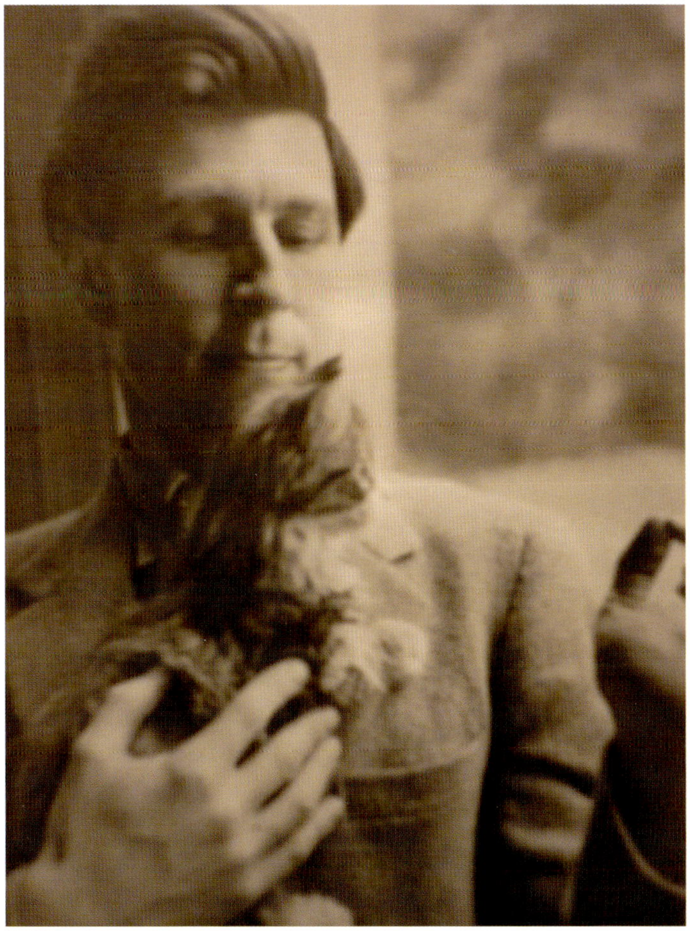

Fig. 1.6 Ivor Roberts-Jones with a kitten, c. May 1940; Image: Courtesy of the HMI, Leeds

that he devoured books about military history while a pupil at St Cuthbert's and had been a keen member of the school's Officer Training Corps.[42] Towards the end of 1940 he was posted to Northern Ireland, as a Lieutenant in the 83rd Field Regiment, Royal Artillery, as part of the 53rd Welsh (Territorial) Division (Fig. 1.7). Monica was allowed to join him. A fellow married officer in the same division, though serving in a different unit, was the writer Anthony Powell (1905–2000) – also very proud of his Anglo-Welsh heritage.[43]

It is not clear whether they met in Northern Ireland, where Powell was stationed from 1940–41, but their paths certainly crossed in 1962, when Ivor met Powell at the memorial service for Augustus John. Over the next five years, behind the scenes, Powell would prove one of Ivor's staunchest supporters during the troubled gestation of his memorial to John for Fordingbridge, Hampshire (unveiled October 1967) (cat. 133), which was his first significant work of life-sized public sculpture in bronze.[44]

It was in Northern Ireland, in August 1941, that Ivor's first child, Mervyn, was born (Fig. 1.8).[45] Both Ivor and Monica dearly loved their son, though he proved a demanding child to bring up: he was severely asthmatic, suffered from epileptic fits and from some type of emotional disorder that meant he would never grow beyond a relatively low mental age.[46]

Ivor showed real ability as a soldier. He was promoted to the rank of captain and posted to Alton Officer Cadet training camp as a gunnery instructor.[47] Towards the end of 1942 he was posted to a jungle artillery unit based first in north-eastern India and then in Burma, and spent much of 1943–45 in combat with the Japanese. It would seem he took part in command of a battery in at least one major battle during the Second Arakan Campaign (January–April 1944) – the so-called Battle of the 'Admin Box' (February 1944). On several occasions the unit to which

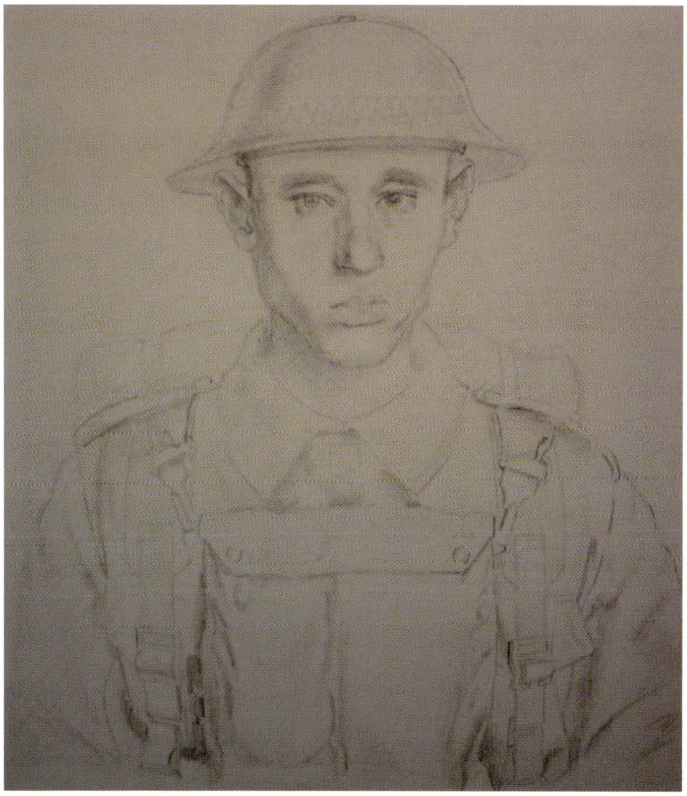

Fig. 1.7 Ivor Roberts-Jones, *Soldier in Full Kit Wearing a Steel Helmet*, 1940, pencil on paper, 39 x 28.3 cm, Private Collection Image: J. Black

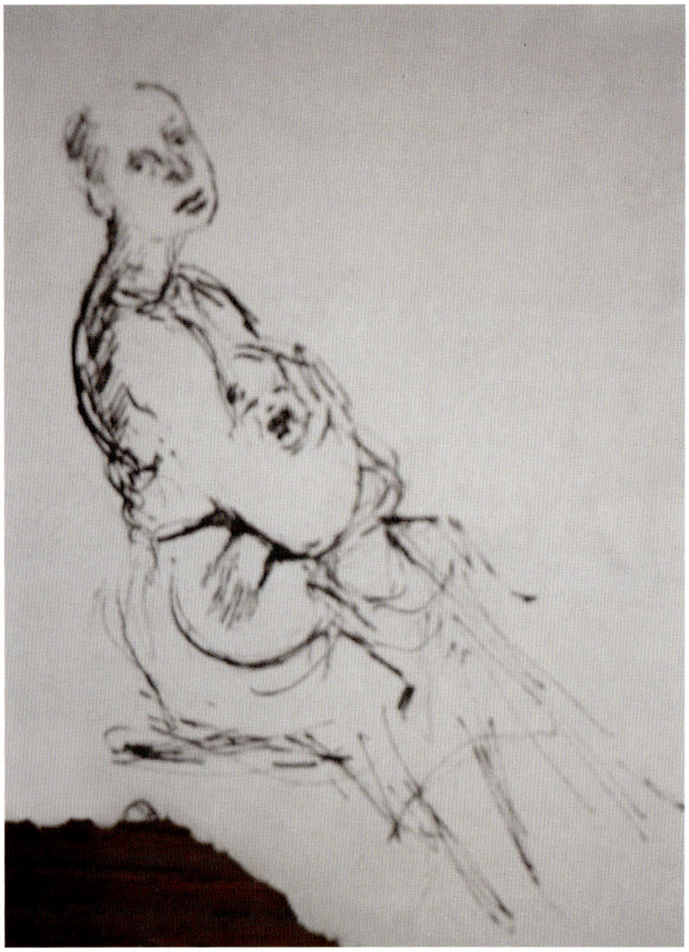

Fig. 1.8 Ivor Roberts-Jones, *Monica holding Mervyn*, 1941, pen and ink on paper, 12.5 x 11 cm, HMI, Leeds; Image: J. Black

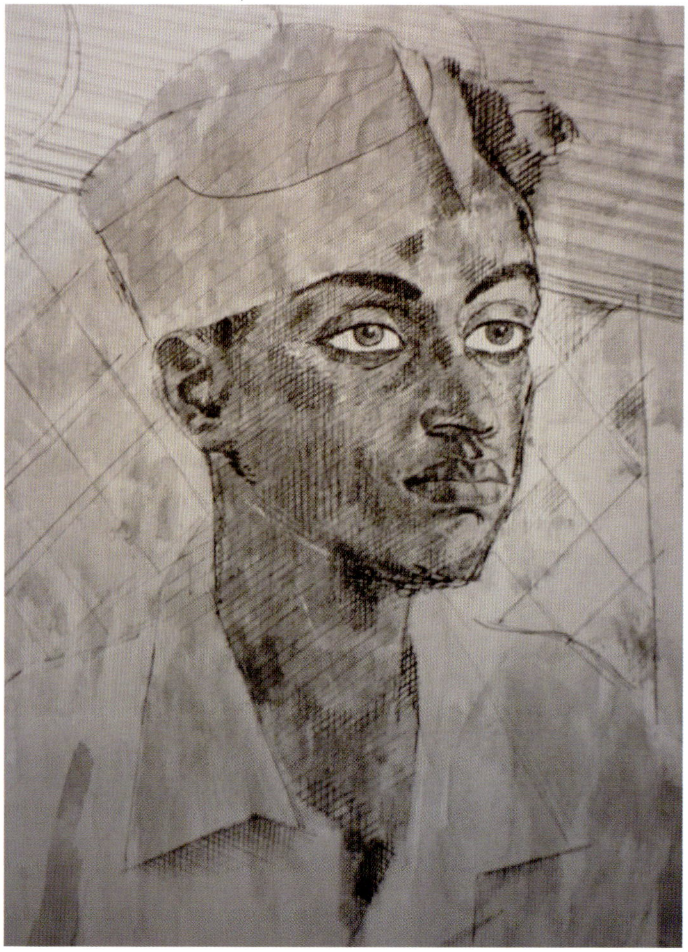

Fig. 1.9 Ivor Roberts-Jones, *Indian Army N.C.O.*, 1944, pen and ink and watercolour on paper, 34 x 38.5 cm, Private Collection Image: J. Black

Ivor's battery was attached, the 7th Indian Division, was surrounded, and infiltrating Japanese troops came close enough to fire upon the guns under his command.[48] It is not clear whether Ivor personally became involved in hand-to-hand combat, but he certainly saw more than his fair share of bitter fighting at close quarters – both in the Arakan and later during the 1945 advance into central Burma. He did have spare moments, in which he produced a number of sensitive portraits, in the manner of his old Goldsmiths tutor Edward Bawden, of Indian soldiers and Burmese civilians he encountered (Fig. 1.9).

He was part of the force that took Mandalay from the Japanese in March 1945 and then advanced to occupy Rangoon early in May. His battery last saw action in July 1945, firing on Japanese troops attempting to escape encirclement by Allied forces at the Battle of the Sittang Bend in the south-east corner of Burma.[49] Japan surrendered to the Allies in mid August 1945 after the dropping of atom bombs on Hiroshima (6 August 1945) and Nagasaki (9 August). Many years later, Ivor hinted that, while by no means anti-Japanese, he had welcomed the American use of nuclear weapons in 1945 for bringing the war to such an unexpectedly sudden end. He suspected that if the war in South-east Asia had continued for much longer, with his battery marked for Operation Zipper – the anticipated invasion of Japanese-occupied Malaysia – he probably would not have survived.[50]

In later life Ivor very much agreed with the argument made by George MacDonald Fraser, a veteran of the Burma campaign in 1945 – including the Battle of the Sittang Bend – in a book that the sculptor read in 1994. Fraser argued that, to British soldiers on the ground in Burma in August

1945, there was precious little sign that their Japanese opponents were in any mood to surrender. The dropping of the two atoms bombs thus ensured that the war came to an end within a matter of days rather than after many months more of bitter fighting.[51]

Ivor never said much about what had happened to him and what he saw in Burma, but the experience evidently marked him deeply. During snatched periods when not in action, or when in reserve, Ivor wrote many powerful poems, which suggest an awareness of the poetry of Wilfred Owen, Dylan Thomas and W. H. Auden, exploring the eerie and disorientating conditions of jungle warfare – shafts of strong light piercing gaps in the thick canopy of trees and jungle vegetation. On rare occasions he would comment of his war in Burma simply that he had never been more frightened, and yet had never felt more alive and observant – to the sudden appearance of Buddhist temples in the jungle and the disturbing sights of jungle creatures on, in and around the artillery pieces in his charge.[52]

In December 1981, attempting to shed some light on what his feelings had been in Burma, he sent Peter Cannon-Brookes fragments of several of the poems he had written there during 1944–45. Of *Arakan*, written in April 1944, he wrote: '[I]n action one would come across small deserted temples – the "single blossom" is probably frangipani ... the idea of light being drawn in to an object is one that has remained with me. I like sculptures like the Indian Buddha that "draw" space as it were in to themselves.' As for 'Limbo/From a Dug In RA Observation Post, Arakan, 1944', he described it as:

> part of a longish poem ... I suppose there is a religious element in it. In the army, especially in action, the neatly painted vehicles, one's carefully chinagraphed maps with at least three colours – the 'brief to the point' telephone instructions with their proper 'responses' as in church – all have the magic of ritual. My spiders seem to have theirs too! ... the ritual is [in] the setting up of the instruments, working out of distances, ranges, angles etc. in my 'house' and the waiting ...

In perhaps one of the most powerful poems Ivor sent Cannon-Brookes, 'Sonnet' (3 June 1945),' he explored:

> the breaking down of the 'ritual' ... this young man, not myself, would have given himself up to the enemy many times. He found such comfort from the sound of the enemy talking amongst themselves during the night as they crept around their outposts – assessing numbers, positions etc. His sergeant must have pulled him back many times. He knew he would be shot of course. He spent much of the rest of the war in hospital. His patrol had been a 'long' one. About two months or so I believe and had failed in its main objective. The Gurkhas developed second sight – it was a strange and 'killing' experience all round.

The poem itself read:

> Out on patrol he felt his resolution
> Slip from a chord to tangent, break the circle
> Pressing through bass of silence extreme caution
> Folded his will like paper. In the cool
> Evening of half-sleep and sweat's remission
> When the mind sometimes expected above the creaking
> Night efforts of jungle some quiet suggestion
> Of friend or woman, he heard the enemy talking
> Only a few yards beyond the track,
> As though to him, some dormitory confession
> Foisting its cool normality in to the night
> But always there was someone to pull him back
> Into the circle of the willed illusion
> Into the forked shadows, the divided light.[53]

His perception of a feared and formidable Japanese opponent was evidently a complex and nuanced one – the enemy were alien, but were also fellow human beings whose very talk could make an isolated infantry officer feel less alone and almost bring with it memories of familiar public school life. Within a month of writing this poem, however, Ivor and his battery were in action against the Japanese at the Battle of the Sittang Bend – contributing to the slaughter of over 12,000 of the enemy, who were attempting to break out to Thailand and continued to fight on fiercely, despite the fact that they had largely run out of ammunition and food.[54]

Ivor was also later quite aware that being a Second World War veteran, with combat experience in one of the most fiercely fought campaigns in the entire war, had stood him in very good stead when he was considered in 1970–71 for the Churchill statue commission in Parliament Square (cat. 135) – a number of influential members of the memorial committee were veterans of both world wars.[55]

Having served in Burma in the Royal Artillery and won the Churchill commission in 1971, he later acknowledged, proved critical in launching his career as a sculptor of large public works – and in securing major commissions towards the end of his career, such as his imposing statue of Field Marshal Sir William 'Uncle Bill' Slim (1987–90) (cat. 153) – commander of the XIVth Army in Burma in which Ivor had served, and commissioned by the Burma Star Association – and that of Field Marshal Sir Alan Brooke (1991–93) (cat. 154), commissioned by Ivor's old regiment, the Royal Artillery. Given the importance of his war service, he may have reflected it would have been rather churlish to deplore the positive effect it would later have on the course of his career.[56]

The war in Burma certainly seems to have had immense significance for him, and yet he does not appear to have harboured any animus towards the Japanese as a people. Indeed, he was later to acknowledge how impressed he had been in the mid 1950s by the work of the avant-garde Japanese Gutai Group.[57] Indeed, many of his former students remember how passionately he recommended eighteenth- and nineteenth-century Japanese woodblock prints to them as models of graceful and harmonious design.[58] During the late 1970s he even tried to design his garden at Cratfield, in Suffolk, so that the viewer would derive a 'Japanese flavour' from it.[59]

On one level Ivor appears to have regarded the war as a test of his masculinity, which he had passed, and as an experience he would have been foolish to avoid. But he was conscious that he would be returning to a Britain that was much poorer than in 1939, and that he would essentially have to start his art career all over again. As he later put it, the war and the destruction of his pre-war sculpture had created a tabula rasa for him – equally discouraging, and yet a stimulus to think afresh and embrace new ideas, new developments in art that he had tended to overlook as an art student at the RA Schools.[60]

In December 1945 Ivor was demobilised from the army and returned to London just in time to visit the last few days of the important *Picasso–Matisse* exhibition held at the Victoria and Albert Museum (1 November 1945–11 January 1946), which he found enthralling. Ever afterwards he would readily admit his admiration for Picasso's inventive energy and versatility.[61]

But he had arrived in a blitzed, depressing and severely rationed city; 31 St James's Gardens had been spared, but much of the rest of the street had been destroyed by the bombing. He was fortunate in October 1946 to obtain a part-time teaching position at Goldsmiths thanks to his old tutor Clive Gardiner.[62] He also found another part-time job for a year to eighteen months, in the stores at the British Museum, unwrapping sculpture from the Ancient Greek, Egyptian and Assyrian galleries, that had been stored in North Wales for the duration of the war.[63]

Evidently, from the sculpture Ivor produced in the late 1940s and during the 1950s, he was considerably marked by some of the ancient sculpture he had helped to unpack at the British Museum, such as carved, seated 'benefactor' figures (Fig. 1.10) from the sixth-century BCE Greek colony at Didyma, in what is now Turkey.[64]

In 1947 Ivor's small terracotta *Winged Figure with Bird* (1946) (cat. 104) was reproduced in Eric Newton's *British Sculpture 1944–1946*. The characterisation of the face, with enlarged, heavily defined eyes, is closely reminiscent of the physiognomy of a number of ancient Sumerian figures in the British Museum, such as that of *Gudea, Ruler of Lagash* (c. 2125–2025 BCE) (Fig. 1.11), which was early on singled out for praise by Henry Moore, in an article published in June 1935.[65] Ivor may also be referencing Picasso's famous painting of a *Child Holding a Dove* (1901), included in the 1945–46 *Picasso–Matisse* exhibition and now on loan to the Courtauld Institute.

The seated female figure certainly recurs in the work Ivor produced in plaster and terracotta in the 1950s, and he may well have returned to the 1946–47 sketches of a standing woman holding a child when, around 1956–57, he was conceiving the figure of a *Woman and Child/Madonna and Child* (cat. 119c) commissioned from him in 1956 for the Anglican church in Ardleigh, Essex (see Chapter 5).

To be included in Newton's survey after barely two years of resuming his sculptural career was a considerable achievement for Ivor. Though he was not mentioned by name in Newton's accompanying essay, the photograph of his terracotta was flanked by those of work by Henry Moore, such as his large elm-carving *Reclining Figure* (1945–46). Newton noted the emergence of Moore as a major figure within British sculpture – indeed, he described Moore as one of its 'leaders', along with Barbara

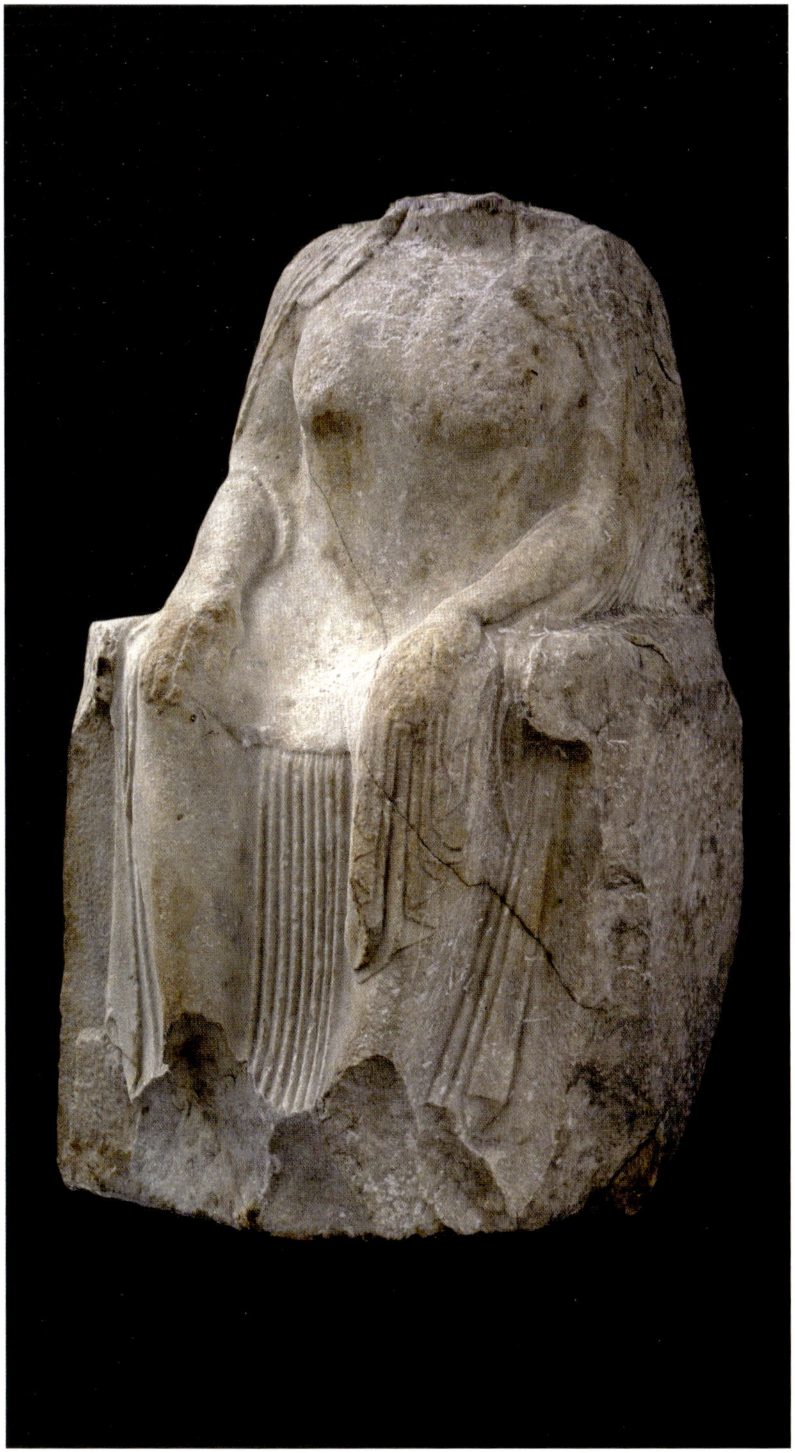

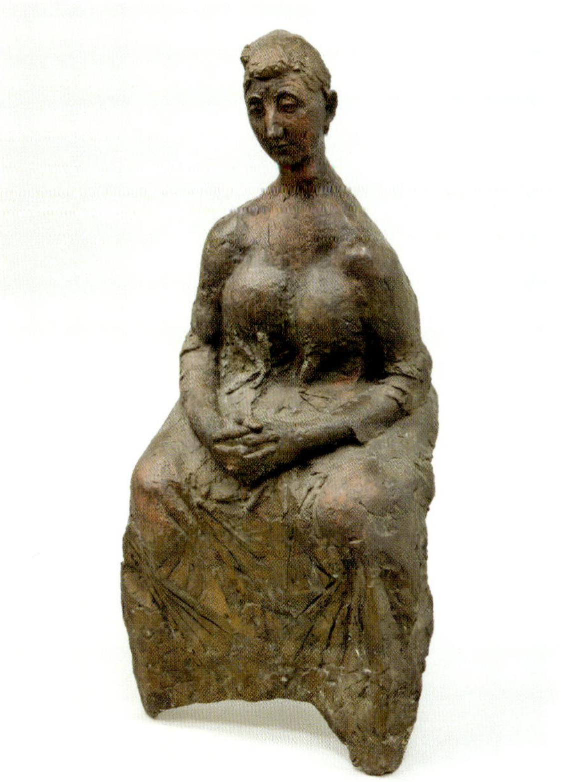

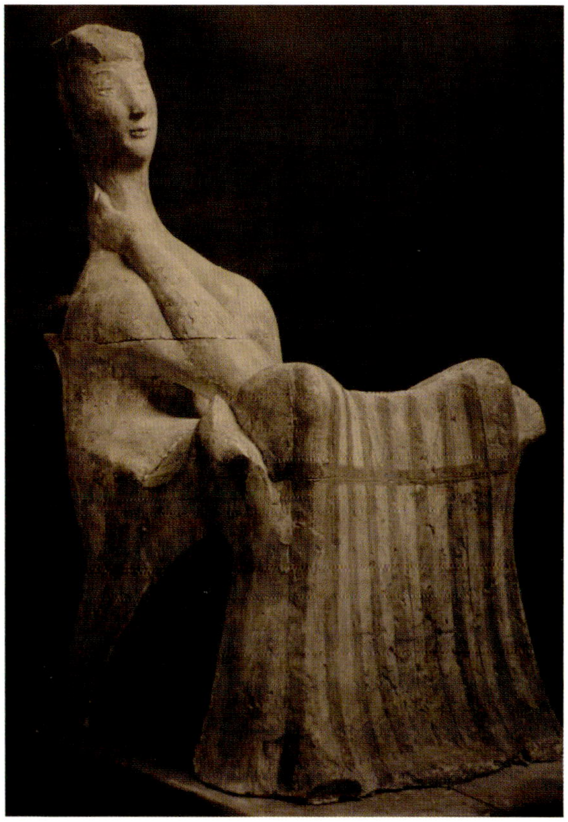

Fig. 1.10 *Seated Figure of a Benefactor*, c. 500 BCE, marble, 70 cm high, British Museum, London; Image: Courtesy of British Museum Images

Top right Cat. 112a, *Seated Woman/Mrs Griffiths*, 1966

Bottom right Cat. 114, *Seated Woman, Head Resting on Right Hand*, 1955–57

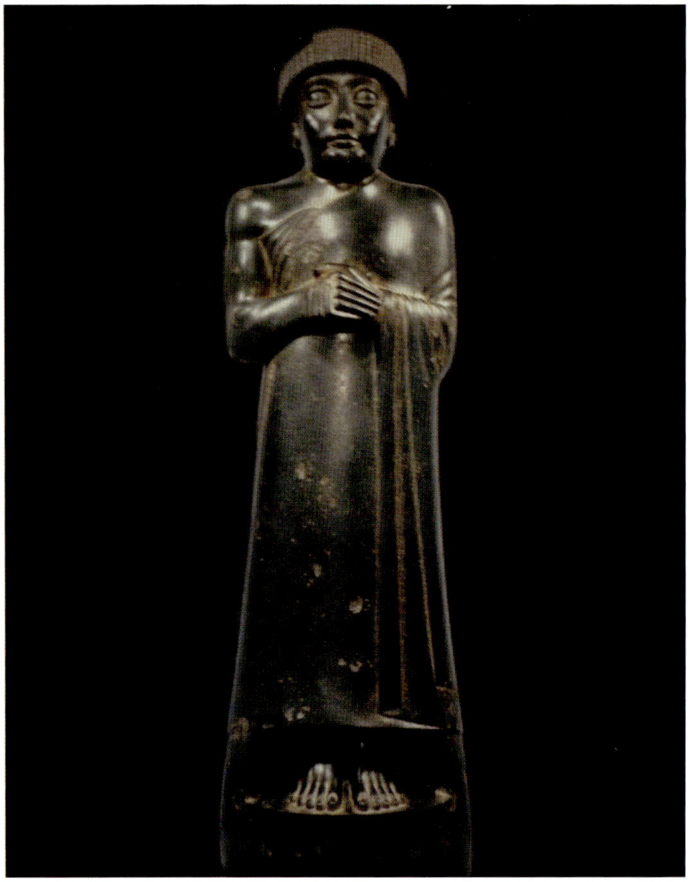

Fig. 1.11 *Gudea, Ruler of Lagash*, c. 2125–2025 BCE, black diorite,75 cm high, British Museum, London; Image: Courtesy of British Museum Images

Hepworth.[66] He predicted, fairly accurately as it transpired, that the form of 'abstracted and simplified' figuration practised by Moore in his 1946 terracotta *Family Group* would grow in popularity – especially for public commissions to adorn the civic buildings within a series of New Towns, the construction of which was soon to commence.[67]

Newton also felt that a form of figuration that explicitly harked back to the sculpture of 'ancient civilisations' and 'classical tendencies', as produced by artists such as Frank Dobson (1888–1963), Karin Jonzen (1914–98) and Dora Gordine (1895–1991), would remain a 'vigorous' strand within British sculpture for many years to come.[68] Ivor's work can be located within this strand of nuanced post-war figuration that remained faithful to a comprehensible form of representation.

A drawing Ivor produced during this period, *Seated Woman/Shelter Angel*, from 1947 (Fig. 1.12) can be identified

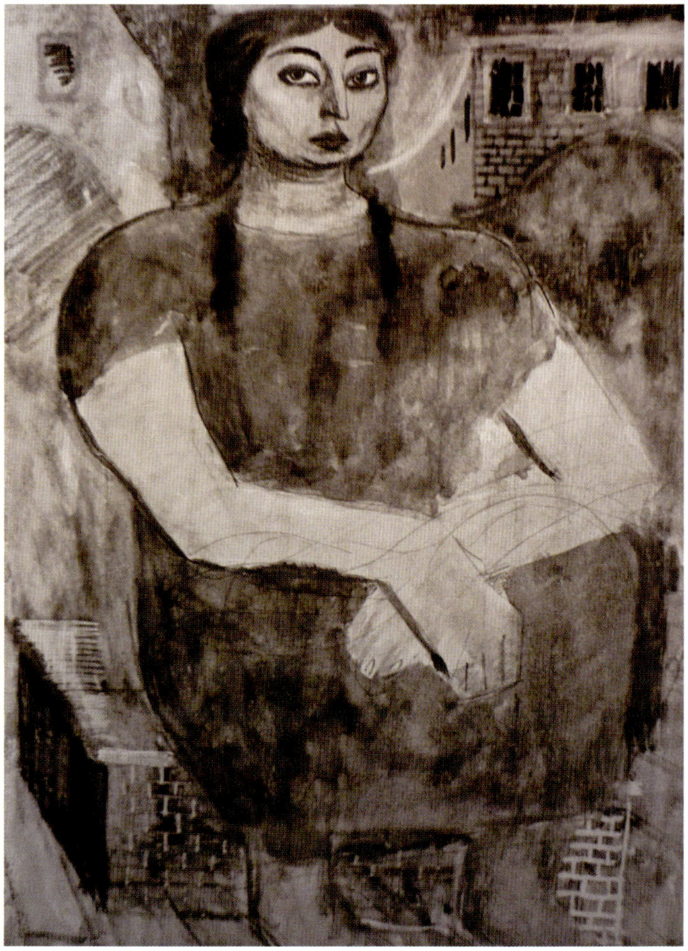

Fig. 1.12 Ivor Roberts-Jones, *Seated Woman/Shelter Angel*, c. 1947, watercolour and pencil on paper, 29.5 x 24.5 cm, Private Collection; Image: J. Black

as evidence for his ongoing fascination with the seated female figure, not only drawing upon recent sculpture on the theme by Frank Dobson – including studies of seated women, which would become the bronze group *London Pride* (1950–51) (Fig. 1.13), destined for display at the Festival of Britain in 1951 – but also harking back to the massive solidity and calmness of the female figures painted by Picasso during his 'classical' phase of the early 1920s. Ivor may have seen examples of the latter early in 1946 at the Victoria and Albert Museum's *Picasso–Matisse* exhibition – as well as those of women and children sheltering from the bombing in the stations of the London Underground drawn by Henry Moore in 1940–41.[70]

Fig. 1.13 Frank Dobson, *London Pride*, 1950–51, bronze, 1.52 m high, outside the National Theatre, London; Image: J. Black

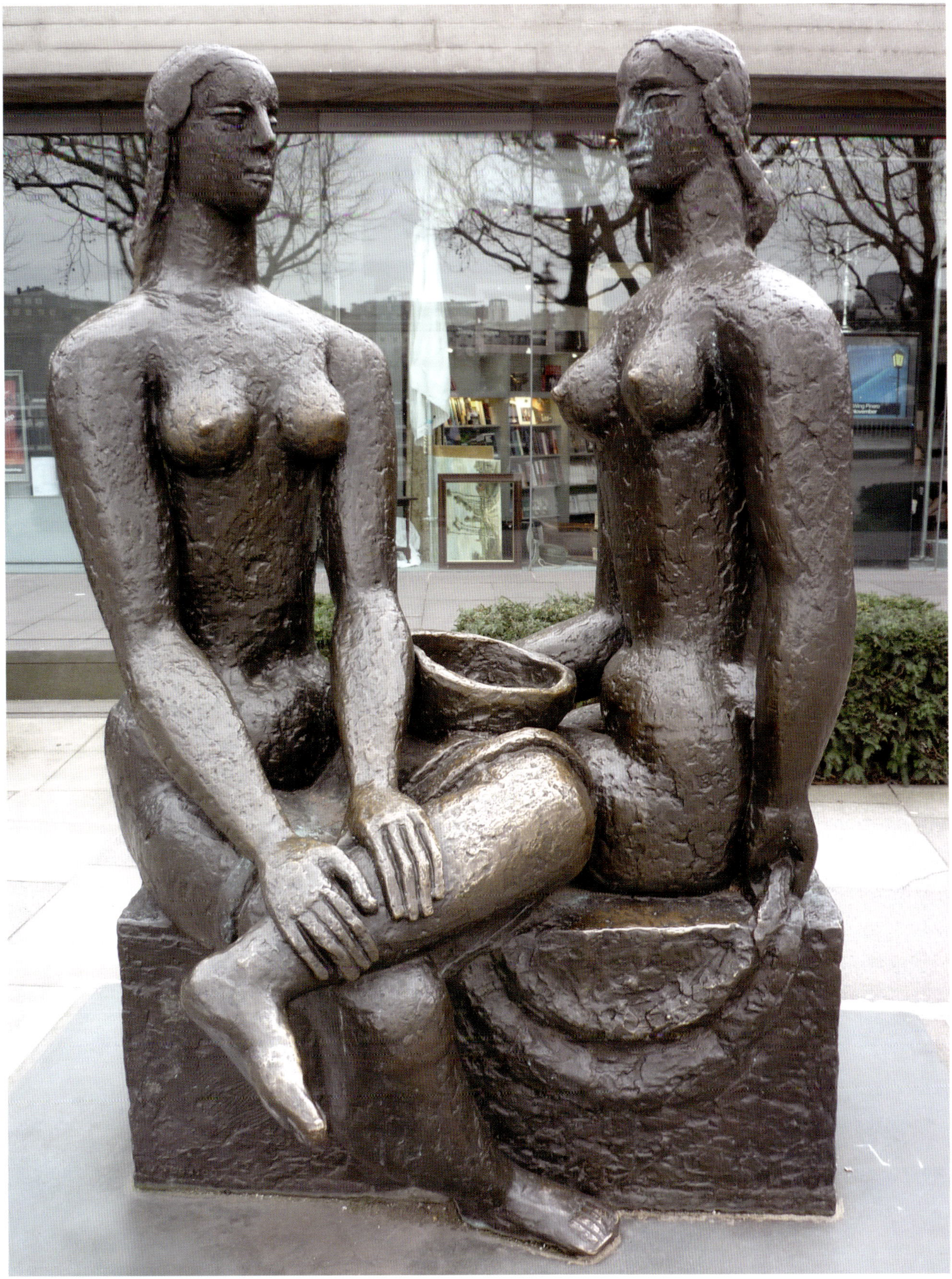

In the late 1940s, Ivor produced a series of small figures of *Clowns* in plaster and terracotta (cats. 107, 109), which may be interpreted as an homage to the poignant acrobats, street artists, characters derived from the *commedia dell'arte* and 'saltimbanques' Picasso painted so memorably during his so-called 'Blue' and 'Rose' periods. Examples had been exhibited at the Victoria and Albert Museum in 1945–46.[71]

The example of carving from Didyma, and particularly of painted terracottas from sixth-century BCE Tanagra

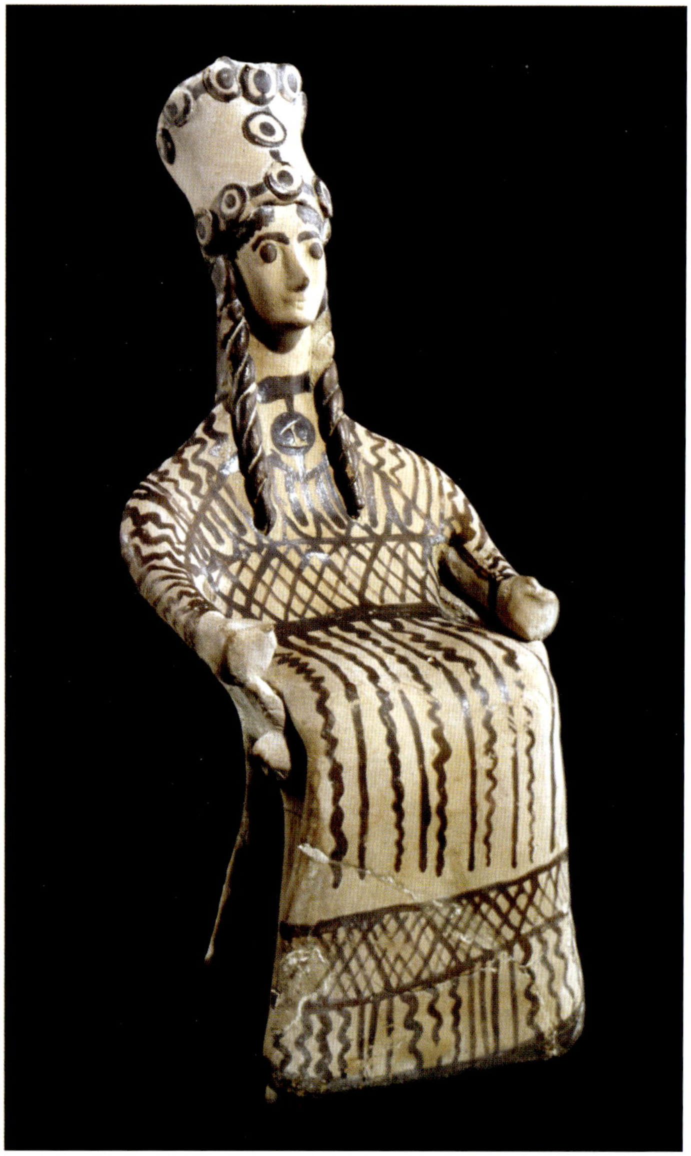

Fig. 1.14 *Seated Figure of a Goddess from Tanagra*, c. 580 BCE, terracotta, 21 cm high, British Museum, London Image: Courtesy of British Museum Images

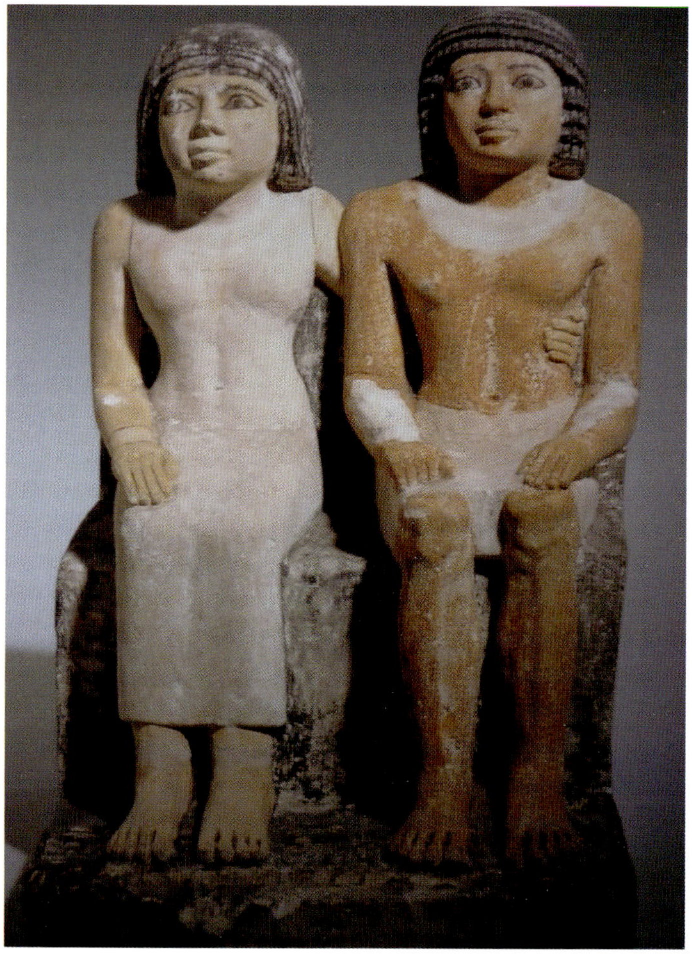

Fig. 1.15 *Katep and His Wife Hetepheres*, c. 2465–2152 BCE, painted limestone, 45.7 cm high, British Museum, London Image: Courtesy of British Museum Images

now in the collection of the British Museum, certainly had an impact on Ivor's formal approach towards the seated female figures and heads in plaster and terracotta, which he exhibited at the Beaux Arts gallery in July 1954, and in his May 1957 solo exhibition held at the same gallery. *Smiling Woman* (1955–57) (cat. 113), for example, exhibited in May 1957, looks to the painted terracottas of a *Goddess* (either Hera or Demeter) also from Tanagra (Fig. 1.14), from around 600–550 BCE, while the figure's rather disconcerting smile is distinctly reminiscent of a *Smiling Female Head* from the sixth-century BCE Temple of Artemis at Ephesus (550–520 BCE, also in the British Museum's collection.

From photographs and postcards he once owned, it is evident that Ivor was interested in carved, seated, painted husband-and-wife groups from Ancient Egypt in the British Museum, such as *Katep and His wife Hetepheres* (c. 2465–2152 BCE – 5th–6th Dynasties) (Fig. 1.15). He would often recommend to his sculpture students at Goldsmiths that their work could only benefit from a couple of hours spent on the ground floor Ancient Egyptian galleries of the British Museum.[72]

In the late 1940s he was introduced by his old friend from the RA Schools, Daphne Hardy, to a convivial circle of Jewish Eastern European intellectuals, writers and musicians, such as Hardy's then partner, the writer Arthur Koestler (1905–83), the cellist William Pleeth and the pianist and conductor Alfred (later Sir Alfred) Brendel. Politically all were on the left. Pleeth seems to have shared Koestler's vehement anti-Stalinism, while Brendel was also very suspicious of the activities of the British Communist Party.[73] No evidence has emerged to suggest whether Ivor shared their political outlook, but it is telling that he later recalled many an enjoyable dinner throughout the 1950s with the three at 31 St James's Gardens – Koestler providing copious bottles of excellent wine and Monica revealing herself to be an excellent cook. Indeed, Koestler maintained that her goulash was just as good as anything he had eaten in his native Budapest, and was convinced she must have some Hungarian blood in her veins.[74] In the early 1950s Ivor produced a finely observed and sympathetic portrait head in plaster of Pleeth (cat. 10), and a decade later one in the same medium of the left-wing though anti-communist critic, painter and writer Sir Richard Rees (1900–70) (cat. 23).[75]

Hardy may have introduced Ivor to her friend Giacometti during a trip they apparently made to Paris in the mid 1950s.[76] There is certainly more than an hint of Giacometti's example in some of the smaller portrait studies Ivor made at that time, such as a plaster *Small Head and Shoulders of Kyffin Williams* (1954–55) (cat. 12) (see Chapter 2).

Ivor later recalled a visit he had made at some point in the early 1950s to Henry Moore, seeking his advice. At this time he was torn between what he then perceived as the sharply conflicting rival claims of representation and what he termed the 'pure abstract element' he so admired in the 'teeming vitality' of the larger figures at Ajanta (a series of caves in the Aurangabad district of the Indian state of Maharashtra, containing massive carvings of

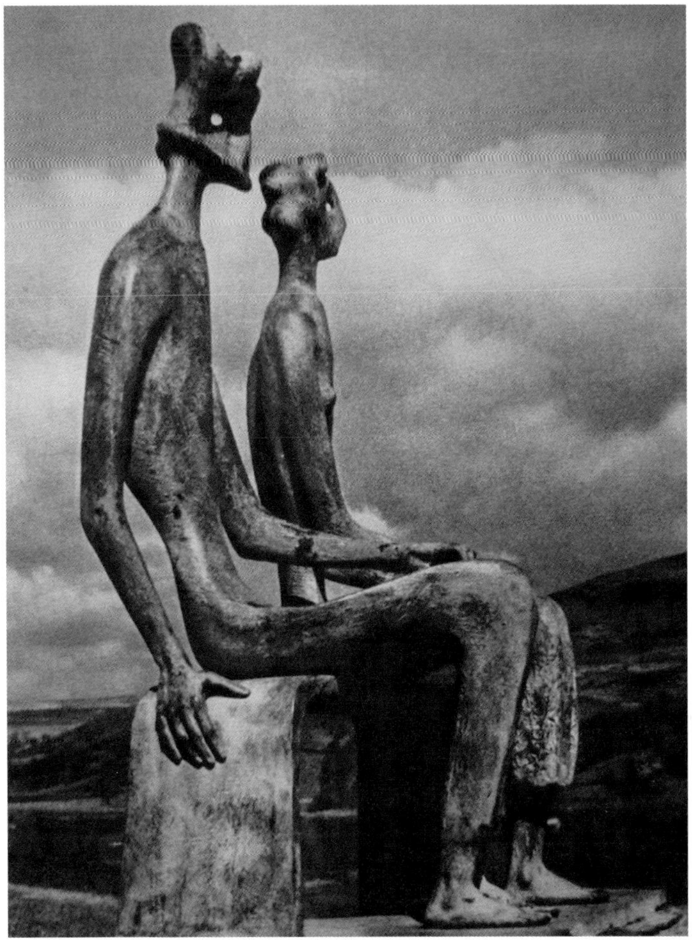

Fig. 1.16 Henry Moore, *King and Queen*, 1952–53, bronze, 1.64 m high, Glenkiln, Dumfriesshire; Image: Courtesy of the HMI, Leeds

Buddha cut into the living rock, dating from c. 480–650 CE). Ivor later recalled that

> Moore saw some photographs of my work at this time and was very understanding about the problem. He said that 'consistency' was only one of the qualities of a work of art … he had been criticised for the mixture of realism and comparatively abstract passages in his [recent] *King and Queen* [1952–53, cast in bronze 1957] [Fig. 1.16]. He was not deeply concerned about it and I found this very encouraging.[77]

In 1983 Ivor pondered whether he had 'ever resolved this' – namely, the tension in his work between the demands of verisimilitude and the 'purer, abstracted element' he had so admired in photographs of carvings at Ajanta.[78] By then he was seventy. Towards the end of that decade, after a health scare, he had come to the conclusion that this tension was indeed a healthy one, to be welcomed rather than comprehensibly resolved.[79]

In the summer of 1953, prompted by the outcry that greeted the award of first prize to Reg Butler in the competition for a 'Memorial to an Unknown Political Prisoner' for his unashamedly angular and non-figurative design to be executed in stainless steel, Ivor joined a group of sculptors who believed in the need to defend the continuing validity of figurative sculpture in forming the Society of Portrait Sculptors.[80]

The following year, he contributed to the July 1954 Beaux Arts Gallery Summer Exhibition, and his seated figure of a *Woman Holding a Cat* (cat. 111) was probably his first piece of sculpture to catch the attention of art critics. *The Times* remarked that it was 'a large and most ambitious sculpture in the modern Italian manner; the design shows a considerable power of invention and there are some sensitive passages of modelling'.[81] Exhibiting alongside Ivor was the painter John Bratby – who within a matter of months would be identified by critic David Sylvester as a leading exponent of the so-called 'kitchen sink' school of painting, while the Beaux Arts Gallery was described as the headquarters of this new movement, and in favour of a general return to an unfussy and 'down-to-earth' form of artistic realism.[82]

The reference to the 'Italian manner' was probably a reference to the growing vogue for the work of Italian sculptors such as Arturo Martini, Emilio Greco, Giacomo Manzu and Marino Marini – particularly the latter, whose bronze *Horseman* (1949) in the 1951 London County Council *Sculpture in the Open Air* show in Battersea Park had been singled out for special praise, while he had held a very well-received solo exhibition at the Hanover Gallery in May–June 1951. Further examples of Marini's portraiture and figurative work had been included in an important exhibition, *New Sculpture, Painting and Drawings by Giacometti, Moore, Manzu and Marini*, held at the Hanover Gallery between June and August 1952.[83]

It is also significant that Helen Lessore at the Beaux Arts Gallery also represented one of the few younger contemporary sculptors who Ivor ever mentioned admiring – Elisabeth Frink,[84] at the beginning of her career, during the early 1950s.[85]

The exhibition attracted the attention of 'progressive traditionalist' architect Raymond Erith, and led to Ivor's first public sculpture commission – a Rodin-inspired figure of *St Francis* receiving the stigmata (cat. 119a) and a tender *Madonna and Child* (cat. 119c), the mother resembling one of Augustus John's many paintings of his partner Dorelia, for the interior of St Mary's Anglican Church, Ardleigh, in Essex (1955–58). This commission will be discussed in greater detail in Chapter 5.

During the second half of the 1950s, Ivor varied his output between the occasional portrait head, such as the impressive *Clive Gardiner* (1955–57) (cat. 11) and the brooding French poet and thinker *Paul Claudel* (1957–59) (cat. 17), and large, expressive, almost Expressionist figures in painted plaster and terracotta, such as *Mrs Griffiths* (cat. 112), *Walking Judas* (cat. 118) and *The Judge* (cat. 117). Indeed, many years later, Ivor acknowledged how indebted he still was to an 'innate Expressionism within my own nature' and imagination.[86]

The Times was particularly taken with these three figures when they were exhibited at the Beaux Arts Gallery in May 1957: '*Walking Judas* and *The Judge* are block-like shapes of a lumbering impressiveness ... while the best of his exhibits [is] the seated figure of *Mrs Griffiths*. This piece has a grave calm which draws the eye, while its modelling indicates character in the sitter and animates the detail without troubling the essential stillness of the whole.'[87] Later, in 1966–67, Ivor would extensively rework *Mrs Griffiths*, and four years later the National Museum of Wales, Cardiff, would pay to have it cast in bronze for its sculpture collection.[88]

In the *Guardian* Stephen Bone was also very impressed by *Walking Judas*: 'a very large statue of a man, striding forward preoccupied with his own sad thoughts and wrapped in some enormous bulky garment that seems to symbolise his imprisonment within them ... a striking and original conception.' Bone also correctly identified the main source for the anguished figure of the *Judge*: 'a torso in a pose reminiscent of Rodin in its violent athleticism'.[89]

In 1956 he made the plaster *Blind Faced Figure* (cat. 121), one of his first treatments of a theme that would recur frequently in his career. He was fascinated by the challenge of convincingly depicting the blind. This theme had already attracted his friend Kyffin Williams. The head of

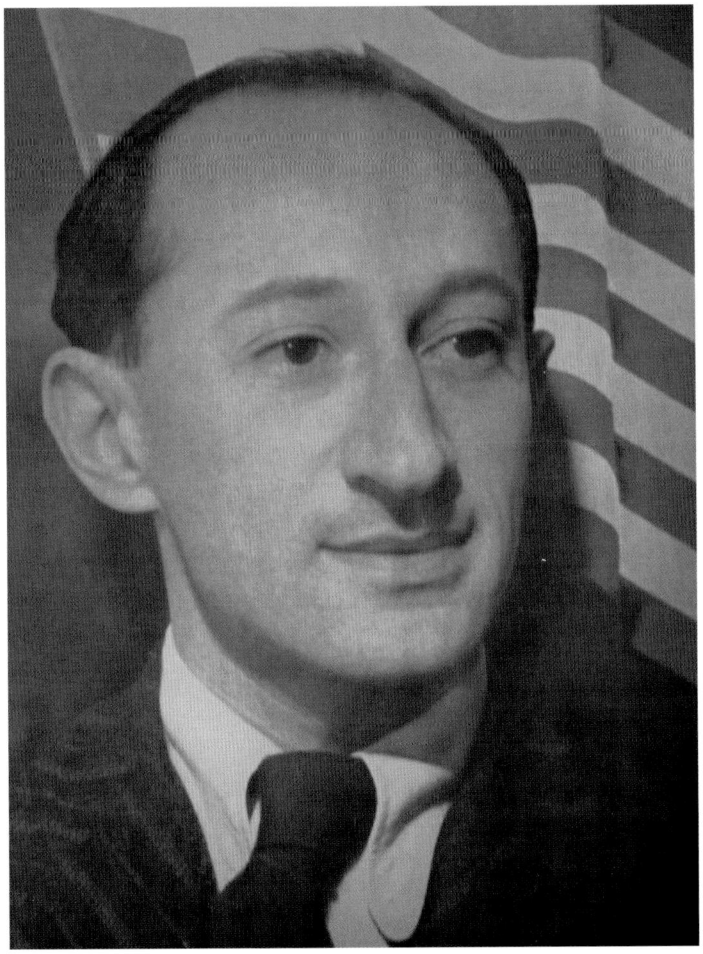

Fig. 1.17 Demetrios Capetanakis photographed in London, c. 1942
Image: Courtesy of the HMI, Leeds

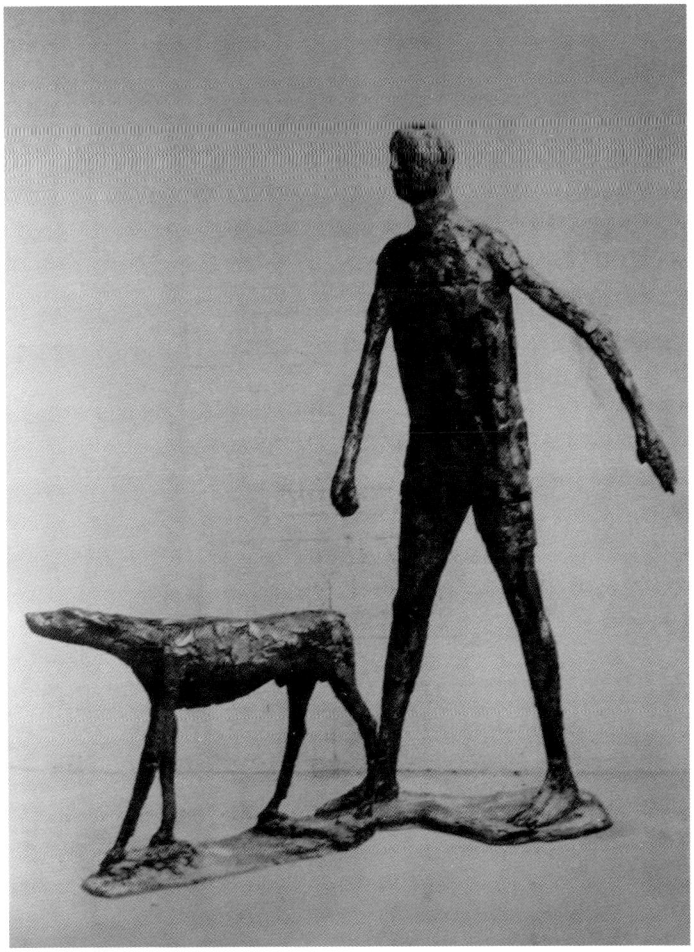

Fig. 1.18 Elisabeth Frink, *Blind Beggar and Dog*, 1957–58, bronze, 1.83 m high, Bethnal Green, London; Image: J. Black

the *Blind Faced Figure* was inspired partly by a photograph taken around 1942 of the London-based Greek poet Demetrios Capetanakis (1912–44) (Fig. 1.17), and reproduced in a book on the poet published in 1947 which Ivor is known to have purchased and read the following year.[90] Years later he described how he was haunted by the photograph of Capetanakis, bearing the faintest trace of an enigmatic smile.[91] He may have been aware that the theme of blindness had also attracted the young and promising sculptor Elisabeth Frink, whose bronze group *Blind Beggar and Dog* (Fig. 1.18) was commissioned in 1957 by Bethnal Green Borough Council and erected the following year.[92]

In the wake of his well-received May 1957 exhibition at the Beaux Arts Gallery, Ivor was greatly encouraged by the positive reaction to this work from Sir Kenneth Clark (then Slade Professor of Art at Oxford) and Sir John Rothenstein (cat. 16) (then Diretor of the Tate Gallery [1938–64][Fig. 1.19]). Clark was apparently keen for Ivor to do a portrait head of his daughter Colette, but the commission did not materialise.[93]

In the late 1950s Ivor caught the attention of veteran bohemian painter Augustus John who, in his capacity as President of the Welsh Contemporary Art Society, suggested in July 1960 that Ivor be commissioned to make a figure of former prime minister Lloyd George for Parliament Square in London.[94] Nothing would come of this particular idea, but befriending Augustus and his partner Dorelia placed Ivor in an advantageous position when it was suggested after Augustus's death in 1961 that he be commemorated with a piece of figurative sculpture. This would later prove to be one of Ivor's most important and yet torturous commissions during the 1960s (see Chapter 5).

The purchase of the heads of his friend *Kyffin Williams* (1918–2006)[96] (cat. 20), and of *Paul Claudel* (1868–1955) (cat. 17) and *Clive Gardiner* (1891–1960) (cat. 11) in 1960 by the National Museum of Wales, Tate Gallery and the Arts Council, respectively, Ivor later recalled, was the first sign of any official support for his career.[96] Williams became one of Ivor's few close friends who was a fellow artist. He would be tireless in promoting Ivor's career. In 1959, for example, he proposed that the NMW, Cardiff, purchase Ivor's bronze head of him, on the grounds that his friend was 'certainly the best portrait sculptor in this country now Epstein has gone'. He acknowledged to the museum's Keeper of Art that Ivor did not do himself justice: 'he [Ivor] doesn't do the rounds of artists' cocktail parties, so he gets no commissions ... in desperation he has even taken up writing plays for TV.[98]

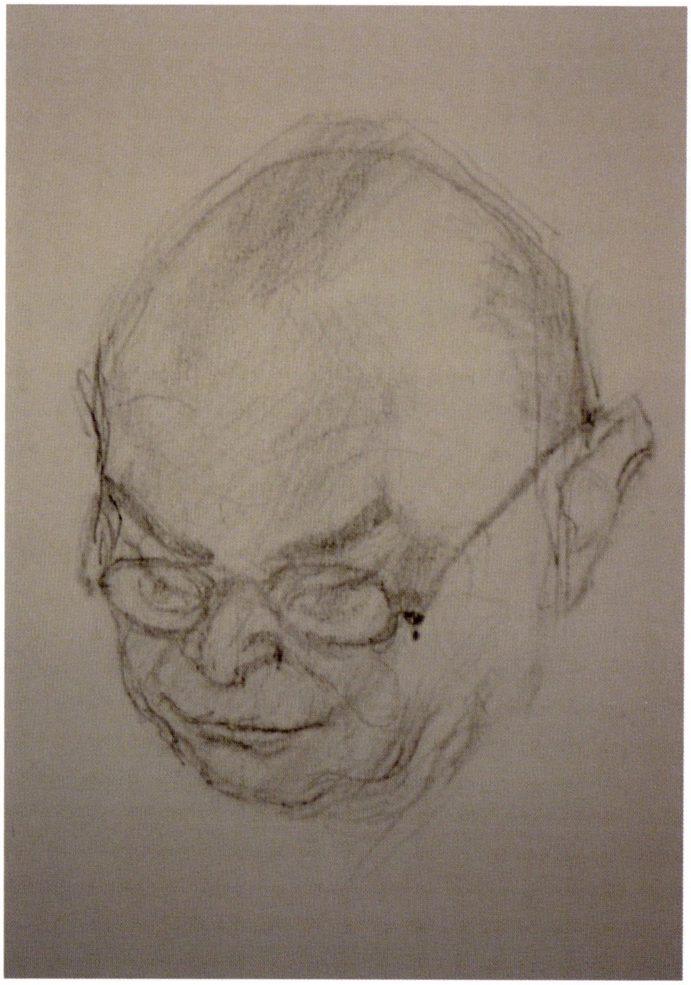

Fig. 1.19 Ivor Roberts-Jones, *Study of Sir John Rothenstein Wearing Spectacles*, c. 1956–57, pencil on paper, 25.3 x 38 cm, Private Collection; Image: J. Black

In 1971 Williams, by now on the NMW's art purchases sub-committee, suggested the museum buy a cast of Ivor's figure of *Augustus John*.[99] Nothing came of that idea – though instead the museum purchased a second version of *Mrs Griffiths* and paid for it to be cast in bronze, as well as a cast of Ivor's head of *Yehudi Menuhin* (1966–67) (cat. 37), a commission from Highgate School that Williams had played a key role in organising.[100]

Shortly before he died, Williams wrote, illuminatingly:

> I first became friends with Ivor after the war ... An immediate point of contact was epilepsy. I am epileptic and Ivor's son, who died young, was a chronic sufferer. Our Welshness, of course, was another bond ... Ivor was small and bird-like,[101] in fact a typical Welshman to look at. However, he did not sound Welsh, if anything he had an Oxford accent. Ivor always had an odd relationship with Wales. He couldn't keep away from the place, yet, he didn't like it ... Our friendship endured until his death. He was the most honest of men and also one of the most sensitive. He was also opinionated and had an inveterate streak of contrariness. Invariably, he would enter my studio and praise the least good work, usually half-hidden behind curtains. Soon, I took to putting my best piece behind the curtain and the worst on the easel ... Like so many Welsh, spontaneity was his thing: the lightning sketch of an animal, the brilliant characterization of a sitter, achieved in one sitting.[102]

Meanwhile, as Ivor befriended Williams (another admirer of Ivor's), the Swansea-born painter Ceri Richards (1903–1971), helped persuade the Welsh Committee of the Arts Council in 1960 to buy a cast of Ivor's *Old Man – Sam* (1960) (cat. 21) – a portrait of his colleague at Goldsmiths, the painter and ex-wrestler Sam Rabin (1903–1991), who taught life drawing at the college.[103]

In 1961 Ivor and Monica suffered a cruel blow, when Mervyn (Fig. 1.20), aged barely twenty, died after an accident at 31 St James's Gardens.[104] His death was not entirely unexpected; his epilepsy and asthma had been getting noticeably worse. The previous year Ivor had had to

Fig. 1.20 Ivor Roberts-Jones, *Mervyn Roberts-Jones*, c. 1958, pencil on paper, 38 x 28 cm, Image: Courtesy of the HMI, Leeds

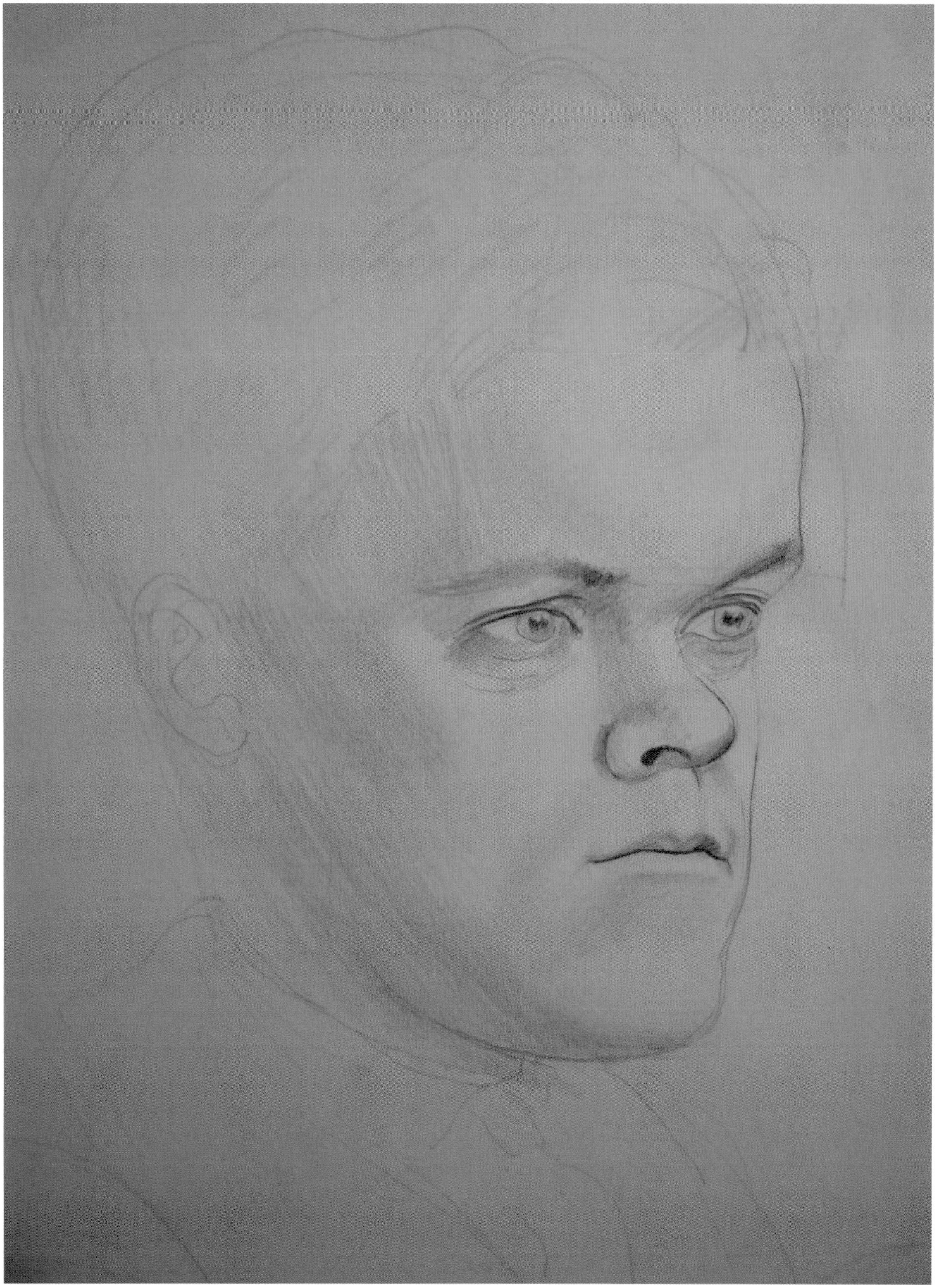

postpone a meeting with Sir John Rothenstein on the grounds that 'At the moment my son, who is a permanent invalid, is with us. I was in fact having a short break when you rang – he is tragically ill ... with epilepsy ... and it is a great strain looking after him.'[105] Many years later he was to admit that Mervyn's death had so affected him that it altered his artistic perception:

> It was a time when a great personal tragedy hit my wife and myself and we had not come to terms with it. My ability to see was almost physically affected. It is strange that the heads are so large – my sight at the time was perfect and this kind of unconscious enlargement is usually the result of failing vision and is not characteristic of my work as a whole. To me they [his portrait heads of the early 1960s] are like works by somebody else.[106]

In the early 1960s Ivor was experimenting with smaller works in plaster and terracotta that referenced recent examples of British sculpture, such as Eduardo Paolozzi and George Fullard. In November 1960, steered by Sir John Rothenstein, he was visited by Gaspero del Corso (1911–1997) and his wife, who, Ivor later wrote to Sir John, 'came over after seeing you and they now want me to have a one-man show at their Gallery "L'Obelisco" in Rome ... They seemed to like my new thing – the *Scapegoat* [1960–61] [cat. 129] figure which is nearing completion and which will be fresh to you'.[107]

Other works from this period, exhibited in July 1961 at the NMW, Cardiff, included *Women in a Wood* (1960) (cat. 124), *Female Torso* (1960) (cat. 122), and *Kite Rider* (1960) (cat. 123). The first work, a bas-relief, harks back to the example of Matisse's series of bronzes of women's backs, not seen together in the UK until an exhibition held at the Hanover Gallery in June–September 1958.[108] Ivor had also taken a keen interest in semi-abstract works by Jackson Pollock, from the late 1930s, recently exhibited in London.[109] The torso referenced cylcladic Greek carvings to be found in the British Museum, which had been favourites of Henry Moore in the 1950s.[110] (Fig. 1.21) *Kite Rider* was Ivor's first known treatment of the 'horse and rider' theme, particularly associated at the time with Marini,[111] and later with Elisabeth Frink,[112] to which Ivor would return in the 1970s, resulting later in the creation of some of his most impressive public sculptures such as *The Lazarus Rider* (1976–80) (cat. 139) and the monumental *The Two Kings/Janus Rider* commission to stand outside Harlech Castle (1979–83) (cat. 144).

A number of plaster 'experiments', including *Fruit Shape* (1960) (cat. 126) and *Flame/Flame Shape* (1960–61) (cat. 125), were also exhibited in April 1961 at the Mullard Sculpture Collection, London. The circular objects he exhibited on that occasion suggest Ivor had been looking closely at Paolozzi's recent works in plaster (Fig. 1.22), exhibited in London in 1958, in which intimations of the organic fuse disturbingly with the mechanical.[113]

Another career milestone occurred in July 1961, when Ivor was included in a major exhibition supported by the Welsh Committee of the Arts Council: *Sculpture 1961*.[114] This constituted the largest exhibition of contemporary sculpture to be held in Wales since before the outbreak of the Second World War.[115] Ivor appeared alongside Kenneth Armitage, Ralph Brown, Barbara Hepworth, F. E. McWilliam, Bernard Meadows and Henry Moore. Ivor's ten exhibits were by far stylistically the least challenging of the exhibits, but, as a number of reviewers noted, for this very reason they possessed an appeal to the general visitor, lacking in

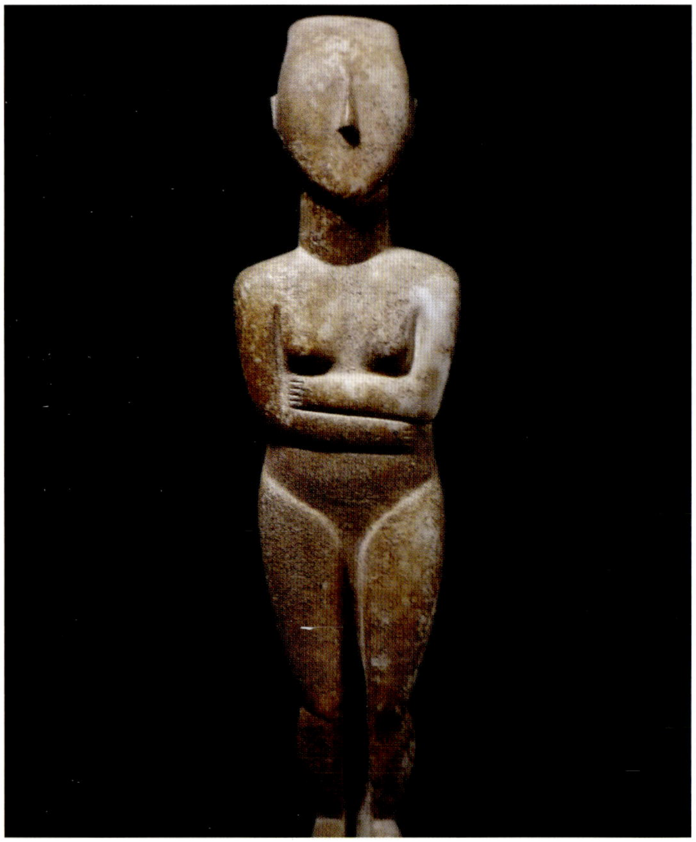

Fig. 1.21 *Cycladic Figurine of a Woman*, c. 2700–2500 BCE, marble, 76.5 cm high, British Museum, London; Image: Courtesy of British Museum Images

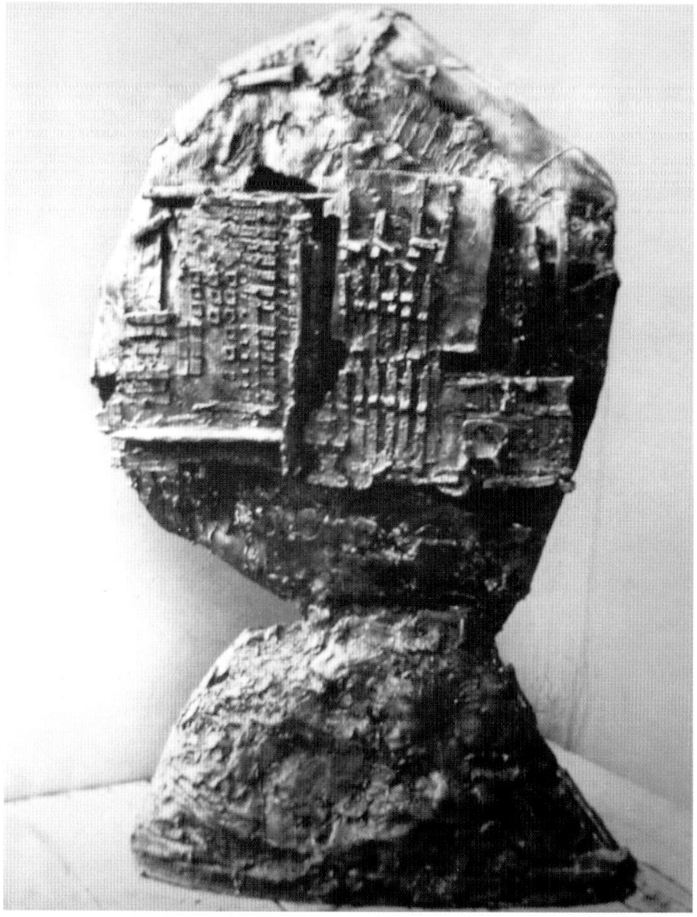

Fig. 1.22 Eduardo Paolozzi, *Krokodeel*, 1956, bronze, 61 cm high, Private Collection; Image: J. Black

the other works on display.[116] Particular favourites proved to be *Reclining Woman Holding a Cat* (cat. 111), *The Scapegoat* (cat. 130) and *Kite Rider* (cat. 123), which one art critic, Maurice Cooke, interpreted as evidence that a 'middle way' had emerged in British sculpture, between the abstraction of Moore and Hepworth on the one hand and the 'wire constructions' of Armitage and McWilliam on the other.[117] Cooke announced that Ivor's inclusion in this exhibition could confidently be taken as proof that he had officially 'arrived'.

Further encouraging news followed when, in the following year, Sir John Rothenstein identified Ivor as 'among the most gifted of the new generation' of British sculptors, alongside Reg Butler, Lynn Chadwick, Elisabeth Frink, Bernard Meadows, Kenneth Armitage and Eduardo Paolozzi.[118] Also in that same year of 1962, he was invited to contribute to an *Open Exhibition of Contemporary Welsh Painting and Sculpture* organised by the Welsh Committee of the Arts Council, while the Arts Council in London commissioned him to make a portrait head of its energetic long-time Secretary-General, Sir William Emrys-Williams (1896–1977) (cat. 28).

Early in 1964, Ivor received promotion at Goldsmiths to become full-time head of the Sculpture Department, and in the spring of the same year he was approached by the family of Augustus John to conceive a life-sized memorial in bronze to that bibulous titan of early twentieth-century painting.[119] He later acknowledged that this commission had helped to establish him as a major sculptor of public memorials, but he could happily have done without the frequently disturbed course of the project, which compelled him abruptly to discard a two-figure concept for the memorial, nearly three years into the project, in favour of a single figure of John.[120] The various phases of this commission will be explored in Chapter 5.

Still, however emotionally draining the John statue commission proved to be, it would seem that the resulting figure, when finally unveiled in October 1967, was judged a success by some particularly influential individuals within the art world, such as Sir Charles Wheeler (1892–1974), President of the Royal Academy, 1956–66, and Sir William Coldstream (1908–87), Principal of the Slade School of Art, 1949–75. Both had been members of the John Memorial Appeal Committee, and in 1969 both successfully nominated Ivor for election as an Associate of the Royal Academy.[121]

This new distinction, plus the high regard felt in many quarters for his figure of *Augustus John* (cat. 133), was soon to place Ivor in contention for what he later admitted was a 'colossal' commission: for a 3.6-metre-high bronze figure of *Sir Winston Churchill* (cat. 135) to stand in Parliament Square. Despite stiff competition from sculptors of the stature of Sir Charles Wheeler, Franta Blesky, F. E. McWilliam and, above all, the Croatian-born Oscar Nemon (1906–85), Ivor was awarded the commission in March 1971.[122] In more ways than one this commission, the details of which will be examined in detail in Chapter 3, proved life changing. Ivor moved from Woodbridge in Suffolk, where he and Monica had been living since 1967, deeper into Suffolk – to Cratfield, near Harlsworth, where Ivor bought a house complete with a large barn, in which he was to work for the best part of two years on the massive figure of Churchill. The commission also made Ivor into a public figure of some renown – especially when the statue was unveiled in November 1973 to generally positive reviews. For example, his old mentor, Sir Charles Wheeler, wrote to *The Times*: 'Mr Roberts-Jones has succeeded in creating a fine statue of a great man. At the time of its inception I thought his task impossible of solution and said so. I must now eat my words. As a character study the sculpture is admirable, its monumentality is very impressive and it is altogether worthy of the historic plot it will occupy for many generations yet to come ... the sculptor by his skill, has handsomely rendered a service to us and to posterity.'[123]

Just a month after the unveiling ceremony, Ivor was elected a full Academician of the Royal Academy,[124] and early in 1975 he was appointed a CBE – largely, he suspected, owing to relief in official circles that his Churchill in Parliament Square 'had not been worse'.[125] To a considerable extent, the figure of Churchill Ivor had created rapidly came to be regarded as a 'classic' interpretation, and led directly to his being commissioned to produce two other figures of the statesman: for Oslo (cat. 136 – unveiled in May 1976) and for New Orleans (cat. 141 – unveiled in November 1977). Both are discussed at greater length in Chapter 4.

Ivor's reactions to the publicity generated by the Churchill in Parliament Square – the 'hooplah', he called it – reveal his ambivalent relationship towards his standing within the art world: he welcomed recognition from his peers, but was profoundly uneasy at the prospect of fame, of becoming a 'public' figure courted by journalists.[126] Perhaps as a reaction to this growing perception of him as the sculptor of 'great men and heroes', from the mid 1970s he turned to projects on a much smaller, more intimate scale – a series of what he referred to as *Little Monuments* (1975–79) (cats. 137–39), inspired by a combination of the 'table top' sculptures of Giacometti, from the early 1930s,[127] and the etched still lifes of Giorgio Morandi.[128] At the same time, he revived the horse-and-rider theme he had started to explore in the early 1960s, initially producing in 1976 a small-scale *Rider* in plaster, which he would later considerably enlarge for installation as *The Lazarus Rider* (cat. 140) in the grounds of Melford Hall, in Suffolk – the home of collector Sir Richard Hyde Parker.

Still, he could not bring himself to retreat entirely from public duties. In 1976 he agreed to sit on the selection committee for a sculpture exhibition in Battersea Park to celebrate the Queen's Silver Jubilee the following year. For the occasion, Ivor produced a slender figure of one of his Goldsmiths students wrapped in a capacious coat, *Vicky in a Long Coat* (cat. 142), the bravura execution of which is worthy of comparison with the gown in which Rodin wrapped his *Balzac* in the 1890s. However, as was noted in reaction to the exhibition, which opened in June 1977, Ivor's contribution rather stood out for appearing to be so traditional and so indebted to the example of Rodin when compared to the majority of the exhibits.[129] As a consolation, perhaps, for his somewhat isolated position, he was later that year awarded a Gold Medal by the Royal British Society of Sculptors. Ivor, however, felt it was only right to acknowledge that what was now being defined as 'sculpture' had changed out of all recognition from when he had been a student at the RA Schools in the late 1930s. That summer he decided it was high time to retire from teaching, as one of his students, perhaps in emulation of Richard Long, wanted to submit a 'hole in the ground' as part of his degree show, while another busily erected a fence 'draped in washing', presumably as a homage to Christo's celebrated *Running Fence* (1977).[130] He also did not think much of some of his younger colleagues who were now in the ascendant in the Faculty of Art at Goldsmiths, such as conceptual artist Michael Craig-Martin (1941–), who had joined the staff of the college three years earlier.[131]

Ivor later stated that he had been happy to 'bow out' when he did, retiring from Goldsmiths as he neared sixty-five, in July 1978. He enjoyed teaching, but had suspected for some time that it consumed a significant amount of his creative energy that should have been devoted to his own work and artistic development.[132]

Before his retirement, he was further cheered by the knowledge that the House of Commons had selected him, from a field of five sculptors – including Franta Belsky and James Butler – to execute a 2.7-metre-high figure of former Labour prime minister Clement Attlee for the Members' Lobby of the House of Commons (cat. 143).[133] The figure was unveiled in November 1979, and gave Ivor the opportunity to meet a politician whose conviction and 'guts' he came increasingly to admire – the recently elected prime minister, Margaret Thatcher.[134] At the same ceremony he was introduced to former prime minister James Callaghan, who on that occasion he did not hold in high regard, deeming him responsible for the strikes and industrial unrest that had plagued Britain in the 1970s: especially during the so-called 'Winter of Discontent' from December 1978 to February 1979.[135] In 1987–88 Callaghan sat to Ivor for a portrait bust (cat. 66) shortly after he had retired from his forty-year service in the House of Commons as MP for Cardiff South, and been raised to the peerage as Lord Callaghan of Cardiff. In close contact with the man, Ivor found Callaghan rather more impressive than he had anticipated.[136]

Meanwhile, as Ivor was about to begin work on the Attlee statue project, the Welsh Arts Council generously offered to hold a retrospective exhibition for him at the Oriel Gallery in Cardiff (July–September 1978). On the whole he was relieved and pleased with the generally positive critical reaction to this exhibition.[137] Moreover, the short exhibition catalogue allowed him to set forth some of his core artistic beliefs, such as his assertion that abstraction and reality had an 'uneasy relationship' in his sculpture: 'All things vividly seen are, as I believe, abstractions, and starting work is the beginning of a move back to reality.'[138]

Furthermore, the exhibition provided a springboard for a number of encouraging developments that would give renewed purpose and impetus to his post-retirement career – he had also been decidedly anxious as to whether he could generate sufficient funds to maintain himself and Monica after giving up teaching.[139] As the Oriel exhibition was coming to a close, the Welsh Arts Council decided to commission a large work from him in bronze to stand outside Harlech Castle.[140] Inspired by a story from the 'tale of Branwen' in the *Mabinogion*, in which 'The old king Bendigeidfran returns from the wars in Ireland bearing the dead body of the young King Gwern – his nephew',[141] Ivor devised an imposing and poignant 'horse and rider', to which he gave the alternate titles of *The Two Kings/Janus Rider* (1979–83) (cat. 144).[142] When the commission was announced in the press, Ivor was flattered to be described as 'one of Wales's most distinguished sculptors', able to produce work on a par with Rodin and with Epstein's *Christ in Majesty* for Llandaff Cathedral (1954–55).[143]

Meanwhile, a new Keeper of Art at the NMW, Cardiff, Dr Peter Cannon-Brookes,[144] commissioned a series of portrait heads from him of past presidents of the museum's Council, such as *The Seventh Marquess of Anglesey* (1984) (cat. 45) and *The Third Earl of Plymouth* (1987) (cat. 65), to be placed in its rather forbidding and slightly creepy Council Chamber.[145] In 1980, prompted by Dr Cannon-Brookes's initiative, two prominent members of the cultural sphere in South Wales – Judge Bruce Griffiths QC (cat. 49) and Sir Alun Talfan Davies (cat. 69) – established the Welsh Portrait Sculpture Trust, in essence dedicated to providing commissions for Ivor to celebrate Welshmen who had achieved distinction in various walks of life, such as former Speaker of the House of Commons, *George Thomas* (1980) (cat. 51) and celebrated opera singer *Sir Geraint Evans* (1983) (cat. 56).[146] As further evidence that he was looked upon with approval by the art establishment in Wales, in 1982 he was appointed a trustee of the Welsh Sculpture Trust (founded in 1981), which opened at Margam, near Port Talbot, the following year. Other trustees included such eminent figures as Henry Moore, Dame Elisabeth Frink, Philip King and the then president of the Royal Academy, Sir Hugh Casson.[147]

Into the 1980s Ivor's health, which had previously been robust, began to falter, while his wife Monica developed a heart condition.[148] He often felt unwell and fought for breath as he prepared an exhibition in the summer of 1983 at Llangefni, on Anglesey, as part of that year's Royal National Eisteddfod – a great honour, as Ivor acknowledged; but it was a pity all his effort was expended for an exhibition that lasted barely a week.[149] However, though on occasion a little sour in his verdict on the Llangefni show, Ivor was actually rather pleased by the praise it attracted – especially for a number of dynamic figures of African animals that he exhibited here for the first time as a group (cats. 90, 93). He had earlier remarked to Sir John Rothenstein: 'I have always been attracted to the great animal sculptures of the past. There is enormous amplitude and force in the small jade creatures of the Far East and Mexico that seemsto make them swell to a great size even as you regard them; a curious working of the sense of scale.'[150]

Isabel Hitchman, the arts officer at the Welsh Arts Council who had first proposed Ivor's exhibition at the Oriel, later recalled that 'the animal sculptures he displayed were ... absolutely delicious. They were small works ... but they had considerable charm in the best sense. Staff said they would walk into the gallery and expect to be leapt at by some cat-like creature on a plinth.'[151] He had long been fascinated by animals he sketched at London Zoo[152] (Fig. 1.23) – and he often found himself diverted by the antics of

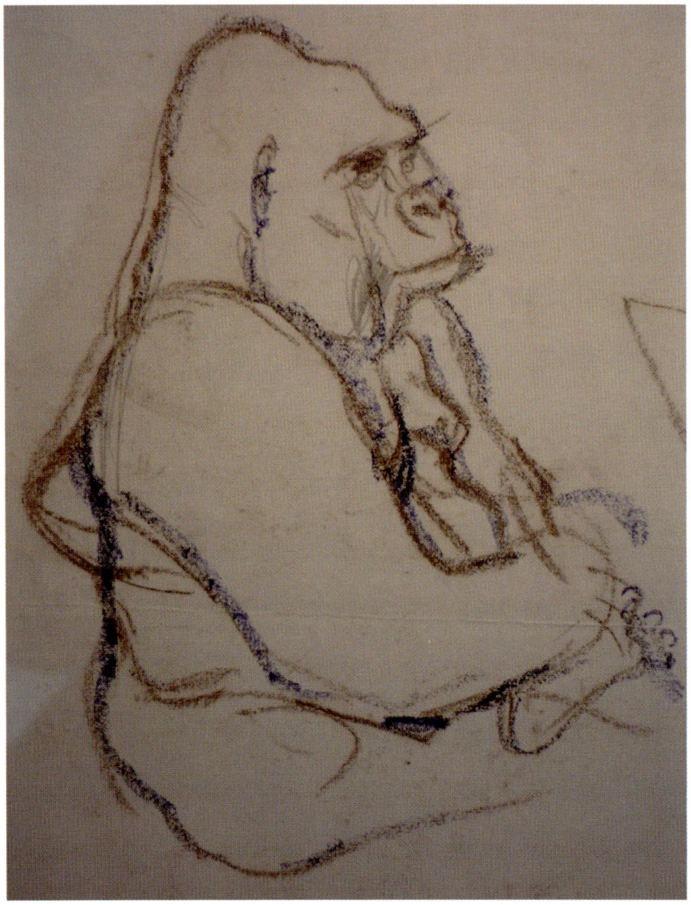

Fig. 1.23 Ivor Roberts-Jones, *Guy the Gorilla at London Zoo*, c. 1977, chalk, pencil and pen and ink on paper, 25 x 21.5 cm, Image: Courtesy of the HMI, Leeds

the birds outside his studio in Suffolk or by the behaviour of his cat 'Duster', when he should have been concentrating on his work or his tax return. Early in 1980 he wrote to an administrator at the National Theatre, as he sought to finalise the details for a commission to make a head of *Lord Chandos* (1979–80) (cat. 48) for the organisation:

> As I look out of the window [at Cratfield] there are bundles of contented sparrow, tits, and even a bullfinch, hanging, immobile thro' stuffing themselves with buds, on our cherry trees. You wouldn't think anything so fat would fly, you can almost hear the air groaning with their weight when they do. They all shack up for the night in the barn roof. They kill each other – and I have to sweep up the bodies in the morning – and those that are left laugh at my cat and me and make my sculptures very dirty. They scream with rage if I work by artificial light – otherwise I am tolerated.[153]

On one occasion the following year he was interrupted in the writing of a letter to Kyffin Williams as: '"Duster" – the cat, doesn't seem to realise that blotting paper is out of date, and has been trying to roll over my letter. She shouldn't be on the table, but with Monica away she takes liberties.'[154]

In the autumn of 1985 he underwent a major operation on his lungs to improve his breathing.[155] The following year he and Monica moved to a smaller property in Shimpling, near Diss on the Suffolk–Norfolk border (Fig. 1.24). Ivor established a studio in a former stable, as he had by no means abandoned hopes of creating large public works. As it transpired, within the space of a few weeks in the spring of 1986 he was approached by Oswestry and Rugby to provide, respectively, a figure with clear local connotations (this became the contentious *Farmer with Ram*, also known as *Borderland Farmer* – cat. 150), unveiled in December 1988,[156] and a life-sized figure of the poet Rupert Brooke in romantically pensive mood (cat. 151), unveiled inSeptember the same year.[157]

Even as he wrestled with these commissions, he won a competition in 1988 from the Burma Star Association to make a 3-metre-high bronze figure of his old commander in Burma, Field Marshal Sir William 'Uncle Bill' Slim (cat. 153), for a prestigious site right in the heart of London, in front of the Ministry of Defence on Whitehall.[158] A group of high-ranking soldiers was so impressed by the figure of Slim, unveiled by the Queen in April 1990, that they commissioned Ivor to produce a figure of *Field Marshal Viscount Alanbrooke* (cat. 154) for site on Whitehall without any prior competition.[159] This commanding figure was unveiled in May 1993 to considerable acclaim; understandably, Ivor was now firmly established in the collective critical mind as the 'last great sculptor of great men'.[160]

Despite his age and growing infirmity, 'ever-present aches and pains' – and the tragic news that his daughter Corinne (Fig. 1.25) had developed terminal leukaemia[161] – Ivor was determined to tackle new challenges, such as the sculptural element for a *National Police Memorial* (cat. 155) he was approached to make early in 1993 by the film director Michael Winner. Two years later, in the summer of 1995, he was approached by the mayor of the Third District of Prague to create a figure of Churchill for the square in the city recently renamed in his honour.[160] Working as hard as ever, he managed to produce a plaster cast of the full-sized model of his *Policeman Mourning a Dead Comrade*

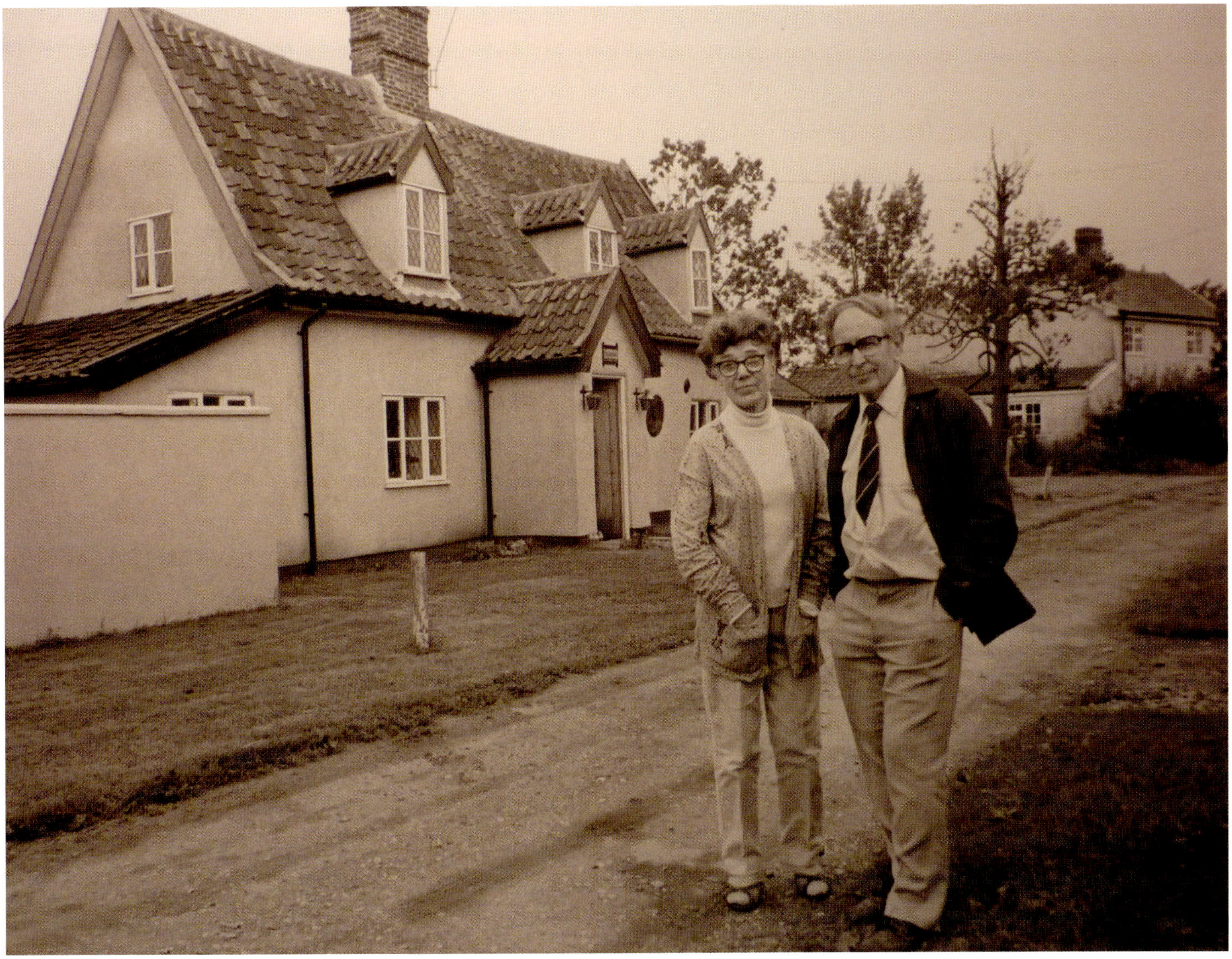

Fig. 1.24 Ivor and Monica Roberts-Jones, Shimpling, Norfolk, c. 1988; Image: Courtesy of the HMI, Leeds

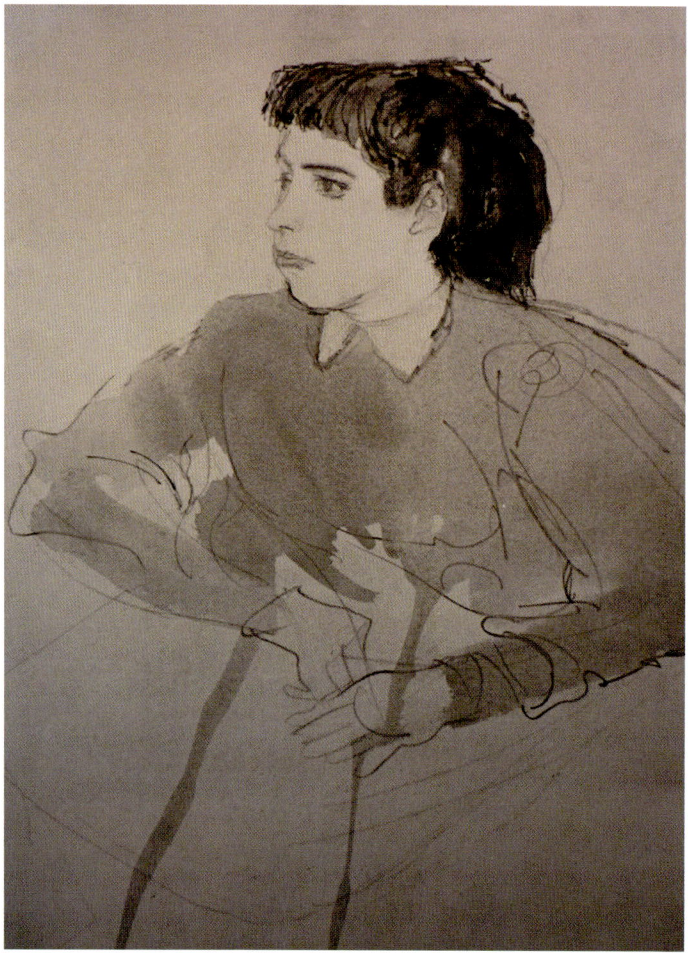

Fig. 1.25 Ivor Roberts-Jones, *Corinne Roberts-Jones*, 1960, watercolour and pencil on paper, 37.7 x 27.5 cm, Private Collection; Image: J. Black

(Fig. 1.26), and a new monumental head and shoulders of Churchill (cat. 156b) he hoped would one day be erected in Prague. The new head was despatched to his preferred foundry, the Meridian Foundry – which he had used since casting the figure of Churchill for Parliament Square – just a fortnight before he died in his sleep, aged eighty-three, in December 1996.[163]

Friends and former students alike were convinced of his significance. Kyffin Williams wrote to Monica of how much he had admired and envied Ivor's

> total commitment to his art, a commitment that made him a great sculptor and the finest portrait sculptor of his generation. It was always good to be with him as his opinions were so challenging and made me think ... Maybe he was the last of his kind for, as you know, sculpture, is something else now and no relation to the tradition that meant so much to Ivor.[164]

Former Goldsmiths student Brian Morley wrote to the *Guardian* describing 'Bobby Jones' as 'small, voluble and energetic with a strong and vivid personality. His opinions on a wide range of subjects were ... lively, occasionally malicious and trenchantly expressed ... To watch him on a portrait head, or a drawing, was a privilege and gave one an understanding that the better teachers can only show you how they see things themselves.'[165]

The general critical reaction was positive, though more nuanced. Ivor was characterised as a gifted portrait sculptor in an age when that type of sculpture was not fashionable, and as a distinguished practitioner of a form of monumental public sculpture that now seemed decidedly old fashioned, if not redundant – especially in the wake of the onward march of conceptual installations, and the sort of objects created by the so-called 'Brit Art' tendency associated with Damien Hirst (whose pieces, by all accounts, Ivor loathed).[167]

To some extent he was, perhaps justly, perceived as a sculptor out of step with the 1990s – a talented, true and faithful heir to the tradition of Rodin and Epstein;[168] a man who created many distinguished monumental public works as well as more intimate and expressively characterful portrait heads that continue to attract the admiration of an engaged public long after the claims of more deliberately contentious and provocatively experimental work have predictably dissipated.

Fig. 1.26 Full-sized plaster model of *Policeman Mourning a Dead Comrade* seen in Ivor's studio-barn, Shimpling, Feburary 1997 Image: Courtesy of the HMI, Leeds

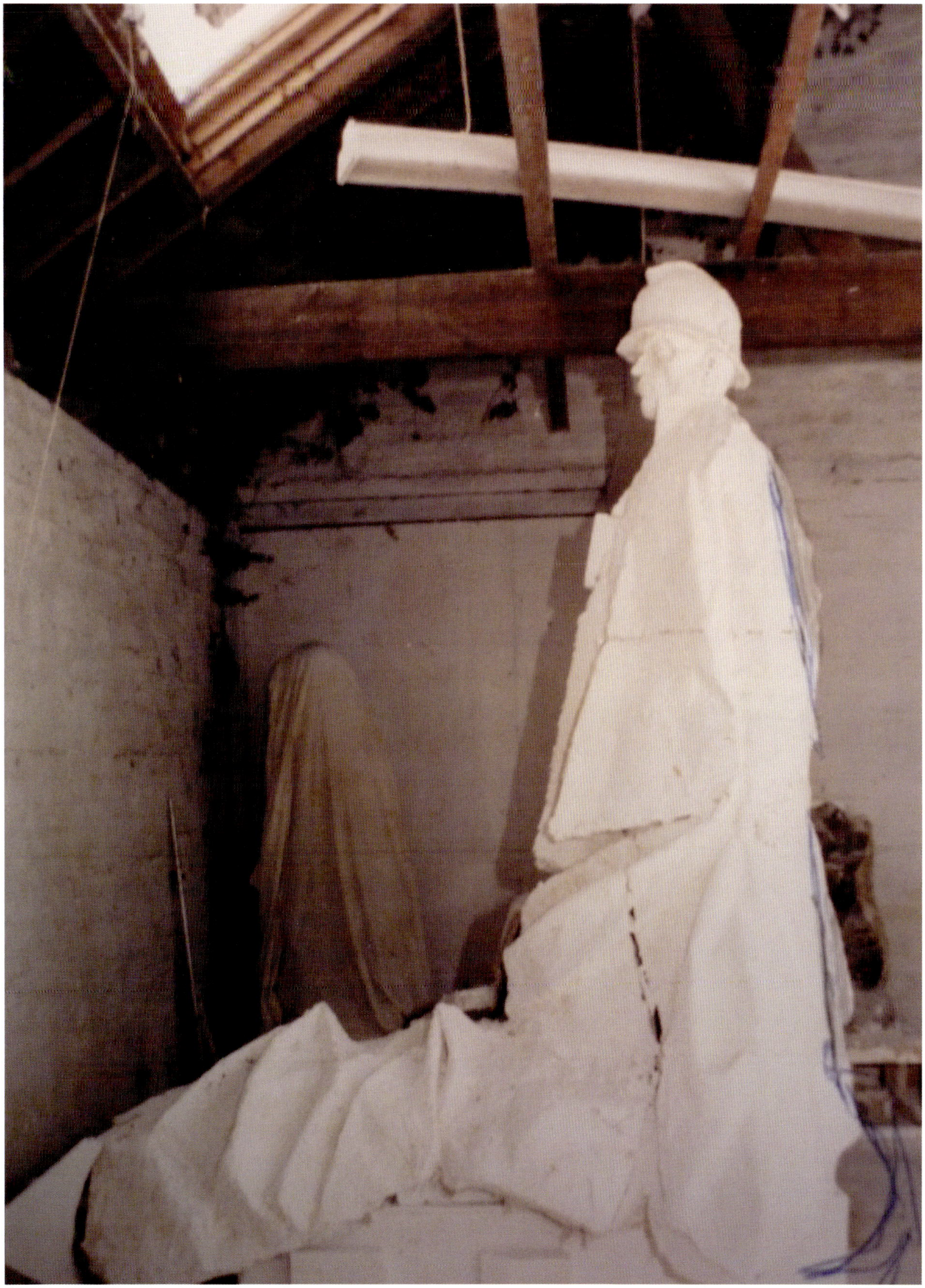

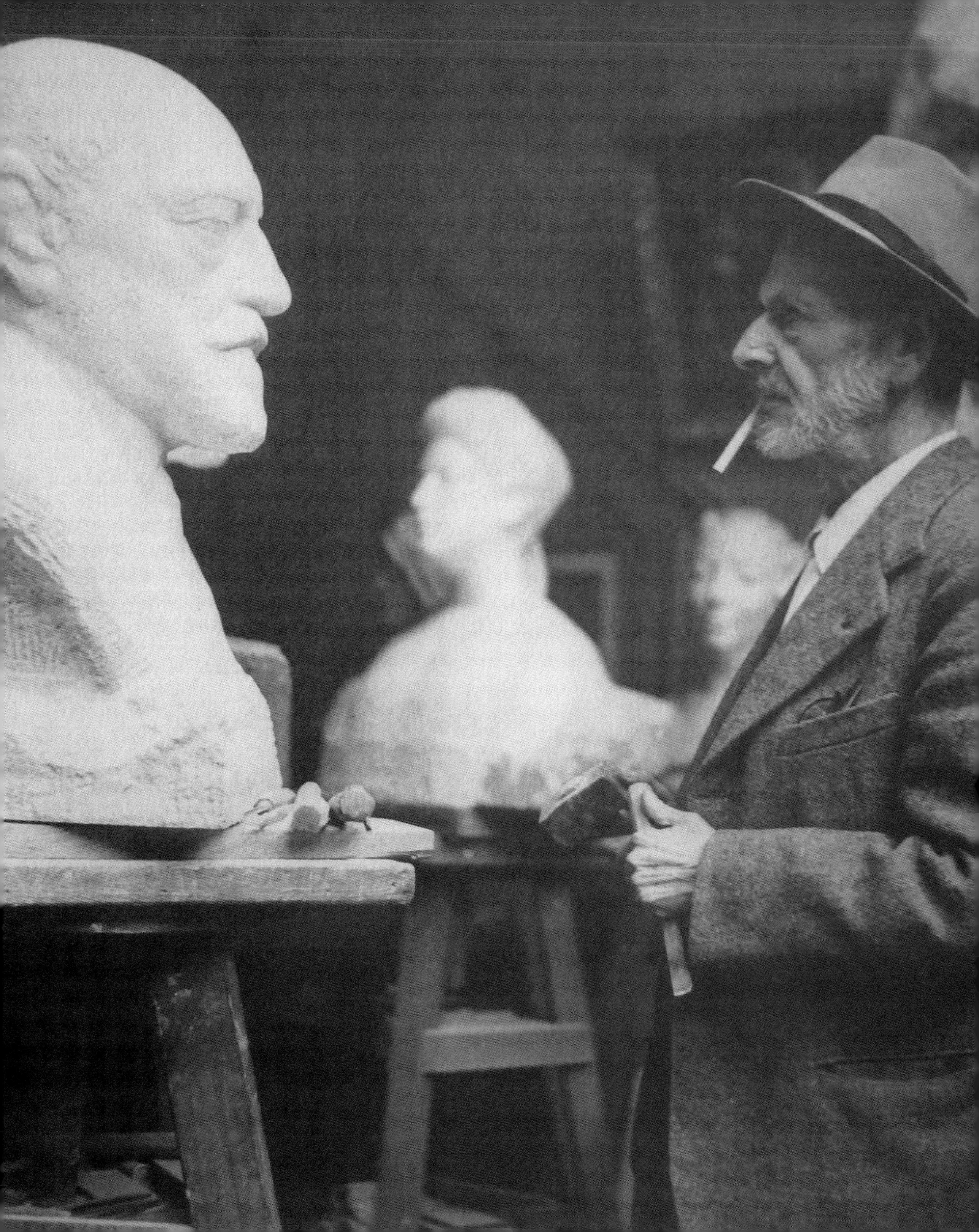

THE DOUBLE EDGE

Ivor Roberts-Jones and the Portrait Head

Jonathan Black

'He liked above all to capture subtleties and ambiguities of character. The many examples of his work in British public collections show how well he succeeded. "A face is a bicycle someone rides", he once said; in his favourite sitters, such as ... *Paul Claudel* and *Somerset Maugham*, that bicycle journey could be traced in vivid detail.'

The Times, December 1996[1]

'Most of [Ivor's] commissioned portraits are dignified likenesses ... *Augustus John*; *Paul Claudel*; *Clive Gardiner*; *Kyffin Williams* and *Sam Rabin* possess a quality of serene, often dreaming, intimacy ...'

Sir John Rothenstein, 1978[2]

'Ivor Roberts-Jones was a very good portraitist ... *Sir William Crawshay* [1973] [cat. 41] ... was an amazingly good likeness but wasn't in any way photographic, or realistic in detail. Ivor had the most amazing ability to detect a persona beneath the skull and the sculpture would be unmistakably the subject – you would recognise him, or her, instantly – but there was something more than that as well. Something about the character came through quite clearly.'

Isabel Hitchman, 2012[3]

Fig. 2.1 Charles Despiau in his studio, Paris, 1920s; Image: Courtesy of the Musée Despiau-Wlérick, Mont-de-Marsan, France

Late in life, Ivor insisted the best portrait sculpture possessed what he referred to as a 'double-edge' – a delicate and hard-to-maintain balance between the abstract and the real, the idealised and the caricatured, with a hint of inner tensions existing alongside serenity.[4] It is not coincidence that the majority of the portraitists he admired were known for the sometimes bitingly caricatural and unsparing edge to their work: Rembrandt,[5] William Hogarth,[6] Goya,[7] Daumier,[8] James Gillray[9] and Egon Schiele.[10] He thought that, as long as there was a human race, portrait heads would be in demand, and he found it extremely puzzling that this type of sculpture was held in such contempt by the wider art world as he grew older.[11] As he stated in 1978, portraiture remained contemporary and yet possessed a timeless quality, stretching back to Ancient Egypt:

> Portraits have always interested me. I think the portrait in sculpture is both complex and exciting. Likeness is only one thing, sculpture is another. The making of an image in the sense of the great dynastic figures of Egypt, or the Kings and Queens of Chartres, is not that far away ... witness the quiet power of the heads of Despiau ... and yet the sometimes haunting quirks of the life cast and the wax-work lie just around the corner.

He had long been attracted to depicting blind people: 'They appeared to be ... drawing the immediate space around them into themselves, as though breathing it in through their white sticks as they tapped out their private geography.' Heads which attracted him had 'this quality, a sort of withdrawal, seeming to attract the space around it towards its centre. Far Eastern sculpture often has this feeling about it.'[12]

He had first discovered Despiau (Figs 2.1, 2.2) when an art student at Goldsmiths College, and later at the RA Schools; but he had also been attracted in his student days by the portraiture of Piero della Francesca, Raphael, Dürer, Rembrandt and Goya that he saw in the National Gallery in London.[13] He was also aware of more contemporary work by Edward Bawden, one of his tutors at Goldsmiths, and Bawden's friend, Edward Ardizzone. Then there was the 'full-blooded melodrama' of an older artist associated with the First World War, Eric Kennington (1888–1960), and his vivid pastel portraits of the Arabs (Fig. 2.3) who had fought under T. E. Lawrence in the desert against the Turks.[14] Ivor was also aware of some of the established sculptors of the 1930s who crossed his path while he was studying at the RA Schools between 1935 and 1939 – so-called 'progressive traditionalists' such as William Reid Dick, Charles Wheeler, Gilbert Ledward and Gilbert Bayes. There are just hints of their presence in the images that have survived of the portrait sculpture he produced during the late 1930s (cat. 1). These presumably were all destroyed when his studio and sculpture store on the King's Road were devastated by a bomb during the London Blitz of 1940–41. In two plaster busts (cats 3 and 4), for which he was probably awarded a prize in 1935–36, one can detect early evidence for his commitment to verisimilitude, however unconventionally 'ugly' – for

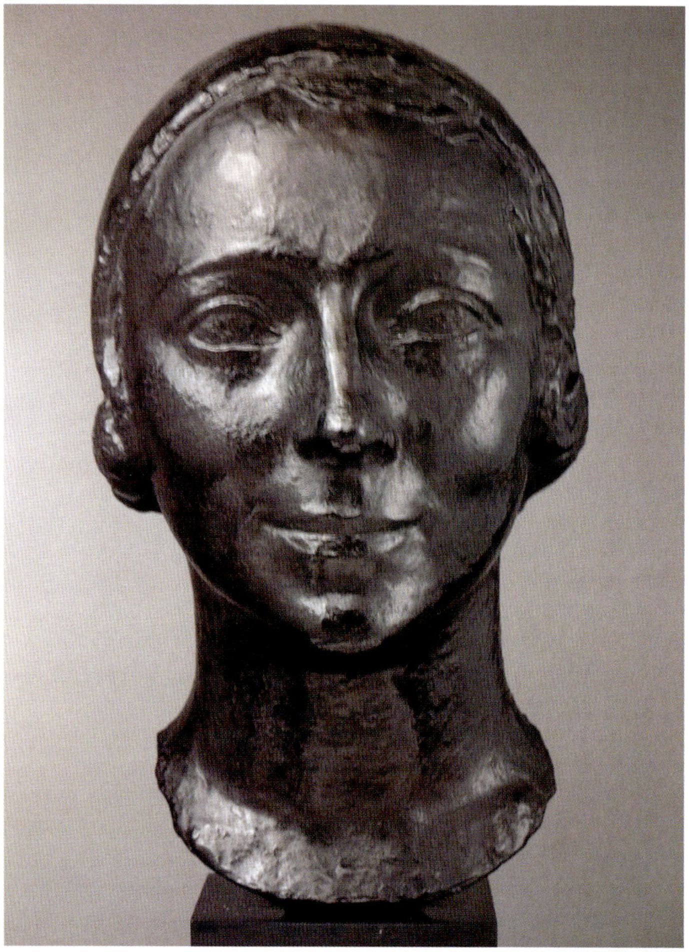

Fig. 2.2 Charles Despiau, *Madame Pomaret*, 1930, 33.5 cm high, Musée Despiau-Wlérick, Mont-de-Marsan, France; Image: Courtesy of the Musée Despiau-Wlérick, Mont-de-Marsan, France

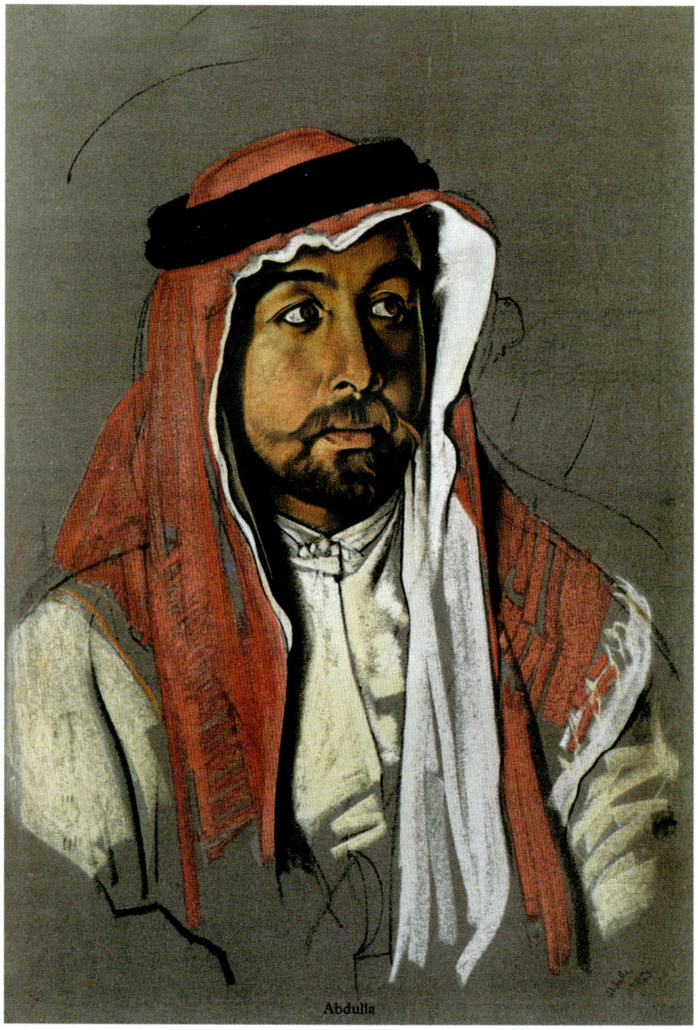

Fig. 2.3 Eric Kennington, *Sherif Abdullah ibn Hussein*, 1921, pastel on paper, 55.9 x 76.2 cm, Harry Ransom Center for the Humanities, University of Texas at Austin; Image: Courtesy of the family of the artist

example, the prominent protuberance on the forehead of one of the self-possessed sitters (cat. 4), while the forehead of the other is heavily furrowed with the lines of a hard, even punishing, life. He is already attracted by those physiognomical bumps and irregularities that he was later to write are so evident in the portraiture of Rodin (Fig. 2.4) – an artist whose notable portraiture he had relatively little to say about until later in life, though he readily acknowledged the power of his public memorials. As Ivor put it in 1983,

> Rodin ... in some of his portraits [left] little pieces of clay ... hanging in the air, proud of the surface, forming little scattered profiles that were never worked in to their sculptural context ... in fact, frequently contradicting the surfaces that slide beneath them ... his sculptures frequently have a sense of perpetually arriving, of their own free will. Memory and immediate impulse appear to have become one thing.

This could be said equally of many of Ivor's best portrait heads: they are possessed with a sense of 'arrival', with the illusion of a vivid immediacy, as if the artist has only just got up from modelling his sitter's head.[15]

He was later to admit that he had also been drawn to the more 'Expressionist' portraiture of turn-of-the-century Viennese artists Egon Schiele (Fig. 2.5) and Oskar Kokoschka.[16] The latter had in fact been friendly with Ivor's close post-war friend Kyffin Williams – himself a talented portraitist – in London in the late 1940s.[17] In the early 1980s Ivor told Keeper of Art at the NMW, Cardiff, Peter Cannon-Brookes, that, on returning to London from the war, his understanding of sculpted portraiture had very much been shaped by admiration for Charles Despiau and Jacob Epstein, and also the American artist Leonard Baskin (1922–2000), who enjoyed a brief vogue in the UK during the 1950s. In Despiau he was attracted by 'the sculptural calm which his finest heads possess'. He made Ivor aware that 'it was important to consider the head as a shape, like an apple, not as a basket of anatomical structures'. As for Epstein, whose reputation was rather in eclipse during the 1940s but experienced a distinct revival during the following decade: 'the structure is more important ... the irregularities and eccentricities of the structure are often greatly exaggerated but as in Despiau their relative assessment adds up to an overall sculptural scheme of great daring.'[18]

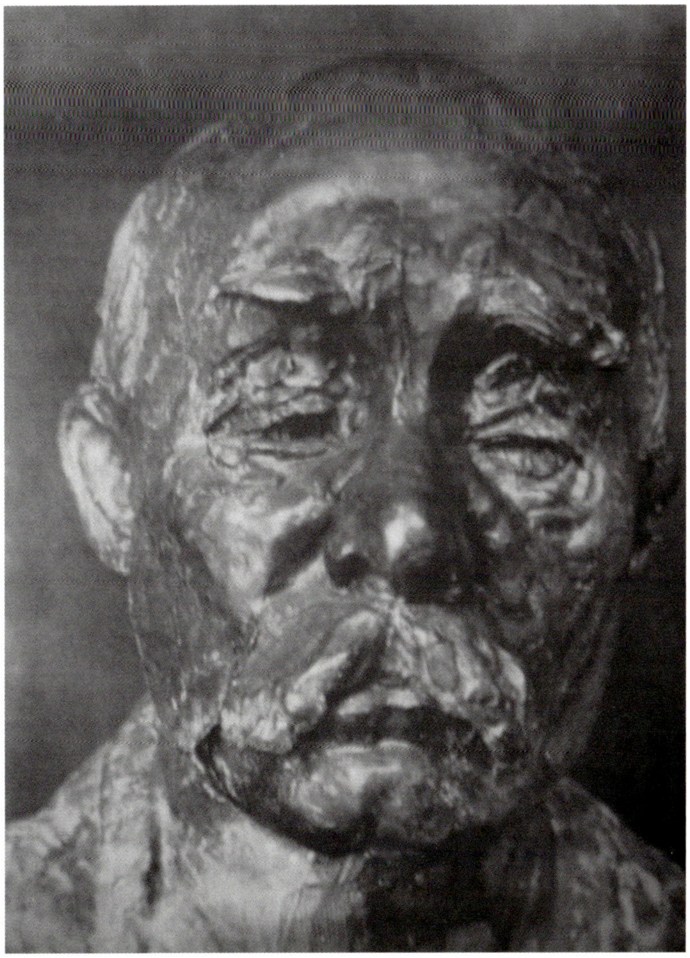

Fig. 2.4 Auguste Rodin, *Georges Clemenceau*, 1911–13, bronze, 45 cm high, Musée Rodin, Paris; Image: Courtesy of the Musée Rodin, Paris

He admitted he had been very taken with Baskin (Fig. 2.6) in the 1950s, but his perception of the man was now more nuanced. In the early 1980s he regarded Baskin's work as 'very uneven but his great overall quality seems to be his humanity and his special awareness of sculptural mass which adds up to a weighty and sombre personal statement'.[19] When it came to portraiture, Ivor was not in the business of character assassination: 'protest is too often shallow and hysterical – shying away from sorrow into rhetoric'.[20] The humanity of the subject must not be overwhelmed. Humanism was as important to Ivor in 1983 as it had been when he mentioned it in 1956 to architect Raymond Erith as a characteristic of his sculpture and general outlook in a usually harsh and hostile world.[21] In the 1950s he was greatly attracted by the approach to Humanism advocated by so-called Existentialist thinkers such as Sartre and Camus – especially the latter, with whom

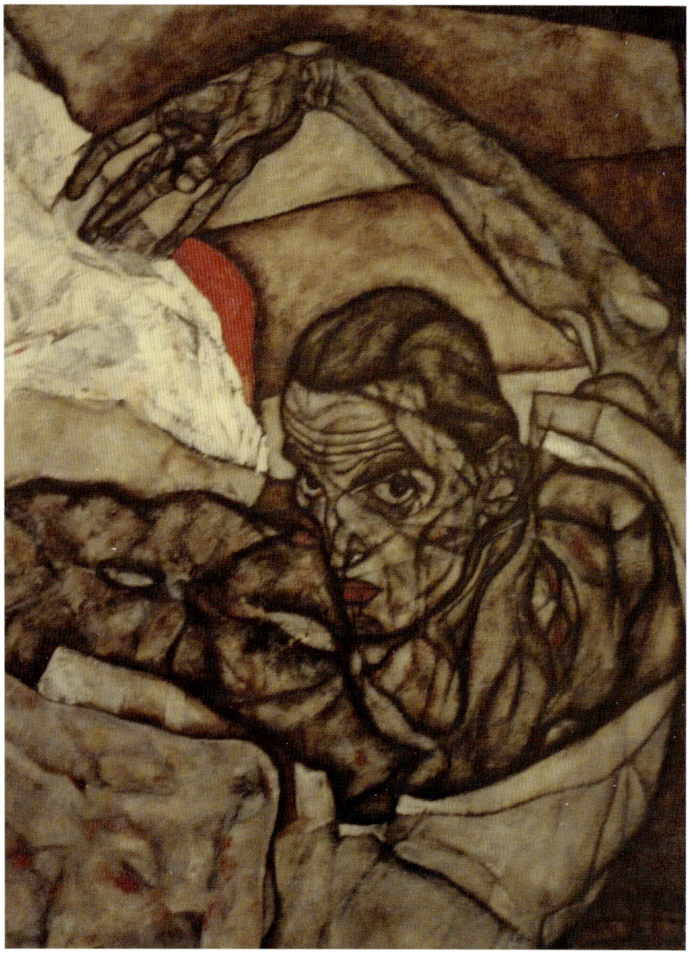

Fig. 2.5 Egon Schiele, detail from *Two Lovers*, 1914, oil on canvas, 44 x 30 cm, Private Collection, New York; Image: J. Black

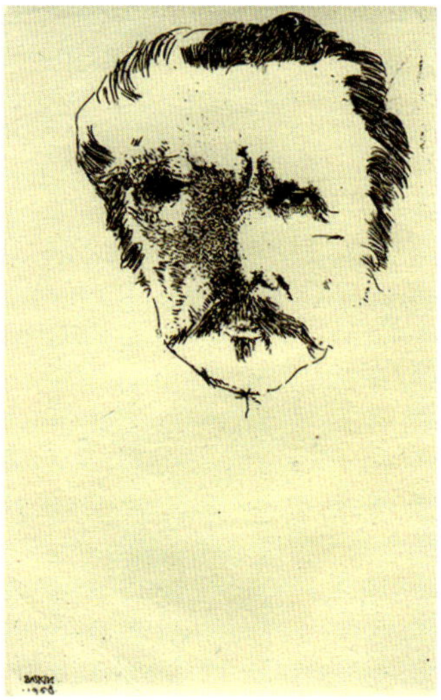

Fig. 2.6 Leonard Baskin, *Eugène Carrière*, 1958, wood engraving, 14 x 11 cm, Private Collection; Image: J. Black

Ivor rather identified as they had been born in the same month of the same year, November 1913.[22]

His sculpted portraiture that survives from the late 1940s suggests he was aware of Frank Dobson's work (Fig. 2.7); between the wars his sculpture was held in high regard, as he was perceived as the 'English Maillol'– Maillol having been widely described as the 'greatest European sculptor' of his day. After the Second World War his reputation began to slip, but his presence can be detected in one of Ivor's earliest known post-1945 portrait heads, *Elizabeth* (1946) (cat. 5), in which the treatment of the eyes and physiognomy also owes a considerable amount to the examples of Ancient Sumerian and Hittite sculpture in the British Museum, which Henry Moore singled out for commendation during the 1930s.[23]

Ivor later mentioned that he had experienced some form of personal crisis – a lack of confidence as to which direction his art should take – in the late 1940s: whether to remain true to his pre-war realism or plunge further into abstraction. A partial answer was supplied by a conversation with Henry Moore, but Ivor also stated how a continued commitment to portraiture had supplied him with some much-needed reassurance and purpose. He recalled that he had produced a number of portrait heads of friends, or people who simply lived near him in Notting Hill or Holland Park, who he encountered during his daily routine. These included portraits of his charlady, *Louise Griffiths* (cat. 9), a friend who was a cellist, *William Pleeth* (cat. 10), and later a woman who was a refugee from Eastern Europe who ran a local junk and curio shop. He later exhibited her head in 1954, entitled *Mother of Judas* (cat. 13) – three years later he was to exhibit the impressive full-sized *Walking Judas* (cat. 117). During this somewhat uncertain time for Ivor, joining the Society of Portrait Sculptors helped to give him confidence and provide a supportive environment among talented fellow portraitists including Dobson, Charles Wheeler (the Society's first president), Jacob Epstein, Franta Belsky (1921–2000), Gilbert Ledward (1888–1960), Lawrence Bradshaw (1899–1978), Wili Soukop (1907–1999), Arthur Fleischmann (1896–1990), Eric Schilsky (1898–1974) Daphne Hardy Henrion (1917–2003) – an old friend from their days together as students at the RA Schools in the 1930s, Josephina de Vasconcellos (1904–2005) and Fiore de Henriquez (1921–2004) – who later in the decade would provide Ivor with a useful introduction to Augustus John.

Some members, such as Henriquez and Wheeler, would be very helpful to Ivor's career in the future; Wheeler, for example, consistently provided him with backing during the many twists and turns of the Augustus John memorial statue project (1964–67) (cat. 133), and smoothed his election to the Royal Academy as an associate member ARA in 1969. Others, such as Belsky and Soukop, would emerge as rivals, often entering competitions for the same projects.[24]

Ivor was to produce only a few portraits during the 1950s – *Clive Gardiner* (cat. 11), *Kyffin Williams* (cat. 20), *Paul Claudel* (cat. 17) and *Old Man/Sam Rabin* (cat. 21) – but they proved very effective in bringing him recognition from the art establishment of the day and attracting the attention and support of some influential figures within that world, such as Sir John Rothenstein (Fig. 2.8) and Sir Kenneth Clark. Rothenstein had seen the plaster cast of *Gardiner*, and was so impressed he asked Ivor whether he too could sit to him. Sir John thought the head possessed an 'Etruscan gravity' and was equal in 'power and seriousness' to recent portraiture by the Italian master Marini, such as heads of *Henry Moore* (1962; Fig. 2.9) and *Igor Stravinsky* (1950; Fig. 2.10).[25]

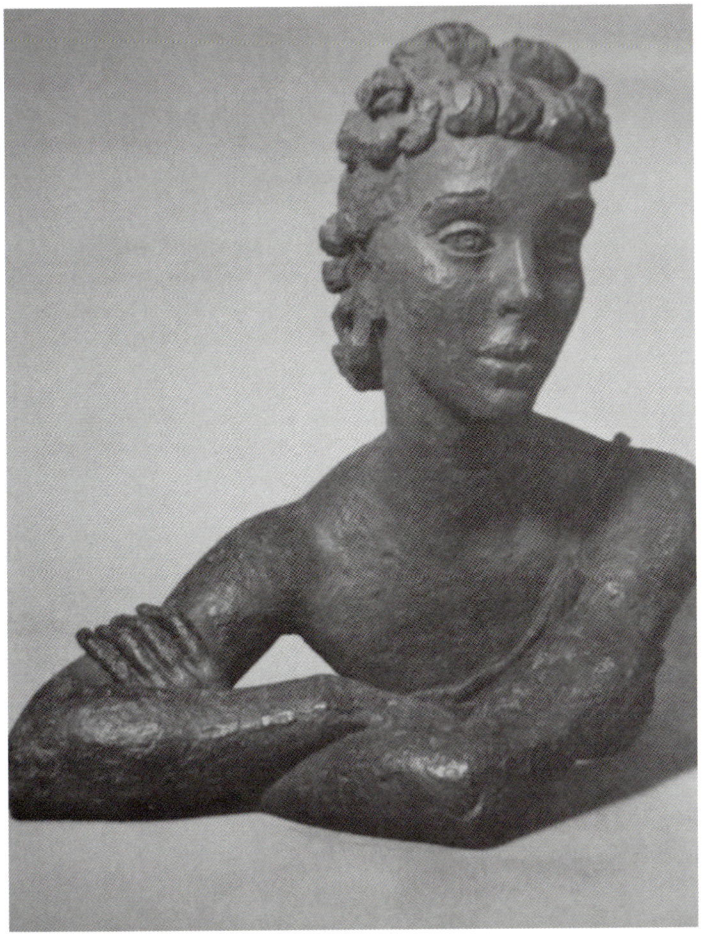

Fig. 2.7 Frank Dobson, *Margaret Rawlings*, 1937, bronze, 57.1 cm high, Tate Britain; Image: Courtesy of Tate Images

Rothenstein was quite taken with the resulting plaster Ivor produced (cat. 16), though he thought it just teetered over the edge into affectionate caricature; he much preferred a portrait of him made later in the decade by Oscar Nemon, which he paid to have cast in bronze. Rothenstein introduced Ivor to Sir Kenneth Clark, who then recommended him to his friend the collector *Elizabeth Watt* (Fig. 2.11; cat. 14). She rather admired Ivor's interpretation of the sometimes spiky and combative Rothenstein, and commissioned a head from the artist. As director of the Tate Gallery, Rothenstein in the late 1950s brought Ivor's heads of *Gardiner* and the French poet and Catholic apologist *Paul Claudel* (cat. 17) to the attention of the Gallery's trustees, and also of the Arts Council. The former purchased a cast of *Claudel* in 1960, and the latter a cast of *Gardiner*. Meanwhile, earlier in 1960, Ivor's close friend, the painter Kyffin Williams – recently appointed to the Art Committee of the NMW, Cardiff – suggested the Museum's art purchasing sub-committee, several of whose members he knew well (and who would later sit to Ivor for portraits) buy Ivor's recently cast portrait of Williams – eyes partially closed, the epitome of the painter as fastidious dandy, communing with an inner voice and oblivious to the distractions of the outside world.

Williams later acknowledged the head was something of a caricature ('He's made me look a grand man ... '), but acknowledged Ivor had succeeded in 'piercing to the heart of who I was then ... at the time I sat to him', as a person who was not at all in tune with the growing popularity of 'rock and roll', which had burst into British consciousness in the mid 1950s,[26] nor at all an 'angry young man',[27] but more interested in British artists working before the outbreak of the First World War[28] (Fig. 2.12). Williams had made his suggestion in November 1959, and by March 1960 the sub-committee had recommended that Ivor's head of the painter be purchased for the museum. At the time Williams indicated to the museum's Keeper of Art, Robert 'Rollo' Charles (1916–1977), that this decision had largely saved Ivor's career. He was so disillusioned with the art world of the day that he was considering giving up sculpture

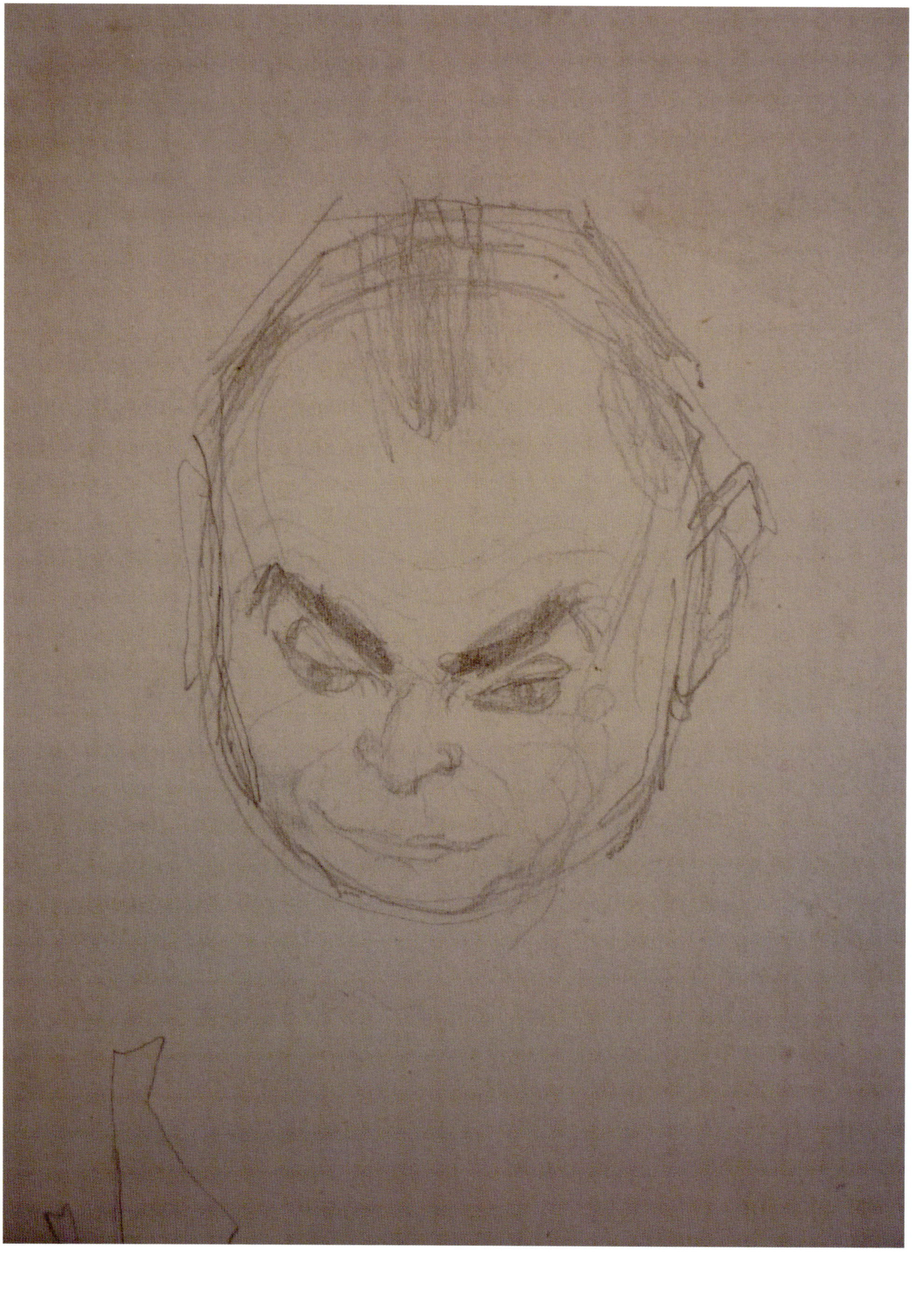

Fig. 2.8 Ivor Roberts-Jones, *Sir John Rothenstein*, c. 1955, pencil on paper, 8 x 5.5 cm, Image: Courtesy of the HMI, Leeds

altogether and trying to establish himself as a scriptwriter for films and television.[29] A letter from Ivor to Williams from the spring of 1960 indicates how much attention he devoted to selecting the most suitable patina for his head of the painter. He had specially arranged for Michael Gaskin at the Art Bronze Foundry – the firm he invariably used from the mid 1950s until around 1972, and initially wanted to employ for the commission of the Churchill statue in Parliament Square – to send the bronze of Williams 'to me ... so I should have a chance to get the patina right – and I will also do my best about the base'.[30]

During his career Ivor would often portray his sitters with their eyes closed, or partially closed. It was an effect which greatly appealed to Williams, though it troubled other sitters. For some years before he sat to Ivor, Williams had been painting portraits of the members of a home for the blind in Cholmeley Park, near to where the painter lived in Highgate, north London.[31] Ivor found these portraits fascinating, and spoke of how he had for many years been intrigued by the whole matter of blindness and how best to depict a sightless person convincingly. Some of the poems he wrote while in Burma, fighting the Japanese as a captain in the Royal Artillery (c. 1944–45), touch on the temporary blindness induced in British soldiers by certain tropical diseases, or by the flash of artillery pieces being fired, or by the dazzlingly white burst of a phosphorous grenade or shell exploding nearby.[32] At least two poems he wrote in the early spring of 1945, as British and Imperial forces closed in on the Burmese city of Mandalay, explicitly refer to blindness in their titles. But only their titles have survived – the poems themselves appear to have been lost.[33]

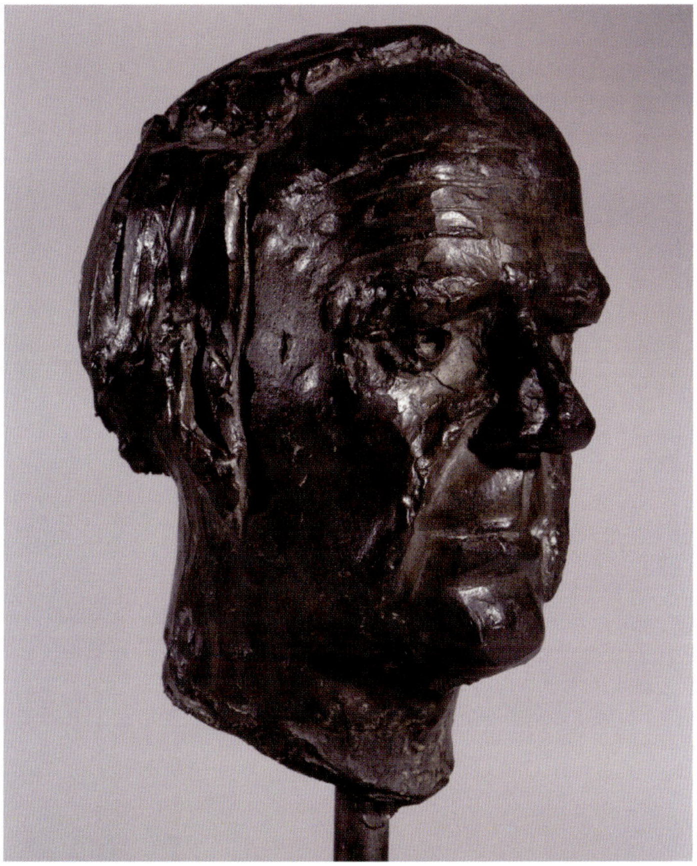

Fig. 2.9 Marino Marini, *Henry Moore*, 1962, bronze, 31.1 cm high, National Portrait Gallery, London; Image: Courtesy of the National Portrait Gallery, London

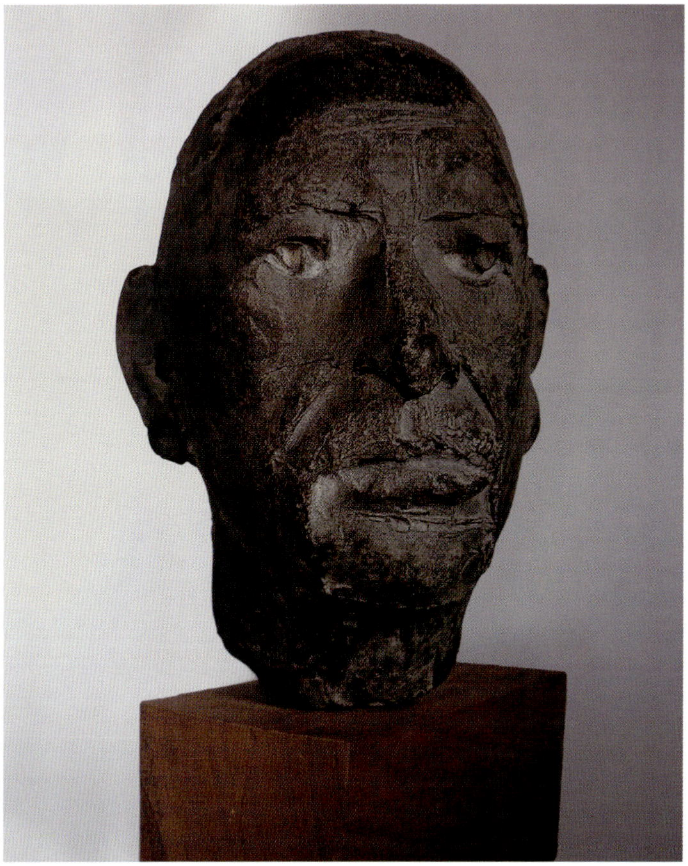

Fig. 2.10 Marino Marini, *Igor Stravinsky*, 1950, bronze, 23.4 cm high, Marino Marini Foundation, Pistoia; Image: Courtesy of the Marino Marini Foundation, Pistoia

Years later Ivor also mentioned how impressed he had been by a photograph of the Greek poet Demetrios Capetanakis (1912–1944) (Fig. 1.17), reproduced in the frontispiece of a memoir about him published in 1947 by publisher John Lehmann.[34] Capetanakis touches on blindness and sight in a few of the dozen or so poems he ever wrote in English. In 'The Return', for example, Capetanakis refers to 'The traveller with empty eyes',[35] while in 'Friendship's Tree' the poet writes of being 'blind and free' and how too much knowledge shared between two friends can actually kill their friendship.[36] Elsewhere in the 1947 memoir, the writer William Plomer touched on how the poet was fascinated by London 'pea-souper' fogs; walking back to Capetanakis's flat,

> It was often a case of the blind leading the blind and even if we had a torch, we should have seen little. [Capetanakis noted how] on certain nervous systems a thick London fog acts like a kind of drug: the absence of perspective, the enfeebled sense of locality and direction, the familiar suddenly turning into the unknown, the muffled or suddenly magnified sounds and lights, occasional voices clearly defined in the absence of traffic – these things help to produce an effect of excited hallucination.[37]

Drawing upon the photograph of the poet, taken around 1942, Ivor imagined him with his eyes closed, and this image served as the model for his large *Blind Faced Figure/Blind Man* (cat. 121), sculpted about 1956. Thereafter, well into the 1980s, Ivor produced a succession of haunting, poignant, usually small, plaster *Blind Heads* (cats 75, 76) – sometimes to be exhibited singly, sometimes in groups – in his top-floor studio at 31 St James's Gardens. By the late 1950s he had produced such heads as gifts to those who had commissioned portraits from him and/or helped his career to progress in some way. He would give small casts of these heads to Rothenstein (cat. 33), Williams (cat. 25), Sir Kenneth Clark, Elizabeth Watt (cat. 24) and the architect Raymond Erith – who in 1956 helped Ivor secure his first public commission, a figure of a *St Francis* (cat. 119a) – who went partially blind after receiving the stigmata towards the end of his life[38] – and also a *Madonna and Child* (cat. 119c) for an Anglican church in west Essex. In the mid 1970s, Ivor returned again to the image of Capetanakis he had formulated in the 1950s, and the Greek poet provided the model for the head of Ivor's enigmatic *Lazarus Rider* (cat. 140), who confidently leaps into space

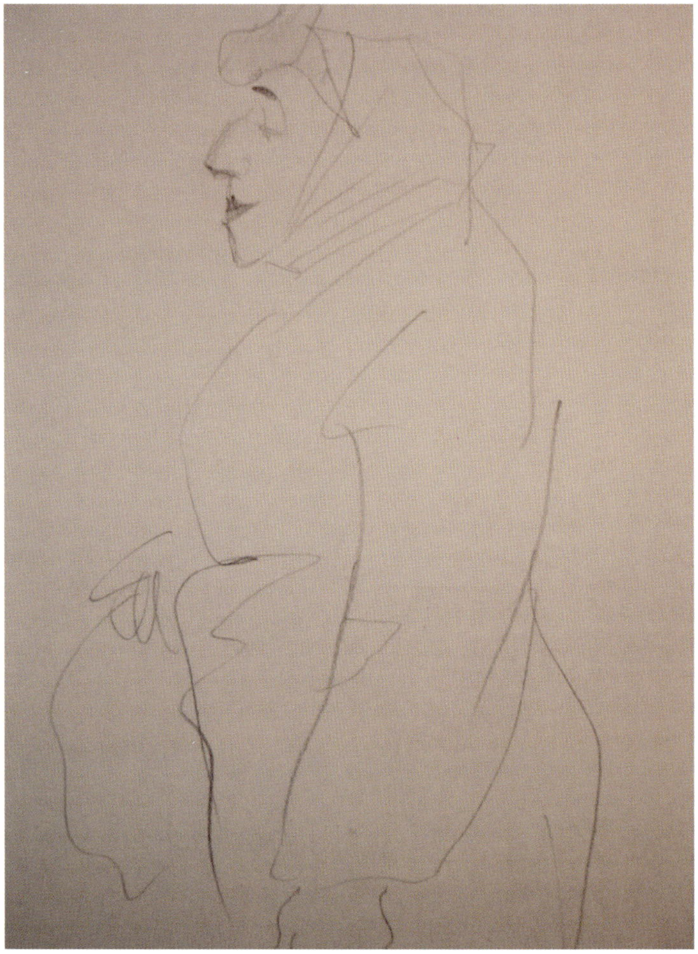

Fig. 2.11 Ivor Roberts-Jones, *Miss Watt*, c. 1957, chalk and pencil on paper, 23 x 17.5 cm, Image: Courtesy of the HMI, Leeds

on horseback with his eyes closed, which he was to work on from 1976 to the early 1980s.[39] In 1978 he told Sir John Rothenstein that he was once more preoccupied with the 1942 photograph of Capetanakis:

> The intense inwardness of his head ... the archaic smile with the lines and muscles around the mouth driving upwards at the corner into the skull, has remained with me up to the present day and led to a series of studies of blind men. The idea of a sculpture drawing force into itself from the surrounding space – looking into itself as it were – like a blind man, has always deeply attracted me.[40]

As it transpired, the NMW's decision occurred as the trustees of the Tate had decided to purchase Ivor's *Claudel*, praised for being a convincing portrayal of a 'voluptuous aesthetic' and a 'cynic who yet wished to have total faith' in the religion which he so passionately promoted to an increasingly heedless and secular world. The purchase of *Claudel* appears to have prompted the Arts Council to buy a cast of *Gardiner* for its collection – and brought Ivor to the attention of what was then termed the 'Welsh Sub-Committee of the Arts Council' (this would soon buy Ivor's robust portrait of his colleague at Goldsmiths, *Sam Rabin*, and commission him to make one of *Sir William Emrys Williams* [cat. 28], shortly to retire as the Council's long-time secretary-general).

The publication of the Tate's purchase of the work and the reproduction of the head in *The Times*[41] also led newspaper tycoon Lord Beaverbrook[42] to ask Ivor to produce a head of the eminent writer *W. Somerset Maugham* (1874–1965),[43] whose memoirs Beaverbrook was about to published with great splash in the pages of the *Sunday Express*.[44] Maugham was also Beaverbrook's neighbour on the Côte D'Azur.[45] The newspaper man had himself already sat to Epstein, and not much enjoyed the experience or the end result; but he felt that Ivor would offer an image of Maugham that would be 'modern yet comprehensible', and that he would be able to exhibit with confidence in the *Daily Express* offices on Fleet Street.[46]

The Maugham head (Fig. 2.13; cat. 27) was Ivor's first really prestigious public portrait commission, but also a rather daunting one, as Maugham had already been memorably depicted by Graham Sutherland (an artist whose landscapes of Pembrokeshire Ivor greatly admired),[47] and in the late 1940s had sat to Jacob Epstein. Maugham was a famously private and fastidious person who rather resented having to sit to Ivor to please Lord Beaverbrook. The writer was also old and not in the best of health. During Ivor's visit to Maugham's villa on Cap Ferrat, the Villa Mauresque, the writer would complain in the artist's hearing to his partner Alan Searle that he had lived for too long, that too many of his friends were dead, and that he now longed for the end.[48] He was preoccupied with his ageing appearance; he even likened himself to 'an iguana sunning itself on the rocks' (Fig. 2.14) and to a 'seedy relic of the Edwardian era'.[49] Furthermore, increasingly paranoid, he had convinced himself that his only child, his daughter Liza, was plotting against him, and indeed was not even really his daughter. He planned to break with Liza and – to spite her further – sell the bulk of his art collection, which she believed he had willed to her, at Sotheby's in London.[50]

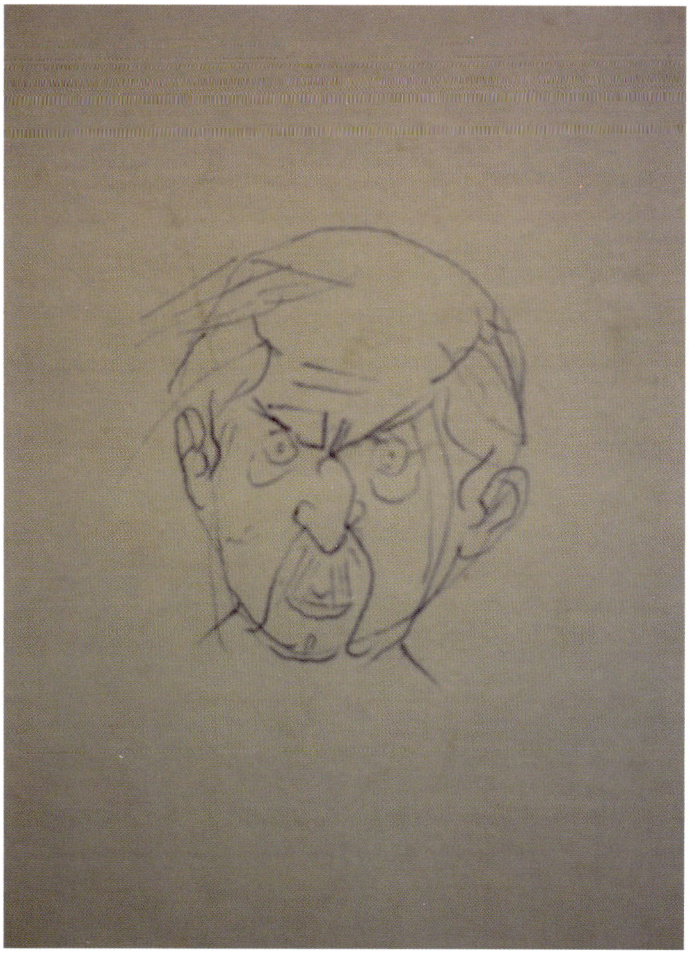

Fig. 2.12 Ivor Roberts-Jones, *Kyffin Takes Issue with an Example of Modern Art*, 1970s, pen and ink on paper, 5 x 3.5 cm, Image: Courtesy of the HMI, Leeds

Despite such unpromising circumstances, Ivor found that, after a bit of 'warming up', Maugham was an engaging and often loquacious conversationalist, happiest talking about himself and his own opinions: how much he disliked Beckett's *Waiting for Godot* (first performed in August 1955)[51] and loathed the writing of 'angry young man' Kingsley Amis.[52] Ivor later recalled, around 1982, that

> it was a great experience staying at Cap Ferrat and working in [Maugham's] villa. Apart from the conversation at lunch my main impression was of his courage. He was 87 [in 1961] and quite indomitable. I had said in the early stages that I would like him to give me one or two sittings on the flat roof in the open air. He had his writing room ... up there but it was a very cold February. He was recovering from ... pneumonia and I

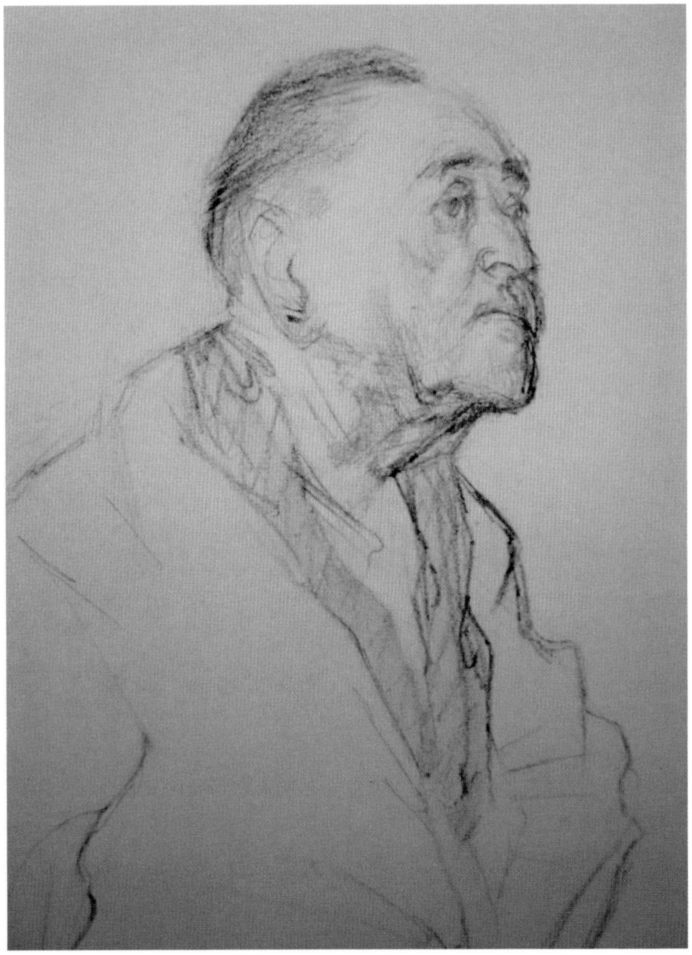

Fig. 2.13 Ivor Roberts-Jones, *Study of Somerset Maugham*, 1962–63, chalk and pencil on paper, 35.5 x 25.3 cm, Private Collection Image: J. Black

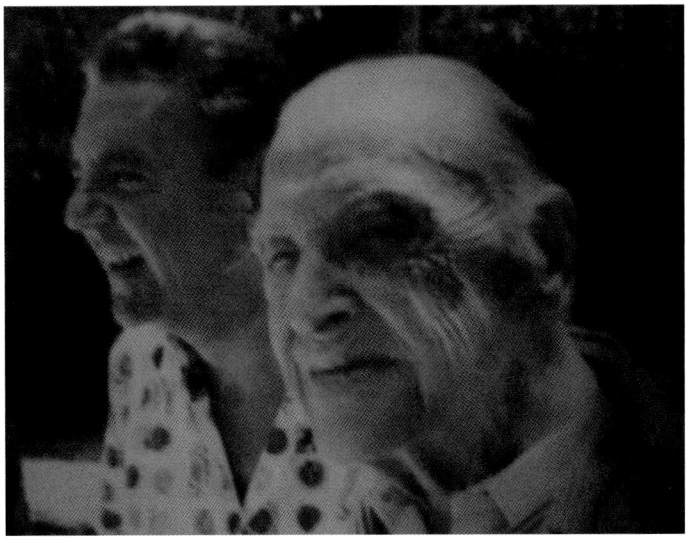

Fig. 2.14 Somerset Maugham and Alan Searle, Villa Mauresque, Cap Ferrat, South of France, 1961; Image: J. Black

> was horrified one day to find him already settled up there, in the open, clutching a hot water bottle to his chest and wrapped up in layers of blanket. He could not be budged. At one stage he went blue – the level of colour dropping down his features as I have seen it do in men suffering from total exhaustion. I moved forward to catch him but the level of colour slowly re-adjusted itself and the sitting returned to normal.[53]

When the head was exhibited at the Oriel Gallery in 1978, it was widely described as one of Ivor's finest portraits. Ian Walker declared in the *Guardian* that Ivor had deftly captured 'both the magnificence and the pettiness of the man'.[54] Ivor long maintained that it was one of 'my finest portraits, alongside *Clive Gardiner* [cat. 11] and *Sam Rabin* [cat. 21]'.[55]

Shortly before his own death, however, Ivor was not quite so positive in his presentation of Maugham:

> During sittings on the roof ... Maugham wasn't in the least bothered. [At one point he got out of his chair and] said: 'I haven't played football for ages' and began to kick his hot water bottle down the steps. Odd people, homosexuals. When I was there news came that Kenneth Clark had suffered a stroke and the two of them, Maugham and his boyfriend, began to jump up and down with glee. 'K. Clark's had a stroke. K. Clark's had a stroke.'[56]

Maugham's opinion of the portrait has not survived, but when his friend the painter Sir Gerald Kelly saw it shortly before Maugham's death in 1964, he remarked sardonically that Ivor had presented the author as a wise Confucian sage rather than the 'madam of a Shanghai brothel', as Sutherland had earlier depicted him.[57]

Photographs of the head of Maugham began appearing in Beaverbrook's newspapers as Maugham's memoirs were serialised in the *Sunday Express*, during September and October 1962.[58] By this time Ivor was already well into his next commission – that of *Sir William Emrys Williams* (1962–63) (cat. 28), for the Arts Council. Progress, as was often the case with Ivor, was swift. But the artist was less than happy with the result – even though the sitter was apparently delighted with Ivor's vision of him.[59] The head was more than life sized, and the treatment of the surface, especially of the initial plaster cast, unusually 'slashed, clawed and agitated'. As Ivor later recalled, he suspected the head of Williams had been distorted owing to a combination of the crushing effect upon him of the death in a sudden accident of his only son, Mervyn, towards the end of 1961,[60] and an overly 'absorbing' awareness of the work of Jean Fautrier (1898–1964) – a series of his celebrated 'hostage' heads (Fig. 2.15) had been exhibited in London a few years previously. He thought, perhaps, that Fautrier's 'portraiture of abjection'[61] – though the Frenchman had subjected the heads of his subjects to far greater flaying and gouging than Ivor – had chimed all too neatly with his intense grief. He thought a slightly later head, of Welsh grandee and past chairman of the Welsh Committee of the Arts Council, Lord Kenyon (1962–63) (cat. 29), also suffered somewhat from a similar effect of 'over-emphasised distortion', which he attributed to his 'disturbed' emotional state following the death of Mervyn.[62]

Later in the 1960s Ivor's time was increasingly taken up with teaching, and with the problem-strewn *Augustus John* memorial statue project for Fordingbridge (1964–67) (cat. 133). He did find the opportunity to produce portraits of friends and colleagues, such as *Helen Roeder* (c. 1965) (cat. 32). She was an old friend from his first days at Goldsmiths, as was her husband, Carel Weight.[63] His portrait of her could be perceived as a rather cruel caricature, but it was well regarded by the sitter and by Weight. Ivor had been convinced she would make a fine portrait subject on the grounds that she could have stepped directly from a late-eighteenth-century drawing by Gillray or Rowlandson.[64] *Paul Drury* (1965–66) (cat. 34) had recently been appointed principal of the Faculty of Art and Design at Goldsmiths; Ivor regarded him as a superb draughtsman whose achievements with a pen or etching needle were all the more impressive for his having only one working eye. According to Ivor, for this reason, Drury did truly see the world rather differently than most people – indeed, he saw more with one eye than the majority blessed with the usual complement of two.[65]

Thanks to his friend Kyffin Williams, a more formal commission came from Highgate School – a head of famous conductor/violinst *Yehudi Menuhin* (1966–67) (cat. 37), who had moved into a house close to the school early in 1960.[66] Three years later he established what would become the renowned Menuhin International School.[67] Menuhin made it clear he could not spare the time for formal sittings, as he faced a punishing schedule of recordings and rehearsals for the Bath International Festival, of which he was the director. Ivor was allowed to sit in on a series of rehearsals and recordings in a studio in Maida Vale. The resulting portrait was modelled from memory, supported by a series of swiftly executed sketches.[68] Menuhin did not like the portrait at all; it apparently exposed a side of him – domineering, self-absorbed and rather arrogant – he was only too aware of but wished to be kept from the public gaze. He much preferred a drawing Ivor had produced of his daughter Hepzibah at the piano (Fig. 2.16). As for the sculptor, he thought he had done his level best to do justice to such a 'magnificent head' – one he later described as a 'withdrawn, inward-looking face',[69] while Williams felt he had successfully caught something rarely seen in portraits of creative minds: that moment when an artist, in this case a conductor, had retreated into himself in order to preserve those elements of a performance that deserved to be retained, while already assessing what aspects must be

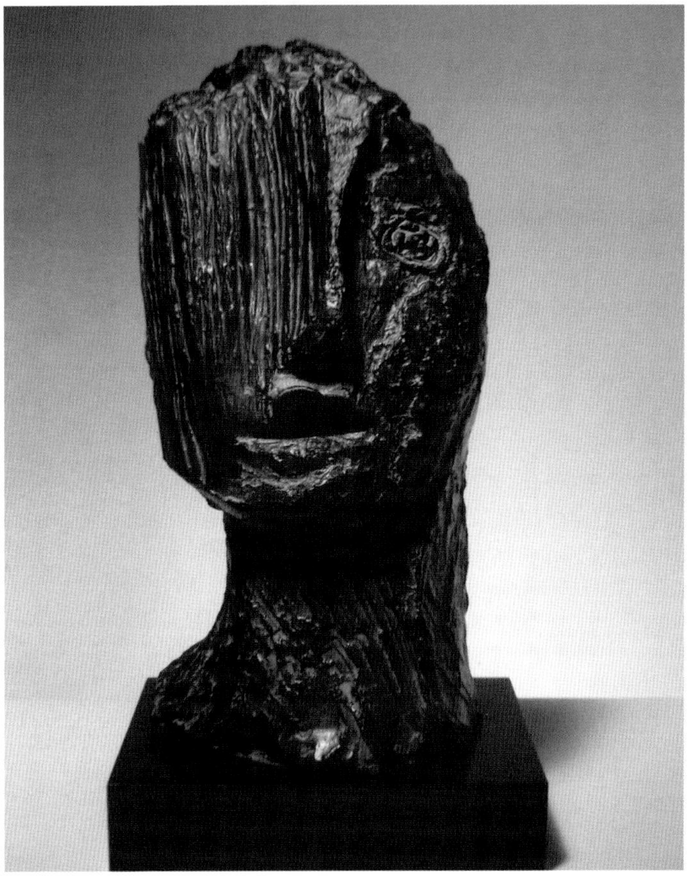

Fig. 2.15 Jean Fautrier, *Head of a Hostage/Large Tragic Head*, 1942, 38.5 cm high, Tate Modern; Image: Courtesy of Tate Images

ruthlessly discarded, to approach perfection as closely as possible when working with fallible human beings.[70]

In the wake of the unveiling of his mammoth figure of Winston Churchill in Parliament Square in 1973 (cat. 135), Ivor was once again in demand as a portraitist: in 1974 he received a commission from the Royal College of General Practitioners (RCGP) to execute a head of its then president, Prince Philip (cat. 43).[71] Ivor did not find the Duke of Edinburgh an easy or restful sitter; he thought him brusque and uninterested in the process of portraiture. The 'Dook', as Ivor named him, bridled at the number of sittings Ivor had requested,[72] and for the first time the artist combined modelling in clay immediately before the subject with taking multiple photographs of the sitter (Fig. 2.17), both to allow the artist to work on the head when the sitter was elsewhere and to provide a useful additional visual aid. The RCGP appeared happy enough with the finished portrait – though the prince complained that Ivor had succeeded in making him resemble a 'Neanderthal man'.[73]

In 1978 Ivor was given a further opportunity to develop his portraiture skills when a new Keeper of Art at the NMW, Cardiff, Dr Peter Cannon-Brookes, came up with the idea that the sculptor produce a series of portrait heads of past presidents of the museum's Council.[74] As it happened, Ivor had recently been asked by Kyffin Williams to make a head of one such past president, the eminent military historian the *Seventh Marquess of Anglesey* (1978–79) (cat. 45), who was an admirer of Williams's painting and also his landlord on Anglesey (Williams had moved to the island from London in 1974).[75]

During the same year the ten portrait heads he included in his retrospective at the Oriel Gallery in Cardiff were greatly admired. Writing in the *Western Mail*, in July 1978, Gerda Roper described his portraiture as

> extremely powerful ... The terrific life force that is disclosed in all of them is due not only to the resemblance to the sitter, but to the handling of the materials. The most brutal slashes through the plaster ones with their ... texturing and bunched and diffused lumps of clay ... are sensitive and acute manipulations of material [that] reveal psychological truths. They are refined to an almost abstract barest of essentials and reveal a wealth of truth.[76]

Over the next decade Ivor produced a number of fine portraits within his series of past NMW Council presidents, including *The Third Earl of Plymouth* (1987) (Fig. 2.18, cat. 65) – Ivor thought he was a 'marvellous subject ... who sat with great restraint and determination'[77] – and the academic *W. A. Twiston-Davies* (1986) (cat. 62), whom Ivor had hoped he had succeeded in presenting as a combination of ancient Welsh bard and modern intellectual.[78] News of Cannon-Brooke's initiative spread quickly within the Welsh art world, and Ivor was soon approached by Aberystwyth University (then a college within the University of Wales) to make a posthumous portrait head of contentious Welsh nationalist academic *Alwyn Rees* (1978–79) (cat. 47). It is an indication of the pains that Ivor was prepared to take over a commission that engaged him, as he put it, 'emotionally and intellectually'[79] – he relished the challenge of producing a convincing portrait of someone he would never meet entirely from photographs and the recollections of those who had known him – that when his first maquette was rejected by one half of the two-man commissioning team from the university, he immediately offered to produce a second free of charge. Oddly enough, the other half of the team – artist Arthur Giardelli (1911–2009)[80] – much preferred the first attempt and paid for it to be cast in bronze; a second cast was subsequently bought by the NMW, Cardiff.[81]

Aberystwyth accepted Ivor's second attempt at the head of Rees, and it was bought by the college. There the head was so admired and appreciated on its unveiling that the National Library of Wales, just down the road from the university, asked Ivor to produce a second cast from the second head for its own collection. Ivor reflected wryly that these tributes were to a man who, in life, had upset many within the university with his steadfast opposition to the college breaking away from the University of Wales organisation to become a university in its own right, while his sarcastic condemnation of the prospect of state support for compulsory Welsh-language teaching in Welsh higher education had won him few friends in the National Library.[82] Such was the fraught and often highly ambiguous nature of nationalist politics in the Welsh cultural landscape in the run-up to the unsuccessful referendum on Welsh devolution held in March 1979.[83]

Fig. 2.16 Ivor Roberts-Jones, *Hepzibah Menuhin at the Piano,* 1967, pencil on paper, 29 x 22.5 cm, Image: Courtesy of the HMI, Leeds

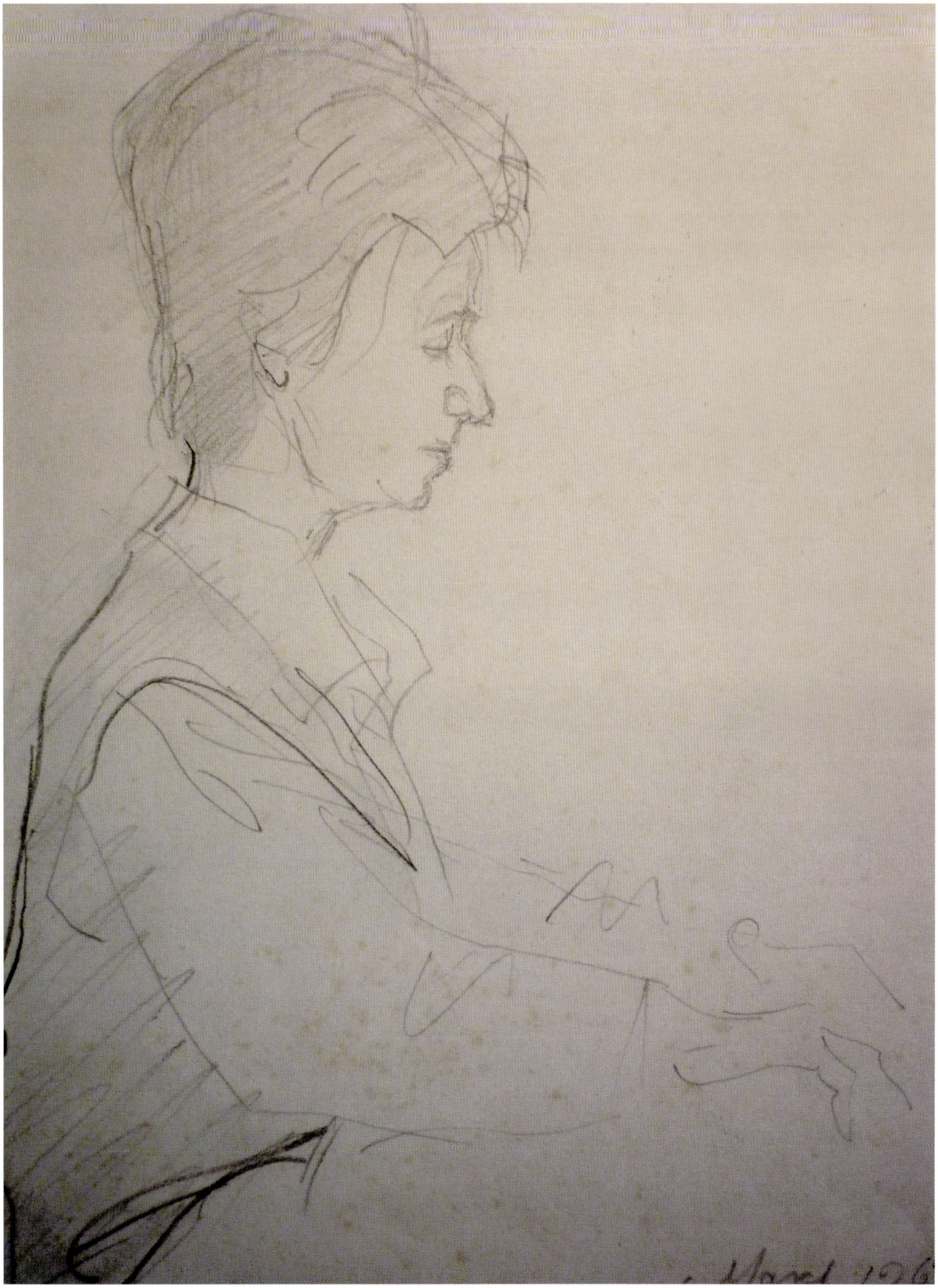

Meanwhile, Kyffin Williams, through Lord Mishcon on the board of the National Theatre, had floated the suggestion early in 1978 that the theatre might wish to pay for a bronze cast of a bust by Ivor of Oliver Lyttelton (cat. 39), the First Lord Chandos (and the National Theatre's first president, between 1962 and 1971), to install somewhere inside its recently opened Lyttelton Theatre. Ivor did eventually succeed in having a head of Lord Chandos placed inside the theatre (1979–80) (cat. 48) – but it was not the original bust he had started just before the sitter's death in January 1972. For once, records have survived that cast light on how Ivor came to make a second portrait of Chandos, and allow one to track the somewhat labyrinthine course it took to being commissioned by the National Theatre board – heading off attempts along the way by Franta Belsky (1921–2000) to have his own head of Lord Chandos accepted instead for the interior of the Lyttelton Theatre.

Belsky believed the National Theatre board wanted to commission a head of Chandos from him, as the Czech-born sculptor had recently produced a portrait of another board member, Lord Cottesloe.[84] Certain key board members, principally Lord Mishcon, were aware of and much preferred the plaster bust of Chandos that Ivor had made in 1972–73 and exhibited at the Royal Academy in 1974.[85] The Second Lord Chandos viewed both portraits in October 1978, and decided he could not really approve either – though he felt Ivor was the better sculptor.[86] At this juncture Ivor offered to make a plaster cast of a new head, drawing upon conversations with and photographs supplied by the Chandos family.[87] The sculptor also took care to keep the National Theatre board informed of his progress. He wrote to the board's secretary in April 1979 that the second head was

> much nearer to what I wanted to do – and I think myself it is very much an improvement on the first one. It is not quite complete yet – but very nearly. I can see what [was] admired in the first head – but I had never felt that I had really shot my bolt over it. Now I do. Of course this in no way involves the National Theatre – or anyone except myself. [The Second] Lord Chandos can see both heads when he comes – but I would just like a little time to complete it. I would like you to let him know what I am doing – as he may be thinking I am being rather laggard about it. In fact it is rather the opposite ... I really had to do [the second head] – and it in no way involves anyone except me. I feel I am nearer to what I wanted to do than I was in the first place.[88]

The Second Lord Chandos and his wife greatly approved of Ivor's second head of his father when they saw it at 31 St James's Gardens in mid June 1979, as did a succession of National Theatre board members who called on Ivor during that summer. However, by the autumn of 1979, Belsky had evidently heard that plans were afoot at the National Theatre to give a commission which he had imagined had been confirmed as his to another artist – whom he hinted to the second Lord Chandos he knew to be Ivor. The Second Lord Chandos felt he had been placed in an invidious position; he knew his father better than most, and it was his opinion that Ivor's second attempt was a much better portrait and the one he would prefer to see commemorating his father inside the National Theatre.[88] He complained, mildly, to the theatre board's secretary, Ms Bird, that Belsky was being somewhat insistent and rather 'pushful' over the matter of 'my father's head'; perhaps tellingly, he added that when he had visited Ivor, the sculptor had been 'patient and obliging'.[90] Ms Bird could only apologise in reply that she was 'appalled to learn that Mr Belski [*sic*] has been worrying you about his own sculpture. He is, I fear, a very pushing gentleman but even so, I would not have thought that he would have gone as far as this.' She could only put it down to the present serious economic climate, which only promised future 'lean times for artists', and reassure him that the board members with whom she had been in contact, including Lords Rayne and Mischon, Sir Peter Hall, and the architect of the National Theatre, Sir Denys Lasdun, had all been impressed with Ivor's second portrait of the First Lord Chandos. It would be the fitting memorial to his key role as the theatre's first chairman.[91]

The new head of Chandos was not unveiled inside the theatre until November 1982. By then Ivor was well underway producing a series of heads of distinguished Welsh individuals for a new organisation, the Welsh Portrait Sculpture Trust (WPST). This was the brainchild of High Court Judge Bruce Griffiths QC, a prominent supporter of the NMW, Cardiff, and friend of its Keeper of

Fig. 2.17 Ivor Roberts-Jones, contact sheet of photographs taken of HRH The Duke of Edinburgh in 1974, Image: Courtesy of the HMI, Leeds

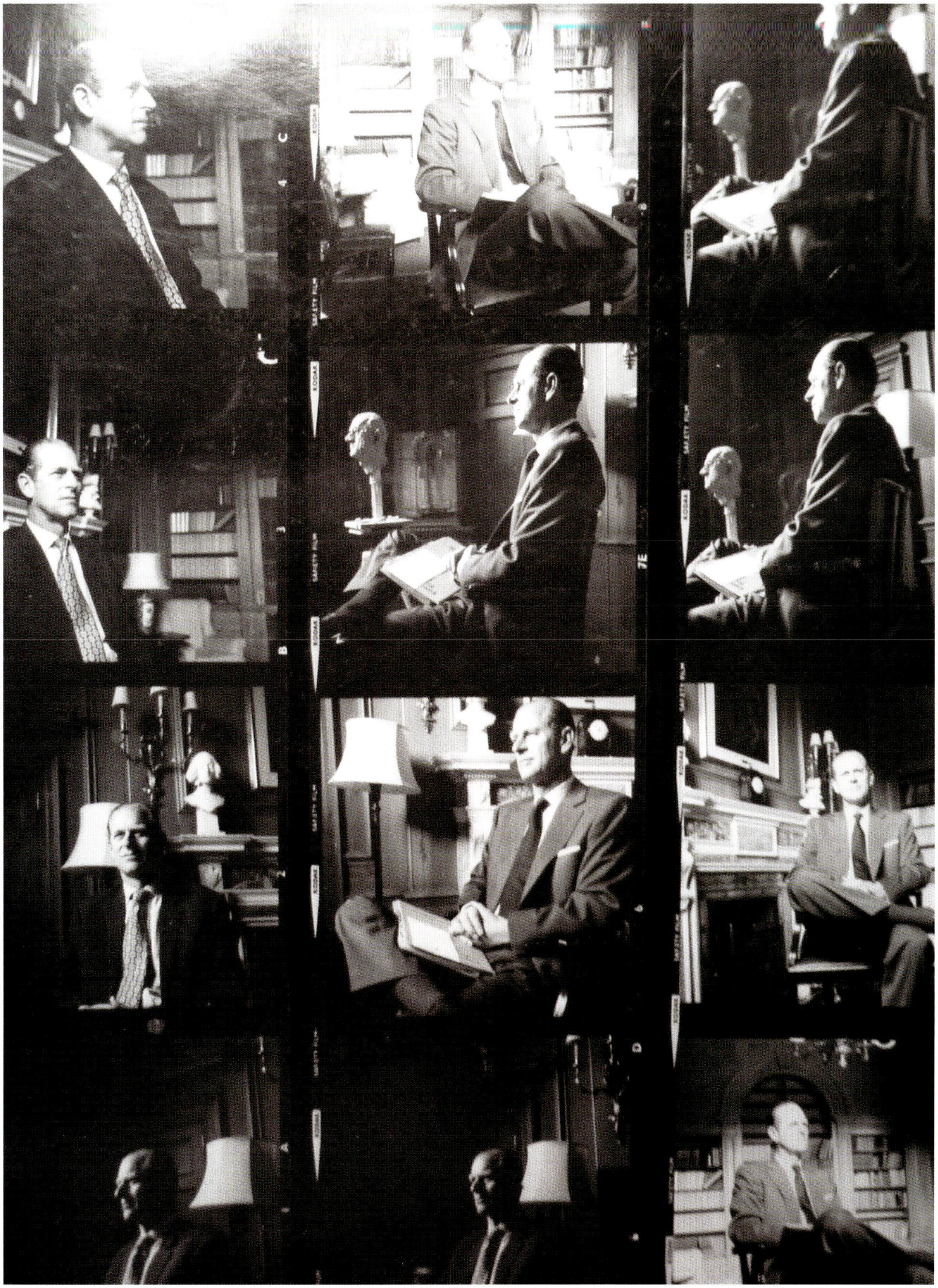

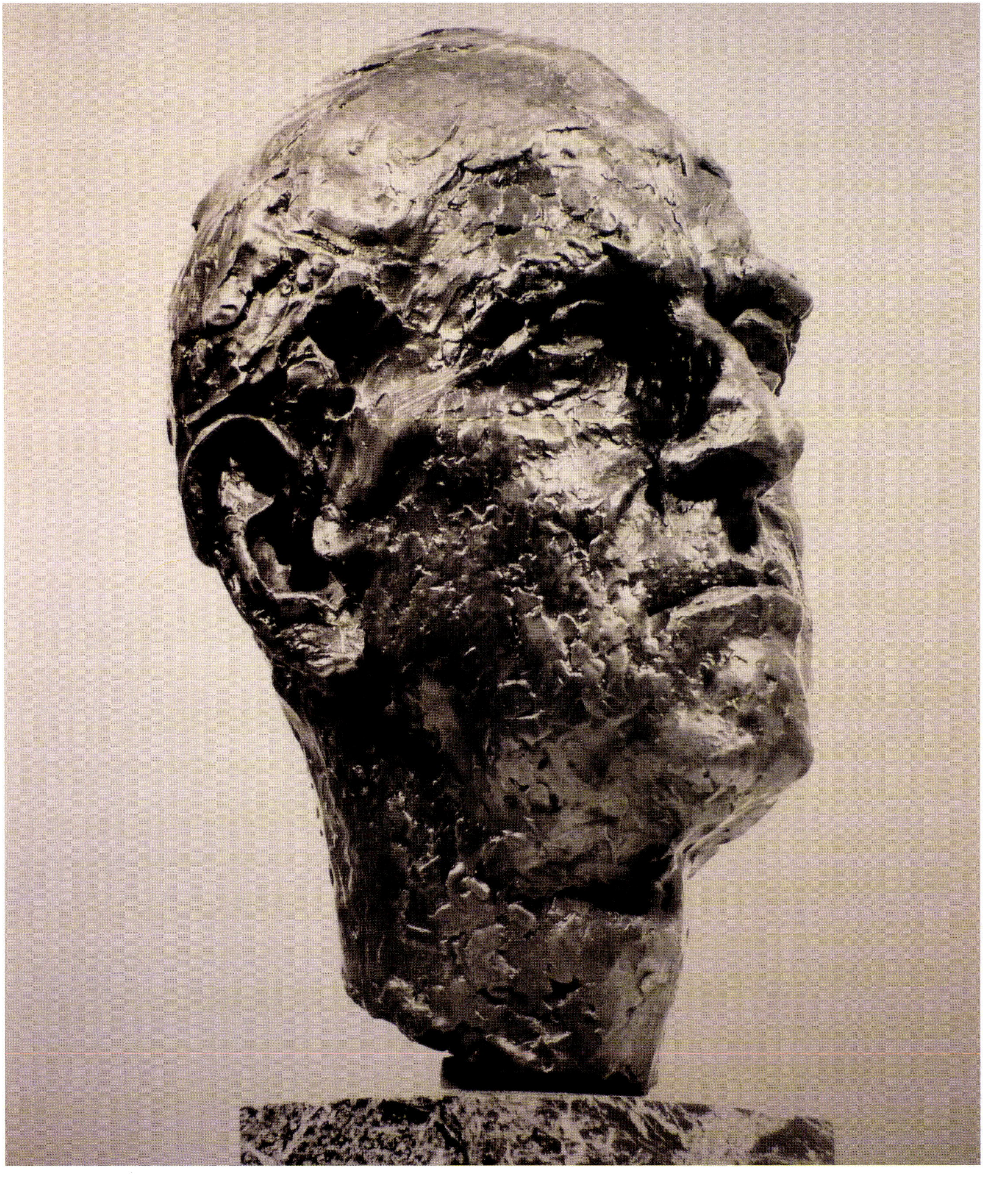

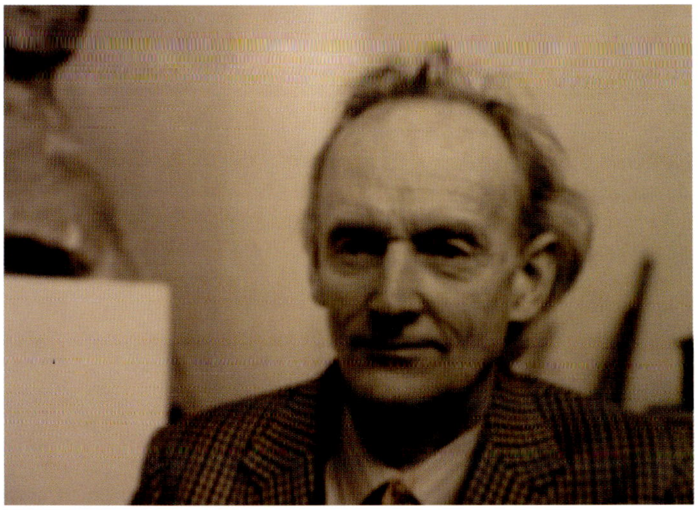

Fig. 2.18 Ivor Roberts-Jones, photograph of the Third Earl of Plymouth taken in 1986 in the artist's studio, 31 St James's Gardens, London; Image: Courtesy of the HMI, Leeds

Art, Peter Cannon-Brookes.[92] Griffiths had seen and been very impressed by photographs of the bust and head of Lord Chandos he had been shown by Cannon-Brookes in 1979–80, wondering out loud why a 'Welsh sculptor' should devote such energy and effort to celebrating an English ex-politician and arts administrator in London. Surely there was no shortage of Welsh people who deserved to be so celebrated? To this end, during the spring of 1980 Griffiths, along with fellow eminent lawyer Sir Alun Talfan-Davies, established the WPST with the aim of commissioning Ivor to produce portraits of distinguished living Welsh individuals for the collection of the NMW, Cardiff; a 'silent' member in the trio of the Trust's principle trustees was the then director of the museum.[93]

Within a matter of weeks, Judge Griffiths had used his contacts to arrange sittings for Ivor with the colourful Speaker of the House of Commons, George Thomas (later Lord Thomas of Tonypandy) (cat. 51).[94] Sittings took place over the summer of 1980 at 31 St James's Gardens. The artist was wary of Thomas at first; after hearing Thomas on the radio he had formed the impression that the Speaker was too self-consciously a performer – too fond of acting the role of ripely orotund Welshman.[95] However, face-to-face with Thomas, Ivor found himself quickly falling under his spell. As he wrote in August 1980 to Yolande Bird at the National Theatre – with whom he was in frequent touch at the time, as the commission for the second head of Lord Chandos ground onwards with painful slowness – Speaker Thomas (cat. 50) was 'a marvellous sitter – like a fine red cockerel brim full of every kind of energy – and he sat, or stood, for two hours at a stretch, so it was all over in four sittings. One's life has its brighter moments.'[96] Ivor was later to describe Thomas as a

> vivid, life-affirming spirit with a head worthy of a sculptor ... of Achnaton's[97] [*sic*] day ... When he is entertaining at Speaker's House, and in public generally, he is extremely charming, almost satyr-like, but at rest and in private his head takes on a weight that was[,] for me anyway, quite a revelation. He seemed indomitable

Cat. 43 *Prince Philip, The Duke of Edinburgh*, 1974–75

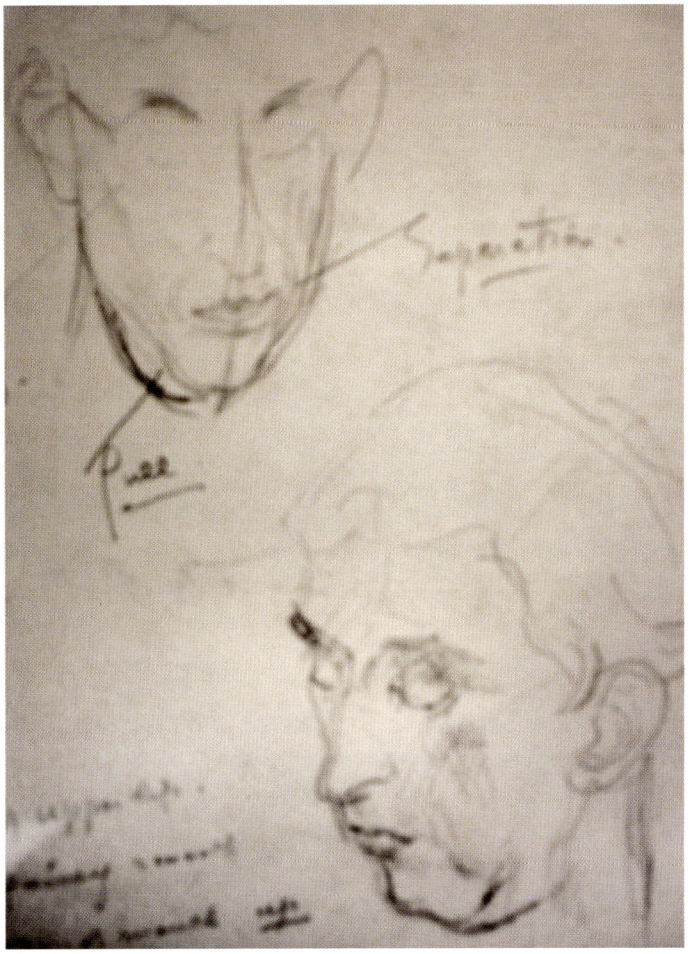

Fig. 2.19 Ivor Roberts-Jones, *Two Studies of HRH The Prince of Wales*, c. 1980–81, pencil on paper, 19 x 13 cm, Image: Courtesy of the HMI, Leeds

and one could easily see where his authority lay ... who could fail not to like George Thomas?[98]

It also considerably helped their relationship to develop on a friendly footing that he saw eye-to-eye with his sitter on contemporary political issues: both admired Margaret Thatcher, though in the summer of 1980 she was heading fast towards the nadir of her unpopularity, and both sympathised with Welsh Nationalism while being convinced that separation of the country from the United Kingdom would ultimately be devastating for Wales.[99] Ivor was not so implacably opposed as Thomas[100] to greater devolved powers for Wales of the sort offered and rejected in the vote of March 1979.[101]

Meanwhile, Griffiths helped arrange funding for a commission from the Contemporary Art Society of Wales for Ivor to produce a head of *Prince Charles* (1980–82) (Fig. 2.19; cat. 52) to occupy a niche inside the entrance hall of the new St David's Concert Hall in the centre of Cardiff (opened in 1983). This proved quite a long-drawn-out commission. Sittings took much longer to organise than had been the case with Speaker Thomas: they had barely started when they had to be postponed as preparations gathered pace for the prince's marriage to Lady Diana Spencer. But Ivor found Prince Charles a much more approachable, intelligent and intriguing individual than his father had been – a curious yet attractive combination of strength and firmly held opinion that was undercut by sudden flashes of petulance and vulnerability. As Ivor was later to remark, it was sometimes the frailties of a person as much as their attractive strengths that made for an interesting and revealing portrait.[102]

During the rest of the 1980s there followed a series of splendid portrait heads and busts commissioned by the WST for the NMW, Cardiff. Sitters ranged from the flamboyant tenor opera singer, *Sir Geraint Evans* (1982–83) (Fig. 2.20; cat. 56), to *Sir Tasker Watkins VC* (1984–85) (cat. 60), war hero and champion of Welsh rugby (he did more than most to ensure funding was available to build a brand new Millennium Stadium for Cardiff, now recognised as an exceptional adornment to the city). Also included were grandees of the Welsh academic and cultural scene, such as *Alun Oldfield-Davies* (1984–85) (cat. 59) – his intellect still razor sharp, though he was in his early eighties, and lips sardonically pursed as if the artist has just revealed in conversation his deficient knowledge of Welsh literature[103] – and Lord Lieutenant of Glamorgan *Sir Cennydd Traherne* (1985–86) (cat. 61). The latter contains a hint of hauteur reminiscent of Epstein's bust of an even more superciliously self-assured and glacially patrician Ninth Duke of Marlborough (1925) (Fig. 2.21).[104]

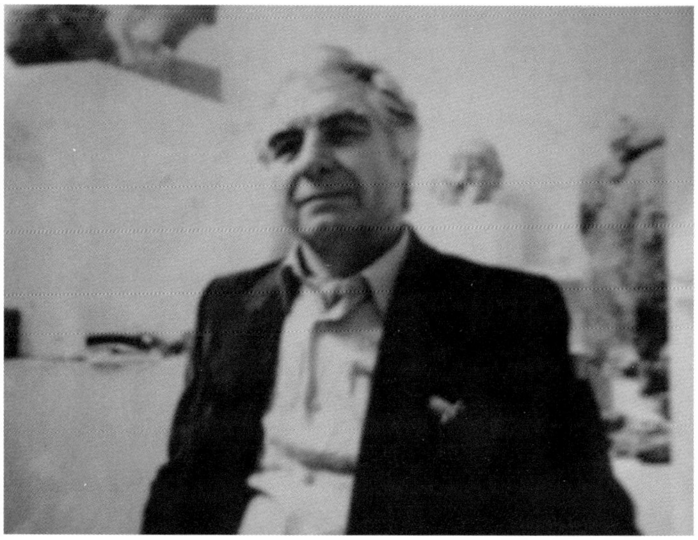

Fig. 2.20 Ivor Roberts-Jones, photograph of Sir Geraint Evans taken in 1982 in the artist's studio, 31 St James's Gardens, London; Image: Courtesy of the HMI, Leeds

As is evident from his correspondence with the NMW, Cardiff, Ivor was conscious of the need to vary his portraits as much as he could – heads with and without necks, an occasional bust, and a variety of different patinas – which he was able to achieve through close cooperation with his preferred foundry, the Meridian Foundry in Peckham, south London. For example, with regard to *Alun Oldfield-Davies* (cat. 59), Ivor wrote to the registrar at the NMW, Cardiff, in January 1985,

> I have a slight surprise for you ... I have made a head and shoulders of Alun Oldfield-Davies ... from my own point of view and I suppose from the museum's, one cannot just have head after head all cut off at the neck. I have made them as varied in pose, length of neck and patina etc. as I could but I thought a full head and shoulders would be a great relief. So, I am giving you a present of a pair of shoulders ... he's one of the best I've ever done.[105]

An artist who knew Ivor during this period of the mid-to-late 1980s, Bridget Heriz-Smith, has recently commented that what has caused her to remain very impressed with Ivor's heads is 'the aggression which he applied to keep the surface permeable. But he combined this brutality with a completely contradictory sensitivity to the fleshy illusion of clay, a tactility almost feminine in its receptiveness.'[106] She now feels that the best of his heads are

> Shakespearean rather than modernist, more tragic than ... utopian or morbid. The vulnerable but dominant inwardness of Ivor's work negotiated contradiction with an overall brutalised form – where ... the form managed to survive whatever bashing, hacking and sawing had been applied ... sometimes the form achieved an inspired presence, possessing a momentum that was both cohesive and expressive in its breadth ... but sometimes it bore witness to frustration maimed, dismembered, wounded. His was a lonely place to be ... stubbornly, defiantly, ambitiously so ...[107]

Commissions also came Ivor's way from elsewhere within the UK. In 1989, largely at the recommendation of his old friend Sir Hugh Casson, and Casson's successor as president of the Royal Academy, Sir Roger de Grey, Ivor received a portrait commission for Sir Nicholas Proctor Goodison (Fig. 2.22; cat. 67), recent chairman of the London Stock Exchange (1976–88) and about to be confirmed as chairman of the Trustee Savings Bank (1989–95). Fortunately, Sir Nicholas made detailed notes at the time on what it was like to sit to Ivor. According to Sir Nicholas, the bust was executed between January 1989 and May 1990. It was commissioned by 'ex-colleagues at Quilter Goodison & Co. ... to mark my thirty years with the firm and my fourteen years of chairmanship'. This was in the autumn of 1988, as Sir Nicholas prepared to leave the firm and to step down as chairman of the Stock Exchange. Sir Nicholas discussed the commission with a then partner of QG & Co. (and in 2000 its managing director), Brian Catchpole. They decided upon a sculptor as the Stock Exchange would be commissioning a portrait of him in oils,

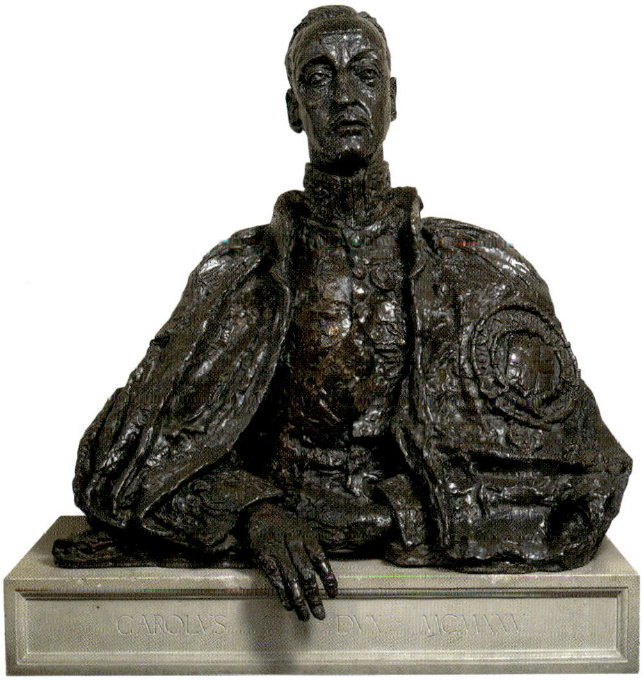

Fig. 2.21 Jacob Epstein, *The 9th Duke of Marlborough*, 1925, bronze, 68 cm high, Private Collection; Image: Blenheim Palace, Oxon, UK/The Bridgeman Art Library

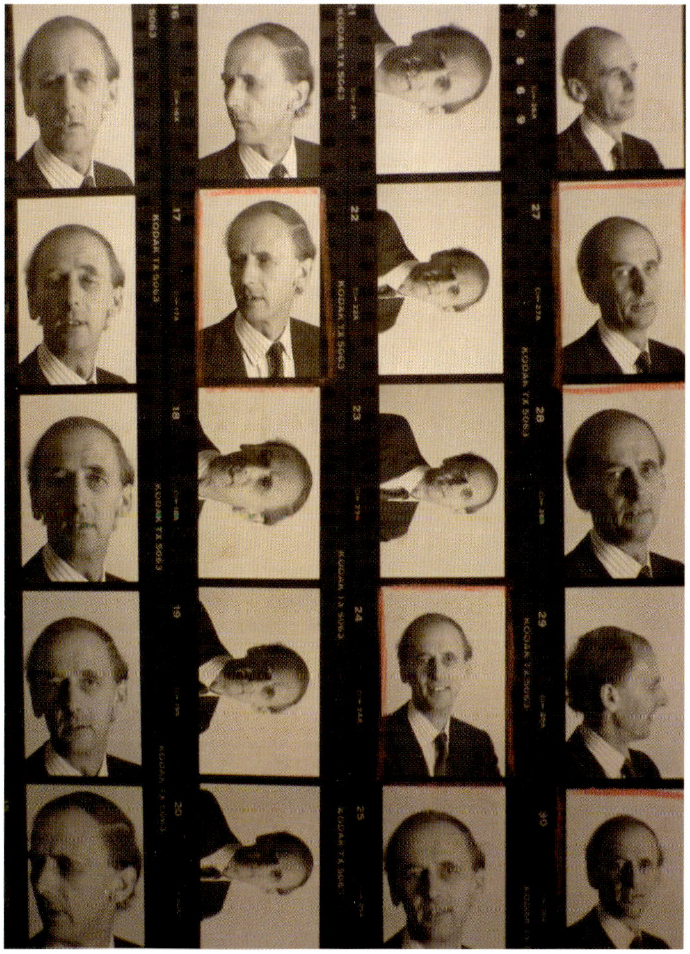

Fig. 2.22 Ivor Roberts-Jones, contact sheet of photographs of Sir Nicholas Proctor Goodison taken in 1989 in the artist's studio, 31 St James's Gardens, London; Image: Courtesy of the HMI, Leeds

and my wife was extremely keen on a three-dimensional portrait. Shortly afterwards I found Hugh Casson and Roger de Grey ... standing together at a reception at the [Royal] Academy and [I] asked them who they would recommend. [At the time Sir Nicholas was on the Academy's Financial Advisory Committee.] They strongly recommended Ivor Roberts-Jones whom thcy regarded as a fine and somewhat overlooked portraitist.

Sir Nicholas first contacted Ivor in November 1988, and his first sitting to the artist took place on 7 January 1989 at 31 St James's Gardens. Further sittings took place between January and April 1989. All the sittings took place on a Saturday, as Sir Nicholas had recently taken over as chairman of TSB, which he found to be 'very demanding'. Sittings invariably commenced at 9.30 am sharp, with the sculptor bringing him a large mug of tea 'brewed in the studio'. Sir Nicholas recalled, 'when I first arrived I remember Ivor introducing me to the clay "lump" veiled in a damp cloth which he had prepared with the help of photographs and unveiling it before me with the flourish of a magician'. A number of plaster portrait heads rested on various shelves 'looking as if they lay where the guillotine had deposited them'.

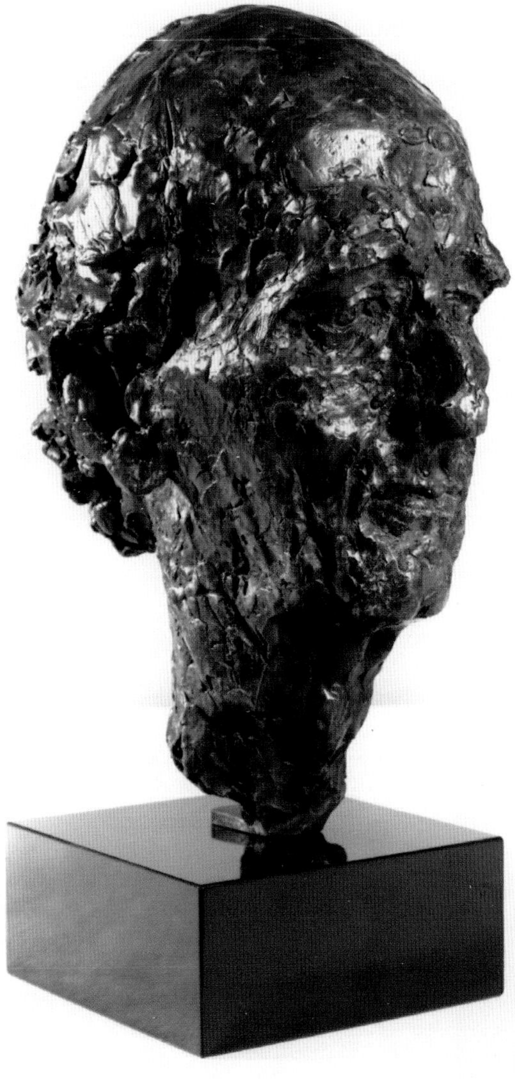

Cat. 67 *Sir Nicholas Proctor Goodison*, 1989–90

Sir Nicholas was especially intrigued by 'the evolution of the portrait which began to take recognisable shape at an early stage ... he worked to establish the shape and exaggerated (or so I thought) the eccentricities – the crookedness of the nose and asymmetric nature of the face'. Ivor did most of the talking.

> First he mentioned the lesson he had received early in his career (later, I learned he had taken this ... from Despiau) that a head can best be discovered by covering it with a cloth and noting its extreme points and then working out the inter-relationship between them, rather than by worrying about the precise structure of the skin and bones between them). Second, he had ruined his work in the past by over-finishing. It was better to rely upon the spontaneity of early impressions.

He recalled discussing with the sculptor 'the Stock Exchange and the radical reforms of 1983–87 and their purpose and effects'. The sculptor had seen Sir Nicholas on television, and was 'surprisingly aware of what we had done and why. He was interested too in the performance of certain stocks and shares which people always assume I know more about than I do.' They talked about the

> world of the arts, about figurative art versus abstraction ... I do recall that we talked about the current under-rating of British artists such as Paul Nash and Graham Sutherland. He acknowledged the value of abstraction but was critical of the view that figurative art had had its day. We speculated on whether an artist such as Carel Weight, whom we both admired, would be seen in a hundred years or so as an artist representative of his age, or whether his work would be as neglected as the Victorian genre artists. He admired Carel both as an artist and as a teacher.

Ivor expressed much interest in Sir Nicholas's work as chairman of the National Art Collections Fund, which he had taken on in 1986. He thought the sculptor was 'adept at getting me to talk. He was like a terrier in teasing out opinions and reactions and seemed to like his sitter to keep talking while he took sightings from various angles and did his modelling. We talked a lot about poetry ... I remember particularly discussing the poetry of Wilfred Owen and his wonderfully condensed use of language ... '

By the last sitting, in April 1989, the head was almost finished and Sir Nicholas was: 'very impressed with it [but] he [Ivor] said that he thought there was something not quite right about the treatment of the top of the nose and its relationship to the recesses of the eyes. He added a small piece of clay and the modelling looked instantly right.' Ivor wrote to Sir Nicholas on 6 October 1989 that he now considered that the head was: 'at last completed'. The sculptor had: 'left it alone for a considerable period without even unwrapping it ... On resuming work things began to fall into place, tho' it did take some time. The strange thing is that, when I do this, the final result seems to be fresher than after, say, four or five sittings.' On 21 May 1990 Ivor wrote to Sir Nicholas that: 'the portrait was now back in the studio in bronze and looking quite at its best.' He was particularly pleased with the head's patina he had obtained from the Meridian Foundry.

Sir Nicholas noted that a second cast of the head had been offered to the National Portrait Gallery early in 1992, and was accepted with alacrity. The second cast had a larger base than the first: 'Ivor preferred the proportions of this base, which were the result of a mistake by the foundry. He told me that he could do with mistakes like that 'just as often as Fate can afford'. The sculptor supposed that 'she [Fate] rations them otherwise the world would be stuffed with genius and would become a claustrophobically brilliant hole'.[108]

For a while the head stood in the Stock Exchange, but when Sir Nicholas retired he was careful to ensure that he was able to take a cast of the head with him. On the request of the then director of the National Portrait Gallery, Sir John Hayes, another cast was purchased for the gallery's collection – the fourth and final work to date by Ivor now owned by the gallery. Recognition by the National Portrait Gallery meant a great deal to him, but it would appear he derived just as much pleasure from one of his later portrait commissions – a posthumous head of the wonderful Welsh character actor and double Oscar winner *Hugh Griffith* (1991) (cat. 69) – largely the doing of his old friend Kyffin Williams, working closely with Anglesey District Council.[109] The head was to celebrate a man who was a native of the island in a new art gallery to stand near Llangefni, which would incorporate a permanent display of William's paintings. The head of *Griffith* was displayed alongside a second head of another old friend of Ivor's, *Lord Cledwyn of Penrhos* (1990–91) (Fig. 2.23; cat. 68), which Ivor produced in part for the NMW, Cardiff, as a commission from the WPST, but on the understanding that a second cast would eventually go to the new Oriel Ynys Môn. Hughes had been Labour MP for Anglesey for many years (1951–79), and in the House of Lords had campaigned strenuously for the Welsh Arts Council to be given adequate funding to realise the construction of the new gallery, which officially opened in 1993.[110] Ivor was a particular admirer of Hughes as a politician, as he had been effective not only on the national level, as secretary of state for Wales (1966–68), but locally within Wales as MP for Anglesey. Furthermore, he was impressed that Hughes had willingly embraced a life in the public eye when the left side of his face was covered by a livid reddish birthmark whose conspicuousness had diminished little with the passage of time. As the artist noted the first time Hughes sat to him, in 1978, in a sculpture there was no need to depict the sitter's distracting birthmark, which tended to divert attention from the innate warmth and sympathetic urbanity of Hughes's character.[111]

Eighteen months later, Ivor's last commission from the WPST – fittingly of one of its founder members, *Sir Alun Talfan Davies* (1994–95) (cat. 70) – was unveiled at the NMW, Cardiff.[112] Though Ivor was now aged 82, and not as mobile as he had once been, the audience at the unveiling agreed that there was absolutely no sign of any diminution in the quality of the portrait he had produced; it was widely judged a 'speaking likeness', balancing as ever the ideal with the credibly imperfect, reinforced by the impression many remarked upon that Sir Alun, famous in his day as a skilled, relentless, probing prosecuting barrister, was about to engage the viewer in some rigorous cross-examination.[113] Ivor was still in demand for portraits; there was talk of a recently arrived commission to portray Placido Domingo (Fig. 2.24), which would involve the artist travelling for the first time to Rome.[114] But Ivor died before sittings could begin.

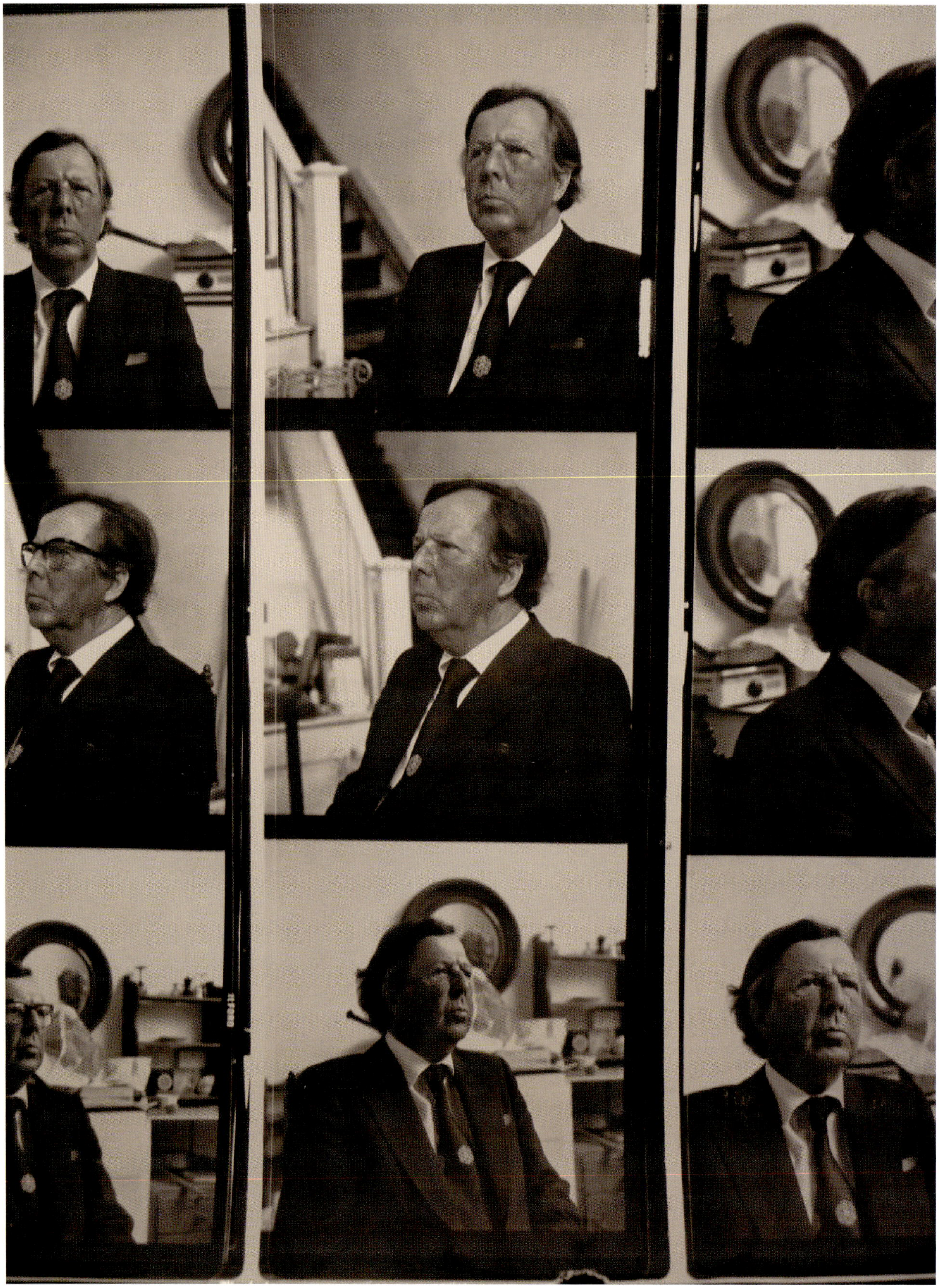

Fig. 2.23 Ivor Roberts-Jones, contact sheet of photographs of Cledwyn Hughes, Lord Hughes of Penrhos, taken in 1990 in the artist's studio, 31 St James's Gardens, London; Image: Courtesy of the HMI, Leeds

Reacting to his death, many of Ivor's obituary writers were in agreement that he had been one of the finest British portrait sculptors of the twentieth century, a worthy devotee of Rodin whose best heads were imbued with a calm, reflective and persuasively intimate power.[115] This perception has only grown in the years since, which have seen a marked revival in the fortunes of the Society of Portrait Sculptors,[116] of which Ivor had been a founder member in the early years of his career.[117]

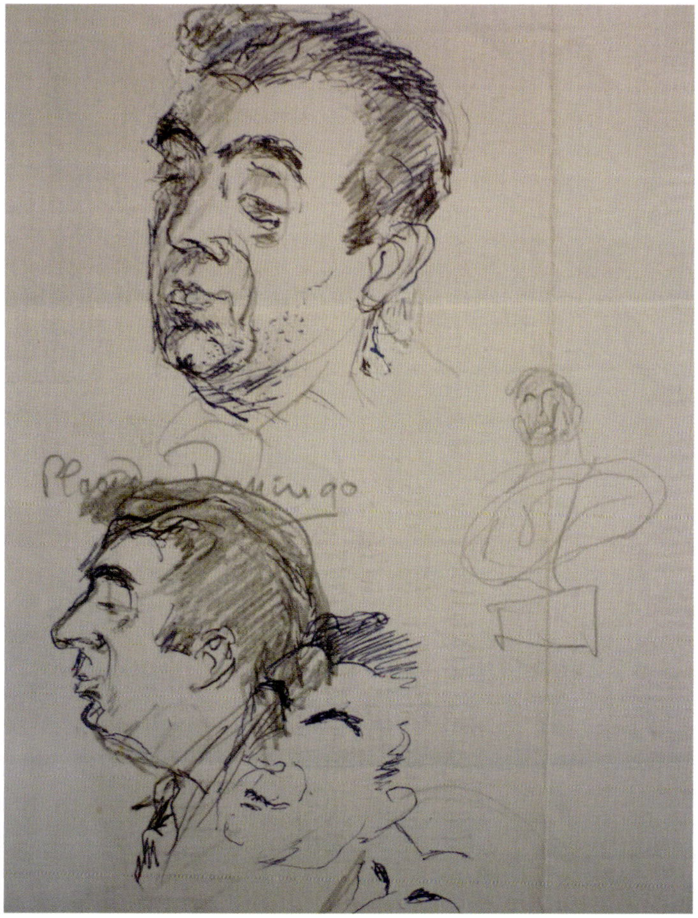

Fig. 2.24 Ivor Roberts-Jones, *Three Studies of Placido Domingo*, c. 1993–94, pen and ink on paper (an invoice from the Meridian Foundry, Peckham), 21 x 10 cm, Image: Courtesy of the HMI, Leeds

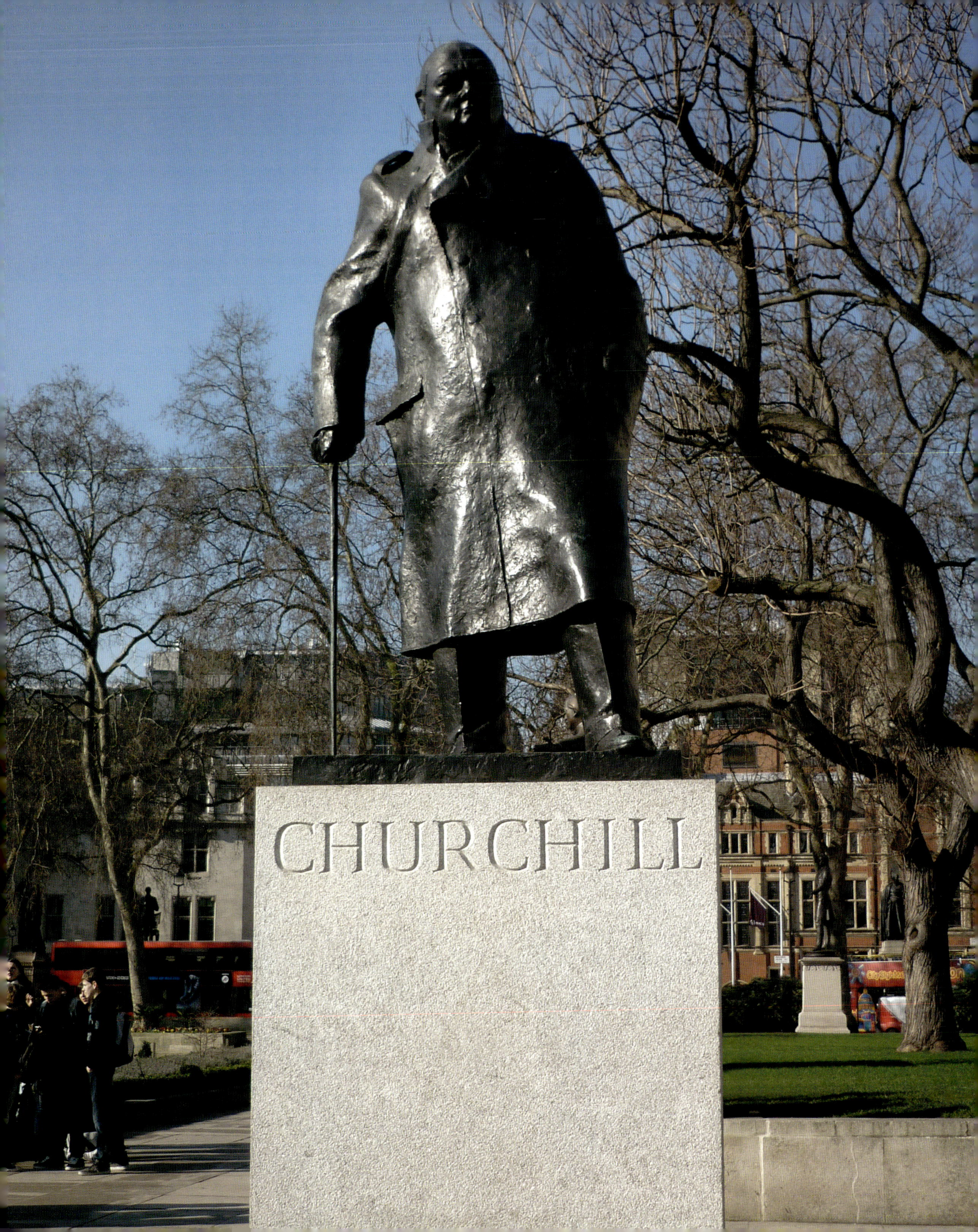
CHURCHILL

MAKING THE ROCK OF GIBRALTAR

IVOR ROBERTS-JONES AND THE SIR WINSTON CHURCHILL COMMISSION FOR PARLIAMENT SQUARE (1970–73)

JONATHAN BLACK

'The best portraits often contain a mixture of love and malice.'

Ivor Roberts-Jones, 1985[1]

'With his statue of Sir Winston Churchill in Parliament Square, unveiled in November 1973, Ivor Roberts-Jones created one of the grandest works of public sculpture in Britain.'

The Times, December 1996[2]

'It is a remarkable statue that manages to capture Winston Churchill's love for the Parliament he spent so many decades in, with the defiant gaze that represents the determination with which he led our country in its darkest and greatest hour.'

Rt Hon. George Osborne MP, June 2013[3]

Cat. 135 *Sir Winston Churchill KG, OM, CH,* 1970–73

After he was awarded the commission to produce a 3.6-metre figure for Parliament Square in March 1971, Ivor was often to speak of the work that brought him to public and critical attention and secured him a mention in *Who's Who.*[4] He welcomed the recognition initially, but as time passed came to perceive the 'Winston outside Parliament' as something of a double-edged achievement – he came to feel its very success actually diverted attention away from his other public works, and from other forms of sculptural activity such as portrait heads.[5] As for Churchill the man, Ivor appears to have harboured decidedly mixed feelings about him. In the years after 1971 he was to describe Churchill as a 'titan', a 'great war leader' and an 'inspiration to the British people in a time of crisis'. He also referred to him in rather less complimentary terms as a 'monster',[6] 'a petulant baby',[7] a man who had resembled a 'boiled sweet'[8] in a uniform with an egg-shaped head that could resemble a 'hairy gooseberry'.[9] He later recalled that he had never seen the statesman at close quarters; he remembered two of his tutors at the RA Schools arguing heatedly about Churchill around 1935: one had described him as a warmonger and reactionary imperialist who was opposed to even the limited degree of self-government that was being offered to Indian nationalists; the other offered the counter-argument that Britain would one day bitterly regret not heeding Churchill's warnings about the future expansionist plans of a resurgent and aggressive Nazi Germany. Ivor reflected both had been right – Winston was a man of many facets, by no means all of them attractive.[10]

It would be safe to say that the sculptor admired Churchill but was certainly not uncritical of him, nor blind to his faults. He later thought it was much to Churchill's credit that 'the great man' took a keen interest in political cartoons, and even collected those by cartoonists such as David Low (1891–1963) and George Strube[11] (1891–1956), whom Ivor also admired, that featured himself – invariably wearing a wide variety of hats that were at least two sizes too small for his egg-shaped cranium.[12] Indeed, Churchill was on record as stating that not being caricatured, however scurrilously, was a clear sign that one's political career was inexorably sliding into oblivion.[13]

The evidence that survives does indicate that Ivor was extremely keen to secure the Churchill commission in 1970–71, partly because he regarded him as such a challenge as a subject for a portrait head that would still seem convincing to a mass audience despite standing high above their heads in Parliament Square. Ivor was also all too aware of the existence of numerous other sculptures of Churchill, who in his lifetime had sat to Sir William Reid Dick (in 1941),[14] Jacob Epstein (1947)[15] and Oscar Nemon in the early 1950s.[16] Later in that decade, Nemon had made a seated figure of Churchill for the Guildhall (unveiled in 1955) and a pugnaciously energetic standing figure of the man for the Members' Lobby of the House of Commons, commissioned in 1967[17] (Fig. 3.1) This would be unveiled in December 1969, but even before the ceremony there were certain Conservative MPs, such as Sir John Tilney[18] and Sir John Rodgers,[19] who were rather dissatisfied with Nemon's conception of Churchill and wanted to commission a full-length figure of the man for Parliament Square, where it would be truly accessible to the public – which was not true of the Nemon figure inside the House of Commons.[20]

In December 1967 Sir John Tilney first raised the question of a statue of Churchill for the north-east corner of Parliament Square, where the statesman had apparently once indicated he would like to be commemorated in sculpture.[21] In July 1969 the then Labour Prime Minister, Harold Wilson, indicated that the government was 'prepared to offer a site in Parliament Square for a statue of the late Sir Winston Churchill'. Wilson then suggested that Tilney form a committee from among members of the House of Commons 'to raise sufficient funds to pay for the proposed statue'.[22]

By late September 1969 a Winston Churchill Memorial Committee (WCMC) had been formed, with Tilney as chairman. Minutes of its early meetings reveal that, while a minority of members – including Churchill's son-in-law and Conservative MP Duncan Sandys,[23] and Labour peers Lord Goodman[24] and Lord Shinwell[25] – thought Oscar Nemon should have first preference for the commission, many others, particularly Tilney, Rodgers, Labour MP George Strauss (chairman of the House of Commons Art Committee)[26] and Conservative peer Oliver Lyttelton, First Lord Chandos (at the time first chairman of the National Theatre) wanted to consider other sculptors, who ideally would be British. Sir John Rodgers, for example, argued that 'before deciding on Mr Nemon, who was a Yugoslav, the Committee should at least consider one, or two, English sculptors'.[27]

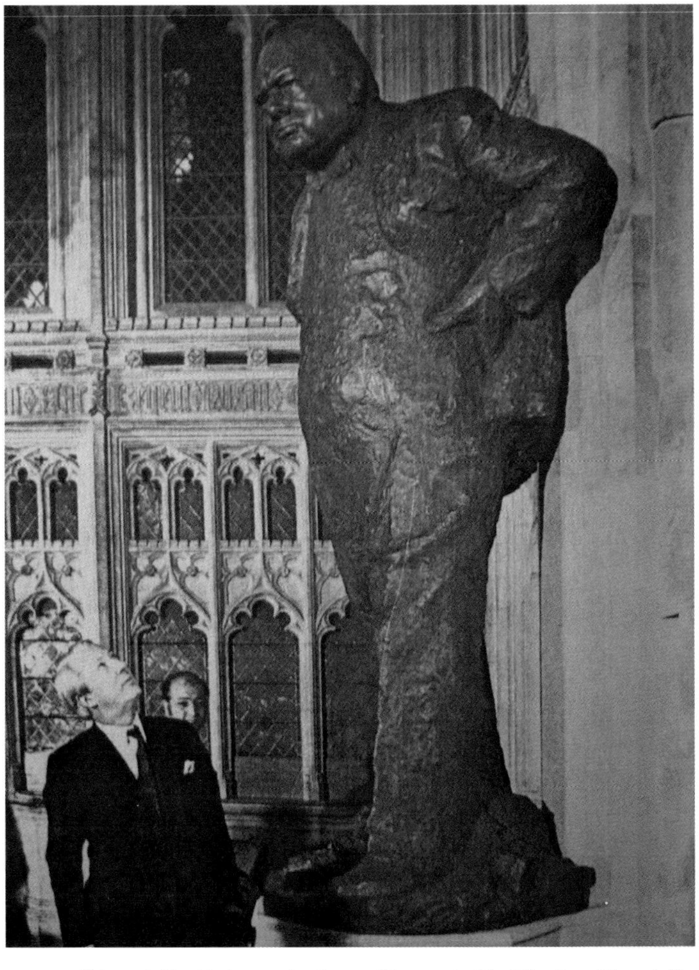

Fig. 3.1 Edward Heath inspects Oscar Nemon's *Sir Winston Churchill*, 1967–69, bronze, 2.18 m high, Members' Lobby, House of Commons, London; Image: Courtesy Churchill Archive Centre, Churchill College, Cambridge

Accordingly, Tilney approached the Royal Fine Art Commission to inspect two maquettes of Churchill that Nemon wished to submit for consideration for the Parliament Square site, and to provide advice as to the selection of a sculptor if Nemon's conception of Churchill proved wanting. The Commission, in turn, asked Henry Moore to inspect Nemon's maquettes, which he did in February 1970. He was not impressed, and made alternative recommendations to the WCMC: Elisabeth Frink, Ralph Brown, F. E. McWilliam and Reg Butler.[28]

By this time the WCMC had formed a smaller Statue Adjudication Sub-Committee, consisting of Tilney, Rodgers, Strauss, Lord Chandos and Richard Crawfurd-Benson, a professional fund-raiser Chandos had recommended be employed by the WCMC. The members of the Sub-Committee had not heard of most of the sculptors Moore suggested, and they did not like the look of the sculpture by those with whom they were familiar, such as Frink and Butler. Tilney decided that, in order to draw up a short-list of likely sculptors, the Sub-Committee should seek the advice of two 'expert assessors' – initially Sir Kenneth Clark and Sir Philip Hendy were considered and approached; they were interested but declined citing the burden of other commitments.[29] Both urged Tilney to approach Sir John Pope-Hennessy (then director of the Victoria and Albert Museum) and the sculptor Sean Crampton (then president of the Royal Society of British Sculptors). The two agreed to help, and by 19 March 1970 had drawn up a short-list of nine sculptors; eight of those approached later that month agreed to participate in a competition for the Churchill figure, and to submit a plaster maquette some 60 centimetres high by the end of June. The eight sculptors in question were, in no particular order, Frederick E. McWilliam, Oscar Nemon, Michael Rizzello, Ivor Roberts-Jones, Anthony Grey, Franta Belsky, Bentley Claughton and Sir Charles Wheeler.[30]

There are hints that Ivor was one of the earlier names to be discussed and to make it on to the short-list. Chandos was an admirer of two portrait heads Ivor had made in the early 1960s for the Arts Council: *Lord Kenyon* (cat. 29) and *Sir William Emrys Williams* (cat. 28), while George Strauss appears to have been aware, via his wife, the collector Patricia Strauss,[31] of Ivor's figure of *Apsley Cherry-Garrard* (cat. 132) and his Augustus John (cat. 133), unveiled by Lord Mountbatten – with whom the Strausses were friendly – in October 1967.[32]

The Sub-Committee considered eight maquettes on 1 July 1970. Its members were not really that happy with any submitted, but the two that showed most promise were by Ivor and Oscar Nemon. Both were asked to go away and submit a reconceived maquette at the beginning of November, in four months' time. In his first effort Ivor had depicted Churchill wearing the bulky and distinctive robes of a Knight of the Garter – awarded in April 1953[33] and conferred in June the following year, when the statesman had been prime minister and was aged nearly eighty.[34] The Sub-Committee felt that Ivor had conveyed all too well how vulnerable and frail Churchill had been at the time, and asked him to depict him wearing some form of uniform that would recall his time as the nation's leader during the Second World War.[35]

Four months later, when the two sculptors submitted their new maquettes, Ivor's proved to be by far the preferred design.[36] In the intervening period – June–October 1970 – he had read widely about Churchill, and had been impressed by the opinion of the statesman offered by Churchill's doctor, Charles Wilson (later Lord Moran). In particular, he noted Moran's interpretation of Churchill's hostile reaction to the portrait of him by Graham Sutherland, an artist whom Ivor greatly admired,[37] which had been presented to Churchill on the occasion of his eightieth birthday in November 1954. In private, Churchill had described Sutherland's portrait as 'filthy and malignant'.[38] Moran thought the painter had in fact 'worshipped [Churchill] too blindly'. Early on in his sittings with Churchill at Chartwell, Sutherland had ruefully told Moran: 'There are so many Churchills, I have to find the right one.' When Moran heard that Sutherland wanted to paint his sitter as 'the lion at bay', he warned the painter: 'Winston is always acting, try to see him when he has got the grease paint off his face.' But Moran felt Sutherland had painted Churchill 'as he pictured him in his own favourite part ... he has accepted the legend for the truth'.[39]

Moran further mused that Churchill had been 'bullied at school', that he was 'not tall', and had been 'un-muscular with delicate hands ... Consequently he had resolved to become tough, to test his nerve under fire. When the war came and he was cast for the part of a tough he knew his lines ... the intimidating scowl ... was made to order.' The nation pictured him 'defying the overwhelming strength of a warrior race. He liked the part, it was the role he had dreamed would fall to him and he was soon playing it for all he was worth.' He felt Sutherland had only offered a 'surface impression' and 'missed the story that lies hidden beneath that fierce façade'. Moran concluded that those who portrayed Churchill all too often missed the fact that his features were 'delicate, almost feminine ... the lips too, they often pout, are delicately moulded'.[40] Ivor took Moran's words to heart. In his portrayal of Churchill he would try to offer a more subtle image of the statesman – of the toughness as well as the delicacy – in order to hint at the tremendous will-power required to play the physically and emotionally demanding role of the embodiment of an entire nation's defiance. As the sculptor was later to put it, the truly effective portrait must provide evidence for both weakness and strength in the character of a subject,[41] and must combine elements of 'love and honesty' and even 'love and malice' on the part of the artist.[42]

The maquette Ivor submitted to the Committee in November 1970 (Fig. 3.2; cat. 135a) presented Churchill wearing not one of the many uniforms he had sported during the war, but in a capacious British Army greatcoat of a type that had first emerged during the First World War, and was known as a 'British Warm'. Churchill had been photographed wearing this greatcoat during a visit he paid to the battle front in Normandy in July 1944, during the Yalta Conference in February 1945 (Fig. 3.3), and in Germany in late March 1945 to observe the crossing of the Rhine by British and Canadian forces. Depicting Churchill in such a coat could also be readily interpreted as a reference to his colourful military career with the British Army – as a second lieutenant in the 4th Hussars (1895–99), when he saw action on the North-west Frontier[43] and, then, in the Sudan, where he took part in one of the last great cavalry charges made by a British Regiment, the 21st Lancers, against the Dervish at Omdurman in September 1898.[44] During the charge he later calculated that he had shot and killed at least five Dervish warriors, and possibly five, at close range.[45] Then, after resigning from the government front bench in November 1915, he had commanded a battalion of the Royal Scots in Flanders, from January to May 1916, when he experienced several close shaves with death.[46] This was an aspect of Churchill's career that does appear to have appealed to Ivor; the sculptor was later to observe that, at least – unlike most politicians who sent young men off to war to be shot at – Churchill did know what it was like to be shot at with bullet and artillery shell.[47]

Ivor later indicated that the pose of the figure had been largely inspired by a famous photograph of a grim-faced and sorrowful Churchill inspecting the smouldering wreckage of the Chamber of his beloved House of Commons on the morning of 11 May 1941 (Fig. 3.4).[48] The Chamber had been largely demolished by two 500kg bombs that had hit the House of Commons during a Luftwaffe raid the previous evening.[49] Much was made at the time of Churchill's determination before the rubble, but the prime minister's actual reaction, as the lobby journalist Guy Eden was later to write, was characteristically emotional,[50] as Eden recalled in 1953:

> I stood with Winston Churchill amid the still-smoking ruins of the House of Commons which had, a few hours earlier, been shattered by Nazi bombs. The Prime Minister gazed silently, a long time. His eyes travelled sadly along the space where the floor of the Chamber had been, to the site of the Table from which he had delivered many a speech ... His jaw muscles were working tensely as he looked slowly around. The end of his walking stick he carried was ground silently and savagely into the powdering cinders that had once been part of the doors leading from behind the Speaker's Chair ... For a full five minutes ... he let his eyes rove ... At last he moved, and in the dim light I could see that tears were running unchecked down his cheeks. Turning abruptly to an official, he controlled his voice with an effort and said quietly: 'This Chamber must be rebuilt – just as it was! Meanwhile, we shall not miss a single day's debate through this!' Brushing the sleeve of his coat across his eyes with the gesture of a schoolboy rather shamefacedly hiding his tears from public gaze, Churchill strode off, back to his War Room ... back to his planning ... for the victory that was to make him, a few years later, the most lauded and cheered man in the land ... and to change the course of history.[51]

His depiction of Churchill wearing the distinctive 'British Warm', Ivor later conceded, owed a great deal to the example in Ancient Egyptian sculpture of high officials wearing tight-fitting robes (Fig. 3.5). Less predictable was the example of a statuette in the British Museum of a hawk, Horus, which Ivor was convinced had exerted a considerable impact on Rodin as he conceived his majestic figure of a tubby *Balzac* (1897–98) wrapped in a dressing gown (Figs 3.6, 3.7).[52] In 1989 the sculptor told the writer John Blackwood:

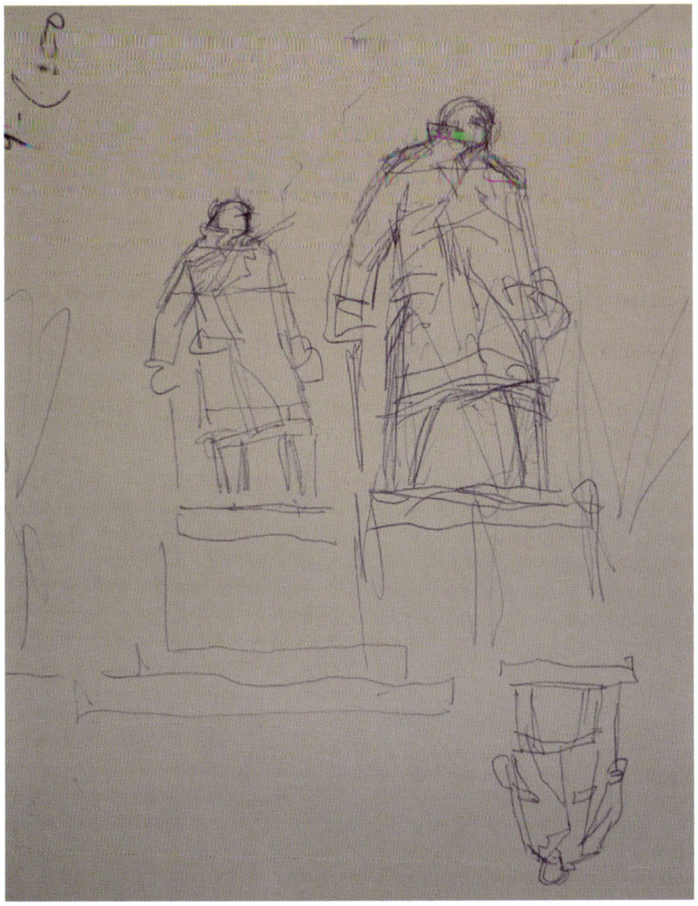

Fig. 3.2 Ivor Roberts-Jones, *Two Studies for his Second Version of Sir Winston Churchill*, 1970, pen and ink on paper, 21 x 14.5 cm, Image: Courtesy of the HMI, Leeds

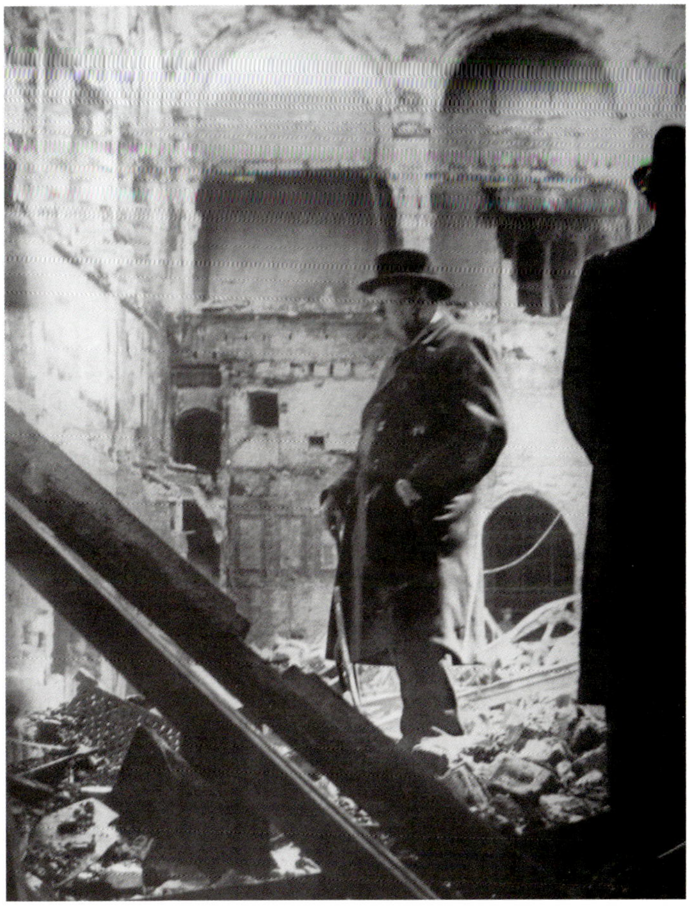

Fig. 3.4 Winston Churchill viewing the ruins of the Chamber of the House of Commons, 11 May 1941; Image: Courtesy of the Churchill Archive Centre, Churchill College, Cambridge

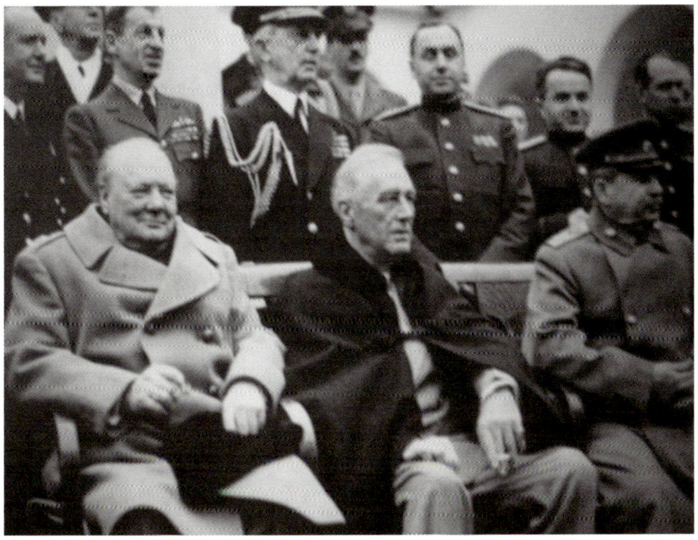

Fig. 3.3 Winston Churchill wearing a 'British Warm' greatcoat at the Yalta Conference, February 1945; Image: Courtesy Churchill Archive Centre, Churchill College, Cambridge

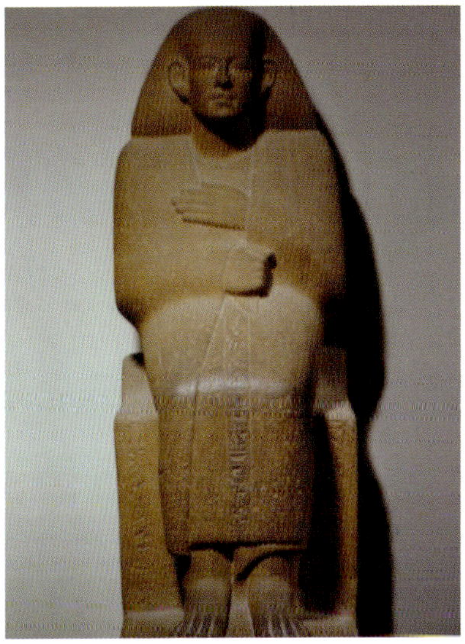

Fig. 3.5 *Seated Figure of a High Official/Ankhrekhu*, c. 1991–1640 BCE, quartzite, 71 cm high, British Museum, London; Image: Courtesy of British Museum Images

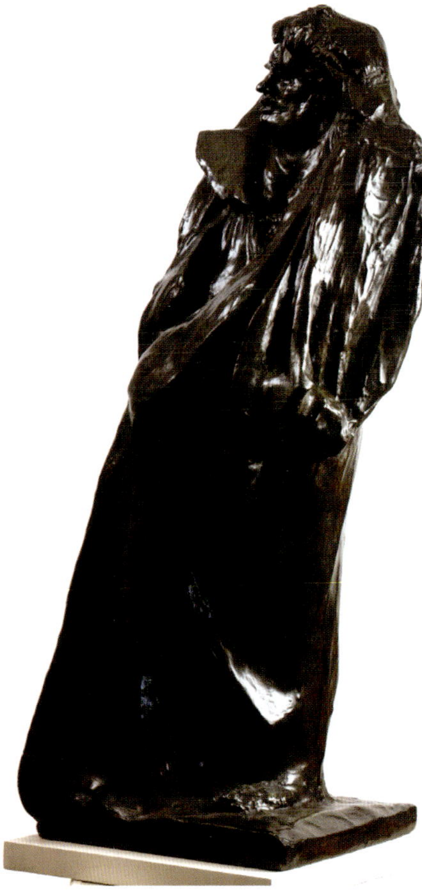

Fig. 3.6 Auguste Rodin, *Honoré de Balzac*, 1896–98, bronze, 1.1 m high, Private Collection; Image: Courtesy of a Private Collection

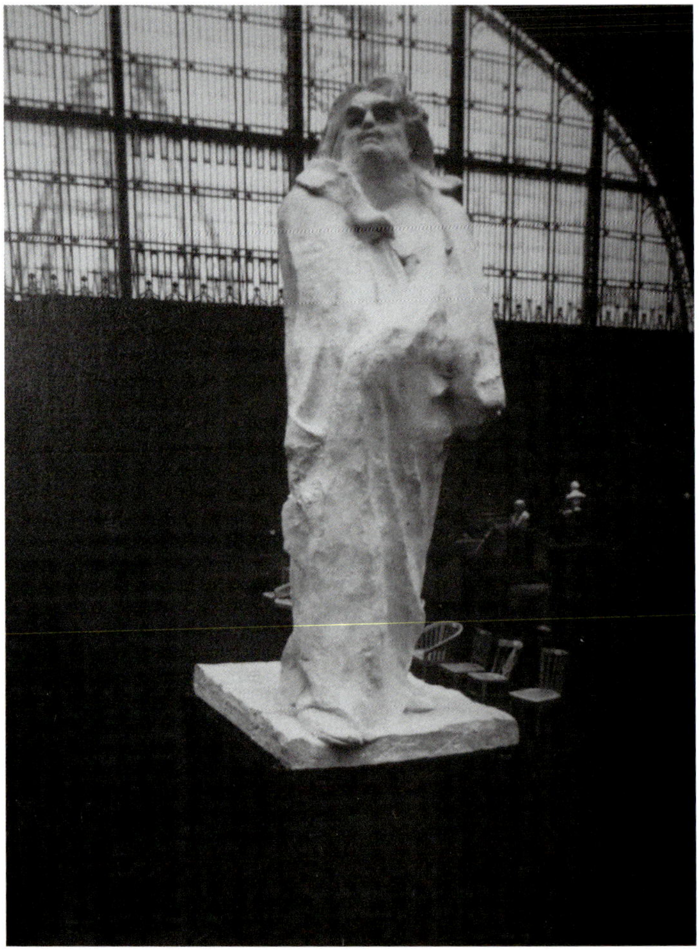

Fig. 3.7 Rodin's full-sized 2-m-high plaster maquette of his memorial to *Honoré de Balzac* on display at the Paris Salon of 1898; Image: Courtesy of the Musée Rodin, Paris

> One of the chief images present in the sculptor's mind as he worked [on the Churchill maquette] was Rodin's famous statue of Balzac in which the looming, yet self-contained bulk of the body, is similarly important. He believed that Rodin was influenced in the making of that statue by a small Egyptian hawk of Horus which he had in his possession (and which is now in the Rodin Museum).[53]

Other similar statues of Horus, also in the British Museum (Fig. 3.8) seemed to him 'to gather up their spiritual fighting energy by resting back on their tails. Accordingly, the figure of Churchill, likewise, leans slightly backwards, as if receiving and absorbing the full brunt of the Nazi onslaught before moving onwards again.'[54]

During the early autumn of 1970, in Paris, he had looked at a statue (Fig. 3.9) of the fiery French First World War prime minister Georges 'The Tiger' Clemenceau (1841–1929) by François Cogné (1876–1952). It had been unveiled in November 1932 near the Métro Champs-Elysées-Clemenceau, fittingly on the Avenue Winston Churchill. Rodin's bronze head of Clemenceau (made c. 1911–13) was one of his favourite portraits by the Frenchman.[55] Nearer to home, he had inspected Hamo Thornycroft's impressive *Oliver Cromwell* (Fig. 3.10), unveiled October 1899, whose pose anticipates that of Ivor's second maquette of Churchill. The right foot of Cromwell is advanced forward, whereas the weight is actually placed on the left foot, the Parliamentary General leaning with his right hand on a vertical object – a sword. Ivor's Churchill presses down for support with his right hand on the type of walking cane he had carried since 1908, when he first achieved a position in government as president of the Board of Trade, under Asquith.[56] The detail rather neatly hints at Churchill's physical frailty – he had been 67 years old in 1941 – and at the same time gives the impression of steadfast resolution, of Churchill braced to receive the onslaught of an oncoming enemy. Ivor also decided to leave Churchill bareheaded – in the photograph he is wearing a homburg – and without his trademark cigar. It is perhaps significant that in the photograph Churchill is not wearing the bulky British Warm but a lighter, less substantial and less sculpturally impressive overcoat – suitable for a fresh spring morning like 11 May 1941.

It became evident early in November 1970 that the Adjudication Sub-Committee was unanimous in its verdict that Ivor was the sculptor equal to the demands of the commission.[57] Its decision was confirmed a week later by the Royal Fine Art Commission (RFAC) in the form of a panel led by its chairman, Sir Colin Anderson. The Commission thereafter wrote to Tilney that it wished to 'congratulate your Committee, the Assessors and the Sculptor on the production of the first stage of what promises to be a very good piece of sculpture. They strongly support your acceptance of it.'[58] Not unreasonably, Tilney informed Ivor of his success and asked him to begin work on a full-sized model in clay of the head of his Churchill statue.[59] The final statue was to be over three metres high, and would be simply too large to make in either his studio at St James's Gardens or at his other residence in Woodbridge – Ivor concluded that he would have to find a larger space to work on the commission.[60]

Meanwhile, Nemon still had his supporters on the wider Churchill Memorial Committee – namely Sandys, Shinwell and Goodman. Possibly through Sandys, Nemon got wind of the decision in favour of Ivor, and early in February 1971 he petitioned the Committee to give him a little more time to submit another maquette.[61] Meanwhile, Churchill's widow and daughter Sarah mobilised on Nemon's behalf – on the grounds that Churchill had actually sat to him, whereas Ivor had not met him and had conceived his maquette using photographs.[62] Sarah Churchill wrote to her mother, copying in Duncan Sandys:

> This urgent note is about Nemon's statue in Parliament Square which so far has been turned down. He was most moved that you should have championed him at this apparently late date. As far as I can gather the Committee for Papa's statue in Parliament Square was not unanimously in favour of the final decision of the RFAC ... I know how anxious you are that the outcome should be a statue that is acceptable to you. You have seen the preliminary large scale study of Papa by Nemon in his studio – which Papa saw and approved. Nemon now suggests that the other sculptor chosen by the RFAC [Ivor] should produce his statue full-size in plaster and that the two should then be compared and that a choice should then be made. The better one would then be easier to determine. If such a solution would be acceptable to [minister of public works] Julian Amery, it would relieve us all from a certain amount of anxiety and distress and also serve to maintain the standard of likeness which we as a family have approved ...[63]

A week later, Nemon followed up with a further plea to Tilney:

> I understand that the maquette of *Sir Winston Churchill*, which I submitted to your Committee, has been rejected because the body was not considered satisfactory but that the head, which would seem to be the most important part for such a statue, received general approval. Since I feel confident that I could produce another design for the body which would be more acceptable, I ask you to allow me to submit a full-sized statue with the same head and another body in plaster for consideration by your Committee before a final decision is taken. If you accept my offer, this work will of course be carried out entirely at my own expense. I am sending copies of this letter to the Minister Mr Julian Amery and to Lady Churchill for their information.[64]

On 22 February 1971 the WCMC met with its two adjudication assessors, Crampton and Pope-Hennessy, the RFAC and the minister of public works to consider once again the merits of Ivor's maquette – this time in relation to a new submission from Nemon. After a couple of hours of often 'heated' discussion, Tilney was to record that the members of the Adjudication Sub-Committee, its two assessors, an overwhelming majority of the larger Memorial Committee and the representatives of the RFAC, 'after viewing the maquettes by Mr Nemon and Mr Roberts-Jones, unreservedly confirmed their support of the Committee's initial selection of Mr Roberts-Jones as the sculptor for the statue'.[65]

Ivor seems to have learned the true extent of all the manoeuvring that had taken place over the statue only some months later – possibly through Lord Chandos, who had indicated a desire to sit to him for a portrait bust (cat. 39). Understandably, he was rather angry about Nemon's behaviour and conceived a distinct animus towards the man, which in later years was to approach paranoia concerning any competition in which both were participating. He also convinced himself that any image of Churchill he produced would fail to satisfy the Churchill family – especially the formidable Lady Clementine.[66]

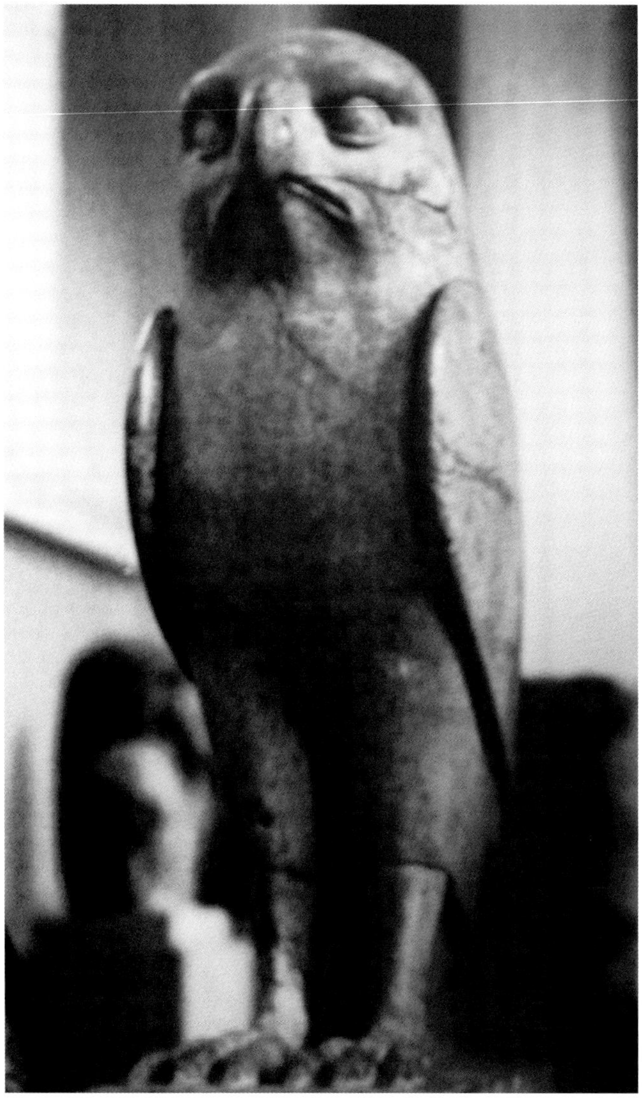

Fig. 3.8 *Figure of a Hawk*, c. 1550–1307 BCE, limestone, 60 cm high, British Museum, London; Image: Courtesy of British Museum Images

But all this lay in the future. In mid March 1971 the WCMC formally announced that Ivor would be the sculptor of a 3.6-metre-high bronze statue of Churchill, costing £30,000 (over £1.2 million today) to stand on a 2.4-metre-high plinth at the north-east corner of Parliament Square.[67] The sculptor's winning maquette was reproduced in the press, to cautious approval.[68] Interviewed by the *Illustrated London News*, Ivor declared, when it came to portraiture,

> If I see an interesting face, a face I like, I just do it and usually it's nobody famous at all. For Churchill, on the other hand, I wanted to make something monumental, large in concept. Obviously, I wanted to get a likeness and I think I have done so but, above all, I wanted to achieve a sculptural quality, not just a society portrait.[69]

Later that spring Ivor bought Orchard Farm, a property near Cratfield in the depths of Suffolk, complete with a 300-year-old tithe barn that was to serve as his new studio, where he would have the space to make the gigantic full-sized model of his Churchill statue.[70] He later revealed that he had even sold his yacht and given up sailing from nearby Woodbridge to concentrate on the Churchill commission.[71]

As it transpired even the barn would not prove large enough. With the help of a local farmer, Ivor built an extension to it from bales of hay covered in polythene.[72] He now had the room he required, though the bales proved a mixed blessing as the hay was an occasional temptation to hungry dairy cows, and Ivor twice found himself having to fend off bovine incursions as he was working on the full-sized clay model.[73]

During the summer of 1971, while Ivor was working on the monumental full-sized head of Churchill in clay in his barn at Cratfield, he evidently also explored the idea of placing the final statue in the centre of Parliament Square. He produced a number of sketches (Fig. 3.11) revealing that occasionally recurring 'Expressionist' aspect to his imagination,[74] in which the figure was 'surrounded by various semi-abstract, rectangular bronze shapes in the grass. These, lit up on special occasions, would represent

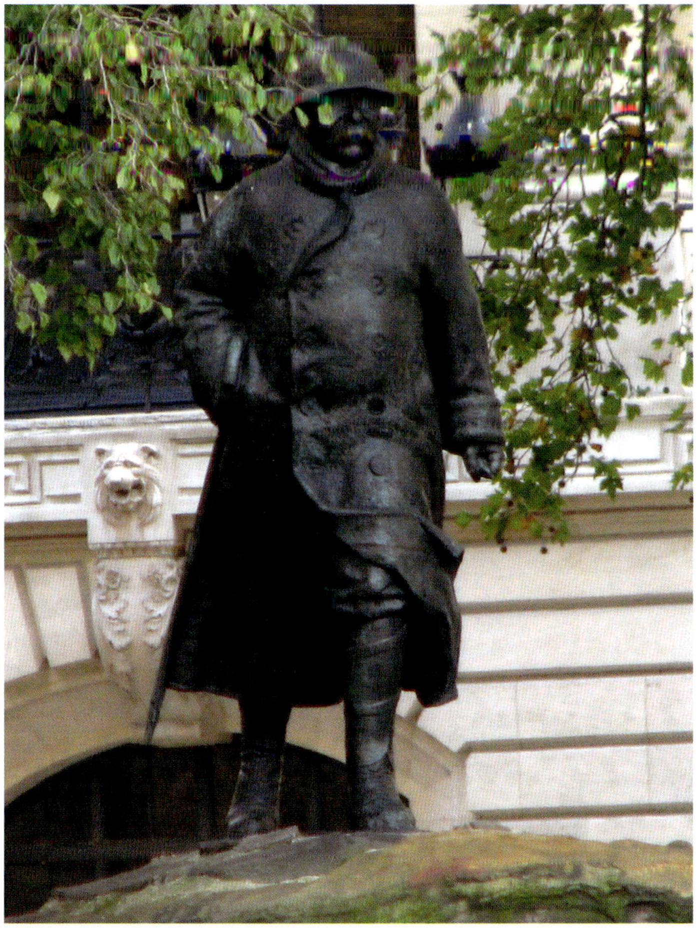

Fig. 3.9 François Cogné, *Georges Clemenceau*, 1930–32, bronze, 2.13 m high, Place Clemenceau, Paris; Image: J. Black

burning beams and so would show Churchill walking through the ruins of London during the Blitz, encouraging and inspiring.' But this would have required expensive relandscaping of the Square and the cutting down of a number of trees, which the Department of the Environment and Westminster Council had made clear they would simply not sanction.[75] Meanwhile, from the outset, Tilney, Rodgers and a majority on the Committee had made it clear that the final statue would be sited in the north-east corner of the Square.[76]

By late September 1971, Tilney was able to report to Duncan Sandys that Ivor had 'completed the full-size head of Churchill and the recent good weather has allowed him to work on it out of doors [at Cratfield] so that he has been able to observe it in all kinds of light'[77] (Fig. 3.12). In addition, he could confirm that the sculptor's fee had been set at £18,000, while Ivor had estimated the statue would cost at least £6,500 to cast. He was hoping the statue would be ready for unveiling by 'May/June 1973'.[78]

In mid-February the following year, Tilney despatched Crawfurd-Benson to Orchard Farm to provide a progress report on the figure of Churchill taking shape inside Ivor's studio-barn. Towards the end of the month he wrote to Tilney:

> The work is still very much in progress. The statue is far from finished although it is well advanced on schedule. The head and shoulders have been cast in plaster and the body is still in clay. Casting the head and shoulders in plaster allows Mr Roberts-Jones to work on them in the open outside his studio barn and does not mean the features are immutable. In fact, he has two full-size heads in plaster ... One has to remember, when looking at the heads at eye level, that they will finally be about 20 feet above the ground. Mr Roberts-Jones has studied the site [in Parliament Square] closely and has assessed that the most advantageous place for viewing this large statue will be on the opposite side of the roadway, approximately 90 feet away. He feels, therefore, that the present downward angle of the head is not quite right and so is considering raising that angle by 5 degrees.

Crawfurd-Benson added:

> At the moment Mr Roberts-Jones has difficulties with light [falling] on the statue. The light in his large studio barn is in fact good. Indeed, when the sun shines it is too brilliant. He cannot, however, get far enough away from the statue to study the effects of light to which the statue will be subject in its final position. When the weather improves, he will move the statue out of the barn – but for that move it will have to be cast in plaster. Rain would wash the clay away. This casting, which it was hoped could be done at Easter, will probably be slightly delayed because Mr Roberts-Jones is not yet satisfied with the complete figure ...

He then proceeded to draw attention to a photograph he had enclosed of Ivor working on the large head and shoulders of Churchill:

> You may notice from the photograph that the collar is raised on the right side of the coat. That occurred quite

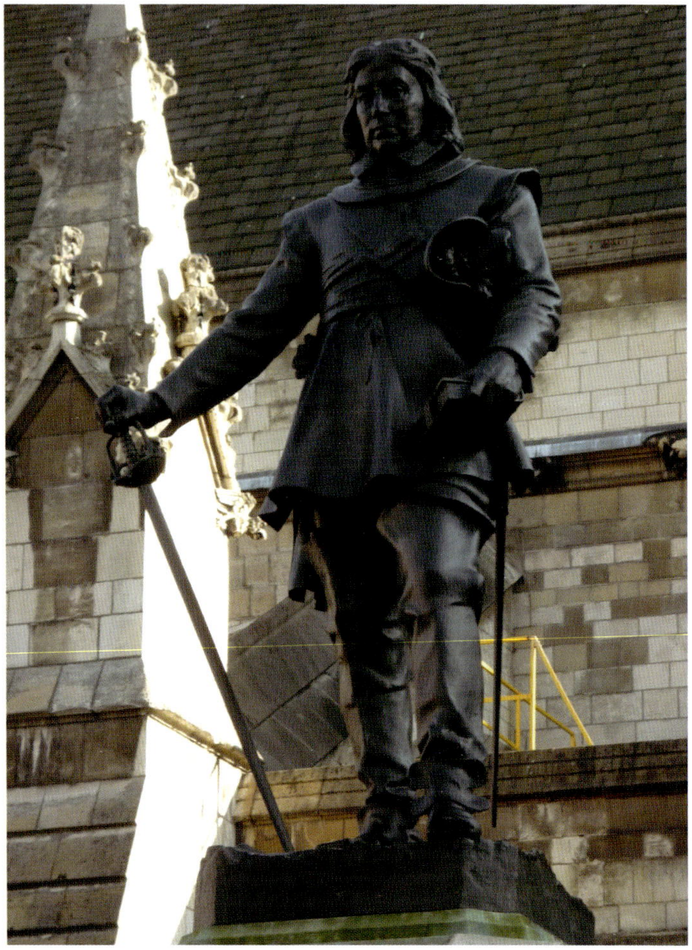

Fig. 3.10 Hamo Thornycroft, *Oliver Cromwell*, 1897–99, bronze, 2 m high, outside the House of Commons, London; Image: J. Black

unintentionally during the work and Mr Roberts-Jones thinks he may retain it in the finished work. When the statue faces New Palace Yard, the lifted right side of the collar would indicate the force of the prevalent south-west wind. Finally, I must record Mr Roberts-Jones's devotion to his work. He has met all his difficulties – there have been some major engineering problems – with cheerfulness and determination. He has not been beaten by them. He has been most patient and agreeable with any suggestions without altering his high artistic standards. His attention to detail, his studies of other statues of Sir Winston and, above all, his enthusiasm are most impressive and, yet, when I mentioned to him that the Committee was due to pay him another instalment of £6,000 at the end of March, he said that he did not think he deserved a payment so soon.[79]

Ivor was later to describe at some length the 'major engineering problems' he had experienced during the commission. Indeed, it would seem that in the autumn of 1971 he asked the advice of the sculptor and protégé of Epstein, David McFall (1919–1988),[80] on how best to tackle the making of such a large full-sized figure of Churchill. McFall had earlier produced an over-life-size figure of Churchill for Woodford in Kent, around 1957–59 – a commission that had proved particularly contentious and drawn-out[81] – and had assisted Epstein with the making of his statue of the South African Second World War leader *Field Marshal Smuts* for Parliament Square (unveiled in November 1958).[82] Ivor also looked to the advice offered by Charles Sargeant Jagger in his 1933 publication *Modelling and Sculpture in the Making* for guidance on tackling such a daunting project from a technical point of view.[83]

In January 1973 the journalist Byron Rogers was to note how the 12-foot-high (3.6-metre) full-sized model of the Churchill statue, 'surrounded by scaffolding and ladders', dwarfed the diminutive sculptor (Fig. 3.13). Ivor described how daunting the process had been of just transporting the sculpture: 'two and a half tons of clay' to make the 'bloody huge' figure in his barn. Rogers described the sculptor as 'a small, quick man, who shins up one of the ladders like a Lilliputian tailor'. Ivor told him: 'When you think of a 12-foot man you just tend to think of something twice life-size: two six-foot men, one on top of the other. But it is not. A 12-foot man is eight times life size. It is the volume.' He had bought the barn specifically to fulfil this commission: 'I wanted room for the statue, and I wanted enough room to get as far back from it as I could, to see it the way a spectator would. I realised I should need even more room. So I had the idea of taking the door away.' Ivor was generous in his praise for the assistance he was receiving from John Dellow, one of his colleagues at Goldsmiths, but added plaintively: 'The Victorian sculptors had marvellous devices like hydraulic lifts. You would press a button and the whole figure would disappear into the floor so that you could work on whatever part you wanted. On the kind of money I am being paid, I could not afford even part of any equipment like that. So I have put all these ladders up. I have to go up and down a hundred times a day.' He admitted that one thing which had 'taken him unawares' during the winter of 1971–72 was the Suffolk cold. 'Clay can freeze, you see. It is full of moisture. And when it freezes it cracks and crumbles. Anyway, it was the winter of 1971 when I first had to face the problem. I knew it was getting dangerous, but I decided to carry on. I was working on the shoulders when suddenly all these tiny icicles formed. You can imagine my feelings. I ran to the house and brought in all the stoves I could find. I made a tent of polythene about the figure [Fig. 3.14]. Amazingly, as it turned out, there was no real damage. The whole thing might have been destroyed.[84]

A month later John Windsor, of the *Guardian*, also commented on the practical challenges Ivor had confronted while making the figure of Churchill:

> Unlike the Victorians, who had statues like we have office blocks, he [the sculptor] had no mechanical lift to take him up and down Sir Winston's effigy. So he rigged up gantries with block and tackle suspended from 300-year-old beams in the tithe barn at Cratfield which he bought specially for the statue. There were four ladders in the top. 'It was rather like climbing the mast,' he said ... He was able to trundle the head and shoulders out of the barn with the help of his improvised derricks, but once out he could not hoist it again. Which is why he often had to lie in the wet, gazing up at it.[85]

Crawfurd-Benson concluded his February 1972 report with the comment that Ivor was ' ... at the moment still working and lecturing at Goldsmiths College, but he has been granted sabbatical leave for the Summer Term. He will then devote all his time to the statue until it is ready to go to the bronze foundry in August or September [1972]. He will probably engage for that work Messrs Morris Singer and Co. of Basingstoke.'[86]

However, by July 1972, having also considered using the Art Bronze Foundry, Ivor had decided instead that the statue would be cast by Jack Crofton of the relatively new Meridian Foundry, which Crofton had established in 1966 beneath a railway arch near Peckham Rye railway station. Ivor never regretted this decision, and would use Meridian thereafter to cast all his work until his death. He would later pen a generous testimonial for Crofton and his partner Megan Thomas in which he stated that in

> the two processes of sand casting and the lost wax process – they have no rival. In all respects their work is of the highest order and artists like the late Elisabeth Frink, F. E. McWilliam and many others have made full use of their skills. Megan and Jack have made a tremendous contribution to my career and I would not hesitate to recommend them for work of any size or complexity.[88]

In March 1972 Tilney asked Crawfurd-Benson to visit Ivor in Suffolk once more, and he did so early in April. On 7 April he submitted a progress report to Tilney, opening with an upbeat comment:

> The whole figure has been completed except for the stick which is represented by a piece of wood at present. The head has been cast in plaster and the body is still in clay. Accordingly, the white of the head draws the observer and the body does not receive at first glance the attention it deserves. When the statue is cast in bronze and mounted on its plinth, the order of observation will be reversed, the pose being seen from afar and the face from relatively close to. The pose of the 2 foot [61cm] maquette has been most faithfully followed. Without seeing the features of the face it is obvious that Churchill stands before you. The figure gives the impression of the power, determination and courage of the great war leader. And yet he does not look as if he is about to step off the plinth. A sense of movement has been most skilfully worked in to the static pose. His legs are quite distinct. There is no suggestion of symbolism of rising from the earth, or sea, or ashes of war such as might have been conveyed by filling in the gap between the legs. The legs are not tree trunks but are not quite right. While I was there Mr Roberts-Jones improved the left leg.

Crawfurd-Benson was particularly impressed with the sculptor's treatment of Churchill wearing the 'British Warm' military overcoat:

> The idea that he is wearing a British Warm ... has been portrayed by emphasising the buttons and the outline of the collar. His clothing does not detract though from the character of the man wearing the clothing. The hang of the coat needs improvement in the front and most particularly in the back. With that improvement and the completion of the upturned right lapel, a real

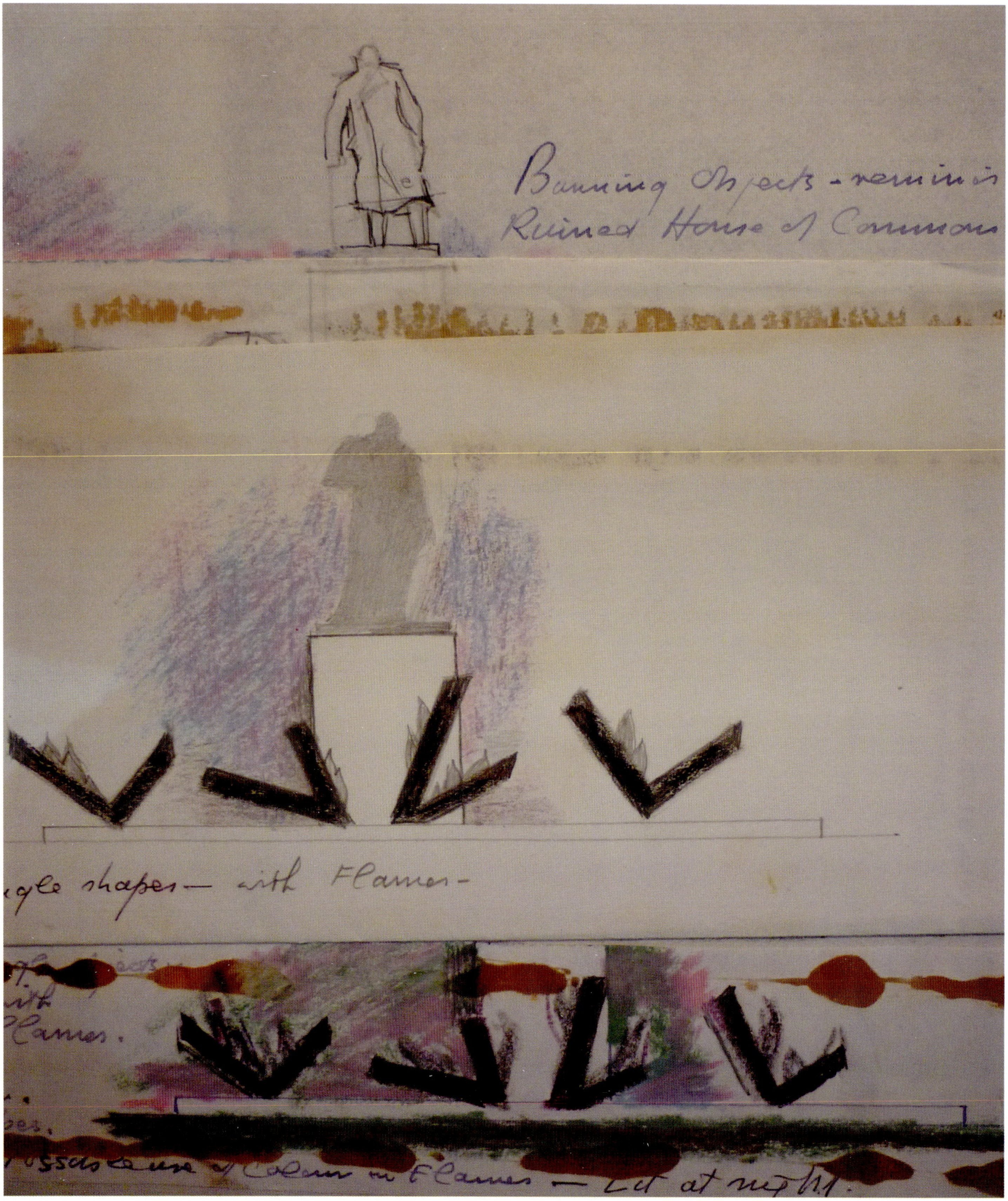
Burning Objects - remini
Ruined House of Commons
gle shapes — with Flames -

> sense of the wind on Churchill's back will be developed. The left arm with the hand in the coat pocket hardly requires any further work, but the right arm with the hand on the stick will receive further treatment. It is a bit thick and possibly too angular at the moment. There is something wrong with the shoulders, particularly the left one. Seen from his left side, Churchill's shoulder and head are not in proper relationship. When I arrived Mr Roberts-Jones was working on that left shoulder and we discussed at length the measures he could take to obtain the correct alignment. If those [details] upon which we agreed give the desired effect, then probably the figure will appear more erect and may gain in dignity.[89]

It seems that Ivor spent considerable time trying to model Churchill convincingly in the British Warm. At one point a colleague from Goldsmiths, Paul Hubbard, along with John Dellow, borrowed from the Imperial War Museum a British Warm reputed to have been worn by Churchill in his July 1944 visit to the Normandy battlefront. Hubbard has recalled how he 'stood for hours in the freezing barn' modelling the coat as Ivor worked alongside on the representation of the coat on the full-sized figure.[90] In 2005 Ivor's old friend Kyffin Williams was to reminisce: 'When [Ivor] was at work on the Churchill monument, I visited him in Suffolk to inspect progress. "You have the coat all wrong", I observed, "I've got my Great Coat in the van. I'll act as your model." At the end of the session, Monica, his wife, appeared and said, "that's so much better".'[91]

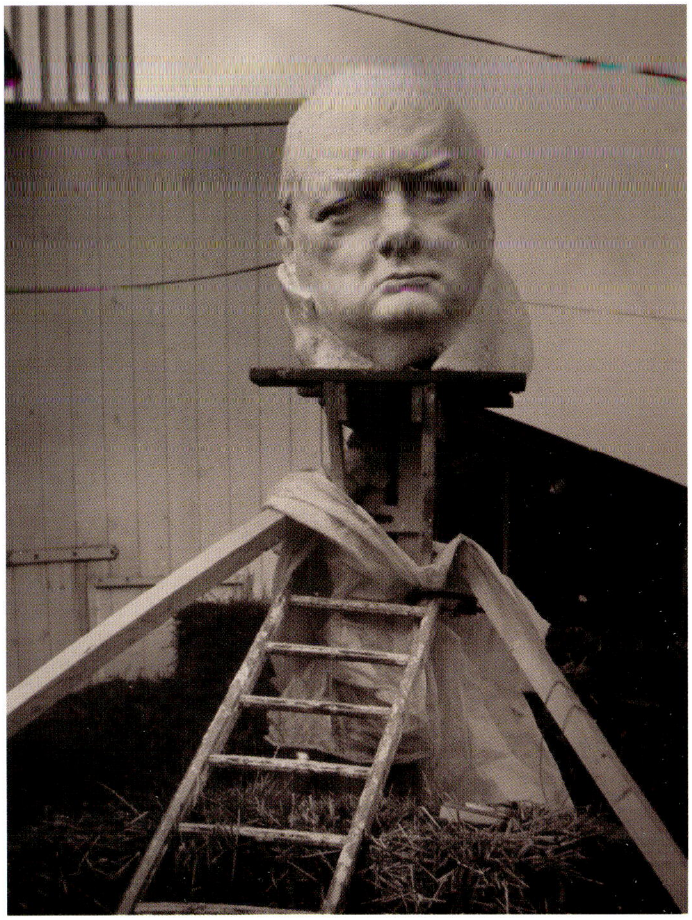

Fig. 3.12 Ivor Roberts-Jones, *Head of Sir Winston Churchill*, photograph taken c. 1971 outside the artist's studio-barn at Orchard's Farm, Cratfield, Suffolk; Image: Courtesy of the HMI, Leeds

In his April 1972 report, Crawfurd-Benson left description of the head of Churchill Ivor had created to the end, as he admitted he had never seen the great man at close quarters. Moreover, since

> Churchill was a man of different appearance at various stages in his long life and he was a man of so many moods, I think Mr Roberts-Jones will be lucky if he satisfies more than 50% of the viewers of the statue. And yet I am convinced he will. At first Mr Roberts-Jones made Sir Winston [look] too old; then he made him too young. Now I believe he is coming round in his deliberations to the right answer. He has created the figure of the war leader. Therefore the head must be of the war leader, or that of a man between 65 and 70. I coaxed him towards reaching that conclusion. At the moment the head is undoubtedly like Churchill but, perhaps, not quite right of him at the pinnacle of his career. The chin, mouth and nose can hardly be improved. The cheeks, the eyes, the forehead, and the top of the head require improvement. I told Mr Roberts-Jones that above the eyes I thought I was looking at Mussolini. This harsh comment he accepted with good will and understanding. He explained how he would remove the dome of the head which would bring about a lowering of the forehead ... This change

Fig. 3.11 Ivor Roberts-Jones, *Sketches of Burning Objects with Figure of Sir Winston Churchill*, c. 1971, pastel, pen and ink and collage on paper, 29.5 x 25 cm; Image: Courtesy of the HMI, Leeds

> will probably cause the cheeks to appear more cherubic and thus bring about a more exact likeness in the features.[92]

Intriguingly, Lord Moran, watching him in 1951 at an election rally in Huddersfield, detected a resemblance between Churchill and the late Italian Fascist dictator. Churchill

> sat apart on the platform as if he were by himself; his head had sunk into his shoulders and, in the hard light of the hall his face and scalp appeared devoid of hair; the monolithic lines of the great skull and jowl were somehow familiar; yes, he was like Mussolini. His eyes gazed vacantly into the distance out of the expressionless mask of a deaf man. There was a political meeting going on, but he was not part of it ...[93]

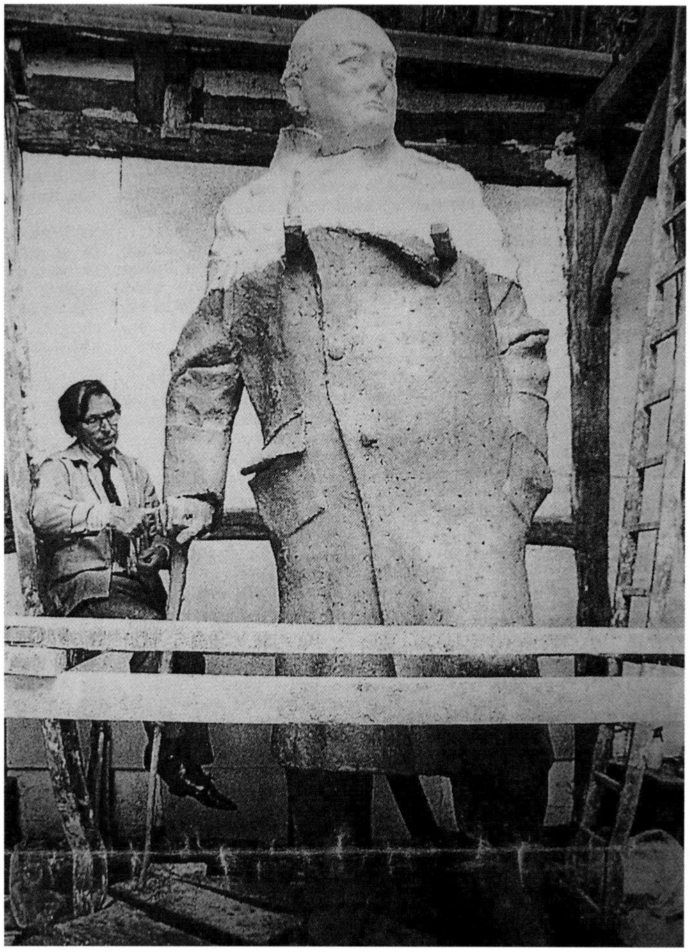

Fig. 3.13 Ivor Roberts-Jones with the full-sized model of *Sir Winston Churchill* inside the studio-barn at Cratfield, c. 1972, Image: Courtesy of the HMI, Leeds

Around the time Crawfurd-Benson was writing his report, Ivor was dipping into the diaries of Harold Nicolson for sightings of Churchill. He noted how Nicolson was often struck by what he referred to as Churchill's 'various "faces"'. During a debate in the House of Commons in September 1939, for example, Churchill resembled 'the Chinese god of plenty suffering from acute indigestion'.[94] Three years later, as the Battle of El Alamein was reaching its crisis, Nicolson again scrutinised a preoccupied Churchill, this time inside Downing Street:

> He gazes around the table with his curious eyes. They are glaucous and look dead. When he gazes at people like this, there is no light either of interest or intelligence in his eyes. There is a faint expression of surprise, as if he was asking, 'What the hell is this man doing here?' There is a faint expression of angered indignation, as if he were saying, 'What damned cheek coming to luncheon here!' There is a mask of boredom and another mask, or film, of obstinacy, as if he were saying, 'These people bore me and I shall refuse to be polite'. And with it all, there are films of stubbornness, perhaps even a film of deep inner thought. It is very disconcerting. Then suddenly he will cease thinking of something else and the film will part and the sun comes out. His eyes then pucker with amusement, or flash with anger. At moments they have a tragic look. Yet these passing moods and phases do not flash across each other: they move slowly and opaquely like newts in a rather dim glass tank.[95]

In his report of April 1972, Crawfurd-Benson had suggested that Ivor had been experiencing problems achieving an accurate rendering of Churchill's eyes:

> particularly the right eye. They convey a rather glowering expression at this stage. Mr Roberts-Jones wants to portray a more resolute expression. Whether that will be achieved by reducing the upper lids, projecting more the lower lids, or, a combination of both ... he does not quite know at present ... by Mr Roberts-Jones's own admission all sculpture is a matter of trial and error. It is the patient process of putting on clay and taking it off, of taking off and putting back. And then

Fig. 3.14 Head and shoulders of *Sir Winston Churchill* inside the studio-barn at Cratfield, partially covered with polythene, c. 1972, Image: Courtesy of the HMI, Leeds

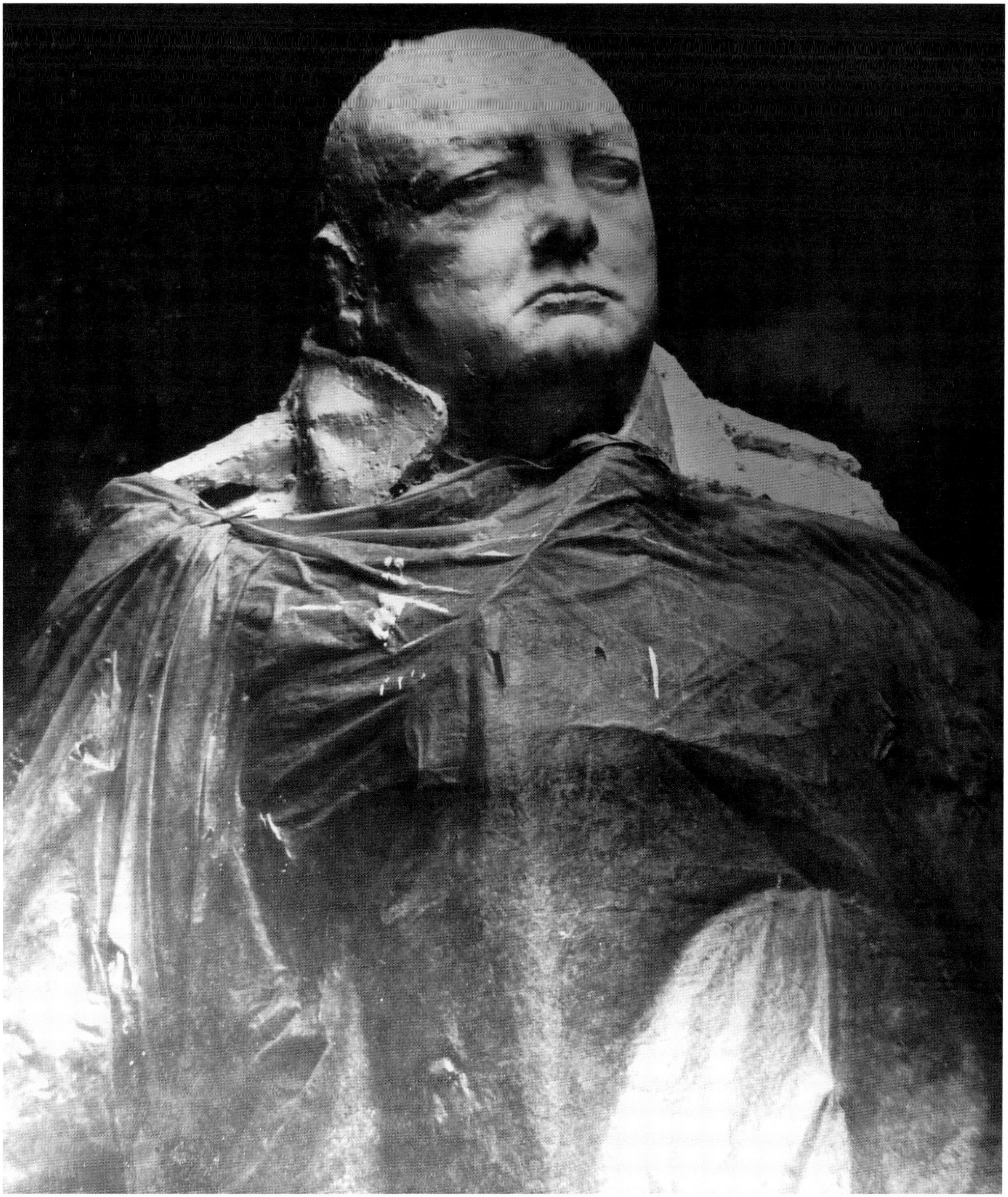

when the statue looks perfect in clay it may turn out different in bronze ... I learned that some of the subtle lines in clay may not come out in bronze, however well the foundry may do its work ... I have been able to point out matters of artistic detail which make a great work, only because such a vast amount of work has already been accomplished. The construction of the largest figure in British sculpture for fifty years has brought most intricate engineering and mechanical problems. They have been solved. As Mr Roberts-Jones has now five months absolutely uninterrupted concentration to give to the statue before it goes to the bronze foundry, I am sure he will produce a statue of which the committee and the nation will be proud. You have knowledge of his dedication and even-tempered reception of comment but I have by the lucky experience of several hours in his company seen Mr Roberts-Jones's meticulous method of working and learned his contempt for anything but artistic perfection.[96]

A month later Tilney felt sufficiently confident to write to Duncan Sandys that Ivor had been making 'excellent progress' with the Churchill statue – particularly with his head and shoulders (Fig. 3.13) – and that the full-sized clay model of the figure should be ready for viewing by the early autumn of 1972.[97] As it transpired, the model was inspected in mid October that year by a delegation comprising representatives from the RFAC, the Department of the Environment and Westminster City Council. All pronounced themselves 'completely satisfied with the statue', and Ivor was given the go-ahead to cast the figure in plaster.[98]

Towards the end of January 1973 Tilney, after paying a visit to Orchard Farm, reported in cheerful mood to the wider WCMC that Ivor had successfully absorbed all the comments and suggestions that Crawfurd-Benson had made the previous April. Indeed, the sculptor had

improved the figure most markedly. He has ... altered the position of the stick a little, making the alignment of the figure more powerful. His slight alterations of the head, particularly about the eyes, have achieved what seems to me to be a remarkable portrait of Sir Winston. The former glowering expression has become one of resolution. The legs and shoulders are better and he has made the back more agreeable and life-like.[99]

Tilney added that Ivor had spent the previous six weeks painstakingly

casting the figure in plaster. In this most delicate operation the clay figure is covered with plaster and then the clay and its supporting wooden armature is cut away from the plaster so that only a plaster mould is left. Into this mould is then poured plaster of a different mixture and finally the plaster mould is chipped away to leave the statue itself in plaster. It can be easily appreciated that through misfortune and not through negligence and inefficiency a plaster statue can look very different from the same statue in clay. It is to Mr Roberts-Jones's great credit that the statue in plaster is, in my opinion, more impressive than in clay.[100]

The huge plaster cast would be divided into eleven sections; the head and shoulders alone were in five segments. The sections would be transported, early in March 1973, to the Meridian Foundry for casting using the lost wax, or 'cire perdu' process.[101] The cast sections would be welded together under Ivor's supervision, and he would also contribute to much of the filing and 'chasing' of the finished bronze in the Foundry situated in a railway archway.[102]

Meanwhile, in late January and early February 1973, the WCMC released the first photographs of the plaster cast of the full-sized model to an expectant press, while Ivor gave a number of newspaper interviews. Perhaps the most revealing was to a young Welsh journalist named Byron Rogers, of the *Daily Telegraph*. The sculptor was adamant that he was

a portraitist, but I have not made a point of doing society portraits ... I did not think about what the scale [of the Churchill commission] would involve. If I had I could have scared myself out of doing it ... A portrait this size has not been done for so long. Basically what you are fighting against is the science-fiction crudity of a large object. If I do it properly it will not dwarf everything. It will just be bigger. If I don't, then what you will get is this science-fiction monster.[103]

Fig. 3.15 Ivor Roberts-Jones with the bronze of *Sir Winston Churchill* at the Meridian Foundry, Consort Road, Peckham Rye, summer of 1973, Image: Courtesy of the HMI, Leeds

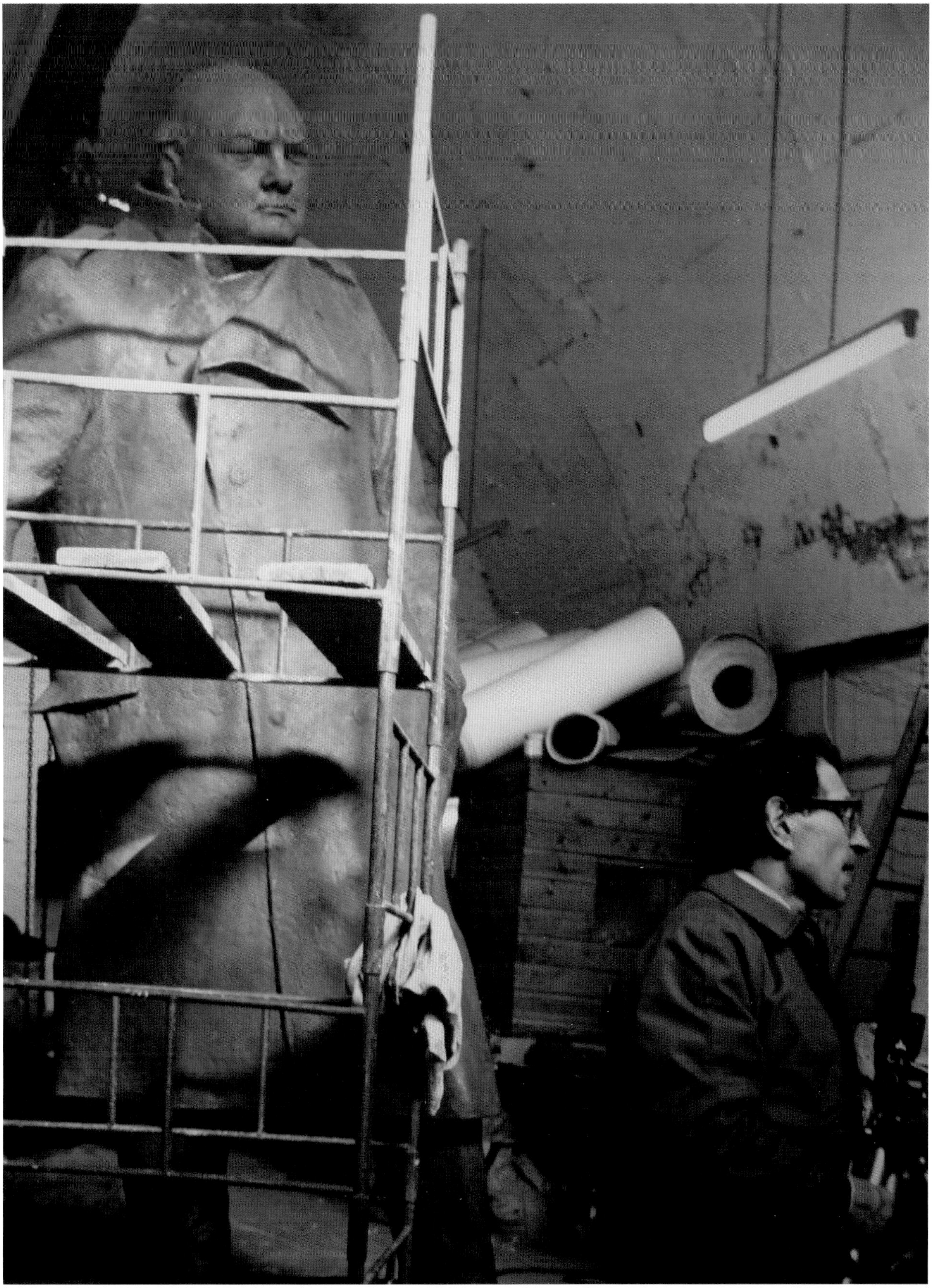

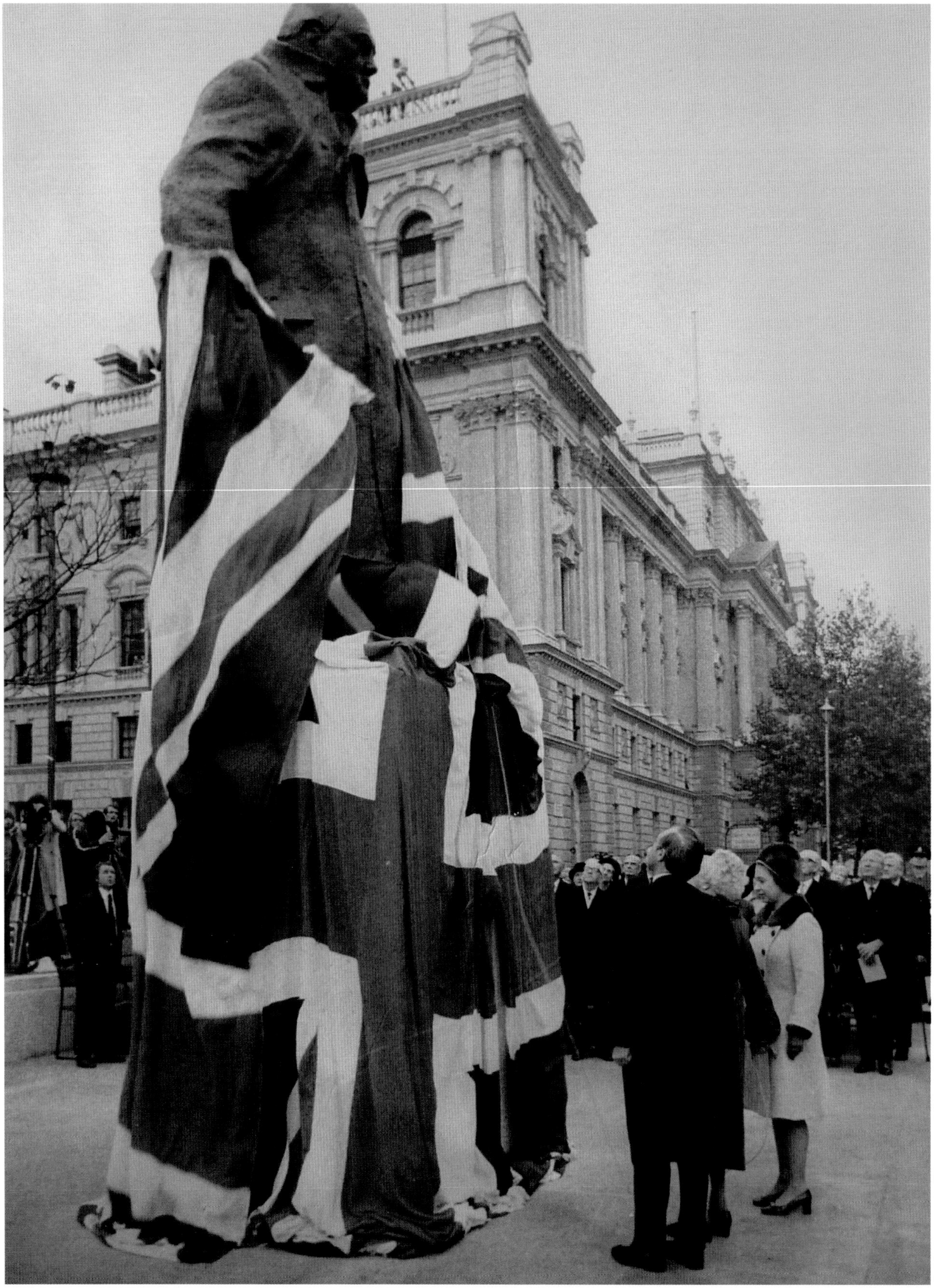

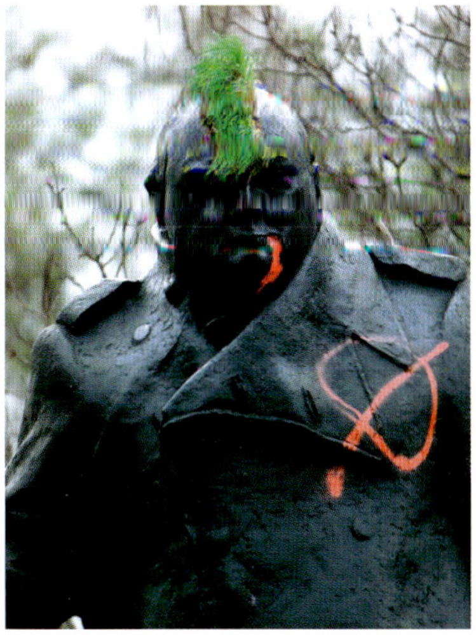

Fig. 3.17 *Sir Winston Churchill* with impromptu 'mohican' hair style, May 2000; Image: Courtesy of the Churchill Archive Centre, Churchill College, Cambridge

The sculptor admitted to Rogers that, 'In his nightmares, [he] had visions of a huge figure in bronze lurching across the lawns of Parliament Square'. Ideally Ivor would have preferred to present Churchill to the public as 'a fragment. A fragment encourages people to look at the shape structurally. But a statue, complete with hands, legs, a crease in the trousers, and people begin to think of it as a man and not as a piece of sculpture.' The sculptor was also very conscious of wishing to convey that his subject was a 'hero' who had lived at a 'tremendous moment' in British history. Not only had the 'scale' of the Churchill figure presented a challenge, but so had retaining

> the intimacy of a portrait as well. I have got to get the head and the monumentality. In addition, the committee wanted him as a war leader. Now, put Winston into ordinary clothes and he looks quite dapper. Put him in uniform and it looks as though a boiled sweet is emerging from the tight clothes. You just can't make a statue out of a boiled sweet ... I wanted to have this overriding mass, with two small legs. I have put the collar up, to make the mass encroach onto the head. I have been criticised for not giving him a uniform hat: but I wanted the bald head. What I have tried for is this indomitable, tense object. Nothing too gesture-ish. He may have been an actor, but he had this contained inner energy. I could not have made Winston into a classical statue. Classical statues stand on one leg with a certain degree of grace. But Winston was a stocky man. So I decided to have him leaning on a stick ... I think it would have been difficult with Churchill to have worked from life. It would have depended a lot on little things like whether he took a liking to you.[104]

Fig. 3.16 *Sir Winston Churchill* unveiled by Lady Clementine Spencer-Churchill, in the presence of Her Majesty the Queen, Parliament Square, London, 1 November 1973, Image: Courtesy of the HMI, Leeds

Rogers felt Ivor had indeed been successful in bringing to the head he had created a suggestion of

> subtlety ... There is an enigmatic expression on his figure's face: not a scowl, not a smile – and not the determined glower that most sculptors give him. Somehow Roberts-Jones has managed an expression of something quite fleeting and secret. The determination is there in the bulk, and in the great knuckles of the right hand grasping the stick. But the face above is quite different: it is a subtle effect.[105]

Towards the end of June 1973 a deputation from the WCMC, led by Tilney and John Rodgers, ventured to Peckham to view the full-sized bronze (Fig. 3.15). They were delighted and considerably relieved with the result – the 'special quality' Tilney had detected in the plaster cast back in January had not been lost in the transition into bronze.[106]

The statue was installed on its plinth in Parliament Square, under Ivor's exacting eye, in mid October 1973. A fortnight later, at noon on 1 November, the work was unveiled by Churchill's widow in the presence of the Queen (Fig. 3.16). On the day itself, Tilney told *The Times* that, of course, 'Not every facet of such an historic character can be captured in bronze. [Churchill] lived so many lives, any one of which any of us would have been proud to have lived. But his grit and greatness are here for all to see.'[107] Philip Howard, the newspaper's own 'special correspondent' for the occasion, who had spoken briefly with the sculptor, wrote that Churchill had been

> portrayed looking east towards Big Ben with his jaw jutting in bulldog resolution and defiance. From behind it looks massive. There is no cigar and no suggestion

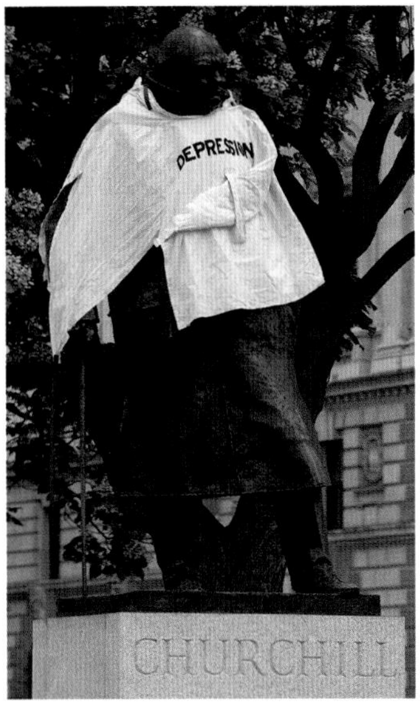

Fig. 3.18 *Sir Winston Churchill* wearing a straitjacket as part of 'Rethink Mental Illness Week', London, July 2012; Image: J. Black

> of the mischievous sense of humour. Mr Ivor Roberts-Jones, the sculptor, told me he has tried to show Churchill as the war leader who inspired Britons in what he insisted were not to be called the dark days but the great days that would be memorable in the history of our race.[108]

Over the next several days the merits or otherwise of the statue would be the subject of intense debate on the letters page of *The Times*: Churchill biographer and Conservative MP Robert Rhodes-James (1933–1999) did not think the sculptor had produced a sufficiently convincing likeness, while a member of the public objected that Churchill's head was 'far too small, arising neckless out of the coat collar like a small egg in too large an egg cup'. But Ivor received stout support from a number of his fellow sculptors, including David McFall, James Woodford (1893–1976) and Sir Charles Wheeler. The latter, in particular, stressed that Ivor had

> succeeded in creating a fine statue of a great man. At the time of its inception I had thought his task impossible of solution and said so. I must now eat my words. As a character study the sculpture is admirable, its monumentality is very impressive and it is altogether worthy of the historic plot it will occupy for many generations yet to come ... the sculptor, by his skill, has rendered a service to us and to posterity.[109]

The sculptor maintained a low profile, but ten days after the unveiling he wrote with only partially simulated asperity to George Pearce, the architect at the Department of Environment who had designed the plinth and setting for the statue, that, whatever else could be said about his conception of Churchill, he had done a damned sight better for him than Epstein with the nearby figure of Smuts.[110] Pearce replied that the sculptor was being unjustifiably modest in his protestations:

> The unveiling was a great occasion, long to be remembered, and your new statue in Parliament Square already seems to have been universally accepted and it would be nothing short of astonishing if there had been no murmur of criticism from any quarter at all. I am quite sure you should feel very happy with the result of your work ...[111]

In the year after its unveiling, Churchill and Ivor's statue of him provided rallying points for those deeply dissatisfied with the state of the country under Labour Prime Minister Harold Wilson, elected with wafer-thin majorities in the general elections of February and October 1974, such as retired General Sir William Walker.[112] During the summer of 1974 Walker had established 'Civil Assistance', an organisation whose volunteers were pledged to prevent by any means the Communist coup in the country, facilitated by militant trades unions, that Walker was convinced was imminent. During 1974–75, the general frequently stated that the country was in the grip of a crisis even more acute than of 1940–41, and was sorely in need of a Churchill figure around whom all patriotic Englishmen could unite to defend the country they loved.[113]

Thereafter, the statue featured occasionally in party political broadcasts for the Conservative Party, thanks to Mrs Thatcher's intense admiration for and identification with Churchill. It briefly appeared, for example, in a broadcast during the general election campaign of June 1987.[114]

In May 2000 the statue assumed a place in British popular consciousness it has never since lost. On the first day of that month Parliament Square was occupied by over a thousand 'anarchist', anti-capitalist demonstrators. One of their number, James Matthews, an ex-Royal Marine, placed a turf 'mohican' coxcomb on top of Churchill's head, while others painted fangs on his mouth from which blood dribbled (Fig. 3.17).[115] Much outrage was expressed at the time at this 'desecration' of the statue, and by extension of Churchill's memory – but the incident did have the unanticipated outcome of making Churchill 'cool' in the eyes of the younger generation, as some historians argued that in the early years of his career Winston had been perceived by his elders as 'bumptious', arrogant and pushy, evoking a degree of alarm similar to that generated by the 'punks' of the late 1970s in the fervid imaginations of their respectable elders. One suspects Churchill would have rather enjoyed the uproar, applying Oscar Wilde's dictum that the only thing worse than being talked about is not being talked about.[116]

The statue was to benefit considerably during the first decade of the twentieth century from the boom in history programmes on BBC television. It was featured in the last episode of Simon Schama's award-winning *A History of Britain*, broadcast on BBC1 in June 2002, and again, five years later, in Andrew Marr's *History of Modern Britain* on the same channel. Another five years later, in mid July 2012, Westminster Council gave permission for Channel 4 and a mental health charity, Rethink Mental Illness, to enclose the Parliament Square Churchill in a straitjacket for a week to advertise the urgent need for a much greater awareness of mental health issues within British society. Churchill was selected as a suitable candidate because he was known to have suffered for much of his adult life from depressive mood swings, which he memorably characterised as 'the Black Dog' (Fig. 3.18).[117]

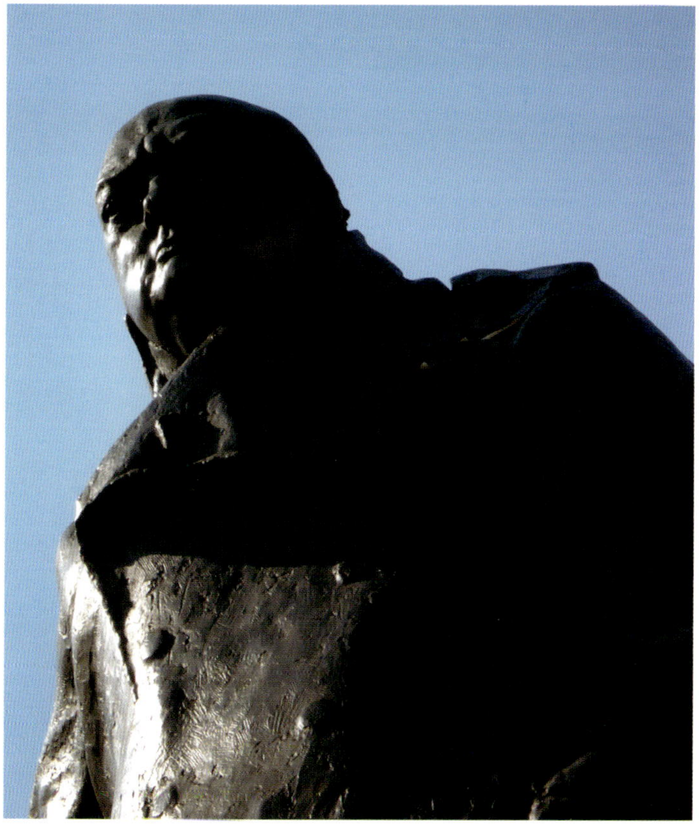

Fig. 3.19 Ivor Roberts-Jones, detail of *Sir Winston Churchill*, 1970–73, bronze, 3.66 m high, Parliament Square, London; Image: J. Black

Perhaps the apogee of the statue's status within the British imagination came on 27 July 2012, when it was prominently featured in the 'Happy and Glorious' section of Danny Boyle's *Isles of Wonder* film, broadcast during the opening ceremony of the London Olympics. In a clip lasting a few seconds, Ivor's Churchill was seen to come to life and vigorously brandish his cane to salute an oncoming 1945-era Avro Lancaster heavy bomber of the Battle of Britain memorial flight that was about to overfly Big Ben.[118]

In later life Ivor almost sounded grumpy, even exasperated, that his Parliament Square Churchill should continue to attract so much attention.[119] Before his death, however, he would gruffly declare that he was only too aware of

> its shortcomings, but you do have to admit you wouldn't confuse him with any other statue in the land. He was, I was told, the Rock of Gibraltar and I gave them the bloody Rock of Gibraltar. I sometimes think I'd like to do him again. But then he used to caricature himself and I'm afraid I did too ... I saw it the other day by accident and I suddenly thought 'you know, that looks rather good'.[120]

As often in the past, the sculptor took self-deprecation too far. Perhaps a more accurate verdict on the statue would interpret it as compelling proof that Ivor had indeed achieved in a truly iconic piece of public sculpture (Fig. 3.19) what he had set as an aim for such sculpture in 1994: truly to 'live', it must possess both 'dignity and caricature, a kind of irony ... an edge and [a] suggestion of an inner life'.[121]

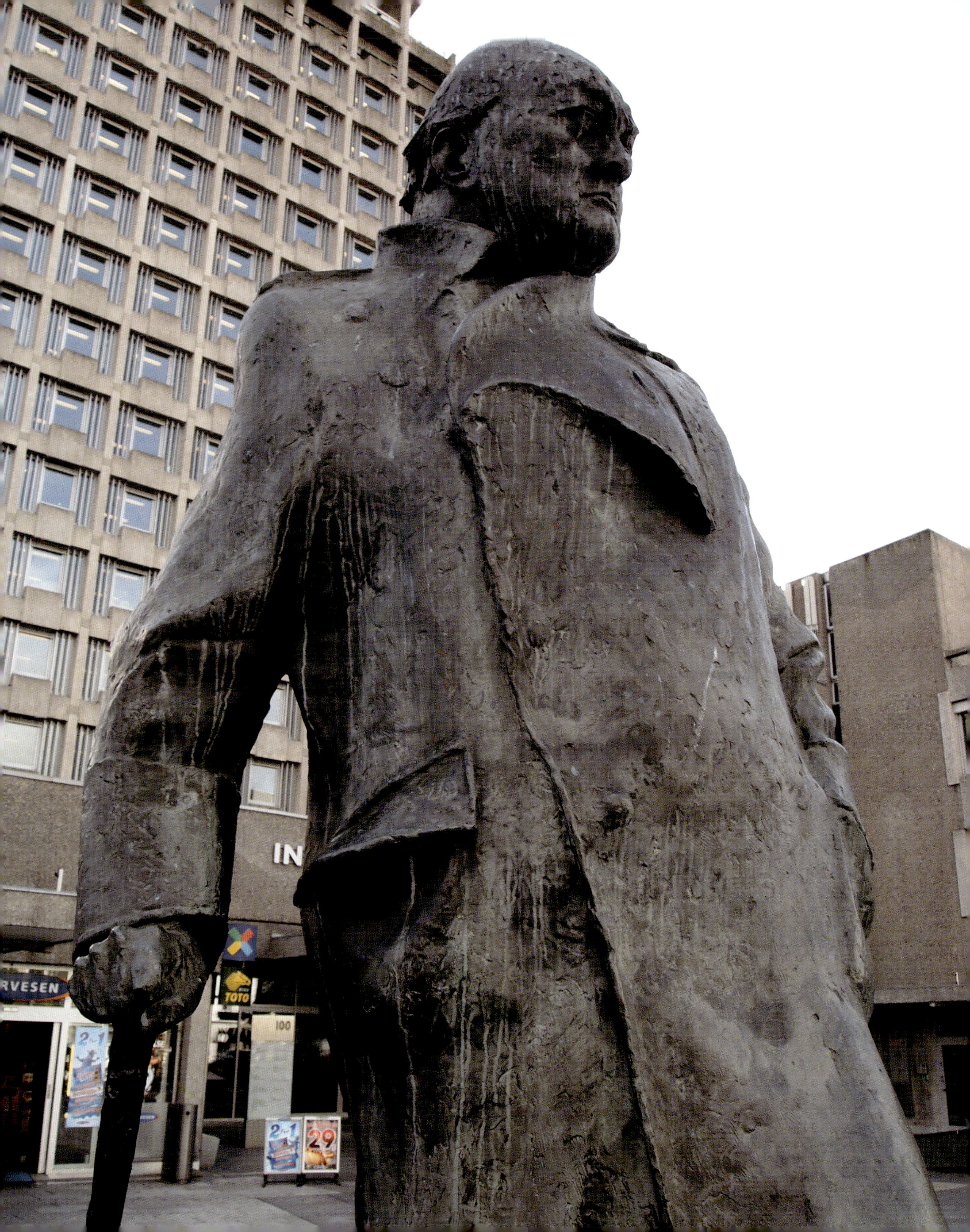
IN
RVESEN
TOTO
100
29

IVOR ROBERTS-JONES'
STANDING BRONZE PORTRAITS OF WINSTON CHURCHILL IN OSLO, NEW ORLEANS AND PRAGUE

SARA AYRES

The unveiling of Ivor Roberts-Jones's statue of Winston Churchill in Parliament Square in 1973 (cat. 135) led to three international commissions for Roberts-Jones to model further statues of Churchill for the cities of Oslo (1975; cat. 136), New Orleans (1977; cat. 141) and Prague (1999; cat. 156).

In addition to shedding further light on Roberts-Jones's sculptural practice, the history of these commissions offers the opportunity to look at three unique moments of place-making, which have in common the Parliament Square *Churchill* as an originating symbol. Roberts-Jones's Parliament Square portrait figure is internationally recognised within its setting at the heart of UK government. Perhaps for this reason, each of the subsequent monumental portraits of Churchill produced by Roberts-Jones lends its place of display a transnational character. The cultural symbolism of the figure of Churchill, or of Roberts-Jones's series of portraits of Churchill, appears remarkably stable in the three international locations in which these statues appear. While the Parliament Square *Churchill* has been subjected to a series of high-profile interventions – iconoclasm or vandalism, depending on perspective – it appears that the international *Churchill*s have settled into the expected, peaceful invisibility characteristic of public monuments.[1] The processes and dynamics of memorial-making in each of these three international locations, although sharing Roberts-Jones's portraits of Churchill as a focal point, were each individually shaped by local personalities and political objectives. These discrete commissioning narratives allow us to situate three richly individual histories of monument-making within wider considerations of place-making and memorialisation in the late twentieth century.

Fig. 4.1 *Winston Churchill* (1975) in Solli Plass, 2012; Image: Sara Ayres

For this research, commissioners from each project shared their memories of the commission, its genesis and its history. These interviews were supplemented with local press coverage and archival material, where available. While the commissioning history of each statue was very different, the objectives for each commemorative monument had aspects in common. A desire to honour Churchill as Britain's wartime leader and the architect of the peace that followed was fundamental to the genesis of each commission. In this respect the monuments are intended to be exemplary and, in Oslo and Prague particularly, record the specific efforts that Churchill is felt to have made on behalf of the commemorating nations. The memorialisation of Churchill's values, conveyed in his wartime speeches, including the determination to fight for freedom and a respect for the integrity of nation-states, was also particularly evident in Oslo and Prague. The statues in these cities publicly materialise the experience of a community and express the inalienable right to national identity.[2] The New Orleans *Churchill* is perhaps the most celebratory of the three statues, and asserts that British influences have shared in shaping the pluralist character of this unique American city. The statues in all locations signify the entwining of the history of

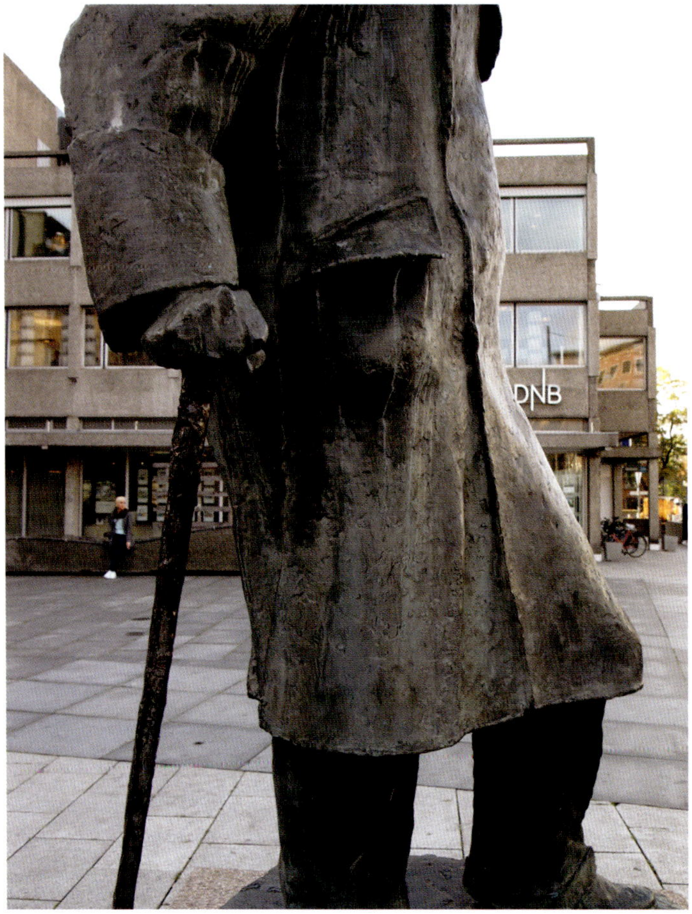

Fig. 4.2 *Winston Churchill* (1975) in Solli Plass, 2012; Image: Sara Ayres

each place (conceived of as city or nation) with that of Churchill's Britain. This set of monuments collectively defines 'Churchill's Britain' as an imagined community that transcends the borders of any one nation-state. This imagined community is situated within a symbolic-historic nexus that increasingly exists within memorials, archives, artworks and media, as opposed to living memory.[3] This lost period, during which the daily experience of individuals across the world fell into synchronicity with others of many nationalities, mediated by the long experience of war and defined by a common enemy, is nostalgically evoked by these statues. Besides the commemoration of the past, the statues are an attempt to orientate the present and future around a shared set of values. For the commissioners, each monument is a deeply felt reminder of Churchill's role in historic events, which resulted in great loss of life, and of the necessity that such events are never repeated. Alongside this fundamental seriousness, the individual histories of each commission are inflected with moments of genuine warmth and humour. Such fragments of levity appear to have the potential to affect collective memory and to be as collectively binding as trauma or tragedy, although they are less routinely documented and archived.

It became clear during interviews with commissioners that the authority of the originating *Churchill*'s location confers upon it its particular power as a work of art. His statue's location, or its context of display, influenced the decision-making of the commissioners, who subsequently asked Roberts-Jones to produce versions of the Parliament Square *Churchill* for their own cities. The desire to materialise a link between places – to assert communal values held transnationally – through the symbolic figure of the Parliament Square *Churchill* seems to have driven the commissioners' choice of artist. Rather than the maker's mark, it is the implicit reproduction of place that creates the guarantee of authenticity or the symbolic weight of these objects, and which anchors Ivor Roberts-Jones's later *Churchills* in their international locations. The originating *Churchill*'s high visibility, its reproducibility in images, and its political and symbolic status within its Parliament Square context in large part facilitated its international cultural mobility.

Oslo

Ivor Roberts-Jones's Oslo *Winston Churchill* (1975; cat. 136) stands on a low plinth in Solli Plass, a square in the Embassy district of Oslo, a short walk from the Royal Palace gardens (Figs. 4.1 and 4.2). The statue's backdrop is architect John Engh's 1964 Indexhuset building, and across the tramlines stands a bronze of Rodin's *Man with Chains*, reproduced from the *Burghers of Calais* group (1889), which was cast as a single figure and erected here in 1902. Between Roberts-Jones's *Churchill* and the National Library of Norway there is a bronze figure of Resistance hero *Gunnar Sønsteby* by Per Ung (2007), complete with the bicycle Sønsteby rode on his many sabotage missions against the Nazi occupation of Norway.[4]

Solli Plass is a relatively small public space, and its wealth of sculptures reflects the fact that the city of Oslo possesses a huge public art collection.[5] Its collection comprises over 21,000 works, mostly by Nordic artists, brought together over the preceding century. Oslo

Kommune, the managing authority of the city, currently dedicates 2 per cent of its annual budget to the care of its collection of public art and to the commissioning of new works for schools, hospitals and other public sites in Oslo and its environs. Oslo's commitment to its public art collection may be seen as more than a simple reflection of the Norwegian nation's wealth. Between 1397 and 1905, Norway had no status as an independent nation. During this long period the roots of Norway's national culture, which had thrived during the Viking Age, before the plague in the fourteenth century decimated the population, were lost. Oslo's investment in public art may now be characterised as an ongoing, creative exploration of a young national-cultural identity.[6]

The Oslo *Churchill* is significantly smaller than the London statue. Roberts-Jones stipulated that the base supporting the Oslo *Churchill* should be lower than one metre, whereas the figure in Parliament Square towers over the other statues located there from its high, monolithic plinth. The surface of the Oslo *Churchill* is pitted and split, much less finished and smoothed than that of the Parliament Square figure, and its head is turned slightly away, as if to signify a conflicted inner state, in contrast to the London statue's front-facing, determined focus.[7]

Roberts-Jones was interviewed by the Norwegian national newspaper *Aftenposten* on 8 September 1975.[8] In the interview he speaks about the similarities in national character he perceives between the Welsh and Norwegian peoples, and also at length regarding his artistic approach to the Oslo *Churchill*. He intended this one to differ from its counterpart in Parliament Square – more human than martial in its bearing, a portrait rather than a memorial:

> Norwegians see Churchill differently than most English people. We see him as a war leader, as a bastion of courage against the danger that directly threatened our nation. For Norwegians, he is more human, the man who strove for freedom and justice overall. For these reasons the London monument has a more architectonic effect and is more a symbol of war ... There should be a different kind of Churchill in Oslo than in London.[9]

Never having had the opportunity to model Churchill from life, Roberts-Jones had again found inspiration in a photograph:[10]

> It was taken soon after a part of the Houses of Parliament had been bombed to bits. He was portrayed there exactly as I represent him in Oslo. He stood in the middle of the ruins, he was not the warrior we are accustomed to seeing, but a human being filled with grief and despair at the measure of what must be endured during a time of war ... Therefore something of sadness grew across the entire attitude of the Oslo figure.[11]

Roberts-Jones also pointed to differences in the working of the Oslo figure's surface: 'Technically there is something rougher in the execution of the Oslo monument, it is more forthright in its detail and carries a stronger imprint of the maker's hands.'[12]

The committee which initiated the commissioning and erection of Roberts-Jones' Oslo *Winston Churchill* was led by Hans Høegh (1926–2010), President of the Norwegian Red Cross from 1975 to 1981, Secretary General of the International Federation of Red Cross and Red Crescent Societies in Geneva and from 1988 to 1993, Deputy Secretary General of the UN. The other three committee members were Anton Smith-Meyer (1919–2011), then the Norwegian consul in Liverpool, Gunnar Sønsteby (1918–2012) and Odd Grann (1930–), from 1981 to 1991 general secretary of the Norwegian Red Cross, now an active campaigner for senior rights in Oslo (Figs 4.3 and 4.4).

Hans Høegh and Odd Grann met in 1949 or 1950, while both were active in the Norwegian Red Cross. Odd Grann first met Smith-Meyer when the latter, then the honorary Norwegian consul for Liverpool, invited Grann to Liverpool to speak to a group of students about the Kontiki expedition. Gunnar Sønsteby was well known

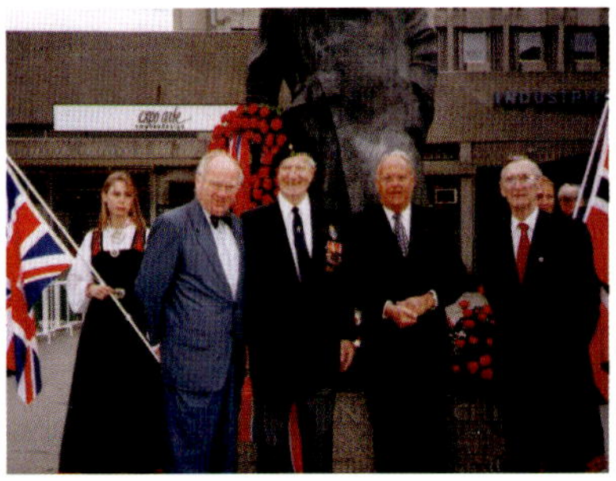

Fig. 4.3 From left to right, Odd Grann, Anton Smith-Meyer, Hans Høegh and Gunnar Sønsteby celebrating 17 May, Norwegian Constitution Day, in Solli Plass, year unknown; Image: Courtesy of Odd Grann

to all three men and throughout Norway, as the most famous of the SOE veterans and a tireless public speaker working to prevent a repetition of trans-European conflict.[13] The committee members were united in their desire to maintain the peace throughout Europe.[14] The idea of creating a statue of Churchill formed in response to the perceived need for a monument to remind Norwegians – especially younger citizens who had no direct memory of the Occupation – of the costs of war and the need for vigilance, in order that Europe should never again be riven by conflict. For these men, the placing of a monument in public space represented a permanent, public affirmation of their commitment to peace and political freedom and to Norway's integrity as an independent state. The Oslo *Churchill* may be characterised as a performance, enacted in bronze, of their commitment to such values.

These commitments were shared by war veterans across Europe, and drove the contemporary development of transnational institutions including NATO and the European Union. The extent to which these issues occupied minds across Europe at this time is reflected in a letter, held in Oslo Kulturetaten's curatorial files, from the Norwegian ambassador to Britain, Frithjof Jacobsen, to the Norwegian government's External Affairs Department, which cited a recent article in the London *Telegraph*. Jacobsen's drawing attention of the government to this article within the context of the commission demonstrates the wider benefits of cultural diplomacy that such a statue might be seen to accrue, yet also underlines the seriousness with which the commitment to peace was viewed in Europe:[15]

> Nato's position ought to be strong, united and conciliatory ... The nations of Western Europe have much in common; at their best, they hold common beliefs in democracy, social justice, a humane approach to life and politics, a belief in the rule of law between individuals and between nations; yet, in the past, they have inflicted the most fearful damage on themselves and others by their disunity.[16]

Odd Grann recalls that the idea for the statue came about around the same time as the centenary celebrations for Churchill, on November 30 1974, yet a memo in the National Archives in London suggests that the project had in fact germinated earlier that year. On 1 March 1974 the Foreign and Commonwealth Western Europe Division received a memo from the British embassy in Oslo.[17] The memo indicates that Høegh had met with the British ambassador to Norway some time earlier regarding the statue. Around the same time, Anton Smith-Meyer had corresponded with Mr Crawfurd-Benson, the secretary of the London Winston Churchill Memorial Statue Committee. According to the memo, Crawfurd-Benson had written to the Norwegian consul-general in Liverpool on 29 January 1974 saying that the statue would take about fifteen to eighteen months to model and about six months to cast. The committee planned to place their order with Roberts-Jones immediately, hoping it would be possible to produce the statue in time for the unveiling planned for 5 May 1975, to coincide with the 30th anniversary of the liberation of Norway.[18]

The committee were aware of the Parliament Square *Churchill*, and decided to ask Roberts-Jones to create a similar figure for Oslo, which they decided should be different from the originating monument in some way to be determined by the artist. Once the committee was formed, progress on the project appears to have been swift. The British embassy in Oslo supplied the name and address of Ivor Roberts-Jones, and Hans Høegh and his colleagues commissioned him by letter and began fundraising.

Odd Grann recalls that fundraising for the statue was straightforward. A letter in the Norwegian National Archives indicates that Høegh wrote to Knut Frydenlund in the Utenriksdepartmentet, or External Affairs Department, of the Norwegian government on 16 December 1974 to request a government contribution of 100,000 kroner.[19] In the letter Høegh states that he has also asked Oslo's City Council for a contribution of 50,000 kroner towards the campaign and is confident of receiving this sum. Frydenlund referred the letter to the Kirke-og Undervisningsministeren, or Church and Education Ministry. On 25 March 1975 the department indicated that it would be pleased to fund the statue, but asked for further details on the costs.[20] (This sequence of letters indicates that Roberts-Jones's fee for the Oslo *Churchill* was 5,000 kroner – about 24,500 kroner in today's money (around £3,000). An official item making a proposal or recommendation to parliament was created on 13 June 1975, suggesting that the payment to support the statue's erection should be made.[21] On 23 June 1975 Alv Heltne wrote formally to Høegh to let him know that the decision to award the grant had been made in the committee's favour.[22]

The committee was strongly supported in its campaign by the national newspaper *Aftenposten*, which launched the campaign to the public on Friday 29 November 1974 – the day before Churchill's centenary – with the announcement that 60,000 kroner had already been raised.

> Churchill's personal efforts meant more to the final victory over Nazi Germany than the new generation can perhaps imagine. As statesman, as inspiration during the darkest times, as leader of the British nation's war effort in a period when the world's eyes were still adjusting … To this man, whom we owe so much, we shall now erect a worthy monument in Oslo.[23]

The article calls on all Norwegians to contribute towards the 400,000 kroner needed to fund the monument. The newspaper reports that the statue's pedestal had already been funded by Tuesday, 3 December 1974.[24] *Aftenposten* listed the names of contributors on Thursday, 5 December and again on Tuesday, 10 December 1974, reporting that contributions to the fundraising campaign for the statue were being received by its offices daily and that the consensus that Norway should honour Churchill was widely supported.[25] The newspaper also reported that suggestions for the siting of the statue had also been received, and that they were passing these on to the state and city governments.[26] On Thursday, 27 February 1975, *Aftenposten* reported that the statue of Churchill was on order with the artist.[27]

Behind the scenes, the commissioning of the statue had developed into a highly controversial and political matter, which would delay the statue's inauguration for another fourteen months:

> At that time, we had I think two Communists on the City board, and they said absolutely no to Churchill. The politicians tried to convince them of the importance of that according to the history of the war [in Norway], and then they said, 'Yes, but we should also have a statue of Stalin.' You can imagine what these guys said to that, 'No question, no question.'[28]

The siting of the statue was also fraught with controversy. Roberts-Jones visited Oslo on several occasions to assess a series of sites. Proposed locations included Frognerparken, near the royal palace; the Akershus fortress, beside the harbour; the Naval Academy at Ekeberg, in the vicinity of the Maritime Museum; and the University on Karl Johans Gate. Collages and drawings produced as a result of these visits are now held in the curatorial file in Oslo's Kulturetaten, curators of the city's public art collection. During one of these visits Roberts-Jones had discovered Solli Plass. Perhaps he noticed Rodin's sculpture – the chained figure from his 1889 *Burghers of Calais* and the parallels between his own London Parliament Square *Churchill*, which is situated near Rodin's *Burghers of Calais*, appealed.[29] In a memo to the City of Oslo and the committee in charge of finding a location for the statue, dated 6 September 1975, Roberts-Jones made a strong plea, possibly even a last-ditch attempt to gain support for the site in front of John Engh's recently constructed modernist Indexhuset:

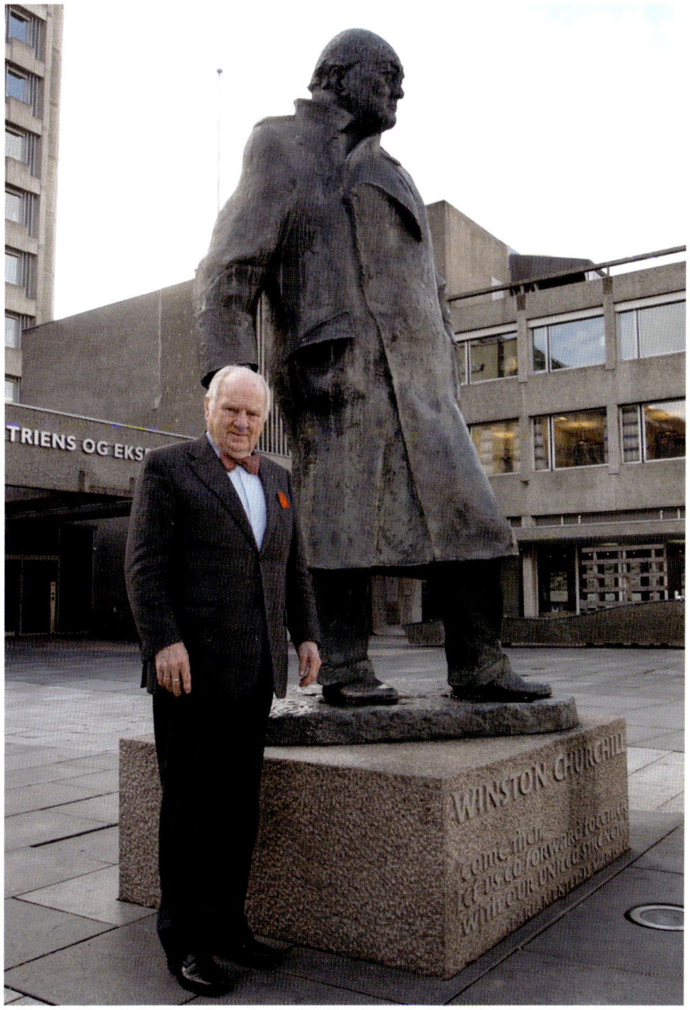

Fig. 4.4 Odd Grann in front of *Winston Churchill* (1975) in Solli Plass, 2012; Image: Sara Ayres

> I would like to add that the idea of placing the statue right in the centre of the City of Oslo, passed by both people on foot and traffic, has a great appeal ... [Instances of suitable locations include] the open space fronting the Import and Export Buildings which seems to be crying out for a sculpture ... Unfortunately [this site seems] to be unobtainable. [It would] of course, from a sculptor's point of view alone, be an excellent site.[30]

Initially, the area council governing Solli Plass, Bydelsutvalg 1, did not support the placing of the statue in front of the Indexhuset. They felt that the statue would not suit John Engh's modernist architecture. They also expressed a preference for statues by Norwegian rather than foreign sculptors.[31] John Engh was duly canvassed for his opinion by Hans Høegh, and supported the placing of the statue in front of his Indexhuset, provided that it was not situated next to the building's entrance, where a frieze by Rolf Nesch was displayed.[32] Dagfinn Austad, curator of the City Council's public art collections, in a letter to Bydelsutvalg 1, also expressed his support for this solution.[33] Further objections were raised by the Bydelsutvalg 1, on the grounds that the site of the statue should be in some way meaningfully connected to the subject of its memorial and should offer enough space to safely allow for large gatherings of people. Solli Plass had been rejected as a potential site by city architect Kjell Lund on such grounds in a letter to Hans Høegh dated 1 July 1975, which suggests that Roberts-Jones had noticed the square on a previous trip and had kept it in mind as an ideal location for some time.[34] Despite these factors, on 5 February 1976, Bydelsutvalg 1 announced they had passed a motion to approve the statue's placement in Solli Plass by nine votes to three. Further objections were raised by the Norwegian national association of sculptors, who stated that Solli Plass, as a centre of commerce not associated with the Second World War, was insufficiently representative and inappropriate for a large, official monument of an important politician.[35] The Norwegian Visual Artists' Association also objected, stating that the impact of the statue on Solli Plass had been underestimated and that the intimate feeling of the square would be disturbed.[36] Both associations' objections were perhaps exacerbated by their lack of an official, consultative role within such decision-making processes, and it is not clear from the file whether their opinions were solicited by the authorities or not. The City Council of Oslo considered the proposal in April 1976; the site and sculpture were approved, and preparations made for the statue's immediate inauguration.

The statue was formally unveiled on Saturday 8 May 1976, exactly thirty-one years to the day after the liberation of Norway from the Nazi occupation (Fig. 4.5). *Aftenposten* reported that King Olav unveiled the bronze in the presence of Churchill's grandson, Winston Churchill Jr, and his wife.[37] Also in attendance were Crown Princess Sonja; the former British ambassador and president of the Anglo-Norsk Society, Sir Michael Wright; the serving ambassador, Charles Peter Scott; Ivor Roberts-Jones and his wife Monica; and representatives of the Norwegian government and parliament. Twelve veterans from the Royal Navy, the British Army and the Royal Air Force, ten Norwegian pilots and ten Norwegian sailors formed a guard of honour.

Odd Grann recalls that events during the unveiling ceremony did not unfold as smoothly as planned:

> We were here the night before the ceremony to check that the statue was okay and properly covered. The next day we instructed the King only to say a few words, but then he saw some war veterans known to him in the crowd and he was inspired and so began speaking in English. He was much more brilliant in English than Norwegian. I think he was going for fifteen or twenty minutes without a loudspeaker. Then he pulled the cord and the coverings didn't fall. I had to climb onto the back of the statue and pull the coverings down and there I was hanging with my arms around the neck of Churchill. Then the King started laughing so that was part of the show.[38]

There is no mention of this irreverent moment of humour in the *Aftenposten* coverage, which notes instead that the crowd broke into spontaneous applause when Winston Churchill Jr stepped up to speak. That Winston Churchill at this time occupied a significant symbolic position within Norwegian cultural history is reflected by this, and further indicated by the fact that, while the committee planned for two thousand people to attend the unveiling of Roberts-Jones's statue, in the event about twenty thousand were present.[39] Odd Grann recalls: 'Everything stopped for him. It was a great day. Churchill for most was the salvation. He was the person who saved Norway from being absolutely part of the German Reich. Many thought he was the man who saved Norway from Germany. He said, "We will never surrender!"'[40]

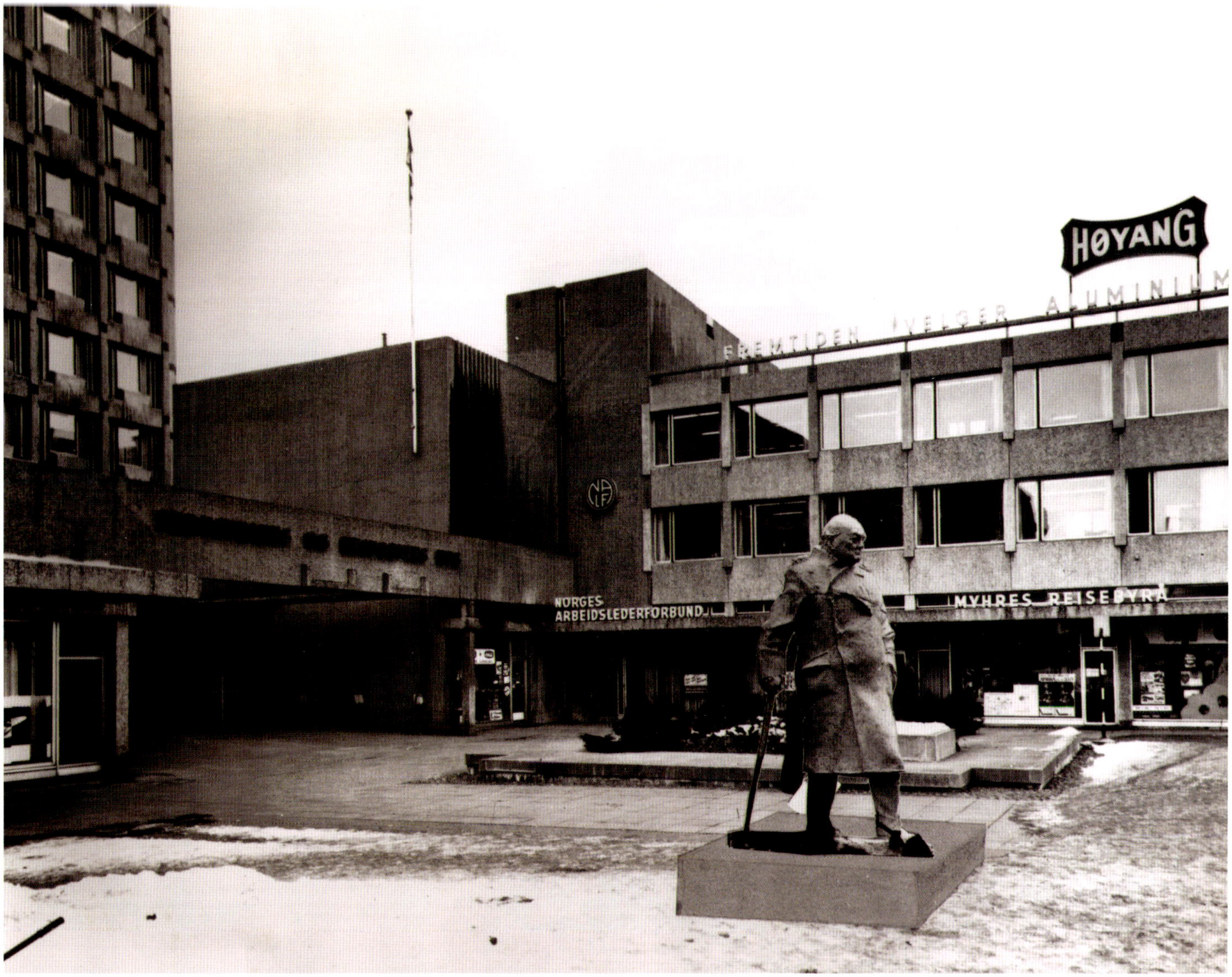

Fig. 4.5 Photomontage by Ivor Roberts-Jones. Image: Courtesy of Odd Grann

New Orleans

> The history of New Orleans has made the city a place where multiple languages, national histories, and traditions collide, conflict, and coalesce ... The poetics of place play a central role ... not just in the links between Africa and America, but also in the connections that link the city of New Orleans and the rest of the Mississippi Delta to the American South, the nation at large, and the world beyond the geographic and juridical borders of the nation-state in the Americas and around the world.[41]

In the summer of 1976 Ivor Roberts-Jones was invited to produce a statue, which would contribute to the creation of a specifically British poetics of place within the richly transcultural city of New Orleans. On 24 August Roberts-Jones wrote to Jack Crofton of the Meridian Foundry in Peckham to obtain a quote for casting:

> There is a firm enquiry – I think that's the best way for me to put it – for another Winston. I think it will probably be about 9ft high – as the Oslo one was. I believe they have already collected the money – so I may be the chap who will decide on the size! It would help me enormously if you could tell me what the price would be for the Oslo Winston as of this moment – and I can work roughly from that. If all goes well it will be a rush job – to be unveiled next Spring – but I remember you were very, very quick over the Oslo one, and so was I! – so I don't see any trouble there. They may stipulate battle dress or something – I really don't know. As things get clearer I'll be in touch – meanwhile the information I've asked for will help me in the first stages – as I must get decisions quickly in order to give us the time we need.
>
> It's for New Orleans. Let's keep our combined fingers crossed.[42]

Some time earlier in 1976 James Coleman Jr, a New Orleans hotel developer, had visited the sculptor in his Holland Park studio to persuade him to undertake the commission for a new Churchill monument for New Orleans. During an interview, Coleman Jr said:

> Well, what impressed me so much was just his total commitment and excitement about what he did as a sculptor. I mean he really was, from beginning to end, very, very intent on hearing from me, what I expected – that he wanted to be sure he was on the right track, even after we met. I saw him in his studio, in his house, and we sat and had tea. We talked for a long time. He told me about what he'd done in Norway. Just a charming guy. Full of energy and interest, and just so excited that he'd havc thc ability to put something in New Orleans.[43]

Following this visit, a drawing and maquette were despatched to New Orleans and duly approved. The New Orleans *Churchill* is perhaps the most martial and celebratory of Roberts-Jones's Churchill portraits. It is also the portrait least inflected by an intent to commemorate the experience of war and the cost of freedom. This *Churchill* was not funded by public subscription, but is rather a corporate commission. Roberts-Jones used the opportunity to try a completely new approach to his subject:

> We gave him the freedom to come up with something he hadn't done before, hence the fact he put [makes victory sign] when he was doing the drawings for us, he showed Churchill's hand in the sign for victory, gave him a mixed uniform with the navy cap and the army coat, and did the wonderful work on his face.

On 3 January 1977, now sixty-five and perhaps exhausted by working in winter conditions, Roberts-Jones wrote to Kyffin Williams, 'It's been a terribly busy Xmas – I have very little time for this Winston for New Orleans, and it has been giving trouble. There is a very tight schedule. I'm rather tired just at the moment.'[44] Roberts-Jones's *Churchill* for New Orleans was unveiled on British Place just eleven months later, on 30 November 1977 – a project span of less than eighteen months (Figs 4.6, 4.7 and 4.8). A commission on this scale would usually be expected to take two years, not including international transport.

The New Orleans *Churchill* differs from its London and Oslo counterparts in that it was created in response to a private commission and then donated with the land on which it was inaugurated to the public realm. The driving force behind the commission was James Coleman Jr, a former Fulbright Scholar whose time at Oxford had been

Fig. 4.6 *Winston Churchill* (1977) in British Place, just before its inauguration; Image: Courtesy of James Coleman Jr

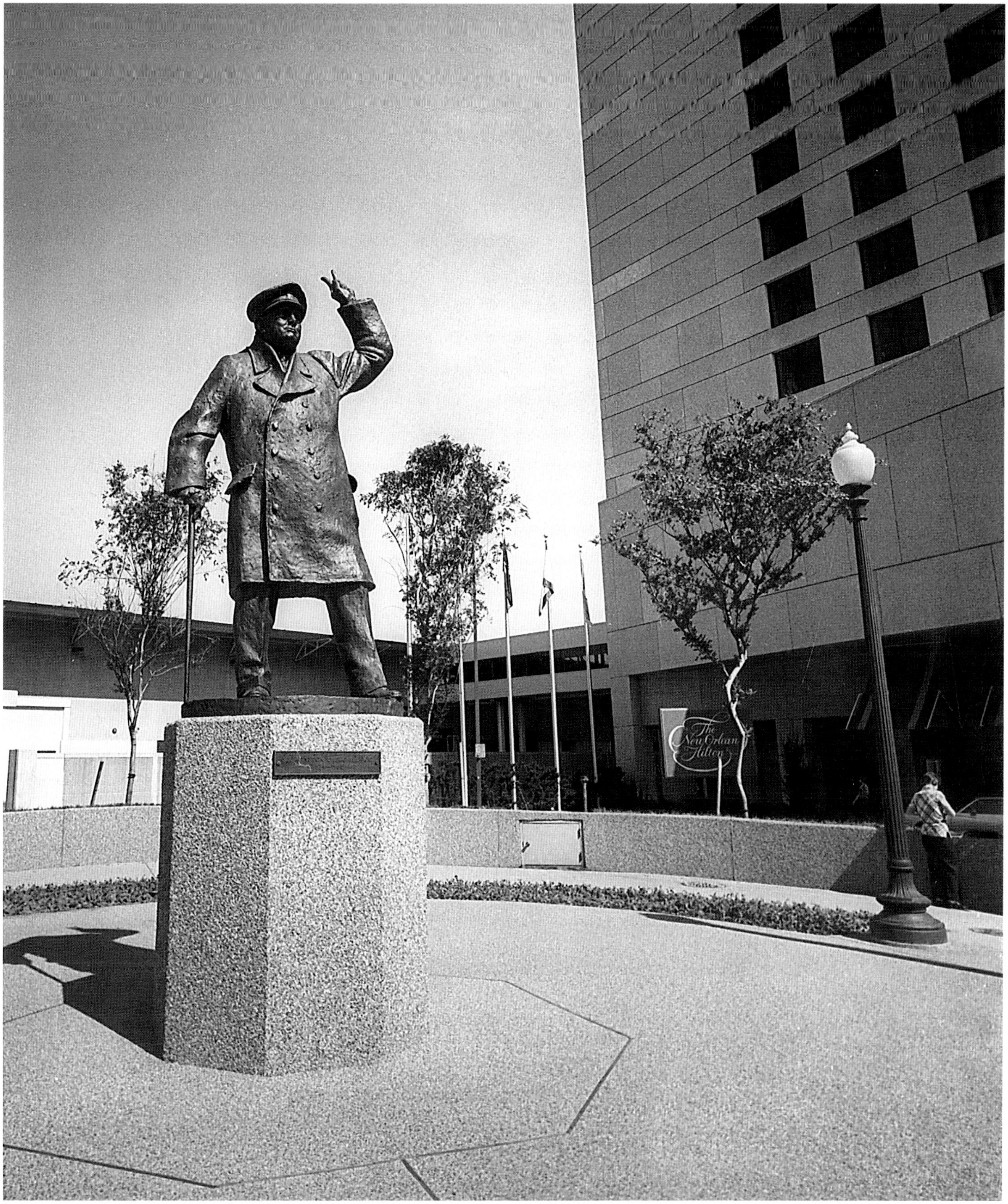
The
New Orlean
Hilton

marked by the forging of close friendships with British students and his membership of the Bullingdon Club. Coleman Jr's time at Oxford coincided with the death of Sir Winston Churchill in 1965. In an interview on 22 October 2012, Coleman Jr reported having been incredibly moved by observing the cortege as it made its way from Churchill's lying-in-state at Westminster to a final private ceremony and burial at Bladon:

> I'd spent two years at Oxford and I'd watched the service and the train [during Winston Churchill's funeral service on 30 January 1965] and told [IR-J] that I'd been very inspired and that I was very pro-Churchill, and to be able to take a French and Spanish city that had been built on that heritage and not recognise the influence of Britain – to change that would be a great challenge and a wonderful opportunity. And, er, 'Oh good, oh good,' he'd get excited like that, like a young guy, really enjoyed it, and then he sent me pictures of the mock-up, and that's how it went.[45]

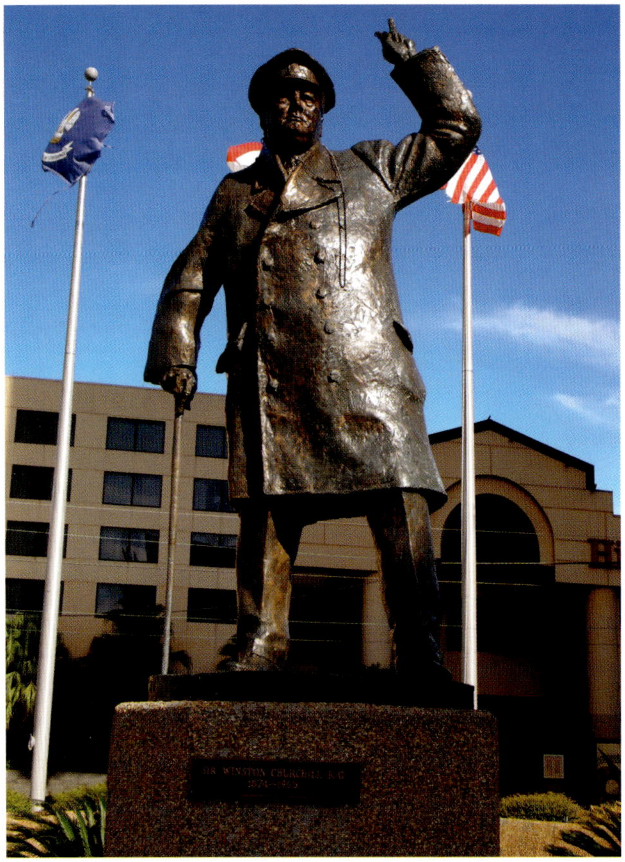

Fig. 4.7 *Winston Churchill* (1977) in British Place, 2012
Image: Sara Ayres

Coleman Jr maintains his links with Britain even today in his capacity as British consul for New Orleans. While his personal affiliation with Britain was undoubtedly central to the genesis of the commission, the creation of a British Place should be seen in the context of the wider development of New Orleans under the stewardship of Mayor Moon Landrieu, who held office in the city between 1970 and 1978. The urban development of New Orleans in the 1970s, much of which was predicated on increasing the city's income from tourism and attracting inward investment, has attracted increasing scholarly attention.[46] The need to attract tourists resulted from New Orleans's ongoing inability to create a firm industrial foothold in the modern, globalising economy of the late twentieth century. Increasing hotel capacity was central to the city's expansion within the tourism and conferencing markets. Coleman and his partner Lester Kabacoff, after whom New Orleans University's Lester E. Kabacoff School of Hotel, Restaurant and Tourism Administration is named, saw their development of the Hilton complex as a means not only of creating that missing capacity, but of opening up the New Orleans riverfront for leisure. They named their project the International Rivercenter.

> The Hilton was one of the great new projects to modernise the city. To bring some more excitement to it, there was nothing like the Hilton. Lester Kabacoff, he was a partner. He handled a lot of the political things and I was the guy who ran the project. We were partners. And then we had the railroads, the Hilton, they were all owners. I was pretty young but I was the managing partner here, and I really wanted to make this thing go. We needed something where you could have a view of the river and enjoy the river, and so this was the first new hotel that had been built, of a size, for a very long time, so this was a big opportunity. And in doing it, it was at the end of a new street that had been created called Poydras, an avenue for new buildings, commerce and industry, headquarters. It opened this wide avenue up and it ended with the Superdome and it started with the river. And the turnaround at the river, it was in this process that we created what we called British Place, and it was a circle with the Churchill sculpture in the middle.[47]

Fig. 4.8 *Winston Churchill* (1977) in British Place, 2012
Image: Sara Ayres

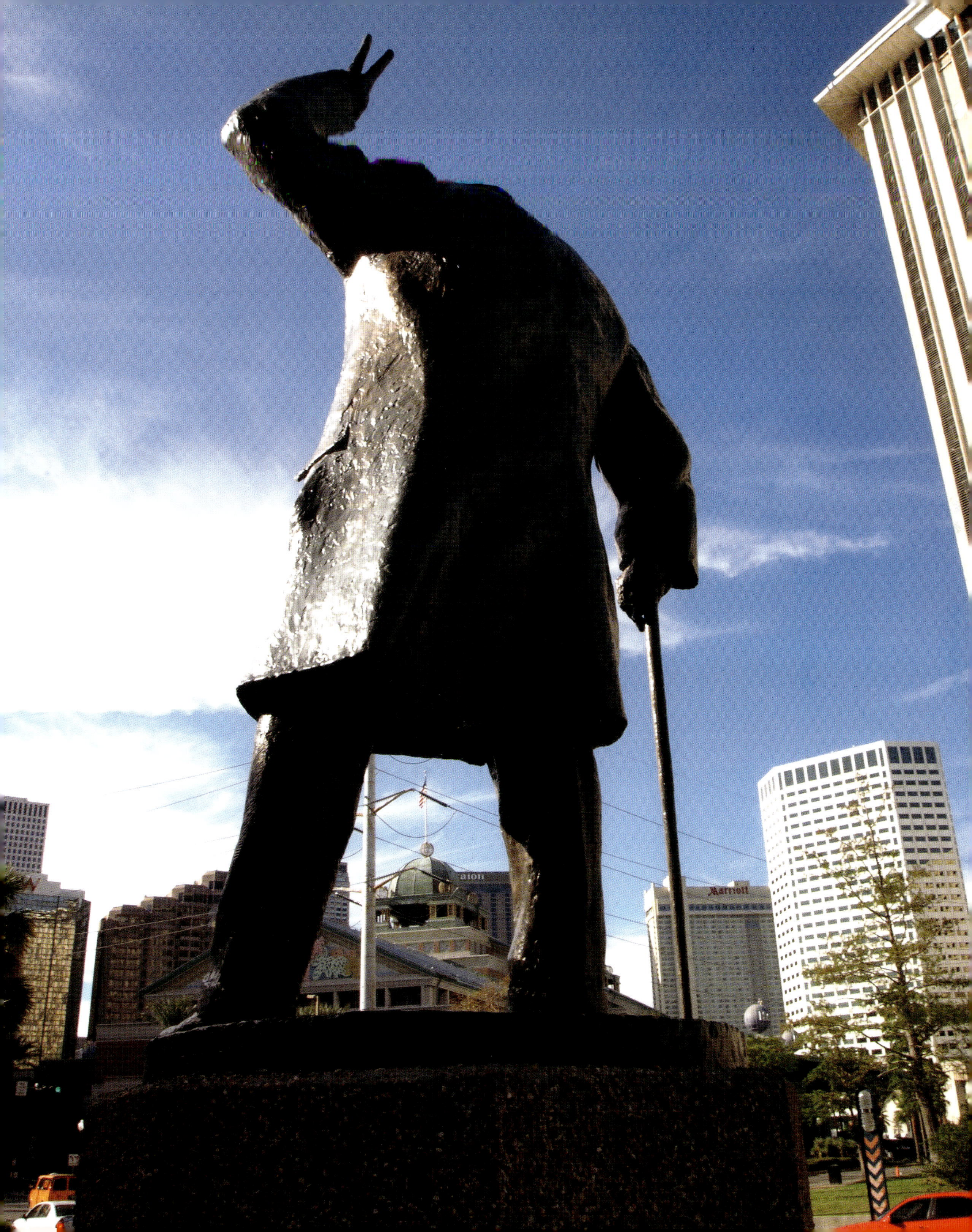
Marriott

Poydras and its environs were developed with an eye on creating international inward investment, but also intersected with the city's unique architectural heritage, which reflects the many cultural influences that have been brought to bear upon New Orleans since its founding in 1718.

> Reflecting the diversity of its people, the built urban landscape of New Orleans was characterized by mixing, hybridization, and the adaptation of materials, architectural styles, and spaces. Currents of Continental European, African, Caribbean, British, and East Coast Anglo-American culture percolated through the city resulting in a place that reflected only fragments of each.[48]

The city's tourism strategy also sought to build on aspects of the melange of international influences sedimented in New Orleans's built environment and culture, as a point of difference securing its destination brand identity, as J. Mark Souther has documented: 'The Greater New Orleans Tourist and Convention Commission promotional imagery designed to lure the American tourist to New Orleans designated it "America's European Masterpiece."'[49] An emphasis on the specifically European character of the city was also central to the development strategy of the area surrounding Poydras Street, of which British Place was a part. On May 27 1976, the Mayor of New Orleans, Moon Landrieu, wrote to the US ambassador in London to ask for her help and advice regarding the sourcing of a British artwork to stand in a planned public space at that time called British Circle:[50]

> a plan being developed by a group of our citizens to name a newly-designed circle at the end of Poydras Street, where it meets the Mississippi River, in honor of Great Britain. The idea is to call it 'British Circle', and hopefully, grace it with a work by a major British artist. It will take its place in our International Center, along with Place de France, Plaza d'España, and the anticipated Piazza d'Italia. Thus, we will be honoring the nations, which have contributed so much to the culture and commerce of our city, as well as its history ... Perhaps you know that the French government presented to us a copy of the famous statue of Joan of Arc for our Place de France; and that the Spanish government has presented us with the spectacular tiles and fountain for the Plaza d'España. The 'British Circle' project is being funded locally, and there has been no request that the British government expend any funds but merely officially endorse the project and help locate an existing statue or other form of monument.[51]

Of all these new public and transnational squares created as part of the Poydras developments, perhaps the most iconic is Charles Moore's Piazza d'Italia, which, despite its period of neglect, remains for many scholars an exemplary instance of postmodernist architecture.[52] Soon after this letter was sent, James Coleman Jr had arranged an appointment with Roberts-Jones, and the project to create a public square that represented New Orleans's historic links with Britain was underway.

Of the three commissions examined during the course of this book, this appears to have been the least complex in terms of its process. Ivor Roberts-Jones's statue was inaugurated in New Orleans on 19 November 1977 (Figs. 4.9 and 4.10). The tongue-in-cheek descriptive account of the ceremony given in the New Orleans *Times-Picayune* newspaper reports the commission's intent to stamp a place within the city with a British character.

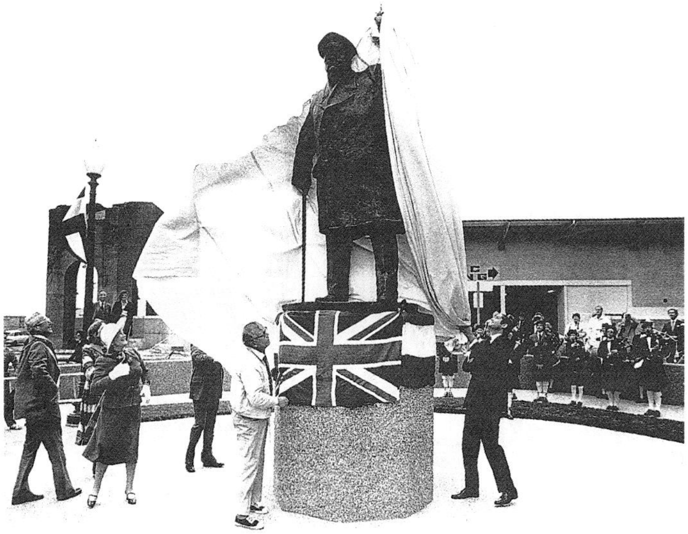

Fig. 4.9 The statue's inauguration. From left to right, Lady Soames, Ivor Roberts-Jones and James Coleman Jr. Image: *The Times-Picayune*

Fig. 4.10 *Winston Churchill* (1977) in New Orleans.
Images courtesy of James Coleman Jr, 1977

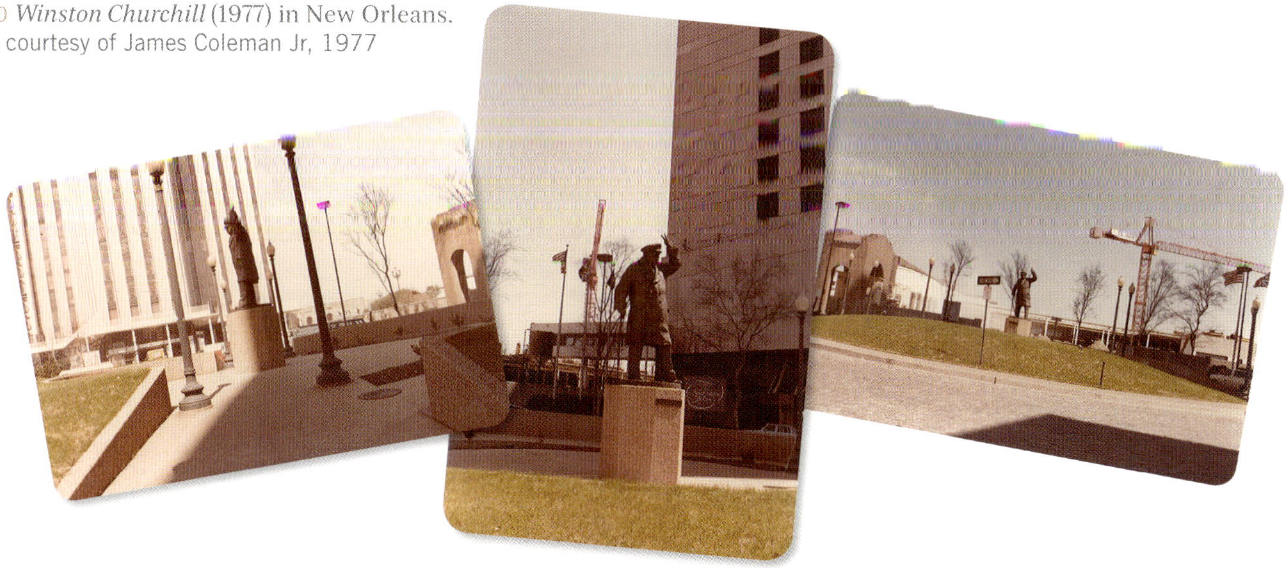

> A bit of New Orleans turned very English Saturday morning for the dedication of British Place and the unveiling of a bronze statue of that man of the century, the late Sir Winston Churchill.
>
> There was no fog, but the weather was London. Dull overcast skies and gales from the Mississippi jangled the flagpole riggings and slashed at the flags in front of the New Orleans Hilton Hotel, site of British Place.[53]

Perhaps mindful of the technical problems attending the unveiling in Oslo, Roberts-Jones took great care over the mechanics for the unveiling of the New Orleans *Winston Churchill*:

> He designed the plinth. So he had to see how that fit together. When he was here he engineered the draping of how the unveiling should be done. He had plans of how the whole thing ought to be covered. He was here early obviously, before the event. And he also had instructions about keeping it up and so on, cleaning it.[54]

In the event, all appears to have run smoothly. Speeches were given by Mayor Moon Landrieu, Louisiana Senator Lindy Boggs, Lieutenant Governor James E. Fitzmorris Jr and James Coleman Jr. A recording of one of Churchill's speeches was played over a loudspeaker. A photograph on the front page of the *Times-Picayune* shows Lady Soames smiling up at the statue as the coverings veiling the statue are drawn off, while Ivor Roberts-Jones anxiously looks on:

> Lady Soames pulls the drape off the statue of her father, the late Sir Winston Churchill. The bronze statue, designed and cast by British artist Ivor Roberts-Jones, was unveiled Saturday at the dedication of British Place between the New Orleans Hilton Hotel and the International Trade Mart. The statue and plaza were gifts to the city from the partners of International Rivercenter, which built the Hilton. Lady Soames and her daughter, Mrs Richard Hambro, came to New Orleans from Great Britain especially for the event.[55]

James Coleman Jr recalls: 'When we had the unveiling, his daughter came, Lady Soames, and when we got it unveiled, she had tears in her eyes. She said, "I can't believe it, this is so wonderful, it's really captured his spirit."'[56]

The *Times-Picayune* was also charmed by Lady Soames, whose speech positioned Churchill as a link between the nations of Britain and the US:

> English pretty with blue eyes and pink cheeks and lips, she looked as if she had walked off a British society page in her cherry red suit, muted print scarf, triple strand of pearls, gold earrings and white upswept hat ... She put on her horn-rimmed glasses to read her speech about how proud she was that her father was chosen to be a symbol of the bond between our two countries and of the mutual 'passionate love of free-dom.' She said his 'ultimate honor' was his honorary American citizenship, given to the man whose mother was an American.[57]

The *Churchill* appears to have been absorbed into the unique cultural life of New Orleans. During the research visit undertaken to support this chapter, Roberts-Jones's statue was found to be wearing Mardi Gras beads. This was explained by James Coleman Jr as a consequence of the previous year's parades. Float riders throw beads as the parades progress through their various routes around the city, and this custom ensures that many aspects of the New Orleans urban environment, from lampposts to architectural decorations, and even trees, are festooned with long chains of multicoloured beads all year round.

> The interesting thing is that Churchill is at the end of most of the parades after they've gone through Uptown or come from Midtown – they all end up on Canal Street. And then they turn at the end and end up by the Hilton, lined up by the Hilton where they ... get off. At the end of the Parade there's a lot of throwing [the] things that they still have and so one of the favourite things is to see if [Churchill's V Sign] can catch it. This is an easy shot.[58]

Prague

Prague's *Winston Churchill*, in Winston Churchill Square, or Náměstí Winstona Churchilla, is flanked by Karel Honzík and Josef Havlíček's Pensions Institute Building (1934), now known as the Trades Union Building, the University of Economics on the eastern side, and the busy thoroughfare of Seifertova on the west (Figs 4.11 and 4.12). To the south lies the city of Prague. The statue's high position offers a wide, clear view of the Old Town and the Castle. Churchill stands with his back to the city, facing the Trades Union Building to the north. Náměstí Winstona Churchilla is located in the third district of Prague, Žižkov, historically a working-class area.

When asked how the project came to be initiated, diplomat Milan Jakobec, who at the inception of the commission was acting as chargé d'affaires in the Czech Republic's London embassy, jokes that renaming squares is a Czech speciality.[59] Náměstí Winstona Churchilla was renamed in 1955, 1977 and 1990. Prior to 1955 it was known as Pensions Institute Square after the building with which it had been constructed. When Tomáš Mikeska became Mayor of Žižkov in the early nineties, the square had already been renamed Náměstí Winstona Churchilla, switching its dedication from that of the second Communist president, Antonín Zápotocký. It was decided that a copy of the Churchill statue located in London's Parliament Square would be the ideal monument for Náměstí Winstona Churchilla.[60]

A committee was formed to raise funds to realise the project. At the time of the inauguration of the statue the committee was headed by Milan Český, then serving Mayor of the Žižkov district, and included David Broucher, the serving British ambassador in Prague; chief economist at Commerzbanka, Kamil Janáček; the Czech ambassador to the UK, Karel Kühnl; a Sebastian A. Leslie; screenwriter and director Václav Marhoul; the serving mayor of the Žižkov district at the inception of the commission, Tomáš Mikeska; cinematographer Miroslav Ondříček; the Czech ambassador to Oslo, Tomáš Pštross; historian and diplomat Pavel Seifter; and political consultant Zdeneck M. Werner.[61] At the beginning of the project, three years earlier, the committee had also included the deputy foreign minister, Pavel Bratinka; Jan Knězínek, chancellor of the Parliamentary Senate; Jan Seger, rector of the University of Economics; and Ondřej Zemina, a member of parliament (Fig. 4.13).[62]

Jan Knězínek, the secretary of the Town Hall at this time and a mutual friend of Mayor Mikeska and Milan Jakobec, put the two men in touch, and work on the project commenced. Following the 1989 Velvet Revolution, the shortage of diplomats able to represent the new republic led to the promotion of dissidents with foreign-language skills but no direct experience of international relations. A signatory of Charter 77, Milan Jakobec unexpectedly found himself in diplomatic service in London in 1994. Soon after, he was charged with finding out how to obtain permission to copy the Winston Churchill statue in Parliament Square, with little experience and few contacts to help him negotiate labyrinthine British bureaucracy.

> This was in the days before the Internet, and I needed to find out who could give us permission to copy this famous statue. I tried the Department of Heritage, the Houses of Parliament, and then the Royal Parks.

Fig. 4.11 *Winston Churchill* (1973, cast in 1999), Náměstí Winstona Churchilla, 2013; Image: Sara Ayres

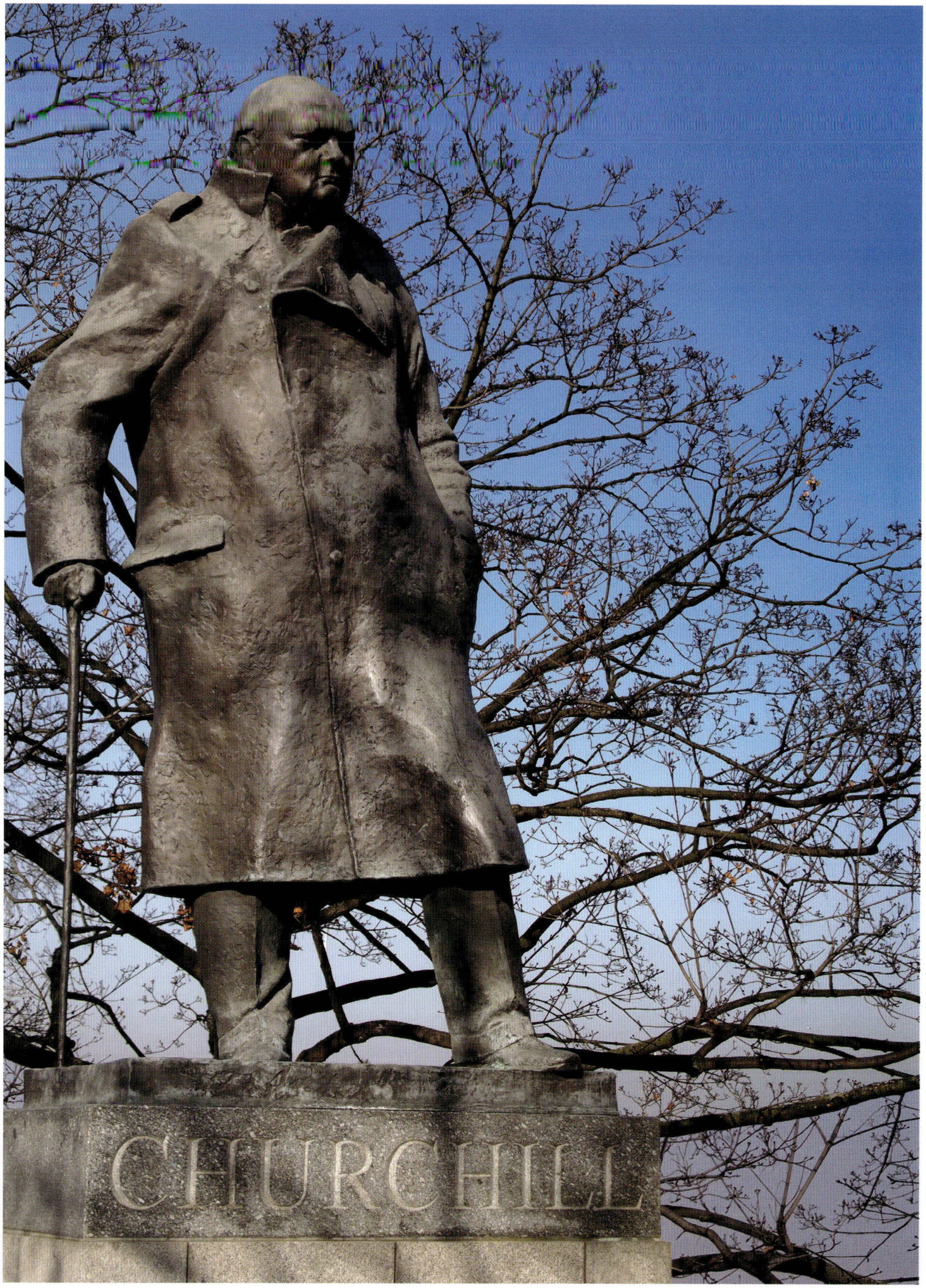
CHURCHILL

They all said, no, not us, although the Royal Parks admitted responsibility for keeping the statue clean and free of pigeon guano.[63]

The Czech sculptor (and longstanding rival of Roberts-Jones) Franta Belsky gave Milan Jakobec the British sculptor's address. Jakobec recalls:

> Franta Belsky was quite jealous. [Belsky] was very diplomatic, but he felt he was a little jealous because he had also sculpted portraits of Churchill. Quite interesting to see, but [Belsky] was very professional. [Belsky] knew that Žižkov wanted a copy of this famous Westminster statue, so he was not trying to fight with us, or to say I'm here and I'm Czech. Also at this time [Belsky] was working on a memorial [for Westminster Abbey] to the Czechoslovak forces who served in the Second World War, and told us he was quite busy and [didn't have] time to create a new Churchill statue. He had also very recently created a bust of Churchill for the British embassy in Prague.[64]

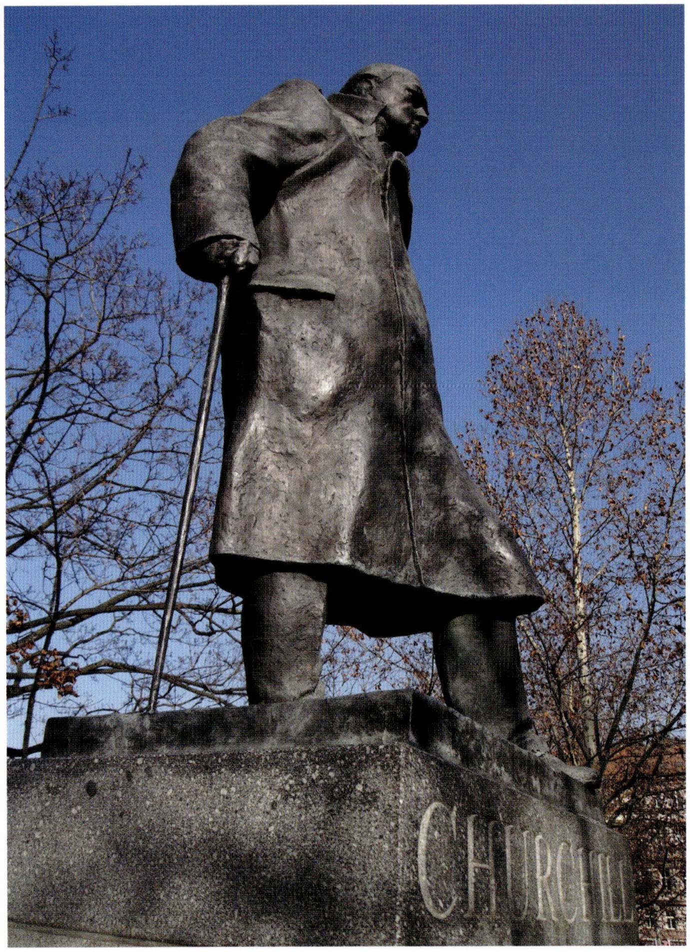

Fig. 4.12 *Winston Churchill* (1973, cast in 1999), Náměstí Winstona Churchilla, 2013; Image: Sara Ayres

In August 1995 Jakobec wrote to Roberts-Jones to enquire about the possibility of making a copy of the Parliament Square *Churchill*:

> I owe your address to our compatriot Mr Franta Belsky, who sends you his warmest regards ... The Prague Borough of Žižkov would like to erect a copy of your famous statue of Sir Winston Churchill in the square [in Prague] that has been given the name of Sir Winston Churchill. Sir Winston Churchill has always been an extremely popular British statesman in the Czech Republic and Prague wants to pay a more visible tribute to him.[65]

Roberts-Jones was keen to create an original standing portrait of Churchill for Prague, as he had done for Oslo and New Orleans. In his response to Jakobec he enclosed a photograph of the Oslo *Churchill* in Solli Plass:

> I am delighted to hear that my figure of Sir Winston has the approval of the authorities in Prague and I would like to help you in this matter. But first I must acquaint you with the facts as they stand at present. Firstly, the original plaster model, from which the bronze at Westminster was moulded and cast, is no longer in existence and the mould itself, after ten years, would be no longer fit for use. This makes the idea of an 'exact' replica by 'mechanical' means out of the question, even if Parliament would give consent. However, this doesn't make the idea of a 'copy' impracticable – but I would have to make it afresh – and it would have to be a 'variation' on the original theme.[66]

This proposal appealed to the Czech commissioners. Letters were followed by meetings, and the project was soon underway:

> We met in London during his visit, then I met him in his atelier in Suffolk with Mr Knězínek, during his visit to London. Ivor Roberts-Jones was very helpful and enthusiastic. He had never been to Prague, but had a photograph of the Jan Hus monument in the Prague Old Town Square – very beautiful and historic, but

> not well known outside of the Czech Republic. He was so enthusiastic about making a new statue. He had begun on the head even without having a signed contract. He told us he admired the traditional baroque sculpting for which Prague is famous.[67]

The Prague committee launched its fundraising campaign with a foundation stone ceremony at Náměstí Winstona Churchilla. This ceremony took place at the empty plinth that was the former site of Antonín Zápotocký's statue. (The statue of Winston Churchill is located in a different part of the square, and stands on completely new foundations.) Landscape architects advising on the siting of the Winston Churchill statue recommended that it would be better located a little further south.[68] The committee's launch was boosted by the involvement of former British prime minister Lady Thatcher, a very popular figure in the Czech Republic. Tomáš Mikeska recalls:

> Lady Thatcher was coincidentally in Prague at the time of the ceremony of the foundation stone. She kindly baptised the stone with her royal touch! She also visited the Town Hall. She was lovely. President Reagan and Lady Thatcher are for us the most important fighters against Communism. According to our views they are the main heroes of the destruction of the Berlin Wall.[69]

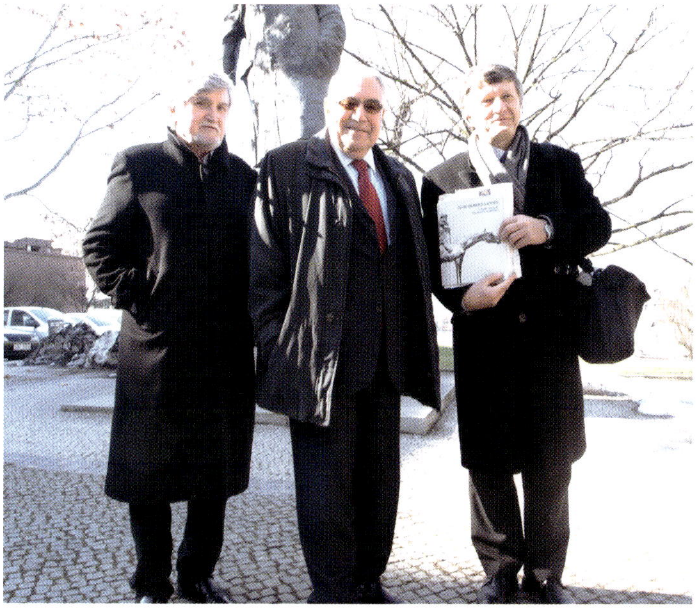

Fig.4.13 From left to right, Tomáš Mikeska, Kamil Janáček and Milan Jakobec in Náměstí Winstona Churchilla, 2013; Image: Sara Ayres

Just five months after the inception of the commission, Ivor Roberts-Jones died suddenly on 9 December 1996. At this point he had completed a new over-life-sized head for Prague's *Churchill* (cat. 156b), and Tomáš Mikeska had made plans to visit the sculptor's studio in order to view it:

> I had a meeting with Ivor Roberts-Jones in London, but the day before this meeting Ivor Roberts-Jones died. We were again at point zero. The fundraising had been very successful, so this was all in place. But we could not now obtain the sculpture we had hoped for.[70]

On 15 January 1997, Milan Jakobec wrote to Roberts-Jones's widow, Monica, to let her know that the committee had not abandoned the project. He confirmed that the Mayor of Žižkov was considering whether to use the new head of Winston Churchill, which Roberts-Jones had made just before his death, 'in combination with the copy of the Winston Churchill Westminster statue body, if technically and legally feasible. At the end of this week I will consult on the feasibility of the project [with] Mr Franta Belsky.'[71]

Both Belsky and Monica Roberts-Jones advised against this plan. Monica initially also refused to allow the creation of a copy of the Parliament Square *Churchill*, knowing this was against her husband's wishes. The head of Churchill, the last work that Roberts-Jones had made, was cast in plaster before he died. The commissioners ordered an edition to be cast in bronze by the Meridian Foundry for Žižkov Town Hall, where it remains on public view today (Fig. 4.14).[72] While this casting was in progress, negotiations on copying the statue continued. During this period Mayor Mikeska's term of office ended, but he remained in an honorary post to oversee the completion of the project. Negotiations regarding the copy had concluded successfully by the close of that year. On 31 December 1997, Monica Roberts-Jones wrote to Tomáš Mikeska:

> Now I am very anxious that my husband's statue of Churchill should be placed in Prague and I quite understand the difficulties over the royalties and payments. I have been in touch with the Royal Society of British Sculptors and told them how I feel about the matter and they agree that in the circumstances I should accept the £20,000 ... My husband would have been so pleased to see his Churchill in Prague, a fine

city which he always admired through photos and books on the sculpture there.[73]

In June 1998, Monica Roberts-Jones signed an agreement with 'The Association for Building a Monument of Winston Churchill', licensing the making of one copy of the Parliament Square Churchill.[74] Production of the copy was handled by the Meridian Foundry and supervised by the sculptor Nigel Boonham.[75] In September 1999 Jack Crofton of the Meridian Foundry wrote to Milan Český to report that the statue of Winston Churchill was 'progressing well'.[76] Despite Meridian's best efforts, the last weeks of the commission were possibly the most stressful for Tomáš Mikeska:

> Meridian made the statue in a relatively short time. On the date when the commission was supposed to be ready, according to our agreement, we sent a truck. But Meridian slightly overran and the truck waited outside for two weeks while the statue was undergoing completion. By summer 1998, Milan had returned to Prague. He was not on the spot for this, and was much missed.[77]

Kamil Janáček involved the British division of Commerzbanka in finalising the details of transportation. Janáček recalls: 'Creating the copy was not the biggest problem; the biggest problem was the logistics of bringing the statue from London to Prague. Commerzbanka representatives in London eventually found a firm that would agree to do the job. The paperwork involved was immense.'[78]

> It was also a great problem to find drivers willing to cross the number of borders between Britain and the Czech Republic. Papers for the transport were not ready by the time the truck was due to leave. I said to the drivers, you *must* transport the statue; we are already two weeks behind schedule and the statue will be inaugurated on 17 November. The drivers were worried that without paperwork they would be suspected of having stolen the statue. Then the workers creating the plinth pretended that they must see London in order to measure up the plinth of the Churchill statue. The planning permission we have actually is for the plinth, not the statue, so from the administrative point of view the plinth is more important than the statue. Communication by telephone wasn't easy, not everyone here speaks English, Jakobec was not in the right place, and finalisation was not easy. But the truck didn't get stopped once; it had a completely clear journey and the statue arrived in time.[79]

On 17 November 1999 the cast of Ivor Roberts-Jones's *Winston Churchill* in Parliament Square was unveiled in Winston Churchill Square, in the Žižkov district of Prague, by Lady Thatcher. The date was chosen to coincide with the tenth anniversary of the Velvet Revolution that had precipitated the end of the Communist dictatorship in the former Czechoslovakia. Tomáš Mikeska remembers:

> For Lady Thatcher there was no way to say no, because she was already a kind of patron for the project. With a hammer she had knocked the foundation stone already a few years before, albeit that was a symbolic gesture and the statue of Churchill is actually located in an entirely different part of the Square. President Bush and Chancellor Kohl, all the great actors involved in the destruction of the Berlin Wall, were also in Prague at this time, so it was certain that Lady Thatcher would have additional meetings on her programme.[80]

The unveiling was reported in the London *Guardian*. The tone of the report was implicitly critical of Thatcher's influence within the Czech Republic:

> Baroness Thatcher was among the cold war leaders in Prague yesterday to mark the 10th anniversary of the 'velvet revolution' which swept away communist one-party rule in the former Czechoslovakia. Unveiling a statue of Winston Churchill in the capital of what is now the Czech Republic, the former self-appointed queen of the cold warriors praised the reforms of the last decade but warned of the need to resist 'socialist attitudes'. Citizens of the Czech and Slovak republics – peacefully divorced three years after the revolution – once glorified Lady Thatcher as a key dismantler of the iron curtain ... In Prague, she told a crowd of about a thousand people in Churchill Square that Churchill had prophesied 'the two catastrophes that overwhelmed your country ... Nazism and communism. These two truly cosmic evils, apparently in conflict ... are mirror images of each other.' Lady Thatcher was accompanied at the unveiling by Churchill's grandson, Rupert Soames, and by the former Czech Prime Minister, Vaclav Klaus, whose Thatcherite reforms are widely

seen to have ended in a botched sell-off of state assets with little reform. The £110,000 cost of the statue was raised over four years from Czech business and private donations by the Churchill Statue Foundation. It is linked to the Thatcher Foundation. Among its activities is the nurturing of Thatcherite parties and politicians in the former eastern bloc.[81]

The associations accruing to Lady Thatcher within the Czech Republic appear to be extremely positive. The Czechs are very aware of this different register of associations held by some groups in Britain, with regards to Britain's first female Prime Minister:

> A few weeks after the ceremony I was hosting people from Great Britain and we had a bottle of champagne and I mentioned, off the cuff, that from these glasses a few weeks ago Lady Thatcher had also been drinking champagne. My visitors looked at their glasses in shock [*laughs*] and so, of course, the acceptance of Lady Thatcher here is a little different! We know that eleven years of her government was very troublesome for working-class people. Did you know that, in 1947, Lady Thatcher studied in Prague for a semester? Even the Social Democrats came with red roses for Lady Thatcher. But Lady Thatcher is something of an icon for President Klaus. He is a born liberal, and the free-trade economy was started here by the economist, President Klaus.[82]

Humour, or 'comic provocation', appears to have developed as a distinct characteristic within post-Communist public discourse, particularly in relation to the expression of political difference:

> When Václav Havel saw the Churchill statue he said he did not like it because its buttocks were turned towards Prague. I don't know if it was the intention, but I suspect that Churchill's position and his direction is a little comic kind of a provocation, because he is overlooking the building of Trades Unions, this famous functionalist building. This was a very powerful Communist institution. Churchill is challenging the Trades Unions! In response during the inauguration of the statue, the Trades Unions put up a poster, saying 'God Save the Trades Unions', a little spin on God Save the Queen! It was a provocation, but a comic provocation.[83]

The marking of political difference by artistic acts and comic interventions, through the use of representation rather than repression, points also to the Czech commitment to human rights, which were of particular concern to the Czech interviewees for this book. As in Oslo, Winston Churchill has specific significance across the Czech Republic as the only senior politician to reject the terms of the Munich Agreement in September 1938, and for his role in building the architecture of the European Union. Churchill was also the first Allied leader to recognise the Czechoslovak government in exile during the Second World War. As Tomáš Mikeska notes,

> For us, Churchill is the symbol of the fight for freedom, not only in times of war but at all times. It is very important to have such a reminder for this country that freedom is fought for, for eternity. He is a bearer of values. We see it as also important for new students coming through the Economic University, that the younger generations see Churchill as a bearer of values. My father was a political prisoner and suffered in a Communist jail for seven and a half years as a spy of the Vatican. These were the sometimes surrealistic claims of the Communist leaders. I am now writing a book about my father's experiences. So Churchill is making good returns for all of us here, saying that the struggle for freedom is not only this fashionable thing.[84]

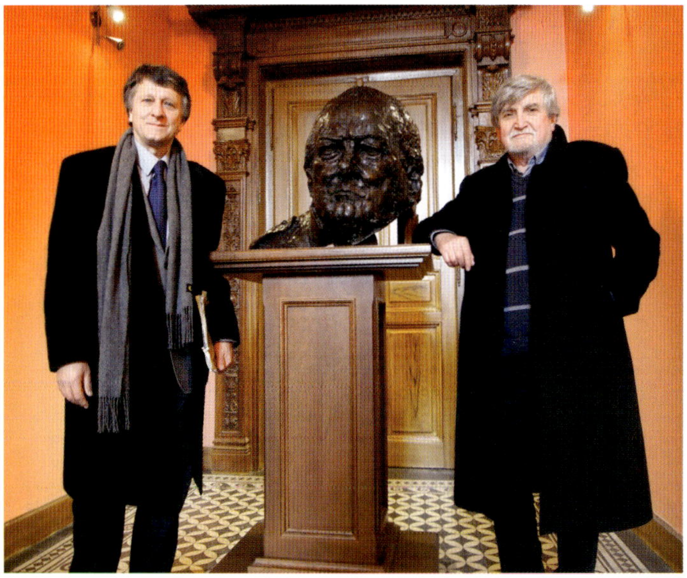

Fig. 4.14 Milan Jakobec and Tomáš Mikeska with *Winston Churchill* (1996) in Žižkov Town Hall, 2013; Image: Sara Ayres

Milan Jakobec agrees: 'My grandfather was also jailed for two years when I was very young, and we visited them. We remember these impressions of these gaols with dogs and walls. And don't forget that before the Iron Curtain came down we had twenty years of democracy, so we knew what we had lost.'

The destruction or erection of a monument, a dedication or naming ceremony, a 'comic provocation': all these actions are symbolic interventions contributing to the transformation of space into place.[86] The commissions examined in this chapter, despite taking place in three very different cities, were created by men who intended the portrait statues to convey broadly similar messages to future generations. Their similarity suggests that the meaning of the figure of Churchill is broadly stable across those specific contexts of display. In Oslo and Prague, this message concerns the political integrity and identity of the young nation-states into which the *Churchill*s were imported. In these different places, the integrity of the nation is expressed through the transnational ideology – symbolised by the bronze bulk of the *Churchill* – in order to secure each nation's assertion of its 'place'. The *Churchill*s embody the nation's right to self-determination, even when that nation has only recently been brought into being. In New Orleans, the *Churchill* signifies the presence of a British element within the pluralist heritage of the city. Across the three sites discussed, the figure of Churchill is iconic, and its symbolism is clear and straightforward. The more controversial aspects of Churchill's career do not appear to have a place within the representational framework of the statue's display and reception internationally, unlike for its Parliament Square originator.

Parliament Square has become one of the most photographed spaces in Britain, partly because it is traditionally a site of protest. Within this context, Ivor Roberts-Jones's *Winston Churchill* (cat. 135) has been, and will probably continue to be, subjected to a series of destructive and creative appropriations. Besides the May Day riots of 2000, which resulted in the much-reproduced photograph of *Churchill* wearing a turf Mohican,[87] in 2012 Channel 4 fitted the statue with a custom-made straitjacket (see Chapter 3).[88] This action was intended to publicise a season of programmes on mental health. Churchill's taste for alcohol has been widely documented,[89] and Channel 4 sought to highlight this aspect of the man as a means of prompting its audiences to think differently about mental illness. Danny Boyle's opening ceremony for 2012's London Olympics featured a film including a section in which the *Churchill* statue was briefly but affectionately animated. As these appropriations of Roberts-Jones's statue demonstrate, Winston Churchill is an iconic, ambivalent and complex figure within Britain. The Parliament Square *Churchill*, as perhaps the 'authoritative' incarnation of Churchill's many public honours, cannot but be a lightning rod for political or publicity-seeking interventions. The infinite reproducibility of this site through photographic, print and now digital media – increased by its visibility as a site for protest – negates any sacrosanct quality to the *Churchill* within its Parliament Square context. Its reproducibility enables the statue to absorb and project infinite meanings, and renders it available for protest.[90]

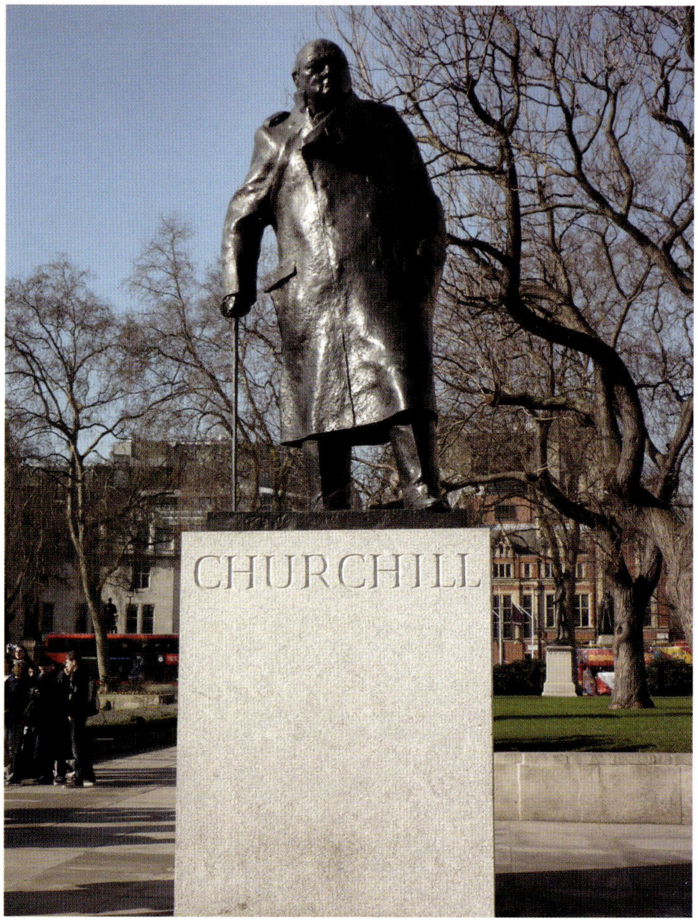

Cat.135 *Sir Winston Churchill KG, OM, CH*, 1970–73;
Image: Sara Ayres

The visibility of the *Churchill* in its place enabled its transnational mobility and significance. Yet, in all three international contexts, the figure of Churchill as represented by Roberts-Jones appears to be received as a less complex and contentious figure than the Parliament Square original. The range of associations attached to the international variants is narrower, and hence has greater stability, than those of the Parliament Square original. Does this imply that the international sculptures have less symbolic charge, are less visible, and consequently more in danger of being forgotten?

Such security as public memorials provide may not be long-lasting. Jay Winter points out that, when such memorialising groups 'disperse or disappear, sites of memory lose their initial force, and may fade away entirely ... In most instances, the significance of sites of memory fades away with the passing of the social groups that initiated the practice.'[91] Whether by a long-term process of forgetting, or by iconoclastic redefinition, he argues, public commemoration is 'both irresistible and unsustainable'.[92]

The history of Antonín Zápotocký's effaced monument in Náměstí Winstona Churchilla may testify to the unsustainability of the public monument. While its name has changed and monuments have risen and fallen, the boundaries of Náměstí Winstona Churchilla have retained their integrity for nearly a century – longer than those of the Czech Republic itself. While the ideologies asserting their presence in the space of this particular public square have been exchanged, the space *as place* has remained, and perhaps become more richly allusive as its contestation has progressed through the historic events of the long twentieth century. If the significance of place is determined by usage, the life of a monument depends on the significance of its place (a point that Roberts-Jones may have had in mind in his preference for the busy Solli Plass, in Oslo). Joined to the wider city by flows of public traffic, and by the history of use, Náměstí Winstona Churchilla has constituted a space for the Žižkov district to work and rework the identifications and differences that articulate its place in the larger world. The aesthetic, material link to the figure of the Parliament Square *Churchill* signifies the district's current affiliation to a transnational political and cultural community – the same community affiliation signified by Roberts-Jones's *Churchill* variants' presences in Oslo and New Orleans.

In this sense, the instances of the *Churchill* series may be characterised as signposts indicating the presence of transnational circuitry or routes through which capital, knowledge, people and ideologies are moved and developed. Significantly, the various international *Churchills* are set against architectural backdrops that may be characterised as 'modernist', or of the International Style. The functions of these buildings are also telling: a House of Industry and Export, an international hotel chain and a University of Economics – all institutions benefiting from and facilitating international flows and connections. The cultural mobility of Roberts-Jones's *Churchill* is indicative of a busy transcultural highway, secured by traditions, ideas, languages and customs held in common across national borders.

Rather than static, eternal and unmoving – invisible – perhaps these sculptural memorials to Winston Churchill should be characterised as mobile components within an ongoing, dialectical process of transcultural exchange and self-fashioning. As long as the originating *Churchill* continues to be a site of contestation and protest as well as commemoration, and its international visibility remains high, the international variants will continue to benefit from this charge, and the transnational links they articulate will retain their significance. Winter is right to state that monuments fade when they are no longer of use to the communities that use their places of display. Rather than fixed tributes of determined but ever-diminishing meaning, perhaps the useful mobility of the *Churchill* series indicates another possibility for the fate of urban monuments.

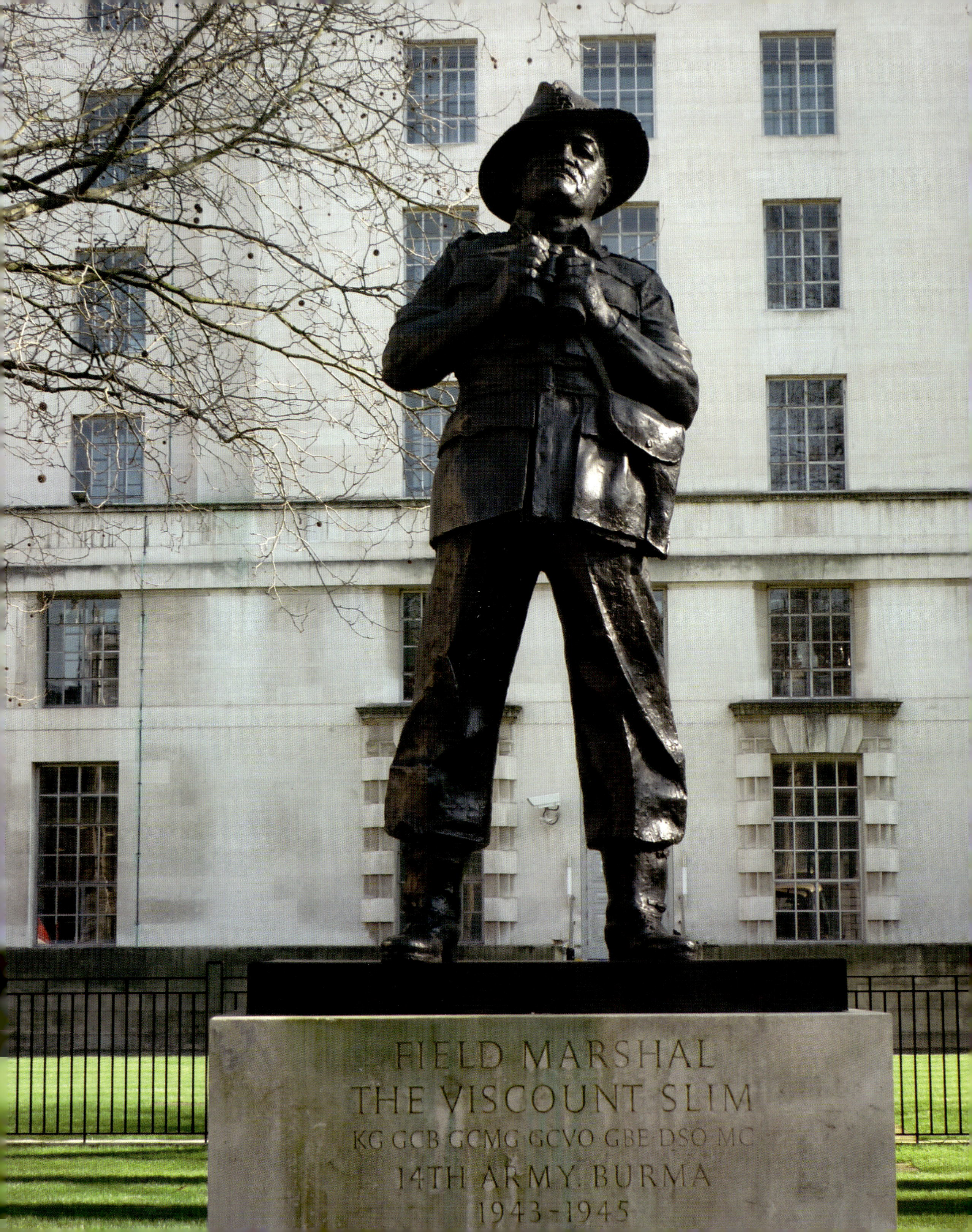
FIELD MARSHAL
THE VISCOUNT SLIM
KG GCB GCMG GCVO GBE DSO MC
14TH ARMY. BURMA
1943-1945

THE LAST ICON-MAKER

Ivor Roberts-Jones and the Public Statue

Jonathan Black

Towards the end of his life, Ivor Roberts-Jones was described as 'the last icon maker' on the strength of impressive public figures such as his *Winston Churchill* in Parliament Square (1970–73; cat. 135), discussed at greater length in Chapter 3; *Clement Attlee* in the Members' Lobby of the House of Commons (1977–79; cat. 143); *Field Marshal Slim* (1988–90; cat. 153) and *Field Marshal Alanbrooke* (1991–93; cat. 154) on Whitehall, in the heart of official London. He often thought in binary paradoxes, so he derived some rather wry amusement that such commissions had in one sense been a great boost to his career, but they also ensured he would be ignored by the wider, fashionable, contemporary art world which, in the main, regarded the type of traditional figurative memorial at which Ivor was such a master with ill-concealed contempt and scorn.

In the 1960s he had experimented with making more formally challenging works that referenced the creations of contemporaries who were regarded as more 'progressive', such as Henry Moore and Eduardo Paolozzi, but in the tension between abstraction and reality he invariably found himself compelled to return to the type of traditional representational sculpture that conspicuously harked back to the example of his great sculptural hero – Rodin. He felt such sculpture still had a powerful role to play in the world – it was still appreciated by the public, and was still being commissioned by committees of the great and good for prominent public spaces.

From his very first public commissions, such as for St Mary's Ardleigh in the 1950s and St Helen's in Wheathampstead in the early 1960s, he was convinced that sculpture, to retain any meaning with the wider public, had to be imbued with a sense of the everyday that was comprehensible, accessible and inspiring. Ivor was both alarmed and intrigued by an article in *The Times* in 1956 which argued that the days of traditionally conceived public sculpture were numbered. It was evident from recent work by artists such as Reg Butler, Alexander Calder and Henry Moore that the public monument could now assume a variety of excitingly innovative forms – and need not be made in bronze or carved from stone, as in the past.[1]

However, as what was meant by sculpture rapidly evolved and diversified out of all recognition from the mid 1960s onwards, Ivor became convinced that the public was being left behind, as the new forms of artistic practice now defined as sculpture were not really interested in commemorating and celebrating the heroic, unusually gifted, individual in a permanent form made from enduring material.[2]

The memorial statues he created brought Ivor a fair measure of recognition – he ended his days an RA with a CBE and two prestigious medals from the Royal British Society of Sculptors – but he was largely unknown in the contemporary art world. He affected to be indifferent to

Cat. 153 *Field Marshal Viscount Slim of Burma, KG, GCMG, DSO, MC*, 1988–90

this state of affairs, but in rural seclusion seethed that art critics, curators and arts administrators appeared to be going out of their way to foster and encourage art that was antithetical to the tradition of Rodin, and to a lesser extent Epstein, which he implacably represented. He mused retrospectively that he should have seen the writing on the wall in 1977, when he was one of the few traditional figurative sculptors included on the selection committee of that year's Queen's Silver Jubilee *Contemporary British Sculpture* exhibition, organised by London County Council and the Arts Council and held in Battersea Park. He took offence at some of the content of the official catalogue – claims in the principal essay that traditional public sculpture was moribund, dead, wince-inducingly irrelevant.[3] In one essay Barry Martin claimed that 'the literary tradition' was simply no longer 'part of the language of sculpture'. The discipline had been 'stripped of any literary or figurative connotations ... the artist has come more and more to rely on the critic to explain his sculpture to the public'. Ivor simply could not agree with this premise or with Martin's assertion elsewhere in the essay that 'architectural and public sculpture' of the traditional stamp should be considered 'essentially dead', while the future for British 'street furniture' lay with the generation of artists who worked in 'welded steel and plastic', and who he claimed had been inspired by the example of David Smith (1906–1965), such as Anthony Caro (1924–), Phillip King (1934–)[4] and William Tucker (1935–).[5]

Ivor took particular umbrage at the fact that there was no mention anywhere in the catalogue of his huge statue of Winston Churchill, unveiled only four years previously in Parliament Square, which had generated a huge degree of discussion and debate in the media and generally been judged a major success.[6] He was perhaps a little hard on Martin, as the latter did acknowledge the existence of impressive recent examples of figurative sculpture by Reg Butler (1913–1981),[7] Elisabeth Frink (1930–1993)[8] and Ralph Brown (1928–), and also affirmed the 'continuing relevance' of Ivor's great sculptural hero, Rodin – in particular, Rodin's *The Age of Bronze* (1877) and *The Walking Man* (1878; Fig. 5.1). One hundred years on from such works, the Frenchman 'personified ... the conventional and time-honoured notion of sculpture'.[9]

Four years later, in 1981, Ivor was further upset by assumptions casually made in the catalogue to the major exhibition *British Sculpture in the Twentieth Century* at the Whitechapel Art Gallery, by Timothy Hyman, that the public memorial as representational statue was no longer viable – indeed, that it was indefensible and even intellectually unhealthy. Hyman had interpreted the lack of traditional figurative sculpture on display in the 1977 Battersea Park exhibition as irrefutable evidence that sculpture of this kind in Britain was in 'terminal decline', though he was prepared to proffer guarded praise for the figuration of Eduardo Paolozzi (1924–2005), George Fullard (1923–1973), John Wragg (1937–), David Wynne (1926–) and Leonard McComb (1930–) – though few examples of their work were actually reproduced in the catalogue.[10] Examples of Ivor's public sculpture, such as his figures of *Augustus John* (1964–67; cat. 133), of *Winston Churchill* for Parliament Square (cat. 135), Oslo (1974–76; cat. 136) and New Orleans (1976–77; cat. 141), and his *Clement Attlee* for the Members' Lobby of the House of Commons

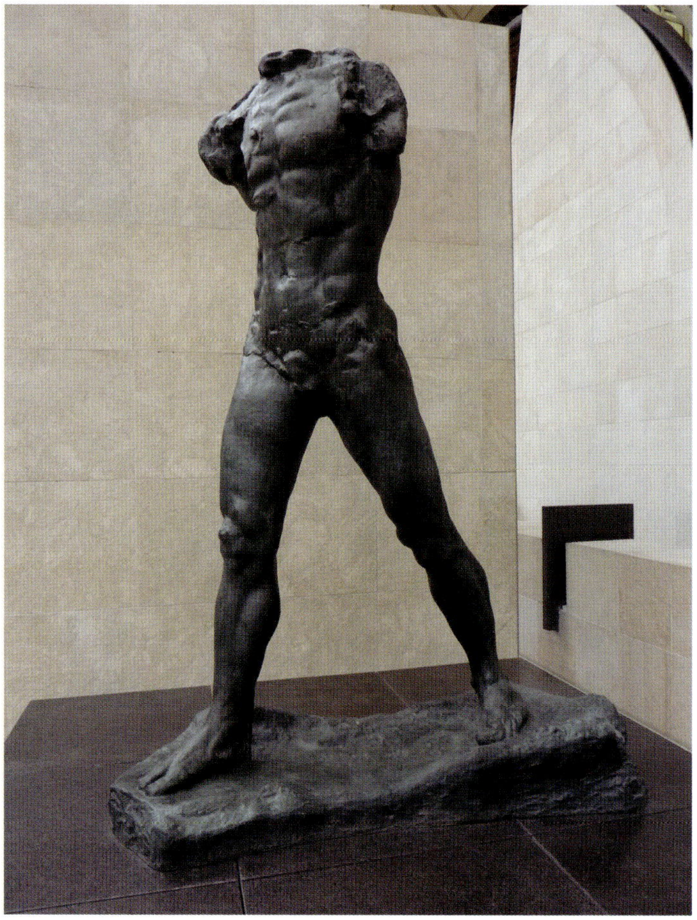

Fig. 5.1 Auguste Rodin, *The Walking Man*, 1878, bronze, 2.13 m high, Musée Rodin, Paris; Image: Courtesy of the Musée Rodin, Paris

(1977–79; cat. 143) are mentioned in the catalogue but not reproduced. In relation to Hyman's list of 'approved' figurative sculptors, it is worthy of note that Ivor had [illegible] work in the late 1950s and early 1960s (see Chapter 1), while in the 1970s he would often find himself competing with Wragg and Wynne for the same commissions – for the figures of *Attlee* (1977) and *Lord Louis Mountbatten* (1981) in the case of Wragg, though the latter was won by Franta Belsky, and for *Mountbatten* and *Rupert Brooke* (1986; cat. 151) in the case of Wynne.

Two years later he took exception to the assertion made by Rudolf Oxenaar (director of the Kroller-Muller National Museum, in the Netherlands) in the catalogue to the exhibition *Sculpture in a Country Park* – the inaugural exhibition of the Welsh Sculpture Trust at Margam, near Port Talbot – that the future of sculpture lay with those he identified as the heirs of David Smith, such as Barry Flanagan (1941–2009), Tony Cragg (1949–), Bill Woodrow (1948–) and Anish Kapoor (1954–).[11] To a certain degree Oxenaar was correct in his prediction, at least for the coming decade: Flanagan was to represent Britain at the Venice Biennale in 1982, was elected an RA in 1991, and made an OBE the same year; Cragg won the revamped Turner Prize in 1988; Woodrow would be a Turner Prize finalist in 1986; and Kapoor was to win the Turner Prize in 1991. Oxenaar, however, did seriously underestimate the future impact of the 'heirs of Duchamp, Gilbert and George and Carl Andre' and the growing respectability of conceptual art and minimalist installations utilising non-traditional materials that would dominate headlines in the 1990s – embodied in the rise of the so-called 'Brit Art Generation'.[12]

Once Ivor became a full Academician, in 1973, he did his best to improve teaching at the RA Schools and encourage an Academy-led revival of interest in the public memorial based upon the figurative sculptural tradition represented by sculptors of the past such as Rodin, Aimé-Jules Dalou, Charles Wheeler and Charles Sargeant Jagger.[13] Until his retirement from the college in July 1978, he would urge his more talented sculpture students at Goldsmiths, such as Etienne Millner, to continue their studies at the RA Schools. Millner did go on to the RA Schools, but was not at all impressed by the standard of teaching. He later felt Ivor's advice on this occasion had proved decidedly faulty.[14]

There is a sense that he did not do his cause full justice, in that his relations with otherwise likeminded champions of traditional figuration in sculpture such as Oscar Nemon, Franta Belsky and James Butler (1931–) were often not good at all; he complained, tongue only partially in cheek, that during his career as a public sculptor he had been pursued by a monstrous Eastern European apparition he dubbed 'Nemonsky' – a diabolic combination of the Croat Oscar Nemon (1906–1985) and the Czech Franta Belsky (1921–2000).[15] Nemon was one of the few among those contemporary sculptors working in a broadly traditional sculptural manner whom he was prepared to disparage in public. Shortly before his death, he described Nemon's head of *Lady Thatcher* in the Carlton Club as 'awful'.[16] In later life, though, he would have opportunity to thank Belsky for recommending him to a committee of his countrymen seeking a figure of Churchill for Winston Churchill Square in Prague (see Chapter 4).[17]

This chapter will now explore some of the distinguished public work Ivor produced from the mid 1950s onwards (his *Churchill* in Parliament Square is discussed in Chapter 3, while the figures of *Churchill* he produced for Oslo, New Orleans and Prague are explored in Chapter 4), his relations with committees and patrons, his attitudes towards the press and public, and his lingering impact on significant spaces in England and Wales, both urban and rural.

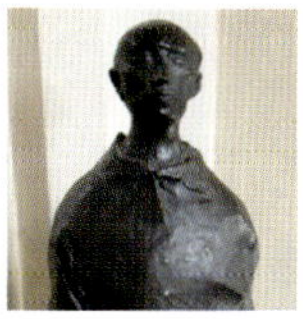

'Rethinking the Sacred': *St Francis* (cat. 119a) and *The Virgin and Child* (1955–58; cat. 19c) for St Mary's Anglican Church, Ardleigh, Essex

This was Ivor's debut public sculpture commission, for which he was very grateful and which he owed to the support of the Essex-based 'progressive Neo-Georgian' architect Raymond Erith RA (1904–1973).[18] Early in November 1955 Erith contacted Ivor,[19] to whom he had been recommended by a combination of Sir John Rothenstein, Charles Wheeler (soon to be elected president of the Royal Academy) and the painter Bernard Dunston RA, who had befriended Ivor through Kyffin Williams in the late 1940s.[20] Erith had been commissioned to remodel the Lady Chapel of St Mary's Ardleigh; £750 for the project had been set aside in the will of Isabella Flynn, a small portion of which was to be spent on two one-third-life-size sculptures to occupy niches within the redesigned Lady Chapel.[21] The bequest already suggested that one of the figures should be of the Virgin Mary, given that the Chapel was dedicated to her; it would seem that it was Ivor who suggested that he also produce a maquette of St Francis.[22] He first devised a figure of the saint wearing a voluminous robe of the single rough-and-ready type Francis possessed, and which he wore during his early years on the road in Tuscany as an itinerant preacher, sustaining himself through begging for alms.[23]

This was an early venture of Ivor in defining a figure through the clothes they wore; at the time he was already working on the more dynamic *Walking Judas* (1955–57; cat. 118), striding forward enveloped in a figure-hugging robe – a device that is probably derived from his long-standing admiration for Rodin's magisterial figure of *Balzac* (1894–97).[24] The pose for the figure, which he adopted very early on in the project, was derived directly from the supplicatory figure of Rodin's *Jehan D'Aire* – part of his *Burghers of Calais* group (1884–89; Fig. 5.2). A cast of this work has stood in Victoria Tower Gardens, near the Houses of Parliament, since 1915, and was one of Ivor's favourite London public sculptures.[25]

At the same time, Ivor was also looking closely at examples of Ancient Egyptian sculpture in the British Museum, where the form of the figure is outlined by a tight-fitting robe or cloak. He later wryly acknowledged that one advantage of using the robe motif was that it covered the saint's feet, which the sculptor did not enjoy working on.[26]

Early in the project Ivor experimented with depicting the Saint wearing a halo composed of circling birds, as a reference to his having reputedly preached a sermon to the 'birds of the air' during his early days tramping the Tuscan countryside.[27] He also initially contemplated including a figure standing next to the Saint representing the ferocious 'Wolf of Gubbio' that had been terrorising the countryside around the town, which the Saint succeeded in turning to more peaceful pursuits with a few gentle words of rebuke.[28] But these two details, after discussion with Erith, were soon discarded.[29] Both decided that the figures should not display expected conventional Christian attributes; rather they would provide an opportunity, as Ivor put it, to 're-think the sacred', to provide a humanist interpretation for an increasingly secular and sceptical world.[30] Ivor had been interested in humanism since the late 1940s, having read discussions of the subject by Sartre and Cyril Connolly[31] – such as the former's influential 1946 essay 'L'Existentialisme est un Humanisme' (translated into English as 'Existentialism and Humanism' two years later),[32] while he was also aware of the importance Henry Moore attached to the 'humanist' quality of much of his recent public sculpture, such as his *Family Groups* for the New Towns of Stevenage (1948–49) and Harlow (1954–55), as well as in relation to his *Reclining Figure* (1957–58), commissioned for the Paris headquarters of UNESCO.[33] Indeed, in October 1956 Ivor explicitly wrote to Erith that, in his opinion, 'sculpture at the present time could do with all the humanism it can get', and that he would attempt to imbue his figures for St Mary's with as much 'humanist feeling' as possible.[34]

It would appear that, in the early stages of the project, the sculptor also had in mind the example of recent Christian imagery by Marini, Manzu and Epstein – particularly the latter's bronze *Madonna and Child* for the Convent of the Holy Child Jesus in Cavendish Square (1950–52, unveiled May 1953)[35] and his aluminium *Christ in Majesty* for Llandaff Cathedral (1954–57, unveiled April 1957).[36]

Shortly after the discussion over humanism and of giving his figures for St Mary's a 'contemporary' appearance, Ivor devised the final version of his figure of *St Francis*, informed by the example of Rodin in the *Burghers of Calais* (Fig. 5.2), and presenting the Saint as having just received the stigmata in September 1224 – hands by his sides, fingers tightly closed over the palms that now bear the sacred wounds, the facial expression suggestive of the mingled pain and ecstasy the Saint is still experiencing moments after God's 'blessing' has been visited upon him.[37] As for his conception for the *Virgin and Child*, Ivor signalled early in the project that he would prefer to depict them as much as possible as a credible, relatively unidealised young mother with an energetically wriggling baby. The mother appears to have been conceived along the lines of one of the neo-Sumerian 'earth mothers' Ivor had created in the late 1940s (cat. 105) and in the manner of his 1947 drawing of a majestically solid *Shelter Angel.*

When photographs of his clay maquettes of the two figures were seen by the church's Parish Parochial Committee – chaired by the vicar of St Mary's, the Reverend Farmiloe – the two designs were speedily approved.[38] But objections to both designs were raised when they were inspected in July 1957 by the local Diocesan Advisory Committee (DAC): it complained that it was not easy to discern whether the Saint Ivor had devised was, indeed, St Francis, while the facial appearance of his Virgin Mother caused considerable disquiet.[39] Her face struck several members of the Committee as 'unhappy ... discontented and ... too experienced'.[40]

In his response to its reservations Ivor revealed that he could be tactful and also combative. He readily agreed to make certain small modifications to his *Saint Francis*, such as adding a cord to the front of his robe to indicate the subject was wearing the sort of robe associated with that of a mendicant friar.[41] However, he was unwilling to change the *Virgin and Child* to any significant degree. He complained to Erith that the DAC was unhappy with his concept of a *Virgin and Child* but could not tell him precisely why. Did it want him to produce a Madonna in the manner of Raphael, Rembrandt or Murillo?[42] The Committee seemed to be suggesting that he make her appear less a contemporary woman than a Virgin Mary in the saccharine style of a Hollywood Madonna, or of the inert, unconvincing and banal New Testament figures regularly exhibited at the Royal Academy. Ivor decided to accept Erith's suggestion[43] that he apply a touch of fin-de-siècle gypsy allure to his Virgin Mary, and rethink her in the guise of one of Augustus John's many pre-First World War portraits of his inamorata, Dorelia McNeil.[44]

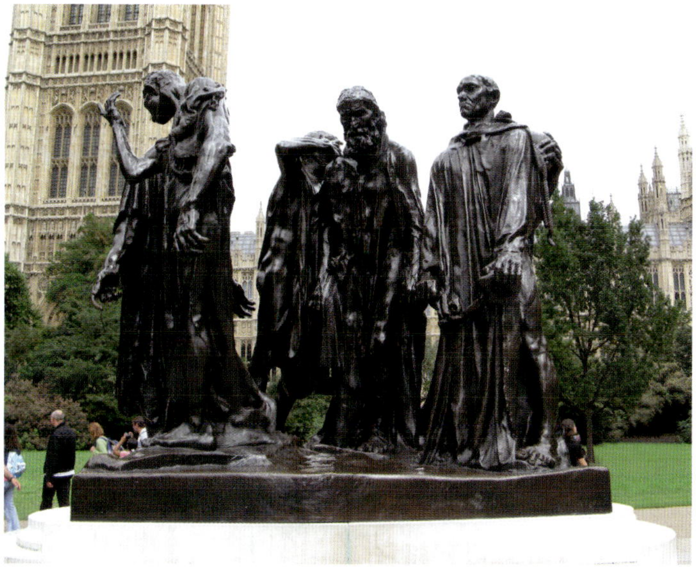

Fig. 5.2 Auguste Rodin, *The Burghers of Calais,* 1884–89, bronze, 2.2 m high, Victoria Tower Gardens, London; Image: J. Black

Indeed, the sculptor was keen not to compromise in still offering a humanistic view of human beings – one that was positive and affirmative rather than doom-laden and pessimistic. He wanted parishioners seeing his *Virgin and Child* to take comfort from the prosaic and yet uplifting joy to be derived in the sight of a young mother holding a healthy baby squirming with life and vitality.[45]

In his discussions with the DAC Ivor was reasonable, doing his best to charm, but was also prepared to deploy some tactical displays of 'temper', as he imagined the Committee would expect evidence of some 'artistic temperament' from a 'proper' sculptor and not some 'third-rate amateur'.[46] In the end he was prepared to compromise only slightly, with little fundamental alteration to either figure when he re-submitted photographs of the two maquettes to the DAC in October 1957. On this occasion the designs were approved with scant discussion.[47] The two figures were cast by Michael Gaskin of Art Bronze Foundry using the lost wax process. Ivor paid particular attention to the patinas given to the works,[48] and how they would be illuminated at night sitting in their niches within St Mary's when installed early in October 1958.[49] In later life Ivor appears to have looked back on his *St Francis* with affection and some pride. This was not the case with the *Virgin and Child*, which he came to regard as an early example case in which he had given too much ground in the direction of sentimentality and 'playing it safe' before the commissioning committee and the architect with whom he was consulting.[50]

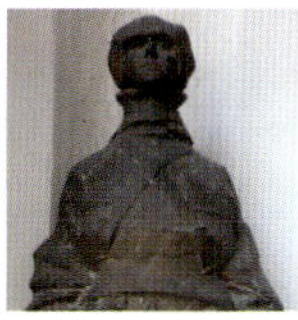

'Heroism to the Verge of Madness': *Apsley Cherry-Garrard* (1960–62; cat. 132) for St Helen's Anglican Church, Wheathampstead, Hertfordshire

In the autumn of 1961 Ivor was approached by Angela Mathias, the widow of Apsley Cherry-Garrard (1886–1959), the polar explorer and author of the best-selling account of his participation in Captain Scott's ill-fated expedition to reach the South Pole in 1912, *The Worst Journey in the World*, published in 1922. Angela had become Mrs Mathias after marriage to a Welsh doctor, Gordon Mathias, but she had been prompted to contact Ivor not on account of his Welsh heritage but as a result of seeing a photograph of his head of *Paul Claudel* (cat. 17), reproduced in *The Times* in July 1960. Her husband had admired the writings of Claudel, particularly on the nature of being tested and the powers of endurance supplied by faith and will.[51] She also felt Ivor would understand something of the nature of suffering, and of the privations caused by the climatic extremes her first husband had experienced, with his years in Burma fighting the Japanese with the 'Forgotten Army'.[52] It also helped Ivor's cause when Mrs Mathias learned through John Rothenstein that the sculptor was an avowed admirer of Rodin, of whose smaller statuettes her first husband had formed an impressive collection.[53]

Mrs Mathias asked Ivor to submit a maquette of her husband wearing Edwardian British polar clothing, in which he had shivered during his time in Antarctica with Captain Scott (1911–12). She lent the sculptor a copy of *The Worst Journey in the World* and several photographs of 'Cherry' taken at Scott's base camp at Cape Crozier in 1911. Ivor quickly settled on a photograph of Cherry (Fig. 5.3) taken shortly before he, Dr Edward 'Bill' Wilson (1872–29 March 1912) and Lieutenant Henry 'Birdie' Bowers embarked on their near-suicidal scientific mission to walk in the depths of the polar winter (average temperature: −33°C) 67 miles from base camp to Cape Crozier, to collect recently laid emperor penguin eggs.[54] It was this mission, achieved despite the fact that temperatures were unseasonably low (on one occasion on their way back it fell to −76°C), that Scott dubbed 'the hardest journey in the world', and that later led Cherry to write his reminiscence of the Scott expedition.[55]

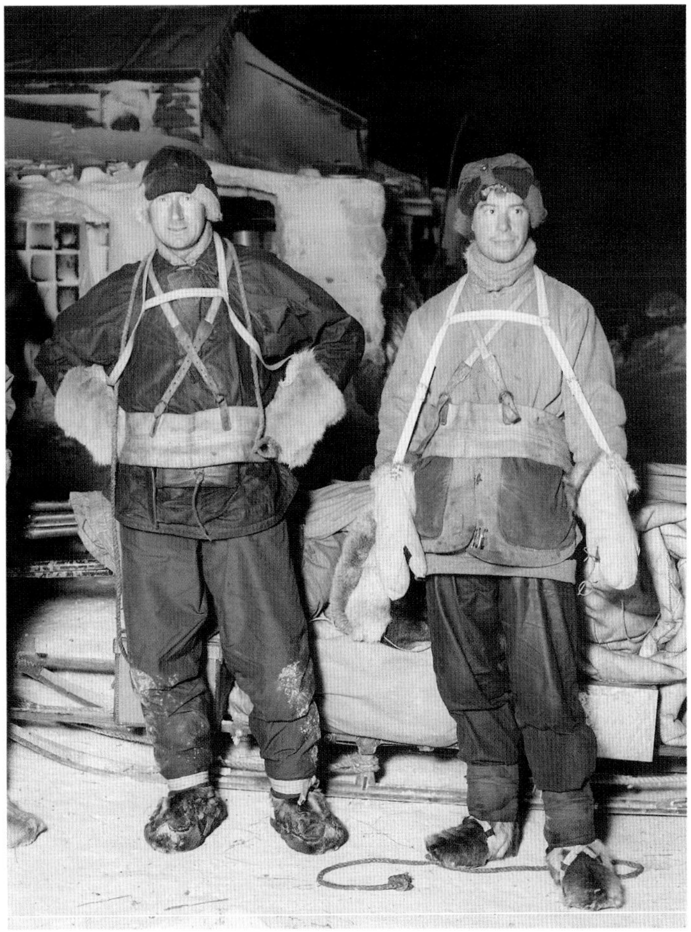

Fig. 5.3 Apsley Cherry Garrard at Cape Crozier, the Antarctic, June 1911 (standing on the right) Image: Courtesy of the Royal Geographical Society, London

Ivor was particularly impressed that, during the painfully slow walk to Cape Crozier, Cherry kept going despite the fact his fingers had been badly frostbitten, many of his teeth had shattered in the cold, and he could hardly see, since the cold prevented him from wearing his spectacles and he was severely short sighted.[56] Without the protection of his spectacles, and unable to wear goggles, which would have reduced what little vision he retained, he quickly succumbed to snow blindness.[57] As Ivor wrote in wonder to the Reverend Roe of St Helena's, the stoic heroism Cherry and his companions had displayed in their walk to and from Cape Crozier 'verged on madness', but he recalled how, as a schoolboy in his teens (presumably at St Cuthbert's) he and his friends had eagerly devoured such tales of incredible British tenacity on the ice.[58] He was also impressed that Cherry did not attempt to conceal the reality that his two companions on the Cape Crozier egg-collecting mission had later frozen to death with Captain Scott in March 1912. When Cherry eventually donated the emperor penguin eggs they had collected to the Natural History Museum, in June 1913, the recipient curators were noticeably offhand and unimpressed when he explained the gruelling circumstances in which the eggs had been obtained.[59]

In conceiving the figure of Cherry in his polar kit, Ivor was aware that his subject had been a highly strung, even neurotic individual, prone to bouts of debilitating self-doubt and crises of confidence.[60] As would often be the case with the subjects of Ivor's public sculpture, who were all male, he had experience of depression but had done his best to overcome his frailties through sheer will power and a sort of desperate determination. The sculptor would be fascinated throughout the rest of his career with the challenge of trying to convey in his public sculpture this amalgam of strength and an element of weakness, the first almost but not entirely obscuring the second.[61] He noted from the pages of *The Worst Journey in the World* that the man-made clothing Cherry and the rest of Scott's party had worn in Antarctica had proved inferior to the natural furs worn by Lapps and Inuit, and which the Norwegian Roald Amundsen had taken with him on his successful bid to reach the South Pole.[62] The sculptor underlined the passage in *The Worst Journey in the World* in which Cherry described how, in the mornings during their journey to Cape Crozier, once he and his two companions had emerged from their tent, in less than 20 seconds their clothes 'froze into iron armour'. They found they could not move from the waist upwards, and their heads quickly froze into one position as they attempted to drag their heavy supply sledge forward. On returning to Scott's base camp, the three men had to be 'cut out of their polar kit'.[63]

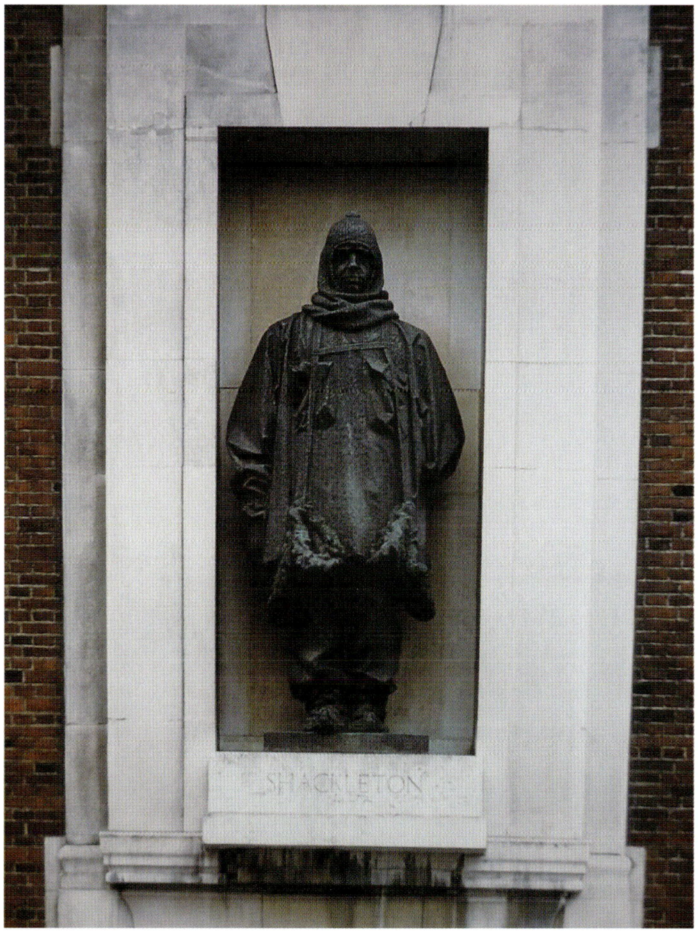

Fig. 5.4 Charles Sargeant Jagger, *Sir Ernest Shackleton*, 1928–32, bronze, 2.59 m high, Royal Geographical Society, London; Image: J. Black

In short order, Ivor devised a maquette of his figure of Cherry which Mrs Mathias immediately found 'appealing' and truthful;[64] in his approach to the figure he consciously referred back to an earlier statue of a hero of polar exploration – not *Captain Scott* as imagined by his wife Kathleen Bruce in Waterloo Place, London (unveiled in November 1915), but Charles Sargeant Jagger's *Ernest Shackleton*, unveiled outside the Royal Geographical Society in London in January 1932 (Fig. 5.4). Cherry was known to have thought well of Jagger's figure,[65] but it was also one of Ivor's favourite works by a twentieth-century British sculptor.[66] Like Jagger, Ivor succeeds in the final version of the figure of Cherry in suggesting that his subject has not only reached the end of his tether, but that he is just barely grasping its last fraying strands and remains upright on account of pure will when every muscle within cries out for him to lie down and welcome a sleep from which he will never awake. Even less of Cherry's face is exposed to the gaze of the spectator than Jagger's *Shackleton*, and yet Ivor convinces us of Cherry's youth and vulnerability, and of his palpable and very appealing sense of innocence. It is as if Cherry is a visitor from another world. Only a year earlier, in April 1961, and wearing garb reminiscent of an Edwardian polar explorer, Yuri Gagarin (1934–1968) had become the first man to orbit the earth.[67]

The work was unveiled in mid October 1962[68] (Fig. 5.5) as the Cuban missile crisis was unfolding (14–28 October 1962); many of the thirty or so participants in the unveiling ceremony must have wondered whether the human race was going to survive until the end of the week.[69]

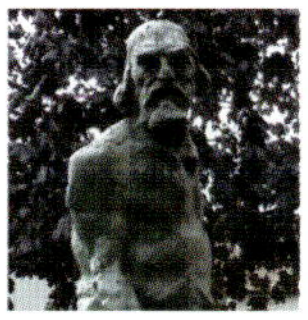

Neglected Prophet: *Augustus John* (1964–67; cat. 133) for Fordingbridge, Hampshire

The celebrated painter and 'titan of Bohemia' may initially have been introduced to Ivor through their mutual friend Charles Wheeler in 1957, around the time of his first solo exhibition, in May of that year, held at the Beaux Arts Gallery. By the late 1950s Ivor appears to have been giving John instruction on how to sculpt and make plaster casts. A year before his death, in October 1961, John wrote to the Contemporary Art Society for Wales, of which he was the president, urging it to contemplate commissioning Ivor to make a statue of former Liberal prime minister

David Lloyd George (1863–1945) to stand outside the Palace of Westminster.[70]

John died in October 1961, and in January the following year Ivor attended the painter's memorial service. It was apparently around this time that an art dealer based in Fordingbridge, Simon Beddoe, suggested to John's widow Dorelia McNeil (1881–1969)[71] that her husband be commemorated with a sculpted figure – though Beddoe had James Butler in mind for the task.[72] Beddoe's idea for a sculptural memorial to John was enthusiastically taken up by a local GP who had looked after the painter in his later years, Dr Aubrey Westlake, and by a long-term John admirer, Gwen, Lady Melchett.[73]

The John family then approached Ivor to conceive a memorial design, as Augustus was known to have 'greatly esteemed his sculpture in his later years'.[74] Ivor was keen to accept the commission, but found his time fully occupied with a series of portrait heads, including *Somerset Maugham* (1961–62; cat. 27) for Lord Beaverbrook, *Sir William Emrys Williams* (1962–63; cat. 28) for the Arts Council, and *The Fifth Lord Kenyon* (1962–63) for the sitter and the NMW, Cardiff.

It was not until the autumn of 1963 that he produced a sketch model of his memorial proposal, to consist of two figures: a seated Augustus John, aged roughly in his thirties and wearing the smock of a professional Edwardian-era painter, painting a standing Dorelia McNeil, wearing the loose-fitting, flowing, full-skirted 'gypsy' dress he had painted her in so often in the years immediately before the First World War[75] (Fig. 5.6). His initial figure of Dorelia (Fig. 5.7) is also decidedly reminiscent of an archaic Greek figure (Fig. 5.8) of a female worshipper of the goddess Artemis wearing a broad-brimmed hat from Tanagra, c. 400 BCE, in the collection of the British Museum, of the type Ivor had studied closely during the late 1940s and early 1950s. This early conception of Dorelia can also be related to Picasso's 'Artist and Model' series of etchings, published in 1931.[76] Ivor's sketch model also calls to mind one of a series of bronze statuettes Manzu produced around 1957–59, with the over-arching title of 'The Painter and His Model', exhibited in the Italian's October–November 1960 solo show at the Tate Gallery[77] (Fig. 5.9).

In a sense, it was quite a brave and potentially contentious move to include a figure of Dorelia in a design for a memorial to John, as she had never actually married the painter. This fact, and her having four children with Augustus, had raised quite a few eyebrows when the couple moved to live a mile from Fordingbridge early in 1927. For many years thereafter, their household at Fryern

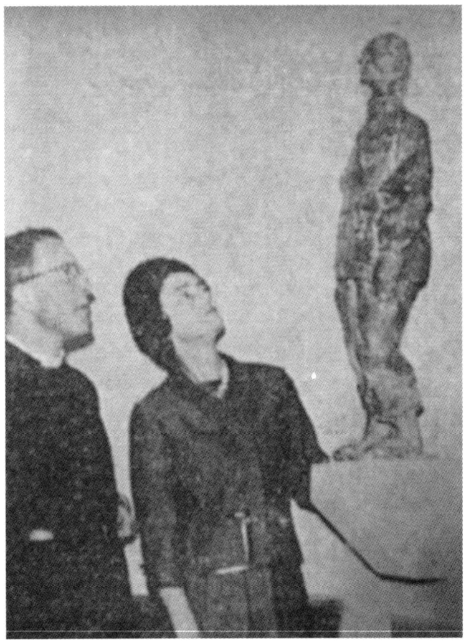

Fig. 5.5 Mrs Angela Mathias and the Reverend G.H.A.T. Roe inspect *Apsley Cherry-Garrard* inside St Helen's Anglican Church, Wheathampstead, Hertfordshire, October 1962; Image: Private Collection

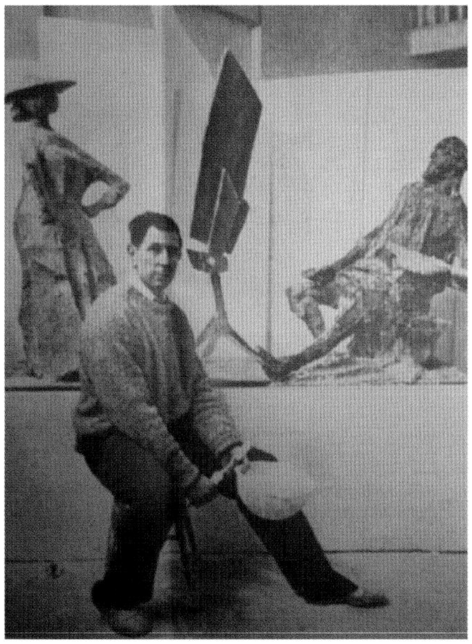

Fig. 5.6 Ivor Roberts-Jones with one-third-scale plaster maquette of his first version of the *Augustus John Memorial* for Fordingbridge, November 1964, Image: Courtesy of the HMI, Leeds

Court was regarded as decidedly 'irregular' by the more 'respectable' inhabitants of Fordingbridge, with much potential for scandal that might damage the reputation of the town.[78]

By the beginning of 1964 the sculptor had made a plaster cast of this sketch model, which had been inspected and approved of by Sir Kenneth Clark and by Dorelia.[79] Dr Westlake saw the maquette a few weeks later, and was 'charmed' by it; encouraged by support for the design from Sir Charles Wheeler at the Royal Academy, Westlake proposed to show it to Fordingbridge Rural District Council (FRDC), of which he was chairman, to seek its approval for the memorial's erection in Fordingbridge.[80] Permission from the FRDC was granted relatively quickly, but Dr Westlake realised agreement for the memorial also had to be given by Fordingbridge Parish Council (FPC). In March 1964 Dorelia McNeil wrote to the FPC indicating that a committee for a memorial statue to her late husband would soon be forming, that Ivor had been approached to undertake the task, and that she would like to see the finished sculpture stand near to Fordingbridge Parish Church.[81]

Two months later, early in May 1964, Ivor was formally commissioned to be the sculptor of the Augustus John memorial by Dr Westlake. Spurred partly by his own initiative at the prospect of beginning such an 'interesting' sculpture, and partly prompted by Dorelia, he had already made a scale maquette of the two-figure group, which was about 76 centimetres high. He planned to use this maquette as a visual aid to help the soon-to-be-formed memorial committee to advertise its appeal to raise funds for the project.[82] His treatment of the two heads was more detailed – especially that of John, depicted as the painter had been described by Lady Cynthia Asquith when he was at the height of his powers in 1917: 'His appearance is magnificent, straight out of the Old Testament – flowing, well-kept beard, hair cut en bloc at about the top of the ear, fine, majestic features. He had on a sort of overall daubed with paint, buttoned up round the throat.'[83]

By July 1964 an Augustus John Memorial Committee had formed, with Lady Melchett as chair and Sir Philip Dunn as treasurer, while other leading members included such prominent art world figures as Sir Charles Wheeler, Sir John Rothenstein, Sir William Coldstream and Sir David Cecil.[84] Ivor informed the Committee that, in his opinion, the two figure memorial scheme would cost at least £10,000 – including his fee of £2,500. He asserted that the overall estimate was quite conservative, warning the Committee and the Parish Council, however, that the planned 'appeal might prove disappointing ... however I do not for a moment believe it will [and] I think the work so important and rewarding in itself that I would certainly do all I possibly could to overcome any difficulties ...'[85]

The memorial appeal was formally launched in November 1964, with publication in the press of photographs of Ivor's one-third-full-sized plaster model of the two-figure group. Ivor's design was described in *The Times* as assuming a 'happy and unusual form' likely to appeal to 'art-lovers in this country and in America', and a 'worthy tribute to so masterly a painter'.[86] Later that

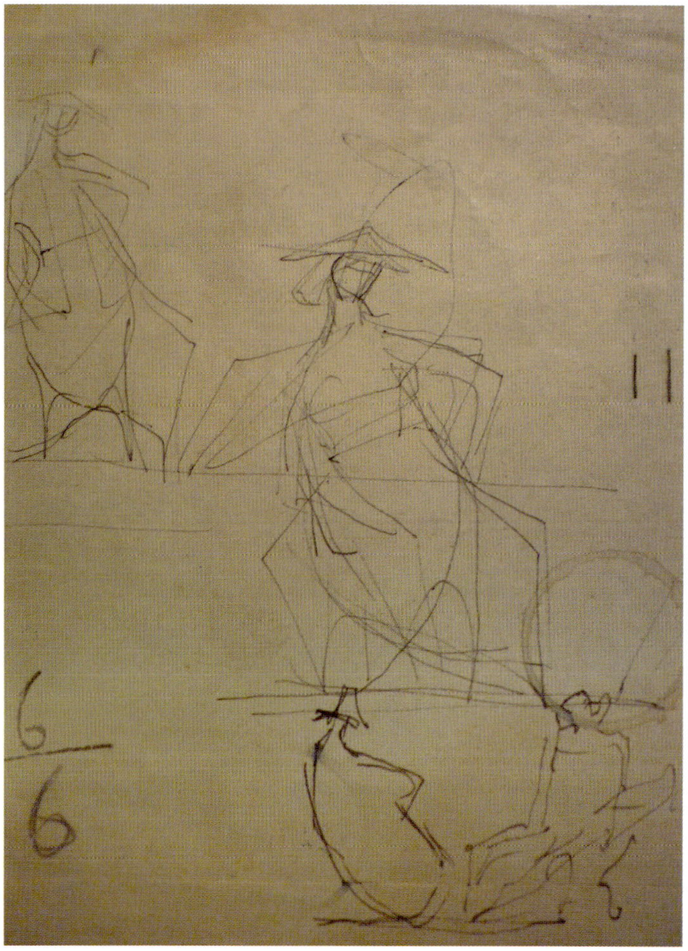

Fig. 5.7 Ivor Roberts-Jones, *Three Sketches of Dorelia McNeil for the Augustus John Memorial*, c. 1963–64, pencil on paper, 23.3 x 29 cm, Image: Courtesy of the HMI, Leeds

same month, the local newspaper for the area around Fordingbridge announced that the FPC had 'offered a site on the edge of the War Memorial Ground on the banks of the River Avon' for the proposed memorial. This site had been approved by the John family and endorsed by the sculptor.[87]

But this news provoked a furious reaction from many quarters in Fordingbridge – not least 52 prominent local businesspeople and traders, who submitted a petition to the Parish Council insisting that the John memorial 'be situated in the town's market place where it would be seen by the greatest number of people and would be of greatest benefit to the town. They also felt that the proposal to include a second figure of Mrs Dorelia John ... seemed unnecessary.' Matters were further complicated when it emerged that the secretary of the John Memorial Commitee, Simon Beddoe, was critical of the choice of Ivor as the memorial's sculptor. He argued that Ivor wanted £10,000 to make the memorial, whereas his suggested sculptor, James Butler, had initially proposed only £750.[88]

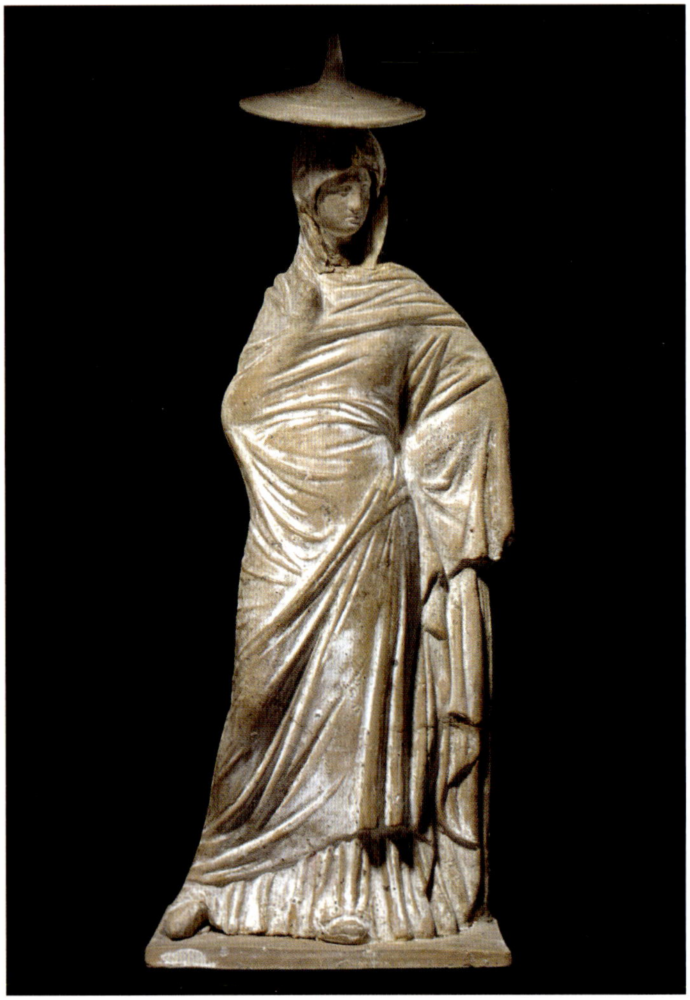

Fig. 5.8 *Woman wearing a Sunhat*, c. 200 BCE, terracotta, 25 cm high, British Museum, London; Image: Courtesy of British Museum Images

Criticism of the design and site of the proposed memorial rumbled on to such an extent that the FPC felt that it had to 'drop the proposal that the proposed Augustus John statue be placed on the site at the Recreation Ground'.[89] Meanwhile, the appeal was not raising as many donations as had been confidently predicted, even though a loan exhibition of John's mural designs and drawings held at the Upper Grosvenor Galleries in London in April 1965 had raised some £700 for the memorial. In the exhibition's catalogue, Sir Charles Wheeler, who had opened the exhibition in his capacity as president of the Royal Academy, argued that, great as John had been as a painter, as a draughtsman he had been

> greater still ... No finer master of the living line has worked in England since Van Dyck ... Fittingly the sculptor Ivor Roberts-Jones has conceived a group of both Augustus and Dorelia for it is scarcely possible, especially when thinking of his drawings, to separate the one from the other. They will live together in bronze at Fordingbridge for centuries to come.[90]

However, that same month it became evident that the British Legion in Fordingbridge did not share Sir Charles's admiration for either Augustus John or the proposed memorial to him. In a 'noisy meeting' held in Fordingbridge Town Hall, Legion members voted by '58 votes to 4 against the Augustus John statue being sited anywhere in Fordingbridge War Memorial Grounds'. A number of speakers pointed out that John had never actually served as a combatant in the country's military during the First World War. Facetious suggestions were made of alternative sites for the memorial – on his grave in the local churchyard, or outside his studio at Fryern Court.[91] After further wrangling, the Memorial Committee announced four months later that it had found another site for Ivor's statue: 'in the Quadrant beside Ashford Water ... between two of the town's bridges', near the parish church of St Mary.[92] Ivor did not regard this new site as ideal, but acknowledged that continued opposition from the British Legion was harming the reputation of the memorial appeal.[93] He was later to write that, by the spring of 1965, he was well aware that '[t]here was little enthusiasm for Augustus's sex life ... among the good folk of F[ordingbridge]'.[94]

Meanwhile, when celebrated society photographer Cecil Beaton, in the presence of Dorelia, formally re-launched the John Memorial Appeal in September 1965, the sculptor produced a painted plaster sketch model of the head of John to use as a prop. In his opening speech Beaton described John as 'one of the most monumental characters we are ever likely to know', while Ivor was a 'brilliant young sculptor' who had so rightly decided to include a figure of Dorelia in his memorial design, as John never tired of 'painting his wife's natural grace and the magical harmonies of her unconscious poses'. He asked those present to give generously, and hinted that if further funds were not forthcoming, 'the sculptor will have to think again, in smaller, simpler terms, and make something less heroic and less monumental perhaps than the occasion demanded'.[95]

The re-launched appeal did not produce the necessary inrush of donations. In April the following year *The Times* announced that the John Memorial Appeal had so far raised £5,000 – only half of what had been hoped – while the site by Ashford Water had fallen through, as the owner could not guarantee it as a permanent one. Ivor stated that, although he had already produced 'several sketches for the memorial which was originally proposed', he now suspected the memorial might have to end as a figure of Augustus John alone.[96] A new site had emerged for the memorial – quite an attractive one overlooking the river Avon at the rear of the Victoria Assembly Rooms – though Ivor was unhappy that it was dominated by a large oak tree that the Parish Council, owner of the site, refused either to have cut down or significantly trimmed.[97] Two months later, what Ivor had anticipated for some time came to pass: the Memorial Committee asked to him to abandon the two-figure memorial design in favour of a single figure of John.[98]

Within just a few weeks Ivor produced a sketch model of a new John, no longer seated, neatly dressed in the Edwardian smock, and in his thirties – but upright, striding forward wearing a simple shirt, rather careworn trousers and barefoot and with a noticeably older face, deeply marked by the ravages of the painter's long, rackety lifestyle (Fig. 5.10). The sculptor was confronting a side of John in later life that was occasionally noted by more perceptive observers: the artist tormented by an awareness of the amount of talent that he possessed and was relentlessly frittering away – pursued by the furies of unfulfilled projects. In the early 1920s John had engaged a new secretary, Kathleen Hale, who later remembered him as 'a bit of a dandy ... broad-shouldered and muscular, who moved surprisingly lightly on his small feet'. He made her think of 'a paralysed giant and ... though he appeared uninhibited, he seemed to me to be always trying to break through tremendous frustration – as if there was a volcano inside him that might erupt any moment'. He was hounded by 'his shyness and despair'.[99] A little earlier, John had admitted to Lady Cynthia Asquith that he often experienced prolonged periods of paralysing depression: 'Rather dreadful that feeling of wanting to go somewhere and not knowing where ... I spend hours of anguish trying to make a move – in some direction.'[100] Perhaps one particular strength of the figure Ivor created of the painter is that its pose suggests John's remaining energy, but also that it is uncertain, undirected and unlikely to result in a work that will ever reach the painter's exacting standards – something of a perfectionist himself, Ivor well knew the feeling.[101]

The figure was conceived in the cramped confines of the topmost room at 31 St James's Gardens – as had been the earlier figures of *St Francis* (cat. 199a), the *Madonna and Child* (cat. 119c) and *Apsley Cherry-Garrard* (cat. 132). For the first time, however, Ivor was required to create a figure that was over life-size, and, given the restricted space he was working in, he divided the figure into three sections: head and neck, chest and arms, and midriff and legs. He would later apply this approach to all his public figure commissions, though he had much more room to work in after late summer of 1966, when he and Monica moved to a detached house on the outskirts of Woodbridge, Suffolk. Ivor set up his new studio in an enlarged shed that he erected at the bottom of the back garden.[102]

With the new figure of John, he started from the head downwards. He first altered the head of the painter, making him distinctly older, more lined by experience and hard living, and more 'ravaged' – as he was later to put it in relation to his head of *Field Marshal Viscount Alanbrooke* (1990–93; cat. 154) – by anxiety and frustration at the reality of fading physical powers and artistic ability.[103]

Ivor appears to have worked extensively from a series of photographs given to him by Dorelia of her husband in the 1930s, in his late fifties and early sixties, but looking considerably older owing to persistent heavy drinking. For the striking posture of the figure, moving as if lurching forward to apply paint to canvas, or possibly a lump of clay to an armature (Ivor anticipating by two decades John's period as a sculptor, which he may have observed at first hand in the late 1950s), Ivor looked back to his earlier *Walking Judas* (1955–57; cat. 118), itself informed by the insistent, driving energy of Boccioni's celebrated *Unique Forms of Continuity of Space* (1912–13). Intriguingly, during the spring of 1966 Ivor was reading a biography of Jackson Pollock – another painter troubled by an over-fondness for alcohol and a noticeable lack of self-discipline – and had been very struck by the series of photographs taken by Hans Namuth of Pollock in the full flow of creating one of his 'drip paintings' – especially those presenting the painter straining forwards over his canvas on the floor, brow deeply furrowed in concentration, paint-coated stick, or brush, in hand[104] (Fig. 5.11).

After a year had passed, the full-sized figure had been personally cast by Michael Gaskin of the Art Bronze Foundry, and Ivor was delighted with the results. In August 1967 he wrote to Simon Beddoe (still secretary of the John Memorial Committee despite his earlier preference for James Butler as the statue's sculptor):

> It really is an excellent cast – and I had it wheeled out and placed facing as it will be and I really was very pleased. There is sometimes a tinge of disappointment when seeing a thing again after a longish break, and in another material, but this time there was no such thing and I was very pleased. I thought I'd let you know and I'd be delighted if you would let the members of the Fordingbridge Committee know because I feel I have so often had to write or ring with some carping query or other – but this is just plain good news. Everything is tied up at this end![105]

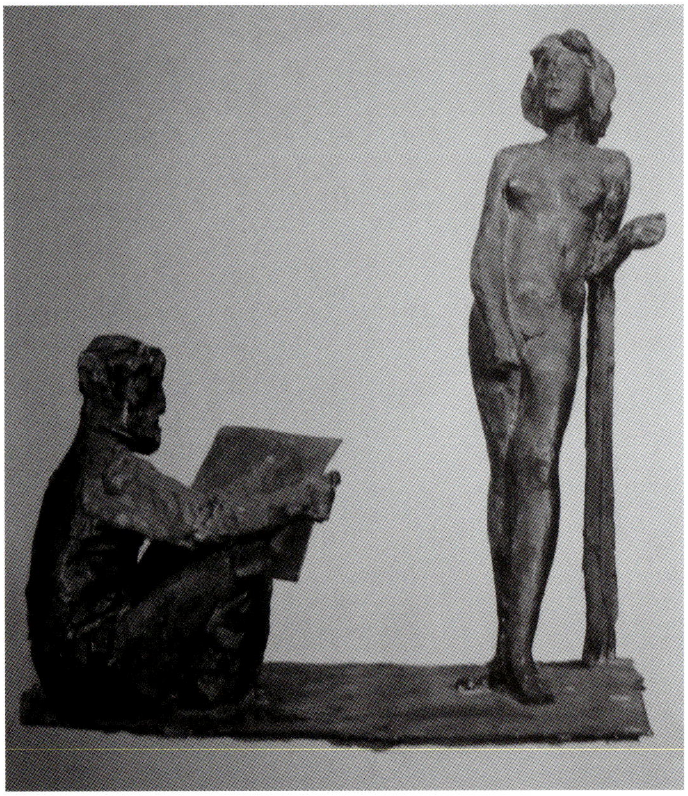

Fig. 5.9 Giacomo Manzu, *Painter and his Model*, 1958, bronze, 65 cm high, Private Collection; Image: J. Black

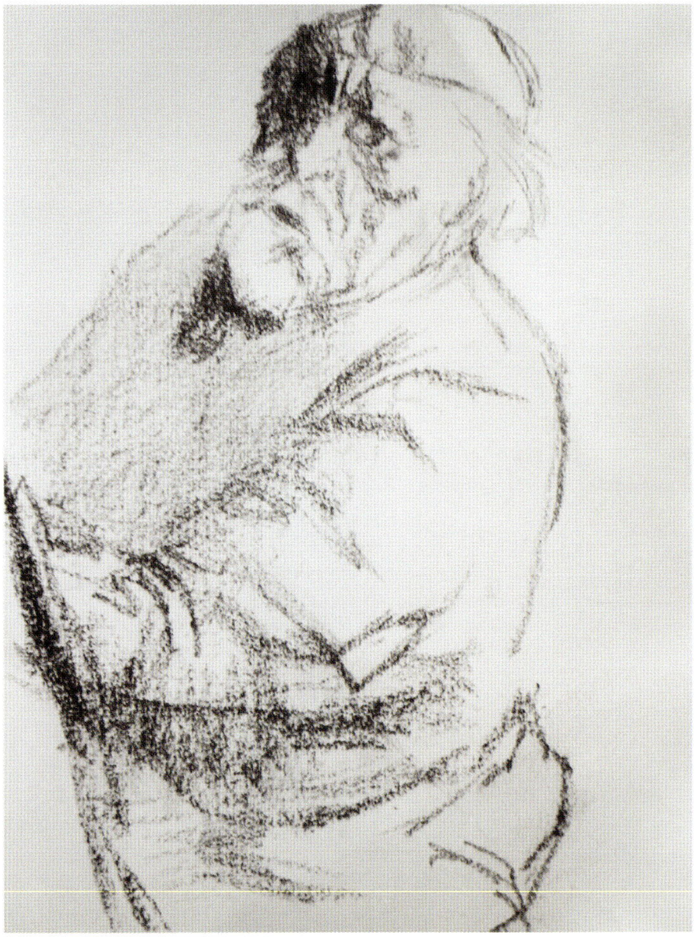

Fig. 5.10 *Study of Augustus John at Work*, c. 1966, black chalk on paper, 38.1 x 45 cm, Private Collection, Image: J. Black

He was also very relieved to have recently heard that the large tree on the Assembly Rooms site that threatened literally to cast his figure of John into the shade had been hit by lightning and 'burnt to a crisp'. Then the one member of the Parish Council who objected vehemently to the remnants of the tree being uprooted and removed from the site had 'died from a stroke'.[106] Ivor later recalled that Dr Westlake had remarked of the departed municipal worthy: 'The poor chap didn't have a chance, with one Welshman down here (pointing at me) and another up there pointing at the sky. This is absolutely true. Fate did indeed take a hand. Augustus must have had a great influence, tho' whether upstairs or downstairs, I wouldn't like to say!'[107]

The statue was unveiled on 1 October 1967 by Admiral Lord Louis Mountbatten, at the invitation of Admiral Sir Caspar John. Mountbatten described the statue as 'entirely faithful to [John's] ebullient personality and to John as … the man of action'. Furthermore, its sculptor had captured 'the John [who] was a formidable man, warm-hearted, liberal, non-conformist in character … [T]his magnificent statue will enhance the beauty of our lovely country and keep alive the personality of a great man whose fame will live wherever his pictures are hung.'[108]

Present in the audience that day were Sir Charles Wheeler, Sir William Coldstream and the writer Anthony Powell. Wheeler informed a local newspaper that the statue was undoubtedly 'a lively sculpture of a truly remarkable man … [H]e felt it would have met with the approval of Augustus John himself.'[109] The often waspish Coldstream remarked in private that Ivor's portrayal of John was a 'shattering' one, likely to put off any devotees of Augustus as well as budding painters in Fordingbridge from any thoughts of 'drink and painting as a career'.[110] Powell thought Ivor had offered a 'compelling' image of John – true to his memory, in the early 1930s, of encountering John lurching down Percy Street in Fitzrovia, and calling to mind an intoxicated Old Testament prophet – if one such had taken to sustained imbibing.[111] Fittingly, years later, Ivor referred to John as a 'prophet' neglected in his own country.[112]

The statue was moved in March 1999 to a site parallel to the River Avon, below the thirteenth-century bridge that gave Fordingbridge its name. Rather appropriately, the impression is given of the painter, having abruptly left a pub across the road, making his determined way on unsteady legs along the river towards his home at Fryern Court. In his previous site, where he had stood since October 1967, he had been positioned facing the River Avon, and left the feeling in many visitors that he was heading purposefully towards its edge to hurl himself in.[113]

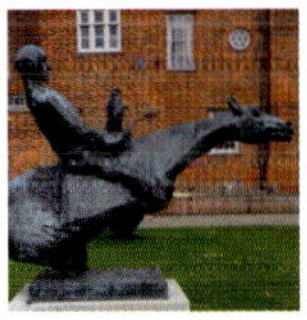

Sculpture in a Landscape: *The Lazarus Rider* (1976–83; cat. 140) for Melford Hall, Suffolk

In the spring of 1976 Ivor exhibited a plaster sketch model of the *Lazarus Rider* at the Royal Academy. He later indicated that the work had been an 'imaginative excursion', after working solidly for much of the previous five years on two huge figures of Churchill: for Parliament Square (cat. 135) and Oslo (cat. 136). Meanwhile, that spring he was already devising an entirely new figure of the statesman for New Orleans (cat. 141).[114] The *Lazarus Rider* was 'something for myself', which referenced earlier explorations of the horse-and-rider theme in his career, such as *The Kite Rider* (cat. 123). Also, when not working on a figure of Churchill, for his own 'sanity of mind', the artist had often frequented the Elgin Marbles at the British Museum.[115] He was especially impressed by the expression of taut equine musculature driven to extremes that was present in the carved pentelic marble relief, *Procession*

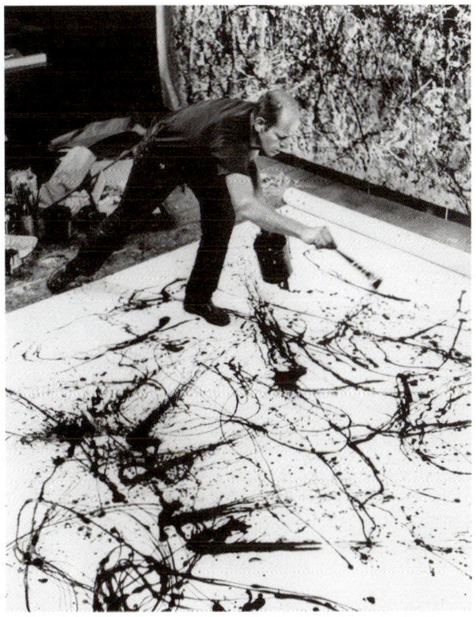

Fig. 5.11 Hans Namuth, *Jackson Pollock creating a 'Drip' Painting*, 1950, photograph, Private Collection; Image: J. Black

of Horsemen, on the Parthenon frieze (c. 443–438 BCE), while he also closely inspected the dynamic head of a horse from the chariot of the Moon Goddess Selene (Fig. 5.12), which had once occupied a position on the east pediment of the Parthenon (c. 438–432 BCE).[116] During this period he also closely studied the depiction of horses under duress in low-relief carvings produced by Charles Sargeant Jagger around 1924–25 for the Royal Artillery Memorial on Hyde Park Corner in London (unveiled October 1925; Fig. 5.13), and paid several visits to inspect a bronze *Horse and Rider* (Fig. 5.14) by Elisabeth Frink, unveiled at the junction of Dover Street and Piccadilly in August 1975.[117] It was clear to Ivor, as it was to many who admired this sculpture, that Frink owed a considerable debt to the example of Marini – one of whose *Horse and Rider* bronzes had first been exhibited in London as early as 1951 (Fig. 5.15).[118] Ivor greatly admired Marini – particularly his portraiture, and the balance he sought to discover between the real and the abstract, between the example of haunting ancient art forms, such as Etruscan sculpture, and the contemporary.[119] But by the mid 1970s Ivor had come to the conclusion that the Italian's treatment of the horse-and-rider theme was just too 'refined' and 'passive';[120] he wanted to present an image of a horse that was grittier and more elemental – harking back not just to the depiction of horses by Ancient Assyrian[121] and Greek sculptors but also to the semi-abstract evocations of horsepower carved so vividly by unknown Bronze Age Britons into the chalk of the English countryside, such as the *Uffington White Horse* in Oxfordshire.

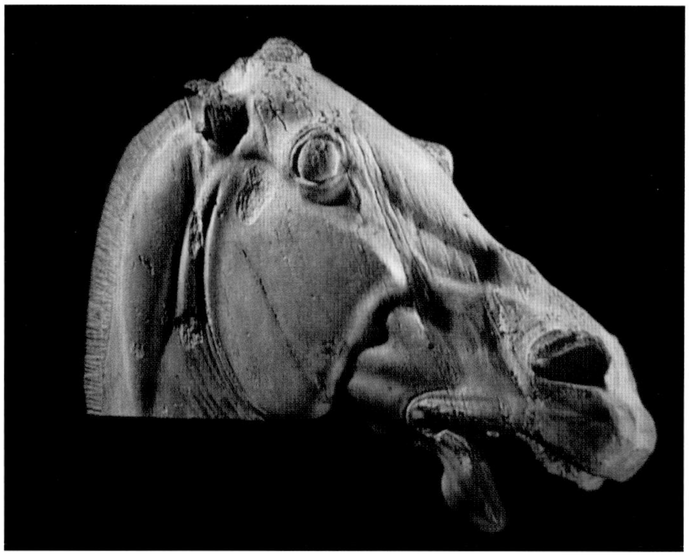

Fig. 5.12 *Head of a Horse of the Moon Goddess Selene*, c. 438–432 BCE, Parthenon Frieze, British Museum, London; Image: Courtesy of British Museum Images

The figure of the rider Ivor devised – alert, dignified, serenely in control of his rearing steed – can be related to the energised fragments of humanity created by Rodin and later Henry Moore, such as the latter's noble, yet by subtle implication clearly doomed, *Warrior with Shield* (1954, bronze), which he admired.[122] The strikingly contemplative head of the *Lazarus Rider* – eyes tightly shut as if rapt in contemplation, or in the grip of some inner vision – harked back to that of the lost plaster *Blind Man* (c. 1955–56; cat. 121), which Ivor later indicated to Peter Cannon-Brookes had been inspired by a photograph of the Greek poet Capetanakis reproduced in a book published in 1947.[123] It would appear that Ivor had been impressed by a description of Capetanakis in the book provided by the poet's close friend Panayotis Canellopoulos, who was especially moved by

> a smile of joy that would often cross his face ... [I]t was an archaic smile. Egyptian Pharaohs, Greek Archaic statues, Etruscan Gods – do not all those strange countenances seem to belong at the same time to childhood and an impossible kind of maturity? It was almost the same feeling that my friend's face gave me. Often, while looking at it, I felt that I was like some one who has to unravel an impossible problem. And the impossible is life itself. I would look at my friend's face and an even graver conviction would come to me: that death itself is what is impossible.[124]

It would also seem that the relationship between the rider and the hawk seated on his wrist can be related to a passage in the 1947 Capetanakis book in which the writer William Plomer mentioned walking with the Greek poet through a thick London fog: 'I told Demetrious how, in a similar fog, a bird had suddenly perched on the handlebar of a bicycle which someone was pushing slowly and had remained there. Characteristically, and rather intensely, he said "How strange!"'[125] At the same time Ivor had become very interested, in the wake of the 'blockbuster' *Treasures of Tutankhamun* exhibition held at the British Museum between March and December 1972,[126] in Ancient Egyptian mythology, and in particular the role of the god Horus, usually represented by a hawk, in leading the spirits of the dead from the world of the living to an

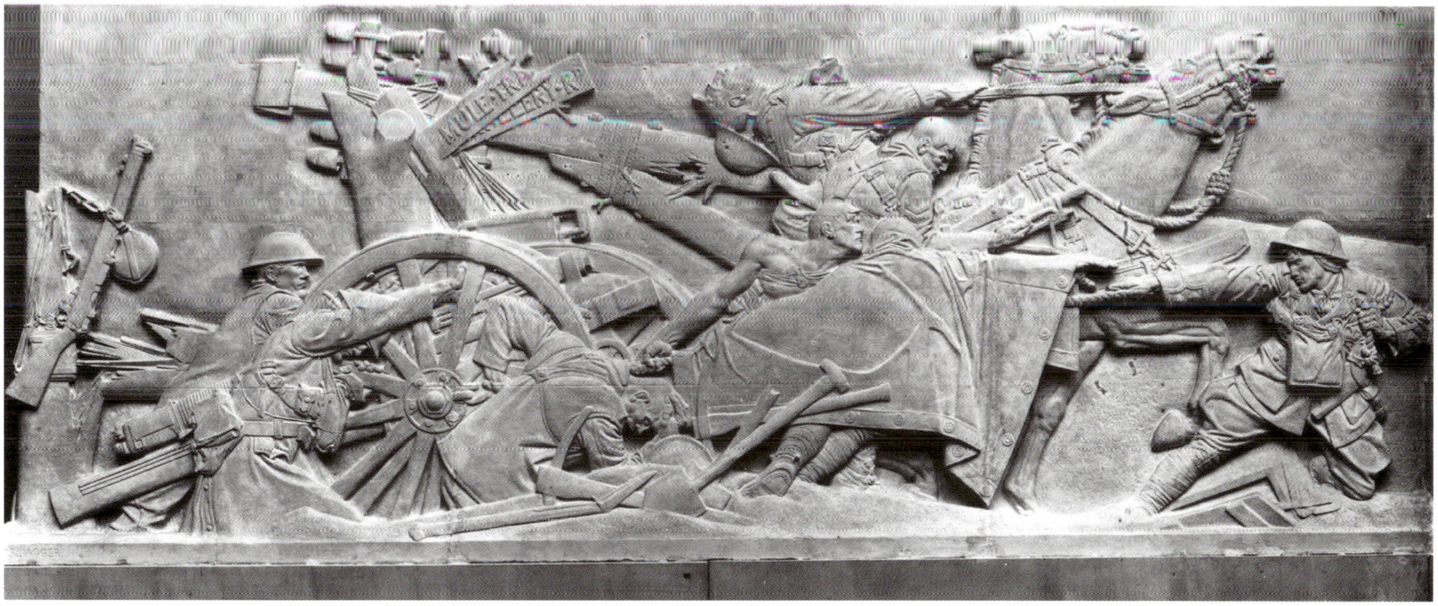

Fig. 5.13 Charles Sargeant Jagger, *Horse Artillery*, 1923–25, Portland stone panel, on the Royal Artillery Memorial, Hyde Park Corner, London; Image: Courtesy of the Estate of Charles Sargeant Jagger

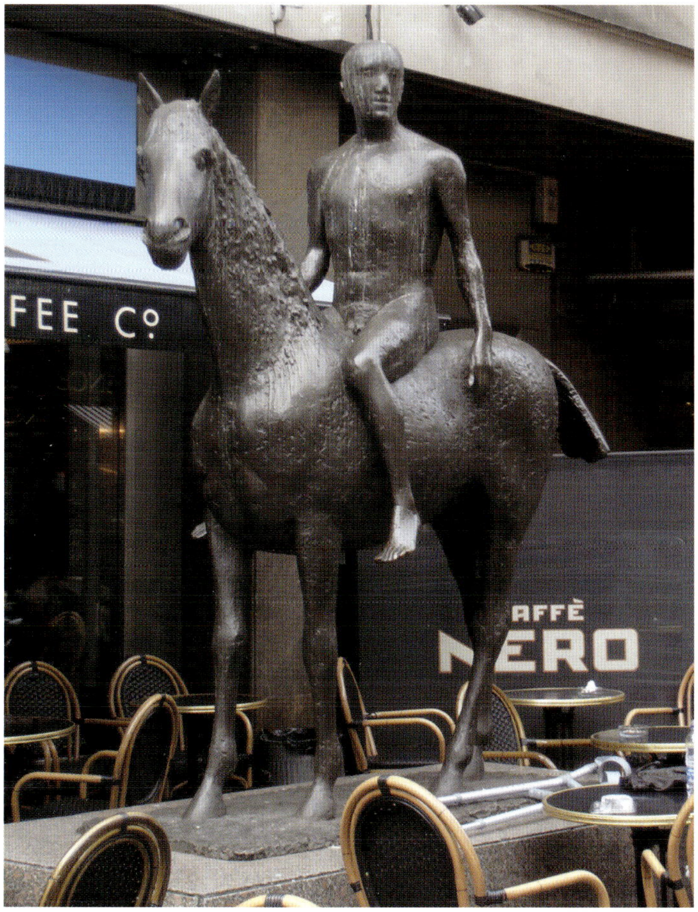

Fig. 5.14 Elisabeth Frink, *Horse and Rider*, 1974–75, bronze, Dover Street, London; Image: J. Black

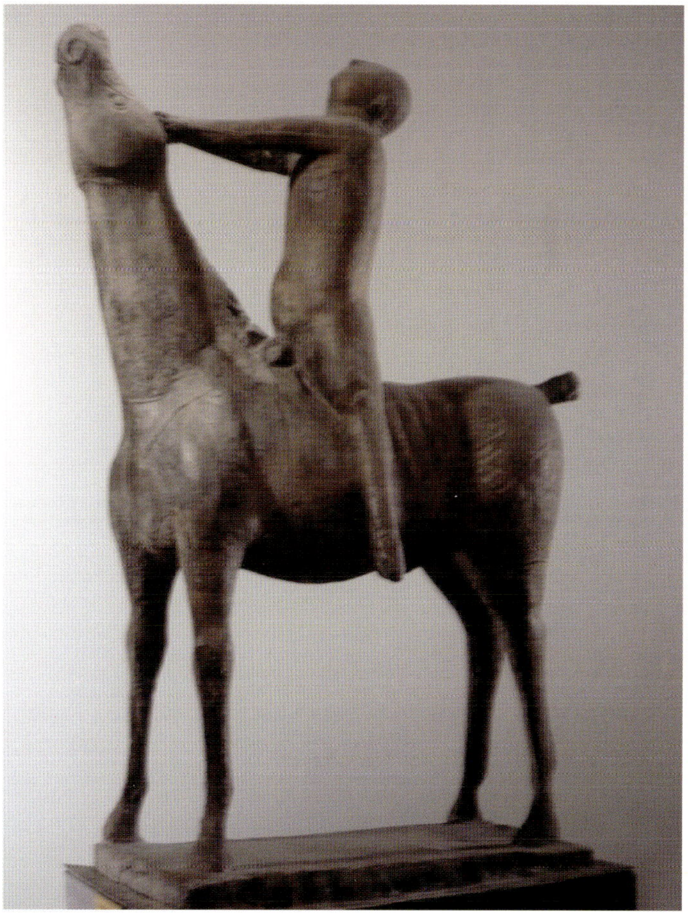

Fig. 5.15 Marino Marini, *Horse and Rider*, c. 1949, bronze, Marini Foundation, Pistoia; Image: Courtesy of the Marini Foundation, Pistoia

often harsh judgement in the afterlife.[127] The eventual owner of the final version of the full-sized *Lazarus Rider*, Sir Richard Hyde Parker, did later quiz Ivor on the 'meaning' of the work. The artist replied at some length, which Sir Richard did not find that illuminating – it was evidently 'very deep stuff' indeed, though the artist was conscious of wishing to inject some new life into a very old tradition of equestrian sculpture in the open air.[128]

Ivor exhibited a larger maquette of the *Lazarus Rider* in his 1978 solo exhibition in Cardiff, where it caught the eye not only of collector Sir Richard Hyde Parker but also of a Welsh Council arts officer, Isabel Hitchman, who was at the time considering possible sculptors for a commission associated with Harlech Castle.[129] Hitchman was so taken with the *Lazarus Rider* that Ivor was soon approached to work on what would become one of his finest public works: *The Two Kings/Janus Rider* (see page 140).[130] As for Sir Richard, he later recalled that, on encountering the plaster of the *Lazarus Rider* in the Oriel Gallery, he 'immediately saw it in bright bronze' standing somewhere in front of his home at Melford Hall in Suffolk.[131] The following year Sir Richard asked Ivor to produce a bronze cast of the work. The artist readily agreed, though he added the proviso that he felt the sculpture 'needed more work' before he would be fully satisfied – particularly in the treatment of the head of the horse and the relationship between its trunk and its 'amputated limbs'.[132]

The sculptor was particularly pleased that the work would be displayed in the open air and be accessible to visitors exploring the grounds of the Hall. Over the next three to three and a half years, as his correspondence with Sir Richard clearly indicates, Ivor was prepared to take infinite pains to ensure the *Lazarus Rider* was mounted and sited to present the work at its very best. In November 1979, for example, he wrote to Sir Richard:

> Monica and I have talked about the placing of the *Lazarus Rider* – and we both feel that the main thing is for you to decide if you like it in itself ... there [are] so many possible sites that it was inconceivable that it wouldn't look absolutely right in one of them – but if you were uneasy about it in any way, then of course it wouldn't look right in any of them. I feel that seen from the Hall and the steps, or terrace, down to the grass area it will look absolutely right – but, of course, against the Hall itself, as in the photo and seen from the Stable Wing, it would require an enormous sculpture to stand out at the full distance. On the other hand, as you approached the Hall, it would read perfectly well – and my suggestion that it should be angled more steeply would certainly make it more commanding.[133]

He later outlined at length how the horse had to be positioned at just such an angle, while its base had to be cast in a certain colour. Ivor was also much concerned with the relationship of the sculpture to the landscaping of its surrounding environment.[134] Indeed, during the period before the sculpture had been installed to his satisfaction, Ivor devoted much thought to how future free-standing sculptures of his, such as *The Sword Form* (1982–83; cat. 145) and *Horned Torso* (1983; cat. 147) might be positioned in the British, and especially Welsh, countryside. He asserted to Peter Cannon-Brookes that sculpture

> should have a special relationship with the landscape ... [I]t would be marvellous to take this relation of sculpture with landscape further and to hang sculpture, like great ideograms, in waterfalls – wedge them between the steep sides of narrow ravines like bridges and suspend them on castle walls. Goodness knows, Wales has her quota of castles. But this kind of adventure requires some sort of dialogue with society and only one, or two, privileged sculptors [Moore?] have this to any degree.[135]

In March 1983 The *Lazarus Rider* was finally installed outside Melford Hall.[136] The work's owner feels he is 'extraordinarily fortunate to possess such a fine work – a distinguished addition to the long history of equestrian sculpture which manages to be both very old and thoroughly up to date'.[137]

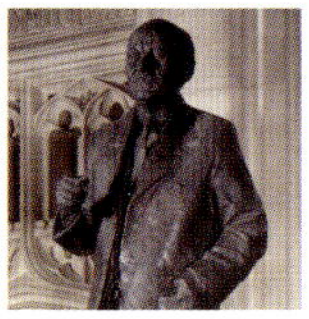

The Meek Man of Iron: *Earl Attlee of Limehouse* (1977–79; cat. 143) for the Members' Lobby of the House of Commons

Ivor was in the UK at the time of the general election of July 1945, but there are later hints that he voted for the Labour Party while he was still stationed with the Royal Artillery in southern Burma.[138] One major reason why he did this was that he was impressed by Clement Attlee's declared determination to build a 'new world' if the Labour Party he led was victorious in the election.[139] In later life Ivor was to mention more than once the colossal debt the country owed to Attlee (1883–1967) for ensuring the creation of the National Health Service in 1948 – an organisation he acknowledged had done its best to provide care for his sick son Mervyn in the 1950s.[140] He also admired the fact that Attlee, despite being physically slight and not that tall – indeed only a little taller than the sculptor, who stood at 5 ft 4 – had an impressive First World War military record to his credit, having volunteered in 1914 as a private and left the army in 1919 a major.[141]

The Earl Attlee Memorial Committee formed in March 1977, and a number of its members were already predisposed to think highly of Ivor's work. The Committee chairman George Strauss, for example – also chair of the House of Commons Art Committee – had been a significant supporter of Ivor during the troubled Churchill commission for Parliament Square. The committee also included Sir John Rodgers, who had voted for Ivor's Churchill maquette in 1971, and Ivor's friend Cledwyn Hughes, MP for Anglesey – who had already agreed to sit to Ivor for a portrait head (cat. 46), which would be executed in 1978. The following month a sub-committee was formed to draw up a shortlist of sculptors to be considered for the commission. This was advised by two individuals Ivor had known for a number of years: Sir Hugh Casson – the then president of the Royal Academy, who four years previously had voted for Ivor to become a full RA – and Michael Rizzello, president of the RBS, of which Ivor had been a member since the mid 1960s and with whom Ivor was quite friendly, or as friendly as he ever was with a fellow sculptor.[142]

In May 1977, when the sub-committee decided on the shortlist, Ivor appeared on it along with Franta Belsky (1921–2000), James Butler RA (1931–), Welsh sculptor Robert Thomas (1926–1999), the then president of the Society of Portrait Sculptors (1972–77), and John Wragg (1937–). All agreed to participate in a competition, and were given until the end of October 1977 to submit a 50–60-centimetre-high plaster maquette. It would seem the maquette Ivor submitted depicted an Attlee who was in his early seventies, wearing the robes of a Knight of the Garter – an honour he had been appointed in June 1956.[143] The Committee was impressed by the maquette and by that submitted by Robert Thomas. The two were given a further three months to submit another attempt, guided by the Committee's stipulation that Attlee not be depicted in ceremonial dress but in a low-key business suit of the type he had worn as prime minister (1945–51).[144] Ivor was also asked to make Attlee appear a little younger.

Ivor's second attempt, which would be chosen as competition winner by the Committee, sought to present Attlee in more informal mode – at ease and yet possessing an unmistakable authority. Ivor, it would appear, had seen Attlee campaigning in London during the general election of February 1950, and had noted that he could be a highly effective speaker before even the most restive large indoor audience.[145]

As was his usual approach, Ivor had amassed a considerable number of photographs of his subject. On this occasion he was struck forcibly by how Attlee had visibly aged between photographs taken of him in 1945 and those dating from the general elections of 1950 and 1951 (Fig. 5.16). Evidently, five years as prime minister, striving to create the 'New Jerusalem' he had promised in 1945, had exacted a punishing physical toll on Attlee. Indeed, for much of 1950–51, the period Ivor seems to have chiefly focused on as the basis for his conception of the head of the prime minister (Fig. 5.17; cat. 143a), Attlee was suffering stoically from the effects of a painful duodenal ulcer.[146]

The Memorial Committee selected Ivor's maquette in March 1978 largely because of the pose he had selected, as well as for the accuracy of the portrait; his Attlee is both at ease and subtly commanding, making a nonchalant,

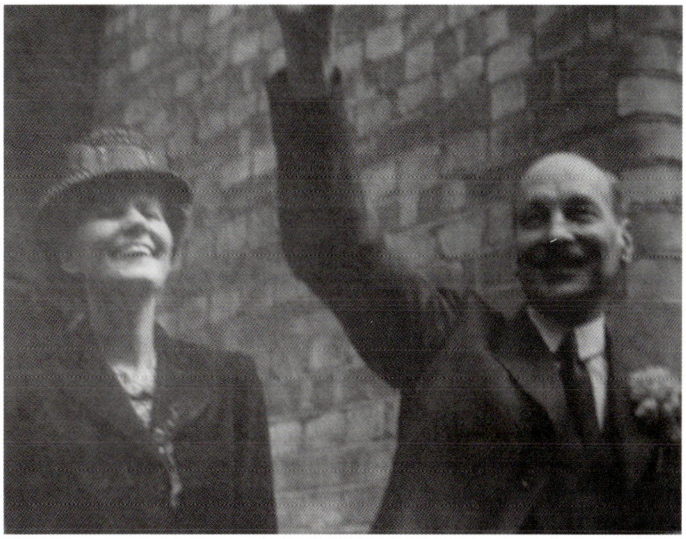

Fig. 5.16 Clement and Violet Attlee in July 1945 Image: J. Black

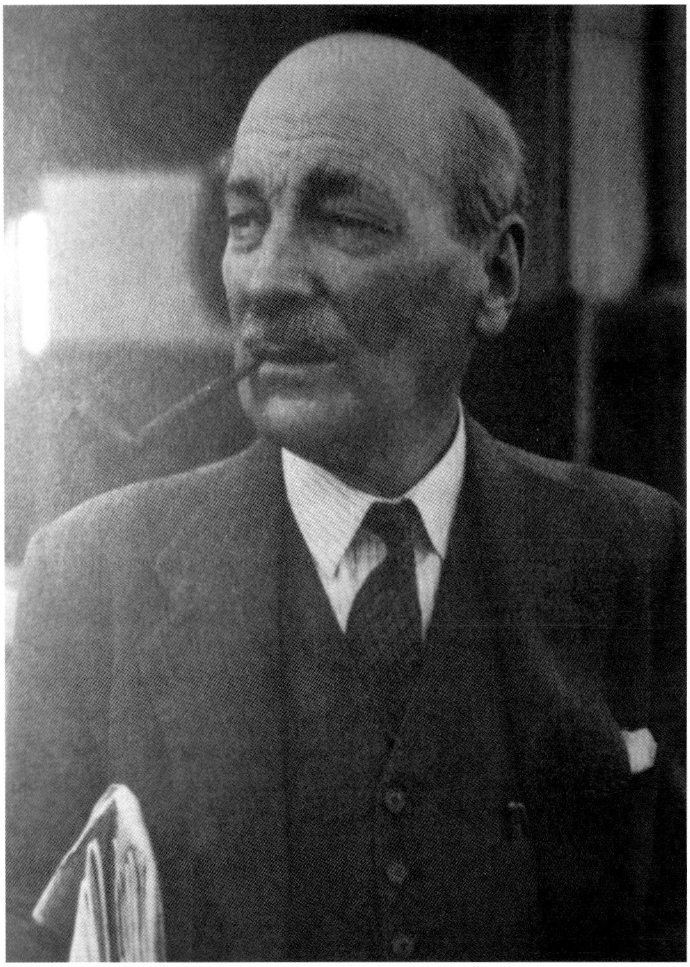

Fig. 5.17 Clement Attlee, 1950; Image: J. Black

conversational point with a finger of his right hand while reaching unself-consciously with his left for his trade-mark pipe in the left-hand pocket of his jacket.[147] One can also just discern, in the version of the statue that was finally erected, the outline of a tobacco tin in the pocket – presumably a tin of the Gold Bar tobacco Attlee habitually smoked. Committee members were somewhat concerned that the image of Attlee they chose would have to hold its own visually against Oscar Nemon's assertive statue of a pugnacious Churchill, facing him directly from the other side of the Lobby.[149] Ivor was well aware that, before and during his prime-ministership, Attlee had been regarded with some condescension by some of his fellow parliamentarians. One story still doing the rounds today, which Ivor encountered during his research for the Churchill commission in Parliament Square, described how '[a]n empty taxi arrived at 10 Downing Street and when the door opened, Attlee got out'.[150] The sculptor thought it was greatly to Churchill's credit that he was angered by the joke, describing Attlee to his private secretary in 1945 as 'an honourable and gallant gentleman who served his country well at the time of her greatest need. I should be obliged if you would make it clear whenever an occasion arises that I should never make such a remark about him and that I strongly disapprove of anybody who does.'[151]

This prior research on Churchill informed his later sculptural conception of Attlee in other ways – for example, in 1977 Ivor referred once more to Lord Moran's celebrated *Diaries*, which he had read in 1971 to provide insights into Churchill's character. In 1959 Moran had noted of Attlee that he was 'so mild mannered and yet this diffident little man [has] ruled his party for six years with a ruthless hand',[152] and Ivor sought to bring a sense of this inner resolve, innate self-confidence and steeliness to his figure of Attlee. One of his portrait subjects from earlier in the decade, Oliver Lyttelton, First Lord Chandos (cat. 39), had also attested to Attlee's dry sense of humour, which had enlivened many a tedious meeting he had chaired during the war as deputy prime minister (1942–45).[153] Above all, perhaps, Ivor was impressed by an observation made shortly after Attlee's death in 1967 by Attlee's personal private secretary: '[T]he Prime Minister did not wear power on his sleeve but kept it in reserve only to be used when necessary ... and wasted not a word.'[154]

The creation of the Attlee statue thereafter proved relatively uncomplicated for the sculptor. One later development in its evolution was that he had to lengthen his subject's legs somewhat to ensure that Attlee would appear to be approximately the same height as the Nemon figure of Churchill. One of the Labour MPs on the Memorial Committee, probably Cledwyn Hughes (cat. 46), who had been greatly in awe of Attlee as a recently elected MP in 1951, was concerned that the figure of Attlee, standing on a smaller plinth than Nemon's Churchill, might still seem overshadowed and even literally looked down upon by the bronze of the Conservative statesman.[155]

Attlee was unveiled in November 1979 by Lord Shinwell, the oldest member of the Houses of Parliament,

Fig. 5.18 Unveiling of the *Earl Attlee Memorial Statue*, Members' Lobby of the House of Commons, London, November 1979
Image: Courtesy of the HMI, Leeds

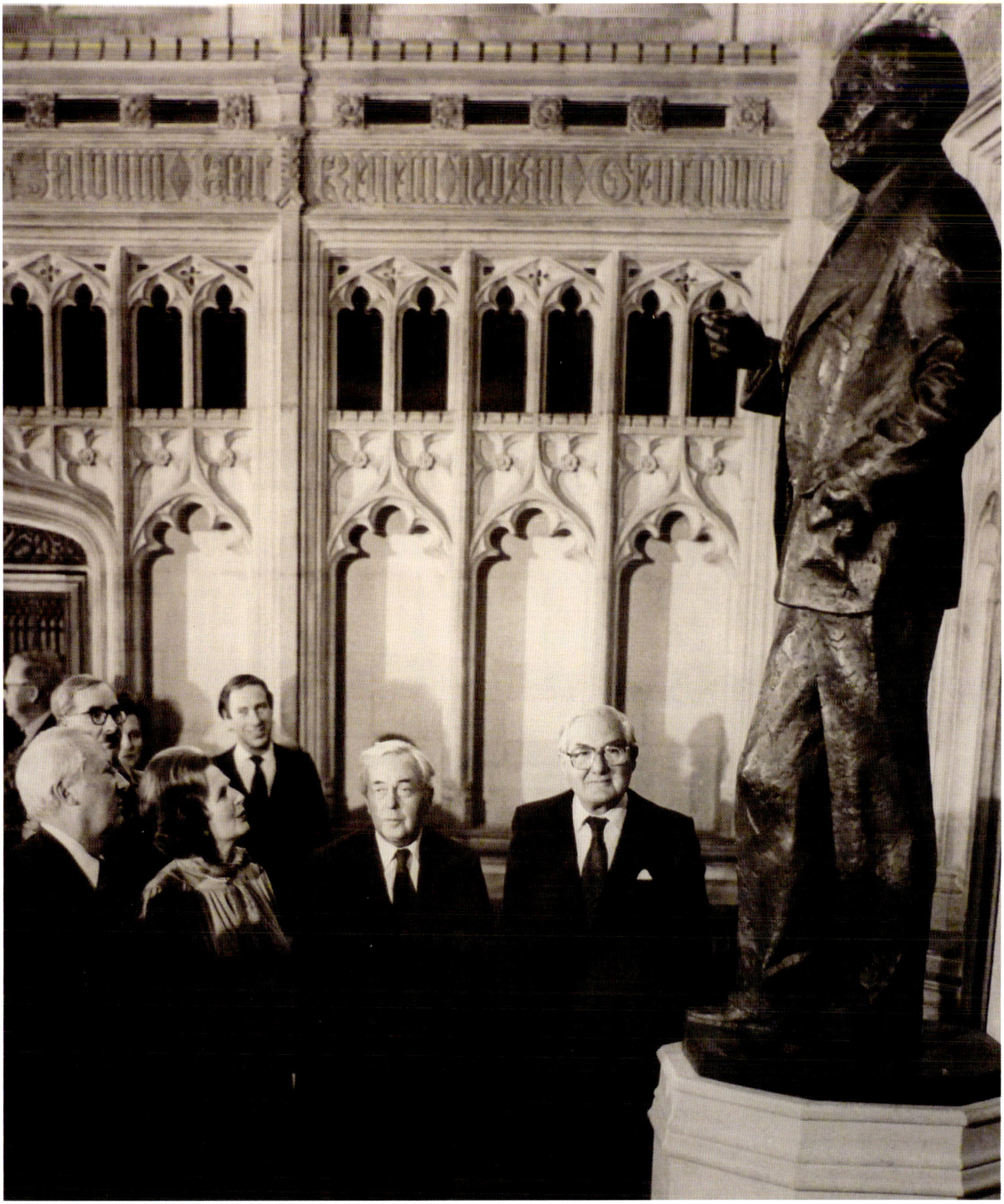

who had served – not always happily – as a minister during Attlee's premiership[156] (Fig. 5.18). Shinwell praised the statue for successfully lending an affable and convivial aspect to the prime minister's character that had only been seen by those with whom he was especially comfortable – the aficionado of the crime literature of Agatha Christie and Raymond Chandler, and conversationalist with a ready repository of amusing clerihews and snatches of doggerel poetry as well as mordantly succinct observations.[157] Perhaps in honour of the sculptor's Welshness, Lord Shinwell somewhat maliciously described how 'Clem' knew well how to deflate the Welsh socialist firebrand Aneurin Bevan with a dry, laconic remark, while he could not abide long-windedness. On one occasion, Shinwell recalled, Attlee had made gentle fun of his Welsh MPs, rasping that one certain way of killing off interest in the House of Commons in any matter under discussion was to be exposed to 'the eloquence of their colleagues from Wales'.[158]

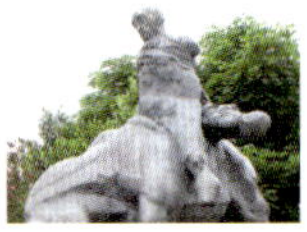

'My Own Kind of Monumentality': *The Two Kings/Janus Rider* (1978–83; cat. 144) for Harlech Castle, Gwynedd, Wales

As we have seen, this commission grew from the success of Ivor's Welsh Arts Council-supported retrospective exhibition at the Oriel Gallery between July and September 1978, and, in particular, from interest generated by his *Lazarus Rider*. On the strength of this work Ivor was invited in December 1978 to produce a sketch model of a major work to stand outside Harlech Castle in North Wales.[159] The intention on the part of the Welsh Arts Council and the Welsh Office appears to have been that Ivor's sculpture would be ready for unveiling in 1983, which would be the 700th anniversary of the beginning of construction of Harlech Castle for King Edward I by the Savoyard architect and mason Jacques de Saint-Georges D'Esperanche.[160] As the sculptor later put it, he was still 'obsessed' with the horse-and-rider theme, but wanted to devise something that was larger, and more sculpturally challenging and complex, than the *Lazarus Rider*.[161] Shortly before Christmas 1978, Ivor's friend the MP Cledwyn Hughes, who was fluent in Welsh and highly conversant with the country's 'national epic', the *Mabinogion*, in its original language, suggested looking at the tale within the poem that was specifically set in the vicinity of Harlech and its nearby mountains:[162] that of the giant king of Britain Bendigeidfran (also known as 'Bran the Blessed'), who left Harlech to invade Ireland to save his sister Branwen from ill-treatment at the hands of her thuggish husband. Bendigeidfran is ultimately victorious, and rescues his sister; but the cost is high. His nephew and fellow king Gwern is killed, along with much of his army.[163] From the early stages of the project Ivor imagined King Bendigeidfran as a physically diminished, mutilated figure, reduced to an armless, legless trunk, his proud head, derived from Ivor's early portrait head of his colleague at Goldsmiths, *Sam Rabin* (cat. 21), scarred and battered. The king is on horseback, with the body of his nephew, King Gwern, slung precariously on its rump – but only just, as his horse is clearly exhausted and on the verge of collapse. The presence of the two kings gave the work its ultimate title – though for a while, around 1979–81, Ivor also called it *The Janus Rider*, since the swaddled form of Gwern looks back to his death in Ireland while Bendigeidfran faces the future and the likelihood of meeting his sister Branwen: an outcome that will never come to pass, as his sister has already died from grief at the slaughter carried out to protect her honour.[164]

Ivor, the veteran of Burma, who knew all too well the dreadful realities of combat, and what he referred to as 'the wastage of war',[165] regarded the sculpture as a warning to future generations not to embark lightly on future wars. And yet the statue could also be read as an acknowledgement that Wales has its own distinct military tradition, standing in the shadow of a castle that had seen no shortage of fighting between the Welsh and the English in the ages of Edward I[166] and Owain Glyndŵr[167] and then of English and Welsh soldiers on both sides during an epic siege of the first so-called 'English Civil War', in 1646–47.[168] Perhaps this inherent duality to the work's message partly explains why Ivor also referred to the sculpture as *The Janus Rider*.

He certainly did not want the sculpture to be interpreted by the public as his pointed lament for the sacrifice of the Welsh Guards at Bluff Cove in June 1982[169] during the recent Falklands War – indeed, he rather admired Mrs Thatcher for insisting that British territory be recaptured from the Argentinian aggressor,[170] and hoped that passersby would also think of British soldiers being killed and maimed at the time in Northern Ireland,[171] and perhaps even grasp something of the redemptive message underlying the work: that after conflict and bloodshed there must follow understanding and reconciliation, while the dead of all sides deserve proper burial and dignified mourning. As he later wrote to Fiona Pearson (deputy keeper of art, NMW, Cardiff), 'The tale, and the death of Branwen, touches on the deepest of themes and the moment depicted parallels the "Lament of King David for Absalom." The sculpture touches on this by the lashing together of the two bodies in the form of a cross, the cross bearing with it the idea of resurrection and hope.'[172]

In addition to Bendigeidfran and Gwern's body on horseback, the sculptor had initially envisaged a much larger scheme incorporating a huge bronze bas-relief, to stand immediately behind the central three-dimensional group, situated within an extensive, carefully landscaped site with a series of flag poles as a backdrop[173] (Fig. 5.19). However, as quickly became evident, this ambitious scheme would have involved much greater expense than the available budget of £8,000 permitted. Thus, sadly, Ivor cut his cloth accordingly to focus on the horse and the bodies it carried. He would spend a good deal of time experimenting with different positions for the horse's head and feet, as well as with the angle of Bendigeidfran's head and trunk and how much of Gwern's face would be exposed from beneath his tightly bound funereal wrappings – which, perhaps deliberately, evoke the mummies of Ancient Egypt (Fig. 5.20).

This was one of the most ambitious works he had ever asked the Meridian Foundry to cast, and progress was slow. However, as he wrote in May 1983, the commission had given him the freedom to experiment with a 'kind of monumentality that was of *my own kind*'.[174] The statue was cast by December 1983, and an unveiling by the secretary of state for Wales was provisionally timetabled for the autumn of 1984.[175] But the Welsh Language Society objected vehemently – not to the sculpture, which its members admired, but to the fact this major commission by Wales's leading sculptor was sited immediately outside an 'English' castle, and symbol of the nation's oppression for centuries by its larger neighbour.[176] Ivor, angry and yet also amused, wondered, if there had been no Harlech Castle to lay siege to in the fifteenth century, what event would have inspired the composing of the song 'Men of Harlech'.[177] The grand unveiling ceremony envisaged was postponed indefinitely, and ultimately never took place.[178] But the sculpture was so popular with staff from the Welsh Arts Council and the local office of the Board of Ancient Monuments – who had initially expressed various

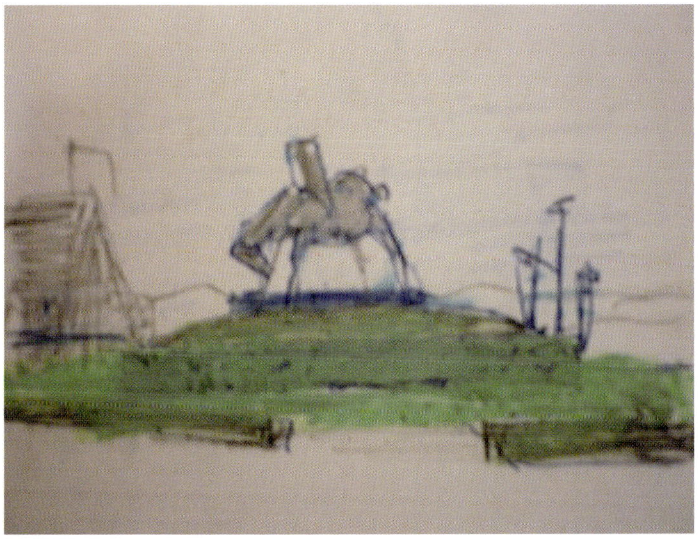

Fig. 5.19 Ivor Roberts-Jones, *Early Study for The Two Kings/Janus Rider*, c. 1979, pastel and pencil on paper, Image: Courtesy of the HMI, Leeds

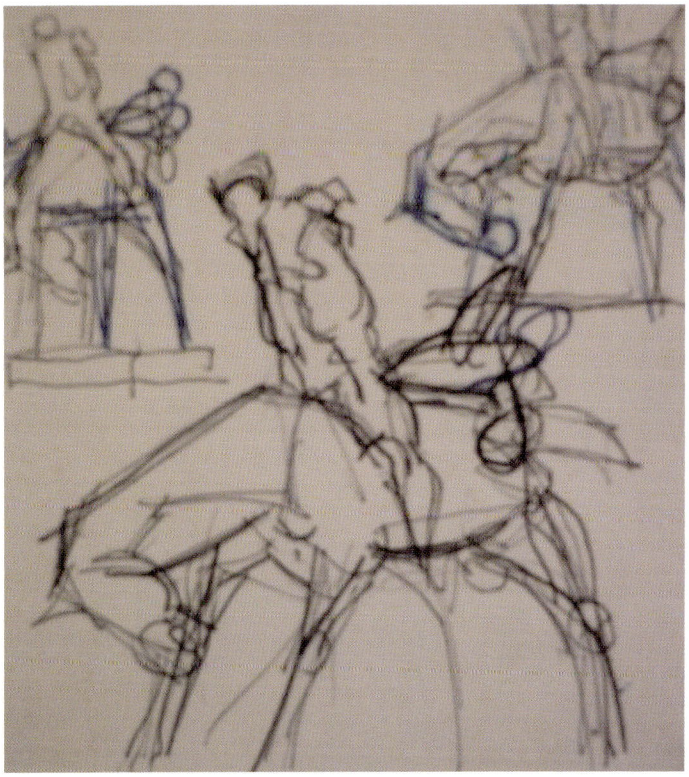

Fig. 5.20 Ivor Roberts-Jones, *Study for The Two Kings/Janus Rider*, c. 1980–81, pencil on paper, Image: Courtesy of the HMI, Leeds

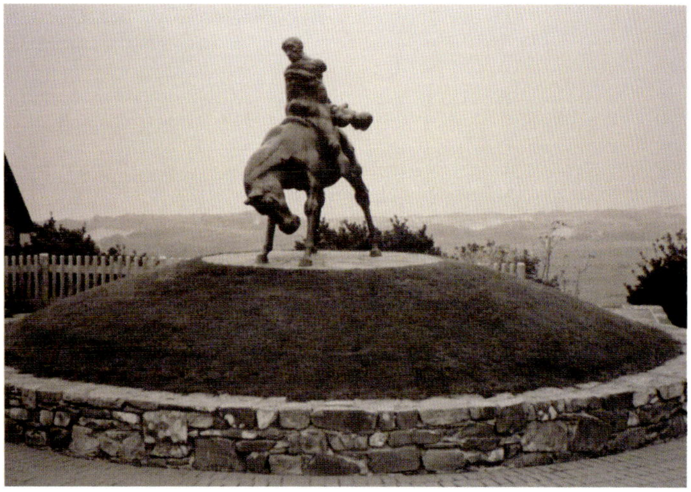

Fig. 5.21 Ivor Roberts-Jones, *The Two Kings/Janus Rider*, 1984, photograph, Image: Courtesy of the HMI, Leeds

guarded misgivings about the project – that they held their own unofficial ceremony for the statue in July 1984. As for the sculptor, averse to 'hooplah' as so often before, he did not attend but sent a message of good wishes and thanks, while writing to Peter Cannon-Brookes that, despite the long gestation of the project, 'working on *Two Kings* has left me with a closer affinity to Wales, which might be thought contradictory – but isn't in fact'. He was not, however, planning to move to the principality: he was happy enough in his Suffolk backwater. Indeed, Ivor seemed to derive a perverse delight from living in what he referred to as 'hermetic rural obscurity'.[179]

A decade later, when his friend and founder Jack Crofton wrote to him in praise of *The Two Kings*, which he had recently inspected, Ivor replied: 'I was delighted when you said you thought of it as one of your best casts, for that gave me the satisfaction of knowing that my own judgement was near the mark. I found after leaving it (in June 1984) that I was still haunted by the black pathos that it exudes and I have thought of it many times since then'[180] (Fig. 5.21).

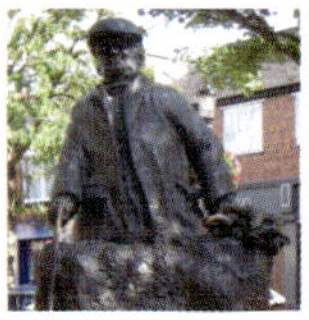

A Welsh Look?: *Borderland Farmer/ Shepherd with Ram* (1986–92; cat. 150) for Festival Square, Oswestry

Some two years after the installation of *The Two Kings*, early in 1986, Ivor was asked to consider a possible commission from his old hometown of Oswestry, which led him to dwell upon his childhood memories of the place and consider what to him had been the town's essence. Was it, indeed, an English or a Welsh town? Historically speaking, the town had lain on the eastern, what was to become the English, side of Offa's Dyke, dug at the command of the Mercian king in the late eighth century.[181] But historians now feel that, by the mid fifteenth century, Welsh was the majority language of the town. This altered with time, and with an influx of English people from elsewhere in Shropshire and other English border counties such as Cheshire and Worcestershire.[182] However, during the thirteen or so years when Ivor was growing up in the town and attending Oswestry Grammar School (1913–26), he later recalled that he had often heard Welsh spoken by the farmers, drovers and shepherds who thronged the centre of the town on market day.[183]

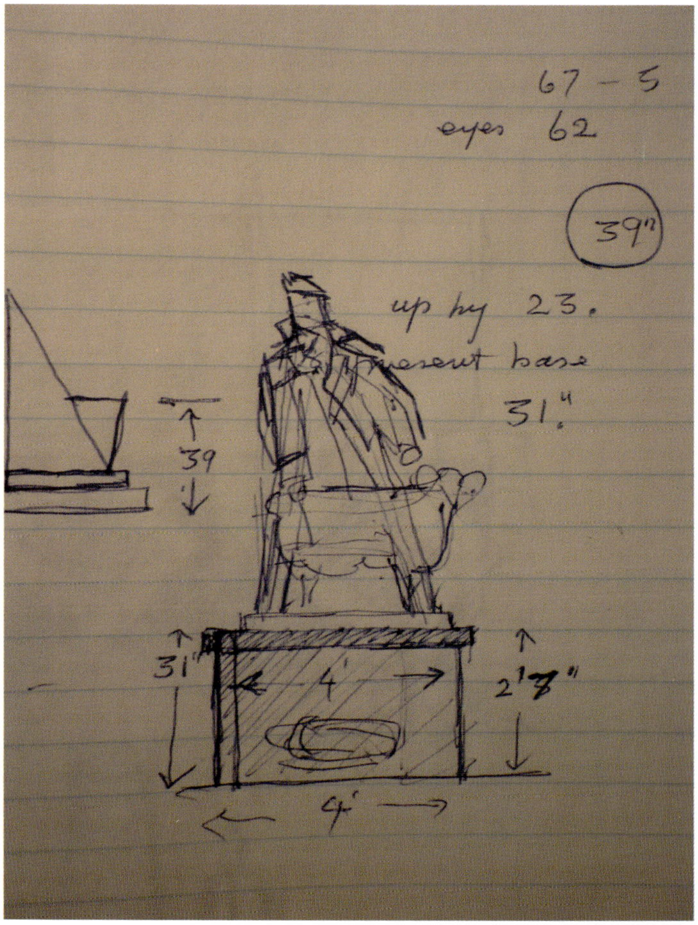

Fig. 5.22 Ivor Roberts-Jones, *Early Sketch for Borderland Farmer/ Shepherd with Ram*, c. 1986–88, pen and ink on paper, Image: Courtesy of the HMI, Leeds

He had initially been asked by the Oswestry District and Civil Society to devise a figure that would have an 'unmistakable local resonance' to stand in the centre of the town's old Cattle Market – soon to be renamed Festival Square.[184] At first he recalled from his childhood the formidable women of the market, 'with brawny forearms and given to salty language', and carrying pigs and geese from pen to pen with a nonchalant ease.[185] After discussing the matter with Kyffin Williams and Cledwyn Hughes, in late 1989 he moved to consider the figure of a farmer, or shepherd, from just over the border in Wales, with his dog, or a sheep (Fig. 5.22). A year later, in June 1990, he decided to replace the sheep with a ram.[186] Earlier in the evolution of the project he harked back in representations of the animal accompanying the farmer to examples of Picasso's sculpture made after the beginning of the Second World War, such as *Man with a Sheep* (1943, bronze, Musée Picasso, Paris) and *The Goat* (1950, bronze, Musée Picasso, Paris), which were exhibited for the first time in the UK at the Tate Gallery in June 1967.[187]

Ivor had also greatly admired the drawings and etchings of gently ruminating sheep that Henry Moore produced between 1972 and 1974, and which were published in 1975 as the *Sheep Portfolio*.[188] But he thought Moore had been all too successful in suggesting the docility and placidity of the animals; he decided that an 'alert ram with its head twisted away from the figure of the farmer – as though "keeping an eye on his harem" ... would add some much needed "tension" to the two figures'.[189] He felt that this 'necessary tension ... even awkwardness and presence of animal personality' was also signally lacking from Elisabeth Frink's bronze group *Sheep and Shepherd* (Fig. 5.23), unveiled in Paternoster Square, London, by a past portrait subject, Yehudi Menuhin, in July 1975, even though he acknowledged that it was in other respects a 'splendid bit of sculpture'.[190]

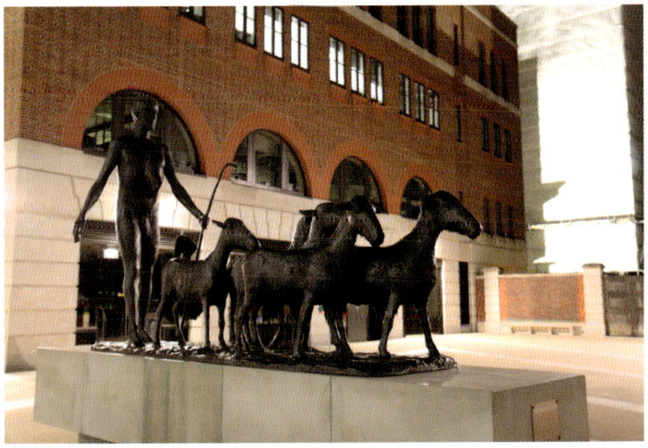

Fig. 5.23 Elisabeth Frink, *Sheep and Shepherd*, 1973–75, bronze, Paternoster Square, London; Image: J. Black

Ivor's ram is shaggier and friskier than the sheep conceived by Moore and Frink – as if to suggest that the beast will prove a lively handful if the farmer attempts to prevent it from breaking away to rejoin the herd. It is possible that he decided to focus on a ram because the project had partly prompted him to reread a lot of First World War poetry by Wilfred Owen, who had been born near and grown up in Oswestry. One of Owen's poems, 'The Parable of the Young Men and the Old' (1918), struck a particular chord with him because of its connection with the Old Testament story of Abraham and Isaac (Genesis 22: 1–18). As he worked on the Oswestry statue, he was also tinkering with a figure of *Isaac* (cat. 148) that was taking shape in his Shimpling studio. In the late 1980s and early 1990s he had still had hopes that he would receive a commission from the Aldeburgh Festival for a figure of the composer Benjamin Britten (cat. 152)[191] – one of Ivor's favourite pieces of classical music was Britten's *War Requiem* (1961–62), which incorporated 'The Parable of the Young Men and the Old' as one of the nine Owen poems Britten had selected to set to music within the Requiem form.[192]

During this 1991–92 period, his old friend and habitual adviser on all matters Welsh, Cledwyn Hughes, introduced Ivor to a sheep farmer called Richards (Fig. 5.24) from the area of Llantysilio Mountain, near Llangollen, not far from Oswestry across the border in Wales.[193] He struck the sculptor as a 'character worthy of the stories of John Cooper Powys'.[194] Another reason why Farmer Richards appealed to his imagination was that he somewhat reminded Ivor of Bruce Bairnsfather's famous First World War cartoon character 'Old Bill' – first seen in the pages of *Punch* in 1915 (Fig. 5.25).

A few months later, Oswestry Borough Council formally commissioned Ivor to make the figure for an estimated £15,000 – with the sculptor's fee set at a modest £5,000.[195] One small bone of contention between sculptor and client was that Ivor wanted to design the base of the work, whereas the Borough Council was insistent that this task should be given to a local firm of architects. Ivor wanted the life-size figure of the farmer to stand on a fairly conventional plinth (Fig. 5.26); the Borough architects were determined that he should be placed on a small mound, broadly suggesting a mountain top. The sculptor was of the opinion that if the architects had their way the figure would resemble a refugee guarding his food supply amid a shattered post-apocalyptic landscape.[196] He felt the setting was not nearly so suitable and attractive as the 'tumulus' feature he had designed the previous decade as the base for *The Two Kings*.[197]

It took a while for the money to be raised in response to the Council's appeal for the 'Festival Square statue', issued early in 1991, by which point the estimated total cost of the project had increased to £20,000. Ivor's final full-sized plaster cast of the *Farmer and Ram* was despatched to the Meridian Foundry – with the sculptor still working directly on the plaster – 'up to twenty minutes before the van arrived'.[198] The work was formally unveiled in December 1992. The figure of the *Farmer* came in for a great deal of criticism from members of the public writing in to the local newspaper, who assumed that the man was Welsh and that the sculptor's depiction of him was innately satirical and malicious. One critic, a J. Elwyn Roberts, accused the sculptor of having created a

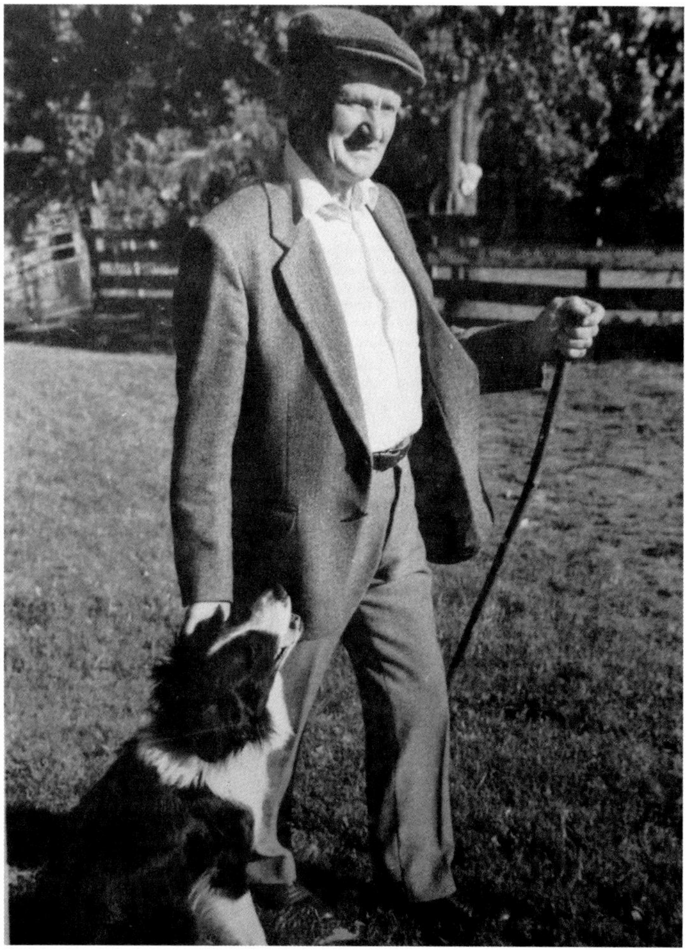

Fig. 5.24 *Mr Richards Sheep Farmer*, 1991, photograph, Image: Courtesy of the HMI, Leeds

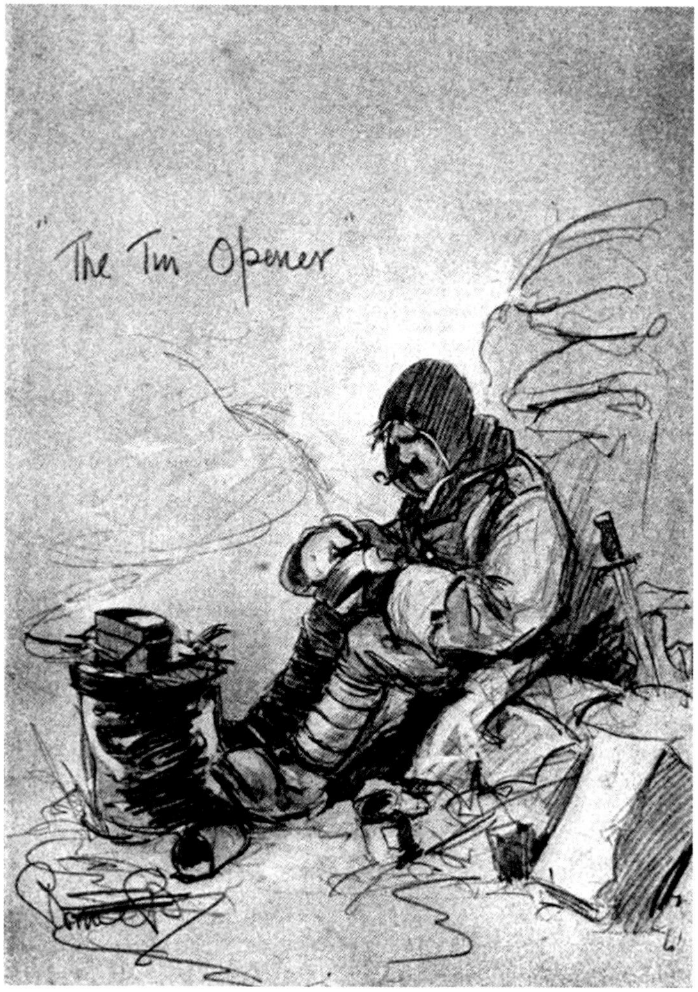

Fig. 5.25 Bruce Bairnsfather, *Old Bill*, 1915, pen and ink and pencil on paper, 60 x 38 cm; Image: J. Black

Fig. 5.26 Ivor Roberts-Jones, *Study for Borderland Farmer on a Plinth Designed by the Artist*, c. 1991, pen and ink and watercolour on paper, Image: Courtesy of the HMI, Leeds

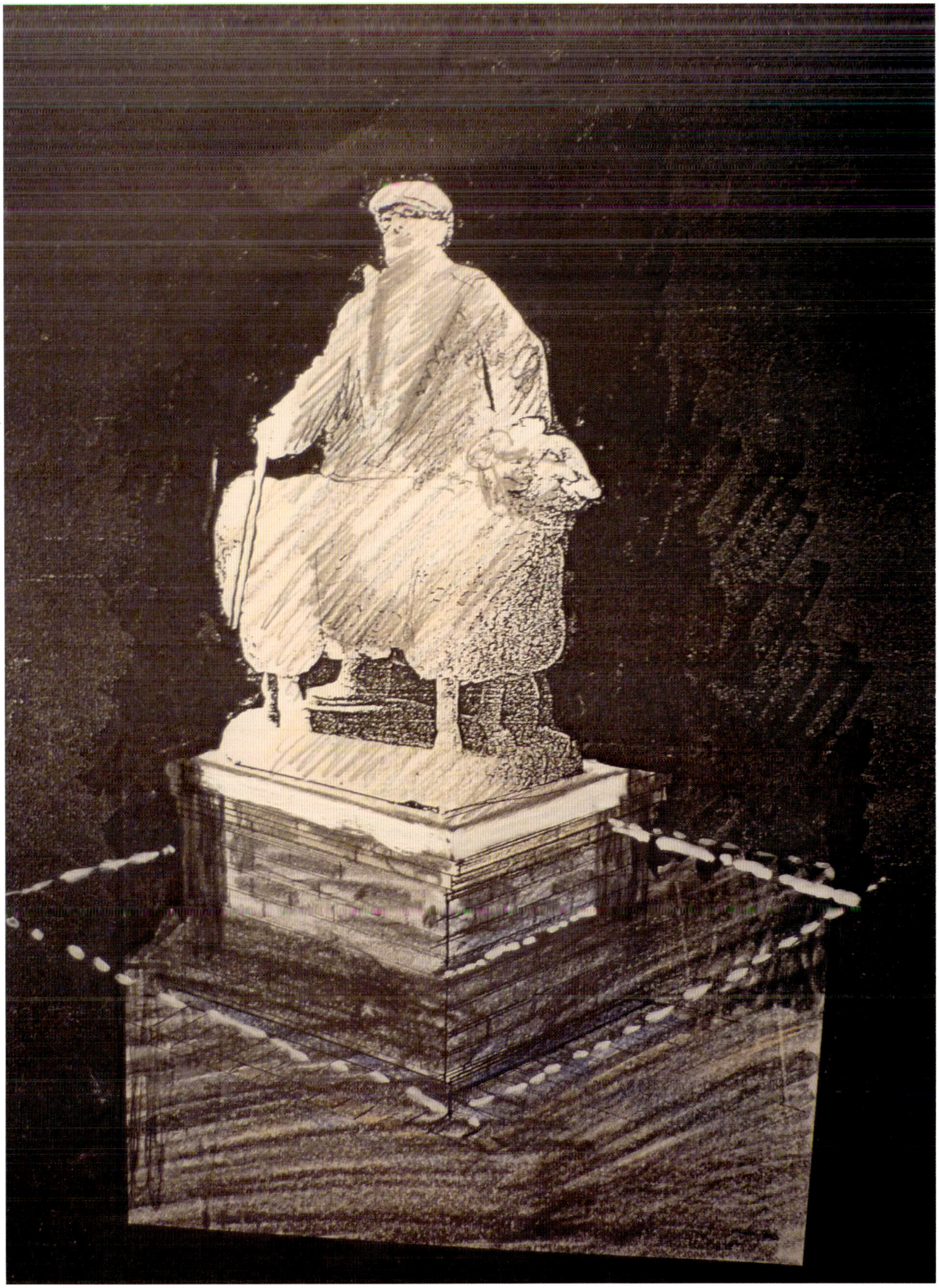

monstrosity ... The farmer looks as if he belongs to a clan of dwarfs and the ram with its thin legs looks as if it suffers from malnutrition ... Any farmer of yesteryear would have been disgusted with it. In fact, it is an insult to the entire farming community. During all my life in Oswestry I have never seen a farmer with a ram. Yes, coming ... with his flock of sheep ... but it was his faithful dog that would be by his side, not a ram.[199]

Ironically, given Ivor's own dissatisfaction with the lack of a plinth for the *Farmer and Ram*, J. Elwyn Roberts was very dismissive of the setting for the sculpture. In a further irony, given how much Ivor admired the poetry of the man, Roberts concluded that the Council would have done much better to have paid for 'a statue in memory of ... Wilfred Owen[. H]e would have been well worth looking up to.'[200]

The following year Ivor protested to Kyffin Williams that, if he had really wanted to, he could have offered Oswestry an 'absolute grotesque' in the figure of the farmer in the spirit of Evelyn Waugh,[201] who had 'outrageously, if hilariously' described the members of a North Wales silver band in his 1928 novel *Decline and Fall* thus:

> Ten men of revolting appearance were approaching from the drive. They were low of brow, crafty of eye and crooked of limb. They advanced huddled together with the loping tread of wolves, peering about them furtively as they came, as though in constant terror of ambush; they slavered at their mouths which hung loosely over their receding chins, while each clutched under his ape-like arm a burden of curious and unaccountable shape ... an elderly man emerged from the back of the group. He had a rough black beard and wore on his uneven shoulders a druidical wreath of brass mistletoe berries ... 'We are the silver band the lord bless and keep you', said the stationmaster [of Llanabba] in one breath, 'the band that no one could beat whatever but two indeed in the Eisteddfod that for all North Wales was look you.'[202]

The passage of time does seem to have diminished the animus felt towards the sculpture. In 2006 a former headmaster of Oswestry School, celebrating the purchase of a number of plaster casts of Ivor's work, noted in passing that *Borderland Farmer* was 'not necessarily his best-loved work'. But it had its defenders, including the writer of the article, who felt the statue was 'an impressive portrait of a man whose tenacity and tough resistance to the fierce weather of the Welsh hills are allied to a genuine compassion for the ram which he holds; the artist was simply observant of certain of those weekly visitors to his home town and it seems to me that this portrayal is an affectionate tribute to them.'[203]

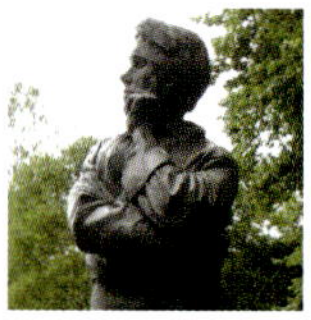

It's Hard To Do Handsome: *Rupert Brooke* (1986–88; cat. 151) for Jubilee Gardens, Rugby

The sculptor read Brooke's poetry as a schoolboy at both Oswestry Grammar School and St Cuthbert's College.[204] He recalled buying a volume of his 'war poetry' shortly before volunteering for the Royal Artillery in September 1939; he did not mention his opinion of the poetry, but it is telling that after his war experiences in Burma (1943–45) he came greatly to prefer the more visceral and unsparing vision of war offered in the later war poetry of Wilfred Owen.[205] Indeed, Owen was raised even further in his estimation when Ivor later discovered that the Greek poet Capetanakis held him in high regard.[206] In terms of book sales, however, Brooke was to remain well into the 1960s Britain's most popular poet of the First World War; it was only then that Owen emerged to supplant him comprehensively in reputation.[207]

Nevertheless, despite his relative decline in popularity, Ivor appears to have been genuinely pleased when he was approached early in the spring of 1986 by Dr Peter Miller, chairman of the Rupert Brooke Centenary Committee, to conceive a 'suitable' figure of the poet for the centre of his hometown of Rugby, to celebrate the hundredth anniversary of his birth, in August 1987.[208] During the previous year the Committee had approached a local sculptor, John Bridgeman, but had been put off by his conception of Brooke as far too effeminate.[209] Miller and his Committee were perhaps particularly sensitive to the question of Brooke's likely bisexuality; around 1909–11 the poet had lightheartedly calculated that he was 'one-quarter homosexual and usually aroused by good-looking boys and youths',[210] and there was considerable and heated debate in the press of the day concerning 'Clause 28' of the Local Government Bill then making its contentious way through parliament.[211] This was to expressly forbid local government bodies from providing tax-payers' money to support any efforts to 'promote homosexuality'. Such legislation, which eventually became law in November 1988,[212] did not affect the Centenary Committee, but a number of its members, including Dr Miller, did sit on the local council, and Miller appears to have correctly suspected that any appeal for funds to pay for a Brooke statue would have to be supplemented with a hefty contribution from the council.[213]

Miller and the committee were keen to keep costs down; they had also approached James Butler to consider the commission, but his initial estimate was judged excessive. Miller approached Ivor partly because the former had recently seen his figure of Churchill in Parliament Square at close quarters for the first time and decided the sculptor of such a 'fine work' would be just the man for the Brooke statue project.[214] Churchill, of course, had played a key role in the creation of the 'Brooke myth' shortly after the poet's death, through his letter published in *The Times* in April 1915 and the emotive eulogy he had given, as only Churchill could, at Brooke's memorial service.[215] In *The Times* Churchill carefully made no reference to Brooke's Fabian past and occasional anti-imperialist jibes, but focused on an encomium to a 'poet-soldier' who 'expected to die' and who

> was willing to die for the dear England whose beauty and majesty he knew and [who] advanced to the brink in perfect serenity with absolute conviction of the rightness of his country's cause and a heart devoid of hate for his fellow-men ... Joyous, fearless, versatile, deeply instructed with classic symmetry of mind and body, he was all that one would wish England's noblest sons to be in days when no sacrifice but the most precious is acceptable and the most precious is that which is most freely proffered.[216]

Ivor quite quickly settled upon a conception of Brooke related to a famous photograph taken of the poet by the American photographer Sherrill Schell in April 1913 – copies of which were available from the National Portrait Gallery in London[217] (Fig. 5.27). The poet rests his chin contemplatively on his left hand, wearing a type of 'Bohemian' wide tie with a soft-collar shirt he can also be seen wearing in some of the other Schell photographs. But Ivor was determined from the outset to place more 'character' in the face of the poet: some suggestion of the emotional turmoil he had experienced in his recent past over unsuccessful love affairs and worries regarding the development of his poetic career should be present in his physiognomy. Thus, he made Brooke noticeably thinner in the face than he appeared in the 1913 series of Schell photographs – gaunter, less blooming with health and more vulnerable. As the sculptor wrote at the time, he had become used to working on portrait heads of much older subjects – with a lifetime of experience present in their wrinkles – and he was finding it hard to 'do handsome' convincingly without descending into trite sentimentality.[218]

Photographs taken of Ivor working in his studio at Shimpling in April 1988 (Fig. 5.28) indicate that by this stage the sculptor had divided the figure of Brooke into two halves: head, shoulders and arms as one portion, trunk and legs as the other. Regarding the latter, he had decided to depict Brooke barefoot, as a reference to what Virginia Woolf dubbed in the summer of 1911 the poet's

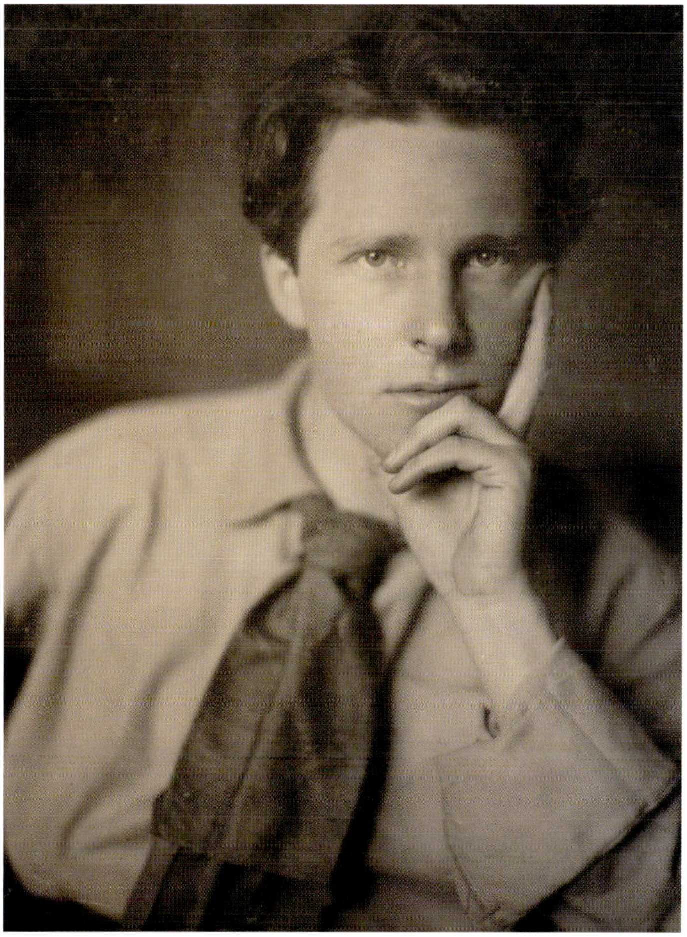

Fig. 5.27 Sherrill Schell, *Rupert Brooke*, 1913, photograph, National Portrait Gallery, London; Image: Courtesy of the National Portrait Gallery, London

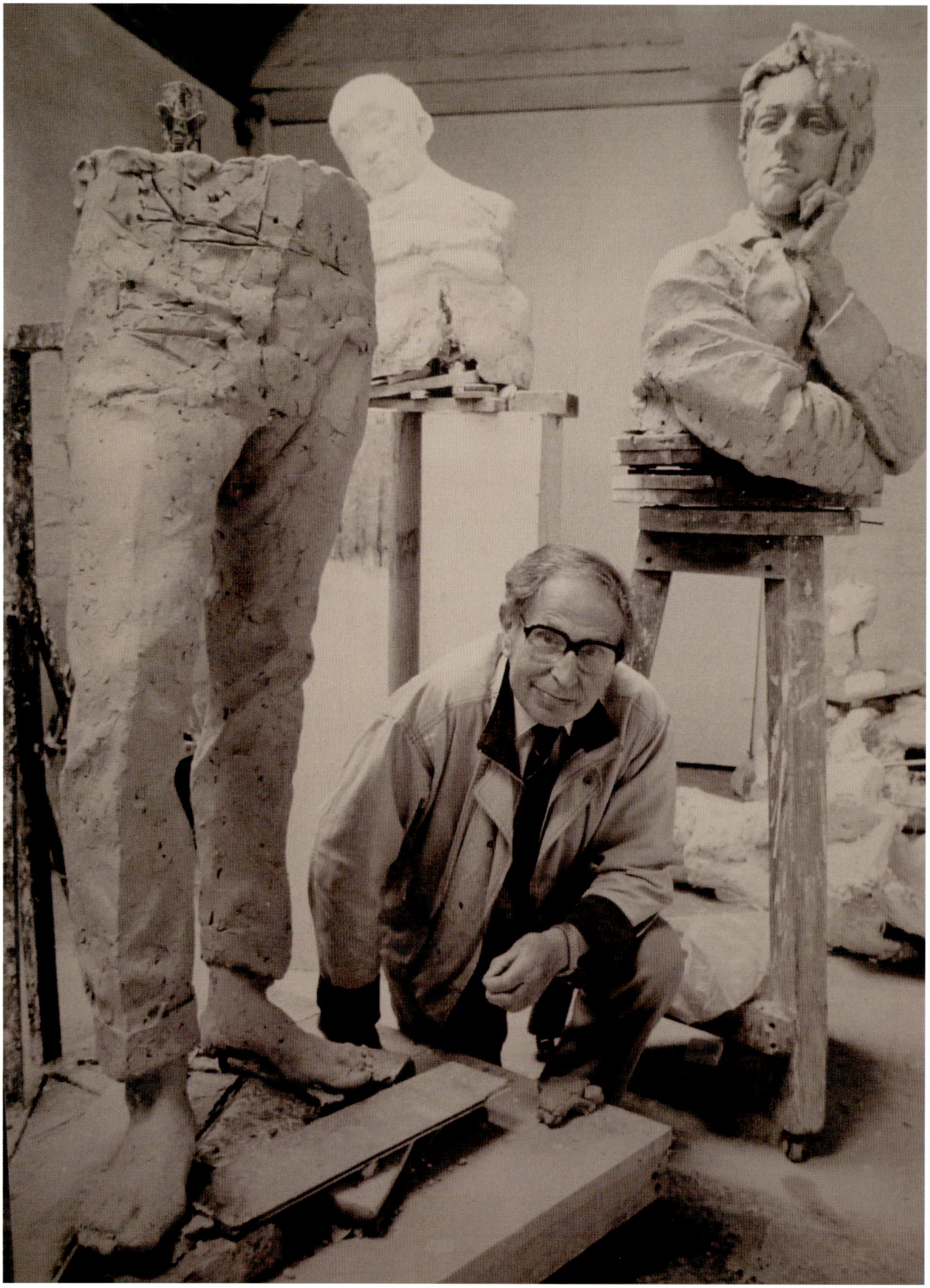

'neo-pagan' period, which embraced Fabian socialism, vegetarianism, 'free love', and generally informal dress, including the conspicuously eschewing of any footwear.[219] The sculptor later declared that 'Brooke the Neo-Pagan' had appealed to him because the poet was then 'care-free', and it was before he had become a 'celebrated Neo-Georgian'.[220]

Brooke, once Ivor had joined the two sections of the figure, was presented not as the soldier in uniform and man of action – the poet of the famous *War Poems* of 1914 – but as the barefoot, unconventional, reflective, even pensive 'neo-pagan': a phase that occupied at most three years of his life, from around 1909 to 1912, while he lived at the Old Vicarage, Grantchester, two miles south-west of Cambridge, to which he had moved in May 1911.[221] During the summer of 1911, Brooke often alarmed his landlords, the Neve family, by sleeping on the lawn (partly to avoid fleas in his rooms at the Old Vicarage), habitually walking around barefoot and conspicuously bathing nude in the nearby River Cam.[222] He also rather shocked the Neves by entertaining guests while only wearing a loose, open-necked shirt (of the sort Ivor depicts him wearing), with either no tie or some suspiciously bohemian cravat, and baggy, un-ironed cricket trousers.[223]

It would be during this 'neo-pagan' period that the poet frequently expressed distinctly anti-traditional opinions and was critical of the British state and empire. He was quite removed from the super-patriot and jingoistic British nationalist who emerges so forcefully from his series of *1914* poems, such as *The Soldier*, which would make him so famous after his untimely death in 1915.[224]

Casting of the full-sized plaster model took place during the summer of 1988, somewhat delayed by Ivor's continuing experiments until the last minute with various combinations for the two sections of the figure. He was unsure, for example, whether the head and chest of the poet would be positioned at right-angles to his legs and feet, or turned to engage the gaze of the viewer more directly. The statue was unveiled in September 1988 by Dame Mary Archer – who still lives in the Old Vicarage, Grantchester, and at the time of writing was working on a book about the period Brooke spent living in the village (1909–13). Dame Mary was full of praise for Ivor's conception of Brooke, telling a crowd of some 500 that Ivor's statue was 'very much like the snap shots of him and I like it ... He had many back-to-nature phases ... and he hated to wear shoes. It is most appropriate that he returns home barefooted.'[225]

With the passage of time, her admiration for the statue has grown. She now detects in the poet's face a subtle hint of anxiety that she missed when she first viewed the work – a suggestion of the anxiety and self-doubt the poet would face after he decided to volunteer for service with the Royal Naval Division in 1914, coming under fire at Antwerp in October 1914, and then the anticipation of participating in the Gallipoli Expedition the following year.[226] Indeed, she has noted the intriguing detail that the placement on Brooke's face of the fingers of his left hand subtly draws attention to the poet's mouth and prominent lips – and it was on the upper lip that Brooke received the mosquito bite, shortly before the Gallipoli landing took place, which was to kill him.[227] Overall, the figure Ivor conceived acknowledges Brooke's physical attractiveness while also hinting at his inner torments, inconsistencies and self-doubt. He is endowed with a heroic aura and yet the idealisation is nuanced, combining frailty and purpose – and ultimately all the more persuasive for suggesting this precarious mixture that was only too true to the poet's fractured personality.

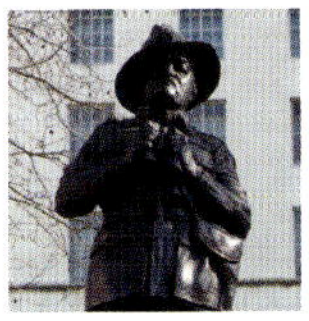

A Homage to 'Uncle Bill': *Field Marshal Viscount Slim* (1988–90; cat. 153) for Whitehall, London

In November 1983 Ivor turned seventy, and as a 'birthday treat' he bought himself a new edition of Field Marshal William Slim's *Defeat Into Victory* (first published in 1956), his classic account of his command of the XIVth Army (the so-called 'Forgotten Army') in Burma from 1943 to 1945. The book he read at the end of 1983 reminded Ivor how much he had admired Slim when he had served in Burma for two and a half years as a captain in the Royal Artillery. Thereafter, every eighteen months or so he reread *Defeat into Victory* and/or Slim's autobiography, *Unofficial History* (first published in 1959). Reading these books reinforced his memory of Slim as his wartime 'chief', known to his troops as 'Uncle Bill', physically brave, as

Fig. 5.28 Ivor Roberts-Jones in his studio at Shimpling, c. April 1988, photograph, Image: Courtesy of the HMI, Leeds

solid as a rock but highly intelligent. According to Ivor, he was 'the one genuine hero I have ever personally laid eyes on ... in a paddy field on the road to Mandalay (in March 1945)'.[229] He liked the fact that Slim, a lower-middle-class grammar-school boy, had started his army career in the ranks, had displayed considerable courage during the First World War, and after the war had earned enough to marry and transfer to a more prestigious regiment by writing thriller novels under the pen-name 'Anthony Mills'.[230] Clearly, as field marshals went, Slim had an unusually rich mental 'hinterland'.

Given this context, Ivor was delighted early in 1988 to be asked by the Burma Star Association (BSA) to submit a maquette for a 2-to-3-metre-high bronze figure of 'Uncle Bill' to stand on Whitehall, just to the north of Lutyens's Cenotaph.[231] It had no doubt helped his standing that he was a member of the Suffolk branch of the BSA, though he had to admit he rarely attended their meetings, as discussing the Burma campaign would in all likelihood 'summon up memories that would not be welcome'.[232] One of the principle 'expert assessors' advising the Memorial Committee on the sculptors to include on its short-list for the memorial competition was an old friend and supporter of Ivor's, Sir Hugh Casson, who had recently stepped down as president of the Royal Academy.[233] Ivor and the other selected sculptors – James Butler RA, Christopher Marvell, Michael Rizzello RBS, and David Norris[234] – were given until the beginning of April 1988 to submit a 60–61-centimetre-high plaster maquette for consideration by the Memorial Committee and its advisory 'panel of assessors', which in addition to Casson now included Sir David Piper, president of the Royal Academy Sir Roger de Grey, architect Sir Philip Dowson, painter Brian Kneale of the Royal College of Art, and art critic William Packer.[235]

The one guideline the sculptors were given by the Committee was an express request from the Second Viscount Slim that they depict his father 'as all the troops who served under his command in Burma will remember him ... in Bush hat[236] and jungle dress'.[237]

As often in the past, Ivor quite quickly conceived the figure he would submit (Fig. 5.29), which would win the competition and be erected with little fundamental alteration in 1990. He amassed a pile of photographs of Slim in Burma from around 1943–45, purchased from the

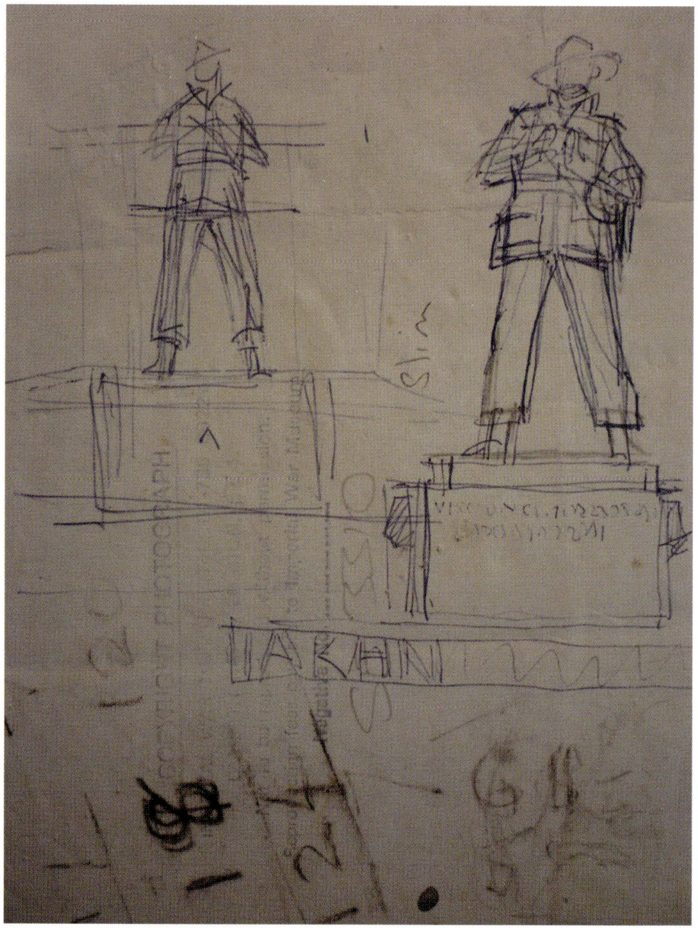

Fig. 5.29 Ivor Roberts-Jones, *Early Sketch for the Field Marshal Viscount Slim Memorial*, c. 1987, pen and ink on paper, 20 x 15 cm, Image: Courtesy of the HMI, Leeds

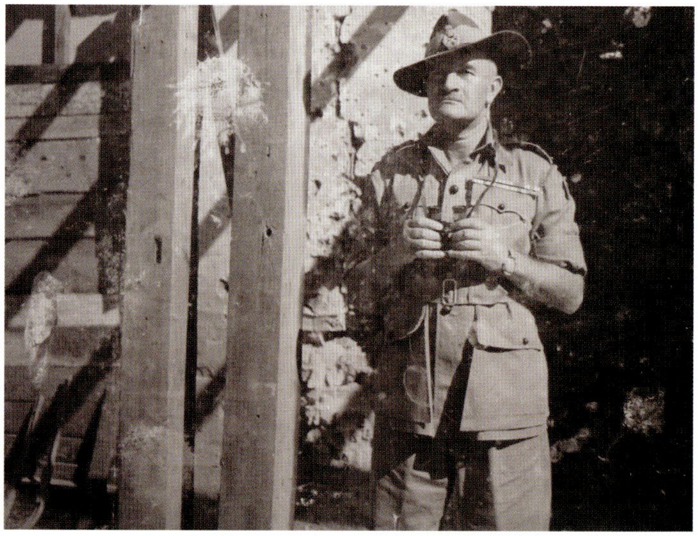

Fig. 5.30 Field Marshal Slim outside his advanced headquarters south of Meiktila, March 1945, photograph, Image: Courtesy of the HMI, Leeds

Imperial War Museum's photography department, with whom he had enjoyed good contacts since the days of his Churchill commission in Parliament Square in the early 1970s. But it would appear that his eye had already been caught by an evocative image of Slim reproduced in the copy of *Defeat into Victory* that he had purchased in 1983. Slim is standing outside his advanced headquarters, on 5 March 1945, as his army closes in on the two central Burmese cities of Mandalay and, to the south, Meiktila, already having destroyed one Japanese army and on the verge of demolishing a second in its path (Fig. 5.30).[238] What had particularly 'stirred the creative juices' was the angle at which Slim was wearing his slouch hat, and the contrast Ivor discerned between the obvious intelligence in Slim's gaze and the physicality of his brawny arms resting on his chest, sleeves rolled up above the elbows, while blunt, purposeful fingers are closed around a pair of binoculars.[239]

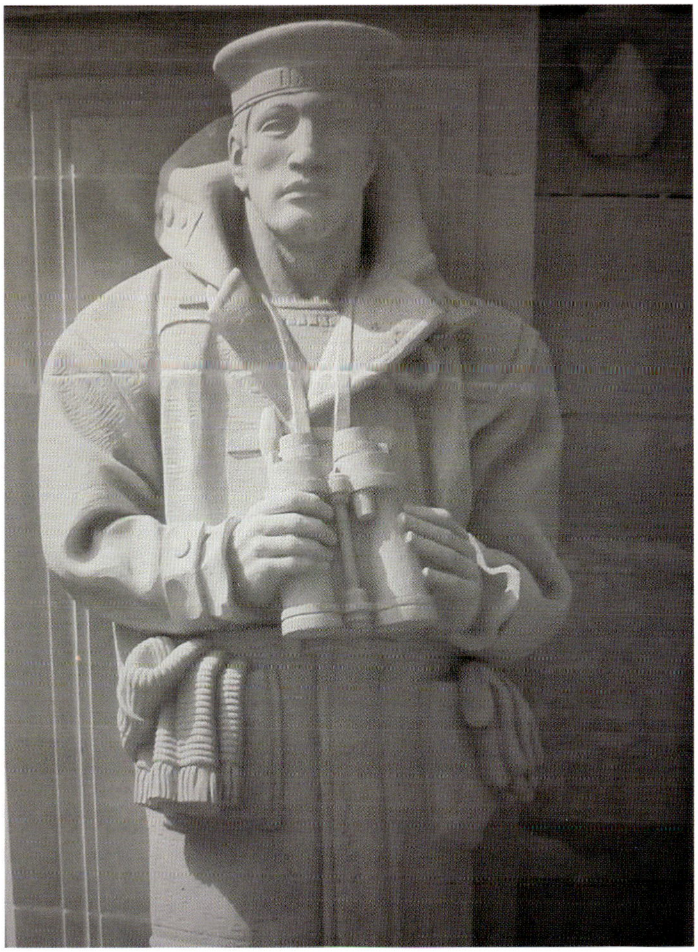

Fig. 5.31 Sir Charles Wheeler, *Royal Naval Rating on Watch*, 1954–55, Portland stone, Royal Naval Memorial, Portsmouth; Image: J. Black

The conception of the figure also owed something to the prior example of a duffel-coated figure of a Royal Navy sailor who grips the binoculars resting on his chest with fierce resolve (Fig. 5.31), created around 1954–55 by Sir Charles Wheeler as part of his *Second World War Royal Naval Memorial* in Portsmouth (unveiled in April 1953).[240] The focus on exposed muscular forearms also recalled the work of another British sculptor Ivor was known to admire greatly, Charles Sargeant Jagger[241] – in particular his imposing figure of a *Shell Carrier* (Fig. 5.32; 1923–25) for the Royal Artillery Memorial on Hyde Park Corner, London (unveiled in October 1925).[242]

As Ivor had often said to a former pupil of his, 'first impressions are often the best', and this is the impression he wanted to communicate in his statue of Slim.[243] After the memorial was unveiled, he read and underlined the following passage in George MacDonald Fraser's well-regarded memoir of his experience as an infantryman of Burma in 1944–45, *Quartered Safe Out Here* (1993). This, he thought, was exactly the Slim he sought to convey in his sculpture:

> Slim was unforgettable ... the only man I've ever seen who had a force that came out of him, a strength of personality I've puzzled over ever since ... His appearance was plain enough, large, heavily built, grim-faced with that hard mouth and bulldog chin, the rakish Gurkha hat was at odds with the slung carbine and untidy trouser bottoms; he might have been a yard foreman who had become managing director, or a prosperous farmer who'd boxed in his youth ... Nor was he an orator ... His delivery was blunt, matter-of-fact, without gesture or mannerisms, only a lack of them. He knew how to make an entrance – or rather he probably didn't and it came naturally ... there was no nonsense of 'gather round', or jumping on ammunition boxes, he just stood ... and talked about how we had caught [the] Japs [in March 1945] off-balance and were going to annihilate him in the open; there was no exhortation, or ringing clichés, no jokes, or self-conscious use of barrack room slang – when he called the Japs 'bastards', it was casual and without heat. He was telling us, informally, what would be, in the reflective way of an intimate conversation. And we believed every word – and it all came true ... You knew when he talked of 'smashing the Jap', that to him it meant not only arrows on a map but clearing bunkers and going in

> under shell-fire; that he had the head of a general with the heart of a private soldier ... And afterwards, when it was all over and he spoke of what his Army had done, it was always 'you', not even 'we', and never 'I'.[244]

In May 1988, the maquette Ivor submitted (cat. 153a) was the unanimous first choice of the assessors and the Memorial Committee. The Second Viscount Slim particularly approved, as did Slim's widow, Lady Aileen, who thought Ivor had 'got Bill's jawline and stance just right'.[245] Shortly thereafter Ivor engaged an assistant, a member of staff and technician at Goldsmiths, Brian Jarvis, on the grounds that he was not getting any younger and would need a good deal of help just to move the huge full-sized maquette that he would create in clay in his studio-barn at Shimpling.[246] As with his earlier statue of Churchill for Parliament Square, Ivor began by creating a full-sized model in clay of Slim's head and shoulders; Brian Jarvis recalls that Ivor seemed to spend 'endless hours' getting the slouch hat at just the right angle, and, when he was happy with the angle, felt he had to trim the brim of the hat back – otherwise, in the final statue, Slim's face would have been obscured by its shadow under direct sunlight.[247]

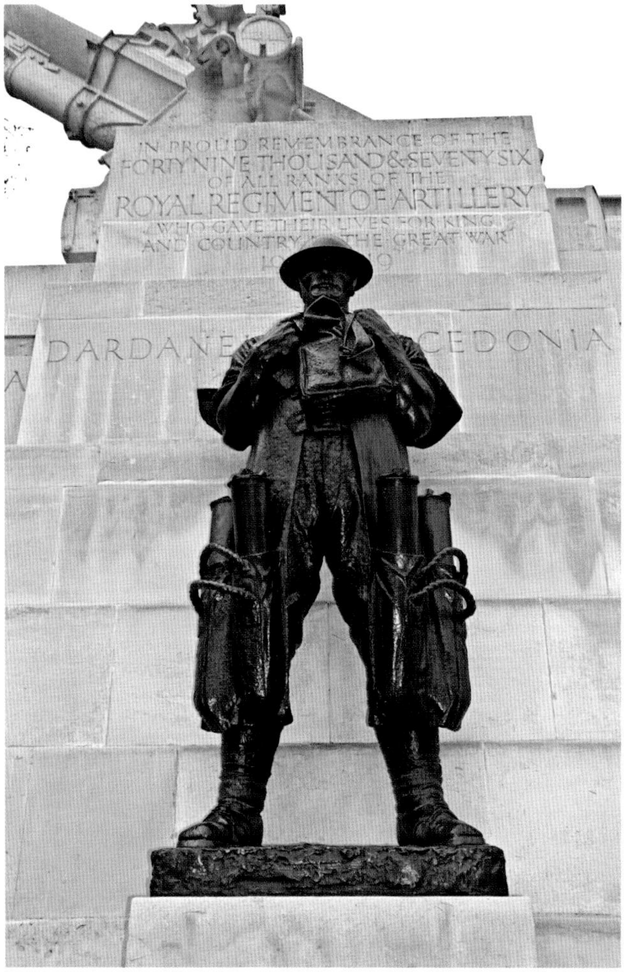

Fig. 5.32 Charles Sargeant Jagger, *The Shell Carrier*, 1923–25, bronze, 2.49 m high, Royal Artillery Memorial, Hyde Park Corner, London; Image: J. Black

When Ivor was satisfied with the clay head – or as close as he ever came to being satisfied with anything he created – Jarvis helped him cast it in plaster. He then winched the plaster head and shoulders onto the main body of the figure, which Ivor modelled in clay in two sections. Even without the head on top, the clay body and feet, when those sections had been attached, were too tall for Ivor to continue working on them. So Jarvis dug a hole in the earthen floor of the studio and carefully lowered the full-sized figure in clay, topped with the head in plaster, into the hole. Ivor was able to work on the statue from the head downwards using a network of 'precarious and rickety ladders', as well as a 'pyramid of packing cases' that he had assembled. This latticework of ladders was all the more unsettling because 'not all the ladders were quite long enough', nor did all of them seem to rest securely on the beams within the roof of the barn.[248] Even after the full-sized model of the figure had been cast in plaster, Ivor continued to work on it; he sawed the figure into two sections, and Jarvis recalls him experimenting with the join between Slim's legs and his torso, and with how far the torso and head could be made to lean backwards before the figure became unstable and threatened to topple backwards, which would have 'finished off' the diminutive sculptor if he had been caught underneath it. It was obvious to Jarvis from the care with which Ivor worked on the Slim figure that it was a 'labour of love', and that the sculptor was 'putting a lot of himself into it'.[249]

Ivor ceased 'fidgeting' with the full-sized plaster cast of Slim just as the lorry arrived in the yard of Ivor's property at Shimpling to transport it to the Meridian Foundry in Peckham.[250] The figure was cast in the autumn of 1989, Ivor taking particular care with the patina so that the figure would not look too shiny and brand-new in sunlight,[251] and was unveiled by the Queen at the end of April 1990[252] (Fig. 5.33). Three years later, as he neared completion of a large figure of another overlooked hero of the Second World War, *Field Marshal Alanbrooke*, Ivor mused in a fragment of autobiographical writing that, if he had fallen under a bus the next day (unlikely given the rarity of bus services in Norfolk), he would have done happily, since he had the statue of Slim 'to be remembered by'.[253]

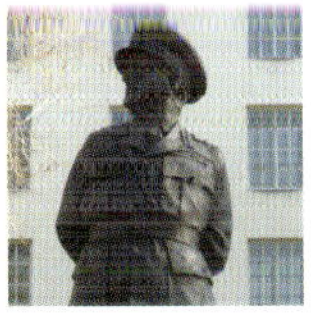

A Memorial for 'Old Shrapnel': *Field Marshal Viscount Alanbrooke* (1990–93; cat. 154) for Whitehall, London

Ivor was to describe the Alanbrooke commission as clear proof that 'success breeds success': the group of high-ranking army officers who were keen to have a statue erected to honour Alanbrooke (Fig. 5.33) – a key figure in British decision-making at the highest level during the Second World War and yet virtually unknown to the general public in 1990 – had been very impressed by Ivor's statue of Slim.[254] Indeed, there is evidence to suggest that the very prospect of the unveiling of the Slim memorial prompted them to seek an Alanbrooke statue in close proximity – in front of the Ministry of Defence building on Whitehall.[255] And by April 1991 they were determined to have Ivor as the sculptor for the new memorial.[256] Even though the sculptor and Alanbrooke, known with qualified affection as 'old Shrapnel', had both served with the Royal Artillery and Ivor had enjoyed reading the abridged edition of Alanbrooke's diaries (published in 1957), he now experienced one of his 'wobbles' of self-confidence. To his assistant, Brian Jarvis, he voiced fear that, at nearly 80, he was simply too 'ancient and decrepit', and that he had 'too many aches and pains' to clamber up the ladders in his studio-barn to work effectively on a full-sized model for the figure, which would stand at over 3 metres in height.[257]

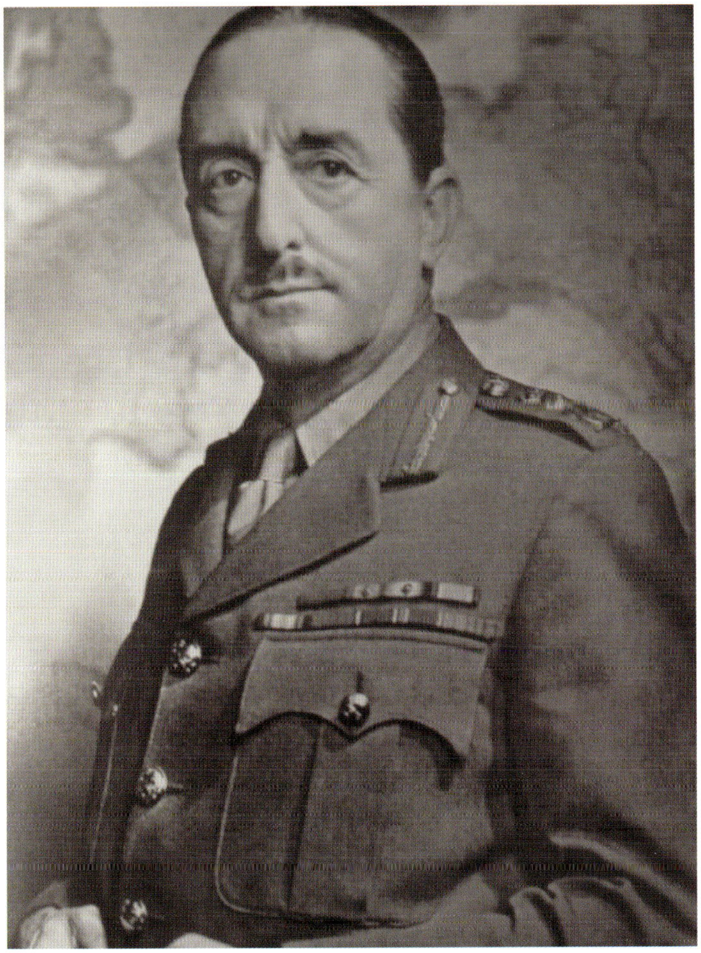

Fig. 5.33 Yousuf Karsh, *General Sir Alan Brooke*, 1943, photograph, National Portrait Gallery, London; Image: Courtesy of the National Portrait Gallery, London

But this 'wobble' proved short-lived, and after a few days Ivor accepted the commission from a Memorial Committee that had close ties to the Royal Regiment of Artillery, which was providing a third of the £150,000 required to pay for the statue and its installation on Whitehall.[258] One reason the sculptor changed his mind was that, while his health remained robust, he had convinced himself that he would not live to see the end of the decade, and a second statue on Whitehall would be a fitting parting shot at more fashionable artists busying themselves with installations and 'piles of bricks'.[259] Another was that he had begun to read more about Alanbrooke, and was becoming increasingly intrigued by his character. He recalled that Alanbrooke had made a memorable appearance in *The Military Philosophers* – one of the later novels of the *Dance to the Music of Time* series by Anthony Powell, with whom he had kept in intermittent contact since Powell had been a supporter of Ivor's during his travails over the Augustus John statue project for Fordingbridge. In the novel, published in 1968, which Ivor read in the early seventies as a respite from working on the statue of Churchill for Parliament Square, the attention of the central character, Nick Jenkins, and that of a portentous War Office doorman is

> unequivocally demanded by the hurricane-like imminence of a thickset general, obviously of high rank, wearing enormous horn-rimmed spectacles. He had just burst from a flagged staff car almost before it had drawn up by the kerb. Now he tore up the steps of the building at the charge, exploding through the inner

door into the hall. An extraordinary current of physical energy, almost of electricity, suddenly pervaded the place. I could feel it stabbing through me. This was the CIGS [Chief of the Imperial General Staff, i.e. Alanbrooke]. His quite remarkable and palpable extension of personality, in its effect on others, I had noticed not long before, out in the open.[260]

Ivor became further interested in Alanbrooke as, during April 1991, he read the most recent biography of the soldier, published in 1982 by General Sir David Fraser,[261] one of the members of the Alanbrooke statue committee. He was impressed by the fact that Alanbrooke had been a more considerable and complex personality even than Powell had implied: able to maintain a glacially impassive and controlled exterior despite being essentially a highly strung and emotional person who, however tired at the end of the day as CIGS, and often vexed in the extreme by Churchill's latest antics, had to write up his diary as a vital safety valve. Ivor's attention was caught by one entry in Alanbrooke's diary, in which the soldier wrote of the imperative he lived with hourly while CIGS 'to maintain "the mask of command" and ... pretend that you are absolutely confident of success when you are really torn to shreds with doubts and misgivings ... once decisions are taken the time for doubts is gone and what is required is to breathe the confidence of success in to all those around'.[262]

The more he read about him in Fraser's biography, the more Alanbrooke emerged as a man of contradictions – the consummate professional soldier who would actually have much preferred to become a surgeon when growing up. While he had displayed considerable physical courage during his First World War service, in his spare time he was happiest bird-watching, fly-fishing, taking photographs of the natural world and collecting cartoons and satirical eighteenth-century prints.[263]

After reading Fraser's biography, Ivor turned to Lord Moran's *Diaries*, which he had previously found so useful in providing illuminating insights into Churchill's character. He noted that, in July 1945, Moran had reflected that 'as the years have passed I have come to respect [Alanbrooke's] character, his complete integrity, his contempt for flattery, his indifference alike to praise and blame and his great longing for peace'.[264] A decade later, shortly after the controversial publication of Alanbrooke's *Diaries*, Moran concluded that the field marshal had, despite appearances, been a 'highly strung, sensitive, apprehensive creature ... who lived behind an iron mask he presented to the world'. And yet he stood equally 'for a sense of proportion, for method, for good sense ... I do not know any other soldier who would have stood up to the Prime Minister so effectively ... He kept Winston on the rails in the conduct of the war. That is his epitaph.'[265]

As was his usual procedure when starting a commission for a major figurative statue, apart from reading as much as he could about Alanbrooke, Ivor amassed many photographs of the subject – from his recent biographer, Sir David Fraser, and from the Imperial War Museum.[266] One photograph he retained (Fig. 5.34), intrigued by the expression on Alanbrooke's face, had been taken while the soldier was Commander-in-Chief of Home Forces

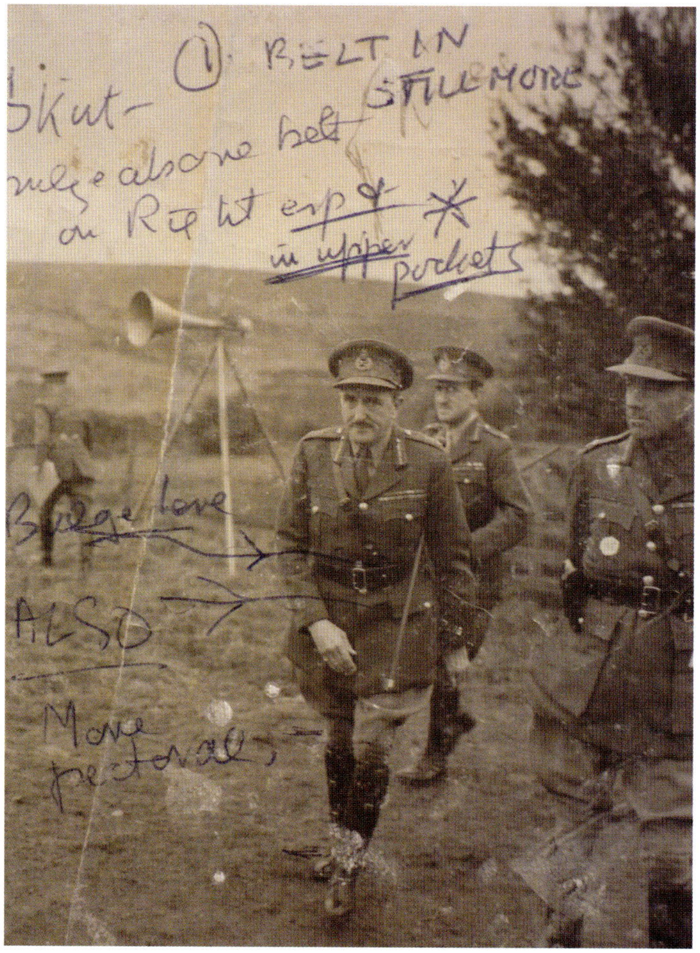

Fig. 5.34 *General Sir Alan Brooke on Salisbury Plain*, December 1941, Image: Courtesy of the HMI, Leeds

attending manoeuvres on Salisbury Plain two months before he was appointed CIGS, in December 1941. On that occasion Alanbrooke had not found it possible to conceal his displeasure at the sight of a large number of poorly designed and poorly maintained British tanks lying inert, scattered across the plain, having broken down.[267] Ivor thought the face of his Alanbrooke must have present in its features some hint of the soldier's impressive capacity for expressing mingled hauteur and exasperation.[268] The sculptor was also struck by Alanbrooke's habitual sartorial elegance in the photograph, by the high polish on his boots – those of a high-ranking artillery officer – and that, whatever the climatic circumstances, he invariably appeared immaculately turned out.[269] Ivor was later to tell a journalist that Alanbrooke had especially appealed to him as a subject for a major statue precisely because he combined in appearance and character 'that mixture of weakness and strength ... that double edge. Alanbrooke ... was a very shy man, a birdwatcher, you know, yet at the same time he was this powerful figure exercising command over people like [Field Marshal] Montgomery.'[270] Ivor had earlier described this unstable but ever-present duality of character which should be evident in the best portrait sculpture as 'the darkness and the light, laid side-by-side together and yet infinitely separate'.[271]

The sculptor also decided, after looking through a generous selection of photographs of the CIGS, that he would not depict Alanbrooke wearing the 'horn-rimmed' spectacles Powell had mentioned in *The Military Philosophers* – however intimidating they might have been in reality, Ivor had come to the conclusion from past experience in portraiture that it was 'hard to make [a sitter] look heroic in specs'.[272]

By June 1991 Ivor had produced a small plaster head of Alanbrooke (cat. 154a) and a clay sketch model of the figure (Fig. 5.35), which delighted members of the Memorial Committee – especially its chairman, Field Marshal Lord Carver, who particularly approved of the pose Ivor had given Alanbrooke – in profile, head raised, as if 'scenting the air for approaching danger ... and keeping an eye out for any passing skylarks in Whitehall'.[273]

Carver thought Alanbrooke's pose 'unusual in a public statue', but that it 'worked as it is true to the man ... in my mind at least'.[274] Ivor had long been an admirer of the Renaissance profile portrait, and while working on the head of Alanbrooke had referred extensively to examples painted by artists such as Piero della Francesca, and in particular his famous portrait of the soldier-condottiere Federico da Montefeltro, Duke of Urbino, in the collection of the Uffizi Gallery, Florence (c. 1465–72).[275] In conceiving Alanbrooke's figure in 1990–91, Ivor was very much indebted to the example offered by the Norwegian sculptor Gustav Vigeland (1868–1943) in his slim, attenuated bronze figure of the poet *Henrik Wergeland* (1906–7; Fig. 5.36), head averted as if in the throes of poetic composition, made for Kristiansand. It is likely that Ivor had visited the Museum in Oslo dedicated to Vigeland's life and work during visits he had paid in 1975–76 to the Norwegian capital in connection with his Churchill statue commission for the city's Solli Square[276] (cat. 136). He was later to state that he had thought long and hard about Alanbrooke's

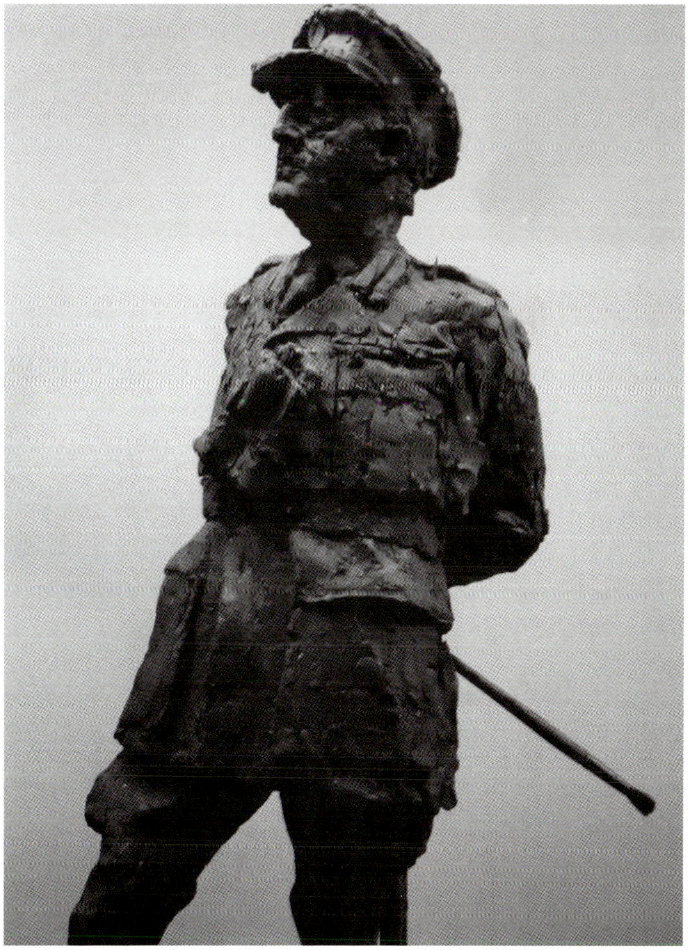

Fig. 5.35 Ivor Roberts-Jones, *Sketch Model for the Field Marshal Viscount Alanbrooke Memorial*, 1991, clay, 50 cm high, lost
Image: Courtesy of the HMI, Leeds

stance, seeking a balance between self-assurance and awkwardness: 'If you notice, Alanbrooke is turning to one side and that could be seen as haughty, but he is also drawing back his head as though exercising command and wishing he wasn't. It is in things like that you can show character.'[277]

In the early autumn of 1991 Ivor's more detailed sketch model of the figure and the full-sized clay head of Alanbrooke (Fig. 5.37) were inspected and approved by a group from the field marshal's memorial committee, and later the same week by a deputation from the Royal Fine Art Commission and English Heritage.[278] The sculptor had worried before the meeting with the Committee that his portrait of the CIGS had become 'too much the caricature "à la Gillray"'.[279] But he knew he was on the right path when one Committee member, on first sight of the clay head, had exclaimed: '"He looks ravaged!" I thought "Thank God. I have got that right."' Ivor hastened to reassure the committee member, probably ex-gunner General Sir Harry Tuzo, that Alanbrooke's head would look different in bronze because it was such 'a very powerful medium'. In bronze, Ivor asserted, he would see 'more of the power' in Alanbrooke's face and figure.[280]

The sculptor was initially confident that he and his assistant would be able within the next six months to produce a full-sized plaster model of the statue for the Memorial Committee to view, and suggest final alterations if they were thought to be required. Lord Carver was keen to see the statue erected as quickly as possible, partly to take further advantage of the glow of success in which the Royal Artillery was basking after its impressive battle performance in the recent First Gulf War. He further calculated that the new statue could only help strengthen the regiment's position in its bid to avoid a new round

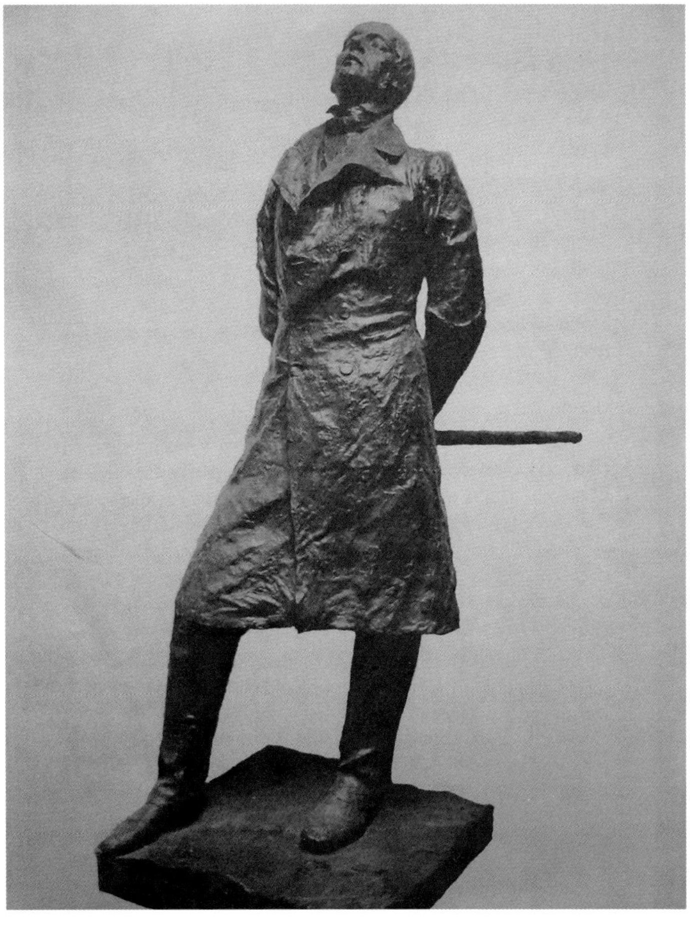

Fig. 5.36 Gustav Vigeland, *Henrik Wergeland*, c. 1906–7, bronze, 2.44 m high, Kristiansand, Norway; Image: Courtesy of the HMI, Leeds

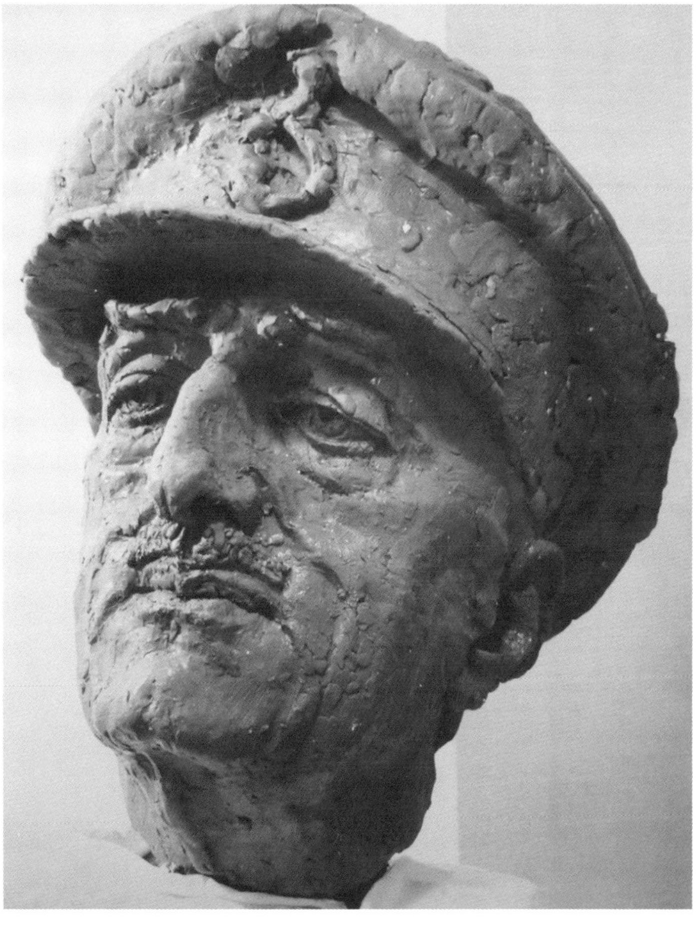

Fig. 5.37 Ivor Roberts-Jones, *Full-Sized Head of Field Marshal Lord Alanbrooke*, 1991, clay, lost; Image: Courtesy of the HMI, Leeds

of swingeing post-Cold War 'peace dividend' defence cuts threatened by the Conservative government of John Major.[281]

As with the previous Field Marshal Slim commission, Ivor positioned a plaster cast of the full-sized head of Alanbrooke on top of the rest of his figure, which took shape in clay as it stood in a hole Jarvis had dug in the floor of Ivor's studio at Shimpling.[282] On this occasion, however, the sculptor was finding it increasingly difficult to manoeuvre around the giant model on the 'network of ladders' and 'pyramids of packing cases' Jarvis had erected for him.[283] Meanwhile, more than usual in this phase of a commission, Ivor experienced violent mood swings between confidence and doubt.[284] As his immediate point of contact with the memorial Committee, William 'Nobby' Clarke wrote to Lord Carver in January 1992, 'the sculptor has just telephoned me to say he feels a lot better today than yesterday. [Jarvis] is helping to make up for lost time. He hopes for a little extra time (in my book that must take us to April 1993) ... he's a weathervane and right now, temperamentally, he's like a bouncing rubber ball. Rings me up full of gloom, then a few hours later changes his mind again.'[285]

Despite thereafter experiencing the occasional further 'wobble' in confidence, Ivor and Jarvis worked solidly to complete the full-sized plaster model of Alanbrooke in September 1992. This was promptly inspected and approved by the Memorial Committee – Lord Carver was amused that the sculptor almost seemed put out that the Committee did not demand any last-minute alterations – and despatched to the Meridian Foundry early in October.[286] The statue was unveiled by the Queen in May 1993 – just a month after the date Clarke had earlier anticipated, and despite the machinations of Lord St John of Fawlsey as Chairman of the RFAC to delay the ceremony until after the area in which the statue was to stand had been extensively re-landscaped (see entry for cat. 154).[287]

During the ceremony the then master gunner of St James's, the honorary head of the Royal Artillery, General Sir Martin Farndale, described the statue as 'magnificent', remarking that it would 'serve as an inspiration to future generations of the value of good strategic planning and leadership'.[288] The day after the unveiling, Sir Robert Fellowes, the Queen's private secretary, wrote to Lord Carver describing Ivor's work as 'a most striking and well-sited statue of a great war leader ... entirely satisfactory and London and Londoners and their visitors will be all the better for it, as will history'.[289] That same day Carver wrote to the artist to convey his heartfelt congratulations:

> Yesterday was a great day for you and all of us who have been involved in the Alanbrooke statue. It was wonderful to see your splendid statue there, where everyone can see it so well with Alanbrooke looking defiantly towards Haig[290] as if saying 'I showed you how to conduct war in a better way!' ... With many thanks and congratulations on a splendid addition to the London scene.[291]

Sir Martin Farndale also wrote in praise to Ivor, describing the statue as

> masterly ... I thought that he looked magnificent ... Alanbrooke was a strong and intelligent man and this you have captured to perfection, along with his characteristic stance. It takes a proud place in the centre of the capital. Your work is such a vital part of our national history and it is wonderful too that you are a member of the Regiment. We all congratulate you again.[292]

The artist replied to both in similar terms, but appeared most pleased by the sentiments Lord Carver had expressed:

> I have enjoyed carrying out the statue – and I am very grateful for the chance to do so. It is only what you all deserve which is a degree of pleasure ... Certainly the site is magnificent ... But it must be those who first conceived the idea and who have been so kind and considerate throughout – that I would most want to please. I am proud to have been chosen to carry it through and very mindful of all the help I have had. Above all I'm grateful to yourself for always being there when things got sticky. I'm sure you will hear a slight metallic mutter of thanks (from Alanbrooke) every time you pass the statue and see a slight slackening of those rather tensed up nostrils.[293]

Ivor was especially touched when, for weeks after the statue's unveiling, he received numerous plaudits by post from many ordinary ex-gunners, often those who had served in the ranks of the regiment, whether in the Second World War or in Korea. Usually not one for retaining correspondence, the sculptor carefully kept these letters, such as one from Robert Smalls, a former bombardier who had served in the Normandy campaign of 1944: '[W]hen the statue was unveiled it was nothing short of a coup. This striking, forceful figure, so poised with a slight air of aloofness but dominant and demanding attention was really special. Part of the coup was its position ... within 80 yards of the Whitehall Cenotaph and there for posterity ... I admired your figure of the Viscount which oozes strength, will [and] depth of thoughtfulness.'[294] A year later Ivor was still rather pleased with his *Alanbrooke*. As he wrote to his old friend Judge Bruce Griffiths, the field marshal was the sort of man 'Daumier would have relished' as a subject; Ivor felt, 'for once, I've been equal to the great Frenchman'.[295]

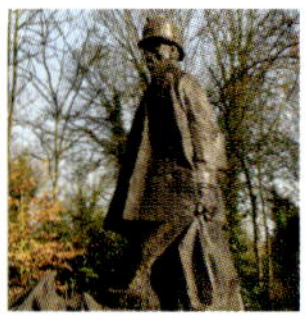

A Policeman's Lot ... *The National Police Memorial Project* (1991–93; cat. 155)

During an impromptu visit to Ivor's Norfolk studio in the late autumn of 1992, Lord Carver found the sculptor surrounded by drawings and 'little models' not related to the figure of Alanbrooke but to 'a memorial to dead policemen'.[296] Carver noted that the sculptor seemed happy enough about progress on the full-sized figure of the field marshal, but his face 'promptly fell' when he asked Ivor about this new project he had 'on the stocks'. Carver observed casually that 'the policeman's lot is not a happy one', to which Ivor replied 'with great vehemence that with some clients ... neither was that of the sculptor!'[296] It is likely that Ivor had the film director Michael Winner in mind as the client who was causing him such vexing trouble. In the spring of 1991, Winner had approached Ivor to provide a sculptural element in profile set within a National Police Memorial to stand at the corner of Horse Guards Road and the Mall in London. Ivor had come highly recommended: the architect Winner had already engaged for the project, Theo Crosby,[298] had warmly approved of Ivor, as did Sir Hugh Casson and his successor as president of the Royal Academy, Sir Roger de Grey.[299]

At heart a traditionalist who believed in the necessity of law and order, Ivor held the British police in high regard. In the past he thought the police had been placed in an invidious position during the miners' strike of 1984–85, while more recently he had sympathised with their position during the Poll Tax riots of March 1990, and had come to feel that the British public did not adequately appreciate the efforts the police were making to protect them from the murderous attentions of Irish republican terrorists. Once he had started work on the project, and for the next five years, he kept a periodic count of the policemen who were killed and wounded in the line of duty – often by IRA or INLA bombs.[300]

Within a few weeks of being contacted by Winner, the sculptor had made a simple sketch maquette for the project (cat. 155a), which already contains the essence of the life-sized plaster model found in his studio after his death in December 1996 (Fig. 5.38). A police constable, wearing the regulation uniform of a British policeman between the early years of the twentieth century and the

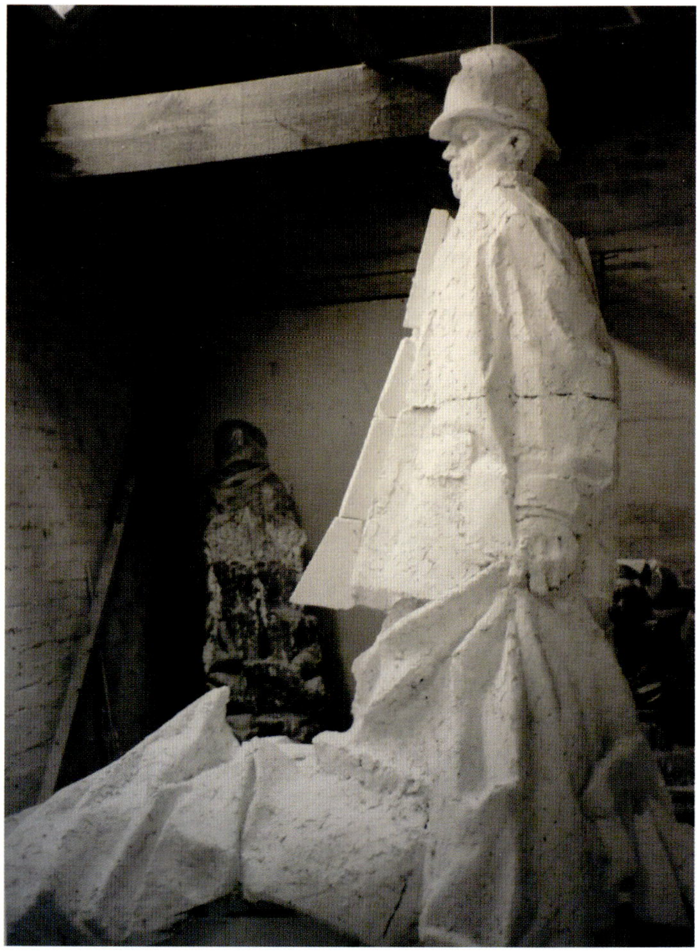

Fig. 5.38 Ivor Roberts-Jones, *Full-sized Model for the National Police Memorial*, 1996, plaster, 2.7 m high, Private Collection; Image: Courtesy of the HMI, Leeds

late 1960s, stands looking sorrowfully down at the body of a dead comrade lying at his feet covered with a police-issue rain cape. This conception of the standing figure of the policeman owes a great deal to the earlier example of Charles Sargeant Jagger's *The Sentry* (Fig. 5.39), enveloped in a rain cape, while the body beneath a covering can be related to Jagger's poignant *Dead Gunner* for the Royal Artillery Memorial (Fig. 5.40, unveiled at Hyde Park Corner, London, in October 1925). In addition, the stylised treatment of the rain cape covering the dead policeman gave Ivor scope for exploring that 'Expressionist' aspect to his work which surfaced from time to time.[301] In this case he had been looking at an early commission by Bauhaus pioneer Walter Gropius, *The Monument to the March Dead* – an innovative architectonic memorial to those killed in Weimar by right-wing forces during the Kapp Putsch of March 1920[302] (Fig. 5.41).

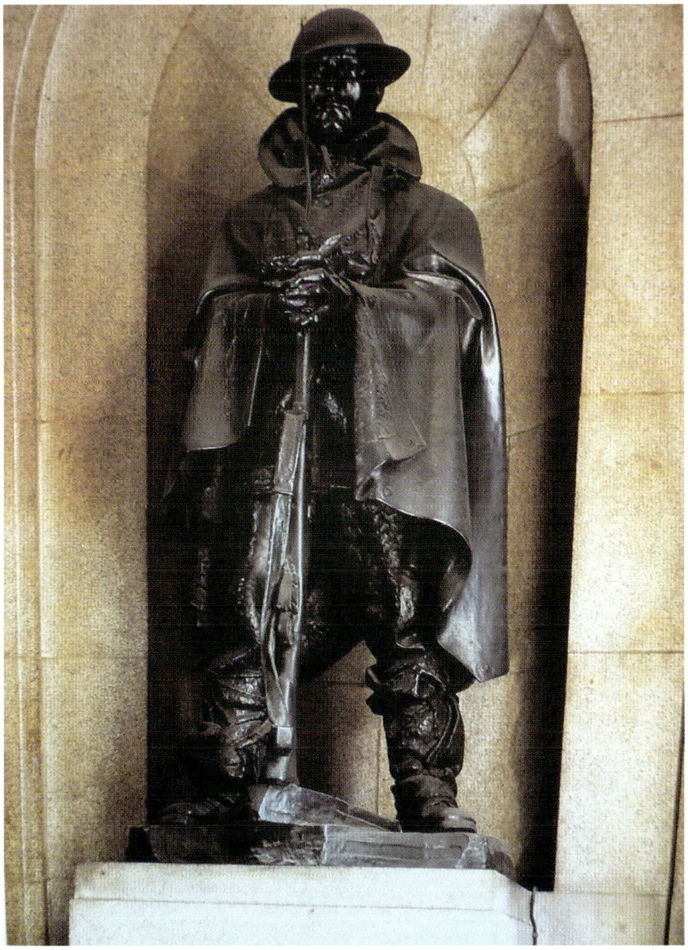

Fig. 5.39 Charles Sargeant Jagger, *The Sentry*, 1921–22, bronze, 2.13 m high, Britannia Hotel, Manchester; Image: J. Black

Over the next two years Ivor was to experiment with the inclusion of a figure of a female passerby, hands raised to her mouth in horror, and a child, playing innocently with a ball, oblivious to the death nearby (Fig. 5.42). Then the woman and the child were removed and replaced at either end of the design's horizontal axis with Alsatian police dogs. Initially, Ivor wanted the heads of the dogs to be raised upwards, mouths wide open exposing impressive jaws, 'as in an Assyrian bas-relief … howling their grief'. However, as Ivor revealed in June 1993, although Winner liked the idea of the two Alsatians, 'the Queen queried this detail on the grounds that they might be too wolf-like. So, the mouths of the dogs were closed'[303] (Fig. 5.43). Within a year the dogs had been removed altogether, as Winner changed his mind about them in the face of criticism of the design from Ivor's old *bête noir* at the RFAC, Lord St John of Fawsley. By this point Ivor's woes had been compounded by taking on the additional task of designing the architectural element of the memorial, since Winner had unceremoniously sacked Theo Crosby as architect after a row in March 1993. Until Ivor's death, many arguments ensued between him and the film director. Sculptors he respected, such as John W. Mills and Etienne Millner, recall long phone calls from Ivor in which he described the Police memorial project as having become a 'nightmare', while Winner was referred to as 'that impossible man, that dreadful man'. The sculptor doubted whether he would ever see his memorial erected, even if he 'achieved the impossible' in simultaneously pleasing Winner and the RFAC.[304]

Winner has since acknowledged that he was not the easiest and most understanding client to work for, though he asserted that Ivor gave as good as he received when it came to invective:

> Now the great thing about Ivor is that he was the most profane, hysterical Welshman you could ever meet. I mean he would turn on me, swear at me and say, 'You are a fucking idiot, you don't know what the fuck you are doing!' But he was … a wonderful man. I loved him. This little Welshman. A great talent. I was very, very fond of him.[305]

Through the rows, tantrums from Winner and a series of often quite petty obstacles raised by Lord St John, Ivor persevered until, about six weeks before his death, the RFAC gave its approval for his latest variant of the policeman looking down at the shrouded form of his dead comrade – Ivor had had to compromise in entirely covering the dead man, rather than leaving a portion of his face visible to the passerby (Fig. 5.44). The full-sized maquette was cast in plaster by the Meridian Foundry and delivered to his Shimpling studio just days before he passed away in his sleep (Fig. 5.38). The sculptor Nigel Boonham discovered the work in the studio after Monica died in 2002, and was immediately bowled over by the undeniable power of this maquette. As one of the trustees of Ivor's estate, he was determined to have the model cast in a more durable material and placed in a fitting setting.[306]

Upon Ivor's death, Winner had turned the memorial project over to architect Sir Norman Foster and the Danish artist Per Arnoldi. Their design proved much more immediately attractive to the RFAC and Westminster City Council, and was unveiled in April 2005. In the meantime, Boonham had tried to interest a number of bodies in commissioning a bronze or resin cast of Ivor's design. For a period in 2004–5 there was a possibility that the work might have been unveiled in the National Memorial Arboretum in Staffordshire. But the charity involved harboured reservations concerning the presence of the dead policeman beneath the cape: would speculation as to what lay under the cape cause distress to the families of bereaved policemen?[307] An impasse appeared to have been reached, until the combined efforts of Boonham and John W. Mills found a resting place for a fibre-glass resin cast (cat. 155) of the sculpture in the new sculpture garden at Renishaw Hall, Derbyshire.[308] Much of the cost of the casting was met by Winner, who was convinced that a major design by 'the man who made the Churchill in Parliament Square' ought to be treated with more respect.[309] According to Winner, interviewed shortly before his own death, he found it baffling that the 'establishment' did not take Ivor's sculpture more seriously.

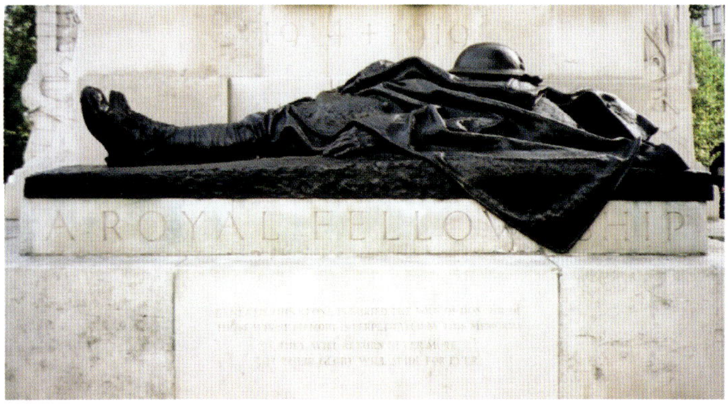

Fig. 5.40 Charles Sargeant Jagger, *Dead Gunner*, 1923–25, bronze, 2.44 m wide, Royal Artillery Memorial, Hyde Park Corner, London; Image: J. Black

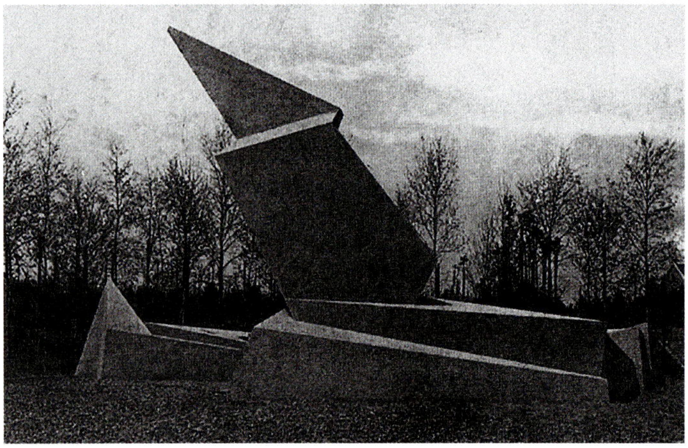

Fig. 5.41 Walter Gropius, *Monument to the March Dead*, 1921, Weimar; Image: Courtesy of the HMI, Leeds

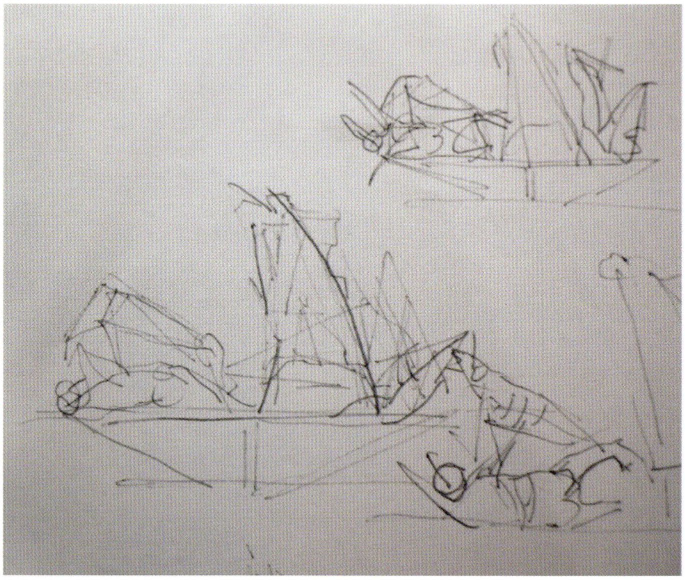

Fig. 5.42 Ivor Roberts-Jones, *Early Sketch for the National Police Memorial*, c. 1991–92, pen and ink on paper, 21 x 29 cm, Image: Courtesy of the HMI, Leeds

He was 'a wonderful sculptor and a wonderful human being ... Paying for the cast to go to Renishaw was the least I could do.'[310]

In his later years Ivor had often pondered why he was not better known and better appreciated by the art world at large. To a considerable degree he did his own cause a disservice, in that he loathed the 'hooplah' of maintaining a reputation – through the regular attendance of openings, private views and 'art world junkets'.[311] However, when in contact with artists he respected, such as Kyffin Williams,[312] John W. Mills[313] and Etienne Millner,[314] he cheered himself up with the thought that traditional figurative sculpture for the public sphere stubbornly continued to be commissioned – despite the scorn of the contemporary art world. He reflected that the services of a number of sculptors for whom he had time, such as Mills, Faith Winter (1927–),[315] Philip Jackson (1944–), Ian Walters (1930–2006) and David Backhouse (1941–) were still very much in demand,[316] having no shortage of entries in their order books. He also derived comfort from the fact that the figure had not been entirely abandoned by younger artists such as Antony Gormley (1950–) – whom Ivor had taught for a brief period at Goldsmiths in the late 1970s – though Ivor thought his penchant for life-casts would, through sheer repetition, soon become tedious.[317] He might indeed have reflected that the human figure had staged something of a revival during the 1990s[318] in the practice of younger artists, such as Gavin Turk (1967–), Ron Mueck (1958–) and Abigail Lane (1967–) – at least in the gallery, if not executed in durable materials for permanent exterior display.[319]

He was convinced that the public was already becoming tired with 'shed-destroyers' and 'sheep-slayers',[320] as he respectively referred to Cornelia Parker's *Cold Dark Matter* (1991)[321] and Damien Hirst's *Away from the Flock* (1994).[322] There was still considerable room, he believed, for the 'icon-maker' in public art, since the public had shown no diminution in its appetite for honouring those individuals it regarded as heroes in the form of statues that Rodin might have saluted, and which they could literally look up to in their streets, squares and parks.[323]

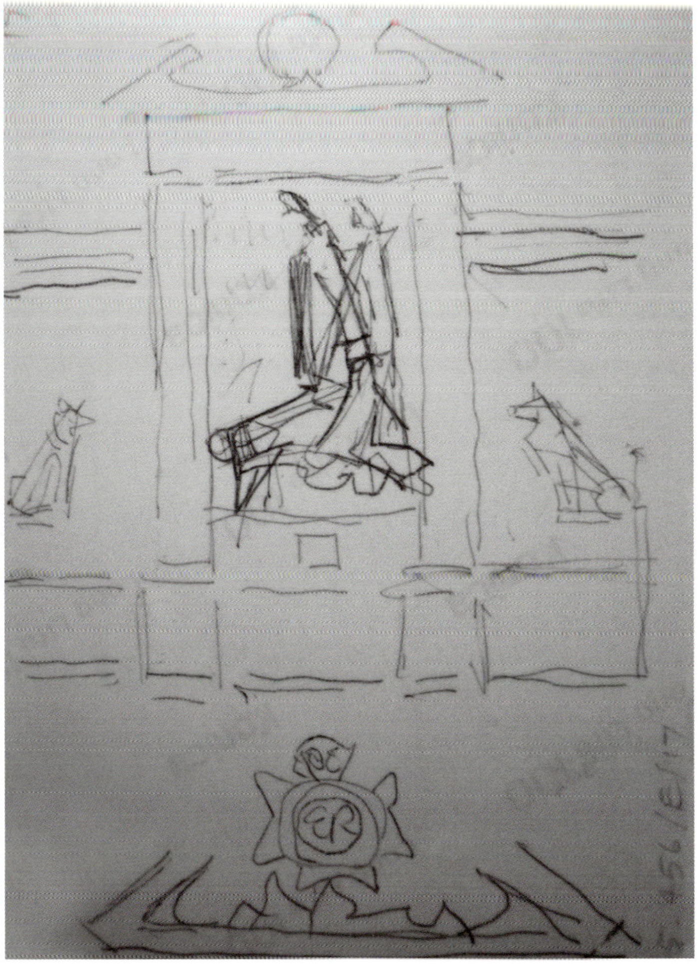

Fig. 5.43 Ivor Roberts-Jones, *Sketch for the National Police Memorial*, 1993, pen and ink on paper, 18 x 13.5 cm, Image: Courtesy of the HMI, Leeds

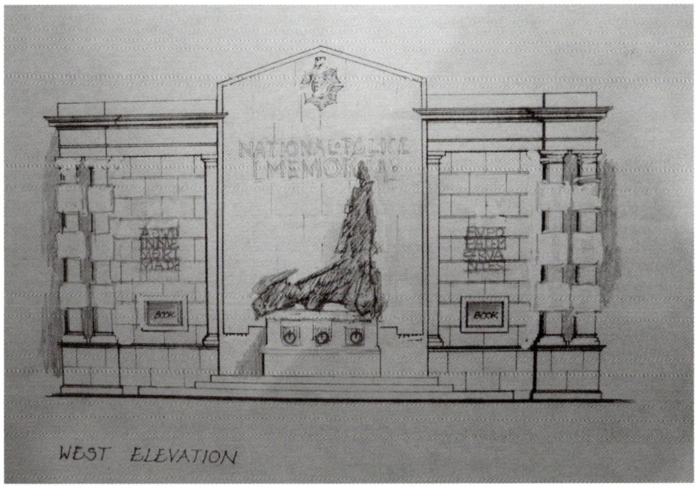

Fig. 5.44 Ivor Roberts-Jones, *Sketch of the Final Version of the National Police Memorial*, 1993, pen and ink on paper, 30 x 21 cm, Image: Courtesy of the HMI, Leeds

IVOR ROBERTS-JONES

CATALOGUE RAISONNÉ OF SCULPTURE

JONATHAN BLACK

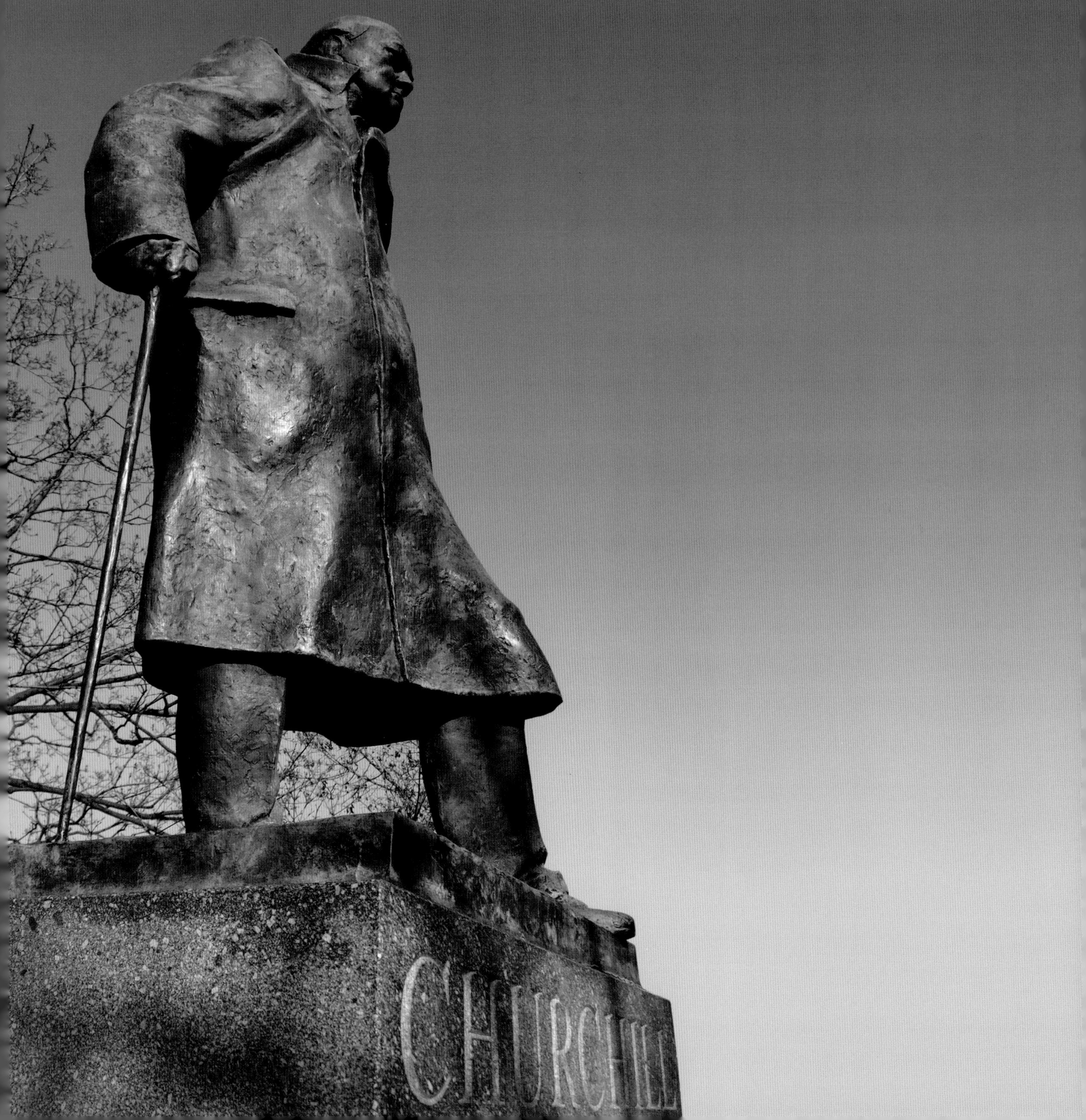

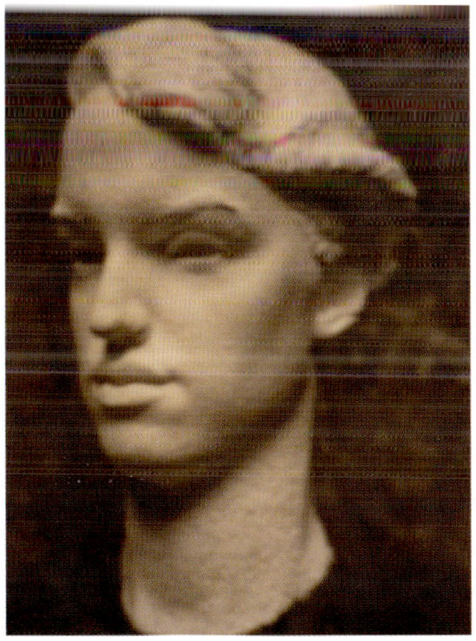

1 *Head of a Young Man*

c. 1935
Plaster
Life-sized
Collection: whereabouts unknown
Exhibition history: unknown

Comments: A photograph of the work in the archive of the Henry Moore Institute, Leeds has 'Thompson, 1935' written on the reverse (F1/1/27, HMI, Leeds).

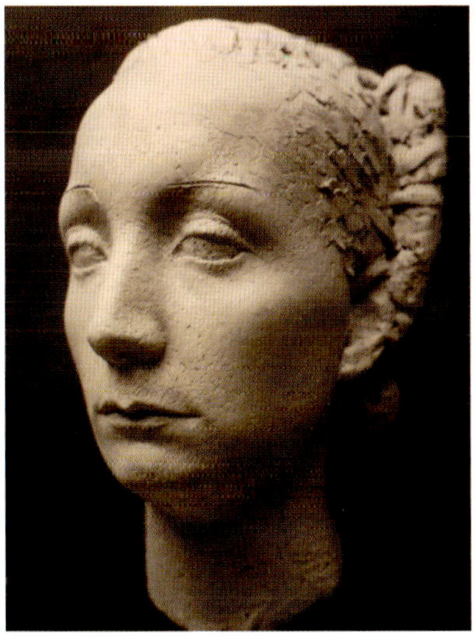

2 *Female Head*

c. 1935–36
Clay
Life-sized
Collection: work was destroyed during the Second World War
Exhibition history: unknown

Comments: A photograph of the work exists in the archive of the Henry Moore Institute, Leeds (F1/1/26, HMI, Leeds).

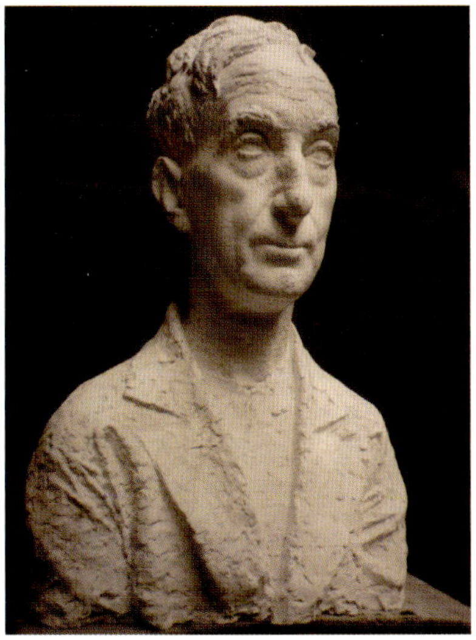

3 *Head and Shoulders of a Mature Adult Male*

c. 1936–37
Plaster
Life-sized
Collection: probably destroyed during the Second World War
Exhibition history: unknown

Comments: This may be one of two busts for which Ivor was awarded a £20 Landseer Prize by the Royal Academy in December 1936 (IRJ File, Lib 2 136, Archives, Royal Academy, London). A photograph of the work exists in the archive of the Henry Moore Institute, Leeds (F/1/31, HMI, Leeds).

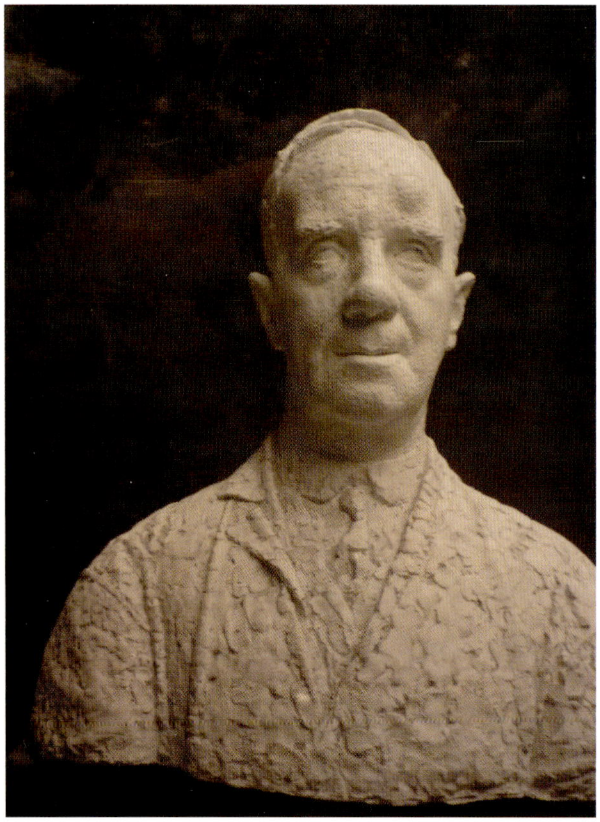

4 *Head and Shoulders of a Mature Adult Male*

c. 1936–37
Plaster
Life-sized
Collection: work was probably destroyed during the Second World War
Exhibition history: unknown

Comments: The head is reminiscent of contemporary portraiture by sculptors such as Sir William Reid Dick (1879–1961) and Sir Charles Wheeler (1892–1974). Ivor later mentioned to Peter Cannon-Brookes that, while a student at the Royal Academy Schools (1935–39), he had met Reid Dick, and for a while there was talk of him working as Reid Dick's assistant to improve his understanding of portrait sculpture (IRJ to Dr Peter Cannon-Brookes, 15 September 1982, IRJ File, Department of Art, NMW, Cardiff). This may be one of two portrait busts for which Ivor was awarded a £20 Landseer Prize by the Royal Academy in December 1936 (IRJ File, Lib 2 136, Archives, Royal Academy, London). A photograph of the work exists in the archive of the Henry Moore Institute, Leeds (F/1/32, HMI, Leeds).

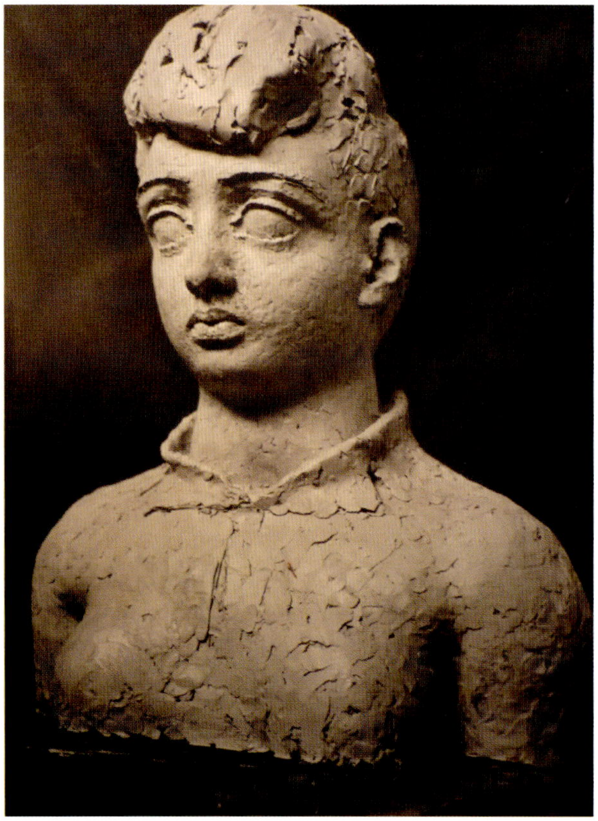

5 *Elizabeth*

1946
Plaster
Life-sized
Collection: whereabouts unknown
Exhibition history: unknown

Comments: This head suggests Ivor was paying close attention to contemporary portraiture by Frank Dobson. A photograph of the work exists in the archive of the Henry Moore Institute, Leeds (F/1/11, HMI, Leeds).

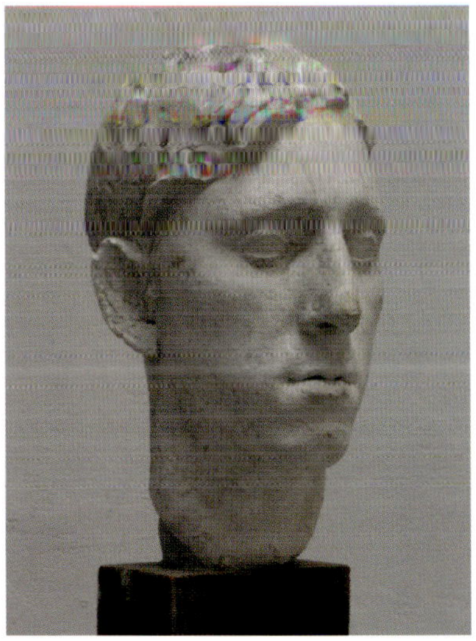

6 *Head of a Boy*

c. 1946–48
Plaster
31.7 x 18.7 x 23.5 cm
Collection: private collection
Exhibition history: Wolsey Art Gallery, Ipswich, December 1999–January 2000.

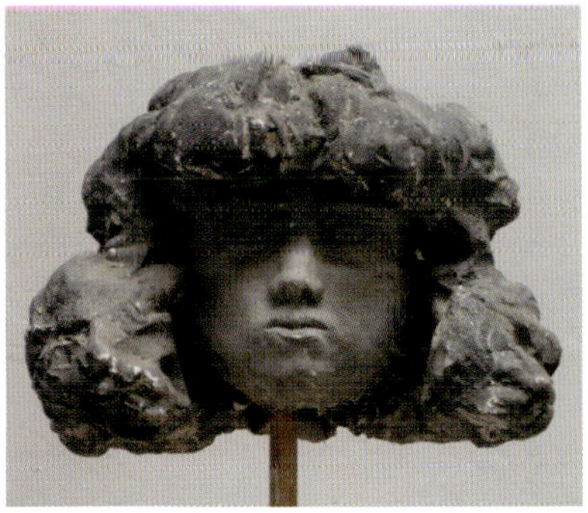

7 *Head of a Woman/Monica Roberts-Jones?*

1950s
Plaster
30.2 x 21.3 x 30.8 cm
Collection: Goldsmiths College, London
Exhibition history: Wolsey Art Gallery, Ipswich, December 1999–January 2000.

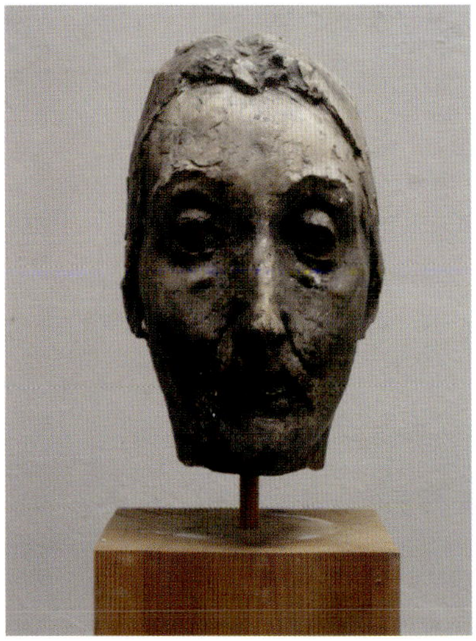

8 *Tacita*

1950s
Plaster
27.3 x 17.2 x 22.9 cm
Collection: private collection
Exhibition history: Wolsey Art Gallery, Ipswich, December 1999–January 2000; Chappel Galleries, Chappel, Essex, July 2000

Comments: The sitter was an Anglo-Italian friend of Monica Roberts-Jones; Ivor was attracted by the 'Egyptian' quality he perceived in her head.

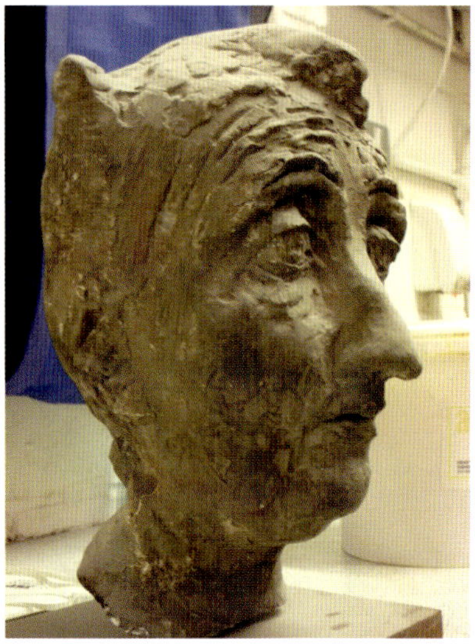

9 *Louise Griffiths*

c. 1952–53
Plaster
31.1 x 20.3 x 22.2 cm
Collection: Goldsmiths College, London
Exhibition history: Society of Portrait Sculptors, Imperial Institute, South Kensington, London, November–December 1953 (88)
Related work: 9a: *Study of Mrs Griffiths*, c. 1950–52, pen and ink on paper, 38.7 x 24.3 cm, HMI, Leeds

9a

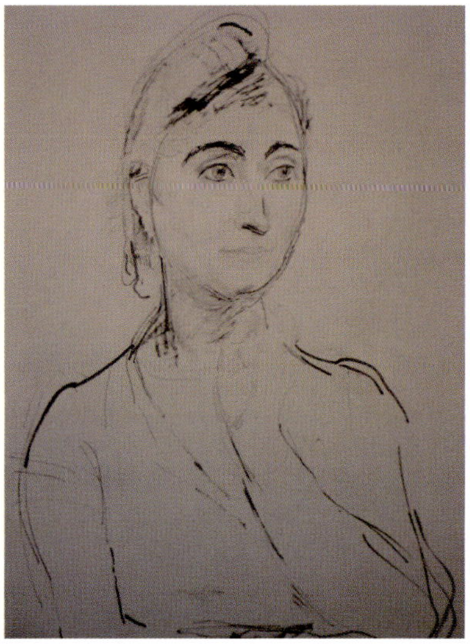

Comments: The sitter was apparently Ivor's much-loved and talkative charlady at his London home of 31 St James's Gardens. Ivor was a founder member of the Society of Portrait Sculptors during the summer of 1953. Other founder members and exhibitors in 1953 included Ivor's old friend and fellow student from the Royal Academy Schools, Daphne Hardy (1917–2003), his future mentor Charles Wheeler (1892–1974), artists he regarded with a wary admiration such as Jacob Epstein and Frank Dobson, established British realists such as Gilbert Ledward (1888–1960) and Lawrence Bradshaw (1899–1978), and a number of émigrés from Eastern Europe such as Franta Belsky (1921–2000), Wili Soukop (1907–1999), Benno Schotz (1891–1984), Arthur Fleischmann (1896–1990) and Eric Schilsky (1898–1974). Also participating in the inaugural exhibition of the Society of Portrait Sculptors were three female sculptors with whom Ivor was friendly: Eva Castle, Josephina de Vasconcellos and Fiore de Henriquez. In the year prior to the exhibition, de Henriquez began giving the painter Augustus John lessons in modelling clay for sculpture, and may have recommended Ivor to the painter as another possible tutor in the technique (Michael Holroyd, *Augustus John: The New Biography* [London: Vintage, 1997], p. 592).

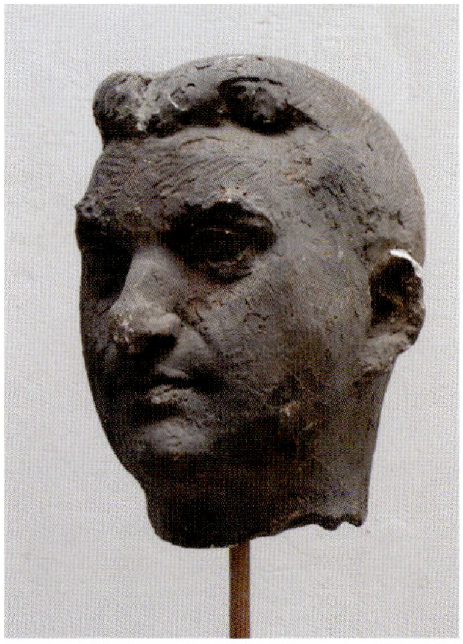

10 *William Pleeth*

c. 1952–53
Plaster
25.8 x 21.6 x 24.8 cm
Collection: Goldsmiths College, London
Exhibition history: exhibited: Society of Portrait Sculptors, Imperial Institute, South Kensington, London, November–December 1953 (76)

Comments: Pleeth (1916–1999) was born in London to Polish-Jewish parents. He studied the cello from the age of six; aged thirteen, in 1929, he won a two-year scholarship to the prestigious Klengel Conservatory in Leipzig. He moved back to London in 1933 and was then appointed soloist of the City of Birmingham Symphony Orchestra. During the Second World War he served in the army, and in 1942 married the pianist Margaret Good. From 1948 to 1978 he was professor of the cello at the Guildhall School of Music, where, from 1955 to 1961, one of his pupils and protégés was the gifted Jacqueline du Pré (1945–1987). In 1952–53 he established the Allegri String Quartet, which he led until 1967. He was also a visiting professor at the Royal College of Music and at the Menuhin School from 1977 to the late 1980s. He was made an OBE in 1980 and died in Finchley, north London, in April 1999. After his death he was described as 'one of Britain's finest cellists ... he was a major artist in his own right whose career might have gone further and higher with greater drive and ambition' (*The Times*, 8 April 1999, p. 25).

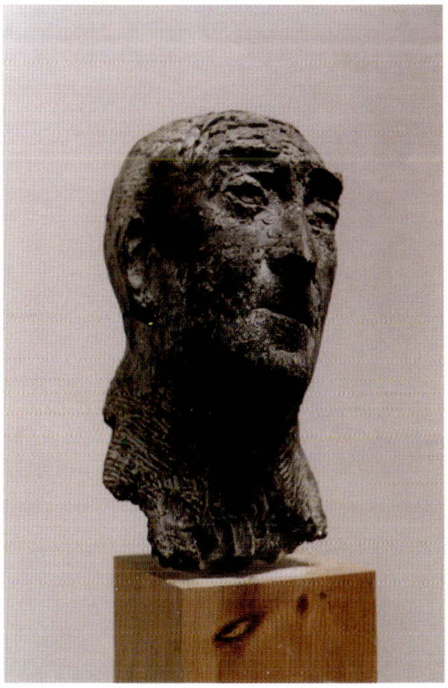

11 *Clive Gardiner*

1953–59
Bronze
40 x 24.2 x 27.3 cm
Collection: Goldsmiths College, University of London; Beaverbrook Art Gallery, Fredericton, New Brunswick, Canada and the Arts Council UK
Exhibition history: John Moore's Exhibition, Walker Art Gallery, Liverpool, 1958; Oriel Gallery, Cardiff, July–September 1978 (15); Wolsey Art Gallery, Ipswich, December 1999–January 2000; Society of Portrait Sculptors, London, May 2006 (54)

Comments: Gardiner (1891–1960) was the headmaster of Goldsmiths School of Art from 1929 to 1958, and was much loved by his students. Born in Blackburn, he studied at the Slade School of Art under Henry Tonks and, between 1909 and 1914, at the Royal Academy Schools. After service in the First World War he started teaching part-time at Goldsmiths in 1918. He provided a series of murals for the Rubber Pavilion at the British Empire Exhibition at Wembley (1924–25), and later for London University's Students' Union. From 1926 he was regularly employed as a poster designer for the Underground Electric Railway and its successor in 1933, the London Passenger Transport Board (LPTB). Between the wars he introduced British commercial art to the rigour of Cézanne, Braque, Derain and Léger, and also did much to encourage the young Graham Sutherland in his early poster work for the LPTB.

In 1936 he held a one-man show of paintings and watercolours, which revealed his love of landscape, and especially of Cézanne. In 1942 the Ministry of Food appointed him as an art adviser to the British Restaurants Mural Programme. In this capacity he worked closely with Lady Clark at the British Institute of Adult Education, and with the Council for the Encouragement of Music and the Arts. At Goldsmiths he encouraged his students to experiment with every facet of art – architectural, decorative, pictorial, illustrative and literary – in pursuit of a common purpose. Gardiner died on 14 May 1960 at his home in Chelsea (*The Times*, 20 May 1960, p. 17). After his death the Warden of Goldsmiths College praised Gardiner for being a consummate talent-spotter, quick to detect ability in promising students such as Sutherland, Eric Fraser and Carel Weight and encourage them to develop. Moreover, he had possessed 'a most warm and charming personality, a quick perception and a penetrating mind and a wonderful sense of humour'. His 'strawberry tea' for the School of Art was the highlight of the year for his students (*The Times*, 24 May 1960, p. 17).

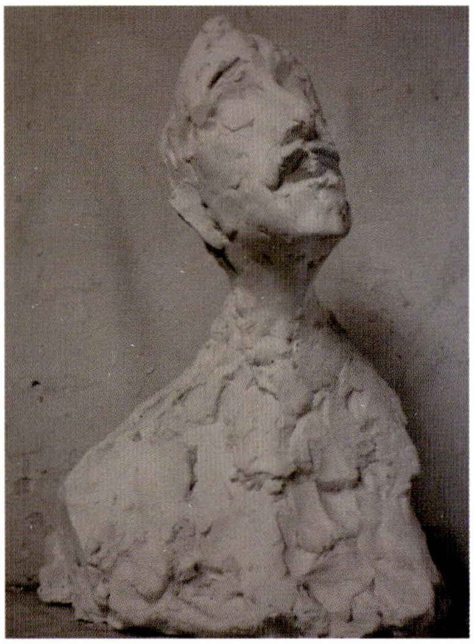

12 *Small Portrait of Kyffin Williams*

c. 1954
Plaster
18 cm high
Collection: private collection
Exhibition history: unknown

Comments: The treatment of this small narrow plaster head, resting on only slightly broader shoulders, is reminiscent of a series of portraits Giacometti produced around 1955–58 of his brother Diego, such as the bronze *Bust of Diego* (1955) which entered the Tate's collection in 1965. It is likely that Ivor knew of Giacometti's post-war sculpture from his old friend from the Royal Academy Schools, Daphne Hardy, who was friendly with Giacometti in the 1950s.

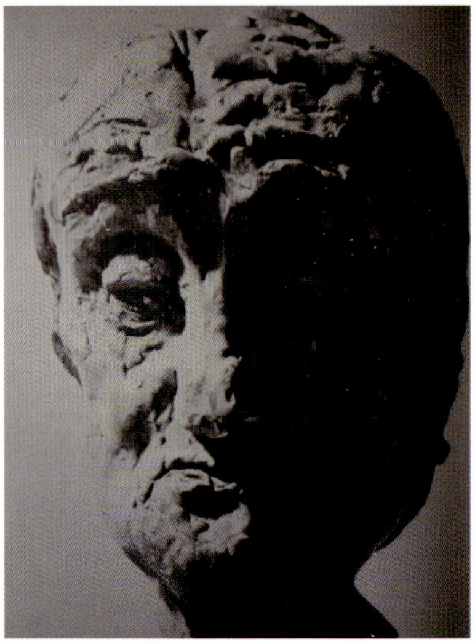

13 *Mother of Judas*

1954
Bronze
40.6 x 35.5 x 22.8 cm
Collection: private collection, Wales
Exhibition history: Summer Exhibition, Beaux Arts Gallery, Bruton Place, London, July 1954; Oriel Art Gallery, Cardiff, July–September 1978 (2); Royal National Eisteddfod of Wales, Llangefni, Anglesey, July–August 1983 (12)

Comments: The sitter was 'a refugee woman who ran a stall in Shepherd's Market, London. The title was derived from late medieval German art, and the 'figure of the grieving woman [was] suggestive of ... miserable tranquillity alongside prolonged sorrow' (Peter Cannon-Brookes, *Ivor Roberts-Jones: The Journey to Harlech* [London: Trefoil Books, 1983], p. 73).

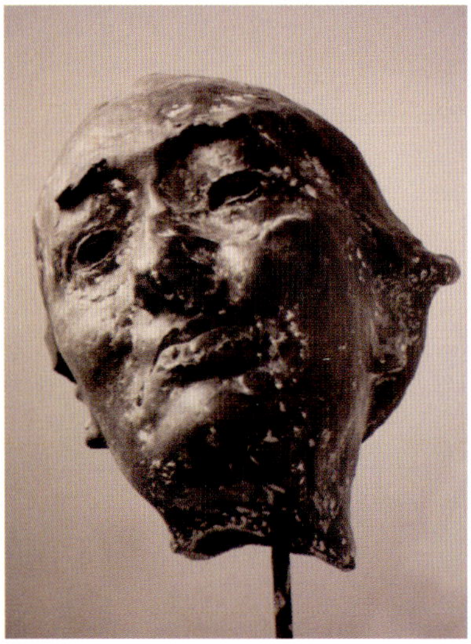

14 *Elizabeth Watt*

1956–57
Bronze
25.4 x 22.8 x 28.9 cm
Collection: private collection, Switzerland; estate of Ivor Roberts-Jones (plaster cast)
Exhibition history: Wolsey Gallery, Ipswich, December 1999–January 2000

Comments: The sitter had worked as Sir Kenneth Clark's secretary. Ivor mentioned the head to the architect Raymond Erith in January 1957. He also mentioned this head in correspondence with the architect Raymond Erith in January 1957: 'Miss Watt is now at the bronze foundry – but hasn't got to the furnace stage yet' (IRJ to Raymond Erith, 26 January 1957, Erith Papers, RIBA Archive, V&A Museum, London).

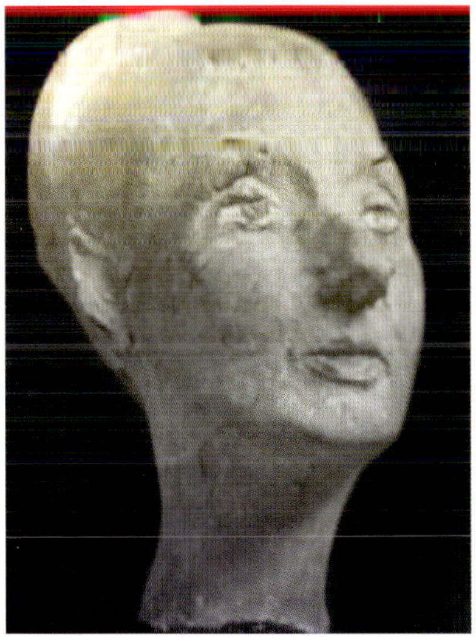

15 *Dorothy*

1957
Bronze
36 cm high
Collection: private collection
Exhibition history: Sculpture in 1961, National Museum of Wales, Cardiff, July–September 1961 (50).

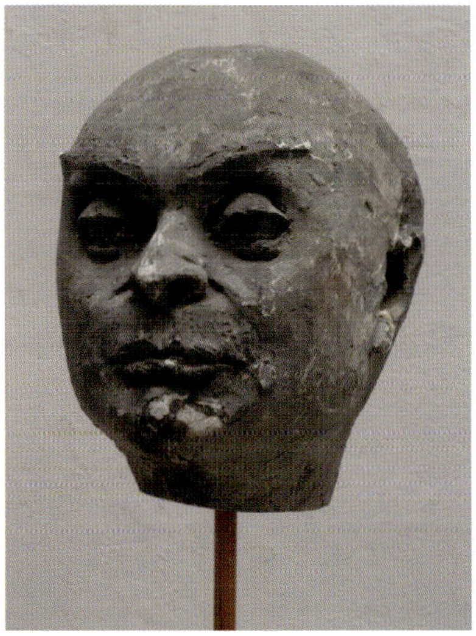

16 *Sir John Rothenstein CBE*

1957
Plaster
24.8 x 20.7 x 24.8 cm
Collection: private collection, London
Exhibition history: unknown

Comments: Sir John Knewstub Maurice Rothenstein (1901–1992) CBE was the son of the eminent painter Sir William Rothenstein (1872–1945), and was educated at Bedales and at Worcester College, Oxford. After meeting a wide circle of artists through his father, such as Augustus John, Eric Gill, Henry Moore, John Piper, Barbara Hepworth, Wyndham Lewis and Stanley Spencer, he was appointed director of the City Art Gallery, Leeds, in 1932. Around this time he converted to Roman Catholicism, and supported the careers of ecclesiastical architects such as Edward Maufe and Raymond Erith. In June 1938 he was appointed director of the Tate Gallery – a post he held until the spring of 1964. Rothenstein was knighted in 1952, but over the next three years had to expend much energy resisting sustained efforts by his trustees – who disagreed with his attempts to purchase the work of contemporary artists such as Moore, Marini, Manzu, Picasso and Giacometti – to have him removed. After his death he was judged to have 'spread the appreciation of a generation of English artists whose work he had known as he had grown up' (*The Times*, 28 February 1992, p. 15).

Ivor wrote to Raymond Erith in May 1957: 'Rothenstein is coming over to have his head "done" – I think I intimidated him because I had a hammer in my hand and was in my shirtsleeves when he came in (IRJ to R. Erith, 15 May 1957, Erith Papers, RIBA Archive, V&A Museum, London). Erith replied: 'I am glad to hear you are doing a head for Rothenstein. Be careful with the hammer!' (Raymond Erith to IRJ, Erith Papers, RIBA Archive, V&A Museum, London). Three years later, in July 1960, Rothenstein played a key role in ensuring that the trustees of the Tate purchased a bronze cast of Ivor's portrait head of Paul Claudel. This was reproduced in Rothen stein's article on him, published in *The Studio* in September 1978. Rothenstein also later owned a bronze cast of Ivor's *Small Head of a Man*.

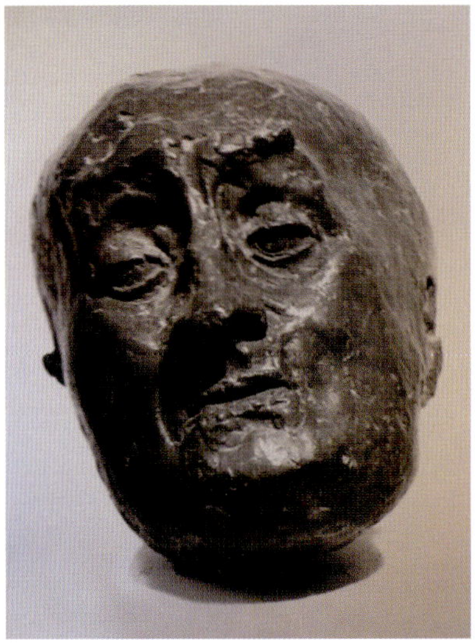

17 *Paul Claudel*

1957–59
Bronze
45.5 x 22.7 x 26.2 cm
Collection: Tate London
Exhibition history: Oriel Gallery, Cardiff, July–September 1978 (19); Royal National Eisteddfod of Wales, Llangefni, Anglesey, July–August 1983 (19); Wolsey Art Gallery, Ipswich, December 1999–January 2000

Comments: Claudel (1868–1955) was a devoutly Roman Catholic poet, diplomat, dramatist and younger brother of sculptress Camille Claudel (1863–1943) – for many years Rodin's mistress. He joined the French diplomatic service in 1893, and soon after began publishing poetry influenced by Rimbaud, symbolism and his intense Roman Catholic faith. He served as French ambassador to Japan (1922–28), then the United States (1928–33) and finally Belgium (1933–36), whereafter he retired. Politically conservative, he loathed National Socialism and Communism equally. After the French defeat in June 1940 he emerged as a prominent supporter of Pétain. However, as Pétain's Vichy regime became more openly anti-Semitic after October 1940, he turned against it and, in 1941, was placed under house arrest. He welcomed General de Gaulle's return to France in July 1944, and two years later was elected a member of the prestigious Académie Française. On his death, *The Times* described Claudel as 'one of the most original and significant literary figures in France' (*The Times*, 24 February 1955, p. 10).

In July 1960 a bronze cast of the head was purchased by the Tate Gallery. Its director, Sir John Rothenstein, wrote to Ivor: 'We hope to have Claudel on view shortly. It is a long time since I have known the Board so unanimously impressed by the work of an artist hitherto unrepresented in the collection' (Sir John Rothenstein to IRJ, 27 July 1960, IRJ File, Archives, Tate Gallery, London).

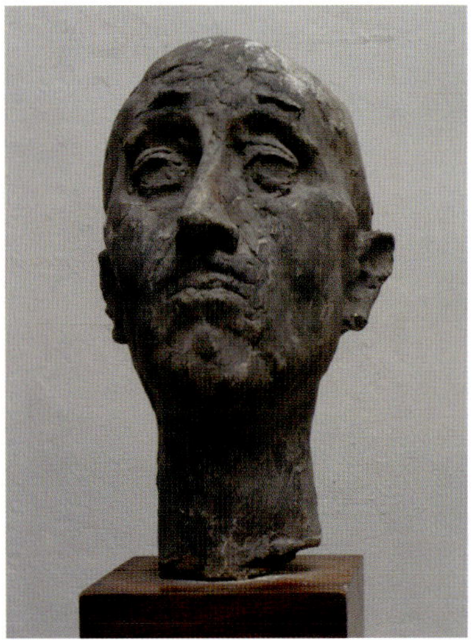

18 *Head of an Adult Male*

c. 1958
Painted plaster
32.4 x 20.6 x 25.4 cm
Collection: private collection
Exhibition history: Chappel Galleries, Chappel, Essex, July–August 2000

Comments: The sitter was a mature evening student at Goldsmiths College, whose military bearing caught Ivor's attention.

18

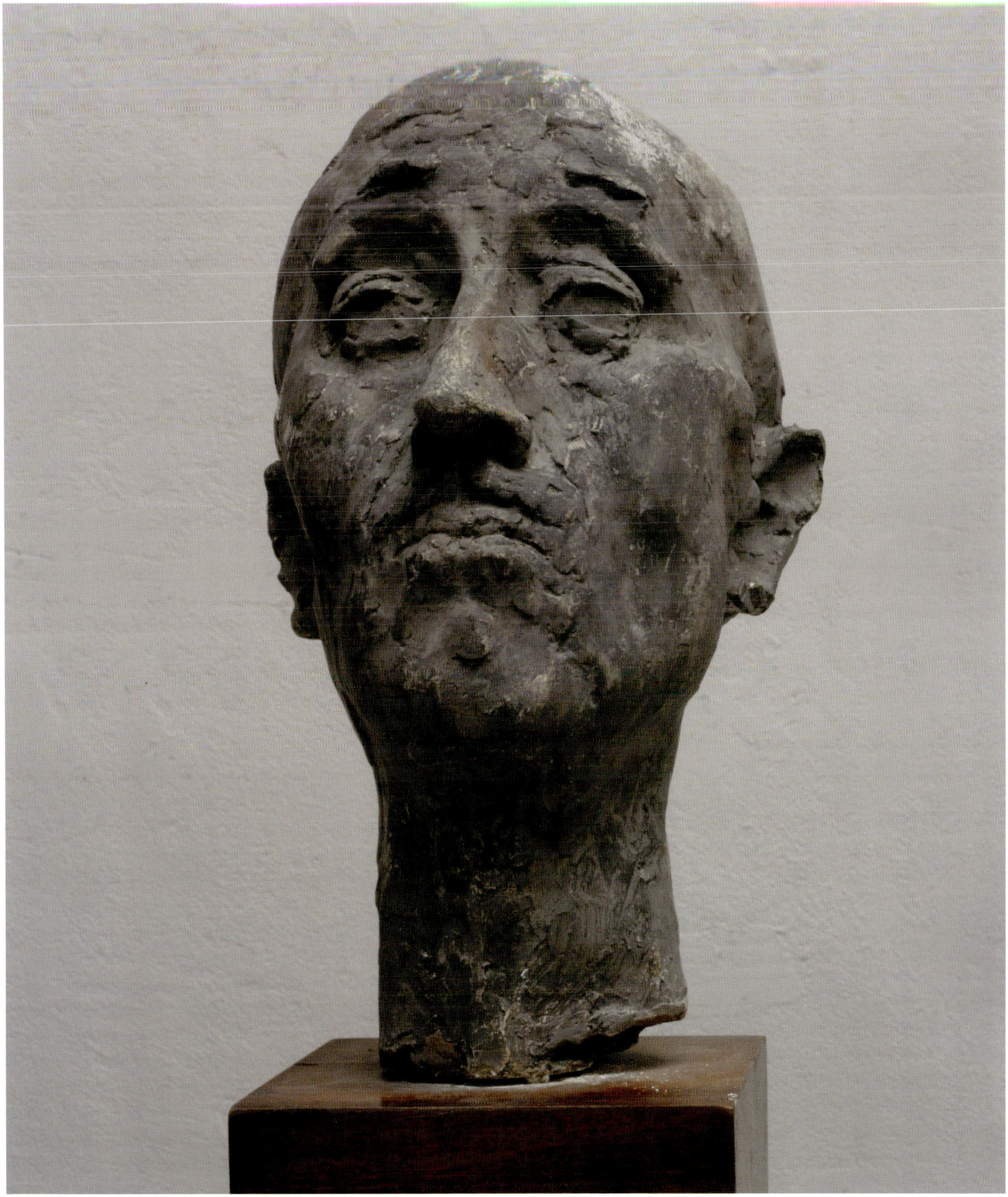

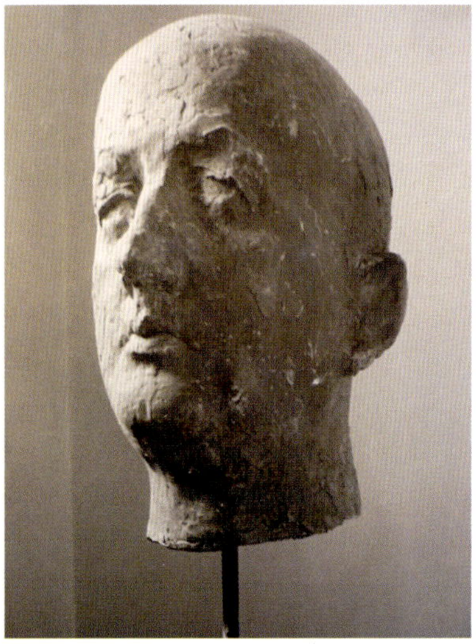

19 *Jack Pullen*

c. 1958
Plaster
Life-sized
Collection: private collection
Exhibition history: unknown

Comments: The sitter was a fellow tutor of Ivor's at Goldsmiths College.

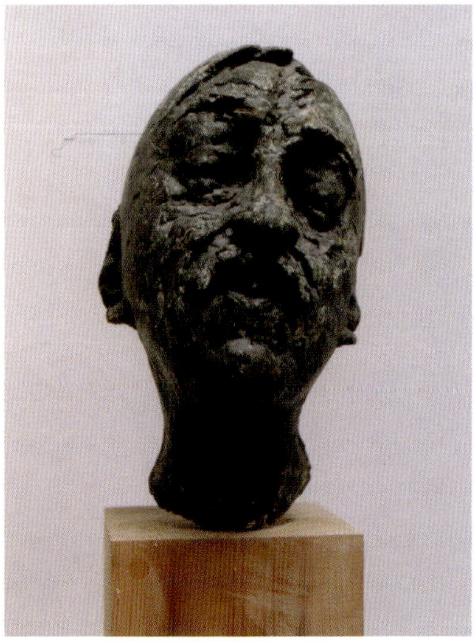

20 *Kyffin Williams*

1959
Bronze
33 x 15.9 x 28 cm
Collection: National Museum of Wales, Cardiff; Oriel Ynys Môn, Anglesey
Exhibition history: Royal Academy, London, May 1965 (1125); Oriel Gallery, Cardiff (16); Royal National Eisteddfod of Wales, Llangefni, Anglesey, July–August 1983 (5); Wolsey Art Gallery, Ipswich, December 1999–January 2000; Albany Gallery, Cardiff, August–September 2008

Comments: Sir John Kyffin Williams (1918–2006) was born in Llangefni, Anglesey, into a family of gentlemen farmers. His father was a bank manager at nearby Chirk. Educated privately at Shrewsbury School, he served first as a private (1936–38) then as a lieutenant in the Royal Welch Fusiliers, until 1941, when he was invalided out of the service with epilepsy. He was advised to take up painting, and trained at the Slade School of Art under Professor Randolph Schwabe from 1941 to 1943. While at the Slade, he fell in love with the art of Piero della Francesca, and years later lamented the failure of art schools to continue to teach rigorous draughtsmanship. In 1944 he was appointed part-time senior art master at Highgate School – a post he retained until 1973. A pupil of his later years recalled that Williams always wore 'a coat of Welsh tweed and a Royal Welch Fusiliers tie', and delighted in reading out the racing stories of Damon Runyon (*The Times*, 6 September 2006, p. 63).

Williams had his first solo show at the Colnaghi Gallery in 1948. His standing as an accomplished painter of the North Wales landscape of Gwynedd was confirmed by his inclusion in the 1949 Arts Council exhibition *Twenty-Five Paintings by Contemporary Artists*. He later took a negative view of most art produced after 1950. In 1968 he was awarded a Winston Churchill Fellowship to paint Welsh ancestors in Patagonia. Two years later he was elected an ARA, and in 1974 was made a full Academician. His paintings greatly appealed to the pillars of the Welsh establishment, such as the Marquess of Anglesey, who helped Williams to move to live on the island in 1974 (Meic Stephens in the *Independent*, 2 September 2006, p. 40).

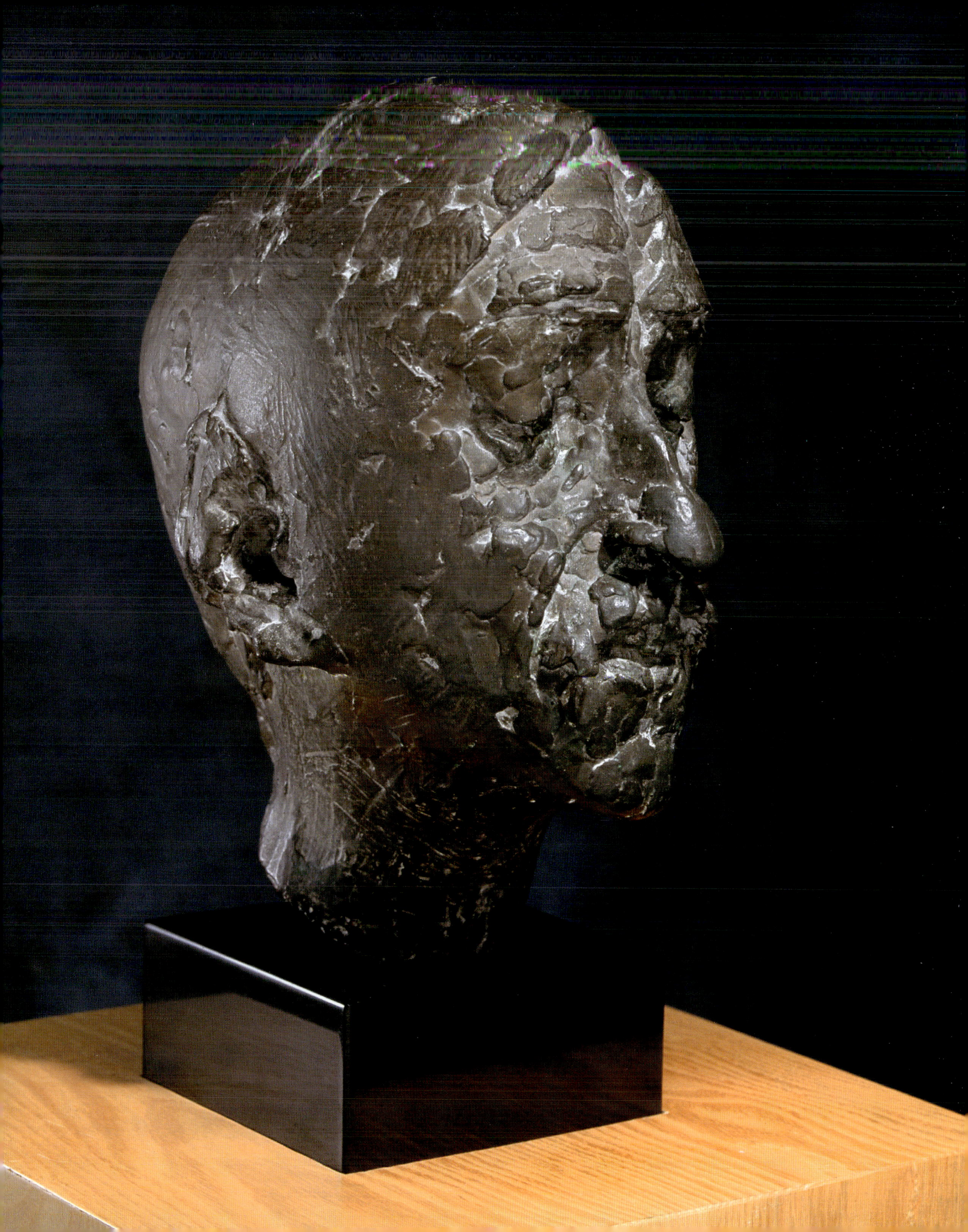

For many years he was president of the Royal Cambrian Academy in Conwy (1969–1976 and 1992–2006); he was awarded the OBE in 1982 and knighted in 2000. He was an early and highly vocal critic of the 'young British artists' of the 1990s. He never learned to speak Welsh, though his mother was a fluent Welsh-speaker (*Western Mail and Echo*, 2 September 2006, p. 2). He struggled with his epilepsy throughout his life and died after a long struggle with cancer. After his death the opera singer Bryn Terfel remarked that 'every true Welsh home has to have a Kyffin' (*The Times*, 2 September 2006, p. 20). He was apparently blessed with 'an iconic scruffiness and a self-deprecating sense of humour ... able to attract a continuing stream of devoted and beautiful women', though he never married (*Western Mail*, 22 August 2008, p. 10). It has been said that he was 'Wales's greatest ever artist', and that 'he saw himself as the first artist the people of Wales could relate to ... He was proud of Wales but bitterly critical of the country's politicians for failing to build a new National Gallery of Welsh Art' (*Western Mail*, 22 August 2008, p. 10).

In the autumn of 1959 it was Williams who suggested to Rollo Charles, the Keeper of Art at the National Museum of Wales, Cardiff, that the museum purchase Ivor's portrait head of him – then on display at the New Art Centre in London (Rollo Charles to Caryl Whineray, the New Art Centre, 41 Sloane Street, 24 November 1959). The head was purchased for £84 (IRJ File, Department of Art, NMW, Cardiff). When he heard his portrait had indeed been bought, Williams wrote to Charles in 1960:

> I am no grand man like Ivor's work. It was a great thing for him to have my head bought by the Museum as he was getting very fed up with his lack of success. He is certainly the best portrait sculptor in the country now Epstein has gone but because he doesn't do the rounds of artists' cocktail parties, he gets no commissions, in desperation he has now taken up writing plays for TV. (Kyffin Williams to Rollo Charles, c. April 1960, IRJ File, Department of Art, NMW, Cardiff).

21 *Old Man/Sam Rabin*

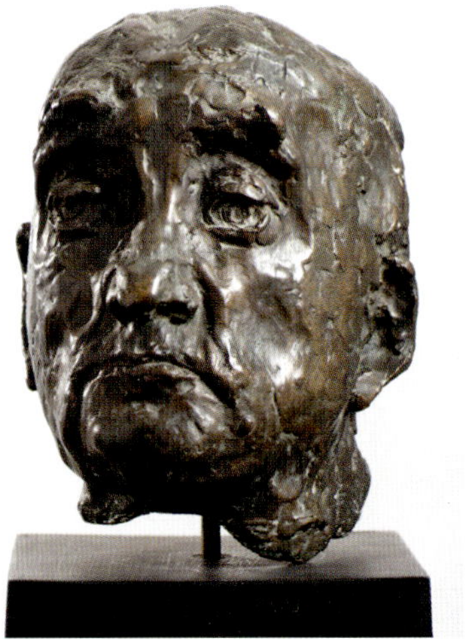

1960
Bronze
40 cm high
Collection: National Museum of Wales, Cardiff (Welsh Arts Council Collection); Beaverbrook Art Gallery, Fredericton, New Brunswick, Canada
Exhibition history: Oriel Gallery, Cardiff, July–September 1978 (17)

Comments: Sam Rabin/Samuel Rabinovitch (1903–1991) taught life drawing at Goldsmiths College between 1949 and 1965. Among his students were Mary Quant, Tom Keating and Bridget Riley. Born to Russian-Jewish parents in north Manchester, he trained first under Adolph Valette, alongside L. S. Lowry and James Fitton, and then at the Slade School of Art (1921–24) under Henry Tonks and John Mansbridge. In the mid 1920s he visited Paris, where he was introduced to Charles Despiau, who encouraged him to take up sculpture full-time. However, between the wars, as he could not prosper as a sculptor, he made his living as a boxer and as the wrestler known as Rabin the Cat. Indeed, in 1928, he won a bronze medal in wrestling for Britain at the Amsterdam Olympics. Five years later he appeared as a wrestler in the 1933 Korda film *The Private Life of Henry VIII*, and as a Jewish boxer in the 1934 film version of *The Scarlet Pimpernel*. Later, in the 1950s he was befriended by William Roberts and Augustus John, both of whom were impressed by his paintings and drawings inspired by boxing matches. In 1960 he held an exhibition of his boxing paintings at the Leicester Galleries in London. Five years later he left Goldsmiths to teach at Bournemouth College of Art. On leaving the college in 1985, he was given a retrospective at Dulwich Picture Gallery. A passionate advocate of rigorous draughtsmanship, he was dismissive of Cubism and abstraction but unstinting in his praise of Degas (*The Times*, 24 December 1991, p. 18).

The Welsh Committee of the Arts Council bought a bronze cast of the head early in 1961. In October of the same year, Lady Dunn (the wife of Sir James Dunn) gave the Beaverbrook Art Gallery, Fredericton, New Brunswick a bronze cast of the work. In April 1978 Ivor wrote to the Curator at the Beaverbrook Art Gallery: 'The Old Man is based on Sam Rabin – who was a very fine lithographer and draughtsman and who was also a good sculptor in his early years. He had also been an Olympic boxer and an "all-in" wrestler in his youth – which I think is rather implicit in the head' [IRJ to Roger Lamb, 8 April 1978, Archives, Beaverbrook Art Gallery, New Brunswick, Canada].

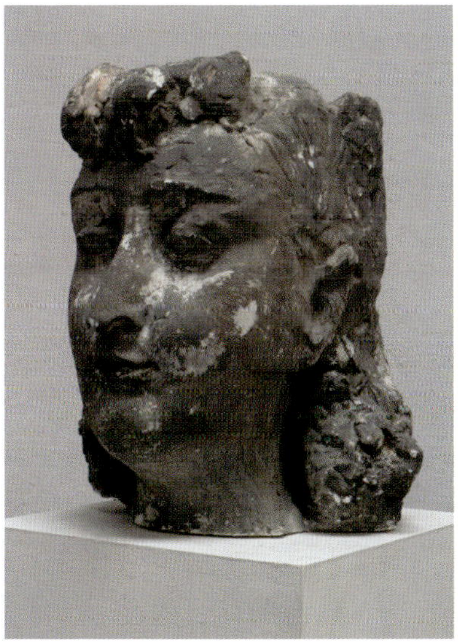

22 *Head of a Young Girl*

1960–61
Plaster
30.5 x 26 x 26.4 cm
Collection: Goldsmiths College, London
Exhibition history: Sculpture in 1961, National Museum of Wales, Cardiff, July–September 1961 (54).

23 *The Hon. Richard Rhys/Rees*

1960–61
Plaster
45.6 cm high
Collection: private collection
Exhibition history: Sculpture in 1961, National Museum of Wales, Cardiff, July–September 1961 (58)

Comments: Sir Richard Lodowick Edward Montagu Rhys (1900–1970), who also used the surname Rees, was an editor, critic, painter and patron of the arts. In particular, he was a great support to an often impecunious George Orwell (1903–1950), one of Ivor's favourite writers, and to the economic historian and

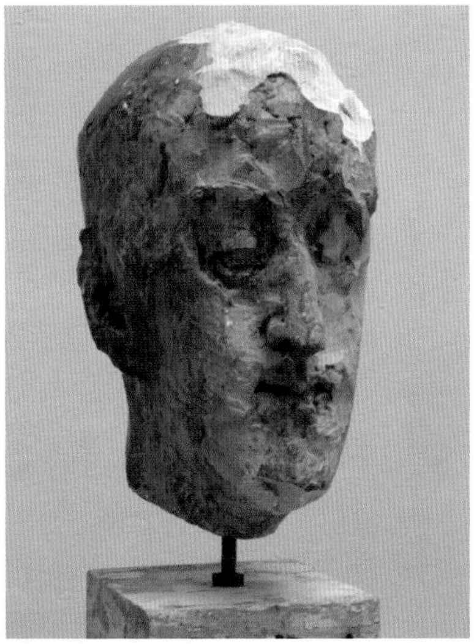

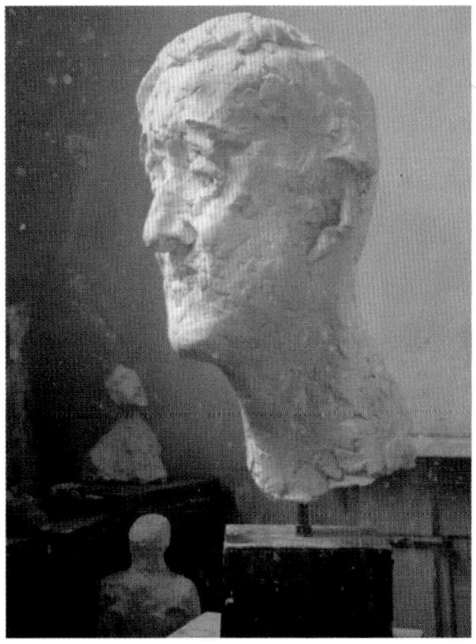

socialist thinker Richard Henry Tawney (1880–1962). From a family with strong Welsh origins, he was educated at Eton and Trinity College, Cambridge. Rees/ Rhys joined the diplomatic service after university, serving as attaché at the British embassy in Berlin in 1922–23. He left the Foreign Office in 1925 to become a lecturer for the Workers' Educational Association for the next two years. In 1930 he was appointed editor of the left-wing *Adelphi* magazine – where one of Orwell's first published articles appeared in 1931 – and remained in the post until 1937. He is reputed to be the model for the character Ravelston in Orwell's 1936 novel *Keep the Aspidistra Flying*. During the Spanish Civil War, Rhys drove an ambulance behind Republican lines, and in the Second World War he served in the Royal Navy. He was awarded the Croix de Guerre for bravery by the French. In 1958 he published a joint study of D. H. Lawrence and Simone Weil, and three years later a revealing biography of his old friend Orwell – of whose literary estate he was one of the executors – entitled *George Orwell: A Fugitive from the Camp of Victory*. Between 1962 and his death he translated many articles and essays by Simone Weil into English. He was also R. H. Tawney's literary executor, and did much to champion his writings and the work of the Workers' Educational Association, of which Tawney had been president from 1928 to 1944 (Peter Davison, ed., *George Orwell: A Life in Letters* [London: Penguin, 2011], p. 520).

Ivor mentioned the head in a November 1960 letter to Sir John Rothenstein, predicting that it was 'going to be one of my best' (Ivor to Sir John Rothenstein, 9 November 1960, IRJ File, Archive, Tate Gallery, London).

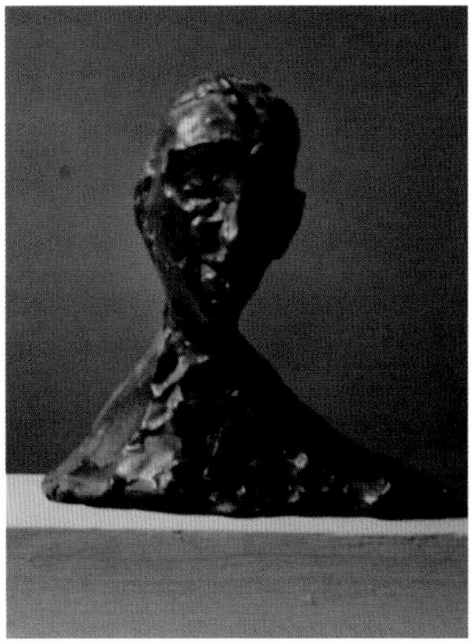

24 *Small Head of a Man*

c. 1960–61
Bronze
12 cm high
Collection: private collection

Comments: The work was made for Elizabeth Watt (q.v.).

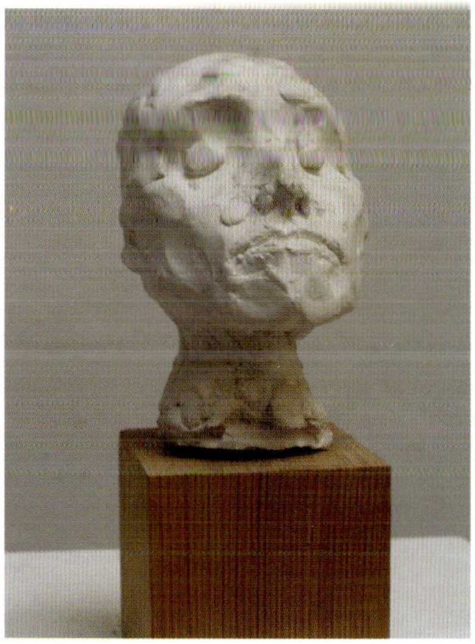

25 *Small Head of a Man*

c. 1961
Plaster
10 cm high
Collection: private collection

Comments: Ivor gave this head as a gift to Kyffin Williams in the early 1960s, to thank Williams for his assistance in ensuring the National Museum of Wales's purchase of a cast of Ivor's portrait head of the painter.

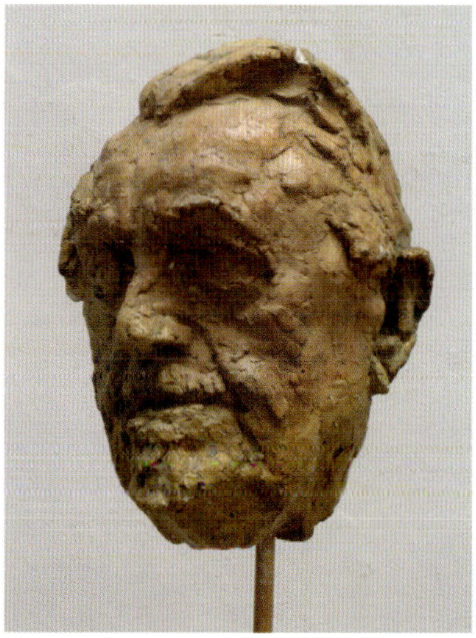

26 *Pat Millard*

c. 1961–63
Plaster
28.9 x 22.6 x 24.8 cm
Collection: estate of Ivor Roberts-Jones
Exhibition history: unknown

Comments: Millard was a colleague of Ivor's in the Faculty of Art at Goldsmiths College.

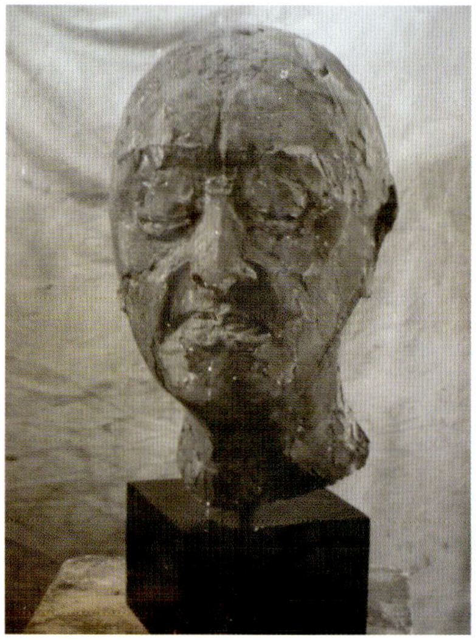

27 *W. Somerset Maugham CH*

1961–62
Bronze
33.7 x 19.7 x 26 cm
Collection: Beaverbrook Art Gallery, Fredericton, New Brunswick, Canada
Related work: 27a: *Skin Study of Somerset Maugham*, 1961–62, plaster, 32.8 x 22.6 x 25.7 cm, private collection
Exhibition history: Oriel Gallery, Cardiff, July–September 1978 (20); plaster cast, Wolsey Art Gallery, Ipswich, December 1999–January 2000

Comments: William Somerset Maugham (1874–1965) was an acclaimed playwright, short story writer and novelist. While training as a doctor at St Thomas's Hospital, Lambeth, he published his first novel, *Liza of Lambeth* (1897). Other well-received publications included *Of Human Bondage* (1915), *The Moon and Sixpence* (1919), *On a Chinese Screen* (1922), *Ashenden, or, the British Agent* (1928), *Cakes and Ale* (1930) and *The Razor's Edge* (1944). In 1962 he published a volume of memoirs,

27a

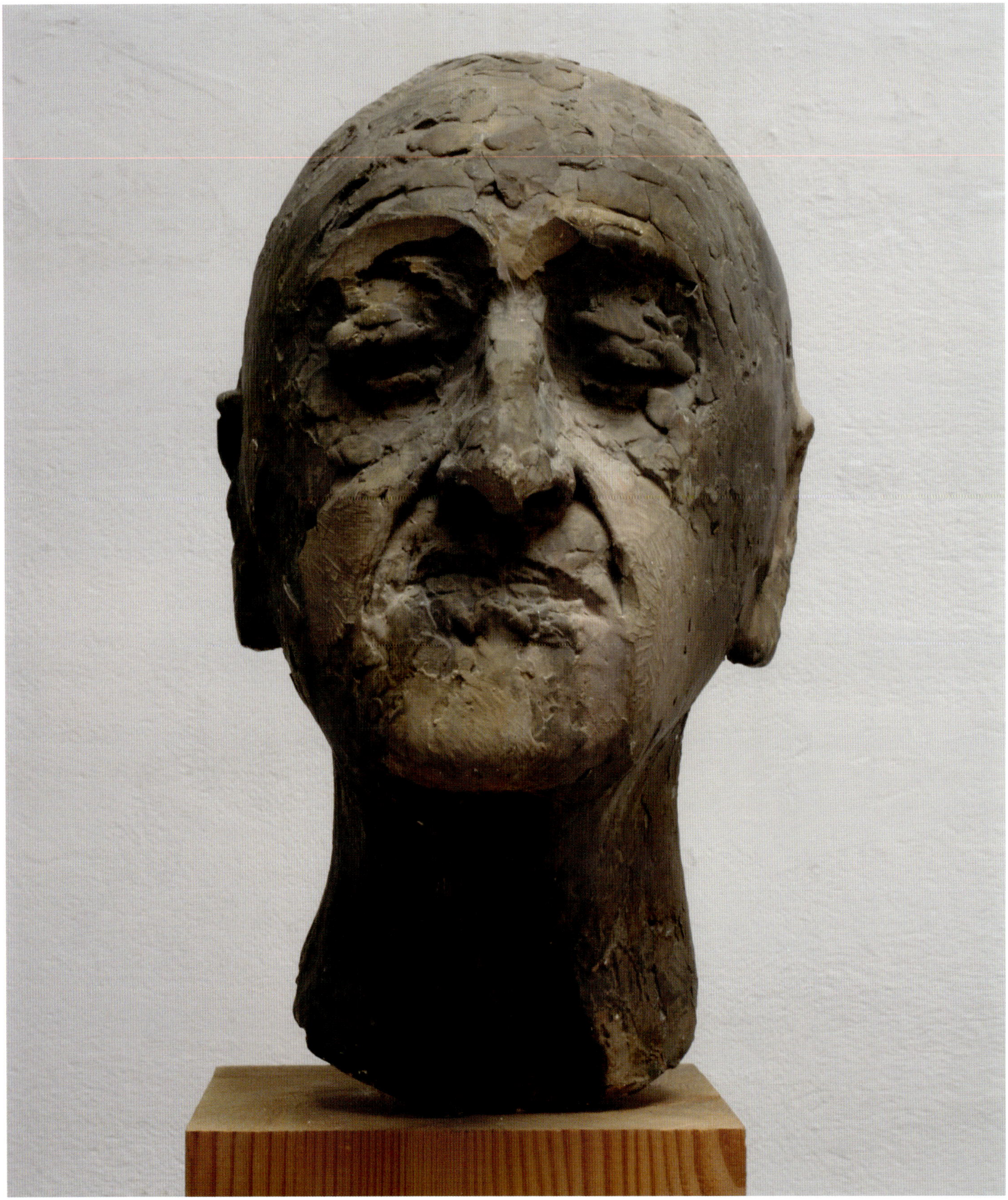

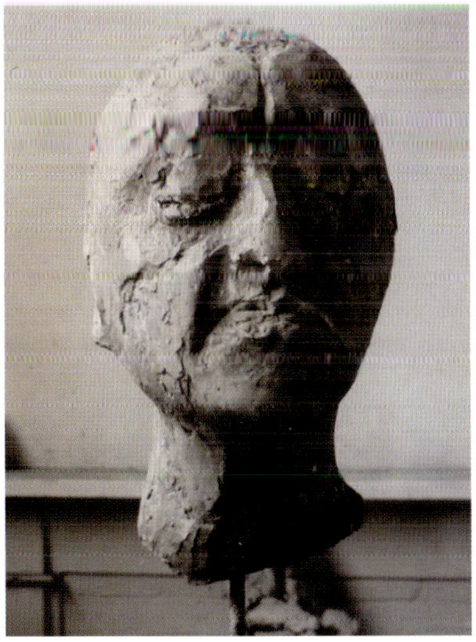

Looking Back, which was serialised in the *Daily Express*, owned by Lord Beaverbrook. A homosexual for much of his life, from 1944 to his death Maugham's constant companion was Alan Searle. *The Times* described Maugham at his death in December 1965 as 'the most assured English writer of his time [and] the most celebrated of English authors. No writer of his generation graced the world of English letters with more complete or more polished assurance.' His writing was notable for 'the detachment and precision of his observation of men and manners, his ironic sense of the human comedy, his worldly good sense and mastery of technical means and ends'. He was also a notable art collector of work by Graham Sutherland, Matisse, Picasso, Renoir and Gauguin. His portrait was also painted by Graham Sutherland and long-time friend Sir Gerald Kelly (*The Times*, 17 December 1965, p. 17).

According to Ivor, writing to the Beaverbrook Art Gallery, Fredericton, New Brunswick, Canada in 1977, the head of Maugham was commissioned directly from him by press baron Max Aitken, First Lord Beaverbrook (1879–1964), owner of the *Daily Express* (from 1916) and the *London Evening Standard*. When his head of *Claudel* (q.v.) was bought by the Tate a photograph of it was reproduced in *The Times*, and this 'prompted Lord Beaverbrook to commission me to do the Somerset Maugham'. He added that he thought that along with *Old Man Sam* (q.v.), Maugham was one of 'my best portrait heads – done at a time when I had few commissions and simply did heads of my friends' (Ivor to Robert Lamb, 8 April 1977, Archives, Beaverbrook Art Gallery, Fredericton, New Brunswick, Canada).

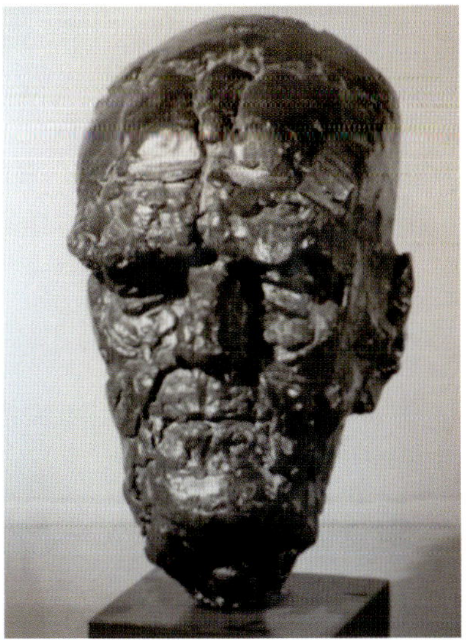

28 *Sir William Emrys Williams*

1962–63
Bronze
36 x 21 x 26 cm
Collection: Arts Council Collection, Southbank Centre, London
Exhibition history: unknown

Comments: A Mancunian of Welsh extraction, Williams (1896–1977) was successively secretary of the British Institute of Adult Education (1934–40), director of the Army Bureau of Current Affairs (1941–45), secretary general of the Arts Council (1951–63) and secretary of the National Arts Collections Fund (1963–70). He was knighted for services to the arts in 1955. The cultural commentator Robert Hewison has described Williams as a 'Welsh–Mancunian who became one of the most powerful cultural mandarins in the country' and as 'the arch-manipulator of patronage in a good cause' (Robert Hewison, *Culture and Consensus: England, Art and Politics since 1940* [London: Methuen, 1997], pp. 80–1).

In May 1984 Ivor wrote to the Arts Council that the head of Williams had been commissioned directly from him 'by the Welsh Arts Council', and that Sir William had

> purchased a copy for himself ... I think it could have been about 1965 (?). Sir William was very fond of the head but I was extremely unhappy about it. At about the same time I did two other heads and they also share the same characteristics – they are all three over life-size, exaggerated beyond my

capacities at the time and, as I came to see later, generally unsatisfactory. One is in the National Museum of Wales [Ivor is referring here to his head of the Fifth Lord Kenyon] and [then] there is this [one] ... [O]n re-seeing the one in Cardiff, I decided to undertake to replace [it]. The sitter was willing and I did so. The other 'got lost' – but Bill's I could do nothing about as he was genuinely fond of it ... I think Bill's is the best of the three but to have so missed out on the irreverent mischief in his head is a terrible failure. (Ivor to Margaret Wagstaff, 2 May 1984, IRJ File, Archives, Arts Council, London).

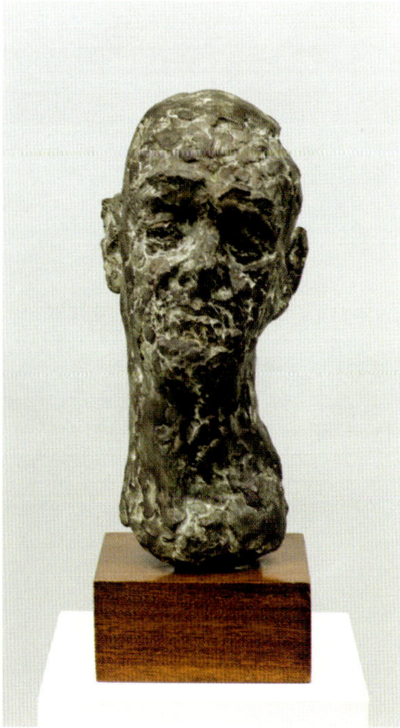

29 *The Fifth Lord Kenyon*

1962–63
Bronze
42.5 x 19.8 x 24.7 cm
Collection: National Museum of Wales, Cardiff
Exhibition history: unknown

Comments: Lloyd Tyrell-Kenyon (1917–1993) was born on the Welsh Borders, the eldest son of the Fourth Baron Kenyon, a courtier to both Edward VII and George V. He succeeded his father aged ten, in 1927. Educated at Eton and Magdalene College, Cambridge, he worked at the Fitzwilliam Museum in the late 1930s as a curator before serving with the Shropshire Yeomanry and the Royal Artillery during the Second World War, until in 1943 he was invalided out of the army with failing eye-sight. After the war he was elected president of the University College of North Wales, Bangor (1947–82), and then served as president of the National Museum of Wales, Cardiff, between 1952 and 1957. In 1966 he was appointed chairman of the trustees of the National Portrait Gallery, London, stepping down 22 years later, in 1988.

Extremely proud of his Welsh heritage, he re-launched the Gregynog Press in 1978, assiduously promoted Welsh poetry and literature, and sat on the Ancient Monuments Board for Wales from 1979 to 1987. During the 1980s he played a key role in establishing a collection of Victorian portraiture and furniture at Bodelwyddan Castle, near St Asaph in North Wales. On his death *The Times* noted: 'Despite a jovial exterior ... Kenyon had his share of calamities in the family and was never in the best of health. He bore everything with a quiet sense of humour' (*The Times*, 20 May 1993, p. 19).

Lord Kenyon presented the first portrait to the NMW, Cardiff, in May 1963, and it was formally added to the collection three months later (Lord Kenyon to Registrar, NMW, Cardiff, 12 August 1963, IRJ File, Archive, NMW, Cardiff). In 1978 Ivor asked Lord Kenyon to sit once again for a portrait, and this was 'acquired by the National Museum of Wales with the assistance of the sculptor on condition that the earlier sculpture should remain in the Museum's study collection during the life of the sitter' (Cannon-Brookes, *Ivor Roberts-Jones*, p. 69).

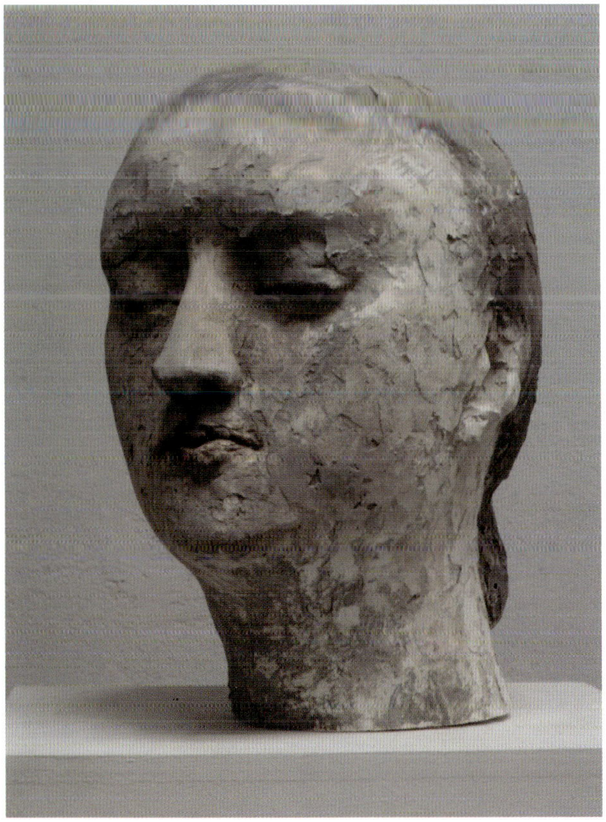

30 *Head of a Young Woman*

c. 1963–65
Plaster
27.3 x 19.7 x 24.5 cm
Collection: The Hepworth Wakefield
Exhibition history: Wolsey Gallery, Ipswich, December 1999–January 2000

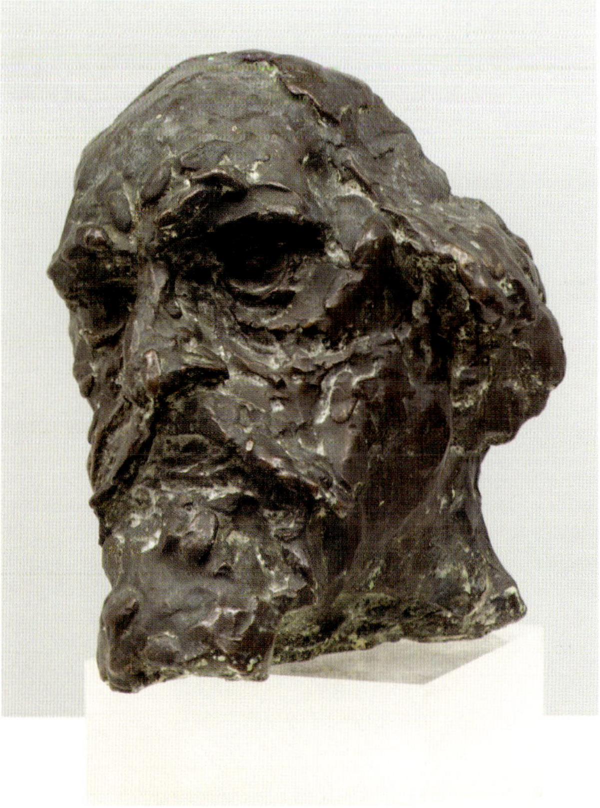

31 *Augustus John OM, RA*

1964–65
Bronze
17.4 cm high
Collection: National Museum of Wales, Cardiff
Exhibition history: Oriel Gallery, Cardiff, July–September 1978 (21)

Comments: This head is an early study for the head of Ivor's first full-length public bronze statue – the *Augustus John Memorial*, Fordingbridge, Hampshire (Cat. 132). This was commissioned from him early in 1964, and was unveiled by Earl Mountbatten in October 1967. The head was used as a focal point to raise funds for the memorial when its appeal was launched in 1965. In the early 1950s John became interested in sculpture, and was given some instruction in portrait modelling by Fiore de Henriquez (Holroyd, *Augustus John*, p. 592). It is possible it was through de Henriquez that John first became aware of Ivor's work: both exhibited at the Society of Portrait Sculptors in 1953, and de Henriquez visited the 1954 summer group exhibition at the Beaux Arts Gallery, which included some of his work. John appears to have heard of him by the time of Ivor's first solo show, held at the same gallery in 1957. In July 1960, eighteen months before his death, John suggested to the Contemporary Art Society for Wales that it commission Ivor to make a bronze statue of the former prime minister David Lloyd George for Parliament Square in London. John had been very impressed by Ivor's head of painter Kyffin Williams (q.v.) he had seen exhibited earlier that year at the National Museum of Wales in Cardiff (D. Brynmor Anthony to Augustus John, 9 July 1960, John Papers, MS 22800E 21, National Library of Wales, Aberystwyth).

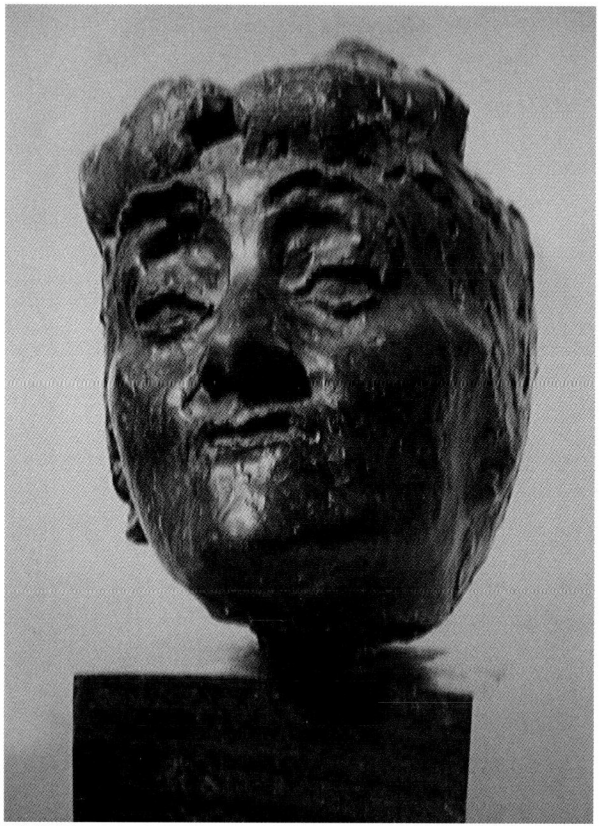

32 *Helen Roeder*

c. 1965
Bronze
27.3 x 21.3 x 33 cm
Collection: private collection (bronze); estate of Ivor Roberts-Jones (plaster)
Exhibition history: Royal Academy, April 1974 (1319); Oriel Gallery, Cardiff, July–September 1978 (14); plaster cast, Wolsey Gallery, Ipswich, December 1999–January 2000

Comments: Painter, poet and short story writer Roeder (1909–1999) was the partner of painter Carel Weight (1907–1997), who had been a part-time student at Goldsmiths College from 1929 to 1932, where his tutor was Clive Gardiner. Weight met painting student Helen Roeder at Goldsmiths in 1929, though they did not get married until 1990. During the 1930s Roeder was secretary to the Industrial Design Partnership of Misha Black, Milner Grey and Partners, and after the war, with her fine command of German, worked as a translator for the Warburg Institute. Weight went on to become professor of painting at the Royal College of Art (1957–73), and was elected to the Royal Academy in 1965 and appointed a Companion of Honour in 1995. In the 1950s Roeder took up painting again, and in 1958 published a well-received study of poet Denton Welch. She exhibited her townscapes and landscapes regularly in London – the last in 1993, with Weight, at the New Grafton Gallery (David Wolfers, 'Helen Roeder', *Independent*, 28 August 1999, p. 24).

Roeder and Weight were part of a social circle that included Oskar Kokoschka and Fred Uhlman (whom Roeder met in the late 1930s as part of her work helping refugees in London), Sir Kenneth Clark, Sir William Coldstream, Ruskin Spear and Leonard Rosoman, with whom Ivor was friendly from the 1950s onwards (Nicholas Usherwood, 'Secrets of the Suburbs', *Guardian*, 15 August 1997, p. 18).

33 *Small Head of a Man/Square Head*

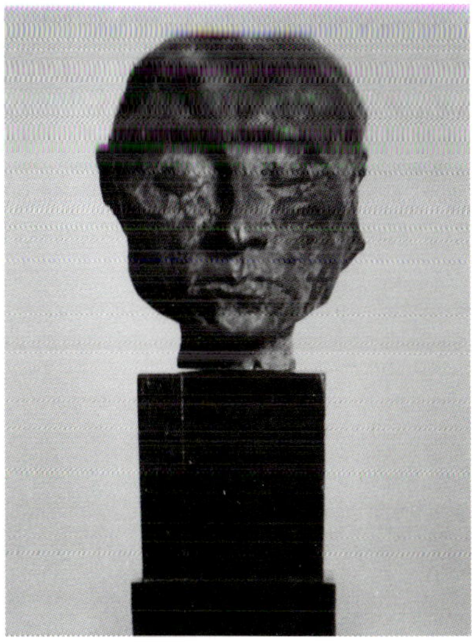

1965
Bronze
9.2 cm high
Collection: private collection x 2
Exhibition history: unknown

Comments: The work was made for Sir John Rothenstein (q.v.), who was impressed by its 'mysterious' and 'Ancient Egyptian' quality (IRJ to Dr Peter Cannon-Brookes, 29 December 1981, IRJ Papers, Archives, NMW, Cardiff).

34 *Paul Drury*

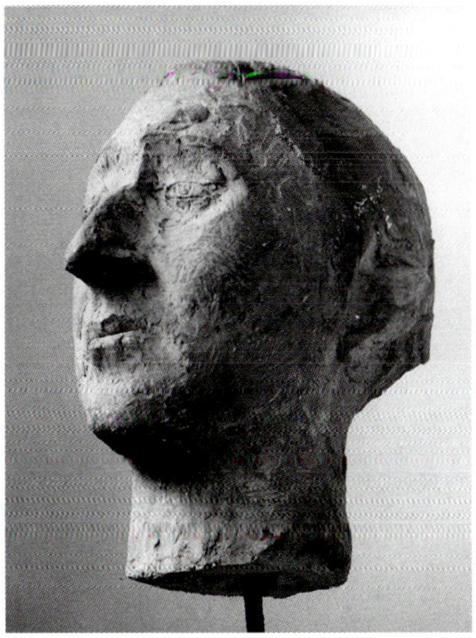

c. 1965–66
Painted plaster
29.2 x 21 x 26 cm
Collection: private collection
Exhibition history: Wolsey Art Gallery, Ipswich, December 1999–January 2000

Comments: Paul Drury (1903–1987) was educated at Westminster School and at Goldsmiths College, where he studied painting between 1921 and 1924. Until the outbreak of the Second World War he taught painting and etching, much informed by his admiration for Samuel Palmer, at the Central School of Art and Design and the Heatherley School of Fine Art. After wartime service in the plaster workshop of the facial reconstruction team at Queen Mary's Hospital, Roehampton, he returned to Goldsmiths to teach in 1947, and in 1966 was appointed principal of the School of Art at the college; he held this post for the next four years. Between 1970 and 1975 Drury was the president of the Royal Society of Painter-Printmakers. He was the son of the accomplished late-nineteenth-century sculptor Alfred Drury (1856–1944), who in his younger days had been a studio assistant to the great French realist sculptor Aimé-Jules Dalou (1838–1903). Apart from the fact that Drury was his boss at Goldsmiths, Ivor may have wished to make a portrait of him since Drury had been blinded in his left eye at the age of ten while playing with an air rifle with his younger brother. After his death Drury was widely praised as a talented early exponent of what became known in the 1940s as 'neo-romanticism' in landscape painting, and as one of the most overlooked of Britain's most distinguished etchers and portrait draughtsmen of the inter-war period (*Daily Telegraph*, 20 May 1987, p. 26).

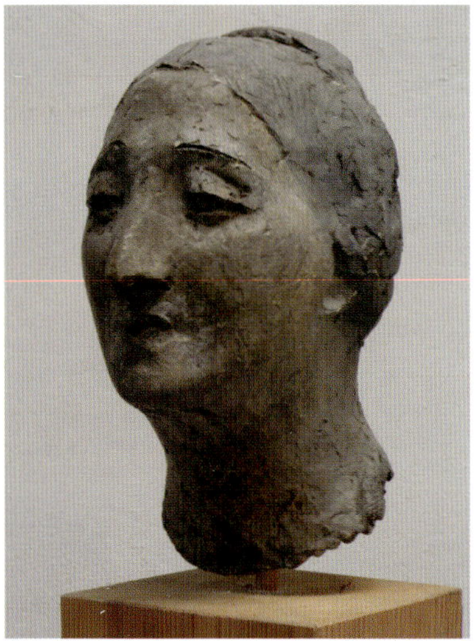

35 *Mrs. Swears*

1966
Plaster
31.7 x 19.4 x 23.2 cm
Collection: private collection
Exhibition history: unknown

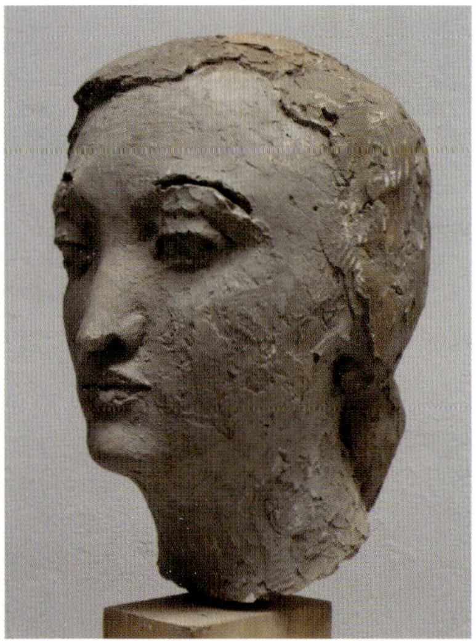

36 *Head of a Young Woman*

c. 1967
Painted plaster
14.7 x 32.7 x 26.3 cm
Collection: private collection
Exhibition history: Wolsey Art Gallery, Ipswich, December 1999–January 2000

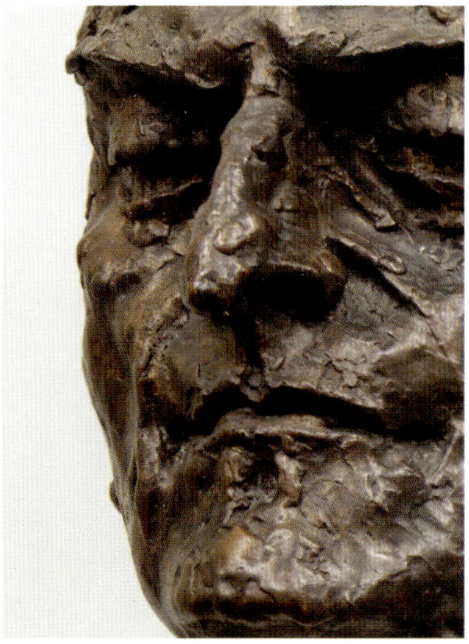

37 *Yehudi Menuhin OM, KBE*

c. 1966–67
Bronze
27.5 x 23.2 x 26.6 cm
Collection: Highgate School, London; National Museum of Wales, Cardiff; National Portrait Gallery, London
Exhibition history: Royal Academy, May 1968 (1150); Royal National Eisteddfod of Wales, Llangefni, Anglesey, July–August 1983 (6); Wolsey Art Gallery, Ipswich, December 1999–January 2000

Comments: A brilliant violinist and accomplished conductor, Menuhin (1916–1999) had his debut concert performance as a violinist in Berlin in 1929, and recorded the Elgar Violin Concerto in 1932 aged only sixteen. Memorably, he was to play at Belsen concentration camp in April 1945, only a few weeks after its liberation by British troops. He took up residence in the United Kingdom in 1958, and was

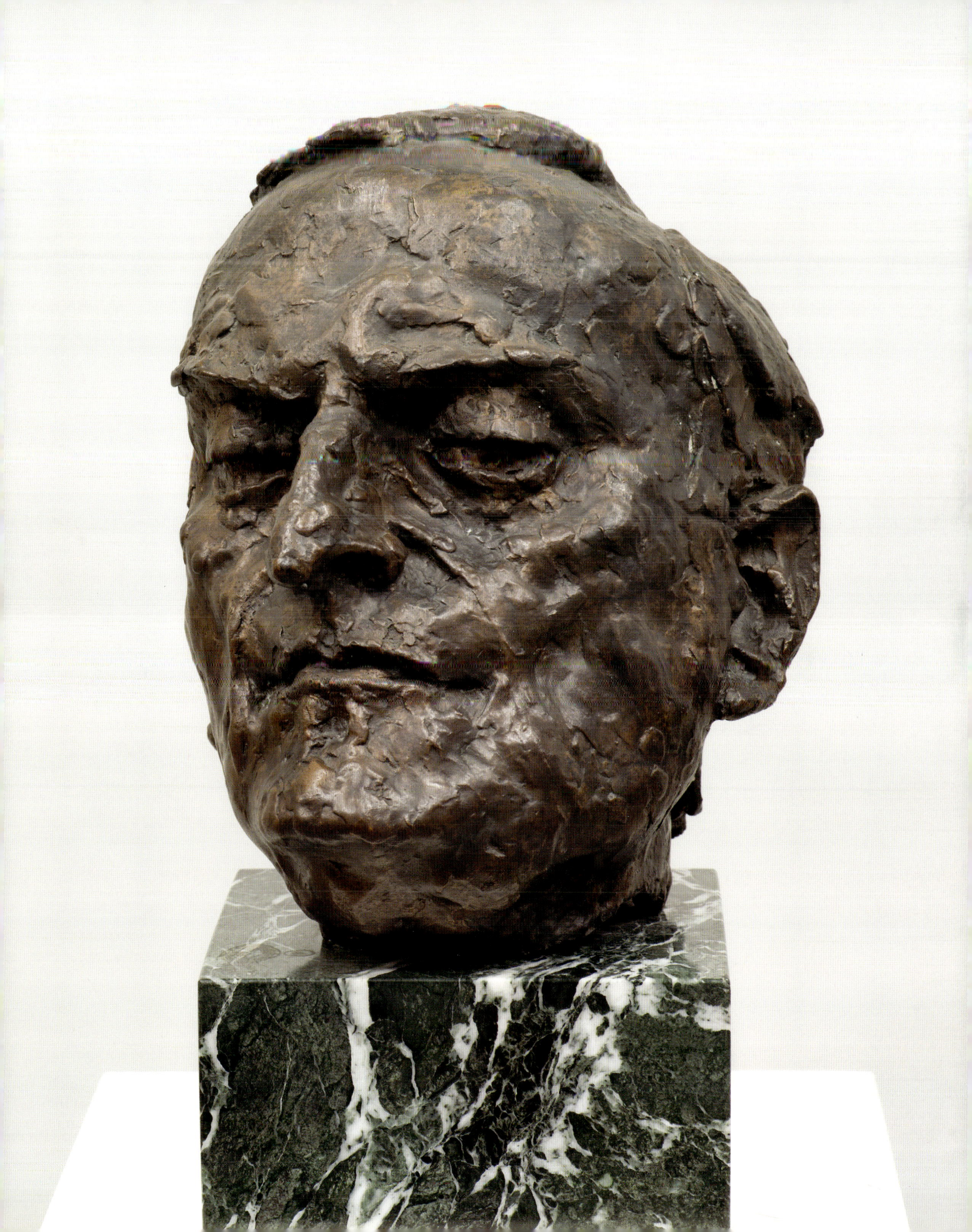

awarded an honorary knighthood in 1965. From 1958 to 1968 he was director of the Bath Festival of Music. In 1985 he became a British citizen, and he was created a Life Peer in 1993 (*Guardian*, 13 March 1999, p. 19).

It would seem that Ivor had Kyffin Williams to thank for this commission, which was for Highgate School where Williams taught. Menuhin made it clear from the outset that no sittings were possible, so Ivor based the head on a combination of his memories and a series of drawings as Menuhin imperiously conducted during rehearsals (Cannon-Brookes, *Ivor Roberts-Jones*, p. 69). Many years later Ivor wrote to Robin Gibson, registrar at the National Portrait Gallery, which had just purchased a cast of the Menuhin head, that

> I did it during rehearsals for the Brahms Trio recordings he did with Barry Tuchwell [*sic*] ... I think the head does suggest the vigour of his attack on certain passages in these performances. It impressed me very much – the extremely charming aspects of his character that rather get in the way of the toughness a musician just has to have at his level hadn't led me to expect this. I was amazed, for instance, at the difference between one 'take' and another, done after a 'playback' when they decided to make the violin passage 'a little stronger'. I expected a subtle alteration – you know something I'd hardly detect. In fact I was very nearly blown out of my seat!

Barry Emmanuel Tuckwell OBE (1931–), was an Australian-born horn player and principal French horn for the London Symphony Orchestra (1955–1968). The Brahms Trio referred to may be the Trio for Violin, Horn and Piano in E Flat Major, Op. 40 – a performance with Menuhin playing the violin was recorded on 18–30 July 1966 and released in March 1968 (IRJ to Robin Gibson, 7 December 1982, IRJ File, Archives, NPG, London). Gibson replied: 'I very much agree with you what you say about the head showing the vigour of Menuhin's attack. I think this was one of the things which impressed me when I saw it in the salerooms' (Robin Gibson to IRJ, 14 December 1982, IRJ File, Archives, NPG, London).

In May 1971 Kyffin Williams suggested to the keeper of art at the NMW, Cardiff, that he 'might acquire a cast of [Ivor's] Augustus John statue for placing somewhere outside the Museum' (Rollo Charles to IRJ, 4 May 1971, IRJ Archive, NMW, Cardiff). The museum decided in the end that it could not afford the full-sized figure of John, but members of its Art Purchasing Committee were very taken with the head of Menuhin that Williams personally brought in to the museum to show them (Rollo Charles to IRJ, 9 July 1971, IRJ Papers, Archives, NMW, Cardiff). The Museum finally bought the head in October 1971 for £1,200, which at that time was the largest sum Ivor had received for a portrait head. The keeper of art at the museum wrote to Ivor: 'I like the head and am glad we're getting it!' (Rollo Charles to IRJ, 7 October 1971, IRJ papers, Archives, NMW, Cardiff).

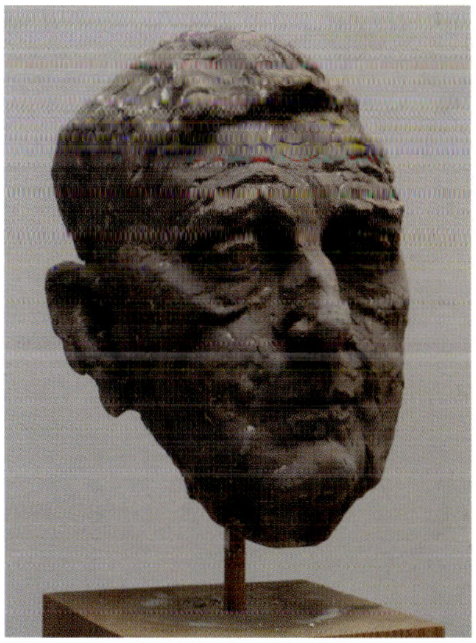

38 *Head of a Man*

c. 1971
Plaster
34 x 20.6 x 25.4 cm
Collection: estate of Ivor Roberts-Jones
Exhibition history: Chappel Galleries, Chappel, Essex, July–August 2000

Comments: There is a related drawing, dated 21 December 1971 (pencil and chalk, 25.2 × 17.5 cm) in the collection of the estate of Ivor Roberts-Jones.

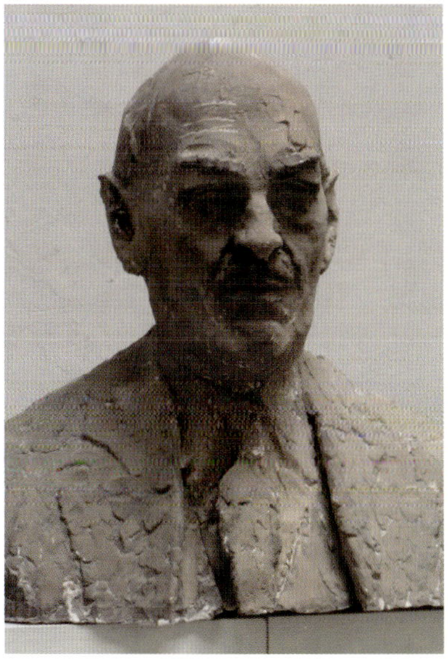

39 *Oliver Lyttelton, Lord Chandos, DSO, MC*

c. 1972–73
Plaster
51.4 x 52.7 x 42.2 cm
Collection: estate of Ivor Roberts-Jones
Exhibition history: plaster (edition of five), Royal Academy, London, May 1974 (1278); Wolsey Art Gallery, Ipswich, December 1999–January 2000

Comments: Oliver Lyttelton (1893–1972) was educated at Eton and Trinity College, Cambridge. During the First World War he saw distinguished service in the Grenadier Guards and was awarded the Distinguished Service Order and Military Cross for bravery and leadership under fire. From the early 1920s he went into business, first becoming managing director of the British Metal Corporation Ltd, and later chairman of Associated Electrical Industries. He was elected a Conservative MP in 1940 and retained his seat until 1954. Highly regarded by Churchill, he was successively minister of state for the Middle East (1941–42) and minister for production (1942–45). Returning to politics when Churchill won the general election of October 1951, he was appointed secretary of state for the colonies. In September 1954 he was ennobled as First Viscount Chandos and moved to the House of Lords. Between 1962 and 1971 he was the first chairman of the National Theatre – where he frequently clashed with Kenneth Tynan (1927–1980), the theatre's literary manager (1963–72). The ground-floor Lyttelton Theatre is named after him in recognition of his huge contribution to the creation and continuing existence of the National Theatre (see *The Memoirs of Lord Chandos*, London: The Bodley Head, 1962, and Simon Ball, *The Guardsmen: Three Friends and the World They Made*, HarperCollins: London, 2004).

In September 1969 Chandos was part of the initial informal Winston Churchill Statue Committee formed by John Tilney MP. At its very first meeting, Chandos argued that Oscar Nemon's statue should not be automatically accepted and that the work of other – British – sculptors should be inspected. A few months later he was part of the four-man sub-committee formed to judge the competition for a statue of Winston Churchill for Parliament Square. In March 1970, after taking advice from the Royal Fine Art Commission, the director of the V&A and the president of the Royal Society of British Sculptors, the sub-committee invited nine sculptors, including Ivor, to take part in the Churchill statue competition. At the July 1970 meeting, which picked Nemon and Ivor's maquettes as front-runners, Chandos was a vocal supporter of Ivor's submission. He voted for Ivor's design at meetings in November 1970 and February 1971. A month later he again endorsed Ivor as the winner of the competition, and urged that his success be promptly announced to the public to stymie any attempt to re-run the competition. It would seem that Ivor, prompted partly by Richard Crawfurd-Benson (secretary of the Winston Churchill Memorial Committee), suggested to Lord Chandos that he sit to him for a portrait, but sittings had hardly started when Chandos died in January 1972. The head-and-shoulders bust Ivor subsequently made was based on a combination of memory and sketches made of Chandos shortly before his death (Richard Crawfurd-Benson to Sir Max Rayne, chairman of the National Theatre Board, 27 November 1973, Archives, National Theatre, London). According to Crawfurd-Benson, Lord Chandos had such faith in Ivor as a portraitist that whatever he produced in the way of

> head or bust [should] be placed in the National Theatre. I believe ... there is to be a Chandos Bar. Unfortunately Oliver Chandos died before any sittings took place, but Roberts-Jones went on with his artistic urge to make the head as a relaxation during his work on the Churchill Statue ... Roberts-Jones is [now] putting the finishing touches to his Chandos bust (Richard Crawfurd-Benson to Sir Max Rayne, chairman of the National Theatre Board, 27 November 1973, Archives, National Theatre, London).

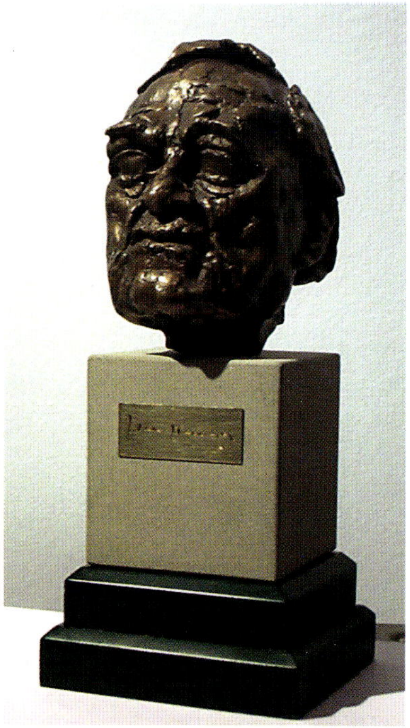

40 *John Grierson*

1972
Bronze
13.3 x 11.2 x 14.2 cm
Collection: Grierson Trust (bronze and plaster cast)
Exhibition history: first awarded December 1972; plaster cast, Wolsey Art Gallery, Ipswich, December 1999–January 2000

Comments: Grierson (1898–1972) was born in Scotland and worked as a film critic in New York during the 1920s. In February 1926, reviewing Robert Flaherty's film *Moana*, he coined the term 'documentary'. By 1929 he was working for the Empire Marketing Board, and that same year made his first film of social commentary, *The Drifters*. In 1933 he joined the General Post Office (GPO) and established a film unit there. In 1936 he produced the famous film *Night Mail* for the unit, but resigned from it in 1937. During the Second World War he worked for the Canadian National Film Commission, but was sacked in 1945 for suspected Communist sympathies. From 1948 to 1950 he spent two frustrating years in the Films Division of the Central Office of Information. Between 1957 and 1967 he made numerous documentaries for Scottish TV.

According to a former trustee and chairman of the Grierson Trust, the 'portrait bust of John Grierson' was commissioned by the then John Grierson Memorial Trust, after his death in February 1972, to be given as an award to those receiving prizes from the Trust. The first such award, for documentary filmmaking, was made

40

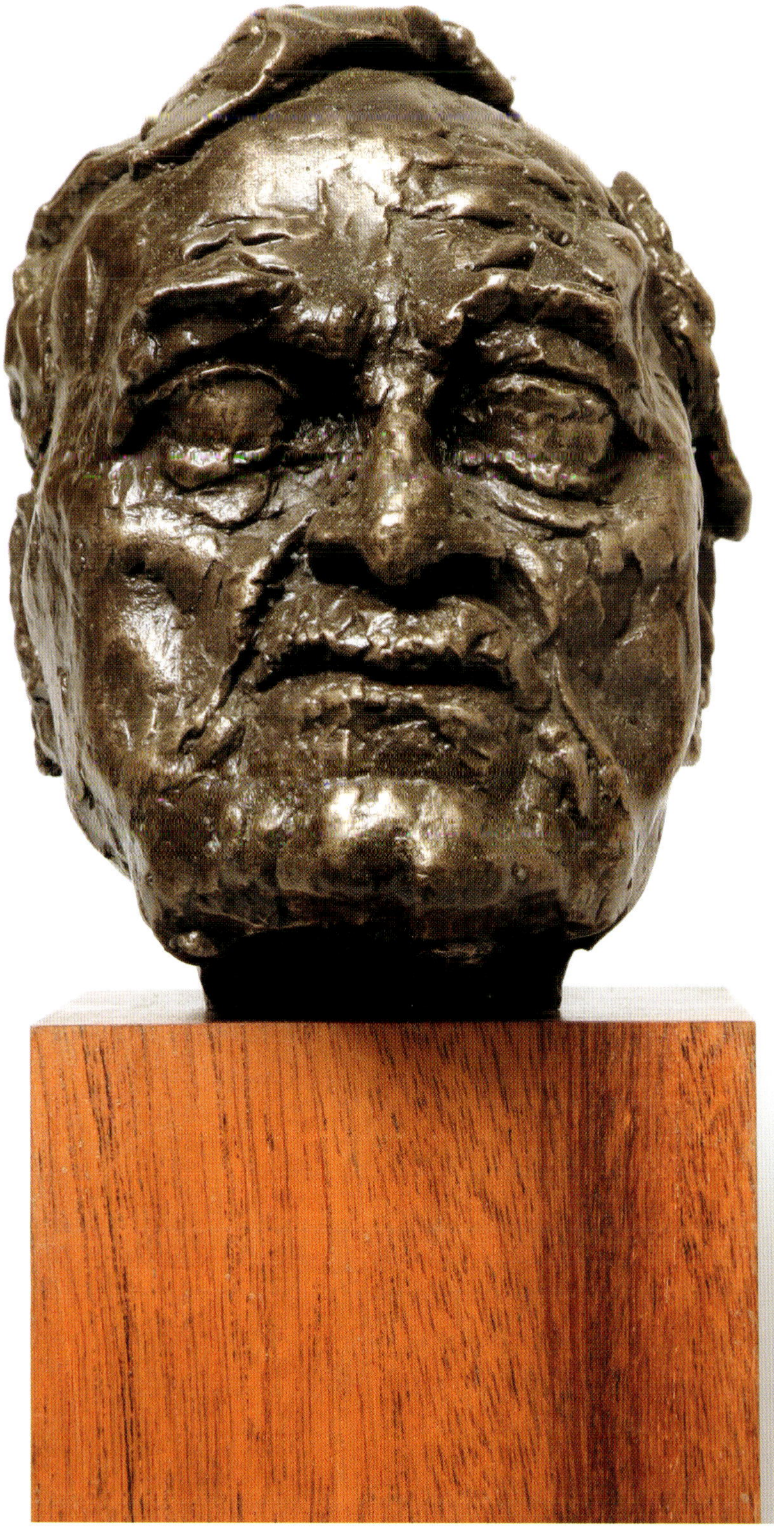

in 1972 to director and activist John Edwards. Ivor was given the Grierson commission by a founder and later chairman of the Trust, the late John Dudley Chittock OBE (1928–2011), media correspondent for the *Financial Times* (1963–87) and editor of *Screen Digest* (1971–96), who lived quite close to the artist in Suffolk. 'The artist worked from photographs of Grierson taken of him in his sixties ... and eight bronzes were struck.' Casts were made from the head in fibreglass resin instead of bronze, to save money. Past recipients of the award have included Nick Broomfield, David Attenborough, Molly Dineen, Sacha Mirzoef, Banksy, Julian Temple, Nick Holt and, in 2011, John Pilger (Murray Weston, Trustee of the Grierson Trust, 1998–2009, and Chairman, 2008–9, to Dr S. Ayers, 31 January 2012).

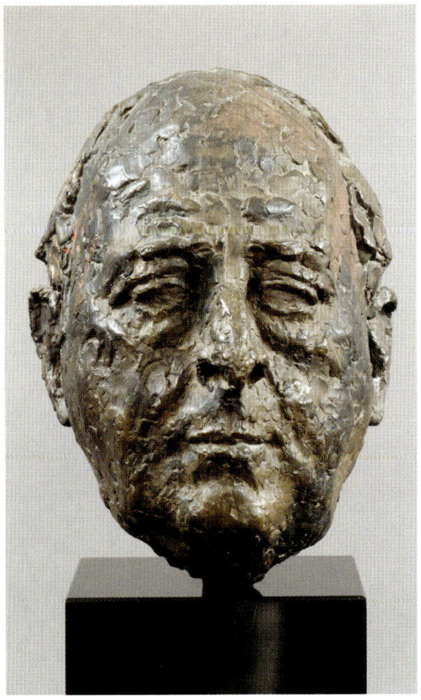

41 *Colonel Sir William Crawshay DSO*

1973
Bronze
28 x 20.2 x 25.5 cm
Collection: Arts Council of Wales and National Museum of Wales, Cardiff
Exhibition history: Royal Academy, May 1974 (472, edition of five); Oriel Gallery, Cardiff, July–September 1978 (23); Royal National Eisteddfod of Wales, Llangefni, Anglesey, July–August 1983 (17)

Comments: Sir William Crawshay (1920–1997) was educated at Eton and University College, Aberystwyth. He was intensely proud of his Welsh roots and of being a direct descendent of the founder of the great ironworks at Merthyr Tydfil. In 1940 he joined the army and served with the 5th African Rifles in Abyssinia, where he was wounded and mentioned in despatches. Four years later he volunteered to serve with the Special Operations Executive in occupied France. In July 1944 he parachuted alone into the Indre Department and organised 17,000 of the Maquis to fight the Germans. He was awarded the DSO and the Croix de Guerre in August for fighting off a column of 2,000 SS troops attacking his mountaintop headquarters. The following year he fought with the Royal Welch Fusiliers in the Netherlands. After leaving the army in 1954 he inherited Llanfair Court, near Abergavenny. Between 1960 and 1974 he served as president of the Royal British Legion of Wales, and was judged a great success in the post – so much so that he was knighted in 1972. He also sat on the Council of the National Museum of Wales from 1952 to 1982, and for the last five years was its president (*The Times*, 4 February 1997, p. 21).

In the autumn of 1971, while sitting on the Art Purchasing Committee of the NMW, Cardiff, he was a keen supporter of the proposal to buy Ivor's bronze head of Yehudi Menuhin (q.v.), as well as a bronze cast of his extensively reworked *Mrs Griffiths* (Cat. 112a) for the museum's collection (IRJ to Rollo Charles, 27 October 1971, IRJ Papers, Archives, NMW, Cardiff). Three years later, Ivor wrote to Rollo Charles, Keeper of Art at the NMW, Cardiff: 'I think Sir William liked his head and Lady Crawshay also I think. A bronze is being made for him and for the Arts Council too' (Ivor to Rollo Charles, Keeper of Art, NMW, Cardiff, c. January 1974, IRJ Papers, Archives, NMW, Cardiff). Charles replied a few days later: 'I am greatly looking forward to seeing your Crawshay head' (Rollo Charles to IRJ, 25 January 1974, IRJ Papers, Archives, NMW, Cardiff). In July 1981, when Ivor's head of George Thomas, Lord Tonypandy, was presented to the NMW by the Welsh Portrait

Sculpture Trust, Crawshay accepted the work with a gracious speech in his capacity as president of the museum. Three years later the museum purchased a cast of the Crawshay head for its own collection. On that occasion Ivor wrote to the registrar at the NMW that the recently cast head of Crawshay 'is not polished and has small areas of colour. I would like, when I next visit the Museum to add a small area of colour or gilding. I like the bronze treated this way for this particular head' (IRJ to Dr Richard Edgecumbe, 12 November 1984, IRJ Papers, Archives, NMW, Cardiff).

For nearly 30 years Crawshay also sat on the Arts Council of Great Britain, and for six years was chairman of the Welsh Committee of the Arts Council, which had been established in 1968. After his death he was described as 'a courteous, cultured and sensitive man' who endured the severe Parkinson's disease he suffered during the last decade of his life with great 'courage and cheerful fortitude' (*The Times*, 4 February 1997, p. 21).

42 *Ralph Edwards CBE, FSA*

1976–77
Plaster
30 x 20 x 24 cm
Collection: private collection
Exhibition history: Royal Academy, May 1977 (134)

Comments: Herbert Cecil Ralph Edwards (1894–1977) was born in Shipston-on-Stour to Welsh parents. His father, the Reverend W. A. Edwards, was the local vicar; his great uncle was the first Anglican archbishop of Wales. Educated at Hertford College, Oxford, he served during 1917–18 in the First World War. In 1921 he joined the editorial staff of *Country Life*. Five years later he was appointed to the Department of Woodwork at the Victoria and Albert Museum. In 1937 he became the department head, and his pioneering study *Georgian Cabinet Makers* was published in 1944. He retired from the V&A in 1954, but continued to serve as an advisor on works of art to both the Ministry of Works and the Historic Buildings Council of England and Wales. For over a decade he sat on the Art Purchasing Committee of the NMW, and in the autumn of 1971 'warily' approved the purchase of a bronze cast of Ivor's reworked *Mrs Griffiths/Seated Woman* (Kyffin Williams to Rollo Charles, 21 November 1971, IRJ Papers, Archives, NMW, Cardiff).

In his later years, despite recurrent bouts of poor health, Edwards travelled widely, becoming an expert on English miniatures, watercolours and drawings. He married Marjorie Brook in 1926, and they had three sons. After his death, his *Times* obituary commented:

> Frail in body, and often clearly unwell, Edwards was an invigorating and combative conversationalist. There were probably few of his friends who did not find themselves in violent disagreement with him at times. But his friendship was well worth an occasional tiff and 'anyway Ralph is very good value' was a judgement many times delivered ... He was indeed a very social person. (*The Times*, 14 December 1977, p. 16).

A few days later the Marquess of Anglesey added that Edwards had 'deeply held, uncompromising, political views. These, regularly expressed in pungent, waspish terms, looked with mounting horror upon what he saw as the slide down the slippery slope towards totalitarian collectivism in this country' (*The Times*, 23 December 1977, p. 12). In September 1979 his son Nicholas (1934–), by now secretary of state for Wales (1979–1987), approved the commissioning of Ivor's design for the bronze *The Two Kings/Janus Rider* sculpture to stand outside Harlech Castle (press release from the Welsh Arts Council, March 1980, Press Cuttings File, IRJ Papers, Archives, HMI, Leeds). At the time Ivor thought that Edwards junior, as far as politicians went, 'seemed a very civilised chap' (IRJ to Sir Richard Hyde Parker, 11 January 1980, Archives, Sir Richard Hyde Parker).

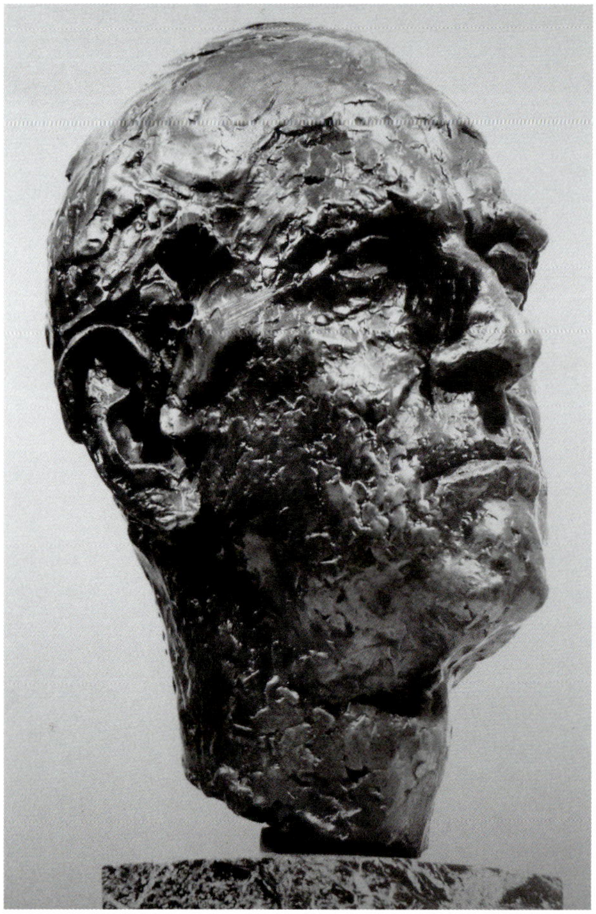

43 *HRH Prince Philip, The Duke of Edinburgh*

1974–75
Bronze
32 x 20 x 26 cm
Collection: Royal College of General Practitioners, London
Exhibition history: unknown

Comments: Born Prince Philip of Greece in June 1921, he served in the Royal Navy between 1939 and 1951 as Philip Mountbatten. In November 1947 he married Princess Elizabeth – the future Queen Elizabeth II (1952–). In 1956 he founded the Duke of Edinburgh's Award Scheme, and in February the following year was made HRH Prince Philip, the Duke of Edinburgh. He has been president of the UK World Wildlife Fund (1961–82) and chancellor of the University of Wales (1964–86). At the beginning of December 1974 Ivor wrote to his founder, Jack Crofton, that he would be 'bringing the Dook's head along shortly' for casting. There is an implication that Ivor would, instead, much rather have made a portrait of jazz great Edward Kennedy 'Duke' Ellington, who had died earlier in 1974 (IRJ to Jack Crofton, 1 December 1974, Megan Thomas Archive). It would seem that Ivor did not greatly enjoy this particular commission. Interviewed by Byron Rogers in June 1993, he testily declared: 'Of course, not everyone likes portraiture either. The Duke of Edinburgh said I'd made him look like Neanderthal Man' (IRJ interview with Byron Rogers, *Sunday Telegraph*, 27 June 1993, p. 5).

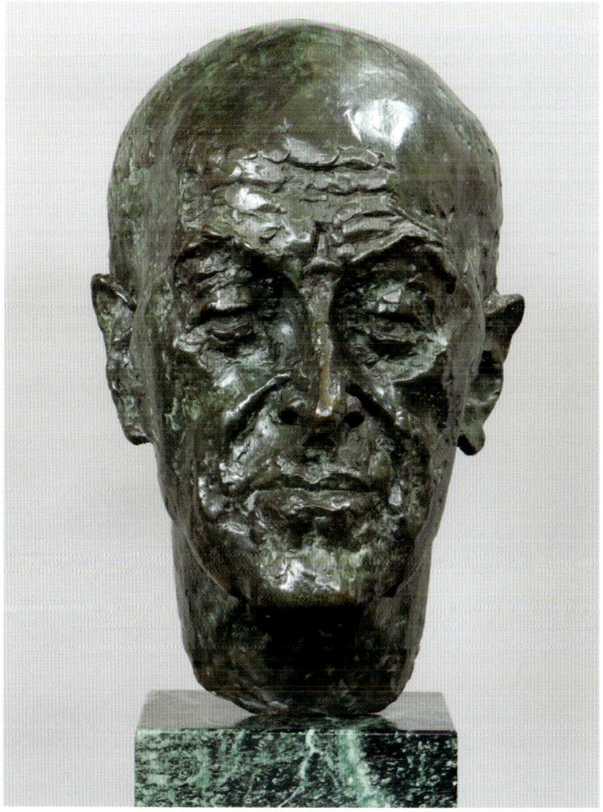

44 *The Fifth Lord Kenyon*

1978
Bronze
42.5 cm high
Collection: private collection and National Museum of Wales, Cardiff
Exhibition history: unknown

Comments: The work was commissioned by the recently arrived new Keeper of Art at the NMW, Peter Cannon-Brookes, who was aware that Ivor was very unhappy with the head of Lord Kenyon he had previously made in 1962 and which the sitter donated to the museum in May the following year (Cannon-Brookes, *Ivor Roberts-Jones*, p. 69). The second head, with which both artist and sitter were very pleased, entered the museum's collection in September 1979 (entry for 14 September 1979, IRJ Diary for 1979, IRJ Papers, HMI, Leeds).

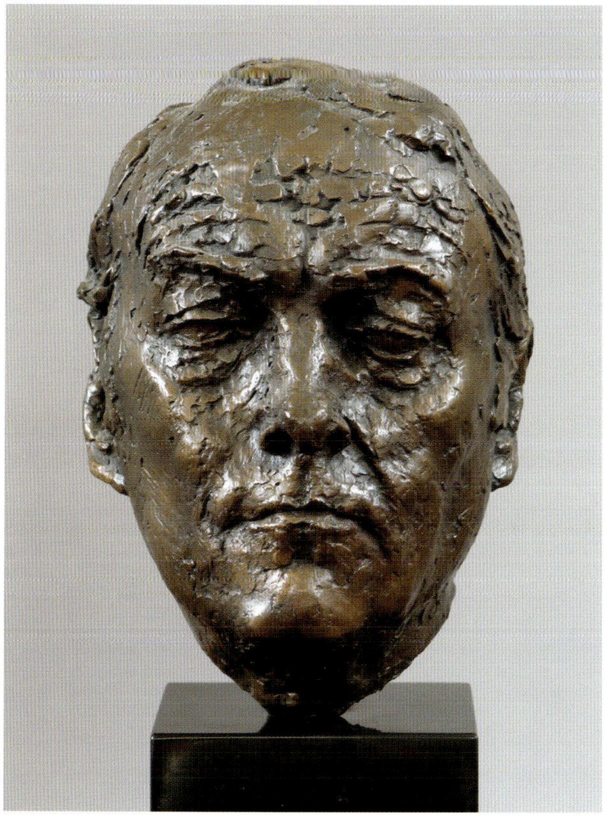

45 *The Seventh Marquess of Anglesey*

1978–79
Bronze
28.5 x 18.5 x 25.5 cm
Collection: private collection and National Museum of Wales, Cardiff
Exhibition history: unknown

Comments: George Charles Henry Victor Paget, Seventh Marquess of Anglesey (1922–2013), was educated at Eton. During the Second World War he served with the Royal Horse Guards, rising to the rank of major. He succeeded to his title in 1947. Serving as Vice Lord Lieutenant of Anglesey from 1960 to 1983 and as Lord Lieutenant of Gwynedd from 1983 to 1989, he also published a critically well-received eight-volume *History of the British Cavalry* (Pen & Sword Books).

At the end of 1978, Ivor noted in his diary for that year: 'I also did a head of Lord Anglesey [this year]' (entry for 30 December 1978, IRJ Diary of 1978, IRJ Papers, Archives, HMI, Leeds). It is possible that his close friend Kyffin Williams had suggested the commission to his friend the Marquess of Anglesey, who had been his landlord since 1974. Indeed, when Williams had indicated he was thinking of retiring from teaching at Highgate School, the marquess had encouraged him to move back to his native Anglesey, to a house on the Paget Estate. The idea for the commission had also been supported by the keeper of art at the NMW, Cardiff, Peter Cannon-Brookes, who hoped one day to acquire a cast of it for the museum (author interview with Cannon-Brookes, 3 May 2013).

In May 1979 Ivor collected the head from the Meridian Foundry and delivered it to the marquess at his home, Plas Newydd, on Anglesey (entry for 22 May 1979, IRJ Diary for 1979, IRJ Papers, Archives, HMI, Leeds).

In July 1984, Cannon-Brookes suggested to the director of the NMW that the museum ought to buy a cast of the head of Anglesey from Ivor, given that the marquess was the current president of the museum's Council (Cannon-Brookes to the director, NMW, Cardiff, 12 July 1984, IRJ Papers, Archives, NMW, Cardiff). This was done for £1,300, and the head cast by the Meridian Foundry early in October. Just prior to the delivery of the head to the museum, early in February 1985, Ivor wrote to its registrar that it was a 'very small and intimate little head – the idea was that it should go in to one of the semi-private rooms at Plas Newydd – on a mantelpiece in fact! On the other hand I like compact objects' (IRJ to Dr Richard Edgecumbe [registrar, NMW, Cardiff], 12 January 1985, IRJ Papers, NMW, Cardiff). The registrar, on the head's arrival, promptly wrote to the artist that it was 'splendid' (Dr Richard Edgecumbe to IRJ, 4 February 1985, IRJ Papers, Archives, NMW, Cardiff).

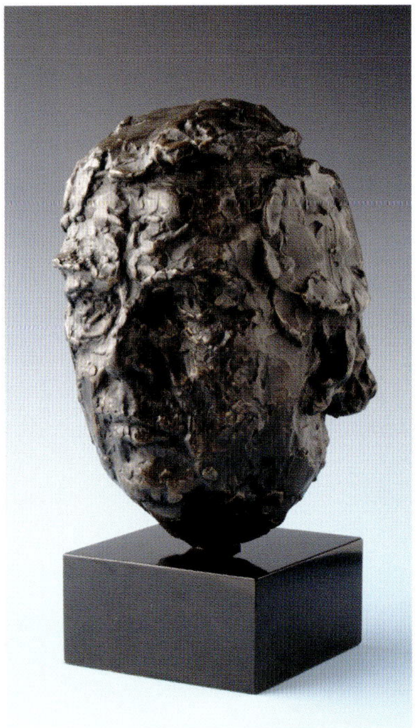

46 *Lord Cledwyn of Penrhos CH*

1978
Bronze
29 cm high
Collection: National Museum of Wales, Cardiff; Oriel Ynys Môn, Anglesey
Exhibition history: Oriel Gallery, Cardiff, July–September 1978 (24)

Comments: Hughes (1916–2001) was born in Holyhead, Anglesey, and educated at the local grammar school and then at the University of Wales, Aberystwyth. After service in the RAFVR during the Second World War he was elected Labour MP for Anglesey in 1951 – holding the seat until May 1979. Under Harold Wilson he was secretary of state for Wales (1966–68), in which position he was succeeded by Ivor's future sitter, George Thomas, and then minister for agriculture (1968–70). In 1969 he advised Prince Charles on Wales, as the Prince was about to be invested as Prince of Wales. On the moderate wing of the Labour Party, Hughes was a key supporter of James Callaghan after he succeeded Wilson as prime minister in April 1976. In 1974 Hughes was elected as a moderate chairman of the Parliamentary Labour Party (PLP), narrowly beating the radical Ian Mikardo, and leading efforts to prevent the PLP from being taken over by political militants.

Between 1977 and 1985 he was president of the University College of Wales, Aberystwyth, and favoured greater Welsh devolution if not outright independence in the referendum vote of March 1979. In June 1979 the outgoing Labour prime minister, James Callaghan, made him Lord Cledwyn of Penrhos, and he took over as leader of the opposition in the House of Lords in November 1982 – a position he held for a decade. During the 1980s he was a notable supporter of Neil Kinnock in his struggle with the extreme left within the Labour Party. Hughes was also a life-long campaigner for the Welsh language in the Commons and the Lords, and in the early 1980s played a key role in persuading the Conservative government to establish a Welsh-language television service. A great admirer of Lloyd George, in 1996 he established a trust to raise a statue to the great Welsh Liberal politician in Parliament Square. In 1999 he spoke in the opening session of the Welsh Assembly in Cardiff. *The Times* described him as 'very much part of the Welsh Establishment' (23 February 2001, p. 25). A few days later *The Times* noted Hughes's passing with regret, describing him as one of the most popular members of the House of Lords:

> one of the great animated conversationalists of politics. But he was also a thoroughly serious politician, shabbily treated by Harold Wilson who excluded him from his 1974 administration ... There are two faces of Welsh politics at Westminster – the sanctimonious, oleaginous one represented by George Thomas, later Viscount Tonypandy, and the mischievous, but rarely malevolent one, symbolised by Cledwyn. I suppose Thomas achieved the greater public fame but Cledwyn always won the private esteem stakes by a canter (*The Times*, 27 February 2001, p. 7).

It would appear that Ivor first asked Hughes to sit to him in the spring of 1975, but sittings had to be postponed as his time was increasingly taken up with the Churchill Commission for Oslo (IRJ to Cledwyn [Hughes], 27 April 1975, IRJ Papers, Archives, HMI, Leeds).

In his 1978 diary, Ivor noted in December: 'During this year, did a head of Cledwyn Hughes – entirely on spec'. He mentions working on the head at the Meridian Foundry in May 1978. It was finally cast to his satisfaction in February 1980 (entry for 1 February 1980, IRJ Diary, ibid.).

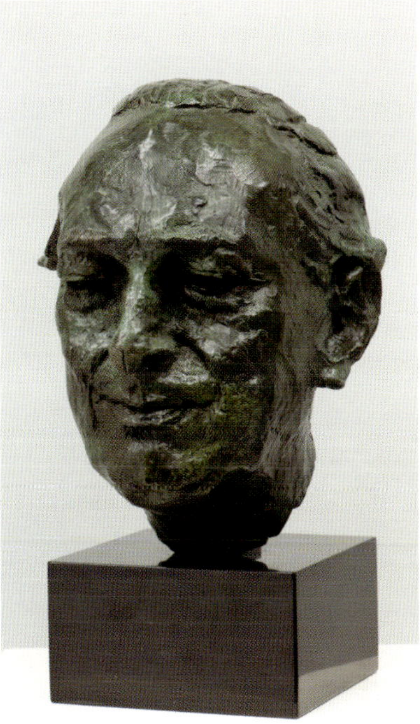

47 *Alwyn Rees*

1978–80
Bronze
28.5 x 22.2 x 26 cm
Collection: University of Wales, Aberystwyth and the National Museum of Wales, Cardiff
Exhibition history: unknown

Comments: Alwyn David Rees (1911–1974) was a social anthropologist and prominent Welsh Nationalist. In his diary for 1978, Ivor noted on 21 June: '[S]tarted work on head of Alwyn Rees', and on 12 December 1978:

> Arthur Giardelli and Brynmor Thomas [both from the University of Wales, Aberystwyth] to 31 [St James's Gardens, Holland Park] to see the Alwyn Rees head. This has been done from photographs. Thomas queries the likeness. [I a]greed to do a second [version] – but refuse to alter the [first]. Giardelli is very fond of it – but Aberystwyth University are to have it, so Brynmor has the last word (Diary for 1978, IRJ Papers, Archives, HMI, Leeds).

In April 1979 he met Giardelli again to discuss the Rees head. A month later he noted in his diary: '31 May 1979: Brynmor Thomas comes to stay and approves

[the] second version of Alwyn Rees [at Ivor's studio in Suffolk] ... 3 June 1979: take 2nd version of Alwyn up to London ... 19 July 1979: Visit to London ... meet Giardelli re 2nd Alwyn Rees head – he approves' (Diary for 1979, ibid.).

The following year he noted: '3 March 1980: 2nd Head of Alwyn Rees completed and mounted. Colour first head of Alwyn for [Arthur] Giardelli' (Diary for 1980, ibid.). Evidently, Giardelli was so taken with Ivor's first attempt at the portrait of Rees that he paid for it to be cast in bronze by the Meridian Foundry. Ivor then applied one of his special patinas to order.

Four years later, in November 1984, the NMW, Cardiff, bought a cast of his second head of Rees from the artist for £1,300. Ivor had a spare, as the Meridian Foundry had apparently cast one 'by mistake' (IRJ to Dr Peter Cannon-Brookes, 8 October 1984, IRJ Papers, Archives, NMW, Cardiff). The cast was bought on the initiative of Dr Peter Cannon-Brookes (Dr Richard Edgecumbe, Registrar, NMW, Cardiff, to IRJ, 16 October 1984, ibid.).

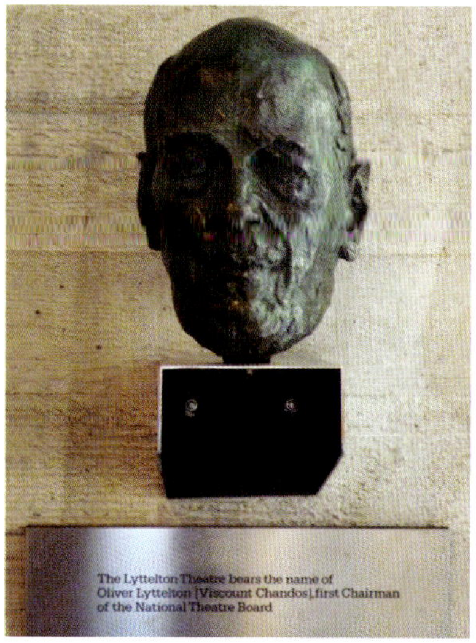

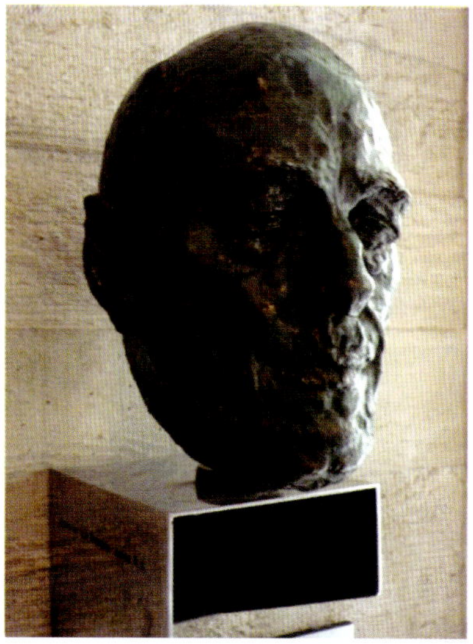

48 *Head of Oliver Lyttelton, Lord Chandos, DSO, MC*

1979–80
Bronze
26.5 x 13 x 19.4 cm
Collection: Foyer, Lyttelton Theatre, National Theatre, London; plaster cast, 32.1 x 22.8 x 27 cm, Goldsmiths College, London
Exhibition history: plaster cast at the Royal Academy, May 1987 (1101); plaster cast, Wolsey Art Gallery, Ipswich, December 1999–January 2000

Comments: During the summer of 1978, the Design Committee of the Board of the National Theatre began toying with the idea of commissioning a bronze head of the First Lord Chandos, its first chairman. Initially, it considered approaching one of Ivor's great rivals, Franta Belsky, with the commission (Yolande Bird [secretary to the Board of the National Theatre] to Lord Mishcon [Lord Victor Mishcon (1915–2006), ennobled 1978, member of the Board of the National Theatre, 1965–90], 3 August 1978, Archives, National Theatre, London). A month later all the members of the Design Committee had seen the head, and most were not impressed. The reaction of Sir Peter Hall (1930– , director of the National Theatre, 1973–88) was rather negative. Lord Reilly (Sir Paul Reilly (1914–1999), director of the Design Council, 1959–1977), who did know Lord Chandos, was not particularly impressed by the head as a likeness; as a work of art he found it somewhat mediocre. Sir Denys Lasdun (1914–2001, architect of the 'brutalist' National Theatre between 1967 and 1976) did not find it a very good likeness – he felt it was 'dead' (Yolande Bird to Lord Mishcon, 18 September 1978, Archives, National Theatre, London). The secretary to the Board then 'mentioned the existence of the head by Ivor Robert-Jones which the Committee viewed just over two years ago ... The current Lord and Lady Chandos indicated they thought Belsky's head of the First Lord was 'rather like a death mask and lacking [in] animation'. The Second Lord Chandos had 'heard from mutual friends that ... the one which was "from life" by the artist responsible for the statue of Churchill in Parliament Square ... was rather interesting. They would be prepared to view the Roberts-Jones one, assuming that it is still available' (Yolande Bird to Lord Mishcon, 26 October 1978, Archives, National Theatre, London).

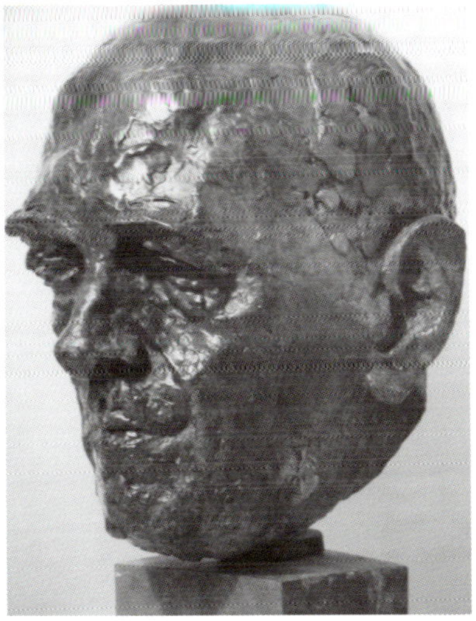

In February 1979 Ivor showed his 1972–73 bust of Lord Chandos to the Second Lord Chandos and to members of the National Theatre Board's Design Committee. While all were impressed by the bust, the Second Lord Chandos thought there was 'something not quite right about it'. Ivor promptly offered to make an entirely new portrait head, 'as I have plenty of photographs and drawings of the first Lord' – which suitably impressed his audience (entry for 13 February 1979, Diary for 1979, 2005.456/B, IRJ Papers, Archives, HMI, Leeds). By early March he had finished the second head and cast it in plaster (entry for 5 March 1979, ibid.). The Second Lord Chandos and members of the Design Committee were very taken with the plaster cast when they saw it at Ivor's London home in mid June 1979. In August the head was viewed by Design Committee member Sir Paul Reilly, who had previously been away. He reported to the Board's secretary:

> [M]y wife and I did manage to call upon Mr Ivor Roberts-Jones ... and saw his new head of the late Lord Chandos. We both liked it both as a portrait and as a piece of sculpture, so I hope the N[ational] T[heater] will now proceed with the commission. His new version is much better than his first attempt. What a nice man Ivor Roberts-Jones is. We enjoyed our hour with him (Sir Paul Reilly to Yolande Bird, 18 August 1979, Archives, National Theatre, London).

With this endorsement, and confirmation of approval from Lords Mishcon and Rayne, the secretary of the Board felt able to contact Ivor to tell him to proceed with casting the head in bronze. The artist was to be paid £2,000 (IRJ to Yolande Bird, 24 January 1980, Archives, National Theatre, London). By midsummer 1980 the head had been cast, and after prolonged discussions with Sir Denis Lasdun a site for the head had been decided upon in the Lyttelton Theatre (IRJ to Yolande Bird, 27 August 1980, ibid.). The bronze was delivered to the National Theatre in September 1980 but was not unveiled on its current resting place until November 1982. Ivor was somewhat put out not to be invited to the ceremony until the last minute (Archives, National Theatre, London).

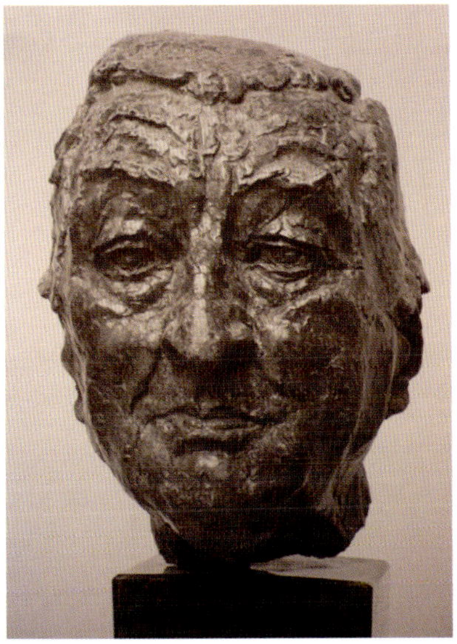

49 *His Hon. Judge Bertrand Richards QC*

1980
Bronze
26.3 x 20 x 27.7 cm
Collection: private collection; plaster cast, private collection
Exhibition history: Bronze (edition of 5) exhibited Royal Academy, May 1984 (no. 1465).
Related work: 49a: *Study for the Portrait of Judge Bertrand Richards*, 1980, pencil on paper, 16 x 17 cm, Henry Moore Institute, Leeds

Comments: Richards (1913–2000) was born in Denbighshire, the son of an Anglican rector, and educated at Lancing and Corpus Christi College, Oxford. During the Second World War he served in the Royal Artillery with the 8th Army in North Africa and during the Normandy campaign of 1944. In 1941 he was called to the bar by the Inner Temple and became a Circuit Judge in 1972. He was known as a 'colourful character', and during one trial, when a police officer in the witness box was being grilled by a barrister, told the lawyer: 'I should warn you that I have a very high regard for the police and have named my dog "Fuzz" in tribute.' He was honorary Recorder of Ipswich from 1975 to 1999. He created uproar in January

49a

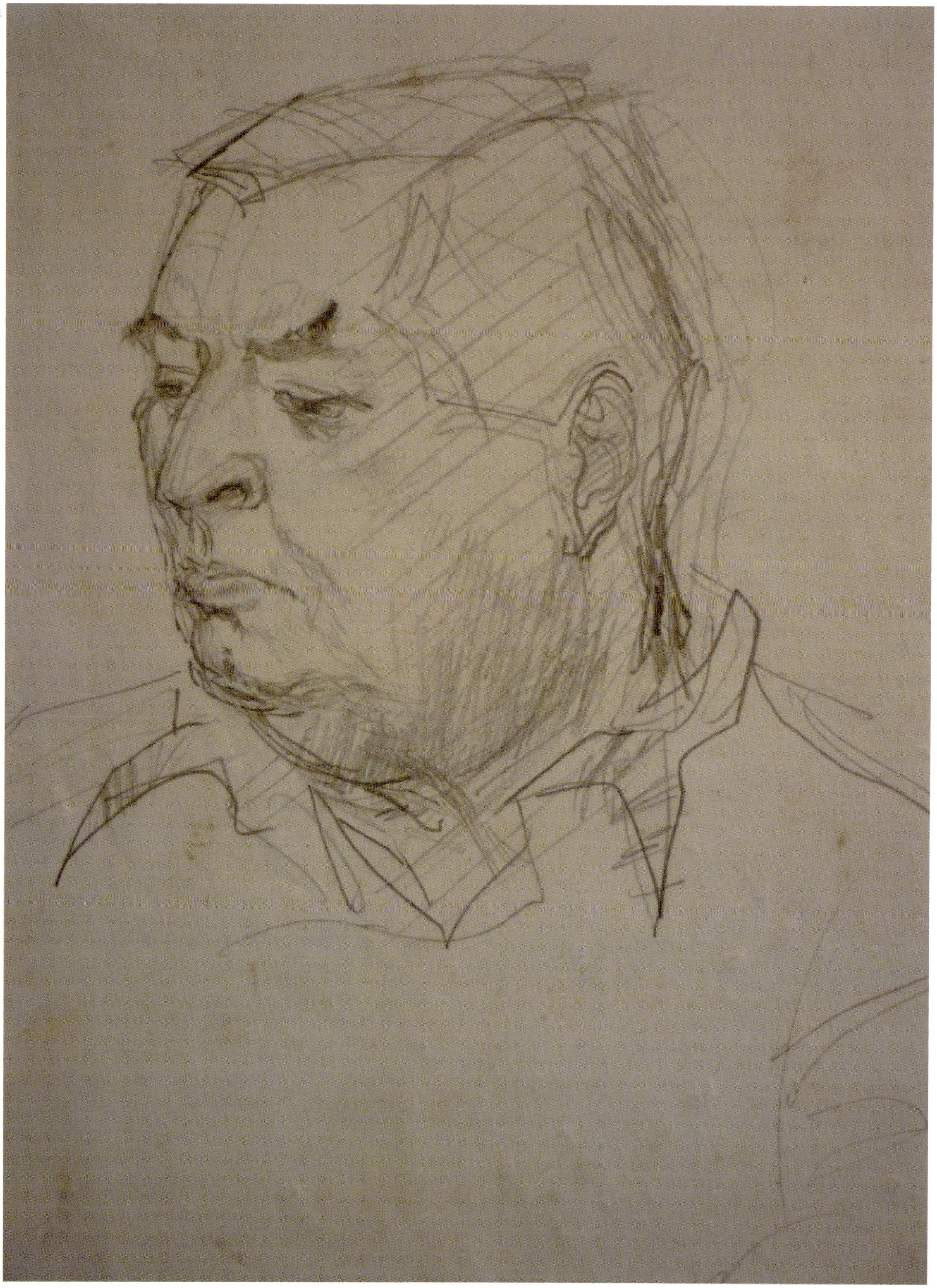

1982 when he criticised a rape victim for hitchhiking at night during a trial at Ipswich Crown Court. He made the comment that she had been 'asking for it'. He fined the rapist rather than giving him a prison term. Such was the outrage that he was banned from taking further sex cases, and retired early from the Ipswich bench in 1986 (*The Times*, 1 September 2000, p. 18). After his death a fellow barrister described Richards as 'most civilised and erudite ... His intellect was such as would, but for certain aspects of his character, have made him a worthy member of the Court of Appeal. He did, alas, always feel compelled to speak his mind. This, combined with a puckish sense of humour, was enough to spike his chances of promotion' (Alistair Sampson to the *The Times*, 8 September 2000, p. 20).

In his diary for 1980, Ivor noted that, during the second half of that year, he had 'also carried out, to the casting stage, a portrait head of Judge Richards who lives locally. This was done at Coppings' (entry for 24 December 1980, IRJ Papers, Archives, HMI, Leeds). In June the following year he wrote to Kyffin Williams that 'Bertrand and Jane [the judge's wife] have now taken possession of the "Head" ... I must say the bronze suited it and I think it one of my best. He had a marvellous head to do. Let's hope I'm helped to persuade him so – but rather doubt it' (IRJ to Kyffin Williams, 29 June 1981, A1/13/38, Williams Papers, National Library of Wales, Aberystwyth).

50 *His Hon. Judge Bruce Griffiths QC*

1980–81
Bronze
28 cm high
Collection: private collection
Exhibition history: unknown

Comments: Bruce Fletcher Griffiths (1924–1999) was born in Barry, Glamorgan, and educated at Whitchurch Grammar School, Cardiff, and King's College, London. After wartime service with the RAF (1942–47), he was called to the bar at Gray's Inn in 1952. The previous year he was a co-founder of the moderate Conservative think tank, the Bow Group, and encouraged rising stars within the party such as Geoffrey Howe and Michael Heseltine. Made a QC in 1970, Griffiths sat on the bench for the Wales and Chester Circuit from 1972 until his retirement in 1986. From an early age he had displayed a keen interest in the visual arts in Wales, and was also an accomplished poet – though he never learned to speak Welsh. He was appointed a member of the Welsh Arts Council in 1972, and chairman of its Arts Committee in 1975. He was also a founder of the Welsh Sculpture Trust in 1980, and its chairman from 1981 to 1992. He was also chairman of the Contemporary Art Society for Wales from 1987 to 1992, and its vice-chair from 1992 to 1998 (*Independent*, 30 January 1999, p. 23). A devout member of the Church of Wales, he was described in his obituary in *The Times* as a 'forceful and erudite' advocate ... always courteous, kind and jovial ... and was the most engaging of men'. He married his wife, Mary, in 1952, and they had two sons and one daughter (*The Times*, 1 February 1999, p. 26).

In his diary for January 1980, Ivor wrote that he had recently been 'getting to know Judge Bruce Griffiths – who is starting up the idea of my doing portraits of George Thomas (Speaker of the House of Commons), Prince Charles and also the writer

David Jones. Famous Welshmen all' (entry for 18 January 1980, IRJ Diary, IRJ Papers, Archives, HMI, Leeds). By the end of the year Griffiths, along with Sir Alun Talfan-Davies, had founded the Welsh Portrait Sculpture Trust, which went on to commission a whole series of bronze portrait heads of distinguished Welsh sitters from Ivor, expressly for presentation to the collection of the NMW in Cardiff. Sittings for the head of Griffiths continued during April and May 1980 (entry for 11 May 1980, ibid.).

In 1981 Griffiths was also a founder member of the Welsh Sculpture Trust, based at Margam near Port Talbot, and two years later was chairman of its trustees – by which time Ivor had been appointed a trustee. By 1983 Griffiths also owned Ivor's early bronze head *Mother of Judas*, which he lent to the solo exhibition Ivor held at Llangefni on Anglesey in July–August 1983.

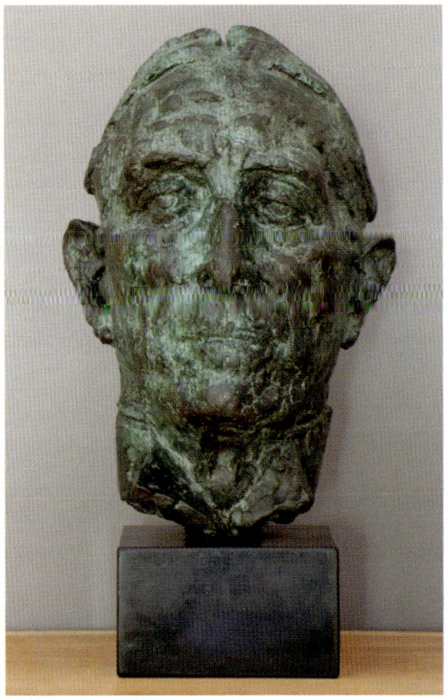

51 *George Thomas, First Viscount Tonypandy*

1980
Bronze
31.8 cm high
Collection: National Museum of Wales, Cardiff; House of Commons Art Collection; National Portrait Gallery, London
Exhibition history: Bronze (edition of five) at the Royal Academy, May 1982 (732), Royal National Eisteddfod of Wales, Llangefni, Anglesey, July–August 1983 (3); Ivor Roberts-Jones Memorial Exhibition, Royal Academy, London, April–August 1997

Comments: Thomas George Thomas (1909–1997) was born in Port Talbot, the son of a Rhondda miner, and was educated at Tonypandy Secondary School and University College, Southampton. He joined the Labour Party in 1925, and in 1936 he led a hunger march from Tonypandy to Cardiff. In July 1945 he was elected Labour MP for Cardiff Central, and then in 1950 for Cardiff West, which he held until his retirement in 1983. He reached the apex of his political career in April 1968 when Prime Minister Harold Wilson appointed him secretary of state for Wales, which position he held for two years. Thomas emerged during this period as a fervent opponent of Welsh Nationalism and of devolution. A fluent Welsh-speaker himself, he opposed any policy that advocated the enforced speaking of the language. In 1969 he made a great success of the investiture of Prince Charles as Prince of Wales at Caernarfon Castle, and befriended the Prince, who later asked him to read at his wedding in July 1981 (*Guardian*, 23 September 1997, p. 16).

Thomas expected the secretaryship of Wales in 1974, but was passed over by Harold Wilson. In compensation he was elected Speaker of the House of Commons in 1976, which office he held for what were generally regarded as seven successful years. With the introduction of radio broadcasts of the House in April 1978, Thomas became a radio star, assisted by his rich Welsh accent and ready wit. He strongly opposed Welsh devolution during the devolution referendum campaign of 1979. He retired as speaker in 1983, and was elevated to the House of Lords by Mrs Thatcher as the First Viscount Tonypandy. In 1983 he became a trustee of the Welsh Sculpture Trust – along with Ivor and Sir Hugh Casson (1910–1999; president of the Royal Academy, 1976–84). Thomas's fluently written memoirs were published in 1985, revealing a marked dislike for Michael Foot and James Callaghan. Though engaged at least twice, he never married, and the strongest influence on him was

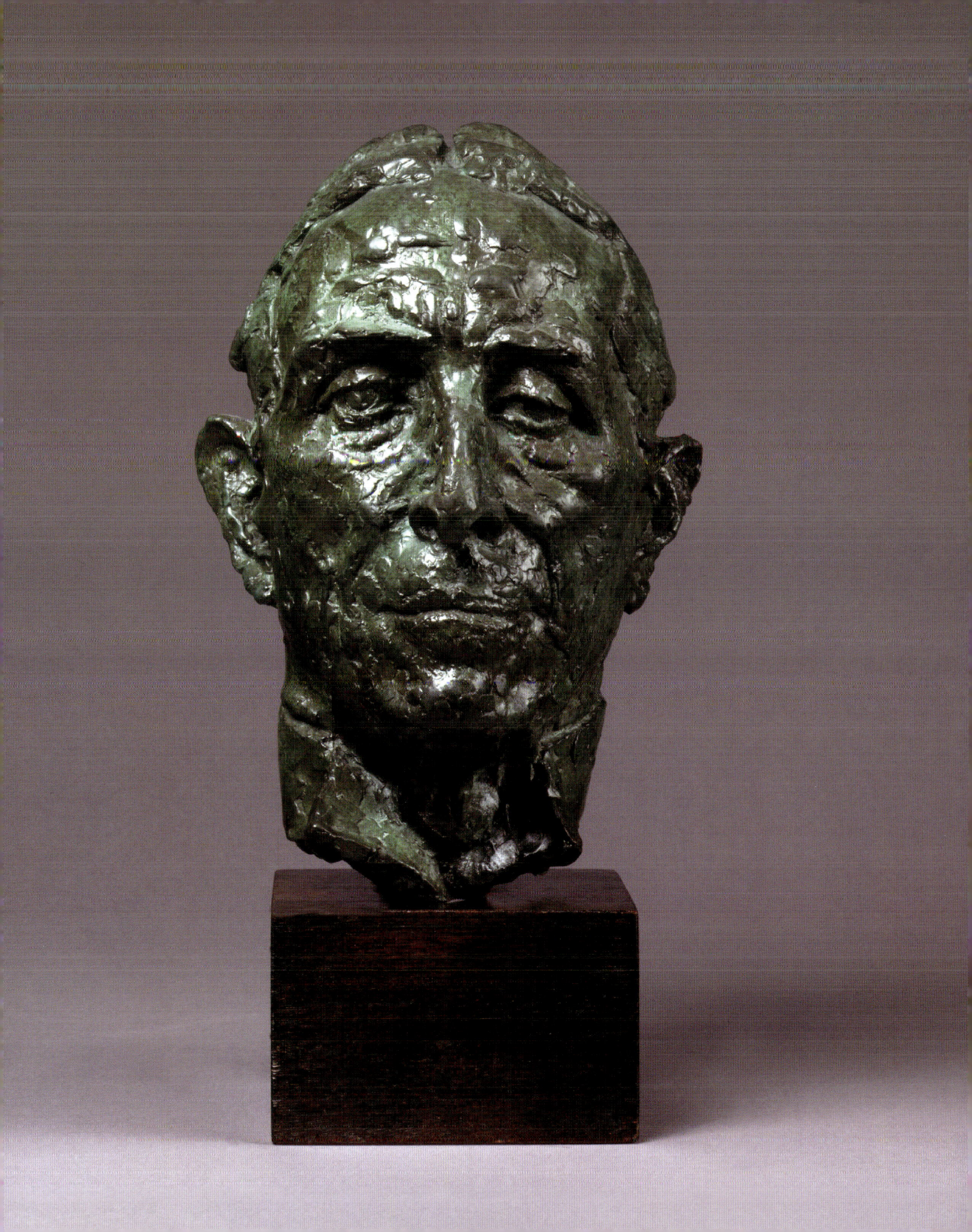

probably his formidable 'Mam', who died in 1972. During the last years of his life he bravely battled throat cancer, and campaigned vigorously against the creation of a separate Welsh Assembly in the referendum of 1997 (*The Times*, 23 September 1997, p. 21; *Daily Telegraph*, 23 September 1997, p. 24).

Though he was respected by many MPs, some did not think highly of Thomas. A month after his death, for example, Conservative MP Robert Rhodes James denounced the late speaker as 'an arrogant, sanctimonious, deceitful and malicious bully ... a fraud and charlatan, eager to bend the knee to anyone above his station and thinly contemptuous of anyone deemed to be below it'. Rhodes James asserted that Thomas's 'legendry Welsh charm concealed a vicious streak' – though he conceded that Thomas had 'charm and wit and wrote well' (*The Times*, 17 October 1999, p. 2).

Early in 1980 a recent acquaintance, Judge Bruce Griffiths (q.v.) suggested that Thomas sit to Ivor for a portrait head (entry for 21 February 1980, IRJ Diary for 1980, IRJ Papers, Archives, HMI, Leeds). In March 1980 Ivor's fee for the commission, from the recently created Welsh Portrait Sculpture Trust, was set at £2,000 (entry for 25 March 1980, ibid.). Thomas sat during June and July 1980 at 31 St James's Gardens (entry for 1 July 1980, ibid.).

Ivor's bronze of Thomas was formally unveiled in the Welsh Office in Cardiff on 31 July 1981. The *South Wales Echo* noted of the event that

> gathered last night in the foyer of the Welsh Office – the Welsh establishment paid tribute to the son of a Tonypandy miner. Among those present were Nicholas Edwards, Secretary of State for Wales, and Michael Foot, Leader of the Opposition. More than £4,000 had been raised by friends and admirers of Mr Speaker and MP for Cardiff West ... Mr Roberts-Jones's bust was unveiled by Nicholas Edwards ... Sir William Crawshay, President of the National Museum of Wales received the bust for the Museum's collection.

After the speeches Ivor told a reporter for the *Echo* that Thomas was 'very, very charming and considerate. I expected all that, but I didn't want to go for that. When he sat in the chair in my studio his head seemed to have a sense of hidden power – and I went for that' (*South Wales Echo*, 1 August 1981, p. 3, Press Clippings Book, Library, NMW, Cardiff).

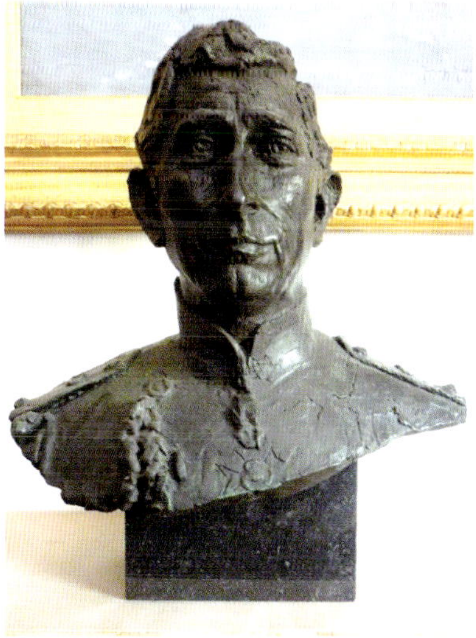

52a *Bust of HRH Prince Charles, Prince of Wales*

1980–82
Bronze
41.7 x 43.2 x 24.2 cm
Collection: private collection
Exhibition history: Chappel Galleries, Chappel, Essex, July–August 2000

Comments: This bust was produced in tandem with 52b, below. Ivor hoped that it might be purchased by the sitter for the Royal Collection, but he was dissatisfied with the patination for the bust in 1982, though pleased with the work as a portrait – emphasising the prince as both 'aesthete and future head of state' (IRJ to Dr Peter Cannon-Brookes, c. September 1982). After the sculptor's death, the Royal Collection showed some interest in buying the bust, but the patina had further deteriorated. The head was re-patinated by the Artisan Bronze Foundry in June 2006 (Dr Peter Cannon-Brookes to Dr J. Black, 3 May 2013).

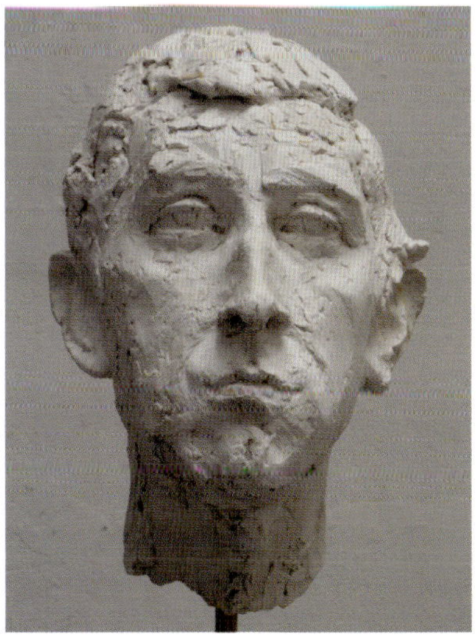

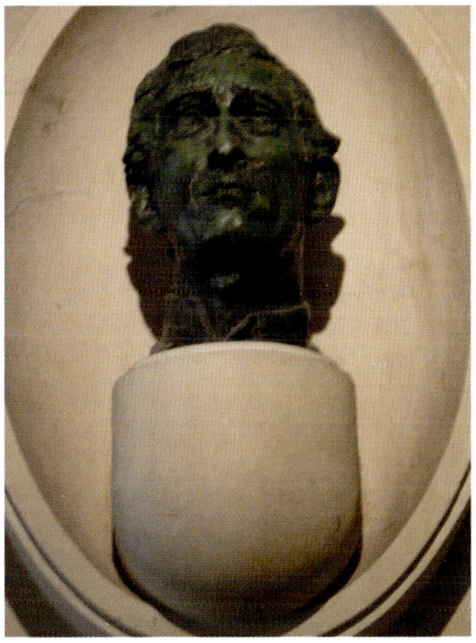

52b *HRH Prince Charles, Princes of Wales*

1980–82
Bronze
32.5 x 23.6 x 25.4 cm
Collection: St David's Concert Hall, Cardiff; plaster cast, 30.5 x 21.6 x 25 cm, private collection
Exhibition history: plaster cast, Wolsey Art Gallery, December 1999–January 2000

Comments: Charles Philip Arthur George Windsor, Prince of Wales, was born in November 1949 and educated at Gordonstoun School and Trinity College, Cambridge (1967–70). He was created Prince of Wales in July 1958, but his official investiture did not take place until 1 July 1969 in Caernarfon Castle. After service in the Royal Navy (1971–77), he created the charitable Princes Trust. From July 1980 he began to look upon Lady Diana Spencer as a future wife – though the prince was still very much involved in an affair that had begun in 1970 with Camilla Shand (from 1973, Parker-Bowles). He proposed to Lady Diana in February 1981, and they were married in St Paul's Cathedral in July of that year. Prince William was born in June 1982, and Prince Harry in September 1984. In the early 1980s the prince emerged as a somewhat contentious champion of traditional architecture; in 1984 he denounced the Royal Institute of British Architects' approval for the design of a new extension for the National Gallery which he famously likened to a 'monstrous carbuncle on the face of a much-loved and elegant friend'. He also championed alternative medicine, homeopathy and organic farming. He was a keen polo player and, coached by Sir Hugh Casson, then president of the Royal Academy (1976–84), he became an accomplished watercolour painter. By 1986 his marriage to Diana was in serious trouble, and the couple were effectively separated by the end of the decade. His formal separation from Diana was announced by Prime Minister John Major in the House of Commons in December 1992.

Ivor noted in his diary in January 1980 that his friend Judge Bruce Griffiths thought that he ought to make a portrait head of the prince (entry for 10 January 1980, IRJ Diary, Archives, HMI, Leeds). By the end of March the commission had been 'fixed, in principle, for £1,500' with the Contemporary Art Society of Wales (entry for 25 March 1980, ibid.). During the summer of 1980 he began 'the long haul of the bust of the Prince of Wales with sittings at Buckingham Palace'. Work on the head was then greatly delayed by the prince's marriage to Lady Diana Spencer; much to Ivor's frustration, he could not resume work on the project until the autumn of 1981. He was partly mollified by the prince's purchase of a bronze cast of one of his 'African big cats' – a puma (IRJ to Kyffin Williams, 29 June 1981, Williams Papers, National Library of Wales, Aberystwyth).

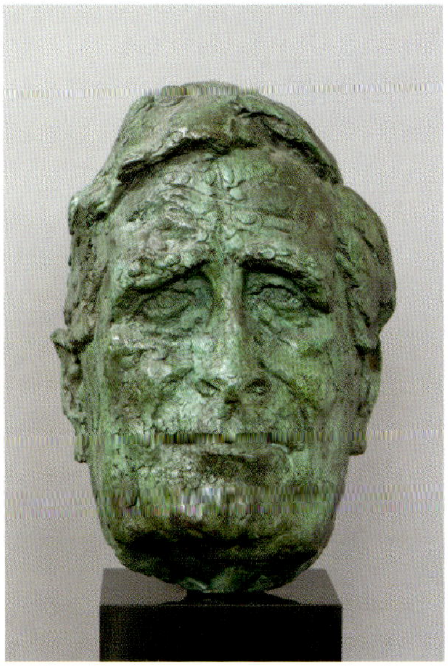

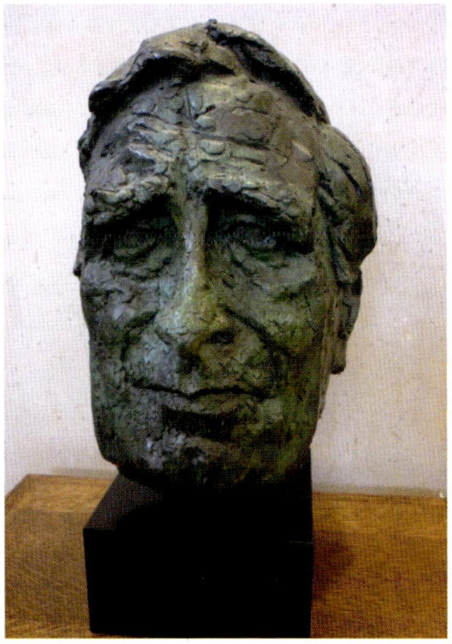

53 *Rt. Hon. Lord Edmund-Davies of Aberpennar PC*

1981–82
Bronze
28.5 x 19.7 x 20.6 cm
Collection: National Museum of Wales, Cardiff
Exhibition history: Royal National Eisteddfod of Wales, Llangefni, Anglesey, July–August 1983 (4)

Comments: Herbert Edmund Edmund-Davies (1906–1992) was born into a working-class household at Mountain Ash, near Aberfan in the South Wales valleys. After studying at Mountain Ash Grammar School, Kings College, London, and Exeter College, Oxford, he was called to the bar at Gray's Inn in 1929. In 1938, rather than pursuing an academic career at the London School of Economics, he moved to practise in Swansea. In 1935 he had married Eurwen, with whom he had three daughters. He served during the Second World War in the Royal Welch Fusiliers, rising to the rank of lieutenant-colonel. In 1943 he was made a KC, and Recorder for Swansea (to 1953), and in 1958 he became a Judge of the Queen's Bench Division. In 1964 he jailed the twelve Great Train Robbers for a total of 307 years.

In September 1966 he chaired the Tribunal of Enquiry into the Aberfan disaster, in which 116 children had been killed when a coal tip fell on their school. He emerged from the enquiry with a reputation as a 'man of compassion as well as of forthrightness' (*Guardian*, 29 December 1992, p. 10). In 1966 he was also appointed a Lord Justice of Appeal, retaining the post until 1974, and from 1969 to 1977 he served as chair of the home secretary's Criminal Law Revision Committee, where he proposed 'a number of radical and wide-ranging reforms ... in the face of opposition from the more Conservative-minded members of the legal profession'. He went out of his way to be fair to the police on the question of their pay. He also wrestled with the question of whether the number of women in the police force should be increased. He decided that present levels were sufficient on the grounds that there were many demanding physical duties for which women were not suited (*The Times*, 29 December 1992, p. 15). From 1974 to 1985 he held the post of pro-vice chancellor for the University of Wales.

After his death *The Times* stated:

> Among his peers Edmund-Davies was remarked not only for the wisdom of his judgements but for a brilliancy of intellect which had shown itself from his earliest days ... On the bench [he] became as noted for the incisiveness of his judgements as he had been for the shrewd nature of his pleadings at the Bar. To this were allied qualities of tact, patience, lucid intelligence and stamina which made him the ideal man to preside over long, complex trials.

Essentially a conservative figure, he always felt that the genuine concern he had for the rehabilitation of prisoners 'ought to be balanced by a concern for society at large and the damage suffered by those of its members who were victims of crime' (*The Times*, 29 December 1992, p. 15). Elsewhere he was widely regarded as 'typifying the best in Welsh intellectual and religious life of his time', and it was thought that he would be 'remembered with affection as a Liberal and humane judge of great academic distinction ... Throughout his life he remained ... conspicuously loyal to his roots and to many friends in Wales' (*Guardian*, 30 December 1992, p. 30).

The bronze cast was presented by the Hon. Sir William Mars-Jones MBE, of Gray's Inn, to Douglas A. Bassett, director of the NMW, Cardiff, 'on behalf of anonymous friends and admirers' on 17 July 1982 (*South Wales Echo*, 28 January 1984, p. 5).

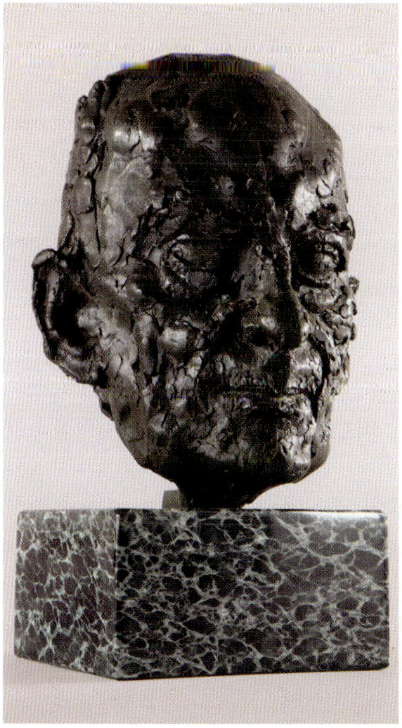

54 *Sir Alex Gordon, President of the Royal Institute of British Architects*

1982
Bronze
26.5 x 15.2 x 17.7 cm
Collection: Glynn Vivian Art Gallery, Swansea
Exhibition history: Royal National Eisteddfod of Wales, Llangefni, Anglesey, July–August 1983 (7)

Comments: Sir Alexander 'Alex' Gordon (1917–1999) was born in Scotland but grew up in Swansea, where his family moved when he was eight. He attended Swansea Grammar School along with Dylan Thomas. In 1935 he joined Swansea Borough's Architects Department. During the Second World War he served in the Royal Engineers as an officer and, after working for the Architectural School within the University of Wales, Cardiff, formed Alex Gordon and Partners in 1960. Two years later he was elected a Fellow of the Royal Institute of British Architects. During the 1960s he built a number of elegant bridges in South Wales, and later the Sherman Theatre in Cardiff and the Werin Theatre in Aberystwyth.

In 1971 he was elected president of the RIBA, holding the post until 1973. He was awarded the CBE in 1974 and knighted in 1988. He retired in 1982 to serve on the Royal Fine Arts Commission (RFAC) until 1987. In his later years he suffered from Parkinson's disease and went blind. A shy man, he never married. Friendly with Kyffin Williams, Gordon was an avid collector of modern art, and was especially pleased to have provided the design of the new West Wing of the NMW, Cardiff. During the 1980s he was also chairman of the Executive Council of the Welsh Sculpture Trust – to which Ivor also belonged from 1983. After his death in 1999, Gordon's art collection – including works by Kyffin Williams, Augustus John, Elisabeth Frink, Ben Nicholson and Barbara Hepworth – was gifted to the Glynn Vivian Art Gallery in Swansea (*Guardian*, 29 July 1999, p. 23).

According to his obituary in *The Times*, Gordon 'was one of the most influential Presidents of the RIBA'. He was 'opposed to both high rise and system building – he saw these as businessmen's buildings and not as architecture at all'. He was also equally contemptuous of the willingness of planners 'to cater for the motor car by tearing up cities and redeveloping them'. As president, he proved 'an outspoken, fearless critic of the scale of mistakes [that had been] made and ... were continuing to be made. Above all, he brought the views of the public into the open' (*The Times*, 29 July 1999, p. 25).

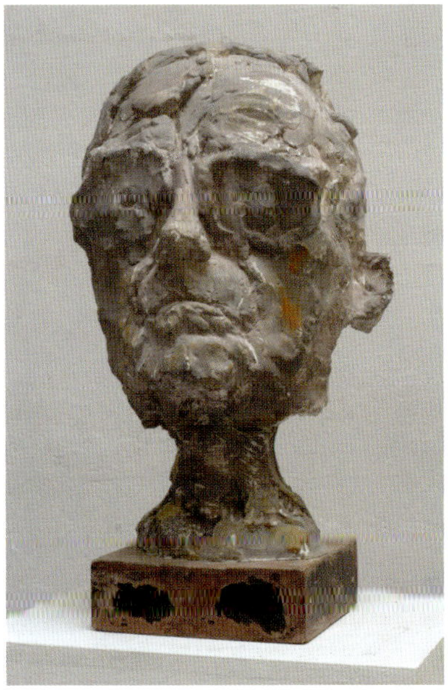

55 *Dmitri Shostakovich*

1982–83
Plaster
34.9 x 22.8 x 27 cm
Collection: private collection
Exhibition history: Royal Academy, May 1983 (1233); Wolsey Art Gallery, Ipswich, December 1999–January 2000
Related works: 55a: *Seven Studies of the Head of Dmitri Shostakovich*, November 1974, pencil and pen-and-ink on paper, 38 x 25 cm, Henry Moore Institute, Leeds
55b: *Small Head of Dmitri Shostakovich*, c. 1981–82, plaster, 9.9 x 9.6 x 12.1 cm, private collection
55c: *Two Studies of the Head of Dmitri Shostakovich*, 1982, pencil on paper, 24 x 25 cm, Henry Moore Institute, Leeds
55d: *Portrait Study of Dimitri Shostakovich*, 1982–83, watercolour, pen-and-ink and pencil on paper, 59 x 42 cm, Henry Moore Institute, Leeds

Comments: The portrait was apparently inspired by a photograph of the celebrated Russian composer (1906–1975), taken in old age, that was reproduced on the sleeve of an LP Ivor bought in November 1974. This inspired him to produce several sketches of Shostakovich in biro on paper. Ivor returned to the subject in 1982–83, possibly after reading the English translation of *Testimony: The Memoirs of Dmitri Shostakovich*, which had been published in 1977. In 1983 the artist told Peter Cannon-Brookes that, on the head of Shostakovich, 'the huge lenses of the spectacles act as a barricade against what he sees outside him and gives the head a sense of inwardness' (Cannon-Brookes, *Ivor Roberts-Jones*, p. 71).

Apart from Shostakovich and Stravinsky, Ivor also encouraged his students to listen to the music of Mahler and Alban Berg. Brian Morley, a student of painting at Goldsmiths in the mid 1950s, later recalled Ivor recommending these composers to his students, as well as the work of British composers who had come to prominence since the end of the Second World War such as William Walton, Michael Tippett, and especially Benjamin Britten (Brian Morley to Monica Roberts-Jones, 12 January 1997, IRJ Papers, Archives, HMI, Leeds).

55a

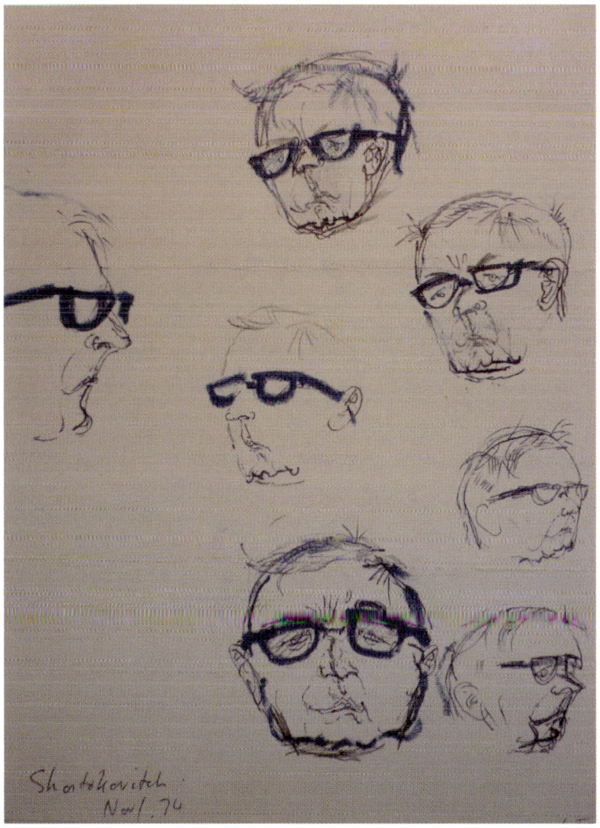

55b

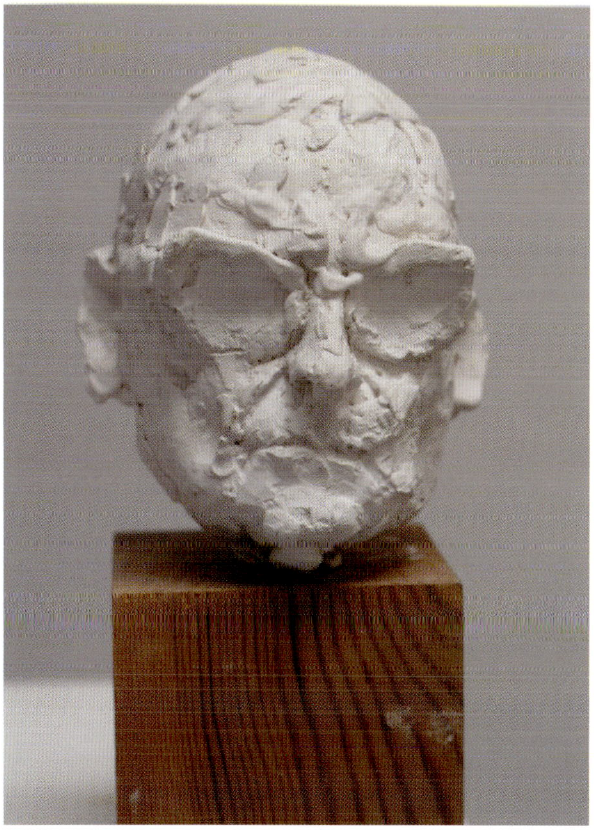

55c

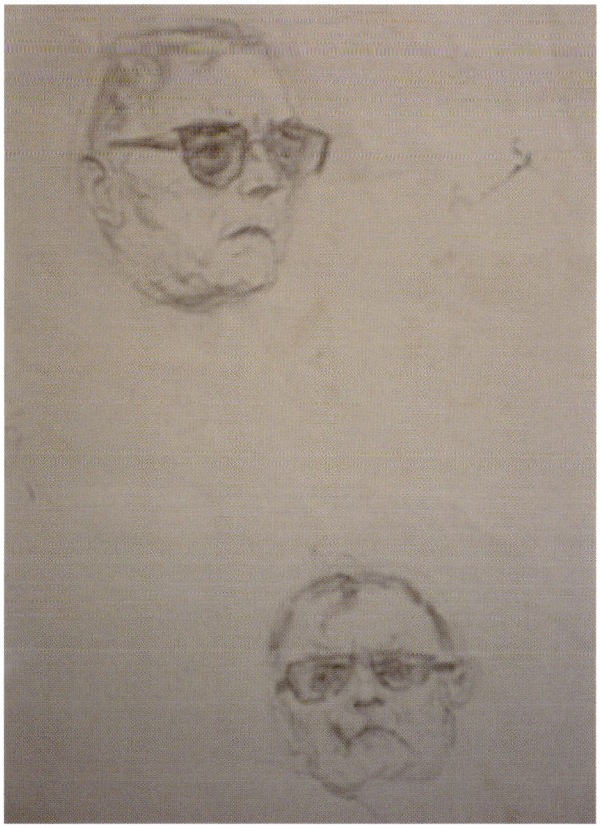

55d

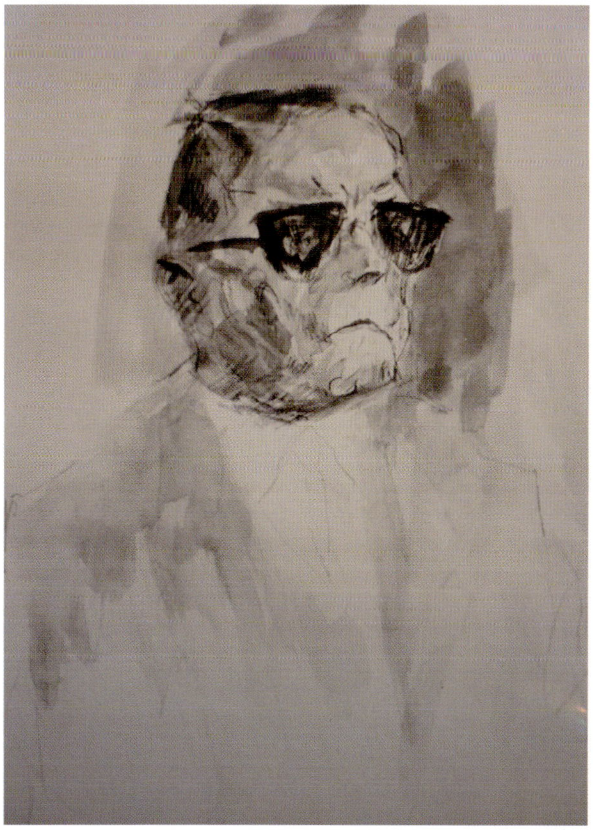

56 *Sir Geraint Evans CBE*

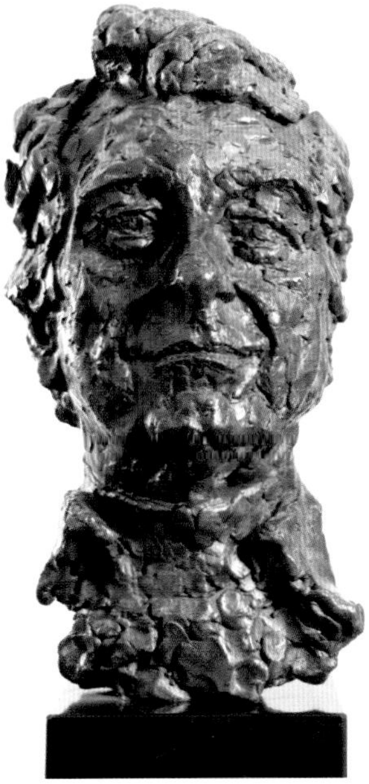

1982–83
Bronze
42.5 x 21 x 27.4 cm
Collection: National Portrait Gallery, London; National Museum of Wales, Cardiff

Comments: Evans (1922–1992) was one of the most talented and celebrated Welsh opera singers of his day – the son of a miner from the small village of Cilfynydd, near Pontypridd. His roots in South Wales remained of huge importance to Evans throughout his life. Both his future close friend and the future Labour home secretary, Merlin Rees, and his future wife, Betty, grew up on his street in Cilfynydd. Evans left school at 14, but his father was determined that his son would not go down the local pit. Instead he found work as a window-dresser in a local woman's fashion shop. Encouraged by a local choirmaster and by his own family, he managed to gain a place at the prestigious Guildhall School of Music and, after service in the RAF as a radar operator during the war, made his debut as a bass baritone at Covent Garden in January 1948.

His vocal talents were highly admired by Benjamin Britten, who insisted he appear in productions of his operas *Peter Grimes* and *Billy Budd*. Evans went on to become famous for his performances as Falstaff, as the 'master-at-arms' from *Billy Budd* and as Figaro. After his death he was described as an 'expert in winning the affection of audiences for his characters ... with a single telling phrase'. A favourite of Prince Charles, Evans was knighted in 1969. His final performance took place at the Royal Opera House in June 1984 (*The Times*, 21 September 1992, p. 17). Shortly before this performance, Evans described himself to John Mortimer as a 'moderate Welsh nationalist' who believed that, while the Welsh and the English could get on, they were two very different peoples: 'The Welsh ... are short and dark, totally different from the English, closer, perhaps, to the people of the Mediterranean' (*Sunday Times*, 13 May 1984, p. 37).

In retirement Evans continued his unstinting support for the cause of classical music in Wales. In 1990 he established a Scholarship Fund, to which he contributed handsomely, at the Welsh College of Music and Drama (WCMD), to help deserving young musicians. The singer insisted on personally auditioning the first group of applicants himself. He was a much loved figure to all for his master classes, provided for professionals and students alike. The principal of the WCMD described Evans as 'the most human of individuals, full of fun, warmth and generosity. Welshmen have a reputation for wearing their hearts on their sleeves; in this respect, Geraint was the epitome. He just did not know how to say "no" to requests for his help and support. Indeed, in some respects this may well have been his undoing' (*The Times*, 28 September 1992, p. 15).

In late February 1983 Ivor wrote to Robin Gibson (registrar of the National Portrait Gallery, London) that he was 'starting on a head of Sir Geraint Evans very shortly' (27 February 1983, IRJ File, Archives, NPG, London). In January 1984 the bronze of Evans was presented to the director of the NMW, Cardiff, Douglas Bassett, by Sir John Tooley, general administrator of the Royal Opera House at Covent Garden. The commission had been paid for by the Welsh Portrait Sculpture Trust; its co-founder, Judge Bruce Griffiths, told a local newspaper that the trust, the museum and the sculptor were all 'keen to commemorate eminent figures in Wales' (*South Wales Echo*, 28 January 1984, p. 5). Since 1981 the trust had commissioned Ivor to make portrait heads of Viscount Tonypandy and Lord Edmund-Davies, the head of Sir Geraint was the next in what Griffiths was sure would be a distinguished series of portraits that generations of visitors to the National Museum would cherish.

Evans interjected that Ivor's head 'looked more handsome than he did ... If this head could break into song, Viscount Tonypandy will always be there to shout "Order, Order" and Lord Edmund-Davies to pronounce: "30 years".' The artist, who was also present, told a reporter that 'Sir Geraint had proved a marvellous sitter and his vivid features had made him an excellent subject' (*Western Mail*, 30 January 1984, p. 8).

Later in 1984, the National Portrait Gallery in London purchased a cast of the head of Evans for its own collection from Ivor for £2,000 (Robin Simon to IRJ, 22 August 1984, IRJ File, Archives, NPG, London).

57 *Dr Benjamin Jones CBE, LLD*

1983
Bronze
Collection: private collection
Exhibition history: bronze (edition of 5), Royal Academy, May 1985 (1386).

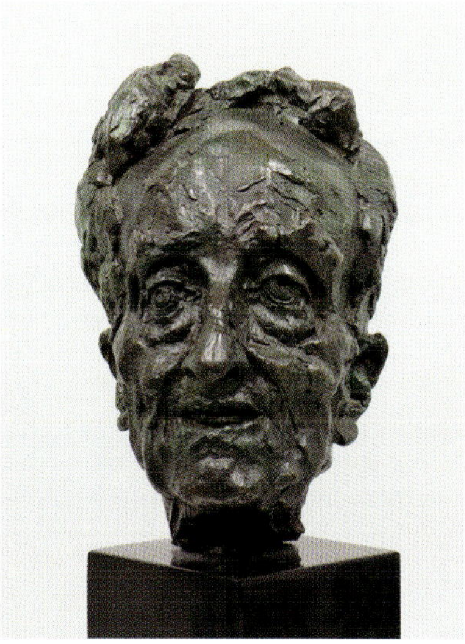

58 *Saunders Lewis*

1983–84
Bronze
30.2 x 19 x 25.6 cm
Collection: National Museum of Wales, Cardiff
Exhibition history: unknown

Comments: When he died, aged 92, Lewis (1893–1985) was described in one obituary as 'The Voice of Welsh Power' (*Guardian*, 2 September 1985, p. 2). An accomplished novelist, poet and playwright, he was a founder member, in 1925, of the Welsh Nationalist Party, Plaid Cymru, and was its first president (1926–39). Lewis was actually born in Wallasey, Merseyside, the son of a Welsh nonconformist minister, and studied English at Liverpool University (1911–14). He served in France during the First World War, where he came under the spell of the writer Maurice Barres, whose influence led him to convert to Roman Catholicism. In his influential *Principles of Nationalism* (1926), Lewis argued that English nationalism was killing

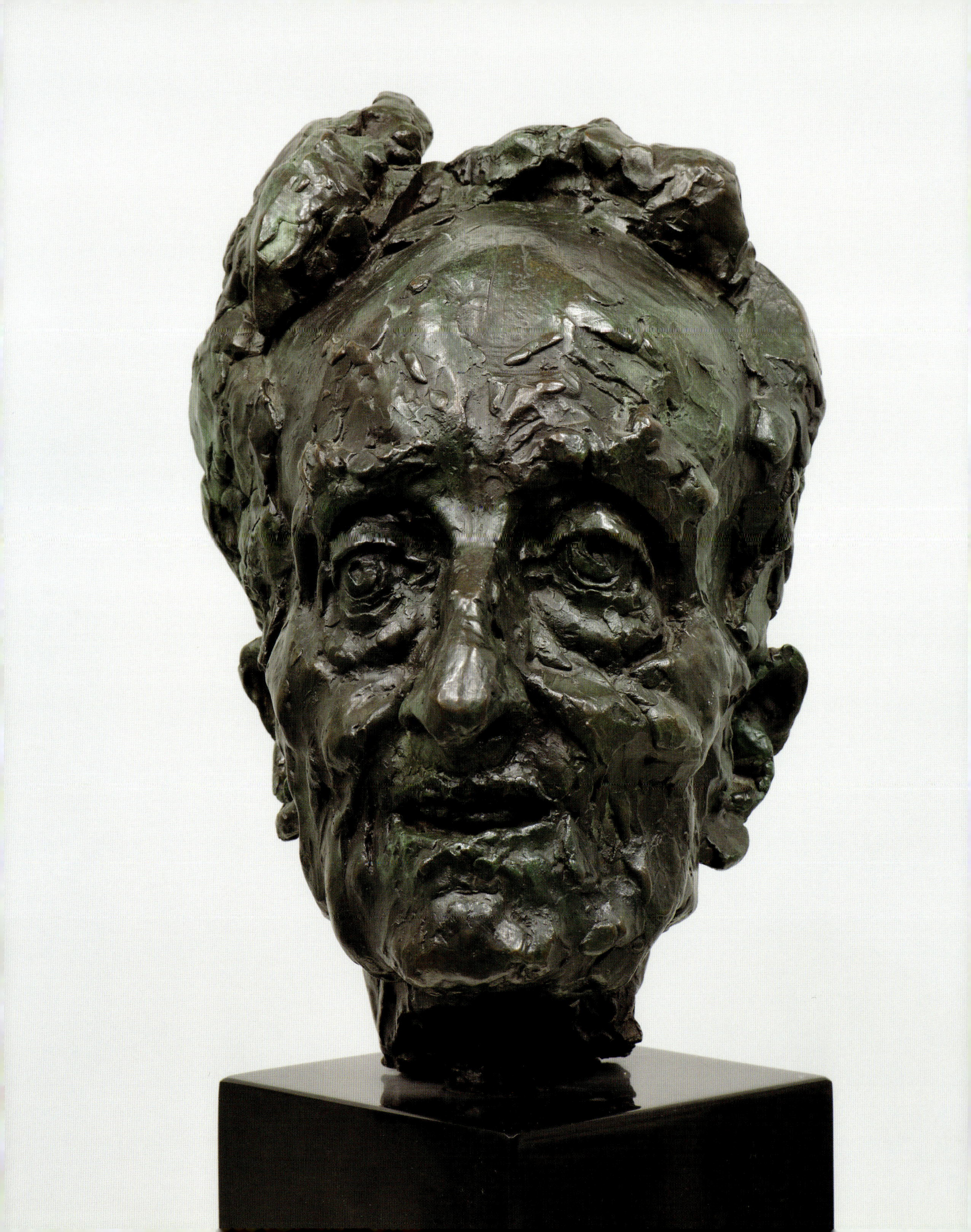

Welsh-speaking culture and that the nation required political autonomy in order to flourish. He admired the traditionalism of the French Catholic right, and particularly the writings of Paul Claudel, but was wary of its admiration for Fascism. After his involvement in burning down three storage sheds at an RAF base on the Llŷn peninsula in North Wales, in 1936, Lewis felt he had taken direct action in defence of Welsh culture, as far as he could. After this act of arson, he quickly gave himself up to the police and was put on trial in Caernarfon. However, the local jury could not reach a verdict. His trial was moved to London, where Lewis was found guilty and sentenced to nine months in prison. Having acquired a criminal record, he was promptly sacked as a lecturer at Swansea University in 1937, and would not find employment in higher education until 1952, when he was appointed a lecturer at Cardiff University. During and after the Second World War his plays were often broadcast on the radio by BBC Wales. In 1962 one of his fiery radio lectures, on 'The Fate of the Welsh Language', helped inspire the creation of the Welsh Language Society. After his death, *The Times* argued that Lewis was 'never the fanatical figure sometimes conjured up by his detractors. He never preached hatred of the English and the sacrifices he demanded were always of the Welsh themselves' (*The Times*, 2 September 1985, p. 12). An Anglican clergyman, Canon Allchin, later declared that Lewis 'must surely stand, with T. S. Eliot and David Jones, as one of the outstanding Christian writers of this century' (*The Times*, 10 September 1985, p. 14).

Lewis was held in very high regard by two writers Ivor enjoyed reading: the celebrated left-wing Welsh historian Gwyn Williams (1925–1995) (*Guardian*, 17 November 1995, p. 19) and the Wales-based travel writer Jan Morris (*Guardian*, 16 July 2000, p. 16).

The head of Lewis was commissioned from Ivor by the Welsh Portrait Sculpture Trust, and was presented to the National Museum of Wales by its co-founder Sir Alun Talfan-Davies on 14 July 1984, Bastille Day – a date the Francophile Lewis would have appreciated (IRJ to Megan Crofton, 26 April 1984, Megan Thomas Archive).

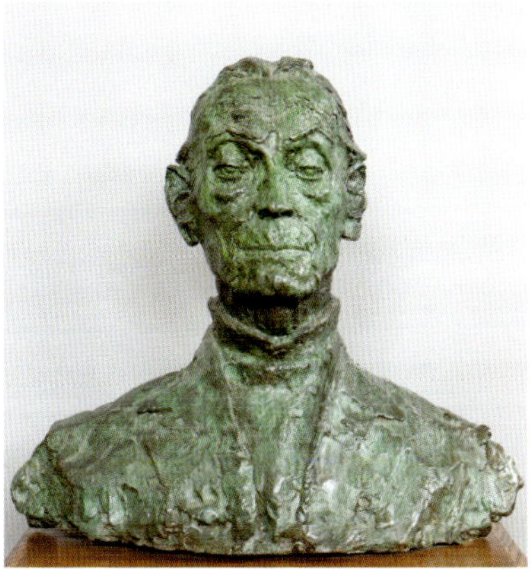

59 *Dr Alun Oldfield-Davies CBE, LLD*

1984–85
Bronze
50 x 55.1 x 28.3 cm
Collection: National Museum of Wales, Cardiff
Exhibition history: Bronze (edition of 5), Royal Academy, May 1985 (1387)

Comments: A longstanding champion of the Welsh language, Oldfield-Davies (1905–1988) was, from 1945 to 1948, the first director of the BBC's Welsh Home Service, then Controller of BBC Wales from 1945 to 1967. For many years he was president of the National Museum of Wales. He was born in Wallasey, Merseyside, the son of a clergyman, and educated at Rhondda County School and the University College of Wales, Aberystwyth. After graduating as a teacher, he taught in a succession of Welsh schools for twelve years before joining the BBC's Education Department in Cardiff in 1937. In 1950, five years after taking over BBC Wales, he was appointed chairman of the Advisory Council to the Welsh Department of

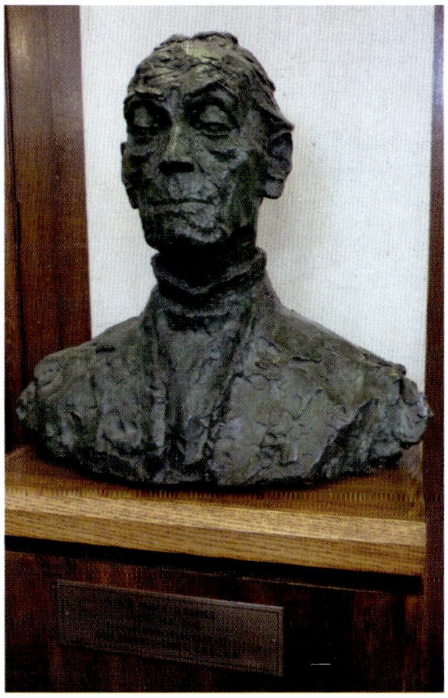

the Ministry of Information. In 1955 he was appointed CBE, and he was made an LLD in 1967, his retirement year, by the University of Wales. At his death, *The Times* described him as 'a first-rate broadcasting practitioner who could command the confidence and regard of Welsh people generally ... [he was] a man of intellectual strength and agreeable personality with a towering presence [and] in a deliberate but friendly way held the ring effectively against the pressures of both the Welsh-speaking and the English-speaking of Welsh society and to build up a programme service in Wales of high standard in both languages' (*The Times*, 7 December 1988, p. 16).

The idea of commissioning Ivor to make a head of Oldfield-Davies appears to have originated with Peter Cannon-Brookes (Keeper of Art at the NMW, Cardiff) in July 1984 (P. Cannon-Brookes to the director of the NMW, Cardiff, 12 July 1984, IRJ File, Archives, NMW, Cardiff). Later that same month, it was decided the commission could go ahead, at a cost of £2,800. Towards the end of August 1984 the prospective sitter had been approached by the museum's director, and had agreed to sit for the portrait. In November Oldfield-Davies, who lived in Llandaff, Cardiff, arranged to stay the weekend with Ivor at his Suffolk house in Cratfield. Ivor wrote to the NMW's registrar that Oldfield-Davies was looking forward to the trip: '[T]he idea of spending one long weekend with us in Suffolk and finishing in one "session" has appealed to him' (IRJ to Dr Richard Edgecumbe, 3 November 1984, ibid.).

Just two months later Ivor wrote to the registrar, Richard Edgecumbe: 'I have a slight surprise for you ... I have made a head and shoulders of Alun Oldfield Davies ... [he] was so tall and his head sprang up from his shoulders so vividly – there was no avoiding carrying him out in that way ... he will shortly be going up to the foundry' (IRJ to Dr Richard Edgecumbe, 12 January 1985, ibid.). After having had a chance to study photographs of the plaster cast of the head, the Registrar replied that 'the shoulders of Alun Oldfield Davies [were] a wonderful idea and your generosity is much appreciated' (Dr Richard Edgecumbe to IRJ, 4 February 1985, ibid.). The bronze was delivered to the Museum in April 1985, and was on public display by the spring of the following year.

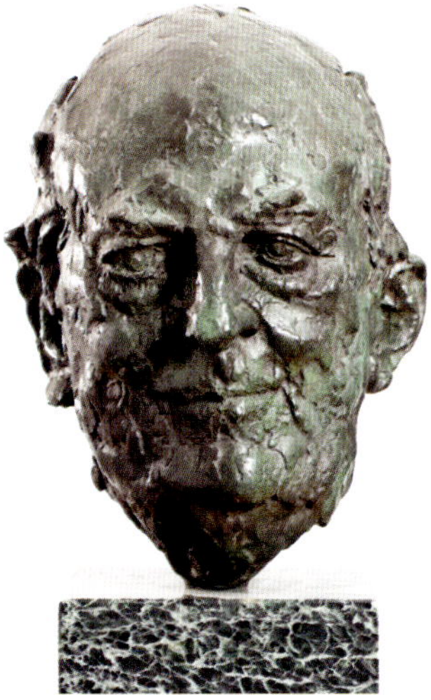

60 *Rt. Hon. Sir Tasker Watkins VC*

1985
Bronze
29.4 x 21.7 x 26.3 cm
Collection: National Museum of Wales, Cardiff
Exhibition history: unknown

Comments: Watkins (1918–2007) was born in Nelson, Caerphilly, and educated at Pontypridd Grammar School. He was awarded the Victoria Cross in August 1944 for taking command of a company of the Welch Regiment, whose first attack on a German position in Normandy had failed. He personally led a bayonet charge that captured two German machine-gun posts at Fresnay-le-Vieum, and then captured a third post on his own, armed with a Bren gun. After the war he studied law, and was called to the bar at the Middle Temple in 1948. He was made a QC in 1965 and knighted six years later. In 1969 he prosecuted extremists of the Welsh

Nationalist Free Wales Army, who had planned to plant bombs at the investiture of Prince Charles as Prince of Wales in Caernarfon Castle.

He was appointed Deputy Lord-Lieutenant of Wales in 1979, and the following year made Lord Justice of Appeal. During the period when he sat to Ivor, Watkins was much preoccupied with how the law should best clamp down on so-called 'video nasties' without impinging on creative freedoms, and also how to frame a new approach in law that acknowledged the existence of marital rape.

In 1988 he was appointed Deputy Chief Justice for England and Wales. After retirement, in 1993, he was elected the forty-sixth president of the Welsh Rugby Union (1993–2004), campaigning tirelessly for the construction of the new Millennium Stadium in Cardiff. Asked in November 2001 about the circumstances in which he had won his VC, Watkins told a journalist:

> I did what needed doing to help colleagues and friends, just as others looked out for me during the fighting that summer ... I didn't wake up the next day a better or braver person, just different. I'd seen more killing and death in 24 hours – indeed been part of that terrible process – than is right for anybody. From that point onwards I have tried to take a more caring view of my fellow human beings and that, of course, always includes your opponent whether it be in war, sport or life just generally (*Daily Telegraph*, 10 September 2007, p. 18).

Peter Cannon-Brookes first raised the idea of Ivor portraying Watkins in July 1984 (Dr Peter Cannon-Brookes to IRJ, 17 July 1984, IRJ File, Archives, NMW, Cardiff). In January the following year, Ivor wrote to the NMW's registrar that he was 'about to start on Watkins and ... that will be another compact head. That is the way I see him' (IRJ to Dr Richard Edgecumbe, 12 January 1985, IRJ File, Archive, NMW, Cardiff). The head entered the NMW collection in the early autumn of 1985.

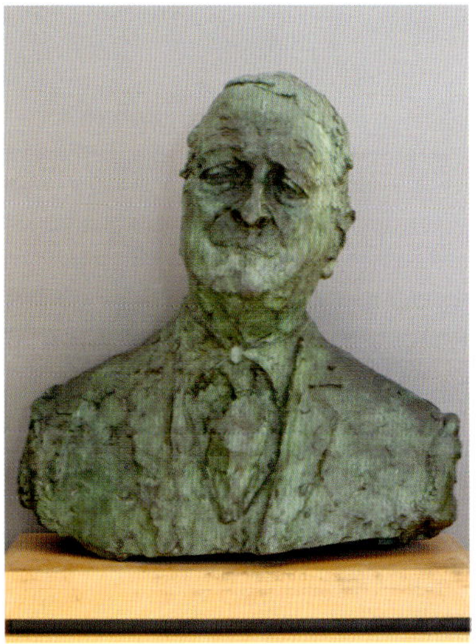

61 *Sir Cennydd Traherne KG*

1985–86
Bronze
52.2 x 51.4 x 31.1 cm
Collection: National Museum of Wales, Cardiff
Exhibition history: unknown

Comments: Traherne (1910–1995) was educated at Wellington and Brasenose College, Oxford, and knighted in 1970. He sat to Ivor having recently retired as Lord-Lieutenant of Glamorgan – a post he held from 1952 to 1985 (*Western Mail*, 28 April 1986, Press Clippings Book, NMW, Cardiff). He had also sat for many years on the Council of the NMW, Cardiff.

In January 1985 Ivor mentioned in a letter to the registrar of the NMW that he was currently 'working on Sir Cennydd Traherne in his Garter Robes as suggested

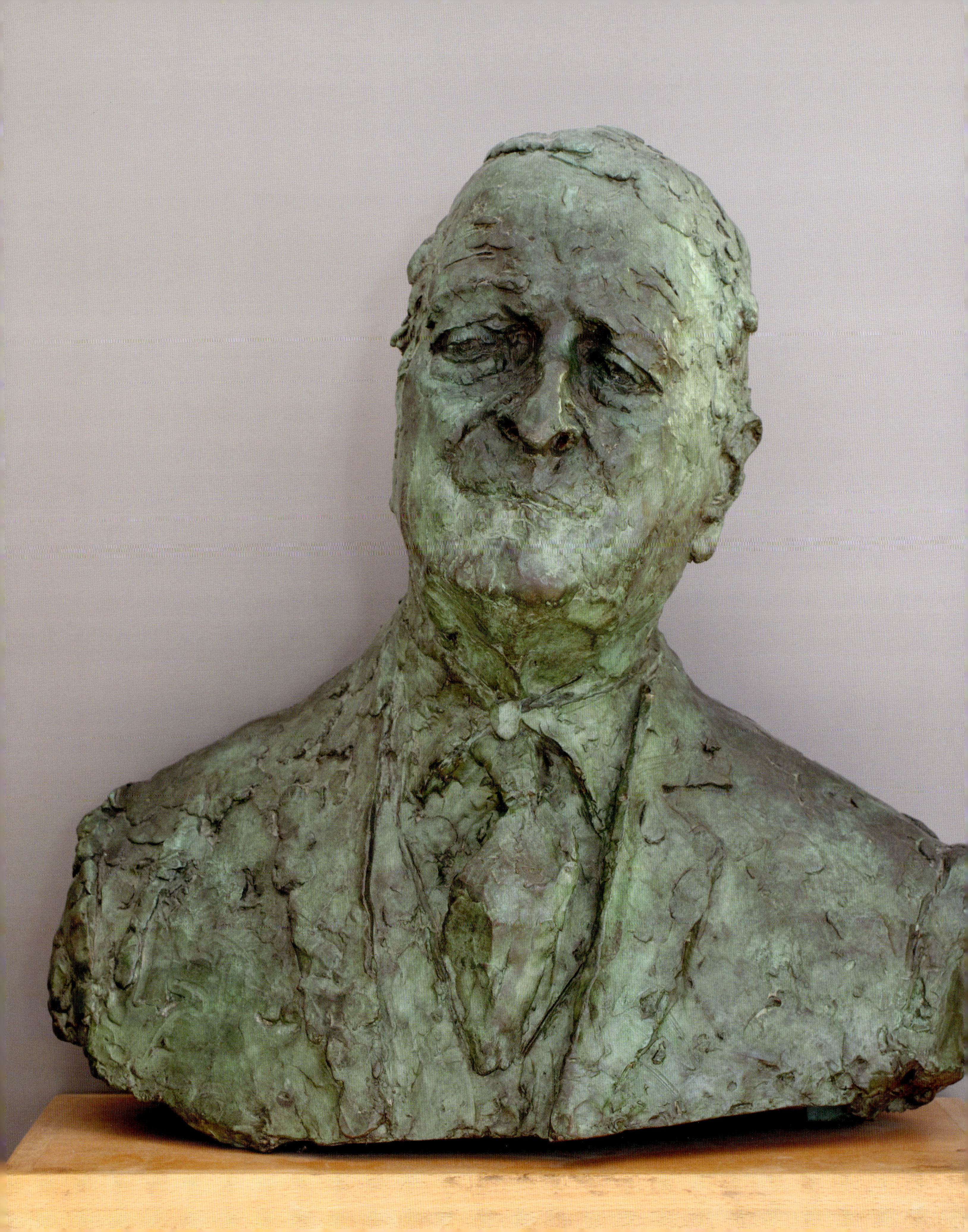

by Bruce Griffiths and Alun Talfan-Davies' (IRJ to Dr Richard Edgecumbe, 12 January 1985, IRJ File, Archives, NMW, Cardiff). Griffiths and Davies constituted the Welsh Portrait Sculpture Trust, and Sir Alun presented the head on behalf of the Trust to D. W. Dykes, director of the NMW, Cardiff, on 26 April 1986. Also present at the ceremony was a man who would soon be sitting to Ivor for his portrait – president of the NMW, W. A. Twiston-Davies (*Western Mail*, 28 April 1986, p. 8). Three years later Traherne would support the idea of the museum commissioning Ivor to make a portrait for it of former Prime Minister James Callaghan (*Western Mail*, 20 November 1989, p. 10).

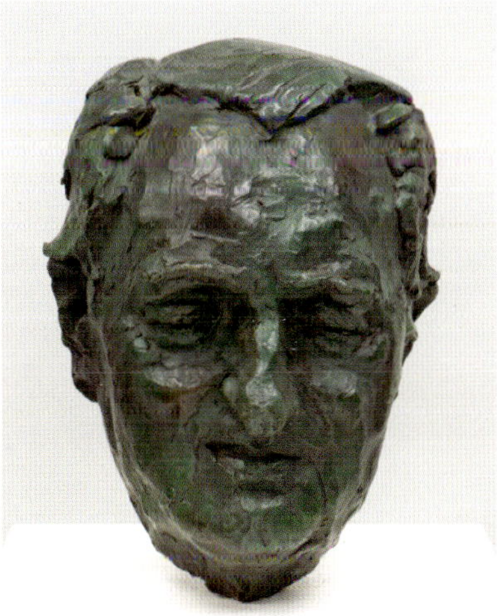

62 *W. A. Twiston-Davies*

1986
Bronze
32.5 x 22.6 x 28.8 cm,
Collection: National Museum of Wales, Cardiff
Exhibition history: unknown

Comments: When he sat to Ivor, Twiston-Davies (1925–1989) was the president of the NMW, Cardiff. In mid July 1986 Ivor wrote to Mark Davis, the new Keeper of Art at the museum:

> I shall be having my last sitting of the head of Twiston on the 19 August and then I shall be sending him up to the Foundry shortly after that. It is virtually finished but I like to leave things awhile so that I can get a rather more detached view of him. Unwrapping it to show Jim Callaghan, who is at present sitting for me, it struck him very forcibly and I don't think there is much more to be done.

The head had been commissioned by Davis's predecessor, Peter Cannon-Brookes, in the summer of 1985 for £3,500 (IRJ to Dr Mark Evans, 22 April 1987, IRJ File, Archives, NMW, Cardiff).

63 *Lord Elwyn-Jones of Llanelli CH*

1986
Bronze
30.7 x 24.5 x 27.3 cm
Collection: National Museum of Wales, Cardiff
Exhibition history: unknown

Comments: Frederick Elwyn-Jones (1909–1989) was born in Llanelli, Carmarthenshire, and studied history at the University of Wales, Aberystwyth, and at Gonville and Caius College, Cambridge. After wartime service, he qualified as a barrister and served as junior British prosecuting counsel during the Nuremburg war trials. In July 1945 he was elected Labour MP for Plaistow and, five years later, for West

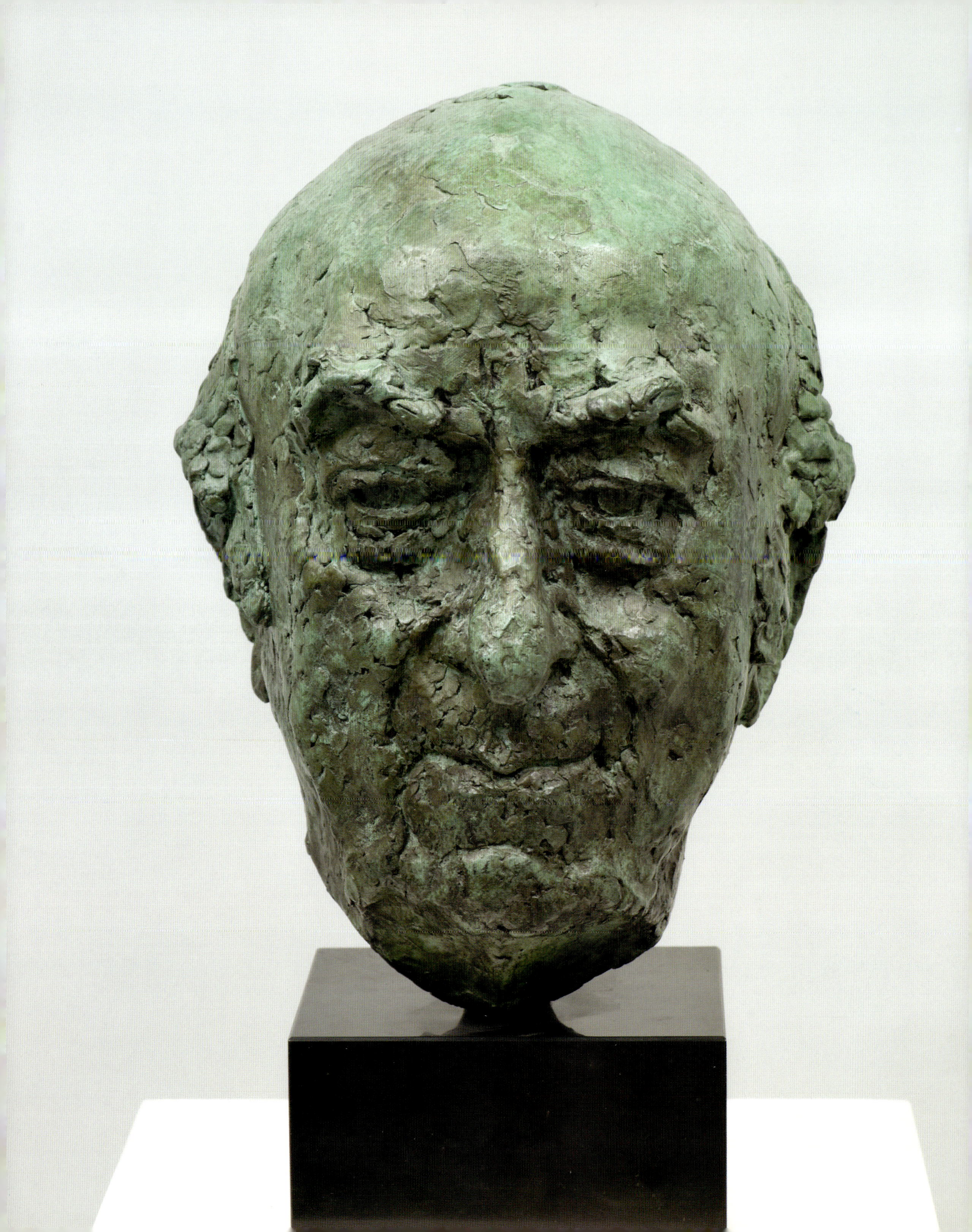

Ham South. In 1964 he was appointed attorney general by Harold Wilson, and held the post until 1970. Four years later he stood down from the Commons and went to the House of Lords as a Labour Life Peer, Baron Elwyn-Jones. From 1974 to 1979 he served as lord chancellor for Wilson, and then James Callaghan, from 1974 to 1979, and in 1976 was made a Companion of Honour. At the time he sat to Ivor, he was president of University College, Cardiff (*Western Mail*, 24 November 1987, p. 8).

The head of Elwyn-Jones had been commissioned from Ivor by the Welsh Sculpture Portrait Trust. It was presented by Judge Bruce Griffiths, on behalf of the Trust to the director of the NMW, Cardiff, on 28 November 1987. The head had been cast over a year previously, but an official presentation ceremony had been repeatedly postponed owing to Elwyn-Jones's poor health (IRJ to Dr Mark Evans, 21 November 1987, IRJ File, Archive, NMW, Cardiff). Indeed, he only lived for a further eighteen months after the head had been unveiled.

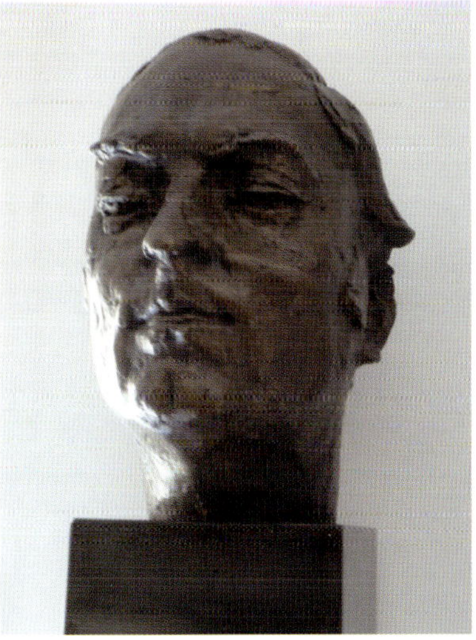

64 *Dr. Peter Cannon-Brookes FRSA*

1986–87
Bronze
30.5 x 22.2 x 26.7 cm
Collection: private collection
Exhibition history: Royal Academy, May 1988 (1097); Royal Cambrian Academy, Conwy, February 1999

Comments: Cannon-Brookes (1938–) was the first Keeper of Art at Birmingham Museum and Art Gallery (1965–78), and also held the keepership of art at the NMW, Cardiff, from February 1978 to May 1986. Between 1979 and 1986 he ensured the Cardiff museum bought seven bronze portrait heads from Ivor. Four of them were commissions Cannon-Brookes had himself proposed: *Alun Oldfield-Davies*, *Sir Tasker Watkins VC*, *W.A. Twiston-Davies* and *The Third Earl of Plymouth*. In 1983 he published the only study of Ivor to appear in the artist's lifetime – *Ivor Roberts-Jones: The Journey to Harlech* – and worked closely with the artist on the exhibition of the same name organised by the Welsh Arts Council and the NMW, Cardiff, and held in July–August 1983, during the Royal National Eisteddfod of Wales at Llangefni, Anglesey.

After the artist's death he curated a display of Ivor's sculpture at the Royal Academy, London, between April and August 1997, and also at the Royal Cambrian Academy in March 1999. In November 1999 he attended the unveiling of the cast of Ivor's Parliament Square figure of Winston Churchill in Prague, representing Monica Roberts-Jones. He also penned the introduction to the catalogue accompanying the exhibition *Ivor Roberts-Jones (1913–1996)*, held in December 1999 and January 2000 at the Wolsey Art Gallery, Ipswich, in which he wrote: 'Ivor Roberts-Jones's portrait sculptures clearly reveal him as the most outstanding British-born sculptor of the second half of the 20th Century.'

Cannon-Brookes was a Trustee of the Welsh Sculpture Trust from 1982 to 1994, and has been the editor of the *International Journal of Museum Management and Curatorship* since 2003.

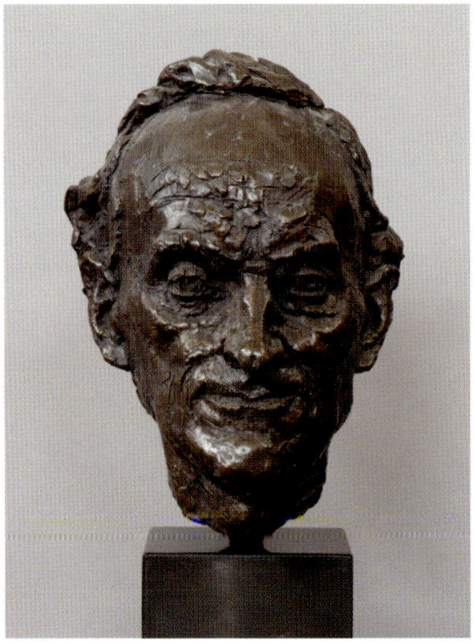

65 *The Third Earl of Plymouth*

1987
Bronze
34.8 x 23.5 x 25.6 cm
Collection: National Museum of Wales, Cardiff
Exhibition history: unknown

Comments: Robert Windsor-Clive, Third Earl of Plymouth (1923–), Viscount Windsor of St Fagan's in the County of Glamorgan, is a major landowner in Wales. For much of the 1970s the earl was president of the Council of the NMW, Cardiff.

The portrait was first mooted to Ivor by Peter Cannon-Brookes in July 1984. This direct commission from the NMW, Cardiff was to be priced at £2,800 (this was raised shortly after to £3,500 – Dr Peter Cannon-Brookes to IRJ, 12 July 1984, IRJ File, Archives, NMW, Cardiff]. The earl agreed to sit for the head early in October 1984; but sittings were delayed by a combination of Ivor falling ill and requiring an operation, his moving house during the summer of 1986, and the demands of his commission to make a full-size figure of Rupert Brooke for Rugby. Eventually, in April 1987, Ivor was able to report to Cannon-Brookes's successor: 'The head of Lord Plymouth is well underway' (IRJ to Dr Mark Evans, 22 April 1987, ibid.).

Two months later he wrote to the new keeper of art that 'Lord Plymouth [was] just about to go to the Foundry' (IRJ to Dr Mark Evans, 28 June 1987, ibid.). The head was ready for delivery to the conference room at the NMW, Cardiff, in January 1988. The artist was pleased to report that the sitter was so taken with the portrait that he had paid for an additional cast for his personal collection (IRJ to Mrs Davies, NMW, Cardiff, 9 June 1988, ibid.).

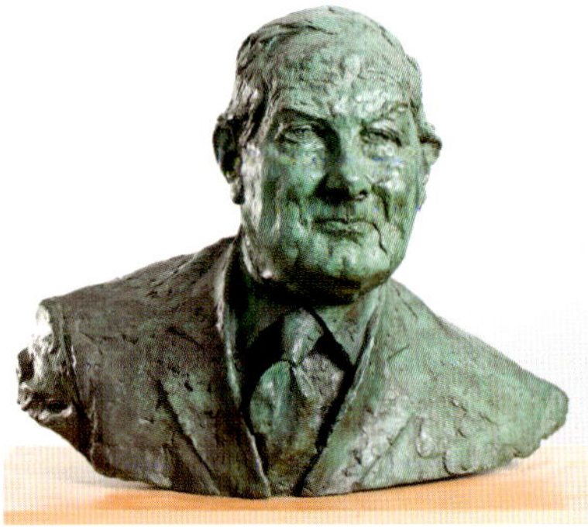

66 *Lord Callaghan of Cardiff KG, PC*

1987–88
Bronze
52 x 53 x 30 cm
Collection: National Museum of Wales, Cardiff
Exhibition history: unknown

Comments: Leonard James Callaghan (1912–2005) was born in Portsmouth. His father was a chief petty officer in the Royal Navy who died when James was just nine years old. Callaghan was educated at Portsmouth Northern Secondary School; he always regretted not having attended university. In 1929 he joined the Inland Revenue as a clerk, becoming a full-time union official in 1936. Four years later, in June 1940, he volunteered to serve in the Royal Navy. In the general election of July 1945 he won the seat of Cardiff South for Labour from the Conservatives. In 1964 Harold Wilson appointed him chancellor of the exchequer, and then home secretary (1967–70) and foreign secretary (1974–76). With the resignation of Wilson, in April 1976, 'Sunny Jim' Callaghan won the ensuing leadership election within the Labour Party, becoming prime minister. For much of his tenure in that office he faced prolonged periods of serious industrial unrest. He signally failed to tackle or resolve the so-called 'Winter of Discontent' of December 1978–January 1979,

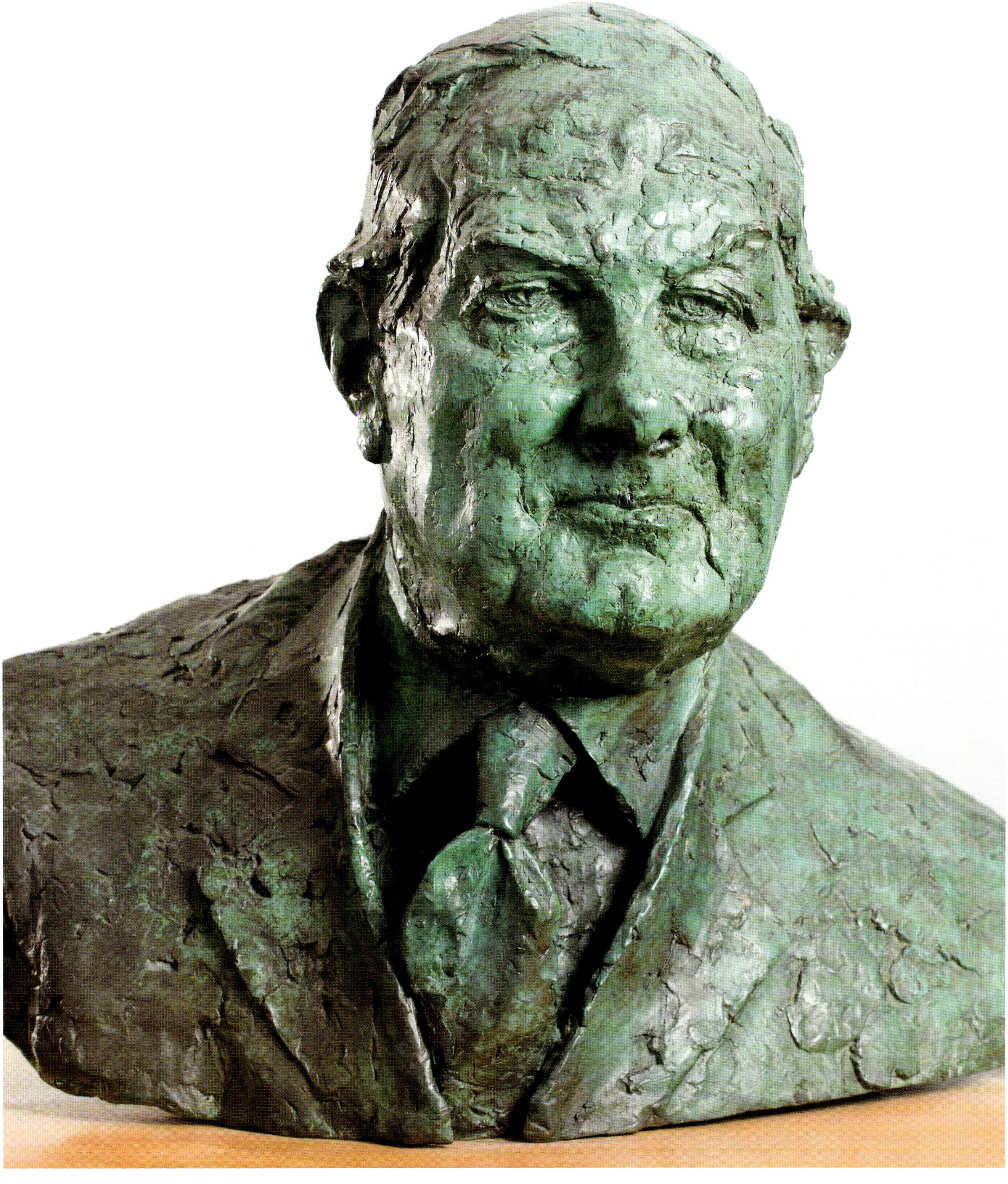

and lost the general election of May 1979 to Margaret Thatcher. He stepped down as leader of the Labour Party in November 1980. Between 1983 and 1987 he was father of the house, leaving his Cardiff seat in 1987 to become Lord Callaghan of Cardiff. In the House of Lords he attacked the Labour Party's commitment to unilateral nuclear disarmament in defence policy, as well as the activities of the extreme-left 'Militant Tendency' in municipal government (*Guardian*, 28 March 2005, p. 17).

This portrait was a commission from Ivor by the Welsh Portrait Sculpture Trust early in 1987, when Callaghan was about to set down as MP for Cardiff South. Ivor's fee on this occasion was £4,000. Sittings began in March 1987; a month later Ivor wrote to the Keeper of Art at the NMW: 'I am finding the Callaghan difficult to complete' (IRJ to Dr Mark Evans, 22 April 1987, IRJ File, Archive, NMW, Cardiff). During their conversations it emerged that, as prime minister, Callaghan had taken a close interest in the course of the 1977–78 competition for the memorial statue to Clement Attlee, which Ivor won. Callaghan also admired the figure of Attlee Ivor had produced, and he was in the audience when it was unveiled in the Members' Lobby of the House of Commons in November 1979. Ivor had also been in the audience at that ceremony, sitting not far from ex-prime minister Callaghan, but there is no evidence to suggest they met on that occasion). By June 1987, however, the sculptor was 'unusually satisfied with the head of Callaghan', and it was soon despatched to the foundry (IRJ to Dr Mark Evans, 28 June 1987, ibid.).

The head was officially presented to the director of the NMW, Cardiff, by Judge Griffiths, on behalf of the Welsh Portrait Sculpture Trust, on 18 November 1989. After the ceremony Callaghan told a reporter from the local newspaper: 'It was a great honour to be depicted by such a talented sculptor ... There is always a risk in being portrayed because artists have strong feelings about their subjects and their subjects very rarely like their own busts. But I am flattered by Mr Roberts-Jones's depiction and the finished bust is a first rate work of art' (*Western Mail*, 20 November 1989, p. 10).

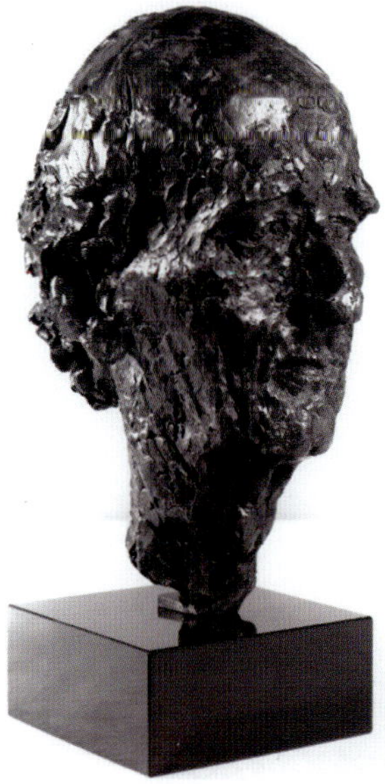

67 *Sir Nicholas Proctor Goodison*

1989–90
Bronze
46 x 17 x 25.5 cm
Collection: National Portrait Gallery, London; private collection
Exhibition history: unknown

Comments: Goodison (1934–) is a financier, a former chairman of the Trustee Savings Bank (1989–95) and of the London Stock Exchange (1976–86). He was knighted in 1982 for services to the nation's financial sector. He is also a con noisseur and collector – at the time he sat to Ivor he was chairman of the Courtauld Institute of Art (1982–2002) and of the National Art Collections Fund (1986–2002). Between 1980 and 1998 he was also vice-chairman of English National Opera. He is an authority on eighteenth- and nineteenth-century English barometers and on eighteenth-century furniture, and is a fellow of the Worshipful Company of Clockmakers as well as president of the Furniture History Society (since 1990).

The head was commissioned to acknowledge Goodison's fourteen years as chairman of the Stock Exchange and thirty years with the firm of Quilter, Goodison & Co. The sitter later recalled that he was advised to select Ivor to do his portrait by two friends he had made through their shared membership of the NACF: Sir Hugh Casson – a recent president of the Royal Academy (1976–1984) – and Sir Roger de Grey (1918–1995), the then president of the Royal Academy (1984–93) (Sir Nicholas Proctor Goodison, 'Sitting for a Portrait', September 2000, copy in IRJ File, Archives, NPG, London).

Several sittings took place at Ivor's London home between January and October 1989. By the end of that period the sitter was 'very impressed with it [but Ivor] said that he thought there was something not quite right about the treatment of the top of the nose and its relationship to the recesses of the eyes. He added a small piece of clay and the modelling looked instantly right' (Sir Nicholas Proctor Goodison, September 2000, copy in IRJ File, Archives, NPG, London). The head was cast in May 1990, and Ivor was 'particularly pleased with the head's patina' (ibid.).

Two years later Sir Nicholas raised the possibility of the National Portrait Gallery in London acquiring a cast of the head with the gallery's director, Sir John Hayes (Sir Nicholas Goodison to Sir John Hayes, 27 May 1992, IRJ File, Archive, NPG, London). Sir John replied in June 1992: 'I was delighted, as I said on the telephone, when we spoke, to see photographs of Roberts-Jones's excellent bust and likeness and I would be very happy indeed to recommend this to the Trustees when they meet on Friday, 16 July' (Sir John Hayes to Sir Nicholas Goodison, 8 June 1992, ibid.).

The trustees' meeting unfolded as Sir John had predicted, and later in July he wrote to Sir Nicholas 'to say that the Trustees were really delighted by the excellent likeness of you by Ivor Roberts-Jones and that, accordingly, the bust has now been added to the National Portrait Gallery's collections. I am extremely grateful to you for ensuring that this excellent bust could be offered to us.' This would be the fourth portrait head by Ivor to enter the collection of the National Portrait Gallery, and it remains the last (Sir John Hayes to Sir Nicholas Goodison, 22 July 1992, ibid.). By October 1992 the second cast had been made by Meridian and delivered to the National Portrait Gallery in London.

68 *Lord Cledwyn of Penrhos CH*

1990
Bronze
29 cm high
Collection: National Museum of Wales, Cardiff
Exhibition history: unknown

Comments: This was Ivor's second portrait of Cledwyn Hughes (1916–2001), who had sat to the artist once before, during the late 1970s. It was commissioned from the artist for £4,500 in the summer of 1990 by the Welsh Portrait Sculpture Trust. According to a leaflet issued by the Trust, dated April 1991, the funds for the portrait head had been raised from a combination of 'the GMB Union, the University of Wales, HTV PLC and the National Museum of Wales, Cardiff' (IRJ Papers, Archive, NMW, Cardiff).

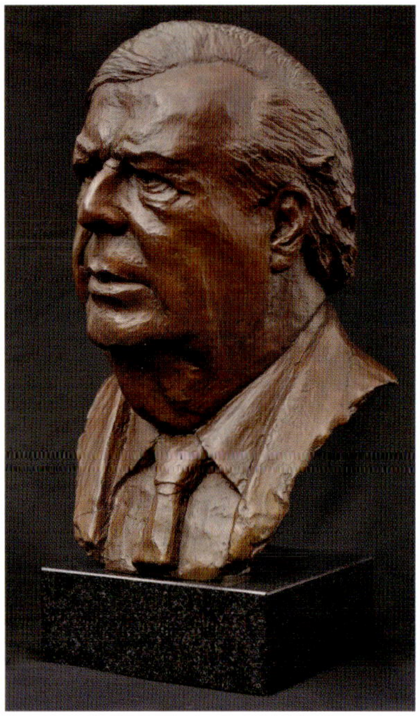

At the time Lord Hughes sat to Ivor he was leader of the opposition in the House of Lords and pro-vice chancellor of the University of Wales (Sir Alun Talfan-Davies to Alistair Wilson [director of the NMW, Cardiff], 17 September 1990, IRJ File, Archives, NMW, Cardiff).

Ivor completed the head in the early spring of 1991, and it was formally presented to the NMW, Cardiff, by Lord Callaghan of Cardiff (who had recommended Hughes's peerage in 1979 – and had also sat to Ivor for a portrait head now in the NMW, Cardiff) on 10 May 1991. In the local press Ivor was described as 'one of Europe's leading sculptors', while the head of Hughes was noted as 'the seventh he has done for the Welsh Portrait Sculpture Fund' and described as 'one of his most characterful' (*South Wales Echo*, 16 May 1991, p. 12).

According to publicity released by the Welsh Portrait Sculpture Trust, the cost of the head of Hughes (£4,500) and of the presentation ceremony had been met by contributions from HTV, the GMB Union, the University of Wales, the NMW, Cardiff, and several private individuals (WPST leaflet, dated April 1991, ibid.). The leaflet concluded:

> In the course of the last ten years the Welsh Portrait Sculpture Trust Fund, by means of the generous support of a large number of friends, has presented to the National Museum of Wales a substantial number of portrait busts by the eminent sculptor Ivor Roberts-Jones of several of Wales's notable contemporaries. These now form a very important and valuable collection (ibid.).

Some eighteen months after the presentation of the head, Lord Hughes gave the opening speech at the debut exhibition in 1993 of Ivor's old friend Kyffin Williams at the recently opened Oriel Ynys Môn on Anglesey. Ivor was invited, but ill health prevented him from attending.

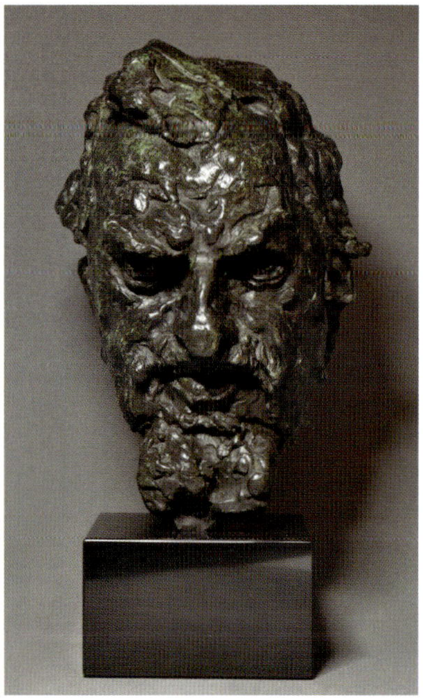

69 *Hugh Griffith*

1991
Bronze
35.5 x 23.5 x 24.5 cm
Collection: Oriel Ynys Môn Gallery, Anglesey
Exhibition history: unknown

Comments: The great character actor Hugh Emrys Griffith (1912–1980) was born in Marianglas, Anglesey, and educated at Llangefni Secondary School. After working in a local branch of the National Provincial Bank, he studied at the St Pancras People's Theatre and won a coveted place at RADA: he came top out of 300 candidates. But he postponed his acting career to volunteer for the army in 1939. In 1943–45 he served in Burma with the Royal Welch Fusiliers – the same period when Ivor was serving in the area with the Royal Artillery. After being demobbed, he graduated from RADA with many plaudits and moved to Hollywood a year later. In 1948 he won his first Tony Award. Thereafter he became a stalwart character actor in many Ealing comedies, including *Kind Hearts and Coronets* (1949) and *The Titfield Thunderbolt* (1953), and in 1957 memorably appeared in the film adaptation of Kingsley Amis's *Lucky Jim*. Two years later he won an Oscar for

Best Supporting Actor in *Ben Hur*, and in 1963 he won a second Oscar in the same category for his performance in *Tom Jones*. By the late 1960s he was suffering from alcoholism – he had been a drinking companion of Richard Burton since the mid 1950s – and parts became increasingly scarce. In 1980, shortly before his death, he was awarded an honorary degree by the University of Wales, Bangor ('Hugh Griffith', *BBC Wales*, 12 January 2009 – copy provided to the author by Oriel Ynys Môn, 25 February 2013).

The head was commissioned from Ivor by the gallery and by Anglesey County Council in 1991 at the urging of Kyffin Williams – who had been resident on Anglesey since 1974. During the commission Williams was frequently consulted – especially when it came to approving the accuracy of the final maquette Ivor submitted to the Council, in the early autumn of 1991. The head was unveiled in a ceremony at the gallery held in November 1991 (Ian Jones to Dr S. Ayres, 13 July 2012).

70 *Sir Alun Talfan-Davies QC*

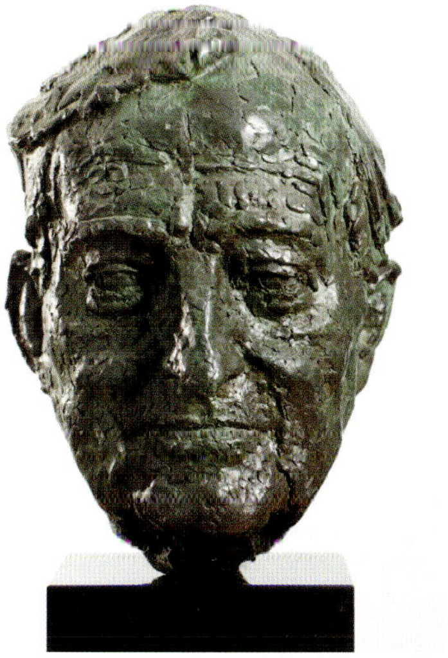

1994–95
Bronze
30.9 cm high
Collection: National Museum of Wales, Cardiff
Exhibition history: unknown

Comments: Sir Alun Talfan-Davies QC (1913–2000) was, at the time he sat to Ivor, chairman of the NMW, Cardiff, and in 1980 had co-founded the Welsh Portrait Sculpture Trust with fellow QC Judge Bruce Griffiths. Davies was born in Swansea and educated at Gowerton Grammar School and at Gonville and Caius College, Cambridge, where he read law. He was called to the bar just prior to the beginning of the Second World War. In his twenties he was a keen Welsh Nationalist. However, in 1940 he joined the Liberal Party, to which he remained faithful for the rest of his life. Apart from his distinguished legal career, he founded a publishing firm to promote poetry written in Welsh, and promoted Welsh-language broadcasting as a vice-chairman of the HTV Group. He was knighted in 1976 for his services to Welsh culture. His elder brother was the poet, critic and broadcaster Aneirin Talfan Davies (1909–1980), head of programmes at BBC Wales and an early champion of the poetry of Dylan Thomas, while his nephew Geraint was controller of BBC Wales (1990–2000) and chairman of the Arts Council of Wales (2003–6). Geraint Talfan-Davies has been the chairman of Welsh National Opera since 2006 ('Obituary', *Independent*, 13 November 2000, p. 24).

It would seem that Ivor often stayed with Sir Alun during visits to Cardiff for meetings and ceremonies at the NMW. The portrait of his host had been suggested to the sculptor by Judge Griffiths in the early spring of 1994 (Judge Bruce Griffiths to IRJ, 6 March 1994, IRJ File, Archives, HMI, Leeds). In July 1994 Judge Griffiths wrote to Ivor: 'I agree that Alun is remarkable ... I hope that his bust is progressing well' (Judge Bruce Griffiths to IRJ, 3 July 1994, ibid.). The head was presented to the NMW, Cardiff, by Griffiths on behalf of the Welsh Portrait Sculpture Trust in November 1995. Ivor was invited to the ceremony but did not feel well enough to attend. The head of Sir Alun was to be his last portrait head to be cast by the Meridian Foundry.

71

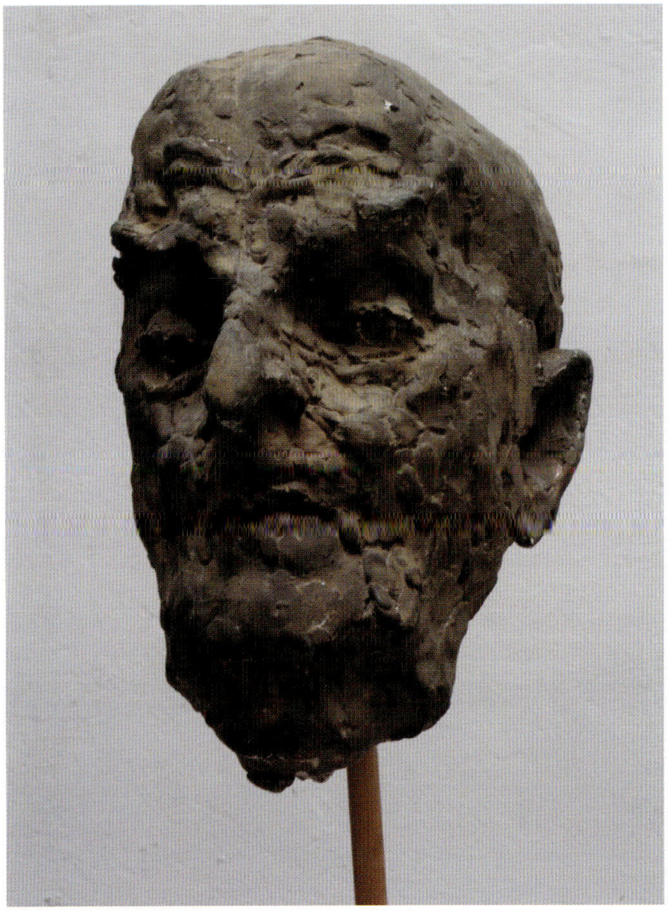

72

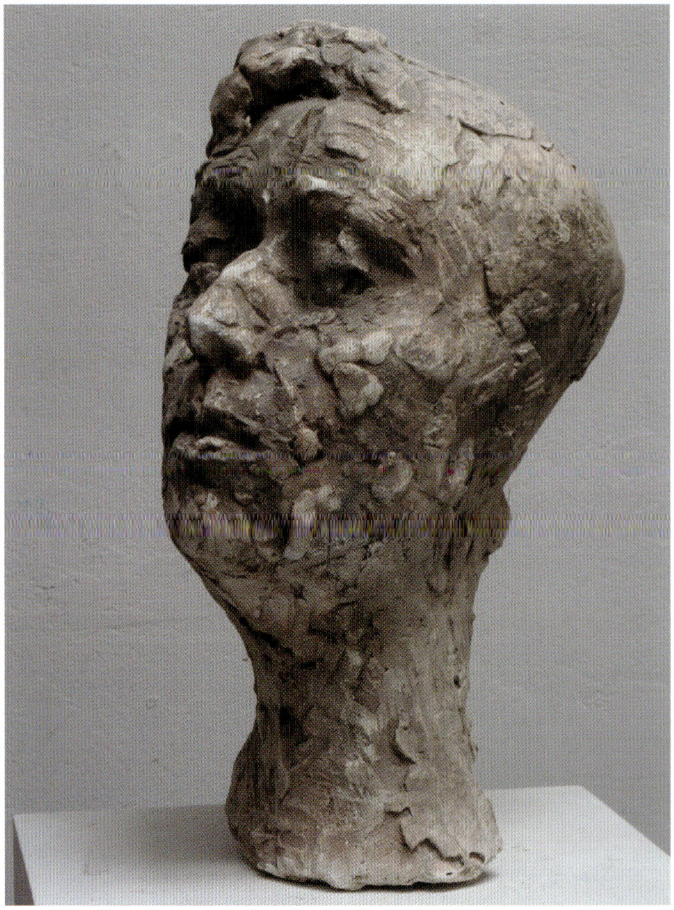

71 *Head of a Man*

1960s–80s
Plaster
29.5 x 20 cm x 25.4 cm
Collection: private collection

72 *Head of a Woman*

1960s–80s
Plaster
38.7 x 19 x 24.8 cm
Collection: Goldsmiths College, London

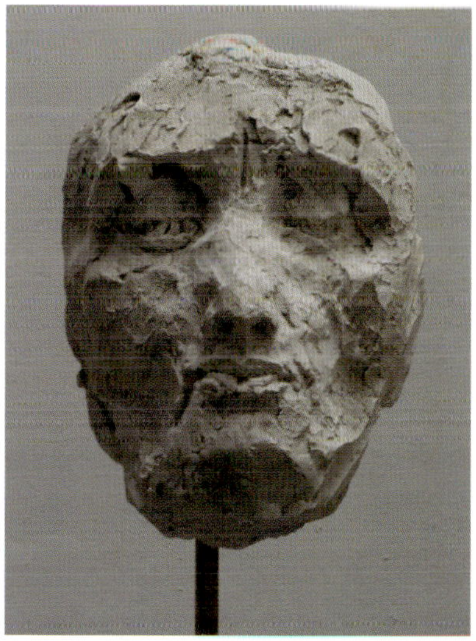

73 *Male Head*

1960s–80s
Plaster
18.4 x 21.6 x 27.6 cm
Collection: private collection

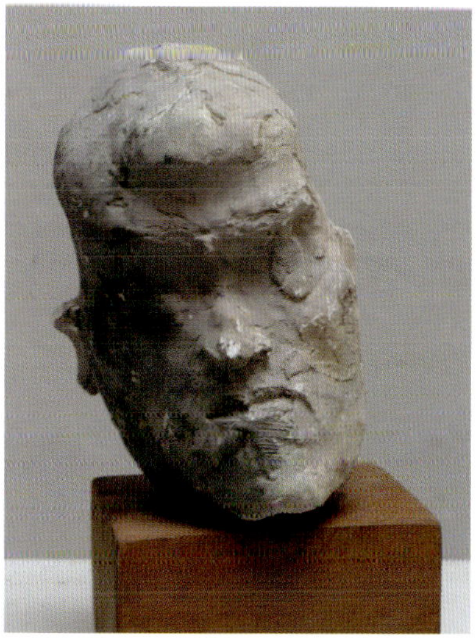

74 *Study for a Blind Head*

1960s–80s
Plaster
15.6 x 10.5 x 15.2 cm
Collection: private collection

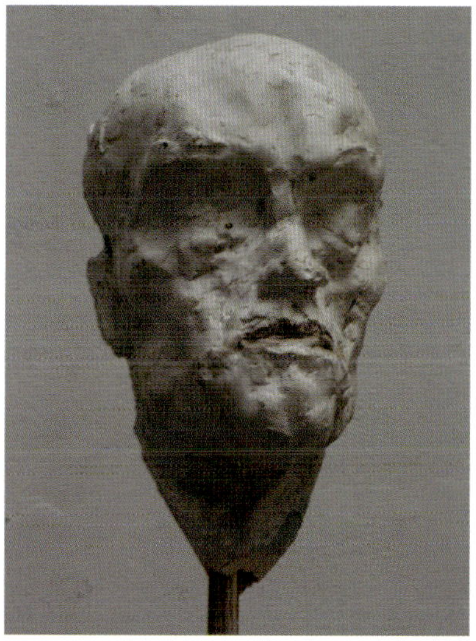

75 *Blind Head*

1960s–80s
Plaster
21.6 x 12.4 x 15.2 cm
Collection: Goldsmiths College, London

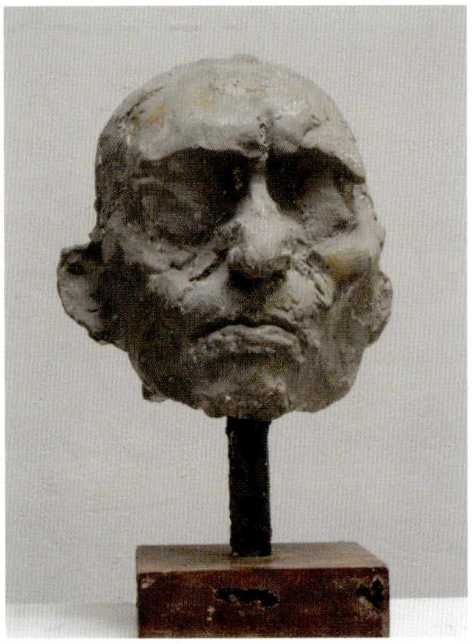

76 *Blind Head*

1960s–80s
Plaster
12.7 x 8.6 x 10.5 cm
Collection: estate of Ivor Roberts-Jones

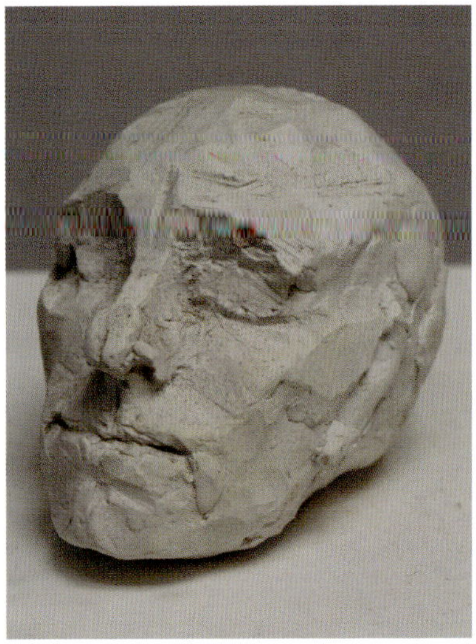

77 *Blind Head*

1960s–80s
Plaster
10.8 x 10.2 x 15 cm
Collection: private collection

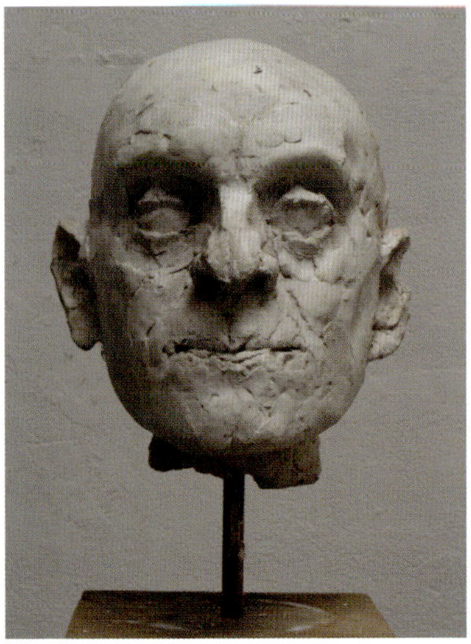

78 *Blind Head*

1960s–80s
Plaster
10.8 x 10.2 x 15 cm
Collection: private collection

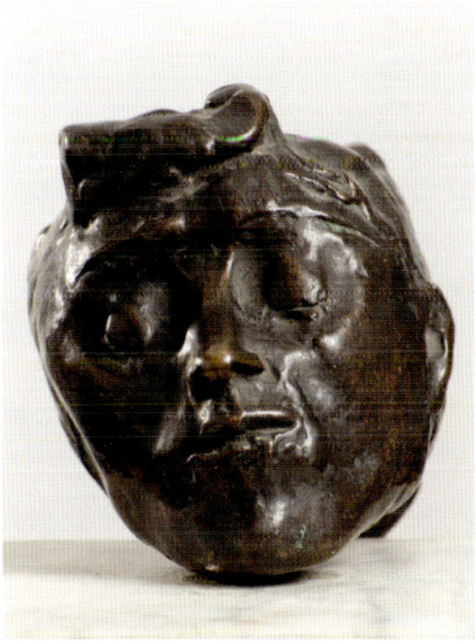

79 *Small Female Blind Head*

1960s
Bronze
13.3 x 11.4 x 15.8 cm
Collection: National Museum of Wales, Cardiff
Exhibition history: Wolsey Art Gallery, Ipswich, December 1999–January 2000

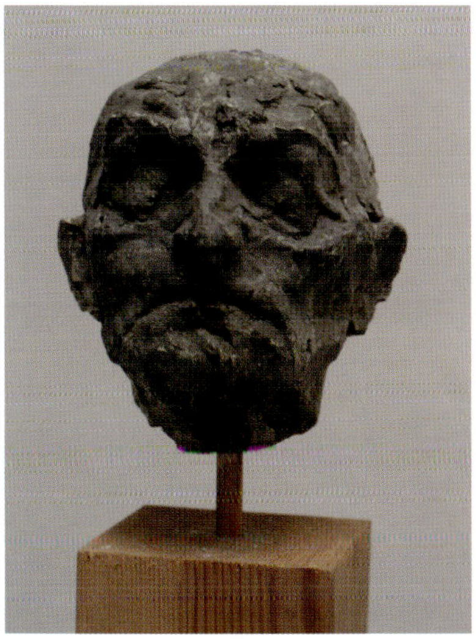

80 *Blind Head*

1960s–80s
Plaster
11.1 x 11.4 x 11.4 cm
Collection: private collection
Exhibition history: Wolsey Art Gallery, Ipswich, December 1999–January 2000; Chappel Galleries, Chappel, Essex, July 2000

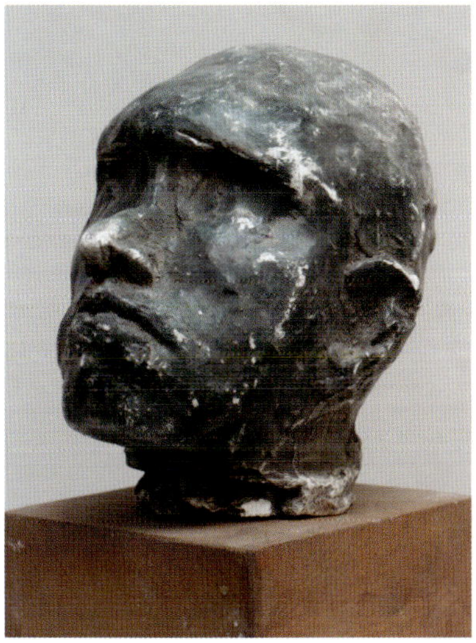

81 *Green Blind Head*

1960s–90s
Painted plaster
12.2 x 11.4 x 12.2 cm
Collection: private collection

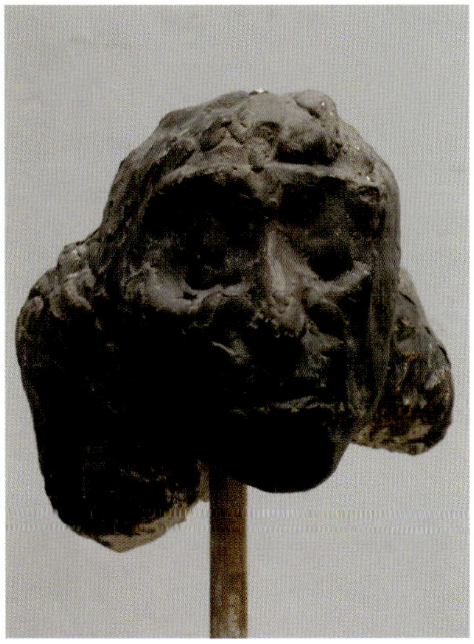

82 *Female Blind Head*

1960s–80s
Bronze
10.2 x 8.9 x 14.6 cm
Collection: private collection
Exhibition history: Wolsey Art Gallery, Ipswich, December 1999–January 2000; Chappel Galleries, Chappel, Essex, July 2000

83 *Female Blind Head*

1960s–80s
Plaster
16.2 x 17.5 x 21.3 cm
Collection: private collection
Exhibition history: Wolsey Art Gallery, Ipswich, December 1999–January 2000

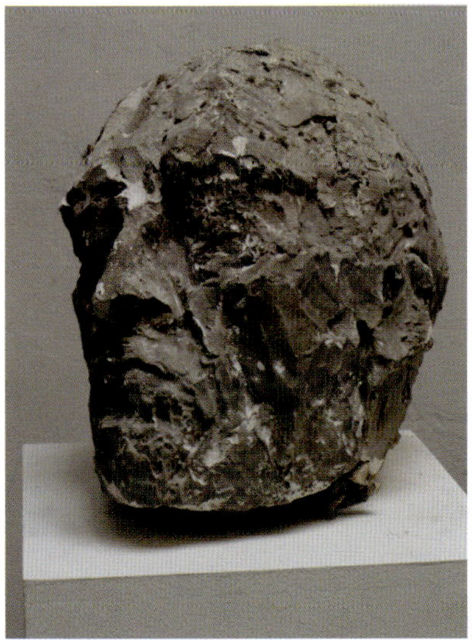

84 *Blind Male Head*

1960s–80s
Plaster
24.5 x 21 x 27 cm
Collection: private collection

85 *Blind Head*

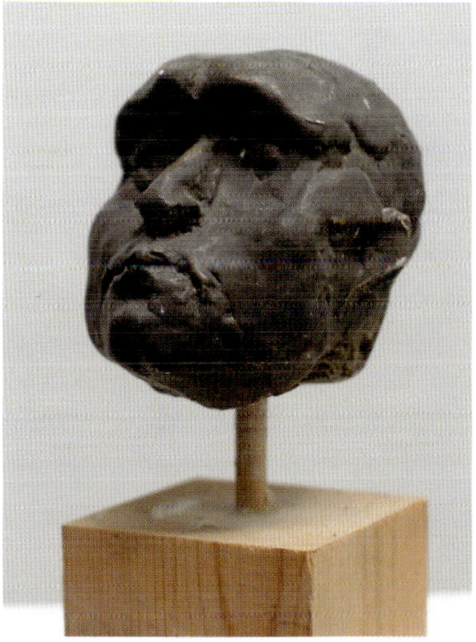

1960s–80s
Plaster
8.3 x 9.2 x 12 cm
Collection: private collection
Exhibition history: Wolsey Art Gallery, Ipswich, December 1999–January 2000

86 *Head of a Woman*

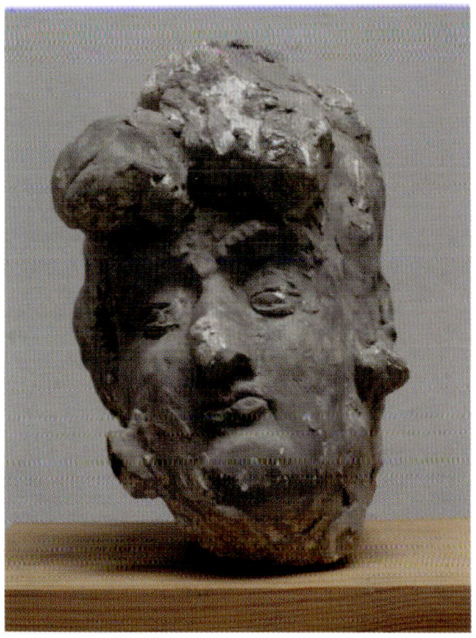

1960s
Plaster
19.4 x 26.4 x 22.2 cm
Collection: Goldsmiths College, London

87 *Head of a Young Woman*

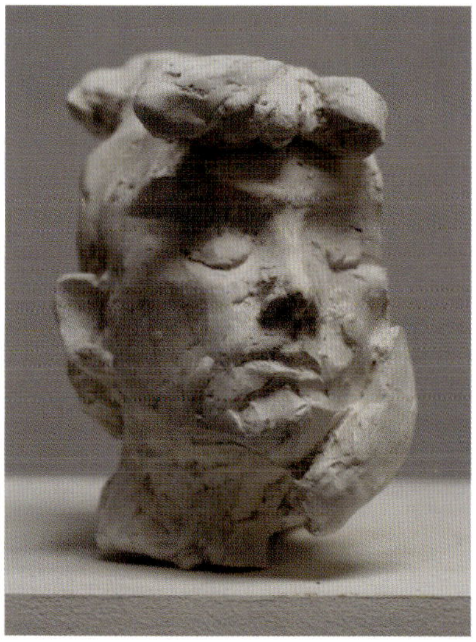

1960s–80s
Plaster
12.7 x 9.6 x 15.2 cm
Collection: estate of Ivor Roberts-Jones

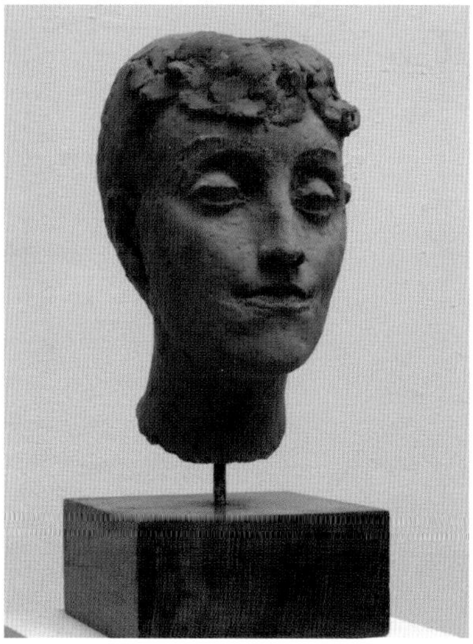

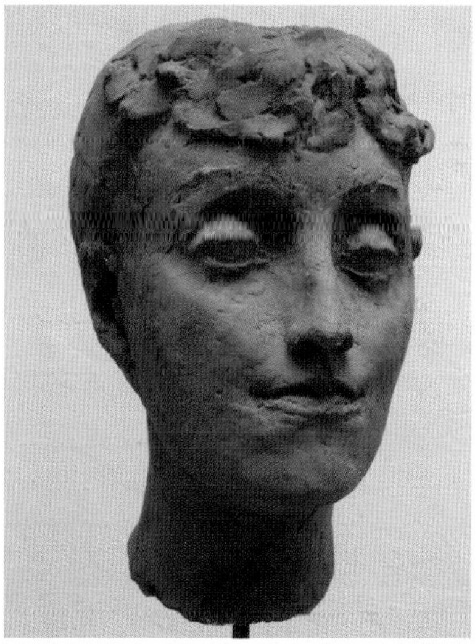

88 *Head of a Woman*

1960s–80s
Plaster
33.7 x 19.4 x 24.8 cm
Collection: estate of Ivor Roberts-Jones
Exhibition history: Wolsey Art Gallery, Ipswich, December 1999–January 2000

89 *Serval*

1966
Bronze
45.7 x 63.5 x 28.6 cm
Collection: private collection
Exhibition history: Oriel Art Gallery, Cardiff, July–September 1978 (25); Royal Academy, May 1983 (1303); Wolsey Art Gallery, Ipswich, December 1999–January 2000

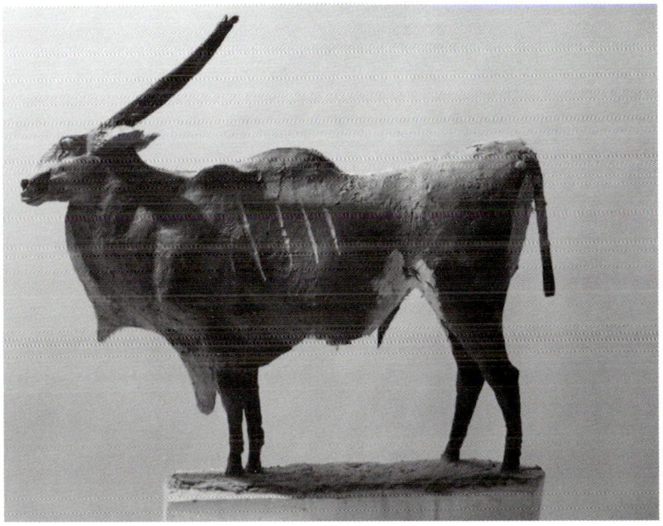

90 *Eland*

1972
Painted plaster
52.7 x 76 x 19 cm
Collection: private collection
Exhibition history: Royal Academy, May 1975 (1340); Oriel Art Gallery, Cardiff, July–September 1978 (26); Wolsey Art Gallery, Ipswich, December 1999–January 2000

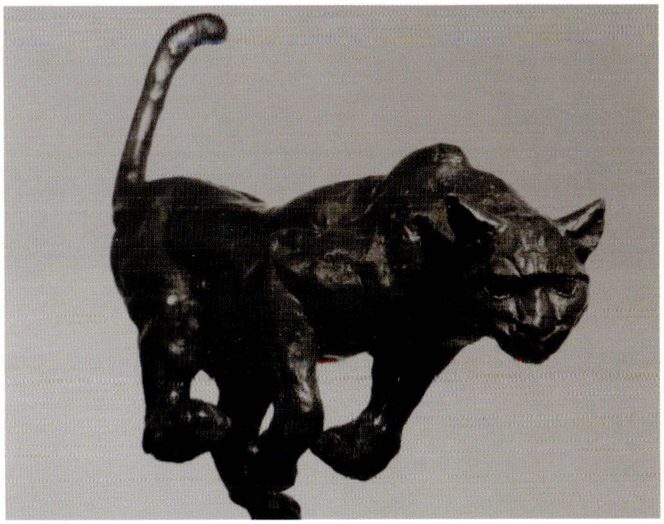

91 *Puma*

1973–74
Bronze
25 x 64.2 x 14 cm
Collection: private collections x 2; plaster, Oswestry School, Shropshire
Exhibition history: Royal Academy, May 1975 (688); Royal National Eisteddfod of Wales, Llangefni, Anglesey, July–August 1983 (9); Wolsey Art Gallery, Ipswich, December 1999–January 2000

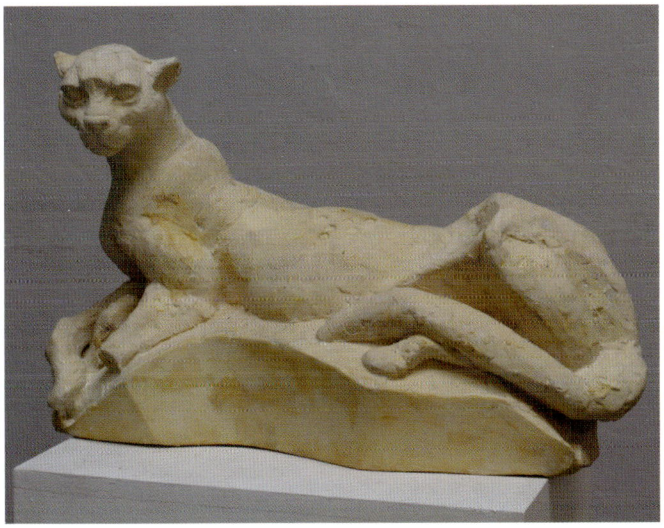

92 *Cheetah*

1974–75
Bronze
32.4 x 43.8 x 21.6 cm
Collection: private collections x 2; plaster, Oswestry School, Shropshire; estate of Ivor Roberts-Jones
Exhibition history: Royal Academy, May 1975 (687); Oriel Art Gallery, Cardiff, July–September 1978 (27); Royal National Eisteddfod of Wales, Llangefni, Anglesey, July–August 1983 (6); Wolsey Art Gallery, Ipswich, December 1999–January 2000

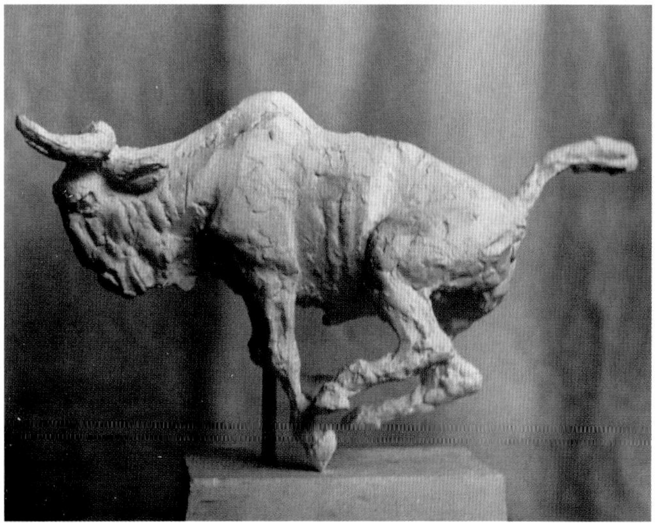

93 *Wildebeest*

1977
Bronze
35 x 45 x 19 cm
Collection: two bronze casts in private collections; plaster, private collection
Exhibition history: Oriel Art Gallery, Cardiff, July–September 1978 (29); Royal Academy, May 1981 (1107); Royal National Eisteddfod of Wales, Llangefni, Anglesey, July–August 1983 (10)

94 *Oryx*

1977
Bronze
36 cm wide
Collection: private collections x 3
Exhibition history: Oriel Art Gallery, Cardiff, July–September 1978 (28); Royal Academy, May 1981 (1106); Royal National Eisteddfod of Wales, Llangefni, Anglesey, July–August 1983 (11)

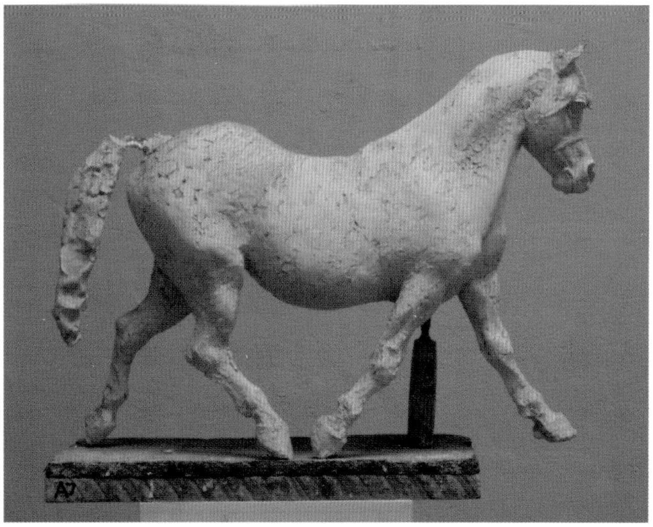

95 *Mountain Pony*

1978–79
Bronze
51 x 61 x 17.8 cm
Collection: private collection, plaster, Oswestry School, Shropshire
Exhibition history: unknown

Comments: In return for making a figure of his daughter's favourite pony, Taliesin, Lord Kenyon agreed to sit to Ivor for a second portrait head in 1978.

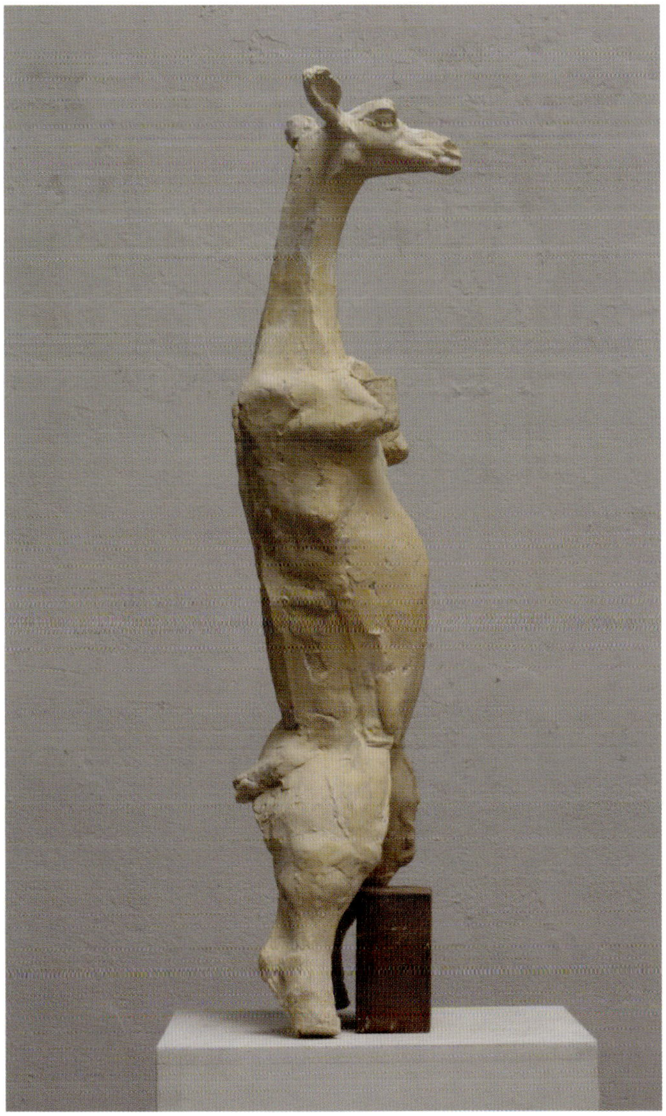

96 *Gerenuk*

1978–89
Bronze
42 x 48.2 x 17.8 cm
Collection: private collections x 2
Exhibition history: Royal Academy, May 1982 (751); Royal National Eisteddfod of Wales, Llangefni, Anglesey, July–August 1983 (20); Wolsey Art Gallery, Ipswich, December 1999–January 2000

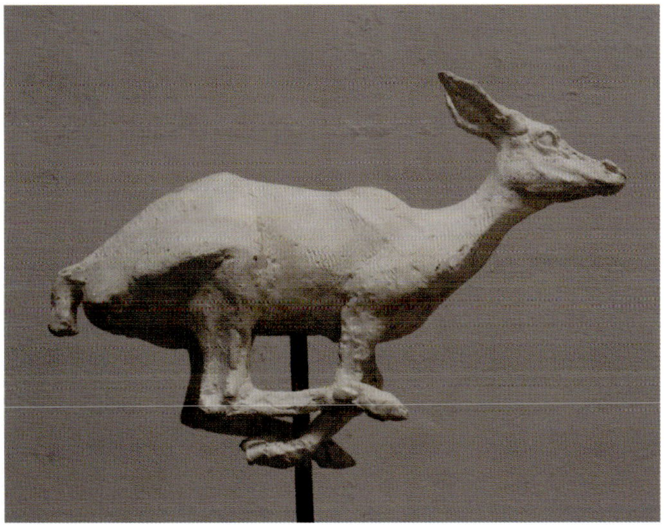

97 *Running Deer*

c. 1978–83
Plaster
21.6 x 36.5 x 11.4 cm
Collection: Oswestry School, Shropshire
Exhibition history: Wolsey Art Gallery, Ipswich, December 1999–January 2000

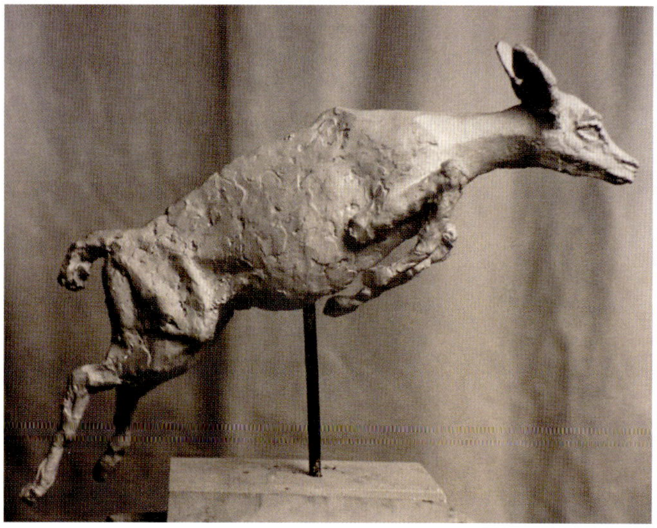

98 *Leaping Gazelle*

c. 1978–83
Plaster
23.2 x 46.7 x 9.8 cm
Collection: Oswestry School, Shropshire
Exhibition history: Wolsey Art Gallery, Ispwich, December 1999–January 2000; Chappel Galleries, Chappel, Essex, July–August 2000

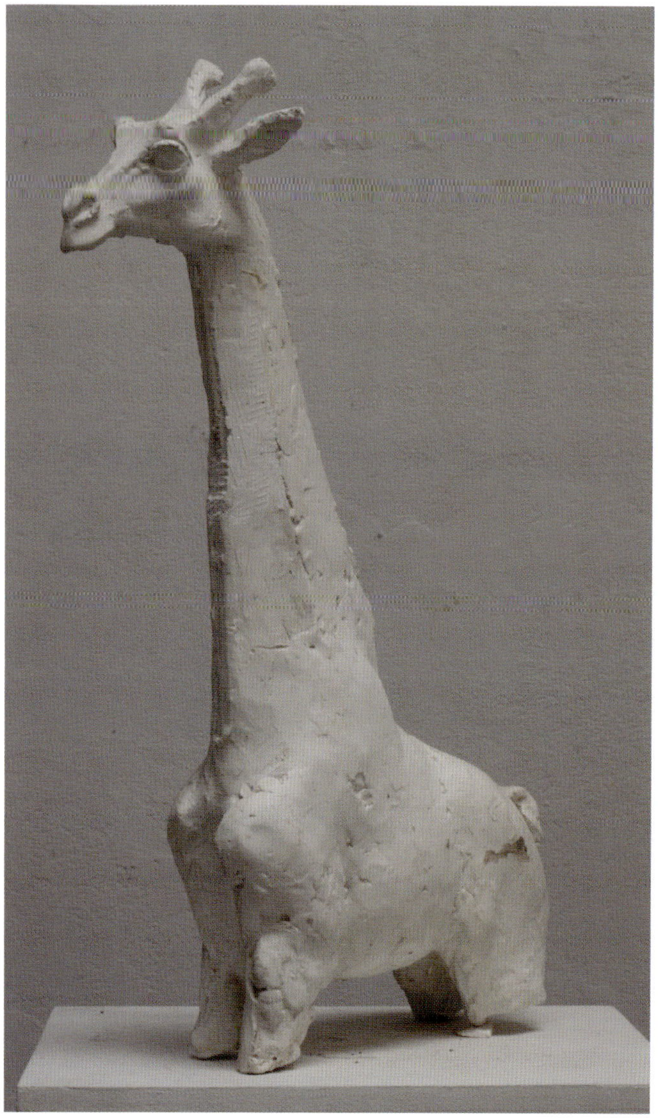

99 *Giraffe*

c. 1978–83
Plaster
45.8 x 24.2 x 15.3 cm
Collection: Oswestry School, Shropshire
Exhibition history: Wolsey Art Gallery, Ipswich, December 1999–January 2000

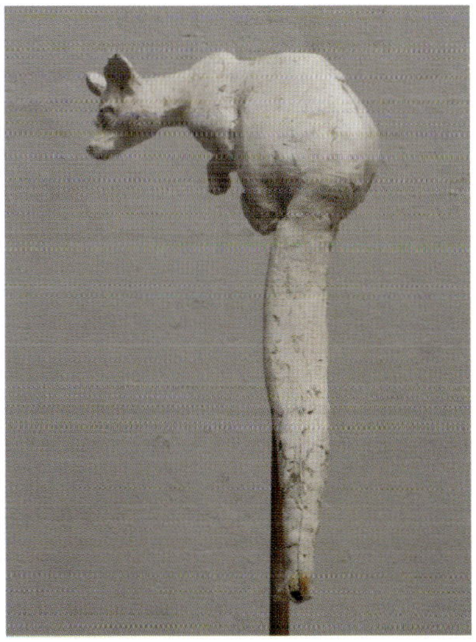

100 *Arctic Fox*

c. 1978–83
Plaster
39 x 16.5 x 9 cm
Collection: Oswestry School, Shropshire
Exhibition history: Wolsey Art Gallery, Ipswich, December 1999–January 2000

101 *Lynx*

1982
Bronze
18.7 x 25 x 10.2 cm
Collection: private collection
Exhibition history: Royal Academy, May 1985 (1325)

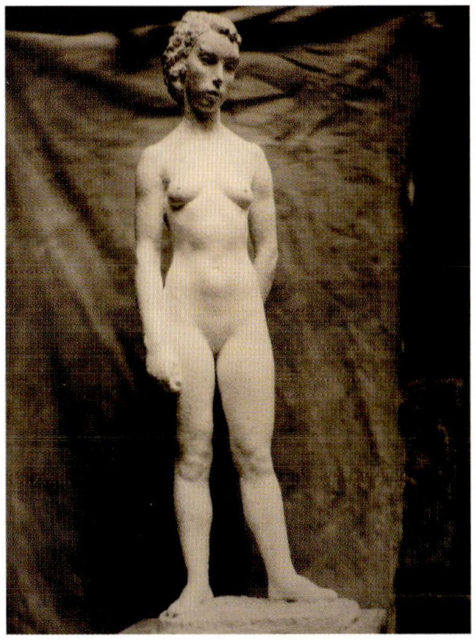

102 *Full-length Figure of a Young Female Nude*

c. 1935?
Plaster
Life-sized
Collection: whereabouts unknown
Exhibition history: unknown

Comments: This figure may be the *Study of a Model* for which, in October 1935, Ivor was awarded a Royal Academy Schools Landseer Prize of £10.

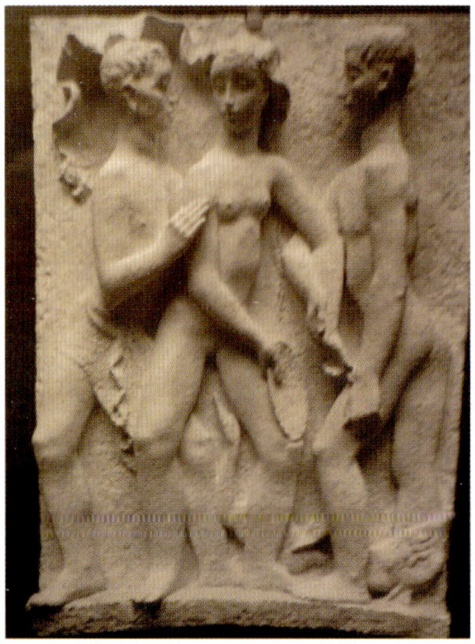

103 *Low-Relief Panel of Three Standing Young Male Nudes*

c. 1935
Plaster
Life-sized
Collection: whereabouts unknown
Exhibition history: unknown

Comments: The panel may be the *Set of Three Models of a Figure from the Life*, for which Ivor was awarded a Royal Academy Schools Prize worth £30 in October 1935 (*The Times*, 25 October 1935, p. 11).

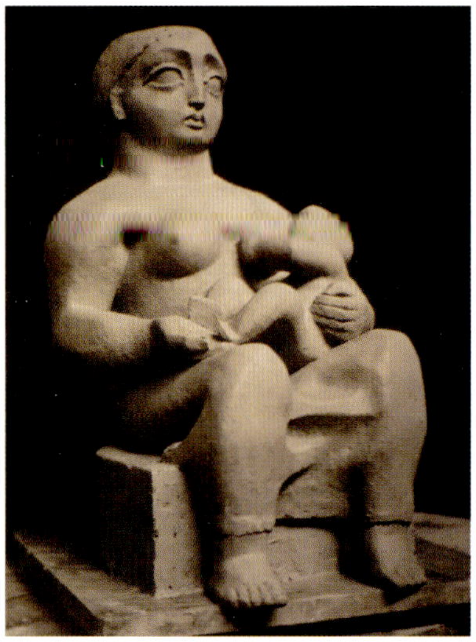

104 *Seated Mother and Child*

c. 1946
Clay?
Dimensions: unknown
Collection: whereabouts unknown
Exhibition history: unknown

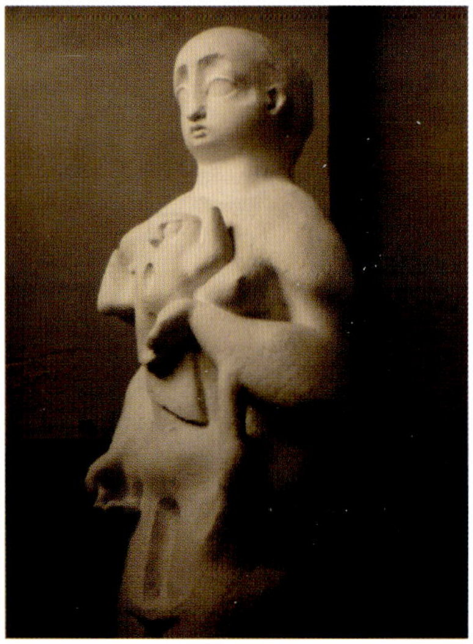

105 *Winged Figure with Bird*

1946
Terracotta
30.7 cm high
Collection: whereabouts unknown
Exhibition history: unknown

Comments: The treatment of the woman's physiognomy and figure suggests that the artist had been closely studying examples of Archaic Greek and Ancient Sumerian and Hittite sculpture in the British Museum. This work was reproduced as Number 49 in Eric Newton's *British Sculpture 1944–1946* (London: John Tiranti, 1947).

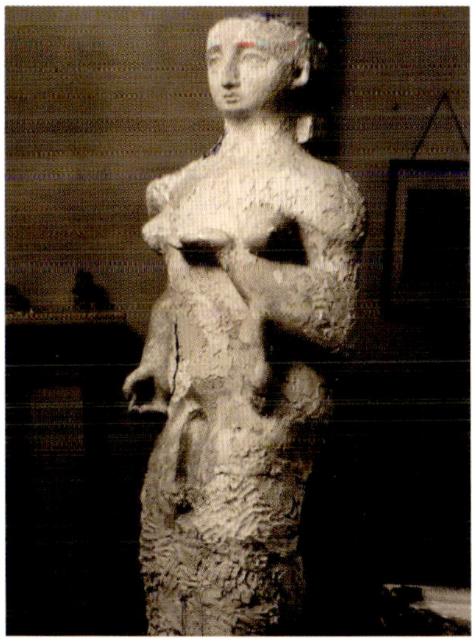

106 *Female Nude*

1947
Plaster
56 cm high
Collection: whereabouts unknown
Exhibition history: unknown

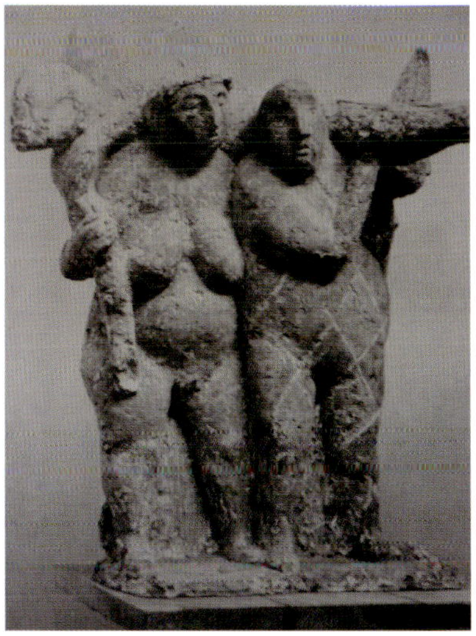

107 *Two Clown Figures Carrying a Third on their Shoulders*

1948–49
Painted plaster
41 x 31.7 x 27 cm
Collection: private collection
Exhibition history: Wolsey Art Gallery, Ipswich, December 1999–January 2000

Comments: Part of a series of figures of clowns in plaster, terracotta and cement that Ivor produced around 1947–49, inspired by Picasso's *saltimbanques* and figures from the *Commedia dell'arte* painted during his so-called 'Blue' and 'Rose' periods, around 1901–6.

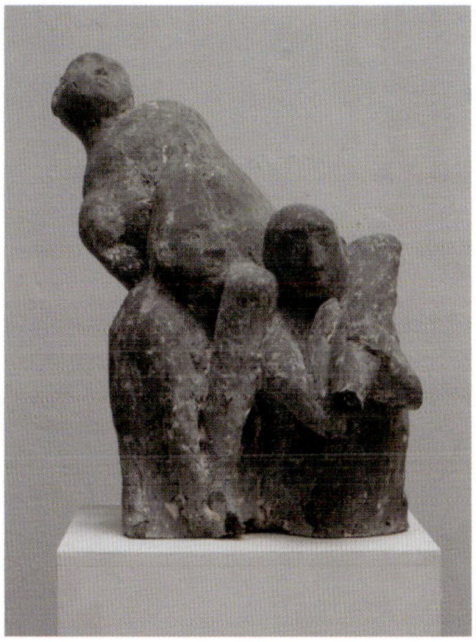

108 *Deposition of a Clown*

c. 1948–49
Ciment fondu
50.8 x 41.9 x 22.2 cm
Collection: private collection
Exhibition history: Wolsey Art Gallery, Ipswich, December 1999–January 2000

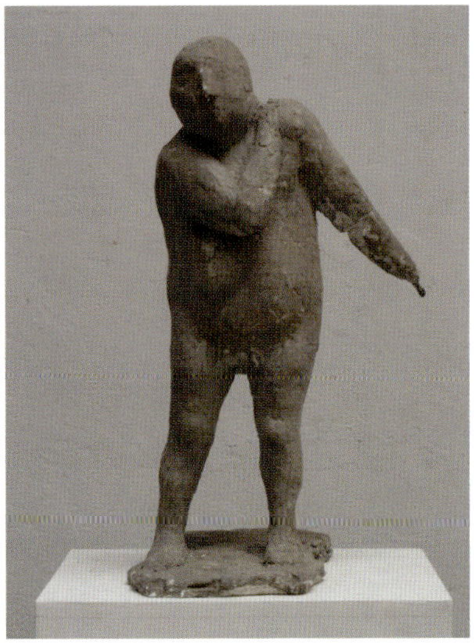

109 *Single Male Clown, Left Arm Outstretched*

1948–49
Painted plaster
40.6 x 23.5 x 21.3 cm
Collection: private collection
Exhibition history: Wolsey Art Gallery, Ipswich, December 1999–January 2000

110 *Male Clown*

1948–49
Painted plaster
Dimensions: unknown
Collection: whereabouts unknown

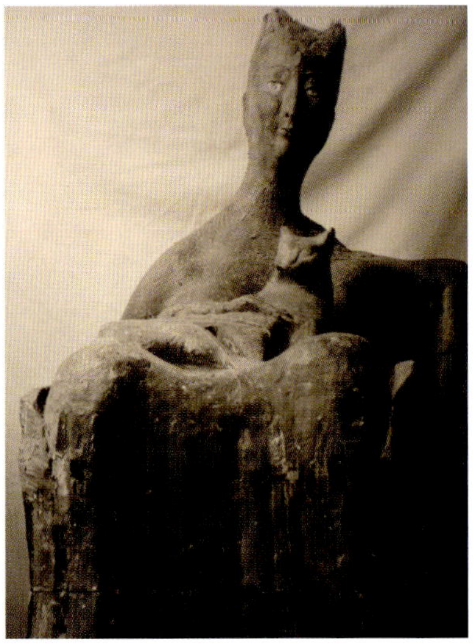

111 *Seated Woman Holding a Cat*

1953–54
Painted terracotta
1.07 m high
Collection: work is no longer extant
Exhibited: Beaux Arts Gallery, London, July 1954

Comments: During the early 1950s Ivor produced a striking series of seated women, often wearing ethereal and rather disturbing smiles, in painted plaster and terracotta. The treatment of their facial characterisation suggests the artist had been looking at the heads of female deities that adorned the Temple of Artemis in Ephesus, in Greek Asia Minor, dating from around 550–520 BCE, while the seated pose and polychrome treatment of the surface are closely reminiscent of carvings in the British Museum of seated female benefactors and goddesses that lined the Sacred Way of Apollo in sixth-century BCE Didyma, also in Greek

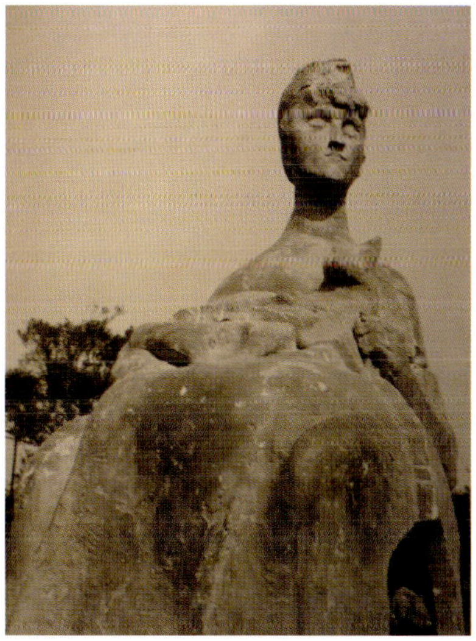

Asia Minor, as well as a number of smaller painted terracotta figurines of goddesses, such as Hera or Demeter, made within the Ancient Greek city-state of Tangara in Boeotia (between Thebes and Athens) around 600–550 Boeotia. (One particular Tanagra statuette appears to have particularly caught Ivor's eye: British Museum GR 1879-6-24-2-4, Terracotta 769. For background to the Archaic Greek sculpture of Didyma and Tanagra, Jenifer Neils, *Ancient Greece: The British Museum Concise Introduction* (London: British Museum Press, 2008], pp. 132–9).

Only the head of this figure now survives (plaster, 36.5 x 18.1 x 22.2 cm, private collection).

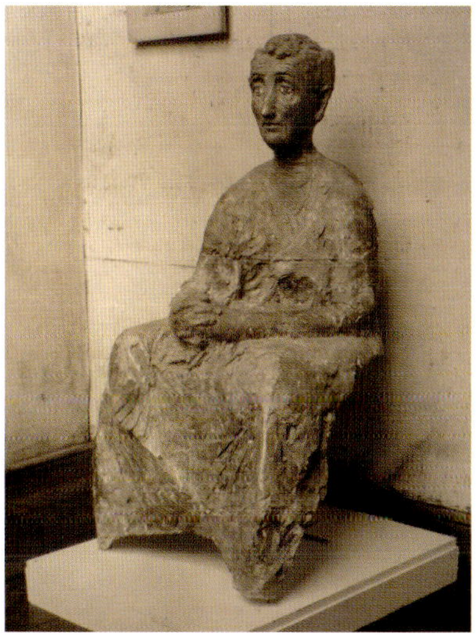

112 *Seated Woman/Mrs Griffiths*

1953–57 (112a reworked extensively in 1966)
Painted plaster and bronze
130.8 x 62.8 x 66 cm
Collection: bronze casts of the second version can be found in: Goldsmiths College, London; National Museum of Wales, Cardiff; Fitzwilliam Museum, Cambridge
Exhibition history: first version, Beaux Arts Gallery, London, May 1957; *Fifth Annual Open Exhibition of Welsh Painting and Sculpture*, Public Library, Wrexham, April 1958; second version: Oriel Gallery, Cardiff, July–September 1978 (1); Royal National Eisteddfod of Wales, Llangefni, Anglesey, July–August 1983 (2)

Comments: *The Times*, reviewing Ivor's May 1957 solo exhibition, commented:

> That the artist can on occasion carry his expressive modelling through a whole figure without losing the abstract power of his original idea is demonstrated by the best of his exhibits, the seated figure of *Mrs Griffiths*. This piece has a grave calm which draws the eye, while its modelling indicates character in the sitter and animates the detail without troubling the essential stillness of the whole (*The Times*, 29 May 1957, p. 3).

The following year, when the work was exhibited in a show in Wrexham, supported by the Welsh Committee of the Arts Council, A.C. Sewter wrote in the *Guardian*: 'The sculpture section, very decidedly more lively than in most shows of this kind, includes two works by Ivor Robert Jones [*sic*] – one of them a full-length life-size portrait of an old lady which seems to indicate an exceptional promise'. (A. C. Sewter, 'Welsh Painting of To-day: Provincial But Sincere', *Guardian*, 17 April 1958, p. 7).

In September 1971 the Keeper of Art at the NMW, Cardiff, Rollo Charles, wrote to his museum's Art Purchasing Committee that Ivor had recently shown him

> a seated figure … this is a re-working of one I saw a few years ago [May 1966] and which I admired when I saw it there. The sculptor himself would rather we bought this than the head [of Yehudi Menuhin] – he would obviously like

112a

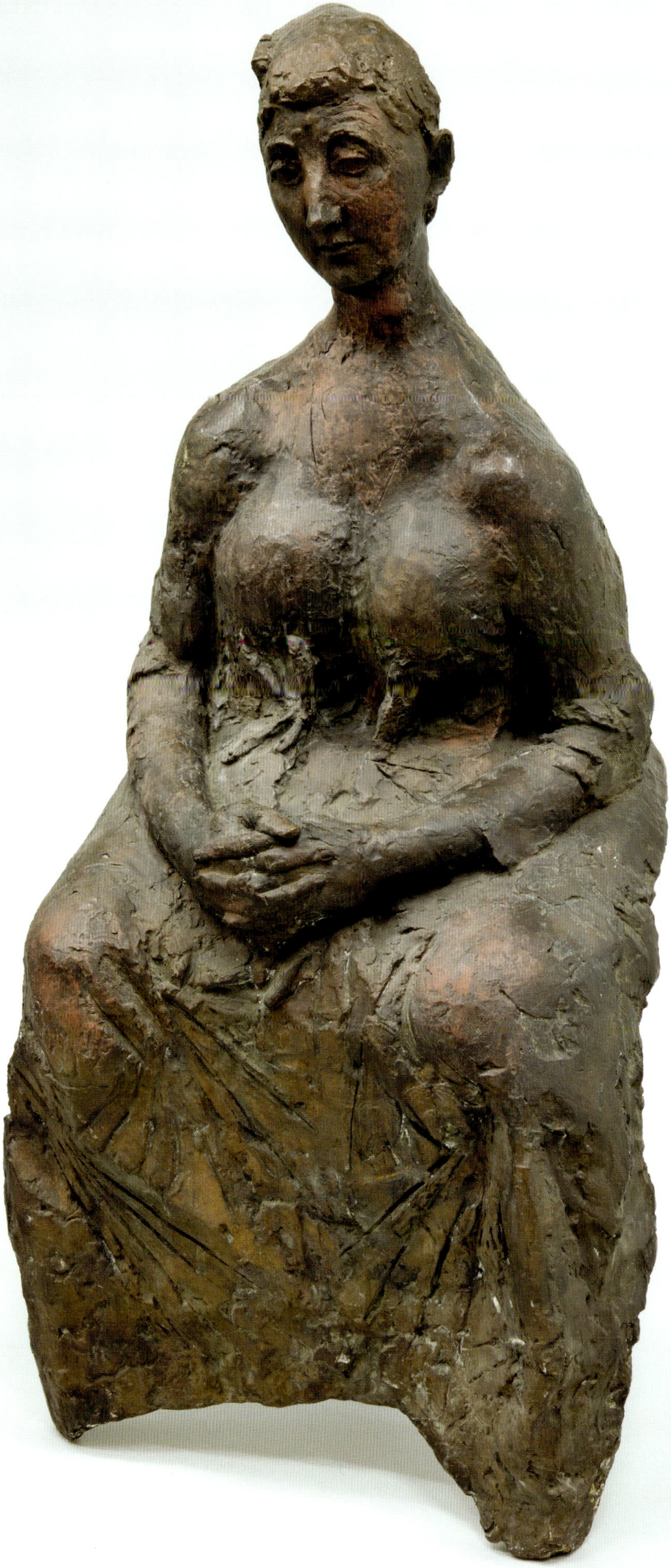

> to be represented here on a large scale and he professes a particular fondness for this work ...

Ivor wanted £2,000 for a bronze cast of this second version of the figure. The keeper's own view was that, 'though the head [of Menuhin] would be a good purchase, the figure would be a very much better one' (Rollo Charles to the Purchasing Sub-Committee of the Art Committee of the National Museum of Wales, 21 September 1971, IRJ File, Archives, NMW, Cardiff).

A month later a member of the committee, the Hon. Hanning Phillips, saw the seated figure in Ivor's studio in London, and wrote to Rollo Charles: 'I thoroughly approve of the Roberts-Jones figure [*Mrs Griffiths*]. I think it is a lovely pose with the clasped hands and serene expression of the face' (13 October 1971).

In November 1971 Kyffin Williams took another member of the Purchasing Committee, Ralph Edwards, to see the seated figure. Williams reported to Rollo Charles that Edwards was '"warily impressed" by the work ... it is certainly a more beautiful thing than the [full-length figure of] *Augustus* [John] and of course very much cheaper!' (Kyffin Williams to Rollo Charles, 20 November 1971, ibid.).

A few days later, Charles was able to write to Ivor with the good news that the Museum was indeed willing to buy a cast of the second version of *Mrs Griffiths*. It took a year to have this done by Michael Gaskin at the Art Bronze Foundry on the King's Road, as Ivor had

> found that on her return from the Royal Academy [in 1966] she had suffered some damage which [was] very perceptible as a hair-line crack ... this without doubt has worsened under the normal manhandling at the Foundry ... Large bronzes are now taking 6 months at the Foundry. There seems to be a very considerable resurgence of bronze casting – and probably rather fewer of the small foundries. I said I would 'shop around' for the casting ... and the result of this was I decided to go to Gaskin's (my usual Foundry) ... My respect for Gaskin has increased and so he is doing the *Seated Woman* (*Mrs Griffiths*). He hasn't the facilities for [the statue of] Winston [Churchill] though, unfortunately ... It's interesting for me that the plaster was by nature rather clumsy and I shall be seeing her for the first time as she really should be. I hope my bronze casting saga isn't too boring – I have it much on my mind. (IRJ to Rollo Charles, c. mid July 1972, ibid.).

The casting was completed in December 1972 and the work delivered to Cardiff in April 1973. Ivor felt that 'Gaskin [had] done an excellent job', and was particularly pleased with the quality of the patination (IRJ to Rollo Charles, early March 1973, ibid.).

113 *Smiling Woman/Seated Woman*

1955–57
Painted ciment fondu
1.35 m high
Collection: private collection
Exhibition history: Beaux Arts Gallery, London, May 1957; *Sculpture 1961*, National Museum of Wales, Cardiff, July 1961 (49)

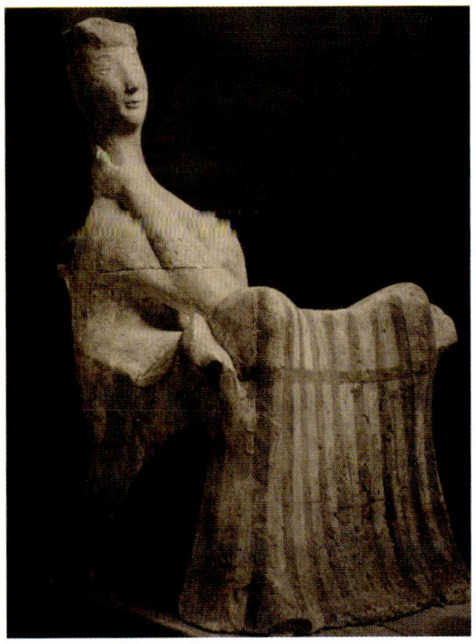

114 *Seated Woman, Head Resting on her Right Hand*

1955–57
Painted plaster
76.2 x 88.9 cm
Collection: no longer extant
Exhibiton history: Beaux Arts Gallery, London, May 1957

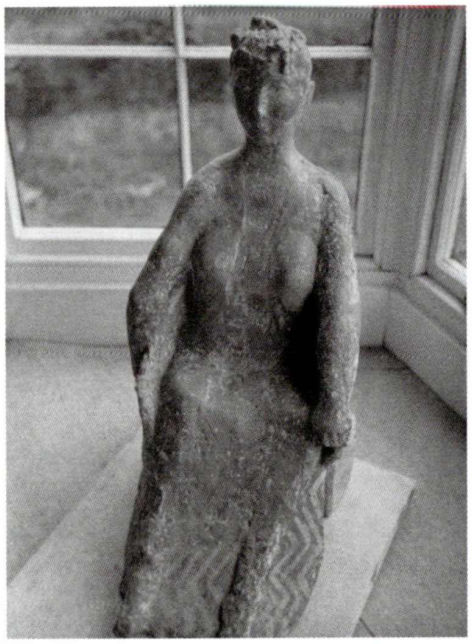

115 *Seated Woman Wearing a Long Skirt*

1955–57
Painted plaster
91.5 cm high
Collection: whereabouts unknown
Exhibition history: Beaux Arts Gallery, London, May 1957

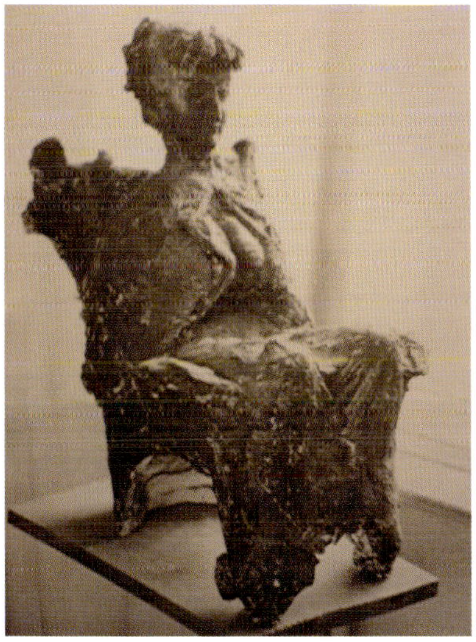

116 *Young Woman Seated in a Chair – Judith*

1955–57
Plaster
41.3 cm high
Collection: whereabouts unknown
Exhibition history: Beaux Arts Gallery, London, May 1957

Comments: The head of 116a, *Judith*, plaster, 15.2 x 10.5 x 15.6 cm, survives in a private collection.

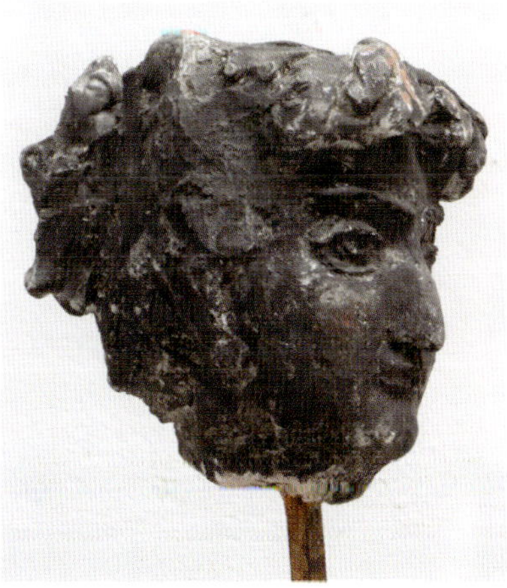

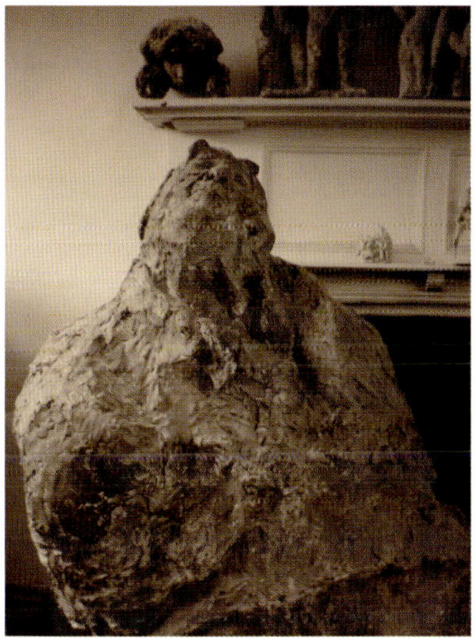

117 *The Judge*

1955–57
Plaster
1.22 m high
Collection: no longer extant
Exhibition history: Beaux Arts Gallery, London, May 1957

Comments: The related work, 117a, *Head of a Judge*, plaster, 23.5 x 23.5 x 13.7 cm, is in a private collection. In the 1930s, Ivor's father William, a solicitor, had wanted his son to become a barrister, and eventually a High Court judge, rather than study at an art school (Sir John Rothenstein, 'Ivor Roberts-Jones', *The Artist*, September 1978, p. 12).

The law, authority, judgement and punishment may have been on the sculptor's mind as, in the late 1940s, he had been introduced by writer Arthur Koestler to the

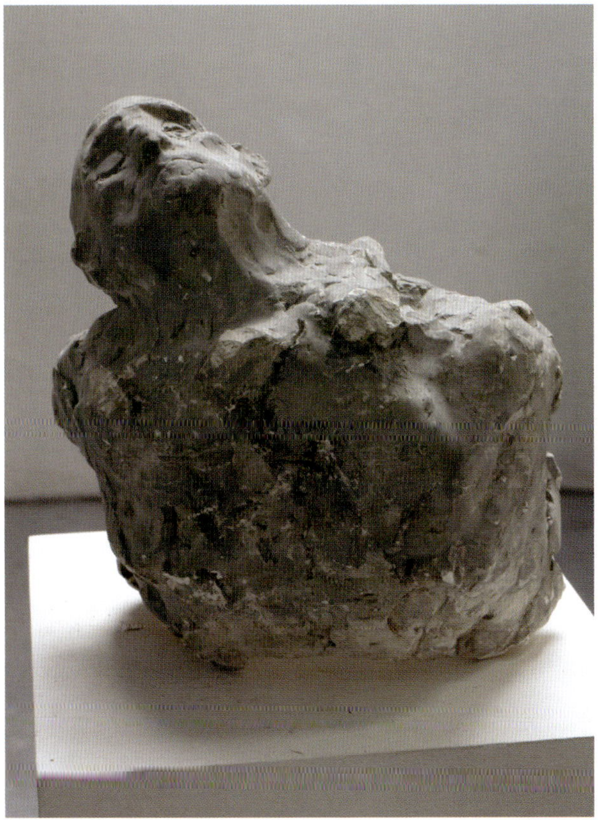

poet and playwright Stephen Spender – whose 1938 play *Trial of a Judge* Ivor may have seen when it was performed at the Group Theatre in London (Valentine Cunningham, *British Writers of the Thirties* [Oxford: Oxford University Press, 1988], p. 323).

Ivor's future wife, Monica, then studying dance and theatre design at Goldsmiths College, had several friends who were part of the Group Theatre – in particular one of its founders, the dancer Rupert Doone, and his partner the painter Robert Medley (David Fraser Jenkins, *John Piper: The Forties* [London: Philip Wilson, 2000], pp. 17–18).

Formally, in terms of the treatment of clay roughly applied to the armature in rough, uneven layers, the appearance of the recumbent *Judge* suggests Ivor's admiration for the particular technique of the Italian sculptor Medardo Rosso (1858–1928), who was much esteemed by sculptors Ivor valued, such as Rodin, Marini and Manzu, and by the Futurists, including Umberto Boccioni (1892–1916), whose *Unique Forms of Continuity in Space* (1913) was for many years a favourite of Ivor's. Indeed, awareness of the Boccioni figure fed into his conception of what would be one of the most imposing works he produced during the 1950s: *Walking Judas*.

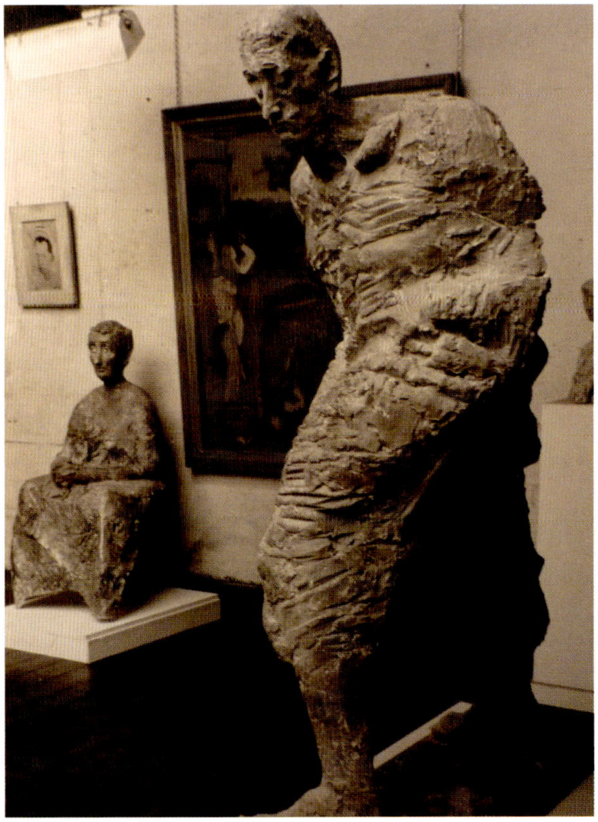

118 *Walking Judas*

1955–57
Plaster
2.13 m high
Collection: no longer extant
Exhibited: Beaux Arts Gallery, London, May 1957

Comment: The deep grooves scored into the surface of the plaster of this figure, evident from photographs taken at the time of its exhibition, suggest that Ivor was informed by the example not only of Jean Fautrier's celebrated series of *Hostages* heads (1944–48), first seen in London in the early 1950s, but also by the battered and maimed figuration of Germaine Richier (1904–1959), such as *Storm Man* (1947–48, bronze, Louisiana Museum of Art), which also had an impact on the so-called 'geometry of fear' generation of post-war British sculptors when it was exhibited at the Anglo-French Art Club in London in 1947 and at the Hanover Gallery, London, in October 1955 (Frances Morris, *Paris Post War: Art and Existentialism 1945–55* (London: Tate Publications, 1993), p. 55).

Ivor seems to have been partial to New Testament themes – in 1954 he produced a powerful head of the *Mother of Judas* based upon an old woman and refugee from Eastern Europe who ran a stall in a market in Notting Hill, close to where Ivor lived at St James's Gardens (Cannon-Brookes, *Ivor Roberts-Jones*, p. 73). The figure of Lazarus was one to which he would turn in the 1960s and '70s; but a figure embodying betrayal, striding confidently forwards with eyes closed, can be related to Ivor's fascination with the so-called 'Cambridge Spies', Guy Burgess and Donald Maclean, who had defected to the Soviet Union in May 1951. However, their defection did not become public knowledge until September 1955, when they surfaced in Moscow and gave a press conference (Dominic Sandbrook, *Never Had It So Good: A History of Britain from Suez to the Beatles* [London: Little Brown, 2005[, pp. 560–2).

Walking Judas was by far the most remarked upon of Ivor's exhibits in his Beaux Arts exhibition, and was taken as heartening evidence that 'younger' sculptors had not entirely abandoned 'realism'. In the *Guardian*, Stephen Bone described the figure as 'the most impressive piece of sculpture in the exhibition ... a striking and original conception (Stephen Bone, 'Judas Imprisoned In His Thoughts: Symbolic Garment', *Guardian*, 20 May 1957, p. 5).

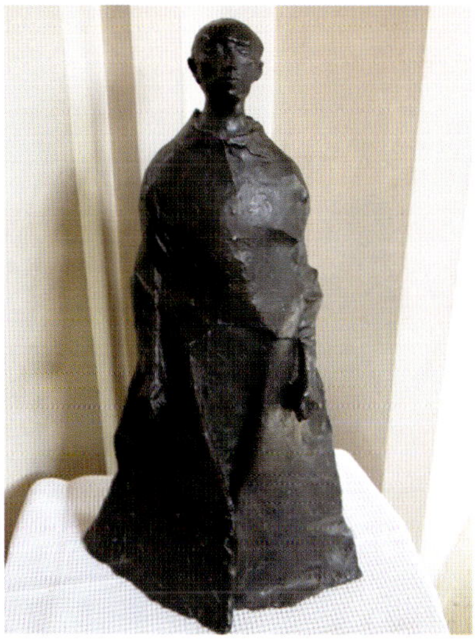

119a *St. Francis*

1955–58
Bronze
68.5 cm high
Located: West Wall, Lady Chapel, St Mary's Anglican Church, Ardleigh, Essex
Related work: 119b Head of St Francis, 1955–57, plaster, 9.8 x 8.9 x 11.1 cm, private collection.

(See overleaf)

119b

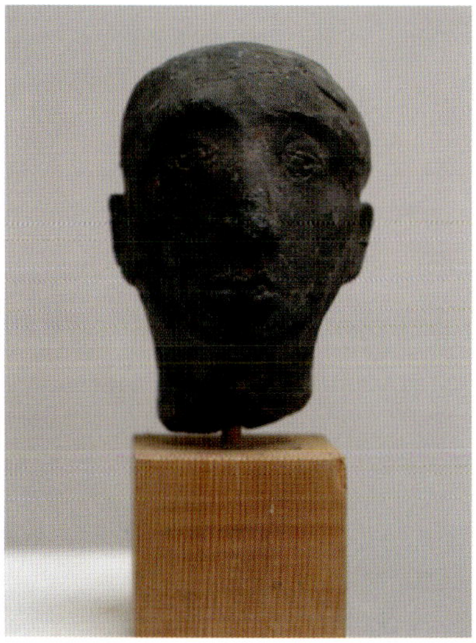

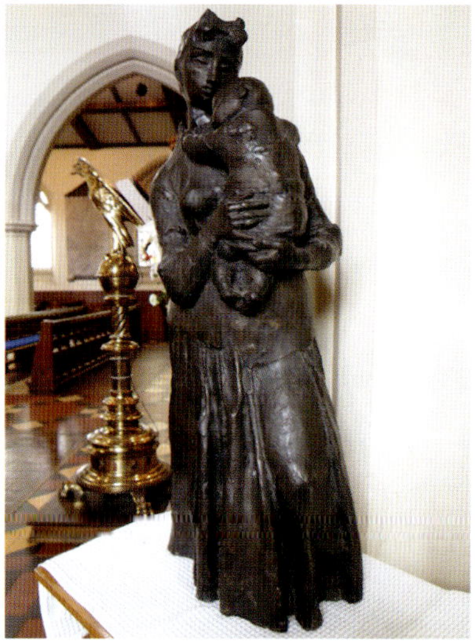

119c *Madonna and Child/Virgin and Christ Child*

1955–58
Bronze
76.2 cm high
Located: East Wall, Lady Chapel, St Mary's Anglican Church, Ardleigh, Essex

Comments: St Francis was born Francesco di Pietro di Bernardone in Assisi around 1181–82. The son of a wealthy silk merchant, he lived something of a playboy lifestyle, displaying a love for fine clothes and rich food, before serving as soldier for Assisi in the early thirteenth century. But in 1205, en route to a campaign against a neighbouring town, he experienced a vision, which instructed him to return to his home town and renounce all worldly goods. He later went on a pilgrimage to Rome, where he begged for alms outside St Peter's Basilica. This led him in 1209 to found a mendicant Order of Friars Minor ('Lesser Brothers') dedicated to a life of poverty and simplicity and to helping the poor in society. The following year the Order was given official sanction by Pope Innocent III, despite the fact that Francesco had not been ordained a priest; the pope also permitted him to establish an enclosed religious order for women, known as the Order of the Poor Clares. Membership of the Order of Friars Minor grew rapidly, and in 1219 Francesco felt inspired to visit Egypt in an effort to convert Sultan al-Kamil, its Islamic ruler – who was impressed by the Italian but not by Christianity. In 1224 Francesco was the first person reported to have received the stigmata – the wounds on the hands, wrists and feet suffered by Christ prior to his crucifixion. He died two years later, in October 1226, and was canonised in July 1228 as St Francis. He was designated the patron saint of animals, as he had apparently preached to the birds – who were suitably responsive – and with the sign of the cross secured the obedience of a ferocious wolf that had been terrorising the countryside around Gubbio (Donald Spoto, *Reluctant Saint: The Life of St Francis of Assisi* (London: Penguin, 2003)).

In 1939 St Francis was named as one of the two patron saints of Italy, and in 1979 as patron saint of ecology. In March 2013, on his election to pope, Cardinal Jose Mario Bergoglio took Francis as his name to signal his commitment to living by the values associated with him (*Sunday Times*, 17 March 2013, p. 24).

Ivor was approached by the architect Raymond Erith (1904–1973) in the autumn of 1955 to provide figures of a St Francis wearing the habit of a monk and a figure of a Virgin and Child for two niches in a Lady Chapel Erith was building for St Mary's Church in Ardleigh (Raymond Erith to IRJ, 12 November 1955, Erith Papers, RIBA Archive, V&A Museum, London).

By December the following year, Ivor had submitted maquettes of two such figures to the local Parochial Church Committee (PCC). He apologised to the architect for the time this had taken, saying that he had been very busy with making work for his first solo exhibition at the Beaux Arts Gallery, which would open in May 1957 (IRJ to Raymond Erith, 17 October 1956, ibid.).

There were no objections to either maquette on the part of the PCC, which approved their design unanimously (Raymond Erith to IRJ, 1 March 1957, ibid.). In July 1957, however, members of the local Diocesan Advisory Committee (DAC) for the Bishopric of Chelmsford found considerable fault with both figures: St Francis 'lacked the normal attributes of the saint', while the *Madonna and*

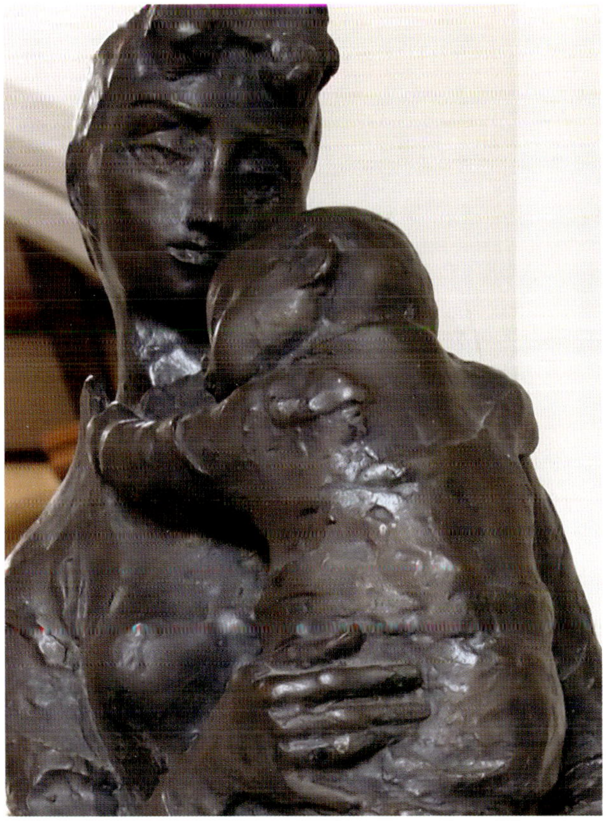

Child was too reminiscent of 'an ordinary mother and child' (Reverend James Farmiloe (Vicar of St Mary's Ardleigh) to Raymond Erith, 8 October 1957, ibid.)

Ivor had admitted to Erith earlier that year that the *Madonna and Child* maquette had proved more of a challenge to conceive, as he was determined that his Madonna should be 'a real woman', and the Christ child 'very much a baby', while the architect had advised him from the outset to 'avoid conventional period costume' (Raymond Erith to Reverend James Farmiloe, 8 August 1957, ibid.).

Early in October 1957, Ivor resubmitted the two maquettes. He had made only slight changes to the *St Francis*, adding a corded girdle to the front of his habit. The *Madonna and Child* had been extensively reworked to make the Virgin Mary look much 'less unhappy and discontented' (Reverend James Farmiloe to Raymond Erith, 8 October 1957, ibid.).

By the end of October the DAC had approved both figures, noting that it was especially appreciative of the artist's having taken the time to submit 'a revised design of the *Madonna and Child*' (IRJ to Raymond Erith, 30 October 1957, ibid.). The two figures were cast over the summer of 1958 by Michael Gaskin of the Art Bronze Foundry, and Ivor supervised their installation in St Mary's late in September that year. He was pleased that this had been accomplished just in time for the feast of St Francis, which falls on 4 October (Mr Bayley [Churchwarden at St Mary's Ardleigh] to Raymond Erith, 7 October 1958, ibid.).

As would often be the case with later works he devised to stand within an interior, Ivor was particularly concerned with how the two statues would be illuminated – especially after darkness had fallen outside (IRJ to Raymond Erith, 16 October 1958, ibid.). Another feature of this commission that would recur in Ivor's public work was the fact that the casting had proved rather more expensive than originally anticipated, and the sculptor found that this ate into the £250 he had been paid in total for the project (Raymond Erith to IRJ, 31 October 1958, ibid.; the two statues together cost a total of £120 to cast).

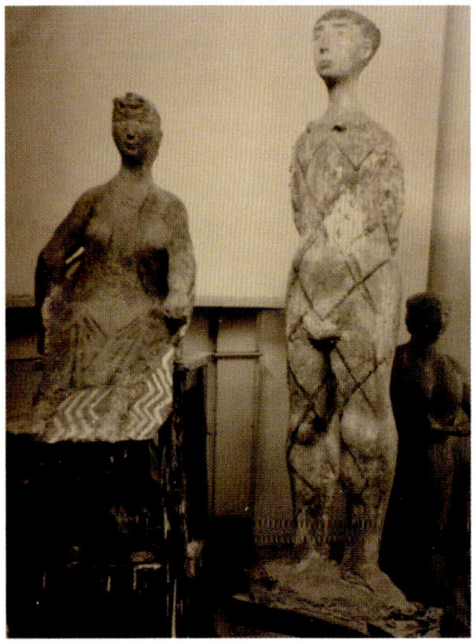

120 *Figure of a Young Man/Spring Figure*

1956–57
Painted plaster
1.52 m high
Collection: Wolsey Art Gallery, Ipswich
Exhibition history: Beaux Arts Gallery, London, May 1957

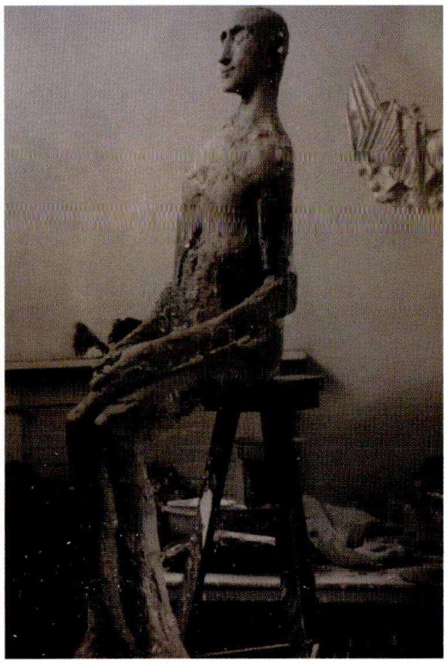

121 *Blind Faced Figure/Blind Man*

1956–57
Plaster
1.52 m high
Collection: only the head of this figure now survives: plaster, 27 x 19 x 21.6 cm, estate of Ivor Roberts-Jones
Exhibition history: Beaux Arts Gallery, London, May 1957; *Sculpture in 1961*, National Museum of Wales, Cardiff, July 1961 (53)

Comments: This statue does not appear to have survived, but constitutes one of the earliest known examples in Ivor's work to explore the theme of blindness. Many years later, in 1981, while preparing for his solo exhibition on Anglesey, Ivor wrote that 'the idea of light being drawn into an object is one that has remained with me from my jungle days [in the Arakan c. 1944–45]. My "Blind Man" of approx. 1953? has something of this quality ... I like sculptures that are like an Indian Buddha that "draw" space as it were in to themselves' (IRJ, December 1981, IRJ 1983 Eisteddfod Exhibition File, Archives, NMW, Cardiff).

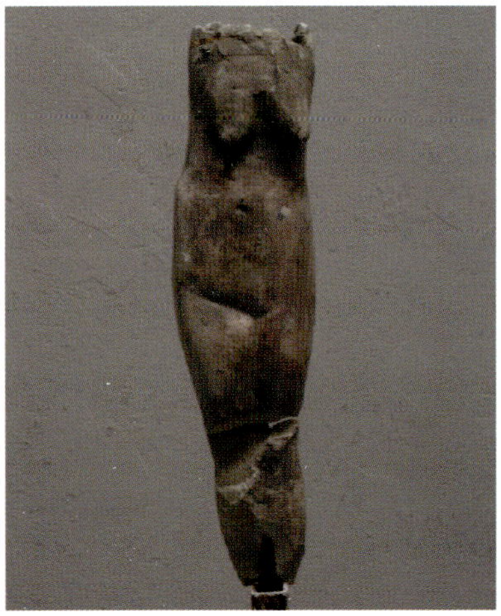

122 *Female Torso*

1960
Plaster
38 cm high
Collection: no longer extant
Exhibition history: Mullard Sculpture Collection, Mullard House, Torrington Place, London, April 1961

Comments: There is a photograph (dated 1960) of this work in the Archives of the Henry Moore Institute, Leeds (2005.456.F/16/2, HMI, Leeds). The *Torso* can be related to examples of Ancient Greek so-called 'knife-figurines' of female subjects, from the Cycladic period, around 2,500 BCE, in the collection of the British Museum. These had first caught Ivor's eye in the late 1940s (IRJ to Dr Peter Cannon-Brookes, 15 September 1982, IRJ File, NMW, Cardiff).

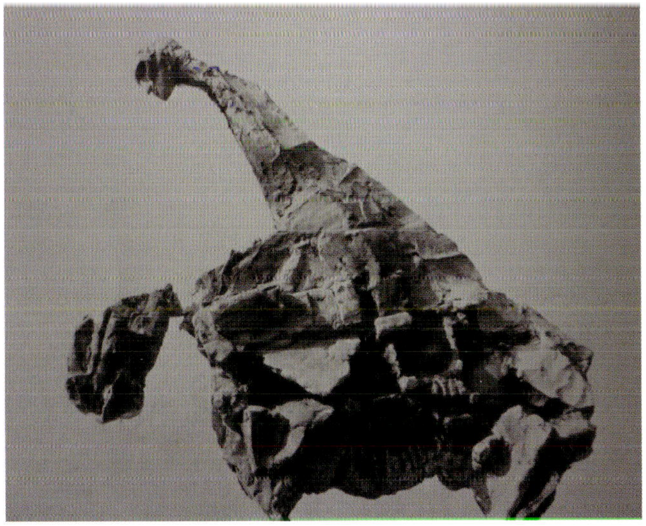

123 *Kite Rider*

1960
Plaster
68.5 cm high
Collection: whereabouts unknown
Exhibition history: Sculpture in 1961, National Museum of Wales, Cardiff, July 1961 (52)

Comments: This marks the first appearance in Ivor's output of the 'horse and rider' theme that would so preoccupy him in the 1970s – for example *The Lazarus Rider* (1976–80) and *The Two Kings/Janus Rider* project for Harlech Castle (1978–83). Reviewing the *Sculpture in 1961* exhibition, *The Times* remarked how well 'Ivor Roberts-Jones holds his own with some elegant plaster figures [such as] a little *Kite Rider* which might well be Don Quixote on Rosinante' (*The Times*, 18 July 1961, p. 13).

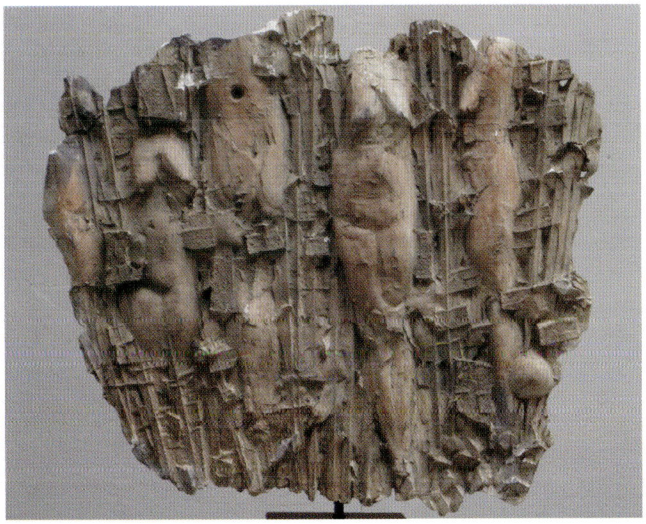

124 *Autumn Relief/Women in a Wood*

1960
Plaster
52.1 x 61.7 cm
Collection: Goldsmiths College, London
Exhibition history: Sculpture in 1961, NMW, Cardiff, July 1961 (55); NMW, Cardiff, July–September 1978 (6)

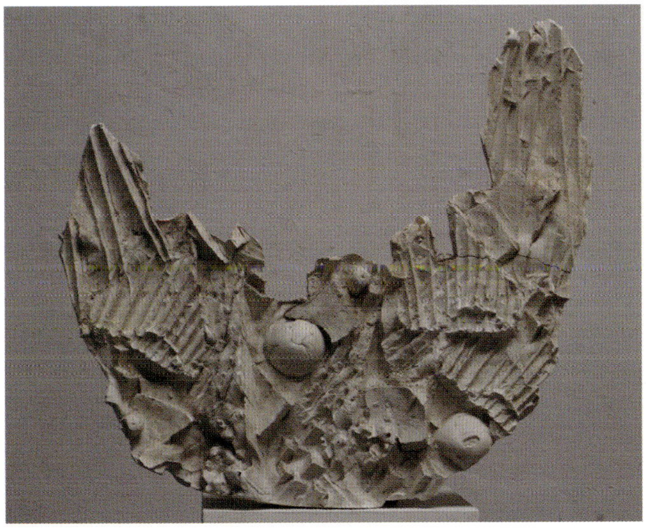

125 *Flame Shape*

1960–61
Plaster
57.2 x 61.7 cm
Collection: private collection
Exhibition history: Mullard Sculpture Collection, Mullard House, Torrington Place, London, April 1961

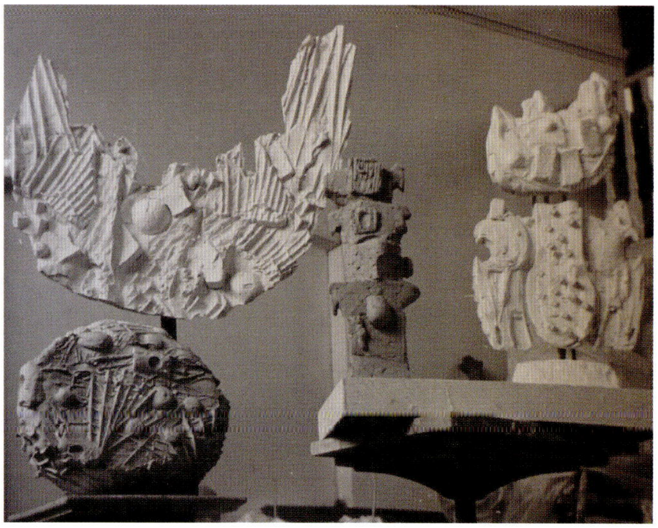

126 *Fruit Shape*

1960–61
Plaster
(far right-hand side)
36 cm high
Collection: whereabouts unknown
Exhibition history: Mullard Sculpture Collection, Mullard House, Torrington Place, London, April 1961

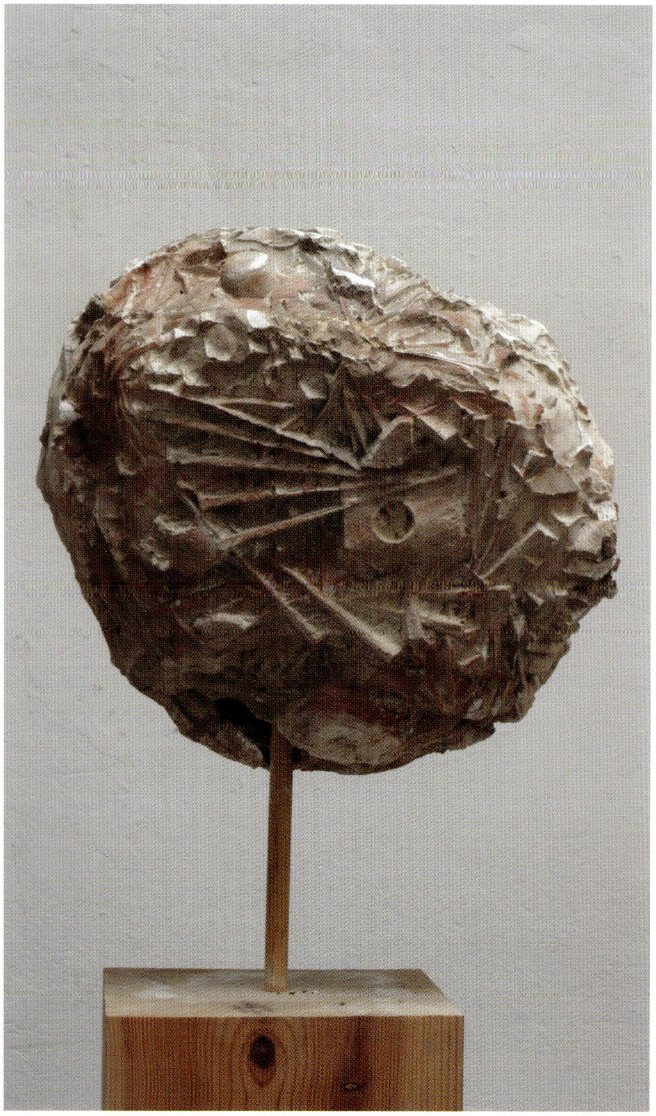

127 *Abstract Relief Experiment*

1960–61
Plaster
40 cm high
Collection: Goldsmiths College, London
Exhibition history: unknown

128 *Tower Relief*

1960–61
Plaster
46.4 cm high
Collection: no longer extant
Exhibition history: Mullard Sculpture Collection, Mullard House, Torrington Place, London, April 1961

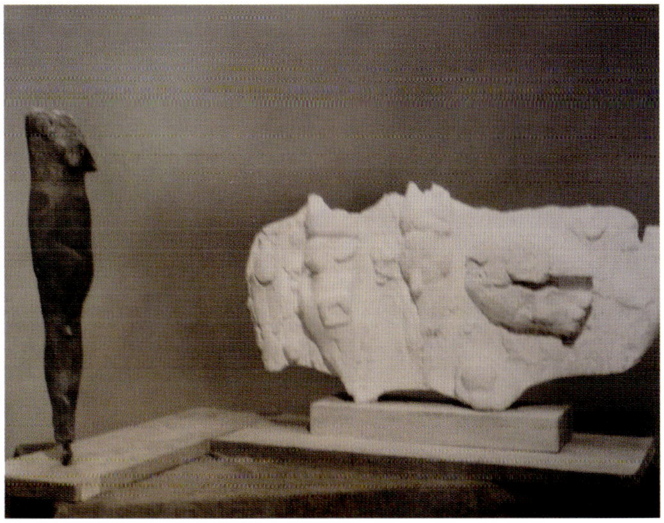

129 *Abstract Low-relief Experiment*

1960–61
Plaster
17.8 x 31.7 x 26.7 cm
Collection: Goldsmiths College, London
Exhibition history: Mullard Sculpture Collection, Mullard House, Torrington Place, London, April 1961

Comments: There is a photograph of this work standing next to *Female Torso* (qv) in the Archives of the HMI, Leeds [2005.456/F/16/1, HMI, Leeds].

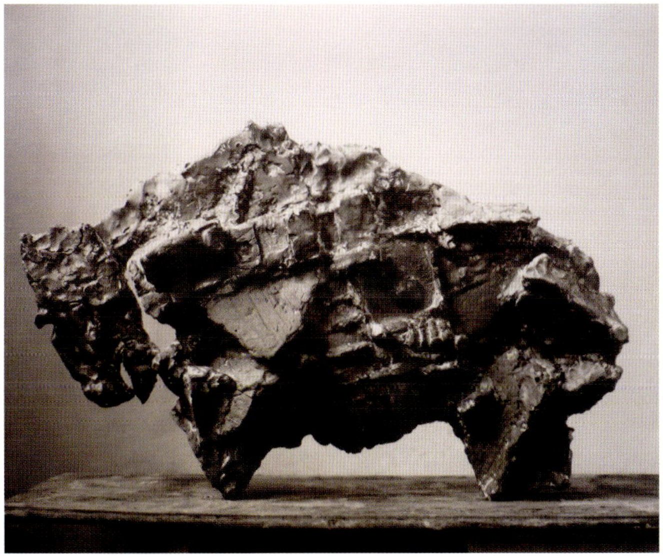

130 *The Scapegoat*

1961
Plaster
68 cm high
Collection: whereabouts unknown
Exhibition history: *Sculpture in 1961*, National Museum of Wales Cardiff, July 1961 (56)

Comments: A work with this title was mentioned by Ivor in a letter written to Sir John Rothenstein, then director of the Tate Gallery, in November 1960 (IRJ to Sir John Rothenstein, 9 November 1960, Claudel Acquisition File, TGA 4/2/890/1). Writing in the *Western Mail*, critic Maurice Cooke identified *The Scapegoat* as 'proof that sculptural talent can be found in Wales. What has yet to be proved is whether that sculptural talent will be supported by Wales' (Maurice Cooke, *Western Mail*, 25 August 1961, p. 12).

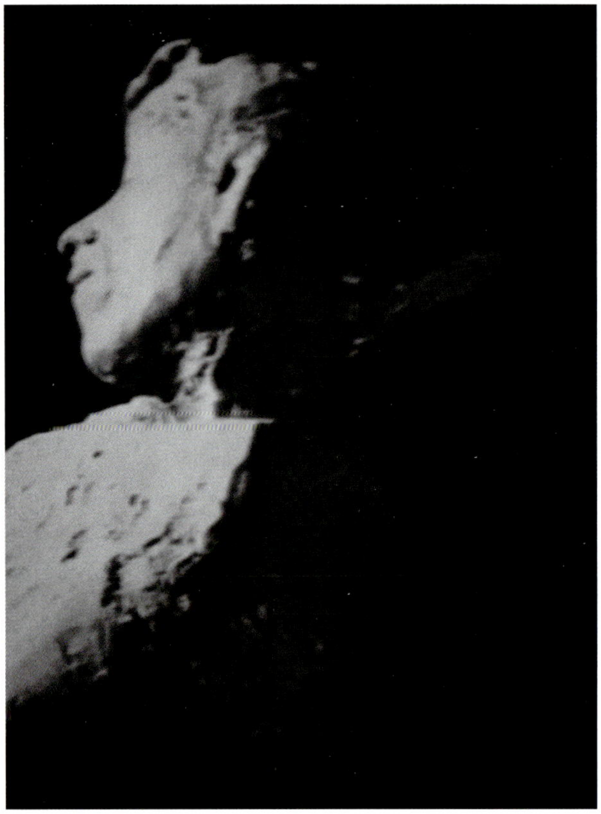

131 *Sleeping Girl*

1961
Plaster
91.5 cm wide
Collection: no longer extant
Exhibition history: Sculpture in 1961, National Museum of Wales, Cardiff, July–September 1961 (57); National Museum of Wales, Cardiff, July–September 1978 (9)
Related work: Small Study of a Female Head, plaster, 13.3 x 11.4 x 15.8 cm, private collection

Comments: The work was mentioned in passing in an article in the *Western Mail*:

> [F]ew of Cardiff's citizens seemed to be appreciating the privilege of this exhibition when I visited it ... Apart from an old man gazing at Ivor Roberts-Jones's *Sleeping Woman* and a young woman looking at Henry Moore's *Fallen Warrior*, the only others there in mid-afternoon were a BBC camera team ... As I left a group of visitors were hovering at the entrance, slightly fearful, debating whether to go in ... (*Western Mail*, 20 July 1961, p. 10).

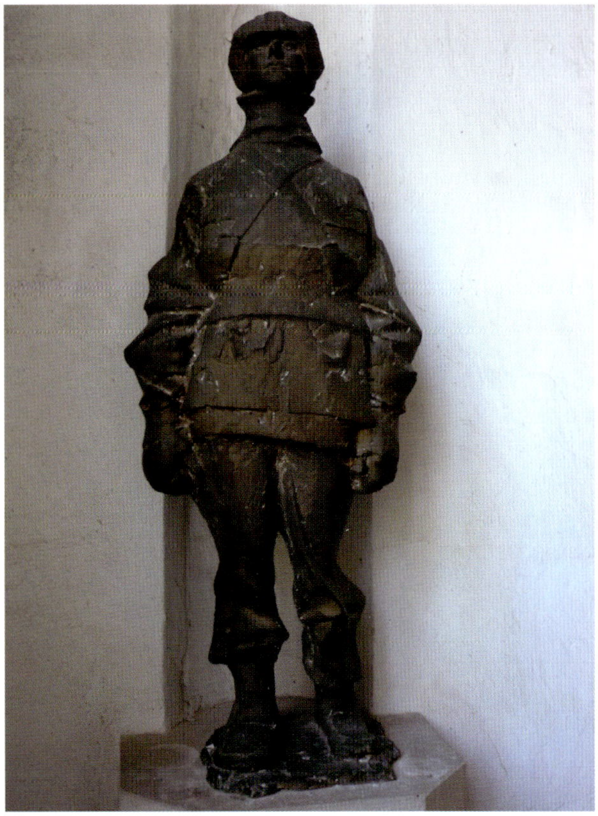

132 *Apsley Cherry-Garrard*

1961–62
Bronze
90 x 32 x 20 cm
Located: north transept of St Helen's Anglican Church, Wheathampstead, Hertfordshire. Inscription reads: 'Apsley George Benet Cherry-Garrard born 2 January 1886, died 18 May 1959. Explorer Antarctic Expedition 1910–1913. Author of *The Worst Journey in the World*.'

Comments: Apsley George Benet Cherry-Garrard (1886–1959) was born in Bedford, the son of Major-General Sir Apsley Cherry. His surname was changed to Cherry-Garrard when his father inherited a large estate at Lamer Park on the outskirts of Wheathampstead in an aunt's will. At the age of 24 Cherry-Garrard was the assistant zoologist and youngest member of Robert Falcon Scott's last expedition to the Antarctic, the Terra Nova expedition (1910–13). In June–July 1911 he endured a gruelling 35-day journey, with his mentor Dr Edward 'Bill' Wilson and close friend Lieutenant 'Birdie' Bowers, to collect the embryos of emperor penguins of the unforgiving Cape Crozier (Sara Wheeler, *Cherry: A Life of Apsley Cherry-Garrard* [London: Vintage, 2002], pp. 106–18). Cherry-Garrard later described this foolhardy trip in a classic of polar literature, *The Worst Journey in the World* (1922).

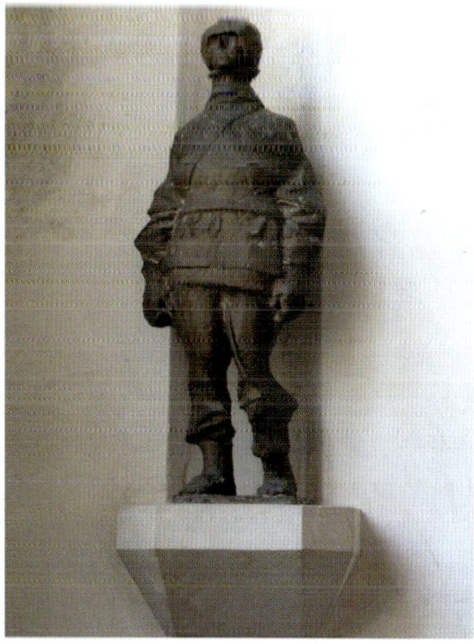

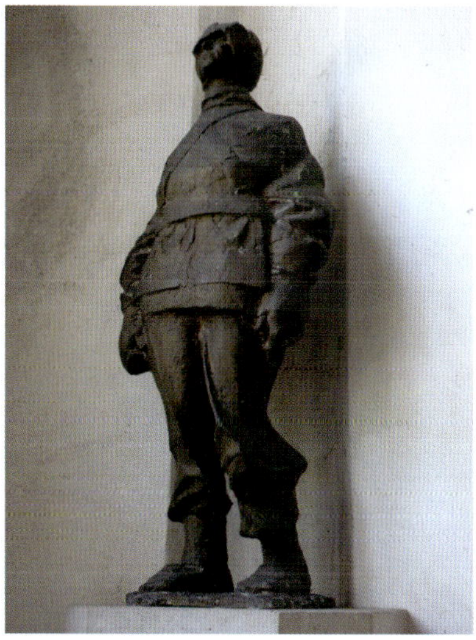

In many senses Cherry-Garrard never really fully recovered from the physical and emotional trauma he experienced in the Antarctic, and was especially haunted by a sense of guilt that he could have done more to save Scott, whom he idolised, and his close friends 'Bill' Wilson and 'Birdie' Bowers from a lonely death on the ice in March 1912 – only a dozen miles from a cache of food Cherry-Garrard had left for the party returning from the Pole. The horror of their deaths was reinforced by Cherry-Garrard being part of the group that found their bodies in November 1912 (Wheeler, *Cherry*, pp. 142–4).

During the First World War he served with the Royal Engineers and the Royal Navy Air Service. With the latter he urged the development of armoured tractors, demonstrating one design, which later evolved into the first operational tank, to Winston Churchill in June 1915. He was invalided out of the RNAS in October 1916 after a prolonged bout of colitis – a condition from which he would suffer for the rest of his life (ibid., p. 192).

In his later years Cherry-Garrard pursued the life of a politically conservative and yet slightly eccentric country gentleman – a benign landlord to his tenants, a friend of George Bernard Shaw (who lived nearby at Ayot St Lawrence), a collector of Rodin and supporter of the ever controversial Jacob Epstein (Cherry-Garrard purchased Epstein's much-criticised *Risen Christ* in 1920) – and pursued a long-running feud with the Church of England on his non-payment of tithes: his protest at what he regarded as the hypocritical attitude adopted by the Anglican Church during the First World War (ibid., pp. 189–92). For many years Cherry-Garrard appeared to be content to remain a bachelor. However, in 1939, much to the amazement of his friends, he suddenly married Angela Turner (1916–2005). In 1948 the couple left Hertfordshire and sold the Lamer Estate to live in London, where Cherry-Garrard could be closer to better medical facilities. He died in London in May 1959, but was buried in the churchyard of St Helen's Wheathampstead, according to the stipulations of his will. Just over a year later his widow, Angela, married his doctor for the last four years of Cherry-Garrard's life, Pembroke-born Dr Gordon Mathias.

It would seem that Cherry-Garrard's widow was determined that her husband should have a memorial in what was then known as the Lamer Chapel in the north transept of St Helen's. Ivor was directly approached by Mrs Mathias in the autumn of 1961. She had been impressed by photographs reproduced in the press the previous autumn of his head of *Paul Claudel*, which the Tate Gallery had recently purchased. By the end of the 1961 the sculptor had submitted a 45-cm-high plaster maquette of Cherry-Garrard in the sort of polar kit he had worn during the Terra Nova expedition to the Parochial Parish Committee, which approved it unanimously (Meeting of the St Helen's PCC, 4 December 1960, Dio-cese of St Albans Archives, Hertfordshire Local Studies, Hertford). Unlike in his irritating experience at St Mary's Ardleigh, the local Diocesan Advisory Committee passed the sculpture's design without demur early in January 1962. Its one caveat was that, as a memorial to a member of the laity, the statue should not take up too much room in the church (Evelyn C. Busby, secretary to the St Albans Diocesan Advisory Committee, to the Reverend G. H. A. T. Roe, Rector of St Helen's, Wheat-hampstead, 12 January 1962, ibid.).

The statue was unveiled by Mrs Angela Mathias on 9 October 1962, in the presence of the rector of St Helen's, the Reverend Roe, and an audience of about 80 people. The sculptor was paid a total of £786 for the commission by Mrs Mathias (*Hertfordshire Advertiser*, 12 October 1962, clipping courtesy of Mrs Ruth Jeavons, churchwarden, St Helen's Wheathampstead).

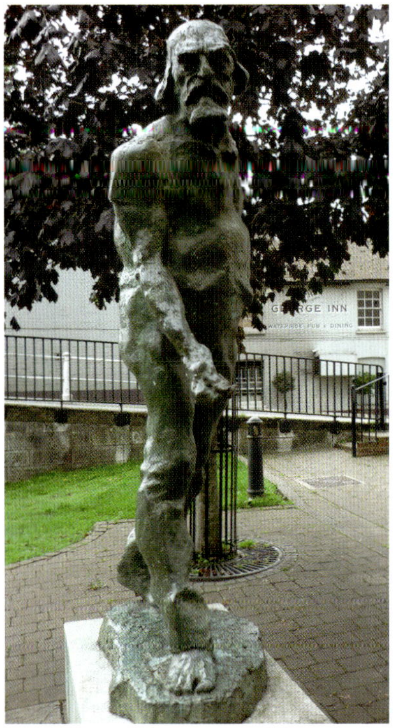

133 *Augustus John OM, RA*

1963–67
Bronze
1.9 m x 49 cm x 1 m
Located: east bank of the River Avon, Fordingbridge, Hampshire
Related work: 133a: *Conversation Piece: Augustus John Painting a Portrait of Dorelia*, c. 1963, plaster maquette, 20 x 24.2 x 10.5 cm, Wolsey Art Gallery, Ipswich, Exhibited: Wolsey Art Gallery, December 1999–January 2000
133b: *Study of Augustus John*, c. 1963–65, plaster, 17.8 x 17.2 x 18.8 cm, Victoria & Albert Museum, London
133c: *Portrait Study of Augustus John*, c. 1963–65, plaster, 24.5 x 16.3 x 14.4 cm, private collection
133d: *Portrait Study of Augustus John*, 1963–66, plaster, 15.9 x 15.3 x 18.4 cm, private collection. Possibly exhibited at the Royal Academy, May 1971 (1023)
133e: *Portrait Study of Augustus John*, plaster, 1963–66, 12.1 x 10.5 x 13.4 cm, private collection
133f: *Dorelia Wearing a Hat*, c. 1963–65, plaster study, 7.3 x 3.5 x 4.7 cm, Wolsey Art Gallery, Ipswich, exhibited there December 1999–January 2000
133g: *Dorelia Wearing a Hat*, c. 1964–65, plaster study, 12.7 x 12.7 x 13.7 cm, private collection

Comments: Augustus Edwin John (1878–1961), the future 'King of Bohemia' and one of the finest portraitists Britain has produced, was born in Tenby, Pembrokeshire, of a Welsh father and an English mother – the latter dying when John was six years old. He studied painting at the Slade School of Art (1894–98), much to the displeasure of his solicitor father. By the time he had left the Slade he had already established a reputation as a supremely gifted if hard-drinking artist. In 1901 he married fellow Slade student Ida Nettleship, who would have five sons: David (1902), Caspar (1903), Robin (1904), Edwin (1905) and Henry (1907). Teaching at Liverpool University in 1901–2, John became increasingly interested in gypsy life, lore and language. By the summer of 1903 John was also in a relationship with Dorothy 'Dorelia' McNeil (1881–1969), and living with both her and Ida in London. In 1905 Dorelia gave birth to John's son Pyramus (d. 1912); she would

133a

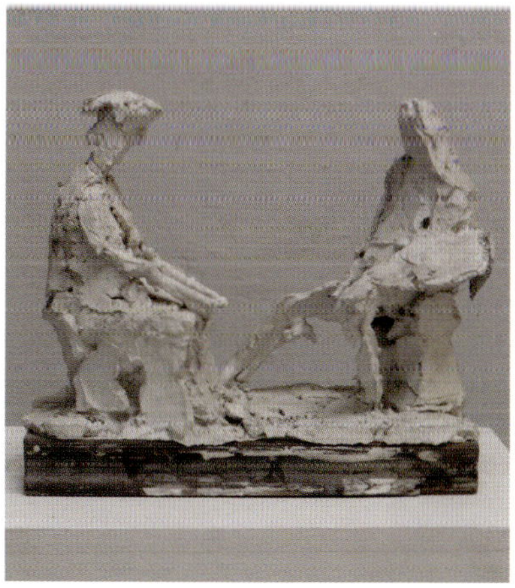

133c

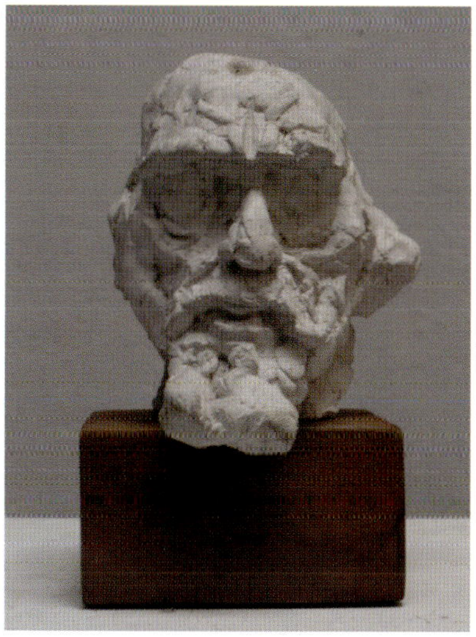

later have two daughters with John: Poppet (1912) and Vivien (1915). Ida died in March 1907 giving birth to Henry. Thereafter, Dorelia lived with John as his partner – they never formally married (Holroyd, *Augustus John*, p. 615). In July 1909 John bought a gypsy caravan for him and his family to tour the south of England; later that summer he stayed in Cambridge, where he met the subject of a future statue by Ivor – *Rupert Brooke* (Cat. 151). In October 1910, John's arrival at the apex of the British art world was signalled by the purchase by the Contemporary Art Society of his portrait of Dorelia, *The Smiling Woman*. In the spring and autumn of 1911 he visited North Wales with James Dickson Innes, and painted some of his finest landscapes.

During the First World War John was an official artist, first for the Canadian War Memorials Scheme (1917–18) and then attached to the British delegation at the Paris Peace Conference (1919); in March 1920 he held a large exhibition at the Alpine Club Gallery, London – one of the last occasions when his work received almost universally approving critical notices (Holroyd, *Augustus John*, p. 617). In March 1927 he moved from Alderney Manor, Dorset, to Fyern Court, close to Fordingbridge in Hampshire. He was elected an RA in 1928, and president of the Royal Cambrian Academy of Art six years later. By the 1930s his heavy drinking had become alcoholism, and in 1937 he was fined for drinking after hours at the Old Mill Club, Salisbury.

In June 1942 John was awarded the Order of Merit, and four years later he was elected chairman of the Contemporary Art Society of Wales. In May 1948 a major retrospective (covering work from around 1933–48) was held at the Leicester Galleries, to mixed reviews. His autobiography, *Chiaroscuro*, was published in March 1952. A year later he became interested in sculpture, and took lessons with Fiore de Henriquez (Holroyd, *Augustus John*, pp. 592–3). Towards the end of his life John joined CND, and in May 1960 he was elected to the new post of president of the Contemporary Society for Wales. In October the next year he died at Fryern Court after catching a severe chill. His nostalgic posthumous autobiography, *Finishing Touches*, was published in November 1964. His muse and partner for over fifty years, Dorelia, died at Fryern Court in July 1969 (ibid., p. 621).

It would seem that Ivor met John, possibly through Sir Charles Wheeler (then president of the Royal Academy), after his 1957 solo exhibition, and, by the late 1950s, was giving John advice on how to sculpt in clay and make plaster casts.

Ivor attended John's memorial service in London in January 1962. It was shortly after this event that Simon Beddoe, an art dealer based in Fordingbridge who had known the painter, suggested that John be commemorated in the town with a sculpture. This idea was then taken up by Dr Aubrey Westlake, a local GP who had looked after John in the late 1950s, and by a long-term John admirer Gwen, Lady Melchett (Augustus John Archive, Fordingbridge Museum, Hampshire). By late 1963 Ivor had been approached by the John family to make the statue. He initially suggested a two-figure statue depicting a seated John painting a standing Dorelia, who would be wearing one of the trademark broad-brimmed hats she had often worn before the First World War. Early in May 1964 he received official confirmation that he had been nominated as the sculptor for the memorial project. He was not to know what a torturous and exasperating commission it would prove to be (IRJ to Dr Aubrey Westlake, chairman of Ringwood and Fordingbridge Rural District Council, 2 May 1964, Augustus John Archive, Fordingbridge Museum, Hampshire).

133

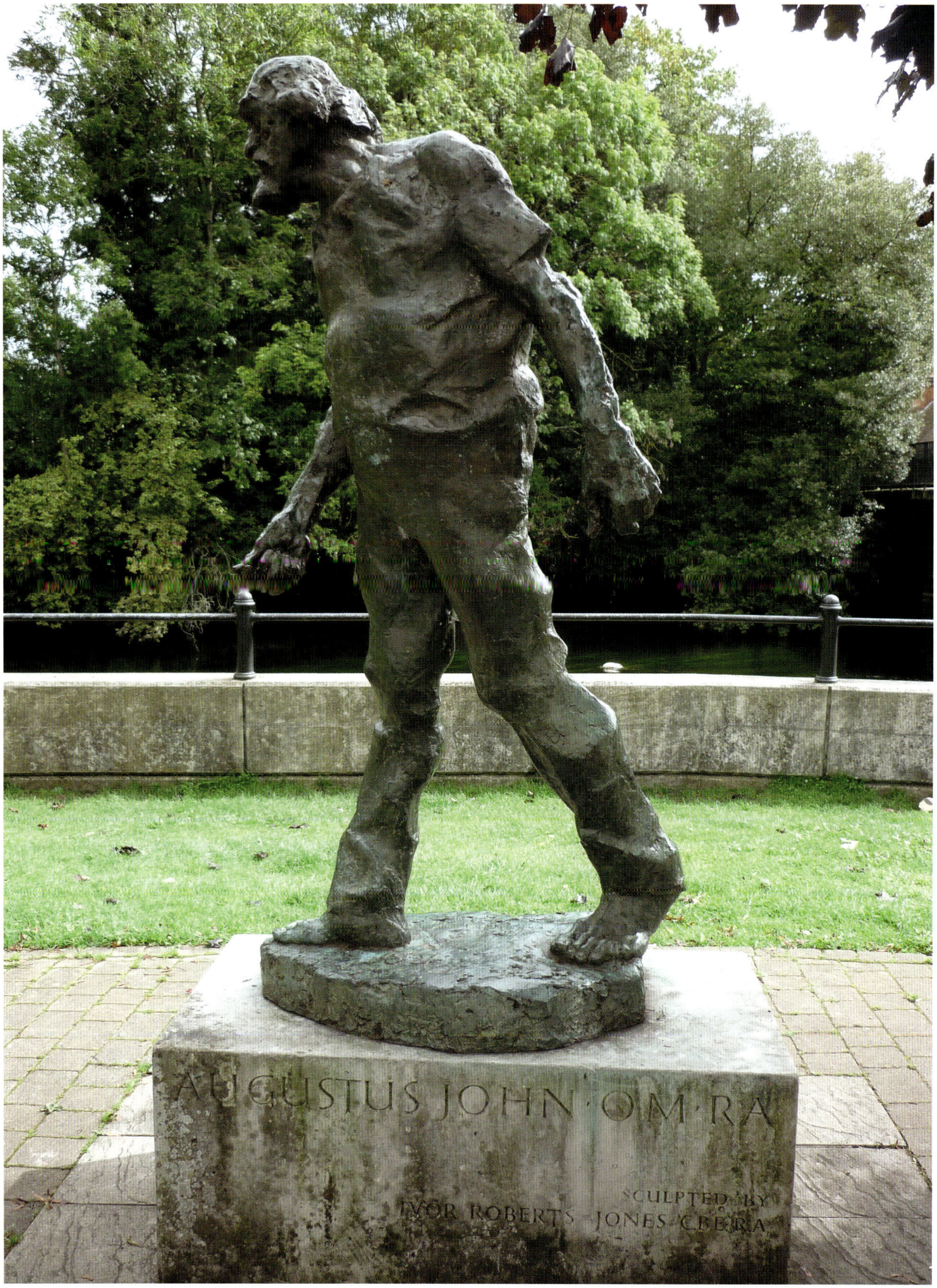

133f 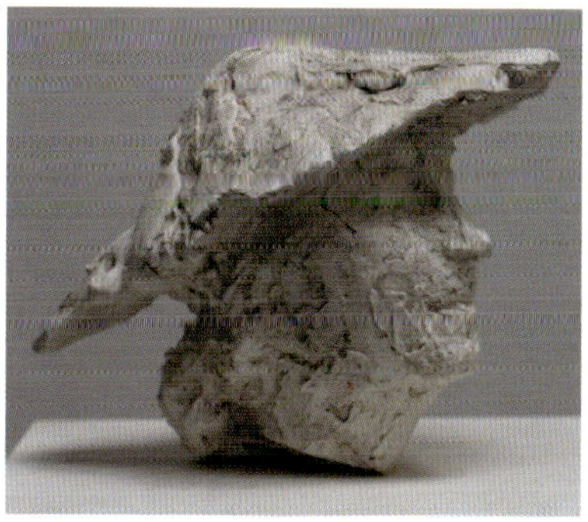

133g 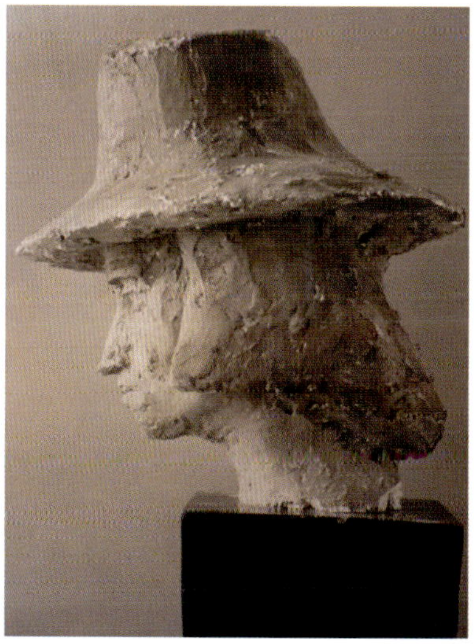

Once a memorial committee had been formed, the project was announced to the press in November 1964, with the simultaneous launch of an appeal to raise the £10,000 thought necessary to realise the statue envisaged (*The Times*, 17 November 1964, p. 11). By September 1965, Ivor had made a painted plaster head of John to serve as a centrepiece for events to raise funds for the two-figure memorial (*Evening Echo*, Bournemouth, 13 September 1965, clipping in Augustus John File, Archives, Fordingbridge Museum, Hampshire). But it became obvious, a year after the appeal had been launched, that nowhere near the required £10,000 had been raised. Meanwhile, there was much argument among the citizens of Fordingbridge and its environs as to where the proposed memorial should be sited (*The Times*, 25 August 1965, p. 10). At least four sites were discussed at length, and then discarded for various reasons over the next eighteen months, until a fifth – on a site near the town's Assembly Rooms – found favour with nearly all concerned during the spring of 1966 (*Guardian*, 8 June 1966, p. 18). By this point the Appeal and Memorial Committees had already been compelled to face the reality that not enough money had been raised to pay for the two-figure memorial design. Ivor now proposed a single figure of a 'walking John', which could just about be afforded in bronze for the £5,000 that had been raised (*The Times*, 16 April 1966, p. 5). This was accepted in May 1966, and the resulting full-sized figure of John was cast by the Art Bronze Foundry in August 1967. The figure, now installed in an area of open ground owned by the Victoria Assembly Rooms overlooking the River Avon, was unveiled by Admiral Earl Mountbatten of Burma on 1 October 1967.

Mountbatten declared that John would have 'certainly approved' of what he described as a 'magnificent statue [that] will enhance the beauty of our lovely country and keep alive the personality of a great man whose fame will live wherever his pictures are hung' (Earl Mountbatten of Burma, 1 October 1967, Augustus John Archive, Fordingbridge Museum, Hampshire).

The fifth site proved not to be the statue's final resting place. In March 1999 it was moved again to its current site next to the River Avon, downriver from the very bridge that gives Fordingbridge its name.

134 *Seated Woman*

c. 1964
Plaster
60 cm high
Collection: whereabouts unknown
Exhibition history: *The Face of Man*, Whitechapel Art Gallery, London, 1965?

135a

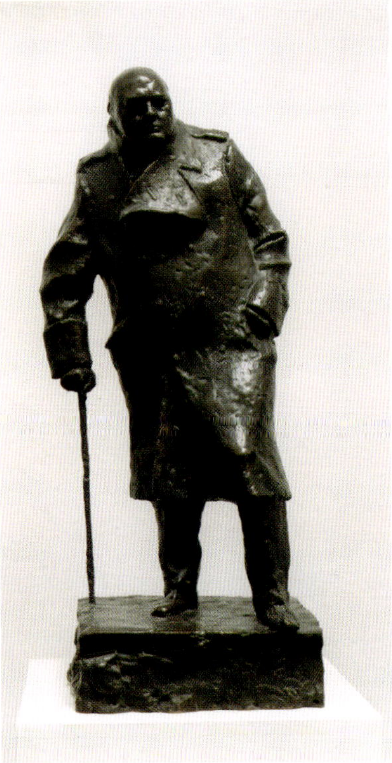

135 *Sir Winston Churchill KG, OM, CH*

1970–73
Bronze
3.66 m high
Located: north-east corner of Parliament Square, London
Related Works: 135a: *Maquette for the Sir Winston Churchill Memorial*, bronze, 1971, 57.2 x 26.7 x 21.6 cm, private collection; exhibited at Wolsey Art Gallery, Ipswich, December 1999–January 2000
135b: *Portrait Study for Sir Winston Churchill in Parliament Square*, 1971–73, plaster, 24.2 x 19.7 x 23.5 cm, estate of Ivor Roberts-Jones; exhibited at Wolsey Art Gallery, Ipswich, December 1999–January 2000
135c: *Portrait Study for Sir Winston Churchill in Parliament Square*, 1971–73, plaster, 14.6 x 11.4 x 14.7 cm, private collection; exhibited at Chappel Galleries, Chappel, Essex, July 2000
135d: *Portrait Study for Sir Winston Churchill in Parliament Square*, 1971–73, plaster, 17.5 x 15.6 x 20.3 cm, private collection; exhibited at Wolsey Art Gallery, Ipswich, December 1999–January 2000
135e: *Portrait Study for Sir Winston Churchill in Parliament Square*, 1971–73, plaster, 15.3 x 11.8 x 13.7 cm, private collection

Comments: Indispensable in the Second World War, something of a mixed blessing when in power at other times, Winston Leonard Spencer Churchill (1874–1965) was born in Blenheim Palace, the son of Lord Randolph Churchill, a younger son of the Seventh Duke of Marlborough and American heiress Jennie Jerome. Educated, unhappily, at Harrow and at the Royal Military Academy, Sandhurst, Churchill saw action on the North-west Frontier, Sudan, and South Africa (1896–1900) as a second lieutenant with the 4th Queen's Own Hussars and as a war correspondent.

He first entered parliament as Conservative MP for Oldham in October 1900; in February 1906 he crossed the floor of the House of Commons and joined the Liberals. Later that same month he was elected the Liberal MP for Manchester North West, and in April 1908 he moved on to become Liberal MP for Dundee, which seat he held until November 1922. In April 1908 he gained ministerial rank when he was appointed president of the Board of Trade; later that same year he married the Hon. Clementine Hozier (1885–1977). They would have four children: Diana (1909), Randolph (1911), Sarah (1914) and Marigold (1918), who died aged two and a half.

In February 1910 Churchill was promoted to become Home Secretary. He held that post until October 1911, when he was moved to take charge of the Royal Navy as First Lord of the Admiralty. In May 1915, in the wake of the growing debacle of the Dardanelles expedition – of which, in the eyes of many, he was the chief architect – Churchill was forced to leave the Admiralty for the lowest possible government position of Chancellor of the Duchy of Lancaster. In the autumn of 1915 he resigned this post to take command of the 6th battalion, Royal Scots Fusiliers, in the trenches of Flanders for nearly a year. With Lloyd George becoming prime minister in December 1916, Churchill correctly anticipated that he would soon return to high office. In July 1917 he was appointed minister of munitions, then secretary of state for war and the air (December 1918–February 1921), and then colonial secretary (February 1921–October 1922).

135

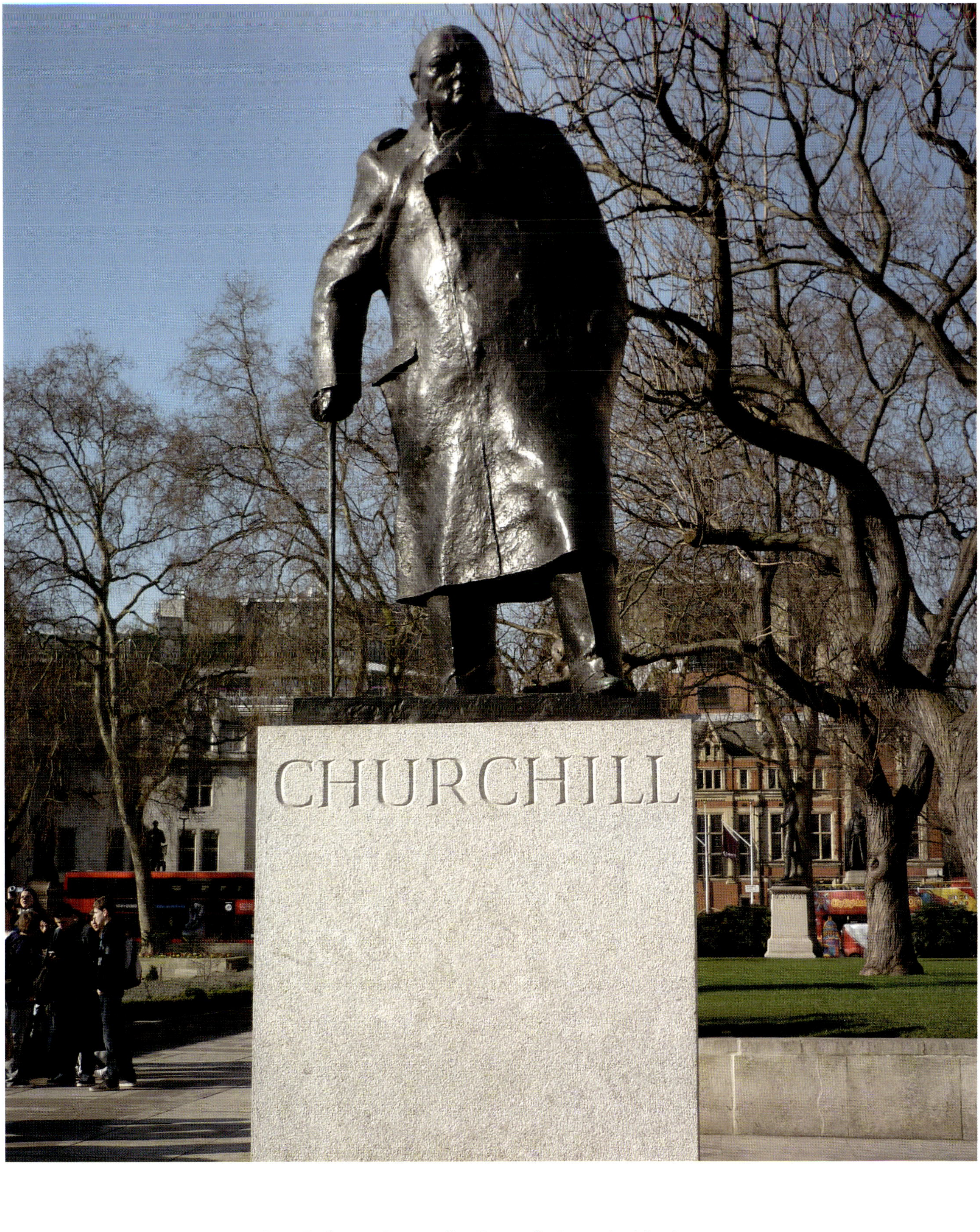

135b 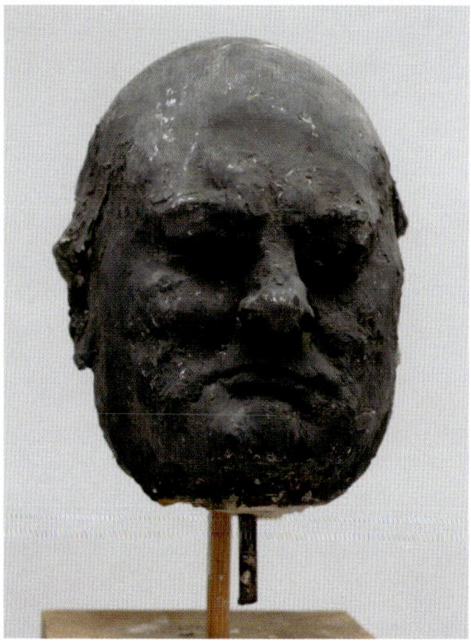

When Lloyd George fell from power in October 1922, so did Churchill – who also lost his seat in the ensuing general election. In 1923 he changed parties again, returning to the Conservatives, and was elected MP for Epping, which he held until October 1964 when he retired from the House of Commons (the seat was renamed Woodford in July 1945). Much to his surprise, the Conservative prime minister, Stanley Baldwin, made him chancellor of the exchequer in November 1924. He occupied this position until June 1929, when the Labour Party won the general election. Within eighteen months Churchill had alienated himself from the leadership of his party, and he resigned from the shadow cabinet in 1931. So began his so-called 'wilderness years', during which he argued for rearmament and warned against the threat posed by National Socialist Germany. With the outbreak of the Second World War he re-entered the government as First Lord of the Admiralty, and then became prime minister in May 1940. He held this post – inspiring many of his people and infuriating many of his military leaders in equal measure – until Germany had been defeated, in May 1945. Two months later he was profoundly shocked to lose the general election to a landslide victory of the Labour Party. He returned to power as prime minister in October 1951, until compelled by old age and failing physical and mental powers to step aside in favour of Anthony Eden in April 1955. In April 1953 the new queen, Elizabeth II, had appointed him a Knight of the Garter, and the same year he was awarded the Nobel Prize for Literature. He died at his London home in January 1965. He was given the honour of a state funeral in St Paul's Cathedral (Richard Holmes, *In The Footsteps of Churchill* [London: BBC Books, 2006])

The idea of a statue of Churchill in Parliament Square was first mooted in December 1967 by John Tilney, Conservative MP for Liverpool Wavertree. He regarded such a work as a publically accessible counterpart to the figure of Churchill that Oscar Nemon was then executing for the Members' Lobby of the House of Commons (Department of the Environment, PWO 1/105 AD, National Archives, Kew Gardens, London). Once he had secured the support of Churchill's widow, and that of over 150 MPs, in July 1969 the proposal for a Churchill memorial was accepted by the Labour prime minister, Harold Wilson, who directed Tilney and his chief supporter Sir John Rodgers, Conservative MP for Sevenoaks, to form an all-party committee to decide who would sculpt the memorial, and precisely where in Parliament Square it should stand (*Hansard*, 3 July 1969, pp. 638).

By late September 1969 such a committee had been formed, composed of Tilney; Rodgers; Conservative peer Lord Chandos; Churchill's son-in-law, Conservative MP Duncan Sandys; Labour peer Lord Goodman; Labour MPs George Strauss and Emmanuel Shinwell; and the Liberal MP Jo Grimond (Minutes of the Winston Churchill Statue Committee, 23 September 1969 [WCSC], DSND 13/8 [1969–1975] Duncan Sandys Papers, Churchill Archive, Churchill College, Cambridge).

In the committee's early discussions a consensus quickly formed that any statue of Churchill ought to be erected in the north-east corner of Parliament Square – a site the great man had once identified as a fitting spot for any future memorial to himself (*The Times*, 5 March 1970, p. 11; 'Resolute and Defiant as Ever, Churchill's Statue is Unveiled', *The Times*, 2 November 1973, p. 2). A minority of members were keen to commission another figure of Churchill from Oscar Nemon, but the majority had not been greatly impressed by Nemon's statue of Churchill, unveiled in the Members' Lobby of the Commons in December 1969 (Minutes of the WCSC, 17 December 1969, ibid.).

135c

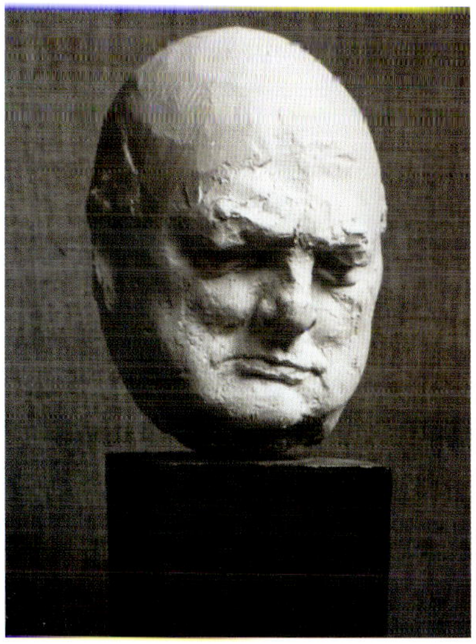

In February 1970 the Winston Churchill Statue Appeal was launched in *The Times* with the aim of raising £30,000 to pay for a suitable statue of Churchill in Parliament Square. Meanwhile, that same month, a panel of experts from the Royal Fine Art Commission inspected Nemon's latest maquette for the Churchill statue and rejected it. They recommended that it hold a restricted competition among a number of invited sculptors (Minutes of the WCSC, 25 February 1970, ibid.).

In mid March 1970, advised by Sean Crampton (president of the Royal Society of British Sculptors) and Sir John Pope-Hennessy (director of the Victoria and Albert Museum), the Statue Committee invited Oscar Nemon and eight other sculptors to submit a maquette of a Churchill figure by the end of June. Nemon and six other sculptors indicated that they were prepared to participate: Ivor, F. E. McWilliam, Michael Rizzello, Anthony Grey, Franta Belsky, Bentley Claughton and Sir Charles Wheeler RA (Minutes of the WCSC, 22 April 1970, ibid.).

Early in July the selection sub-committee viewed the submitted maquettes and decided those by Ivor and Nemon appealed the most – though it was felt that both required more work. The two sculptors were asked to go away and submit a second maquette within three months' time (Minutes of the Adjudicating Sub-Committee of the WCSC, 1 July 1970, ibid.).

When the selection committee viewed these new maquettes, early in November 1970, it unanimously selected Ivor's (Minutes of the Adjudicating Sub-Committee of the WCSC, 3 November 1970, ibid.). A fortnight later this decision was seconded by a panel from the RFAC (F. Fielden, secretary to the RFAC; John Tilney, chairman of the Executive Committee of the WCSC, Minutes of WCSC, 17 November 1970, ibid.). But a number of members on the larger Churchill Statue Committee – led by Duncan Sandys – still preferred Nemon's maquette. Ivor was asked to undertake further work on his maquette, and also to make a four-foot-high clay model of Churchill's head (John Tilney to Duncan Sandys, 10 December 1970, ibid.).

By February 1971 Ivor's latest version of the Churchill maquette, and photographs of the new large head in clay, had been closely inspected by members of the WCSC, a panel from the RFAC, and the minister of works. The sculptor's latest conception of Churchill – essentially as the statue stands today in Parliament Square – was enthusiastically approved by all parties (Sir John Tilney to all members of the WCSC, 16 February 1971, copy, ibid.). But a few members of the wider Statue Committee, led by Sandys and supported by Churchill's widow, his daughter Sarah, and his grandson, Winston Churchill junior, still held out for Nemon to be awarded the commission (Sarah Churchill to Lady Clementine Spencer-Churchill, 8 February 1971, NEMO 2/6, Papers of Oscar Nemon, Churchill Archive, Churchill College, Cambridge, and Minutes of the WCSC, 22 February 1971, ibid.).

This lingering opposition to Ivor's conception for the statue was in vain, as he was formally confirmed as the sculptor of the commission in mid March 1971; his fee would be £18,000 (Richard Crawfurd-Benson, secretary of the WCSC, to Duncan Sandys, 11 March 1971, ibid., and press release issued by the WCSC, 16 March 1971, ibid.). Ivor quickly proceeded to buy a property at Cratfield, in rural Suffolk, which had a large barn attached. Ivor decided this building would serve as an excellent studio in which to construct the armature of the huge figure of Churchill – to stand over three metres high on a nine-foot plinth (Bryon Rogers, 'Churchill Rises in the Barn', *Daily Telegraph*, 12 January 1973, clipping, ibid.).

135d 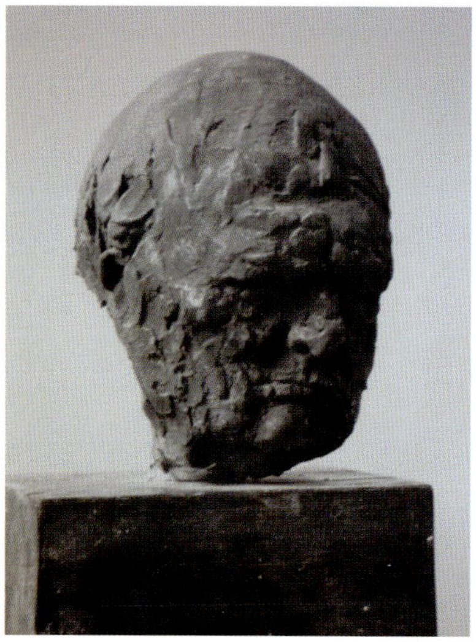

By February 1972 the WCSC's secretary had reported that Ivor's work on Churchill's head and shoulders was well underway, while the artist was experimenting with depicting Churchill wearing a British army greatcoat, known as a 'British Warm', which he had only sketched in 'lightly' on the maquette he had submitted the previous year (Richard Crawfurd-Benson to Sir John Tilney, 24 February 1972, copy, ibid.).

The full-sized clay model was viewed by a deputation from the WCSC and the RFAC in mid October 1972; six weeks later the entire figure had been cast in plaster (Sir John Tilney, progress report to members of the WCSC, 22 January 1972, ibid.). The plaster figure would then be divided into eleven sections to be cast separately by the Meridian Foundry in Peckham, which Ivor had chosen in preference to his initial suggestion of Morris Singer in Basingstoke. The sculptor would then supervise the reassembly of the sections to create the full-sized bronze figure (Richard Crawfurd-Benson to Winston Churchill MP, 10 March 1973, ibid.).

In June 1973 Sir John Tilney reported to the Statue Committee that the eleven parts of the plaster cast of the full-sized statue had been safely delivered to the Meridian Foundry. Casting of the pieces into bronze and their reassembly would not be completed until, at the earliest, the end of August (Sir John Tilney to the members of the WCSC, 11 June 1973, ibid.).

The statue was cast to Ivor's exacting standards on schedule, and installed upon its plinth about a month before the work was unveiled by Lady Spencer-Churchill, in the presence of the Queen, on 1 November 1973 (ibid.). Regarding the statue, Sir John Tilney told a reporter from the *Times*:

> Not every facet of such an historic character can be captured in bronze. [Churchill] lived so many lives, any one of which any of us would have been proud to have lived. But his grit and greatness are here for all to see ... this heroic statue of the man who walked with destiny has arrived in its proper home in the heart of London, in the precincts of Westminster, where it will become an emblem and a spectacle for generations not yet born ('Resolute and Defiant as Ever, Churchill's Statue is Unveiled', *The Times*, 2 November 1973, p. 2).

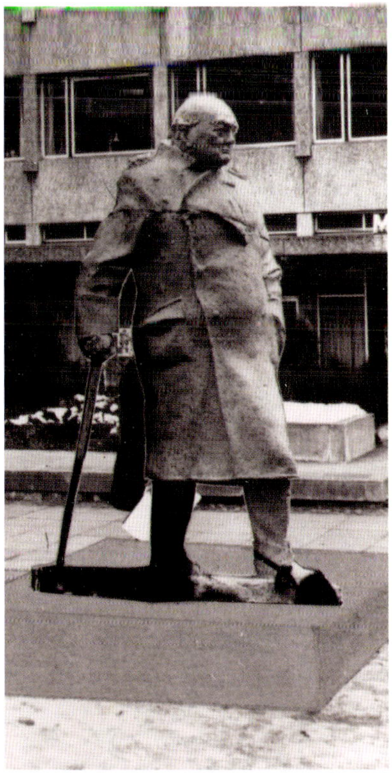

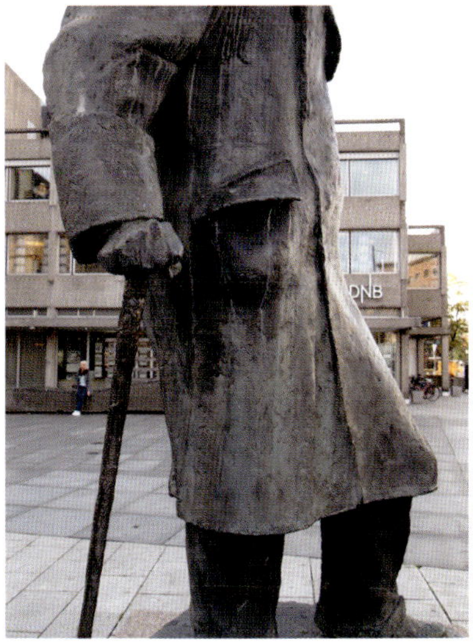

136 *Sir Winston Churchill KG, OM, CH*

1974–75
Bronze
2.74 m high
Located: Solli Square, Oslo, Norway
Related work: 136a: *Study of a Statue of Sir Winston Churchill for Oslo*, 1974, painted plaster, 16.8 x 17.2 x 18.4 cm, estate of Ivor Roberts-Jones

Comments: The idea for a monument to Churchill in central Oslo appears to have originated early in 1974 with a Norwegian businessman, Hans Hoegh, and another Norwegian admirer of Churchill, Odd Grann (currently the head of Oslo's Old Age Pensioners Council) as well as an Oslo-based British diplomat, Anthony Smith-Meyer. Their group was soon joined by the celebrated Norwegian Resistance hero Gunnar Sønsteby DSO (1918–2012) (*Daily Telegraph*, 10 May 2012, p. 12). All four had been extremely impressed by the figure of Churchill Ivor had produced for Parliament Square. The original hope had been that the sculptor would be able to make a variant of the Parliament Square *Churchill* to unveil in Oslo in November 1974 – the centenary of Churchill's birth. This proved far too optimistic: as ever, the process of raising the 250,000 Norwegian kroner necessary to pay for the statue took much longer than anticipated. An appeal was launched in the main Oslo newspaper in August 1974; the aim was now to have the statue ready for unveiling on 5 May 1975 – the thirtieth anniversary of the liberation of Norway from German occupation (*Aftenposten*, 29 November 1974, p. 1).

Work on the statue was further delayed when the Commissioning Committee informed Ivor that, while it was happy to have the body of the *Churchill* in Parliament Square, it was keen for the sculptor to make a new head of the British statesman – more fitting for a man of 'peace and reconciliation' (IRJ to Sir John Rothenstein, c. September 1985, Rothenstein Papers, Archives, Tate Britain). A further complication proved to be securing permission for a suitable site in Oslo (Odd Grann to Dr S. Ayres, September 2012).

Plans for an unveiling in May 1975 had to be abandoned; it was not until the autumn of that year that the full-sized plaster figure – complete with remodelled head – was cast by the Meridian Foundry. The bronze was unveiled by the King of Norway in Solli Plass (Square), Oslo, on 10 May 1976 (*Aftenposten*, 10 May 1976, p. 52). Somewhat late in the day, the Commissioning Committee had the following inscribed on the base of the statue: 'Come then let us go forward together with our united strength.' This was taken from the closing lines of a famous speech Churchill gave in the House of Commons on 13 May 1940, as it became clear that the Germans would soon overrun central Norway, in which he defiantly announced: 'I have nothing to offer but blood, toil, tears and sweat.'

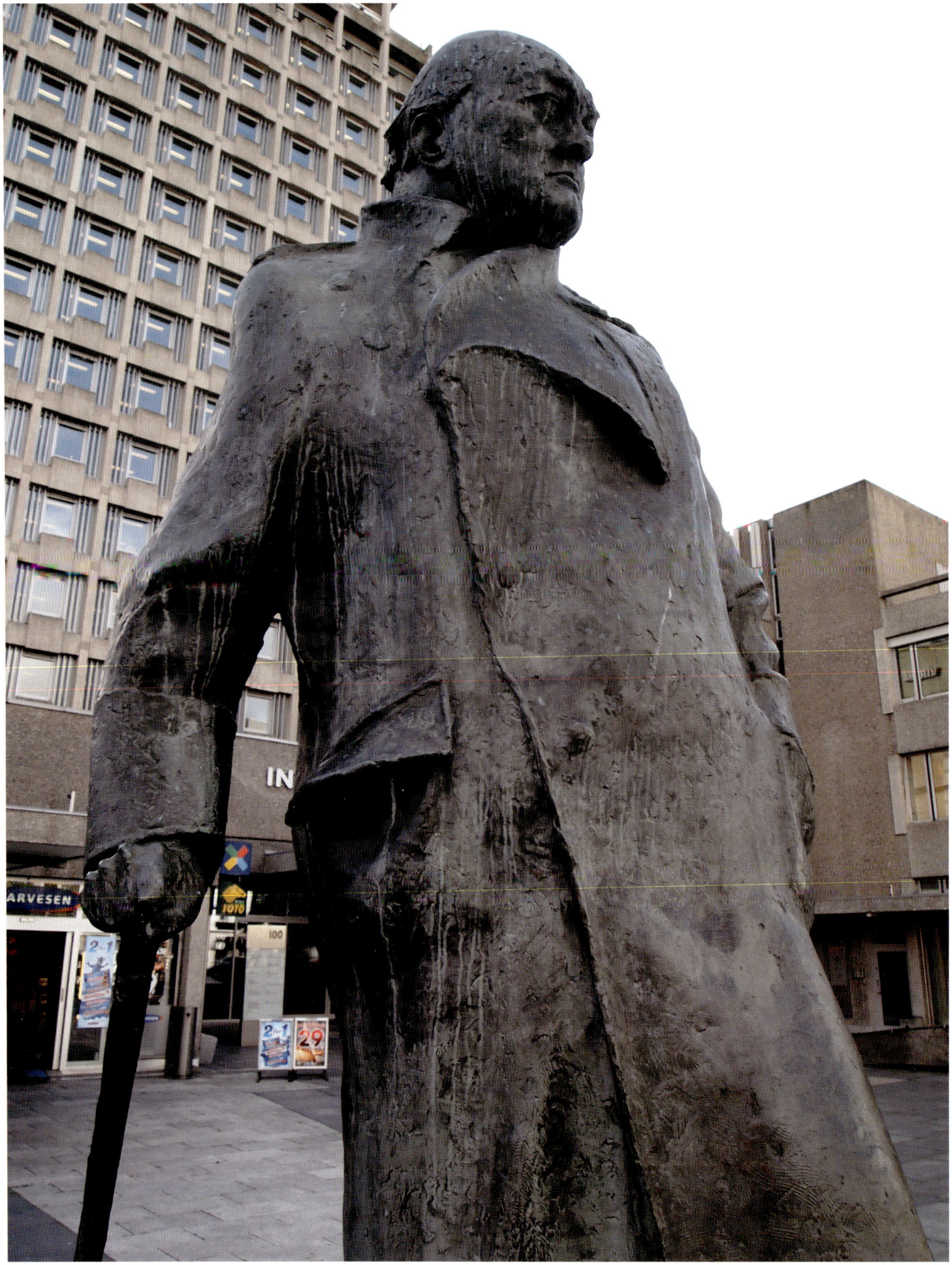
ARVESEN
IN
100
29

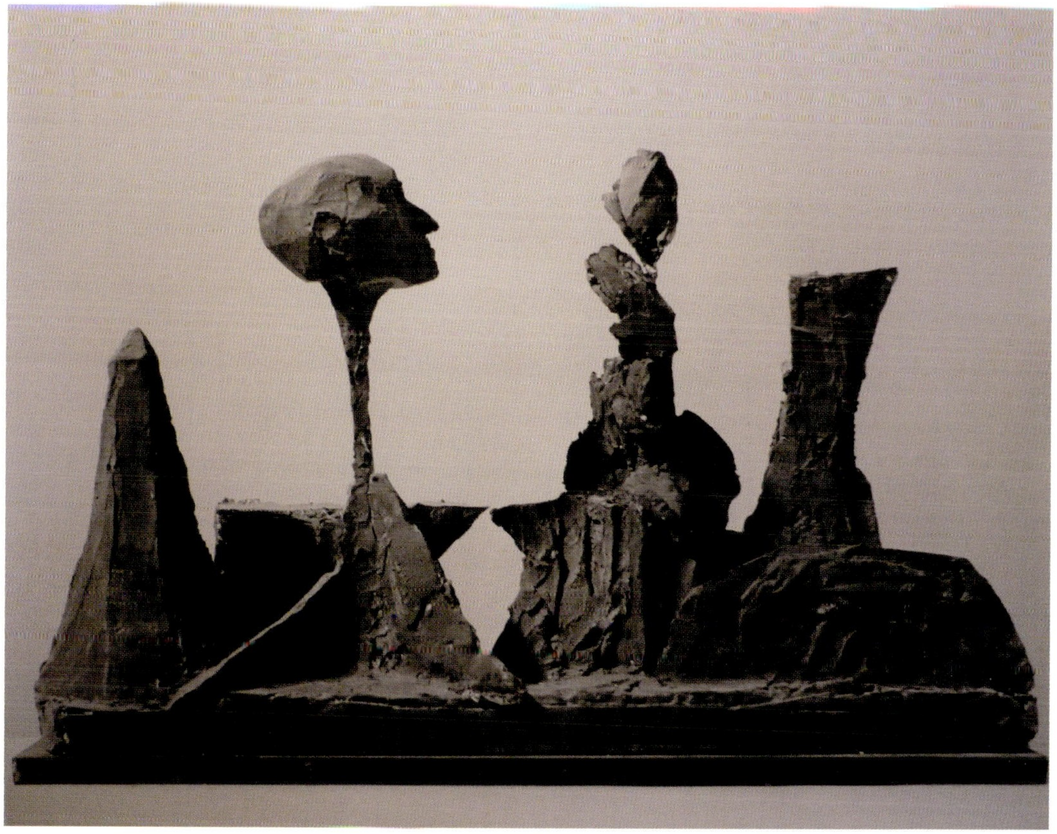

137 *Little Monument I/Still Life, Homage to a Poet (Capetanakis)*

1976–77
Plaster
61 x 38 cm (width x depth)
Collection: private collection
Exhibition history: Oriel Art Gallery, Cardiff, July–September 1978 (10)

Comments: The first in a series of what Ivor variously referred to as 'Little Monuments', or 'experiments in still life', inspired by his respect for the still-lives of Giorgio Morandi (1890–1964) and by his reading of the poetry of the Greek poet Demetrios Capetanakis (1912–1944) who died in London. A posthumous volume of his poems exploring the experience of wartime and human existence was translated into English and published in London in 1947 as *Demetrios Capetanakis: A Greek Poet in England.* At some point in the late 1940s Ivor had bought a copy, dipped in to it, and been greatly impressed. Thirty years after the end of the war, Ivor reread *A Greek Poet in England* with even greater relish, as he found that he detected additional layers of overlooked wisdom in the poems, as the passage of time had left him with a more complex and nuanced understanding of life (Sir John Rothentsein, 'Ivor Roberts-Jones' in *The Artist,* September 1978, pp. 13–14).

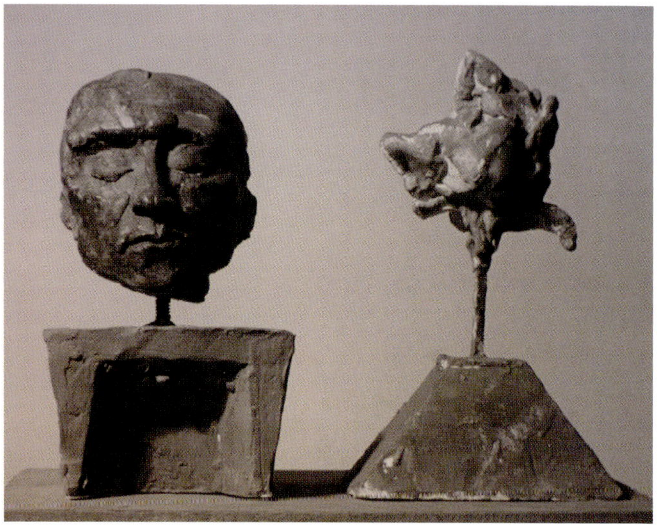

138 *Little Monument II/Still Life*

1976–77
Plaster
23 x 15 cm (width x depth)
Collection: private collection
Exhibition history: Oriel Art Gallery, Cardiff, July–September 1978 (11)

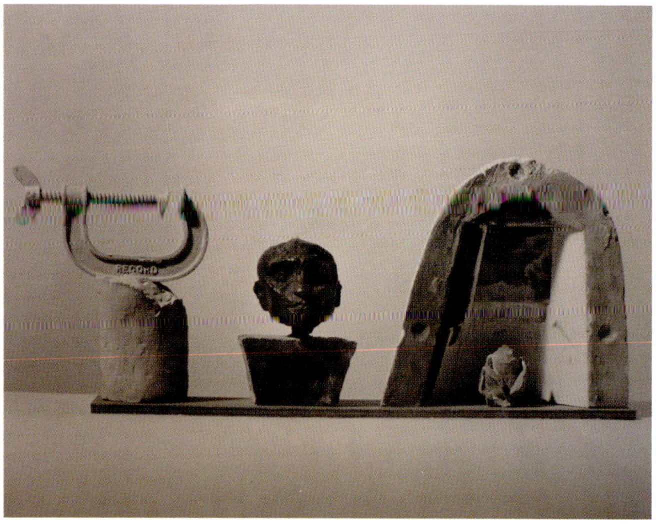

139 *Little Monument III/Still Life – Memorial to a Poet*

1976–78
Painted plaster
61 x 21.5 cm (width x depth)
Collection: private collection
Exhibition history: Oriel Art Gallery, Cardiff, July–September 1978 (14)

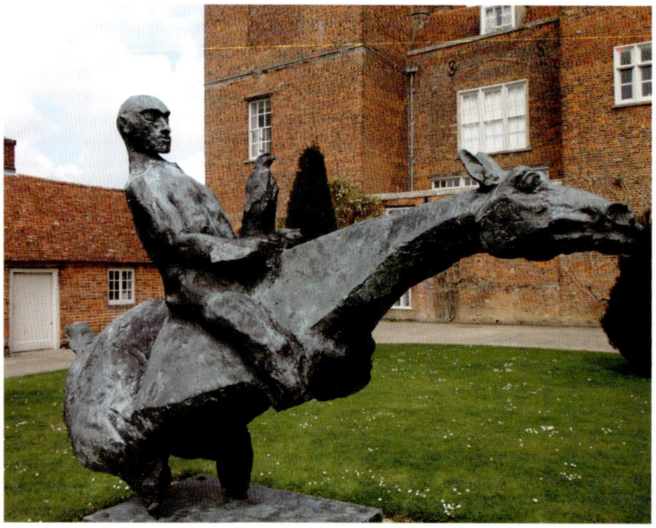

140 *The Lazarus Rider*

1976–80
Bronze
152.5 x 101.5 cm
Collection: Sir Richard Hyde Parker, Melford Hall, Suffolk
Exhibition history: (sketch model in plaster) Royal Academy, London, May 1976 (96); (plaster maquette of second version) Oriel Gallery, Cardiff, July–September 1978 (13)
Related work: 1140a: *Study for the Head of the Lazarus Rider*, c. 1979–80, plaster, 30.5 x 22.8 x 23.5 cm, private collection 140b: *Study for the Lazarus Rider*, c. 1980–82, pencil and collage on paper, 52 x 33.6 cm, Henry Moore Institute, Leeds; exhibited at Wolsey Art Gallery, Ipswich, December 1999–January 2000

140a

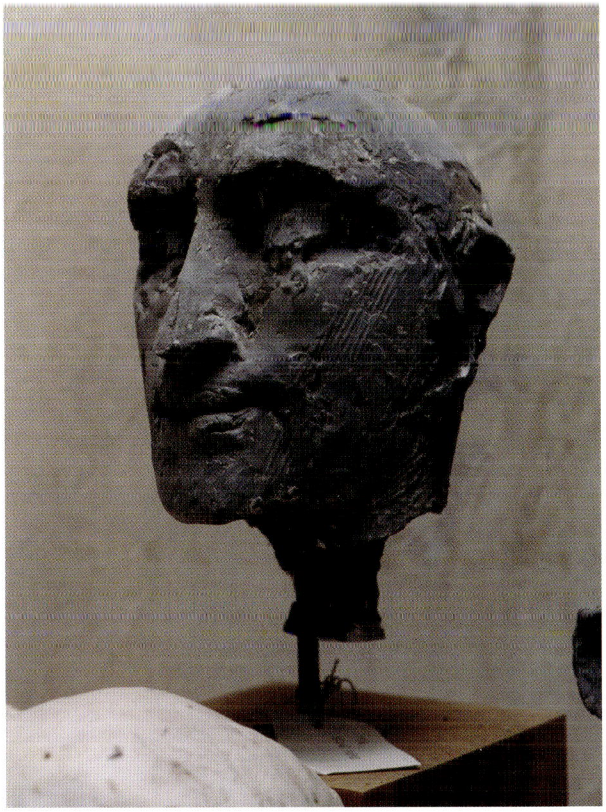

140b

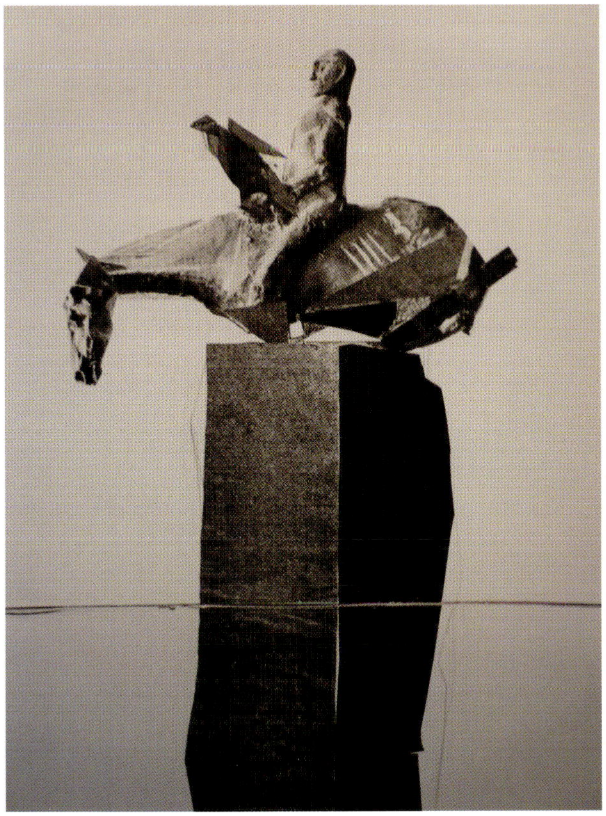

Comments: In Chapter 11 of the Gospel of John, Lazarus of Bethany was raised from the dead by Jesus after he had lain for four days in his tomb. This work harks back to Ivor's earlier *The Kite Rider*, from around 1960–61, and to his admiration for the series of *Horse and Rider* sculptures produced during the 1930s and '40s by Marino Marini (Marina Lambraki-Plaka and Giuliano Scrafini, *Marino Marini: An Archaic Sculptor of Modern Art* [Athens: National Alexandros Soutzos Museum, 2006], p. 261).

The head of the rider, eyes tightly closed with a hint of a smile on his lips, is reminiscent of that of the *Blind Man* Ivor had first modelled in the mid 1950s. The sculptor later wrote: 'The sculpture I like best has ... a sort of withdrawal, seeming to attract the space around it towards its centre. Far Eastern sculpture often has this feeling about it and I tried for this in works like the ... *The Lazarus Rider* ...' (*Ivor Roberts-Jones: Sculpture*, Oriel Welsh Arts Council, Cardiff, 27 July–2 September 1978, unpaginated). The hawk or falcon on the rider's wrist may be symbolic of the soul, freed from the restraint of bodily encasement, and refer to the mythology of Ancient Egypt.

After the second version of the work had been exhibited in Cardiff in 1978, Sir John Rothenstein commented that the *Lazarus Rider* embodied 'energy, poetry and originality. It is not a work easy to forget and should find a place in an important collection' (Sir John Rothenstein, *The Artist*, October 1978, p. 33).

As it transpired, *The Lazarus Rider* had been seen in Cardiff in September 1978 by landowner, collector and patron of the arts, Sir Richard Hyde Parker. In November the following year he wrote to the artist that he would very much like to buy a bronze cast of the plaster he had seen on display at the Oriel Gallery to stand outside his home at Melford Hall, Norfolk (Sir Richard Hyde Parker to IRJ, 1 November 1979, Sir Richard Hyde Parker Papers). Ivor promptly replied that he would be delighted to oblige but, as would so often be the case, he took Sir Richard's interest as a very welcome opportunity to 'modify and improve' the existing plaster of *The Lazarus Rider* (IRJ to Sir Richard Hyde Parker, 3 November 1979, ibid.). The 'new and improved' version had been completed, almost to Ivor's satisfaction, by September 1980, and the following month the new plaster cast was despatched to the Meridian Foundry (IRJ to Sir Richard Hyde Parker, postmarked 10 October 1980, ibid.). The work was finally erected in front of Melford Hall during the summer of 1982 (IRJ to Sir Richard Hyde Parker, 17 July 1982, ibid.). Typically, Ivor had lavished a great deal of time and effort in designing what he felt to be the most fitting base for the statue (IRJ to Sir Richard Hyde Parker, 16 March 1983, ibid.).

141a

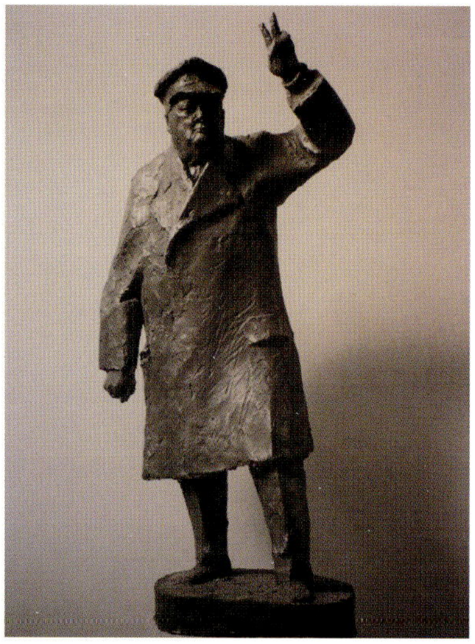

141b

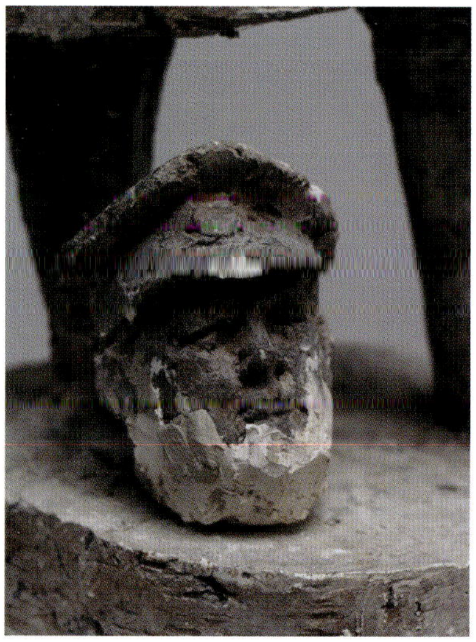

141c

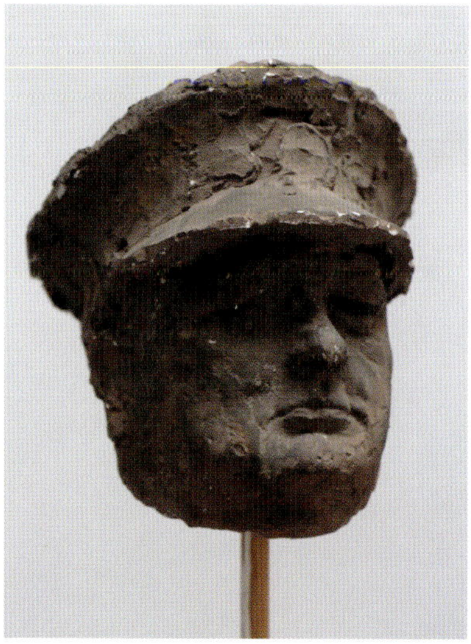

141 *Sir Winston Churchill KG, OM, CH*

1976–77
Bronze
2.74 m high
Located: British Place, between the New Orleans Hilton Hotel and the International Trade Mart, Riverside, New Orleans, USA
Related works: 141a: *Maquette for Sir Winston Churchill in New Orleans*, 1976, plaster, 40.7 x 21.3 x 12.7 cm, private collection
141b: *Portrait Study for Sir Winston Churchill in New Orleans*, 1976, plaster, 9.5 cm high, estate of Ivor Roberts-Jones
141c: *Portrait Study for Sir Winston Churchill in New Orleans*, 1976, plaster, 16.8 x 17.2 x 18.4 cm, estate of Ivor Roberts-Jones

Comments: The idea for this commission originated early in 1976 with anglophile James J. Coleman Jr, at the time the honorary British consul for Louisiana and managing director of the International Rivercentre in downtown New Orleans. In his mind's eye he imagined an inspiring figure of Churchill by Ivor, standing in a small park in front of the new 1,200-room, 30-storeys-high Hilton Hotel (James J. Coleman Jr, interviewed by Dr S. Ayres, 22 October 2012).

In the spring of 1976 Ivor wrote in some excitement to Jack Crofton at the Meridian Foundry:

> There is a firm enquiry ... for another Winston. I think it will probably be about 9ft [2.74 metres] high – as the Oslo one was. I believe they have already collected the money! ... it will be a rush job – to be unveiled next spring [1977] – but I remember you were very, very, quick over the Oslo one ... and so was I! – so I don't see any trouble there (IRJ to Jack Crofton, c. May 1976, Megan Thomas Archive).

Coleman met the sculptor in the summer of 1976, during a visit to his alma mater, Oxford University, and Ivor quickly came up with the idea of depicting Churchill wearing the distinctive cap and coat of an 'Elder Brother' of the Trinity House Corporation of Watermen, Lighthousemen and River Pilots (the corporation had been established at Deptford by Henry VIII in 1514. The honour had been bestowed upon Churchill four hundred years later, while he was First Lord of the Admiralty [1911–15]). This was the garb he had worn when he first met President Roosevelt at Plancentia Bay, Newfoundland, in August 1941 (James J. Coleman interviewed by Dr S. Ayres, 22 October 2012). It also recalled the pseudonym Churchill had adopted when writing to Roosevelt shortly after becoming prime minister, in May 1940, as 'A Former Naval Person' (Max Hastings, *Finest Years: Churchill as Warlord, 1940–45* [London: Harper Press, 2009], p. 15).

To give the figure a touch of added animation, Ivor suggested that Churchill be sculpted giving his trademark 'V for Victory' sign with the fingers of his left hand, which he had begun making in public from mid 1941 onwards (Jock Colville, *The Fringes of Power. Downing Street Diaries, 1939–1955* [London: Phoenix, 2005 (1985)], p. 384). Coleman also asked Ivor to make a head of Churchill which was unmistakably that of 'a great leader of the Western World' (IRJ to Sir John Rothenstein, c. September 1985, Rothenstein Papers, Archives, Tate Britain).

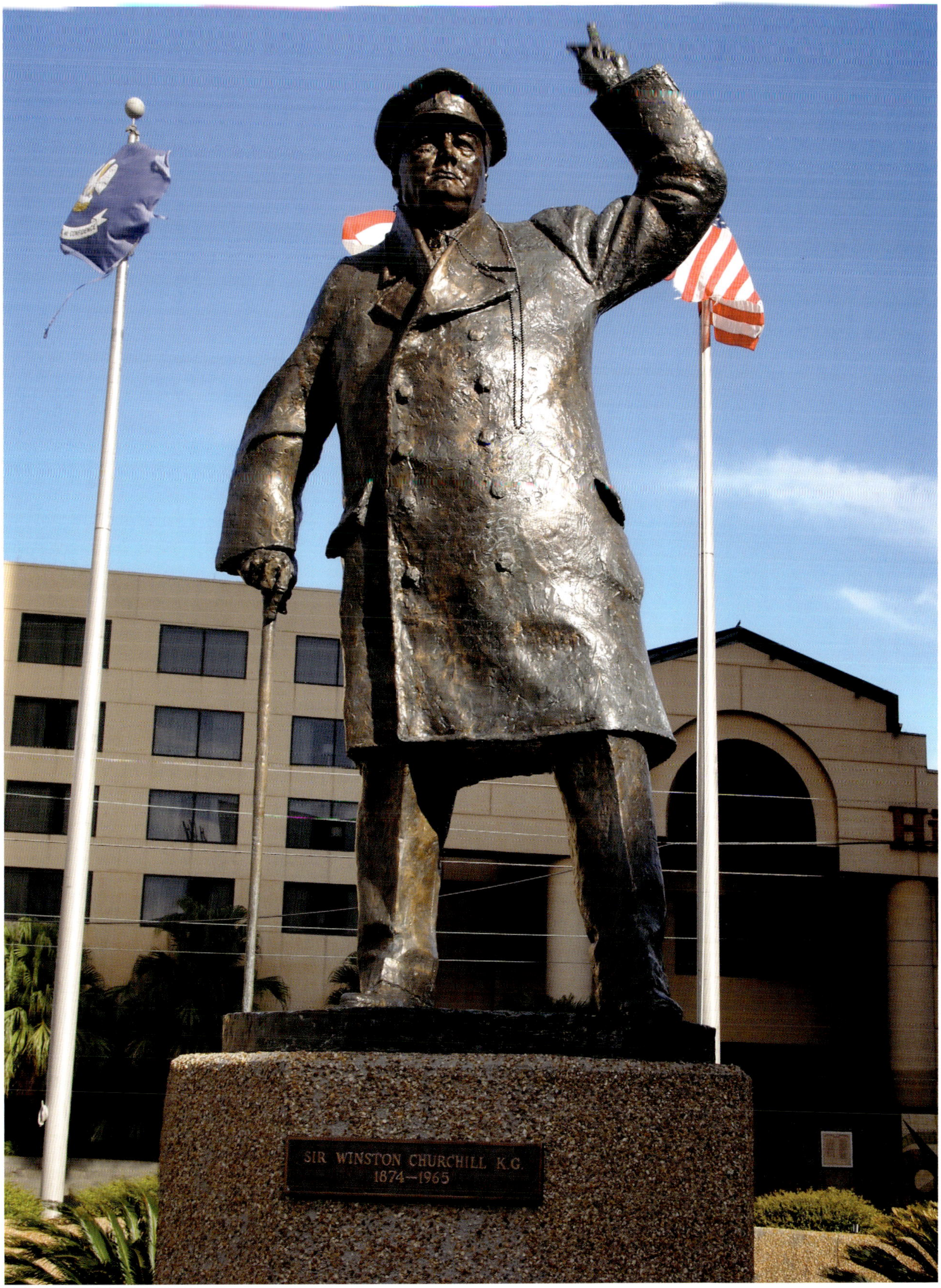
SIR WINSTON CHURCHILL K.G.
1874–1965

This proved an unusually trouble-free commission for Ivor. Coleman and the statue committee, drawn from the partners of the International Rivercenter of New Orleans, were delighted with the scale maquette, and the full-sized work was cast in the spring of 1977 and unveiled by Churchill's daughter, Lady Mary Soames, on 19 November 1977 (*Times Picayune*, 20 November 1977, p. 1).

Four months after the unveiling ceremony, the honorary vice-consul for Louisiana wrote that Ivor's statue had 'won wide acclaim. Everyone agrees it portrays Sir Winston as the sturdy, indomitable, character he was and which gave us all such hope during those trying days. Lady Soames was particularly pleased with the statue ... those of us who lived through his inspirational leadership realise how badly the world today needs someone of his stature' (Ray Samuel, hon. British vice-consul to New Orleans, to Dalton Newfield, past president of the International Churchill Society, Sacramento, California, 10 February 1978, papers of James J. Coleman OBE, hon. British consul for Louisiana).

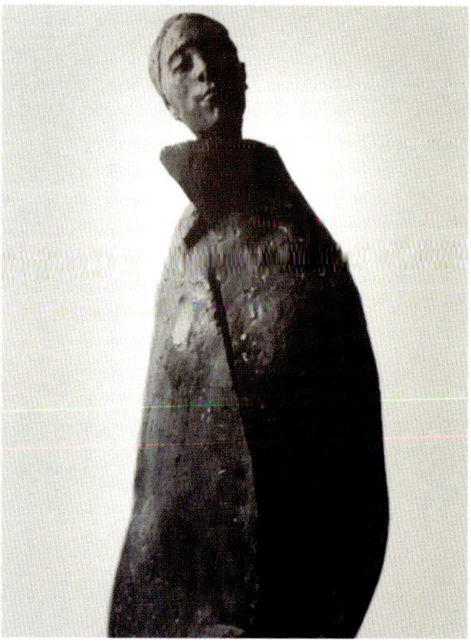

142a
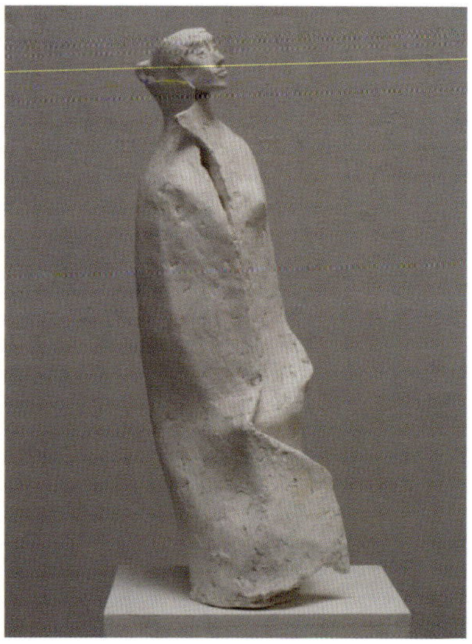

142 *Vicky in a Long Coat*

1976–77
Plaster
1.56 m x 55.7 x 40.7 cm
Collection: private collection
Exhibition history: Royal Academy, London, May 1977 (92); Contemporary British Sculpture, Battersea Park, June–September 1977; Oriel Gallery, Cardiff, July–September 1978 (12); Royal National Eisteddfod of Wales, Llangefni, Anglesey, July–August 1983 (13)
Related work: 142a: maquette, c. 1976, plaster, 57.2 x 17.8 x 21.9 cm, estate of Ivor Roberts-Jones
142b: *Two Sketches for Vicky in a Long Coat*, c. 1976, pen-and-ink on paper, 21 x 20 cm, Henry Moore Institute, Leeds

Comments: 'Vicky' was Victoria Reynolds, a sculpture student of Ivor's at Goldsmiths College around 1975–77 (author interview with Etienne Millner, 16 January 2012). Writing in 1978, Sir John Rothenstein commented that this figure 'displayed a broader sense of form' than had been previously the case in Ivor's work. Moreover, the face possessed 'an enigmatic subtlety while the ample rhythmic folds of her cloak, with its high collar, arrest your attention and remain in the memory' (Sir John Rothenstein, *The Artist*, October 1978, p. 33).

142b

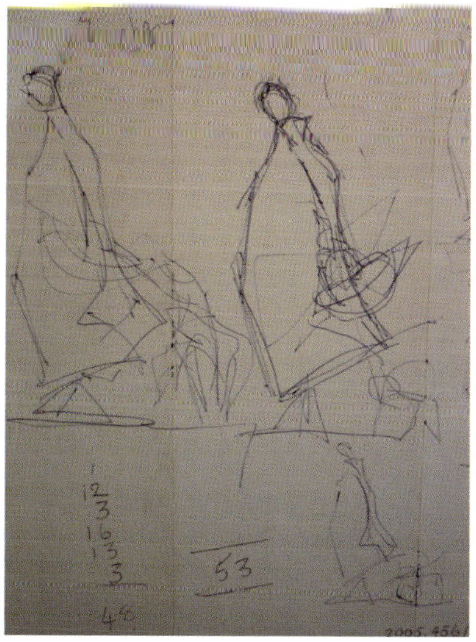

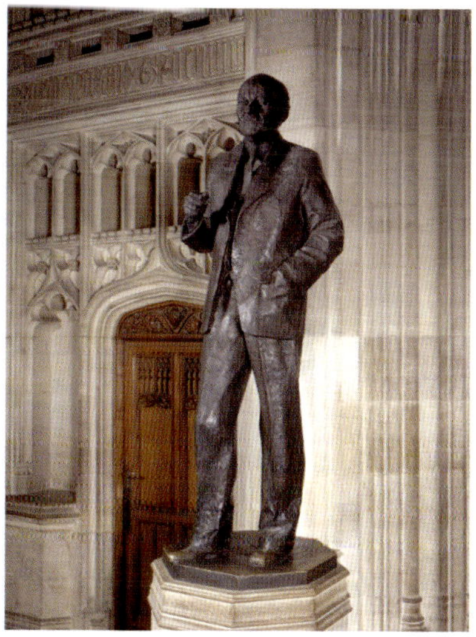

143a

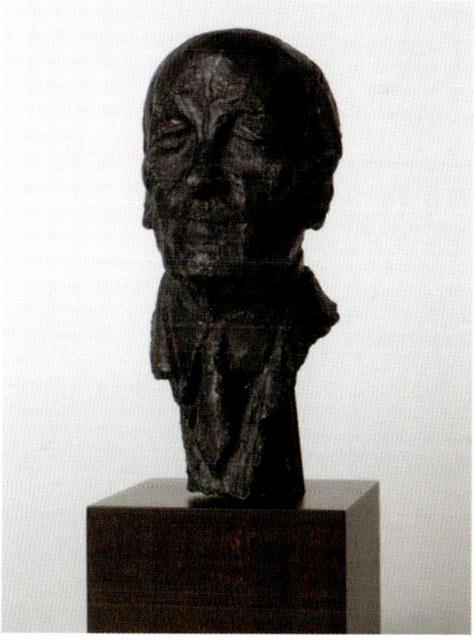

143 *Clement Attlee, First Earl Attlee of Limehouse, KG, OM, CH*

1977–79
Bronze
2.74 m high
Location: Members' Lobby of the House of Commons, Palace of Westminster, London
Related work: 143a: *Portrait Study of Clement, Earl Attlee*, 1977–78, plaster, 17.2 x 7.9 x 10.2 cm, Government Art Collection, London
143b: *Sketch Maquette of Clement, Earl Attlee*, 1977–78, plaster, 92.7 x 31.8 x 26 cm, private collection

Comments: Clement Richard Attlee (1883–1967) was born in Putney, south-west London. His father was a solicitor. He was educated at Haileybury Public School and at University College, Oxford, where he read history. However, after leaving Oxford he studied law, and in 1906 qualified as a barrister. After two years, appalled by the deprivation he witnessed daily as the manager of a charitable club for working-class boys in Stepney in the East End of London, he joined the Independent Labour Party. At the outbreak of the First World War he promptly volunteered for the South Lancashire Regiment. Rising to the rank of captain, he commanded a company of the South Lancashires at Suvla Bay, Gallipoli, before he was evacuated with severe dysentery. On recovering, he served with the South Lancashires in Mesopotamia in 1916, and was seriously wounded in action – a wound that would cause him discomfort for the rest of his life. He returned to active duty early in 1918, having been promoted to the rank of major, and fought in the closing offensive of the British army on the Western Front – where he was wounded again. After demobilisation he ran for office for the first time as 'Major Attlee', and in 1919 was elected the first Labour mayor of Stepney. Three years later he was elected as Labour MP for Limehouse – a seat he would hold until 1950, when it was renamed Walthamstow West (which he held for Labour for another five years, after which he left the House of Commons and was raised to the peerage) (Kenneth Harris, *Attlee* [London: Weidenfeld & Nicolson, 1995]).

His rise within the Labour Party thereafter was steady, if not particularly spectacular. After the party split over the creation of a national (coalition) government in 1931, Attlee remained with the majority faction, which opposed the new government. In the ensuing election Attlee retained his seat while many of his colleagues lost theirs. In 1933 he was appointed deputy leader of the party, and two years later, to the surprise of many, he emerged as the leader. He would hold the post until 1955. In May 1940 he played a critical role in ensuring the fall of Neville Chamberlain as prime minister and his replacement by Winston Churchill. In gratitude, Churchill appointed him lord privy seal, and then, two years later, deputy prime minister with special responsibility for the conduct of policy on the home front. In July 1945, much to the amazement of many – including Churchill – Attlee won that month's general election in a landslide. Over the next five years he established himself as one of the most effective prime ministers Britain had ever had – his government passing legislation that made the welfare state and the National Health Service a reality, and disentangled Britain from the running of India (1947) and Palestine (1948). Indeed, in 2004, a poll of nearly 200 British historians voted him Britain's greatest prime minister of the twentieth century – even ahead of Churchill (Nicklaus Thomas-Symonds, *Attlee: A Life in Politics* [London: I.B.Tauris, 2010], p. 4). Modest and quiet by nature, Attlee was much tougher and shrewder than appearances suggested – indeed, he would deftly see off attempts by Herbert Morrison in 1945, and Stafford Cripps in 1947, to force him to step aside as prime minister (Peter Hennessy, *Never Again: Britain 1945–1951* [London: Vintage, 1993], p. 336).

In many ways, however, Attlee was a traditionalist (ibid., p. 436) – he continued to regard Britain as a great power, and despite the enormous cost involved decided that Britain must have its own atomic weapons programme and make a significant contribution alongside the United States in South Korea – after that state was invaded by the Communist North in June 1950 (ibid., p. 406). Nevertheless, he made it clear he would not agree to the use of nuclear weapons by the United States in Korea when mooted in 1950.

The economy suffered, Attlee lost key colleagues such as Sir Stafford Cripps and Ernest Bevin, and the Labour Party was defeated in the general election of October 1950 – even though the party won more votes than the Conservatives (David Kynaston, *Austerity Britain 1945–51* [London: Bloomsbury, 2007], p. 316).

For the next five years Attlee struggled on as leader of the opposition, doing his best to prevent the Labour Party from lapsing into one of its favourite pastimes – bitter internecine faction-fighting. Attlee himself acknowledged he was past his best, lacking in energy and troubled by his old wounds from the First World War. In December 1955 he left the House of Commons and was made the First Earl Attlee. In 1959 Churchill's doctor, Lord Moran, reflected that posterity would judge Attlee favourably, and noted how often he had been underestimated. On the one hand, he seemed so 'mild mannered and yet ... this diffident little man ruled his party for six years [1945–51] with a ruthless hand' (Lord Moran, *Winston Churchill: The Struggle for Survival, 1940–1965* [London: Sphere, 1968], p. 792).

Even in the House of Lords, Attlee had by no means completely abandoned his zeal for reform, and in 1958 established the Homosexual Law Reform Society. He died from pneumonia in an NHS hospital in October 1967 (Harris, *Attlee*, pp. 562–3).

The years immediately after Attlee's death saw various proposals to buy a bronze bust of Attlee, by either David McFall or Anthony Grey, to be located inside the House of Commons. But the general feeling was that it would be better to wait

143

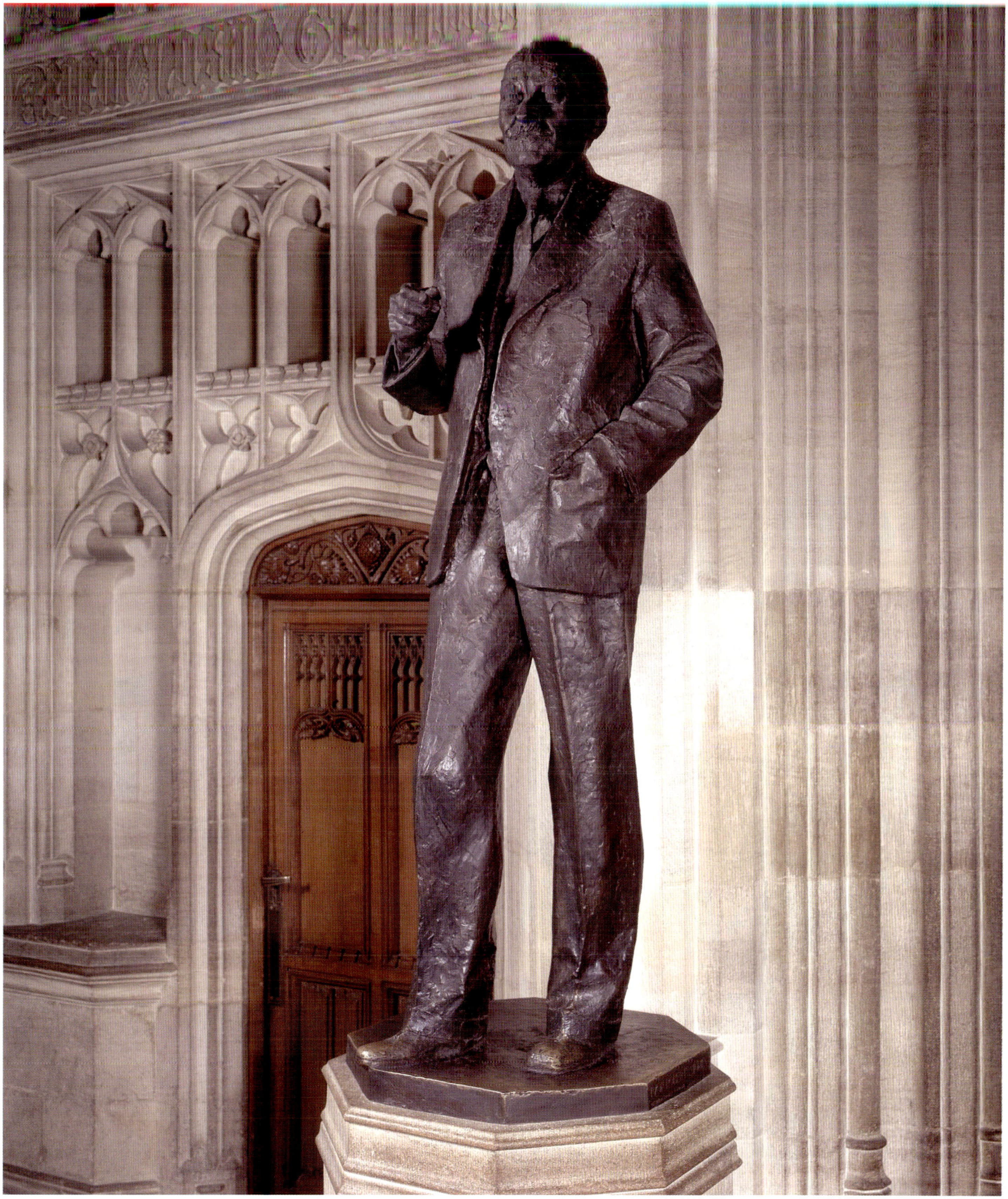

until the 'ten-year-rule' would apply – i.e. until ten years after the death of Attlee before erecting a memorial (Prime Minister Harold Wilson to Arthur Bottomley MP, 2 October 1975, Earl Attlee Statue File, PWO/2/35, Archives, House of Commons, London).

In September 1976, Labour MP Michael Foot, as lord president of the Privy Council, suggested to Prime Minister James Callaghan that, as the following year would be 'the tenth anniversary of Attlee's death [it] would, I think, present a suitable opportunity for the erection of a memorial to him in the Palace of Westminster' (Michael Foot to James Callaghan, 22 September 1976, ibid.). Three months later, Callaghan proposed in the House of Commons that 'an humble address be presented to the Queen'. This was swiftly passed by an overwhelming majority in the House, and in January 1977 it voted to set aside a provisional £18,000 for the Department of the Environment to pay for the future Attlee statue (Earl Attlee Statue File, 20 December 1976, ibid.).

Early in March 1977 an 'Earl Attlee Memorial Committee' was established, chaired by the chairman of the House of Commons Art Committee, Labour MP George Strauss – who had been a great admirer of Ivor's *Churchill* for Parliament Square – and including Attlee's son, the Second Earl, Ivor's old friend the Labour politician Cledwyn Hughes (MP for Anglesey, who sat to Ivor for a portrait in 1978 and would do so again twelve years later) and Sir John Rodgers, another enthusiast for Ivor's work since his membership of the Parliament Square *Churchill* statue committee five years before (Meeting of the Earl Attlee Memorial Committee, 9 March 1977, ibid.). A month later, a small 'selection sub-committee' within the larger memorial committee considered a shortlist of sculptors submitted to it by Sir Hugh Casson (1910–1999), the president of the Royal Academy (1976–84), and Michael Rizzello, the president of the Royal Society of British Sculptors (Meeting of the Earl Attlee Statue Selection Sub-Committee, 5 April 1977, ibid.).

After some six weeks of deliberation this subcommittee decided to invite five sculptors from the list of eight submitted by Casson and Rizzello to participate in a competition for the Attlee statue, which it had been decided would stand in the Members' Lobby of the House of Commons. The five were Ivor, Franta Belsky, James Butler, Robert Thomas and John Wragg, and they were given until the end of October to submit a maquette and drawings. The sub-committee recommended that the whole project cost £23,000, and this was approved by parliament shortly thereafter (Meeting of the Earl Attlee Statue Sub-Committee, 17 May 1977, ibid.).

Towards the end of November 1977, the five maquettes were examined by the full statue committee. The members were most impressed by those submitted by Ivor and Robert Thomas, but felt that both designs needed a lot more work. The sculptors were asked to submit re-worked maquettes by the end of January 1978 (Miss Alda Milner-Barry to Andrew Wicks, 21 November 1977, ibid.). A month later the full committee met again to consider the two rival maquettes, and unanimously selected the one submitted by Ivor. The statue would be a 'full-length work' and stand on 'the vacant plinth at present standing to the East of the arch leading to the Commons Corridor, opposite the statue of Lloyd George' (Meeting of the Earl Attlee Statue Committee, 22 February 1978, ibid.).

In April 1978 Ivor was formally invited to make a figure of Attlee based upon the maquette he had submitted in January, but with one alteration: he was to make the head significantly larger and the legs a little shorter. The sculptor promptly accepted the commission (IRJ to Mrs B. A. Mason, Department of the Environment, 23 April 1978, ibid.). Just over a year later, towards the end of June 1979, Ivor's full-sized plaster cast of his Attlee figure had been seen and approved by the full statue committee – casting by the Meridian Foundry would take place during July (Note by Alda Milner-Barry, Secretary of the Earl Attlee Memorial Committee, 26 June 1979, ibid.).

The bronze was formally unveiled at noon on 12 November 1979 by Lord Emmanuel Shinwell – then aged 95, and the oldest member in the House of Lords. Also present in the audience were Speaker George Thomas – who within eighteen months would be sitting to Ivor for a portrait head – and former prime minister James Callaghan, who would sit to Ivor for a portrait bust in 1987. Also in the audience was the new prime minister, Margaret Thatcher, elected in May 1979; twenty years later she would unveil a cast of Ivor's Parliament Square *Churchill* statue in the third district of Prague (clipping from the *Guardian*, 13 November 1979, ibid.).

144 *The Two Kings/Janus Rider*

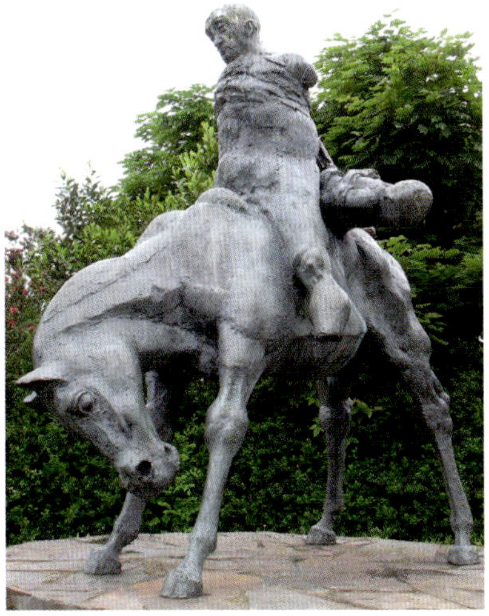

1978–83
Bronze
244 x 122 x 244 cm
Location: outside Harlech Castle, Gwynedd, North Wales
Related work: 144a: *Small Sketch for Harlech Group*, 1979–80, plaster, 61 x 71 x 25.7 cm, private collection, exhibited at Royal National Eisteddfod of Wales, Llangefni, Anglesey, July–August 1983 (18)

Comments: In early September 1978, Ivor noted in his diary: 'Oriel exhibition is now over. Result: one direct purchase; but also the very likely possibility of a largeish commission from the Arts Council and the Society for the Preservation of Ancient Monuments' (entry for 2 September 1978, IRJ Diary for 1978, IRJ Papers, Archives, HMI, Leeds). It would appear that the Welsh Arts Council first considered 'commissioning an artist ... for a design adjacent to Harlech Castle' in the autumn of 1976 (Isabel Hitchman to Dr Peter Cannon-Brookes, 17 June 1983, IRJ File, Archives, NMW, Cardiff). A year later the sum of £8,000 was allocated for 'a major sculpture ... near Harlech Castle', and since 'mention is made of the castle in the *Mabinogion* story of Branwen, daughter of Llyr, the Historic Buildings Commission [the precursor organisation to the Welsh Arts Council] would like to see the site used to reflect the legend' (ibid., Harlech Castle has a long and incident-packed place in Welsh history).

The Welsh Arts Council had supported Ivor's exhibition at the Oriel Gallery in Cardiff, and while visiting it a number of its members had admired his large plaster cast of *The Lazarus Rider*. This led, as Ivor noted in his diary, to discussion of a 'largeish commission'. Shortly before Christmas 1978, Ivor visited Harlech Castle to study various sites for the proposed work, and to 'drink in the atmosphere' (entry for 12 December 1978, IRJ Diary, IRJ Papers, HMI, Leeds).

Early in the spring of 1979 Ivor suggested a bronze 'horse and rider' group inspired by a story within the Second Branch of the *Mabinogion*, in which Bendigeidfran, the giant king of Britain, invades Ireland to rescue his sister, Branwen, and nephew, Gwern, from mistreatment at the hands of the Irish king. Bendigeidfran wins a major victory over the Irish but is badly wounded, while Gwern is killed. The sculptor wanted to focus on Bendigeidfran's return to Wales with the dead body of his nephew strapped to his horse. He was to hand over the corpse to Gwern's mother, Branwen, who would die of grief (Isabel Hitchman, Art Officer, Oriel, Welsh Arts Council, to Dr Peter Cannon-Brookes, 17 June 1983, IRJ File, Archives, NMW, Cardiff). In September that year Ivor's proposal for what he alternately referred to in correspondence as *The Two Kings* or *The Janus Rider* was placed before the Ancient Monuments Board and approved by the secretary of state for Wales, Nicholas Edwards. The work was to be commissioned by the Welsh Arts Council on behalf of Edwards and the Welsh Office (Isabel Hitchman to Dr Peter Cannon-Brookes, 17 June 1983, ibid.).

By late January 1980 Ivor was writing to his old friend Kyffin Williams that he was now hard at work on

> a fairly large model of the *Janus Rider* – about five feet long [1.5 metres] – and it's going very well. It represents Bendigeidfran returning from the wars in Ireland – bearing at his back the body of a young man representing the 'wastage' of the Wars. In silhouette it looks like a Roman 'Janus Figure' on a horse ... I think it will be weightier and more sculptural than anything I've ever done (Ivor Roberts-Jones to Kyffin Williams, 24 January 1980, Williams Papers, A1/12/3, National Library of Wales, Aberystwyth. In ancient Roman mythology *Janus Bifrons* was the god of beginnings and endings, a two-headed deity who simultaneously looked to the past and the future. The month in which Ivor was writing, January, takes its name from Janus).

Two months later, with considerable fanfare, the Welsh Arts Council announced that Ivor had been chosen for a major sculptural commission, costing £8,000, adjacent to Harlech Castle. He was extremely flattered to be described in the Council's official press release as 'Wales's most distinguished and best-known living sculptor ... The commission, moreover, will afford the sculptor his first and real opportunity to show the personal work of which he is capable' (*Western Mail*, 20 March 1980, press cuttings file, IRJ Papers, Archives, HMI, Leeds). Ivor's fee for the sculpture was to be £5,000.

As so often, however, the commission did not run as smoothly as the Arts Council predicted. At the end of 1980 Ivor noted how the 'the last quarter of the year marks the beginning of the very arduous work on Harlech for too little money and, consequently, very little assistance. It has ... been a tremendous strain on my health and even my state of mind' (entry for 24 December 1980, IRJ Diary, ibid.). It would be another two and a half years before his final design of *The Two Kings/ Janus Rider* would be approved, and Ivor could contemplate having the full-sized plaster model cast by Meridian Foundry (IRJ to Sir Richard Hyde-Parker, 17 July 1982, Sir Richard Hyde Parker Papers).

144a

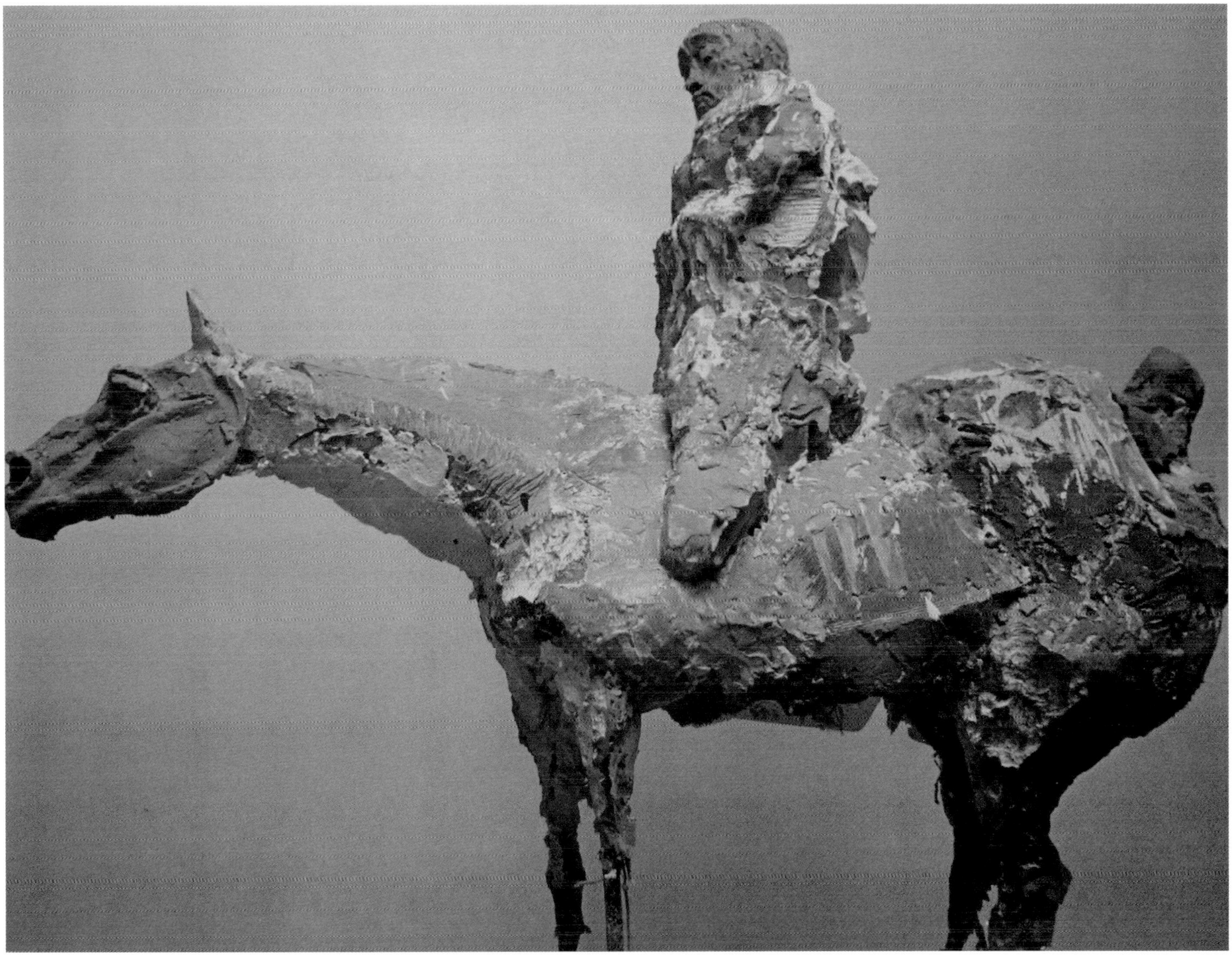

Casting of the work did not begin until December 1982, and was completed by June the following year. It was one of the most complex challenges the foundry had ever faced (Isabel Hitchman, Art Officer, Oriel Art Gallery, Welsh Arts Council, to Dr Peter Cannon-Brookes, 17 June 1983, IRJ's 1983 Exhibition File, Archives, NMW, Cardiff). The sculptor also designed a setting for the work to his usual exacting and time-consuming standards, and it was not until a year later that he felt able to write to the Keeper of Art at the National Museum of Wales, Cardiff:

> The *Harlech* Group is now on site – it was quite exciting putting it there. It is covered up and awaits all the hoo-ha of the ceremonies contingent upon such events. The design of the base has worked out very well and I am very glad that I stuck to the 'tumulus' idea ... the small 'dry' wall and the mound put all this right.

Revealingly, he added: 'strangely enough there is a closer affinity to Wales which might be thought contradictory – given all the difficulties over Harlech ... but isn't in fact' (IRJ to Dr Peter Cannon-Brookes, received 19 June 1984, ibid.).

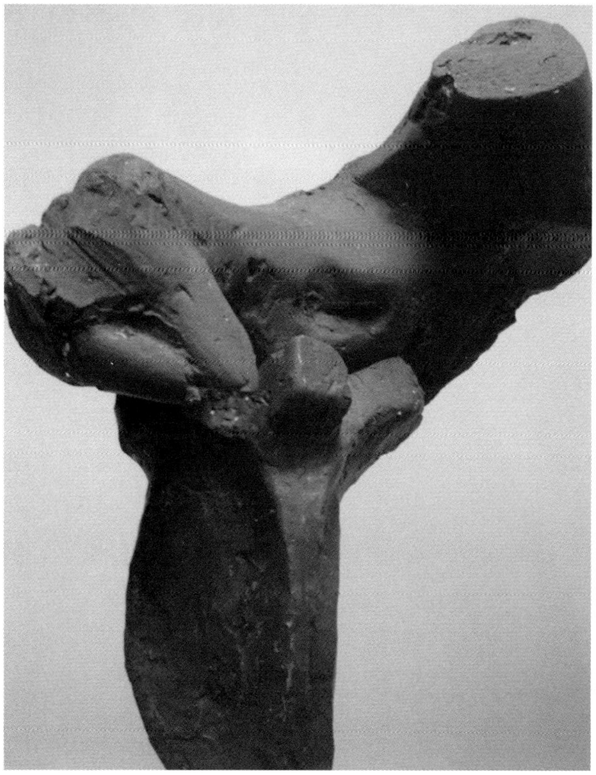

145 *Sword Form*

1982–83
Plaster
60 cm high
Collection: private collection
Exhibition history: In May 1983 the work was considered for inclusion in Ivor's solo show at the RNEW exhibition at Llangefni, but in the end was left out

Comments: The cast was reproduced in Cannon-Brookes, *Ivor Roberts-Jones* (p. 92).

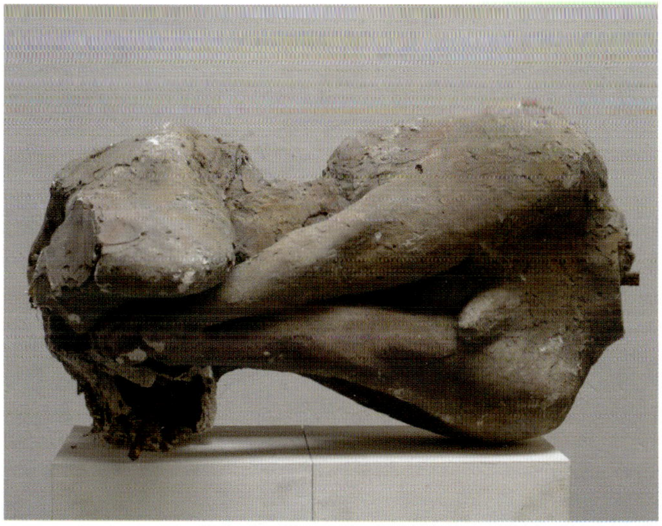

146 *Stretching Torso*

1983
Plaster
67.3 cm wide
Collection: private collection
Exhibition history: unknown

Comments: The work is reproduced in Cannon-Brookes, *Ivor Roberts-Jones* (p. 92). It is reminiscent of the dramatic body fragments Rodin produced in plaster and bronze throughout his career, such as *Iris* (1890–91), derived from preparatory sketches for his *Monument to Victor Hugo*, in which muscles are stretched and flexed to extremes.

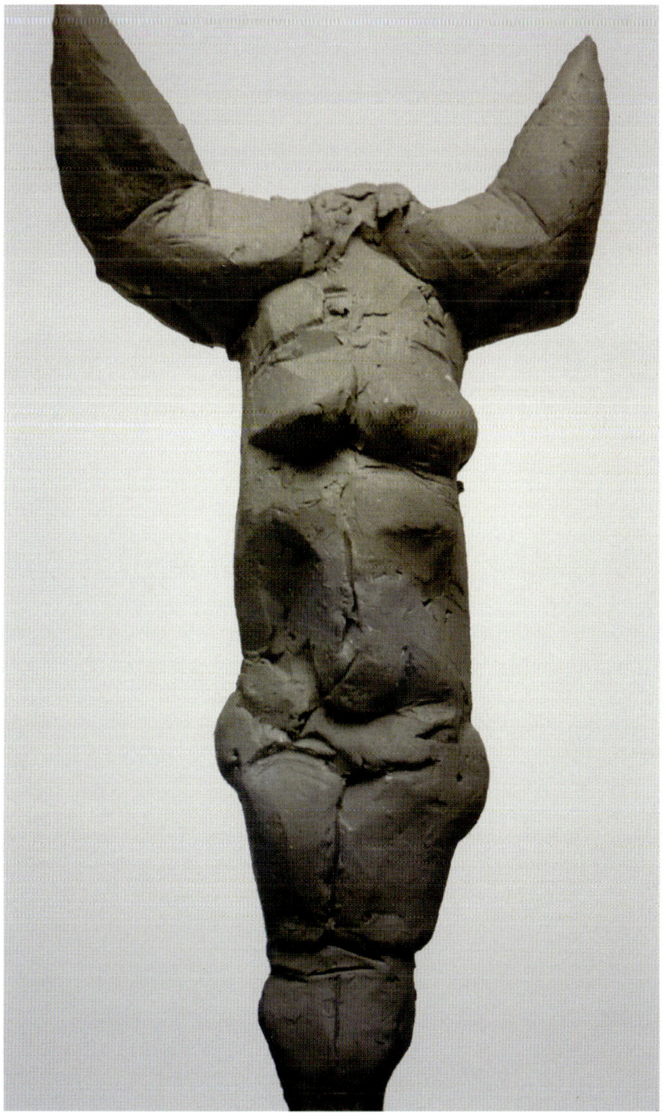

147 *Horned Torso*

1983
Plaster
65 cm high
Collection: whereabouts unknown
Exhibition history: unknown

Comments: Ivor sent a photograph of this work to the National Museum of Wales, Cardiff, in mid June 1983. It was considered but rejected for inclusion in Ivor's exhibition at the Royal National Eisteddfod of Wales, Llangefni, Anglesey, which opened at the end of July 1983 (IRJ to Dr Peter Cannon-Brookes, received 16 June 1983, IRJ File, Archives, NMW, Cardiff). The appearance of the sculpture recalls the examples of Ancient Minoan and Archaic Greek carving in the British Museum, in which Ivor had taken such a keen interest in the late 1940s and early 1950s (IRJ to Peter Jones, Director, Welsh Arts Council, received 17 June 1983, ibid.).

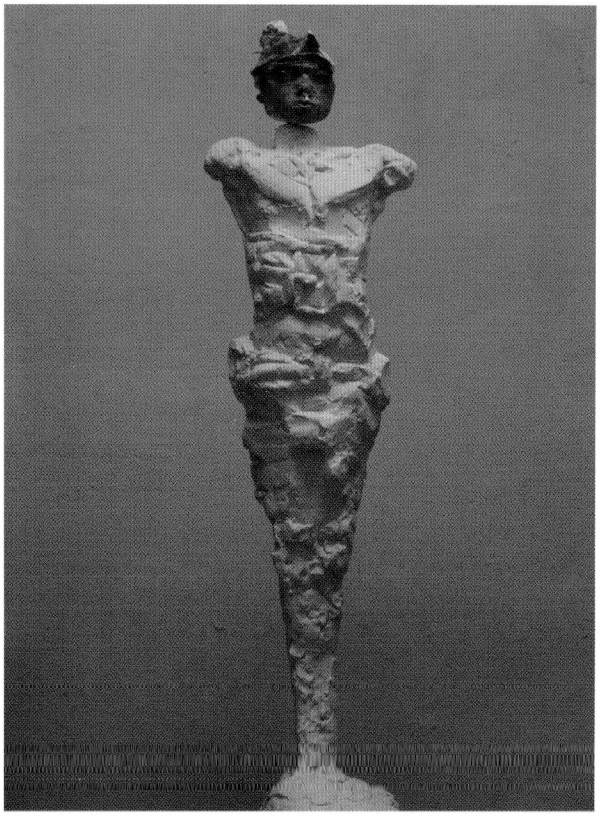

148 *Isaac Figure/Requiem for Isaac*

1984–88
Plaster
135 x 42 x 35 cm
Collection: (headless fragment), private collection
Exhibition history: unknown
Related work: 148a: *Head of Isaac*, c. 1984–88, plaster, 19 x 16.5 cm, private collection
148b: *Study for Requiem for Isaac*, c. 1985–86, pen-and-ink on paper, 20.2 x 15 cm, Henry Moore Institute, Leeds

Comments: In an interview Ivor gave early in 1994, he mentioned that he had been working on a figure of the Old Testament character Isaac as part of a group he referred to as a 'Requiem for Isaac', for 'nearly a decade'. He hoped one day to have the work cast in bronze and installed in 'Snape marshes as a joint tribute to Benjamin Britten and Wilfred Owen' (*Eastern Daily Press*, 4 January 1994, p. 6). The figure represented an evolution of the totemic and term-like figures which hark back to Classical Greece he had been experimenting with in the early 1980s. In a relatively finished form, the work appears in the background in photographs of the artist working in his studio on the full-length figure of *Rupert Brooke* (q.v.), taken in 1987.

148b

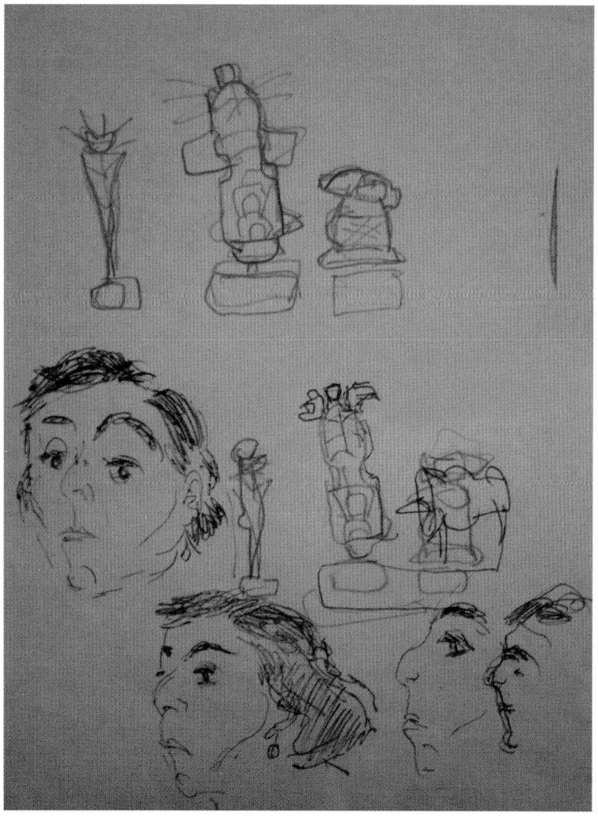

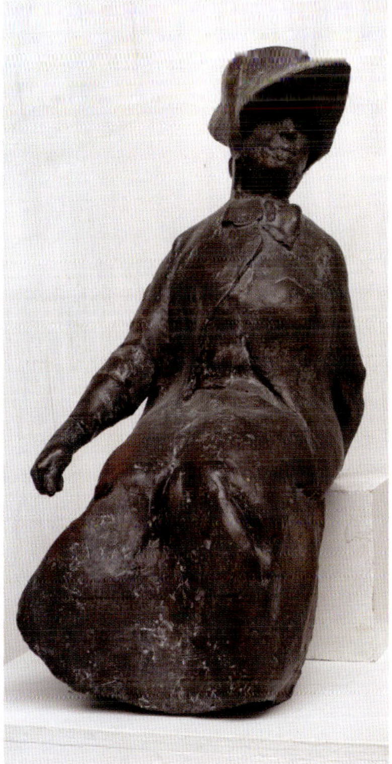

149 *Statuette of Dame Freya Stark DBE, CBE*

1984–85
Bronze
62.2 x 29.5 x 38.1 cm
Collection: private collection; Oswestry School, Shropshire
Exhibition history: Bronze (edition of five), Royal Academy, May 1987, (1108)

Comments: Dame Freya (1893–1993) was an intrepid and celebrated explorer and travel writer. She grew up in Devon and in northern Italy in an upper-middle-class family that was often short of money. During the First World War she served with an ambulance unit in Italy and witnessed the rout of the Italian army after Caporetto. After studying at SOAS, London University, she made her first trip to the Middle East – to Lebanon and Syria – in 1927. Two years later she travelled alone from Beirut to Baghdad, followed by three journeys to the wild and remote region south of the Caspian Sea. In June 1933 she was awarded the prestigious Black Memorial Prize by the Royal Geographical Society, London, for her first travel book, *The Valley of the Assassins*, which focused on Syria and Lebanon. She taught herself to become a competent surveyor and an accomplished photographer.

Three years later, in May 1936, she published her account of a trip she made to the deserts of Yemen in 1934–35 – *The Southern Gates of Arabia*. This was instantly hailed a classic, became a bestseller, and earned Stark the Mungo Park Medal for Exploration from the Royal Scottish Geographical Society in December 1936. Two years later she published her account of exploring southern Arabia: *Seen in the Hadhramout*. During the Second World War she promoted British interests in Egypt, Aden and Iraq (she was caught in the April 1941 Baghdad embassy siege by Rashid Ali's pro-German insurgents). After Italy's surrender in September 1943 she returned to live in Italy, working for the British embassy in Rome (*The Times*, 11 May 1993, p. 17).

Over the next 30 years she published a series of well-received autobiographies, plus studies of ancient Anatolia, Iraq (*Riding to the Tigris*, 1959) and of Alexander the Great (*Alexander's Path*, 1958). She was made a CBE in 1953; in 1951 the Royal Central Asian Society awarded her the Sir Percy Sykes Memorial Medal; and in 1972 she was made a Dame of the British Empire. She built a huge house for herself on a hillside in Asolo in 1962. In 1947 she married British diplomat Stewart Perowne, a homosexual; they separated amicably five years later.

According to her *Times* obituary, she was 'an attractive personality in print ... her style characterised by strong sensitivity to places, people and humour and with a clear narrative'. Moreover, she had 'great curiosity and no narrow prejudices; she liked people, treating them as equals without condescension or diffidence'. She was 'unconventional while cherishing the traditional British virtues of courtesy, restraint and self-reliance ... She was, in fact, like her father a High Tory anarchist as well as an artist.' She possessed 'a will of iron, infinite patience and powers of persuasion [and] a sublime egoism that ... overcame all obstacles ... She believed most men and women were capable of distinction and they responded accordingly. Only the deliberately second rate angered her. She regarded the world as an arena thrown open for individual achievement and she herself achieved much' (*The Times*, 11 May 1993, p. 17).

In mid-September 1984 Ivor mentioned, in a letter to Dr Peter Cannon-Brookes, that he would shortly be 'off to Asolo to do some studies from Freya Stark; this is with the NPG [National Portrait Gallery, London] in view ... for a little figure in their collection' (IRJ to Dr Peter Cannon-Brookes, 11 September 1984, IRJ File, Archives, NMW, Cardiff). Early in November he was back in Suffolk, and wrote to the registrar of the National Museum of Wales: 'I'm just back from Italy and Freya Stark. A marvellous but disquieting experience and I promptly went down with a virus on my return to the cold days of Suffolk! I'm working on a small figure [of Stark] which goes quite well so far' (IRJ to Dr Richard Edgecumbe, 3 November 1984, ibid.). The resulting statuette was exhibited at the Royal Academy three years later, but did not attract the attention of the National Portrait Gallery. Interviewed about portraiture in 1993, Ivor remarked to Byron Rogers: 'Among my sitters, my favourite was Freya Stark. In her fifties she was a round, dumpy little thing and didn't blossom out until her late sixties when the outrageous hat came and she was wonderful' (IRJ interview with Byron Rogers, *Sunday Telegraph*, 27 June 1993, p. 5).

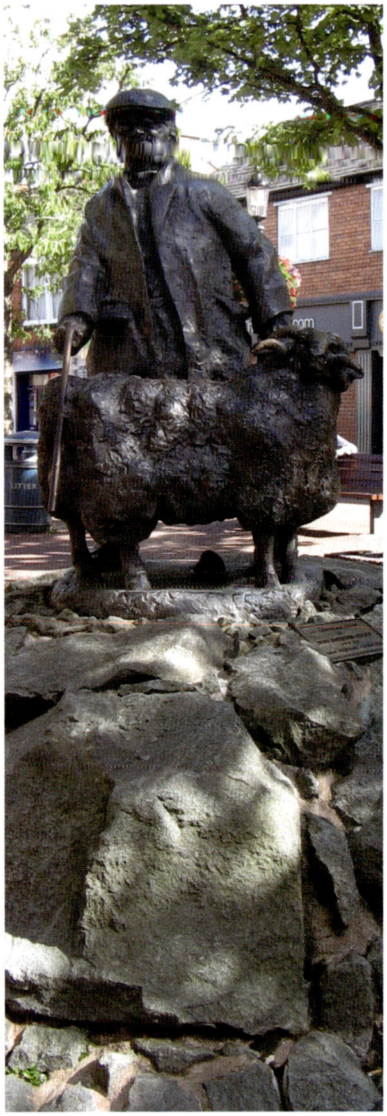

150 *Borderland Farmer/Shepherd with Ram*

1986–1992
Bronze
1.67 metres high
Located: Festival Square, Oswestry, Shropshire
Related work: 150a: *Study for The Head of the Borderland Farmer*, c. 1988–90, unfired clay, 12.1 x 9.6 x 11.4 cm, private collection, exhibited at Wolsey Art Gallery, Ipswich, December 1999–January 2000

Comments: Early in 1986 Ivor was approached by the chairman of Oswestry District and Civil Society (ODCS) to produce a sculpture for his home town, ideally to stand on or near the site of the old cattle market – renamed Festival Square. The sculptor offered to make a life-sized bronze figure of one of the local farming characters he recalled from his childhood. He agreed to charge only £14,000 in total – with his own fee at £5,000 – for a piece that should have cost in the region of £50,000 to £60,000 (*Oswestry Advertiser*, 23 September 1992, p. 3). After a delay of over two years, early in 1988 Oswestry Borough Council (OBC) formally commissioned him to produce a life-sized bronze statue for Festival Square. By 1989 the figure of a farmer with a sheep had emerged from discussions between the sculptor and representatives of the ODCS and OBC, as it was thought that such a figure would 'emphasise the town's connections with farming and the market' (*Oswestry Advertiser*, 16 December 1992, p. 2). Early in the summer of 1990 Ivor decided to replace the sheep with a ram (IRJ to Jack Crofton, 19 June 1990, Megan Thomas Archive). As he later explained to the ODCS, the ram would be more alert, 'with its head twisted away from the figure of the farmer – as though keeping an eye on his harem' (IRJ to Bernard Mitchell, ODCS, c. September 1990, IRJ Papers, Archives, HMI, Leeds).

His desire to replace the sheep with a ram can be linked with his ongoing interest in the Old Testament story of Abraham and Isaac (Genesis 22: 1–18), in which God tests Abraham's loyalty by demanding he sacrifice his first-born son, Isaac. At the last minute the Almighty has Abraham stay his hand and instead sacrifice a ram that is conveniently trapped in a nearby thicket.

Early in 1991, OBC approved the design of the statue in clay to be cast in plaster, and then bronze. But no decision had been reached as to the design of the base. Meanwhile, disquiet was expressed in the local press as the cost of the project began to rise – it now stood at an estimated £20,000 – though the sculptor's fee remained at £5,000, as agreed in 1986. Finally, in July 1992, OBC decided it had raised enough, and that *Borderland Farmer* could be cast in bronze, while Ivor, and the local architects, had agreed on a design for the base of the work. Two months later, the two figures were cast by the Meridian Foundry, and unveiled by the mayor of Oswestry on 2 December 1992. The public reaction to the statue was mixed: the appearance of the farmer was interpreted by some as a racial slur against the Welsh, while the design of the base and the overall cost of the work – at a time of widespread cuts in municipal spending – were also criticised (*Oswestry Advertiser*, 9 December 1992, p. 16).

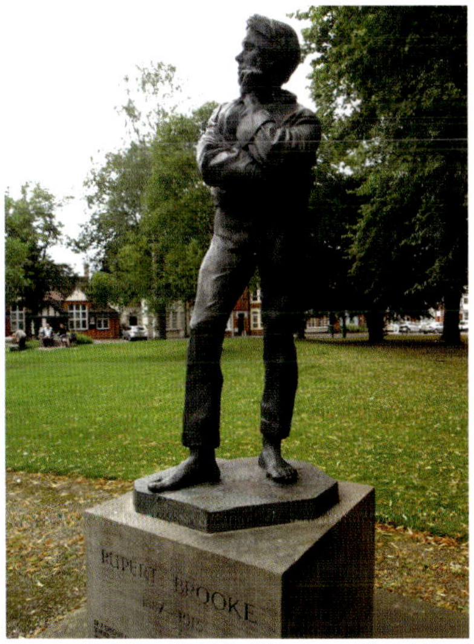

151 *Rupert Brooke*

1986–88
Bronze
1.67 m high
Located: Jubilee Gardens, Regents Place, Rugby
Inscription on base: 'If I should die, think only this of me, that there is some corner of a foreign field that is forever England.'

Comments: Rupert Chawner Brooke (1887–1915) was born in Rugby, Warwickshire, and educated at Rugby School (founded 1567) and at King's College, Cambridge. His first book of poetry was published in 1911, and he contributed to *Georgian Poetry 1911–1912*, which he co-edited with Winston Churchill's personal secretary, Sir Edward Marsh. This was published to great acclaim in 1912. Brooke promptly joined the army at the outbreak of the First World War, and served with the Royal Naval Division at Antwerp in October 1914. He died from septicaemia on the afternoon of 23 April 1915, on a hospital ship lying off the island of Lemnos in the eastern Aegean. He was buried on the nearby Aegean island of Skyros. Winston Churchill's fulsome obituary, published in *The Times* on 26 April 1915, played a key role in establishing Brooke's colossal posthumous fame. The inscription on the statue plinth is derived from Brooke's poem *The Soldier*, written around December 1914–January 1915, which was first published in 1915 in a collection entitled *1914 and Other Poems* (Nigel Jones, *Rupert Brooke: Life, Death and Myth* [London: BBC Books, 2003], pp. 401–2).

The origins of the statue went back to the spring of 1985, when a committee chaired by local councillor Dr Peter Miller met to discuss erecting a memorial to Brooke in Rugby in time for the hundredth anniversary of the poet's birth, in August 1987 (*Rugby Advertiser*, 8 September 1988, p. 17). Initially, the Brooke Centenary Committee approached a local sculptor, John Bridgeman, to devise a figure of Brooke. However, it was not impressed by his suggestions and so, early in the spring of 1986, Dr Miller contacted Ivor, as he was impressed by the figures of *Augustus John*, *Churchill* in Parliament Square and *Clement Attlee* that he had made previously (*The Times*, 15 May 1986, p. 4).

150a

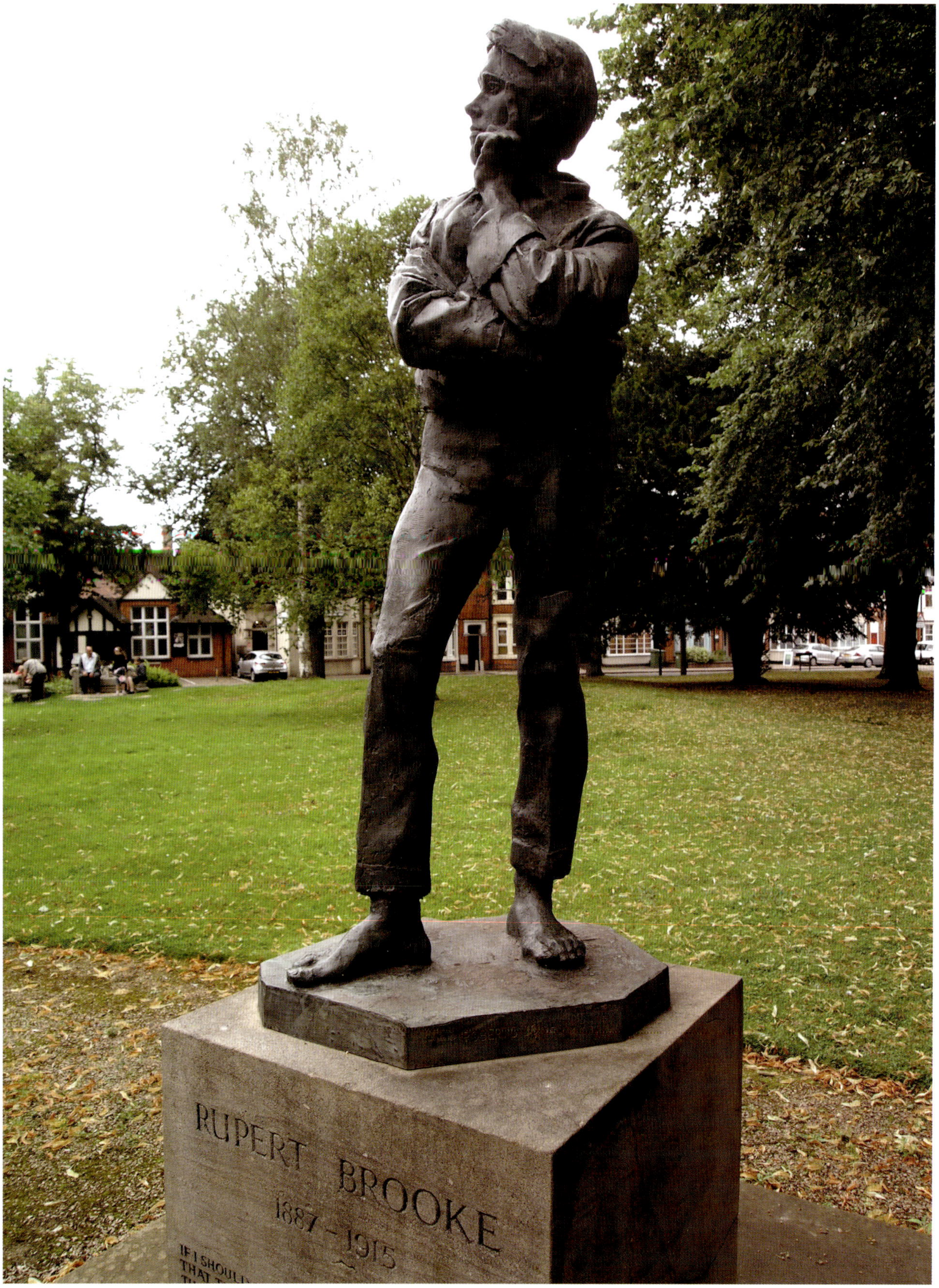

Ivor quickly produced a sketch model of a contemplative and barefoot Brooke, inspired by photographs taken of him in his Bohemian 'neo-pagan' phase of around 1909–12 (*Rugby Advertiser*, 11 August 1988, p. 3). Early in January 1987 the Brooke Centenary Committee launched an appeal to raise the £12,000 needed to pay for the statue, after Rugby Council had voted to donate £3,000 to the project. One year later, however, only a small percentage of the money required had been raised, and the centenary of Brooke's birth had come and gone (*Rugby Advertiser*, 28 January 1988, p. 1). A month later there was uproar when Rugby Council voted to give a further £4,000 (thus increasing its overall contribution to £7,000) to restart the stalled statue project. Dr Miller defended the donation, insisting:

> Ivor Roberts-Jones ... is world famous ... He is foremost among portrait sculptors and we are very fortunate to have his work at an entirely concessionary price ... The sculptor could have easily charged double the £7,000 he had asked for ... Incidentally, he has told me that most public-subscription statues are under-subscribed and cites [an] example, among his own works that have encountered financial difficulties – that of the bronze of Augustus John (*Rugby Advertiser*, 4 February 1988, p. 12).

The local newspaper printed a number of letters that were hostile to the very idea of a statue to Brooke, one critic predicting: 'this statue will be the biggest pink elephant Rugby Council has ever been involved with' (*Rugby Advertiser*, 4 February 1988, p. 12).

The full-sized plaster cast of Brooke was sent to the Meridian Foundry early in June 1988. Two months later the sculptor was on hand personally to supervise the installation of the bronze in a site he had selected in the recently landscaped Jubilee Gardens. Apparently, Ivor was anxious to ensure that the statue would be 'orientated correctly so that it will be adequately lit by the transverse of the sun' (*Rugby Advertiser*, 11 August 1988, p. 3).

On 3 September 1988 the statue was unveiled by Dr Mary (later Dame Mary) Archer, who lived in the Grantchester vicarage immortalised in one of Brooke's poems and had a son studying at Rugby School (*Rugby Advertiser*, 12 May 1988, p. 7). The artist, who was present among a crowd of some 500 at the ceremony, told a local journalist that he had initially thought the statue 'might be a little short but now [Brooke] is standing there in all his glory, I am quite happy ... you cannot really tell until you have seen it in all kinds of light and weather' (Sue Lary, *Rugby Advertiser*, 8 September 1988, p. 17).

152a

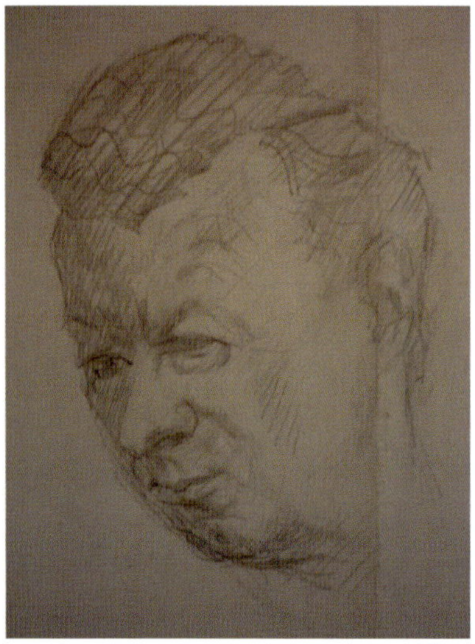

152 *Benjamin Britten*

1987–90s
Plaster
84 x 36 x 43 cm
Collection: the figure was found in Ivor's studio in such poor condition that the body had almost entirely crumbled away. The head survives in a private collection.
Related work: 152a: *Study of the Head of Benjamin Britten*, c. 1987–88, pencil on paper, 13 x 9 cm, Henry Moore Institute, Leeds

Comments: Britten (1913–1976) was born in Lowestoft, Suffolk, the son of a dentist. He was educated at Gresham's School and the Royal College of Music, from which he graduated in 1934. The following year he composed the accompanying music to *Night Mail*, made by the GPO Film Unit – the head of which was John Grierson, who was the subject of a posthumous portrait head Ivor created in 1972. Ivor appears to have loved Britten's music from the late 1940s onwards, such as his operatic successes *Peter Grimes* (1945), *Albert Herring* (1947) and *Billy Budd* (1951). But he did not agree with Britten's decision, on returning to the UK in April 1942 after three years in the United States, to become a conscientious objector and stay out of uniform. After the premiere of his opera, *The Turn of the Screw* (1954), Britten branched out into ballet, with *The Prince of the Pagodas* (1957), and then into a series of quasi-operatic 'parables', incuding *Curlew River* (1964) and *The Prodigal Son* (1968). The latter was dedicated to his close friend, and a composer Ivor much admired, Dmitri Shostakovich. In 1961–62 Britten composed his celebrated pacifist *War Requiem*, drawing extensively on the war poetry of Wilfred Owen, for the dedication, in May 1962, of the new Coventry Cathedral.

In 1948 Britten, his partner the tenor Peter Pears (1910–1986), and the writer Eric Crozier established the Aldeburgh International Music Festival. Twenty years later, Britten created a permanent base for the Festival with a new concert hall at Snape Maltings, five miles from Aldeburgh – and a short drive from Ivor's home near Halesworth where he was living in the early 1970s. Britten's last opera, *Death in Venice*, was performed in 1973, at a time when he was suffering from increasingly poor health. Three years later he was awarded a life peerage, becoming Baron Britten of Aldeburgh. He died in December 1976 (Humphrey Burton, *Benjamin Britten: A Biography* [London: Faber & Faber, 1992]).

There are only a few references to this work in Ivor's papers. In April 1987, writing to the Keeper of Art at the National Museum of Wales, Cardiff, he mentioned that he was 'hoping to start shortly on a figure of *Benjamin Britten* for Aldborough [*sic*]' (IRJ to Dr Mark Evans, 22 April 1987, IRJ File, Archives, NMW, Cardiff). Early the following year, he hinted in an aside to the *Rugby Advertiser* that plans for his statue of Britten had been indefinitely postponed owing to a general failure to raise funds from either the general public or the Arts Council (*Rugby Advertiser*, 4 February 1988, p. 12).

Five years later, during a visit to Ivor's studio in Shimpling in June 1993, journalist Byron Rogers noticed in one dusty corner

> a small and exquisite figure of Benjamin Britten, just three feet high, intended as a memorial to the composer at Snape but marooned here by some obscure dispute, the clay cracking now ... The sculptor had wanted this seated on a low

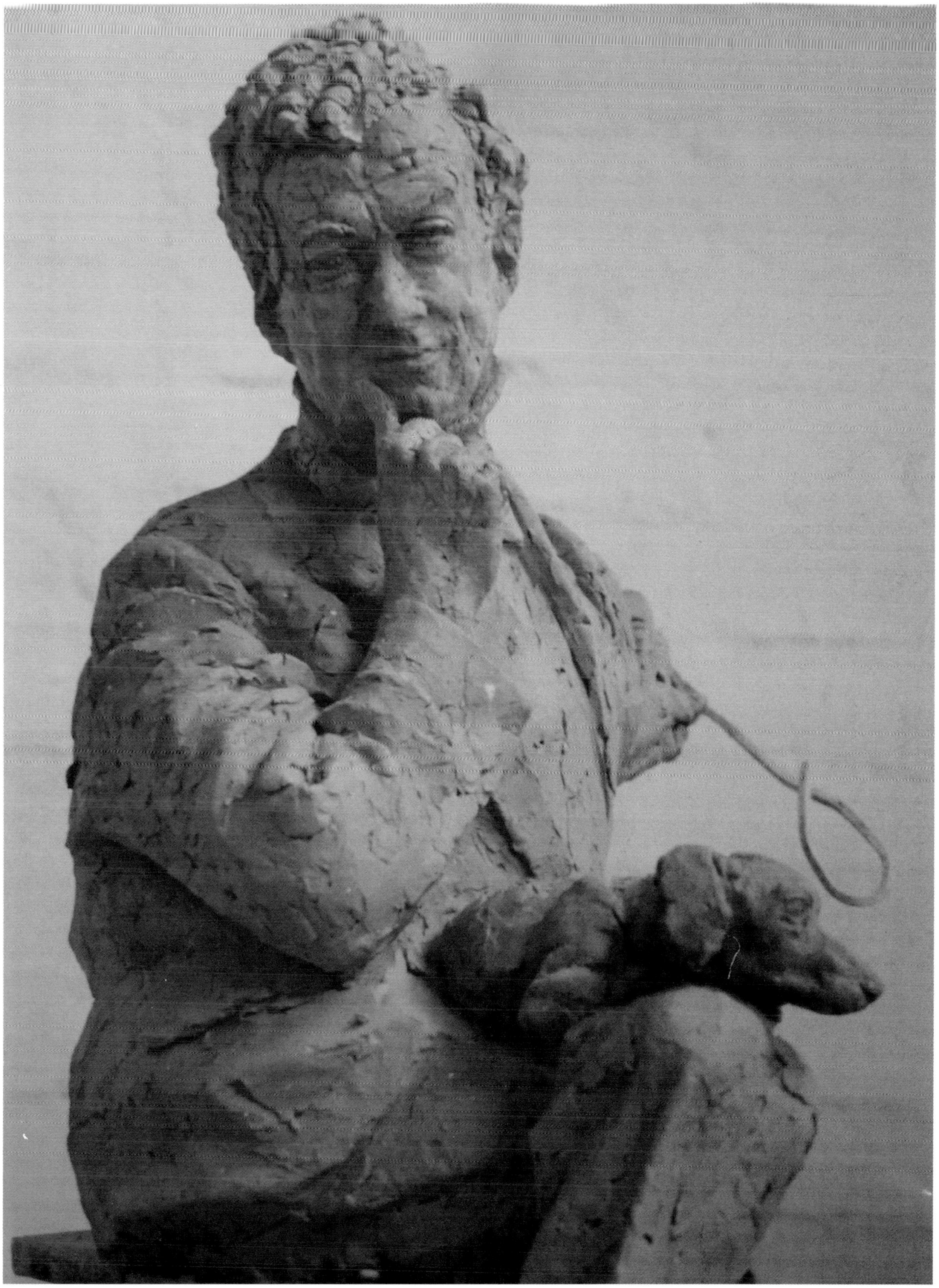

> wall overlooking the marshes that Britten loved, with the figure of Peter Pears striding towards him, the intention being to convey the nature of each man. This could have been the most imaginative tableau of the late twentieth century, yet it is probable that all will come of it is the crumbling little figure, a great lost statue of our time (Bryon Rogers, 'Ivor Roberts-Jones', *Sunday Telegraph*, 27 June 1993, p. 5).

One can only speculate about what Ivor would have thought of Maggi Hambling's sculpture dedicated to Britten, composed of two 3.6-metre-high interlocking steel scallop shells, which was unveiled on Aldeburgh beach in 2003. It is unlikely that his verdict would have been positive.

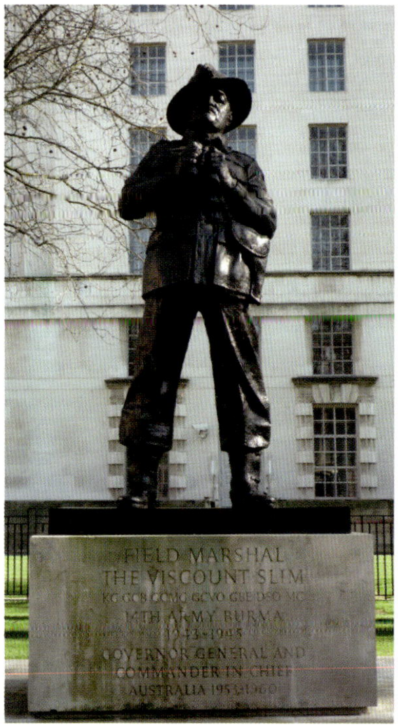

153 *Field Marshal Viscount Slim of Burma, KG, GCMG, DSO, MC*

1988–1990
Bronze
2.75 m high
Location: Whitehall, London
Related work: 153a: *Sketch Model of Field Marshal Viscount Slim*, 1987, plaster, 69.6 x 26.4 x 21.6 cm, Leeds Museums and Art Galleries, exhibited at Wolsey Art Gallery, Ipswich, December 1999–January 2000

Comments: William Joseph 'Uncle Bill' Slim (1891–1970) was born in Birmingham into a lower-middle-class family. After studying at King Edward's Grammar School he worked as a primary school teacher and a clerk in an iron foundry. At the outbreak of the First World War he volunteered for the Royal Warwickshire Regiment. At Gallipoli in 1915 he was seriously wounded as a second lieutenant serving with the Royal Warwicks. In October 1916, after obtaining a regular commission from the West Indian Regiment, he returned to the front in Mesopotamia, where he was again seriously wounded in 1917. For his bravery on that occasion he was awarded the Military Cross in February 1918. In May 1919 he transferred as a captain to the 6th Gurkha Rifles in the Indian Army. At the outbreak of the Second World War he was made a brigadier and commanded the 10th Indian Brigade in the East African Campaign of 1940–41. Later in 1941 he was promoted to the rank of major-general and placed in command of the 10th Indian Division, and distinguished himself during the brief Syria–Lebanon Campaign.

In January 1942 the Japanese invaded Burma, and Rangoon, the capital, fell to them in March. In that month Slim, promoted to lieutenant-general, was given command of the 1st Burma Corps, which attempted to hold the centre of the country. However, by May 1942 it had retreated into India after having been thoroughly mauled by the Japanese. Slim survived this debacle to be given command of the 15th Army Corps within the Eastern army of Lieutenant-General Noel Irwin, with whom he did not get on at all. Slim commanded the 15th Corps during the disastrous First Arakan Campaign (December 1942–April 1943), and was very fortunate to avoid being sacked. Irwin went instead, and Slim became commander in May

153a

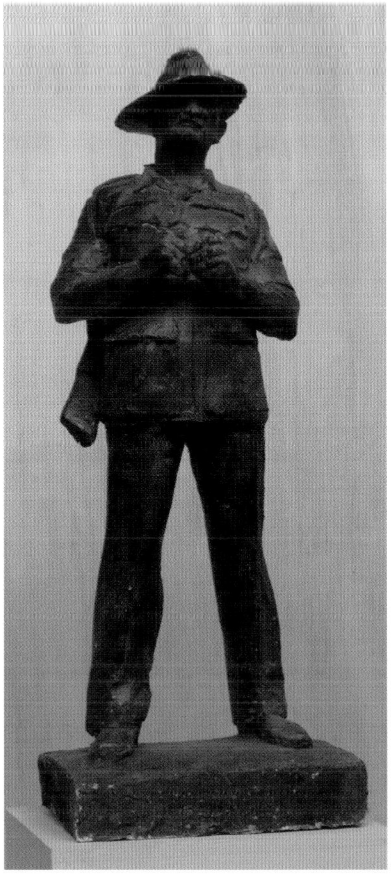

1943 of the new 14th Army, later dubbed the 'Forgotten Army', composed of the 4th, 15th, 23rd and 24th Army Corps.

His dispirited troops were thoroughly retrained and remotivated by Slim, and the new tactics they had been taught to employ proved effective against the enemy in the Second Arakan campaign of January–March 1944 – in which Ivor took part as an artillery captain. The Second Arakan campaign did not achieve its overall objectives, but the Japanese suffered much heavier casualties and British confidence was restored.

In March 1944 Japanese forces invaded Assam in northern India, advancing on the towns of Kohima and Imphal. Fourteenth Army units were surrounded near both towns, but Slim ensured they were successfully supplied from the air. By early July 1944, Slim's 15th Army had pushed the Japanese back across the border into Burma; their invasion had been decisively defeated. In February 1945 Slim masterminded the invasion of central Burma. Within six weeks the central urban centres of Meiktila and Mandalay had fallen to the 15th Army, while Rangoon had been taken by the end of April. During June and July 1945, almost an entire Japanese army was destroyed along the Sittang River as it attempted to escape Slim's encircling units.

In 1946 Slim was appointed overall commander of Allied Land Forces in South-east Asia. Two years later he became chief of the Imperial General Staff. In 1953 he was promoted to the rank of field marshal, and appointed governor-general of Australia until 1959, when he retired from the army. He published his memoirs, the well-received *Defeat Into Victory*, in 1956, and in 1960 was ennobled as the First Viscount Slim. During the last six years of his life he was a popular governor of Windsor Castle (Ronald Lewin, *Slim: The Standardbearer* [London: Wordsworth Editions, 1999], and Max Hastings, *Nemesis: The Battle for Japan, 1944–45* [London: Harper Press, 2007], pp. 590–1).

For many years after the war, the men of the 14th Army felt their trials and achievements in Burma had been overlooked, and referred to themselves as 'the forgotten army'. Slim campaigned forcefully on their behalf, and in February 1951 was a founder member, with Earl Mountbatten of Burma, of the Burma Star Association. Today Slim is widely judged to have been one of the great British commanders of the Second World War, leading an army that achieved much with fewer resources than those accorded to Field Marshal Montgomery, and that faced a truly formidable enemy (Michael Burleigh, *Moral Combat: A History Of World War II* [London: Harper Press, 2010], pp. 343–4).

The Burma Star Association began contemplating a memorial statue of Slim during the summer of 1987. It was to stand on Whitehall in front of the Ministry of Defence, a short distance from Oscar Nemon's statue of Field Marshal Montgomery, which had been unveiled in 1980. The Association also hoped the figure would be erected in time for the thirtieth anniversary of Slim's death (W. H. P Clarke to Sir David Piper, 26 January 1988, Sir David Piper Papers, Archives, HMI, Leeds). In the autumn of 1987 Ivor was contacted by W. H. P. Clarke, a fellow member of the Burma Star Association – its vice-president for the south-east of England and senior fundraiser. He had been recommended to Clarke by the Royal Academy, the Royal Society of British Sculptors and the Royal Fine Arts Commission. Clarke wanted to know whether he would be willing to participate in a 'limited competition for a memorial to Field Marshal Slim', and submit a maquette 'about 60 cm high' to a committee that was forming by the beginning of April 1988. Ivor readily replied that he would be delighted by any opportunity to honour 'Uncle Bill' Slim – who he was careful to point out had been his commander for two years in Burma (copy of undated letter, IRJ to W. H. P. Clarke, enclosed in W. H. P. Clarke to Sir David Piper, 10 February 1988, ibid.).

By early February 1988, the Association had assembled a 'panel of experts' to select the winning maquette, including Sir Hugh Casson (recent president of the Royal Academy), Sir Roger de Grey (current president of the Royal Academy), Sir David Piper (recently director of the Ashmolean Museum, Oxford, and director from 1964 to 1967 of the National Portrait Gallery, London), the architect Sir Philip Dowson (president of the Royal Academy from 1993 to 1999), Dame Elisabeth Frink (who agreed to sit, but then had to withdraw owing to illness) and Slim's son, the Second Viscount Slim (W. H. P. Clarke to Sir David Piper, ibid.).

Apart from Ivor, invitations to participate in the Slim memorial competition had been despatched to the following, also recommended to the Association by the Royal Fine Arts Commission and the Royal Society of British Sculptors: James Butler RA; Christopher Marvell; Michael Rizzello (soon to be elected president of the Royal British Society of Sculptors) and David Norris. All recipients had signalled their willingness to compete, the deadline for the submission of maquettes was extended to the middle of May 1988.

The Association's statue committee and the panel of experts duly assembled in a central London hotel in May 1988, and after a morning's discussion selected Ivor's maquette. On that day the panel of experts was augmented by the professor of sculpture at the Royal Academy, Bryan Kneale (1930–) and the art critic and painter William Packer. It would seem the Second Viscount Slim was a particular admirer of Ivor's maquette, while Piper and Casson both thought it was 'streets ahead of the rest of the field'. It was evident from Viscount Slim's conversation that morning with Casson and Piper that none was well disposed to the work of Oscar Nemon (Sir Bernard Chacksfield, Chairman of the Burma Star Association, to Sir David Piper, 24 May 1988, and Sir David's reply, 26 May 1988, ibid.).

In the following month the Burma Star Association launched an appeal in the press, seeking to raise £100,000 from the public to pay for the statue of Slim (*Independent*, 28 June 1988, p. 8). The public response was emphatic: the donations rolled in, and by the spring of 1989 almost all the money had been raised. After a period of illness Ivor was able to focus on the statue project, and by the end of the year the full-sized plaster model of the figure was awaiting transport to the Meridian Foundry. The work was unveiled by the Queen on 29 April 1990, and the reception from general public and critics alike was very favourable.

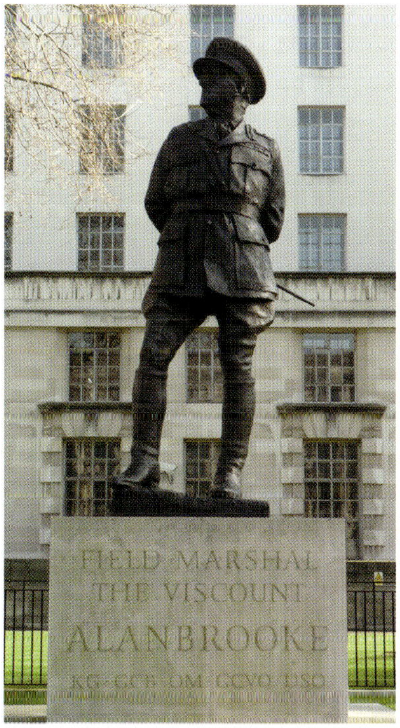

154 *Field Marshal Viscount Alanbrooke KG, GCB, OM, DSO and Bar*

1990–93
Bronze
3.05 m high
Location: Whitehall, London.
Related work: 154a: *Study for the Head of Field Marshal Viscount Alanbrooke Memorial*, 1990–91, plaster, 16.2 x 13 x 14.3 cm, private collection
154b: *Study for the Field Marshal Viscount Alanbrooke Memorial*, c. 1991, pencil and black chalk on paper, 37 x 23 cm, Henry Moore Institute, Leeds

Comments: Alan Francis 'Old Shrapnel' Brooke (1883–1963) was born in the South of France, but grew up in Ulster the youngest son of Sir Victor Brooke, Third Baron Colebrooke. Educated privately, he joined the Royal Artillery in 1902 and studied at the Royal Military Academy, Woolwich. During the First World War he rose from the rank of captain to that of colonel, and such was his talent for planning effective artillery bombardments that he was twice awarded the DSO. By 1918 he was in command of the entire artillery component of the First British Army in France (David Fraser, *Alanbrooke* [London: Hamlyn, 1983]).

At the outbreak of the Second World War he was placed in command of II Corps within the British Expeditionary Force in France and Belgium. He successfully organised the fighting retreat and evacuation of his Corps to the UK in May –June 1940. In recognition of his manifest ability, Churchill appointed him Commander-in-Chief of United Kingdom Home Forces in July 1940. In that role he impressed everyone, and especially the prime minister, with his energy, steely determination and grasp of detail. Consequently, in December 1941, Churchill had him appointed Chief of the Imperial General Staff (CIGS) – a post he held through many gruelling and exhausting years, until early 1946. Brooke was Churchill's senior and most respected military adviser during the war. His primary gift as CIGS lay in his ability to curb Churchill's often militarily unsustainable enthusiasms and penchant for devising poorly planned operations. During his time as CIGS, Brooke would often return from Downing Street bemoaning Churchill's latest brain wave, muttering: 'Impossible, quite impossible ... That man! That man! ... Then a tired but infectious smile would touch his austere features and he would quietly say: 'But what would we do without him?' (ibid., p. 211).

Early in 1944 Brooke was bitterly disappointed to be passed over as commander of Operation Overlord in favour of Eisenhower, but was mollified by his promo tion to the rank of field marshal. He retired from the army as Viscount Alanbrooke early in 1946, though he held the honorary post of master gunner, St James's Park – the ceremonial head of the Royal Regiment of Artillery – from 1946 to 1956. Brooke was a complex man – far more highly strung than his habitually icily impassive demeanour would ever have suggested. Well read, cultured, a lover of a wide range of poetry, he had been a passionate bird-watcher since before the First World War, and in retirement became president of the London Zoological Society (1950–54) and was a long-standing vice-president of the Royal Society for the Protection of Birds (ibid., p. 127).

Brooke's heavily censored wartime diaries, edited by Sir Arthur Bryant, were published between 1957 and 1959, and still caused a storm with their often sharp

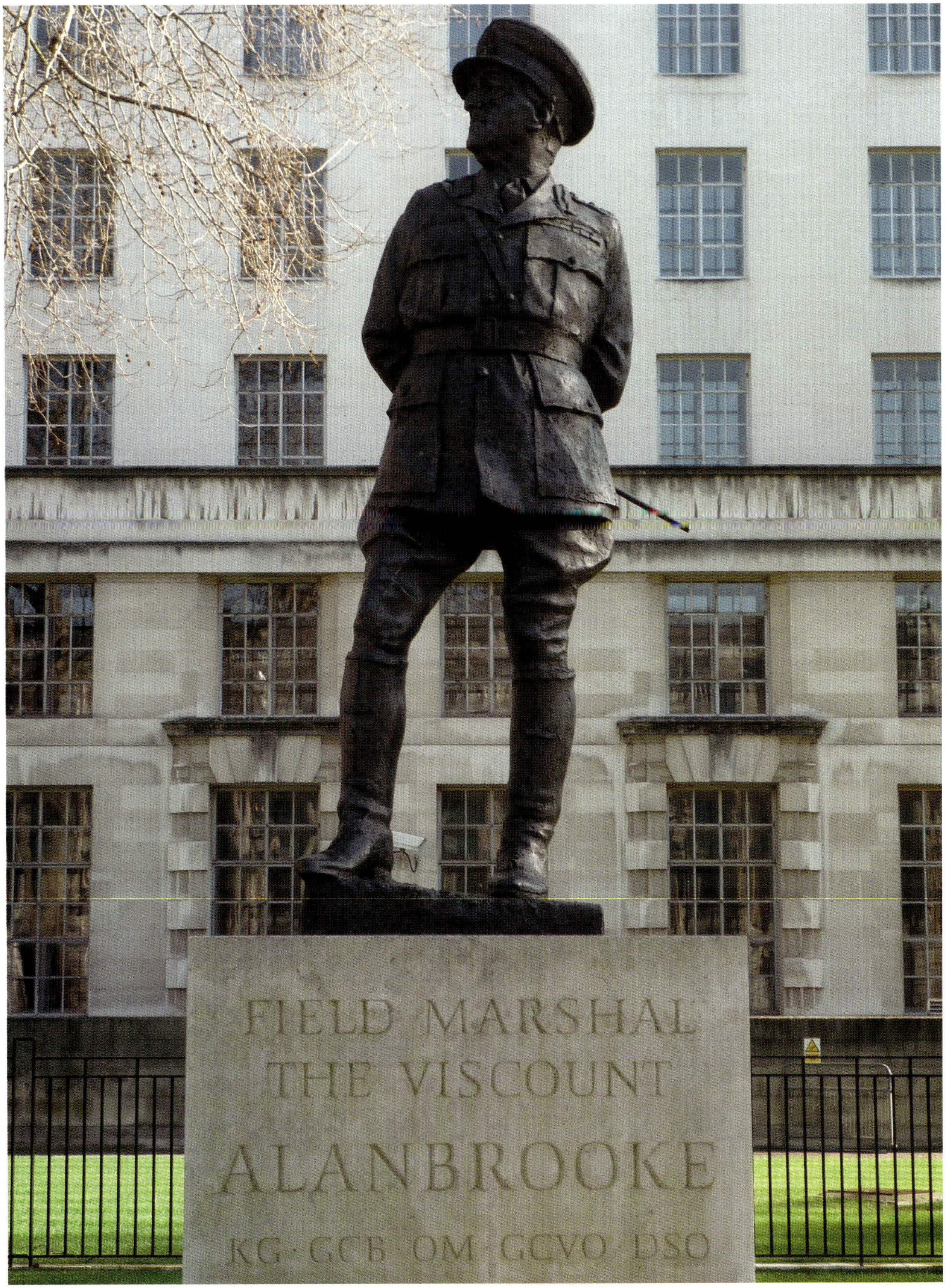
FIELD MARSHAL
THE VISCOUNT
ALANBROOKE
KG · GCB · OM · GCVO · DSO

criticism of Churchill's fumbling and overly emotional conduct of the British war effort. The unexpurgated version, published in 2002, proved an even greater sensation.

The Alanbrooke memorial appears initially to have been the brainchild of the eminent soldier and former Chief of the Defence Staff, Field Marshal Lord Carver (1915–2001). Prompted by the imminent unveiling of Ivor's statue of Field Marshal Slim, Carver contacted Sir Martin Farndale, a senior gunner, arguing that the Royal Regiment of Artillery, Alanbrooke's old regiment, ought to launch an appeal for a statue to him in 1991, as this would be the 50th anniversary of his appointment as CIGS (Lord Carver to General Sir Martin Farndale [1929–2000], 20 March 1990, 15/1/1990–94, Alanbrooke Statue Commission, Alanbrooke Papers, Liddell Hart Centre for Military Archives, Kings College, London).

Farndale replied that plans were already afoot for the regiment to commission a memorial statue of Alanbrooke, which it was estimated would cost some £150,000. Moreover, Farndale intended to contact the 'sculptor of the Slim memorial' about taking on the commission after it had been unveiled (General Sir Martin Farndale to Field Marshal Carver, 11 April 1990, ibid.).

Later in 1990, Carver and Farndale lobbied General Sir John Chapple, the chief of the Defence Staff, for a site on Whitehall to be set aside for a future Alanbrooke statue (General Sir John Chapple to Major-General Sir Martin Farndale, 9 February 1991, 15/1/1990–1994, Alanbrooke Statue Commission, Alanbrooke Papers, Liddell Hart Centre for Military Archives, Kings College London). Meanwhile, in the autumn of that year, Ivor was approached by W. H. P. Clarke, secretary of the Alanbrooke Memorial Project Campaign, to be the sculptor of the work. After some initial reluctance on Ivor's part, on the grounds that he might be a little old (he was coming up to 77), he accepted, and by early February 1991 had sent Field Marshal Carver photographs of a clay sketch model of the statue, which greatly impressed Carver as well as other members of the Alanbrooke Memorial Committee (Field Marshal Carver to Major-General Sir Martin Farndale, 22 March 1991, ibid.).

By June 1991 Ivor was hard at work on a one-third-full-size maquette of Alanbrooke, about 90 cm high, to show members of the Memorial Committee, including its president, General Sir Edward Burgess (1927–) and its two vice-presidents, Field Marshal Carver and General Sir Harry Tuzo (1917–1998). The latter did not live far from Ivor, and was in fact the deputy lord-lieutenant of Norfolk. After a visit to the sculptor's studio, at Shimpling near Diss, towards the end of June 1991, they were happy to confirm Ivor officially as the sculptor for the project: his fee would be £54,000 (Field Marshal Carver to W. H. P. Clarke, 27 June 1991, ibid.).

Meanwhile a fund-raising team was constituted under the leadership of W. H. P. 'Nobby' Clarke – who had previously masterminded the efficient campaign that raised the money to pay for Ivor's statue of Field Marshal Slim. Indeed, there is a hint that it was Clarke who first suggested to Sir Martin Farndale, in the spring of 1990, that if the Royal Artillery was thinking of commissioning a statue of Alanbrooke, Ivor ought to be the first sculptor it should contact. The sculptor had served in the Second World War and, moreover, in the Royal Artillery. He was on the 'same wavelength as the Army ... unlike so many younger men' (W. H. P. Clarke to Field Marshal Carver, 28 June 1991, ibid.).

154a

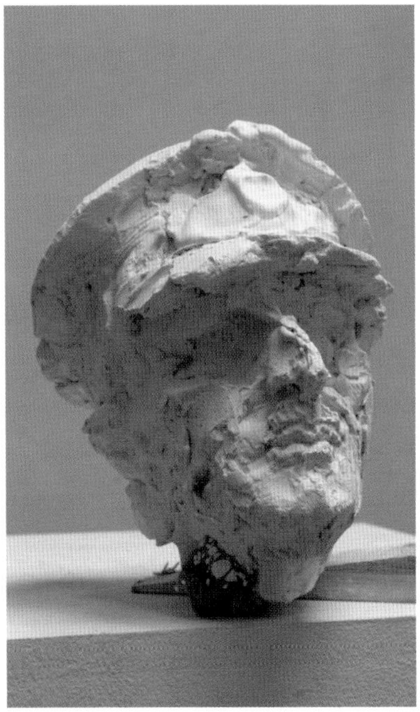

By late September 1991, Clarke reported to Field Marshal Carver that Ivor had

> completed a full-size plaster cast of the statue's head ... He is now beginning to work on the full-size body in clay. Once this is ready in a few weeks time the original team [Field Marshal Carver, General Burgess, General Tuzo and Sir Martin Farndale, with Clarke] will have to meet once again with the sculptor at his studio at Diss for final examination (alteration if any) and acceptance of the full size statue prior to it being sent to the foundry for casting. Please note that casting takes about five to six months. (W. H. P. Clarke to Field Marshal Carver, 1 October 1991, ibid.).

Agreement for the statue to be sited on Whitehall, in front of the Ministry of Defence and between the existing statues of Field Marshals Slim and Montgomery, had been secured from the RFAC, English Heritage, the Ministry of Defence, the Department of the Environment, and Westminster City Council. But Clarke added a note of warning: 'The Chairman of the RFAC, Lord St John of Fawsley, wants either the MoD, or the DoE, to completely re-vamp the site and move the statues about – which will cost at least £65,000 per statue.' If Lord St John had his way and the site had to be extensively redeveloped first, the eventual unveiling of the Alanbrooke statue would be considerably delayed (W. H. P. Clarke to Field Marshal Carver, 1 October 1991, ibid.).

The Alanbrooke statue appeal was launched in the media early in October. In the midst of a severe economic downturn, however, donations arrived in a steady stream but were not nearly as generous as had been hoped (Field Marshal Carver to W. H. P. Clarke, 23 January 1992, ibid.). Meanwhile, the sculptor had been experiencing problems with completing the full-sized plaster cast of the statue, and had to report that, owing to a combination of this and likely casting times at the Foundry, the full-sized bronze figure would not be ready until at least April 1993 (W. H. P. Clarke to Field Marshal Carver, 20 January 1992, ibid.).

Given these developments, Carver decided to ask Sir Robert Fellowes, the Queen's private secretary at Buckingham Palace, whether her unveiling of the Alanbrooke statue could be postponed from the previously arranged November 1992 until April or May 1993. Fellowes signalled that this was feasible, while Carver hoped this display of encouragement from the Palace would help him head off any attempt by Lord St John to delay the installation. Not for the first time, Carver displayed a formidable grasp of the best tactics to deploy to ensure success within the Whitehall jurisdictional jungle (Field Marshal Carver to Sir Robert Fellowes, 13 February 1992, ibid.).

In the autumn of 1992, Lord St John did indeed try to order a halt to any activity on the Whitehall site, prior to its being assessed for a major re-landscaping project. However, when he learned that this would prevent the unveiling of the statue by the Queen – a ceremony already set in her diary – he quickly abandoned his efforts to hold up proceedings. A fervent royalist, the last thing he wanted would have been to inconvenience his monarch (W. H. P. Clarke to IRJ, 14 January 1993, ibid.).

In September 1992 Clarke was able to write to Field Marshal Carver: 'The plaster model of the statue will be going to the foundry for casting into bronze during the first week in October.' He could also report, on a happy note, that an attempt by

154b

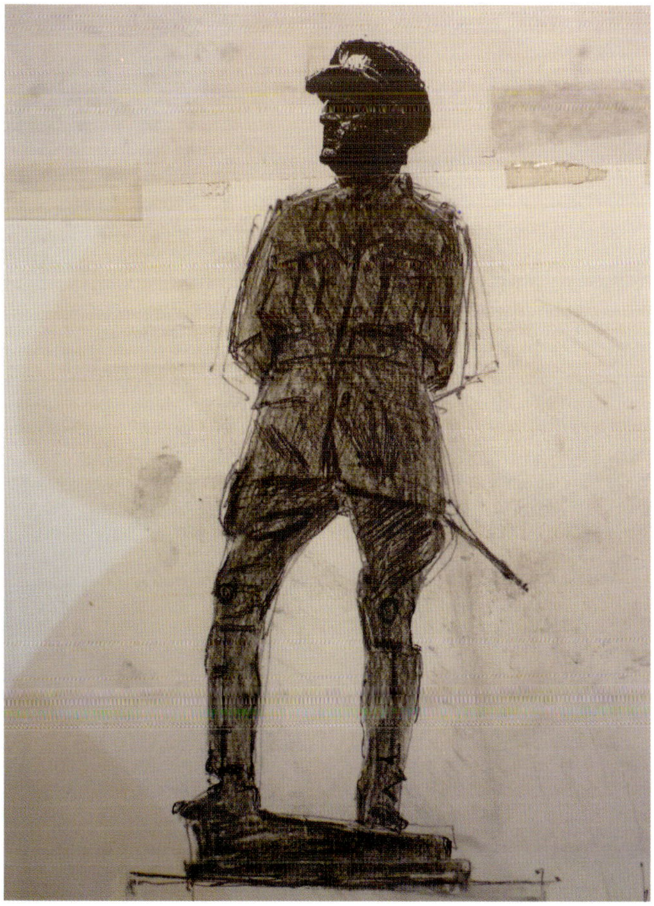

the RFAC to surround the statue with a protective fence had been foiled: '[Ivor] and I ... had strong reservations about completely cutting off the General Public from close examination of the statues ... Mr Roberts-Jones was upset at this idea since the merits of his sculpture, particularly at close quarters, will not be seen by the public as a whole' (W. H. P. Clarke to Field Marshal Carver, 14 September 1992, ibid.).

The statue was unveiled by the Queen on 25 May 1993, before a large and appreciative crowd.

Towards the end of June 1993 the sculptor received his final payment for the statue – in total he had received just over £74,000 for his labours, the most he was ever paid for a sculpture (W. H. P. Clarke to IRJ, 24 June 1993, ibid.). The project cost a total of £155,640, and between October 1991 and June 1993 Clarke and his team raised just under £190,000 (final statement of the Alanbrooke Memorial Campaign Project, 27 August 1993, ibid.).

However, as W. H. P. Clarke was later quick to point out to Field Marshal Carver,

> Mr Roberts-Jones has, if anything, considerably undercharged his old regiment ... he has done ... the Royal Artillery a tremendous favour and consideration when deciding to do the Alanbrooke at the same cost that he charged the Burma Star Association for the Slim ... the Royal Society of British Sculptors advise me that were such an Alanbrooke statue to be commissioned today by a sculptor of Roberts-Jones's considerable reputation, he would have charged at least £85,000 plus VAT! So we did the Alanbrooke just in time!' (William Clarke to Field Marshal Carver, 26 August 1993, ibid.).

155

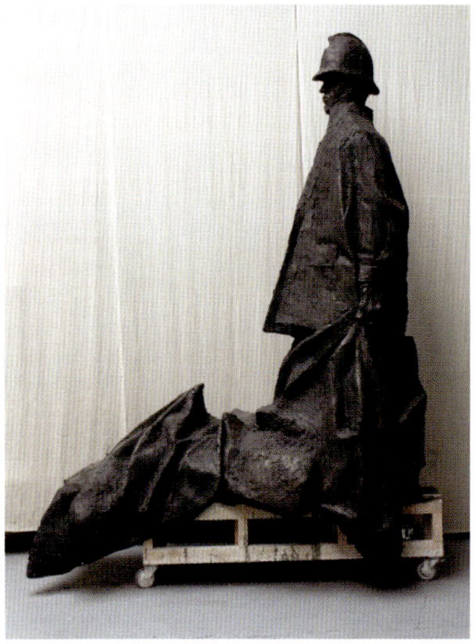

155a

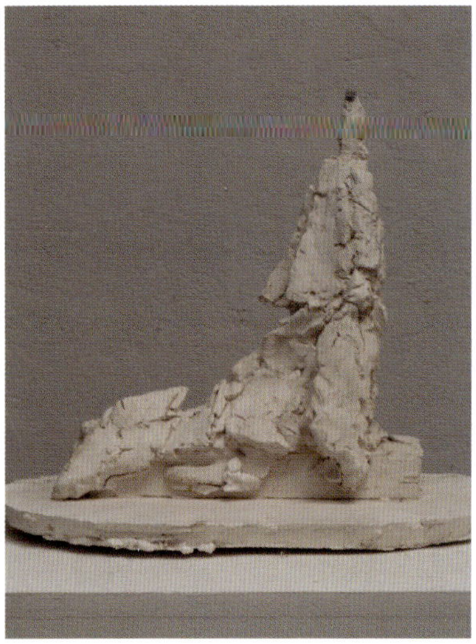

155 *National Police Memorial Project/Policeman Mourning a Dead Comrade*

1991–2006
Fibreglass resin
270 x 66 x 211 cm
Location: Sculpture Gardens, Reinshaw Hall, Derbyshire
Related works: 155: Prior to transportation to Renishaw Hall, 2007
155a: *Small Maquette for the National Police Memorial*, 1991–93, plaster, 22.8 x 26.7 x 14.3 cm, private collection
155b: *Study for the Head of the Policeman, National Police Memorial*, 1993–96, plaster, 29 x 15.5 x 14.3 cm, Wolsey Art Gallery, Ipswich

Comments: This commission was the brainchild of flamboyant film director Michael Winner (1935–2013), who in May 1984 founded the Police Memorial Trust, following the shooting dead of 25-year-old WPC Yvonne Fletcher in April of that year outside the Libyan embassy in St James's Square, London. Her killer has yet to be brought to justice. By the late 1980s, Winner felt that the police richly deserved a National Police Memorial in a prominent central London location. In the spring of 1991 Winner contacted Ivor to discuss the possibility that the sculptor might provide a work in bronze for a National Police Memorial, which had been designed by architect Theo Crosby. Ivor had been recommended to Winner by Crosby, who had known the sculptor for 'many years', and by the president of the Royal Academy, Roger de Grey (Michael Winner in the *Independent*, 4 April 1993, p. 18).

Ivor agreed to undertake the sculpture, and quite quickly focused on the central component of a design in which a policeman wearing an old-fashioned 1950s-issue helmet and waterproof cape looked sorrowfully down at a dead comrade, killed in the line of duty, whose body has been covered with another rain cape (Ian Collins, *Eastern Daily Press*, 4 January 1994, p. 6).

Over the next two years, other possible elements were considered and then discarded. Winner eventually secured provisional agreement from the RFAC to site the memorial on The Mall, near Horse Guards Parade. However, during the last two years remaining to him, Ivor described the whole project as turning into a 'nightmare'. He found Winner a particularly exasperating client, who would pronounce himself satisfied with a new variation to the basic design Ivor had suggested, only to raise a barrage of detailed objections and suggested modifications shortly thereafter (author interview with John W. Mills, 10 May 2011).

Meanwhile, matters were not improved when Winner, in March 1993, suddenly sacked the architect Crosby and asked Ivor to design the memorial's architectural setting as well (IRJ to Byron Rogers, *Sunday Telegraph*, 27 June 1993, p. 5). This had the result of further adding to the sculptor's woes. Though Ivor produced a simple and tasteful design, it would not receive approval from the RFAC, whose chairman, Lord St John, raised a series of objections to aspects of Ivor's sculpture for the memorial – such as whether or not any portion of the recumbent dead policeman should be left exposed (IRJ to Michael Winner, c. April 1996, IRJ Papers, Archives, HMI, Leeds).

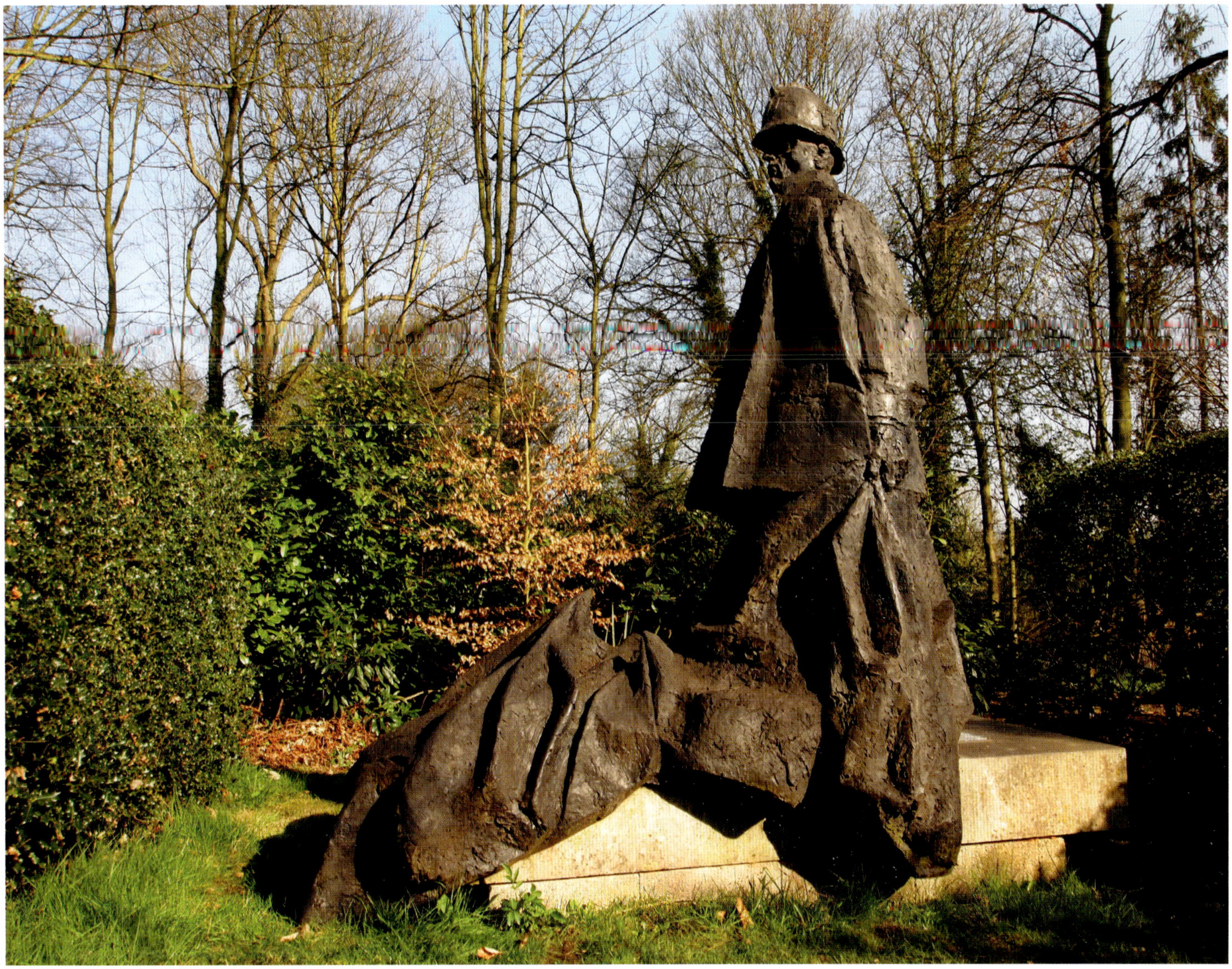

155b

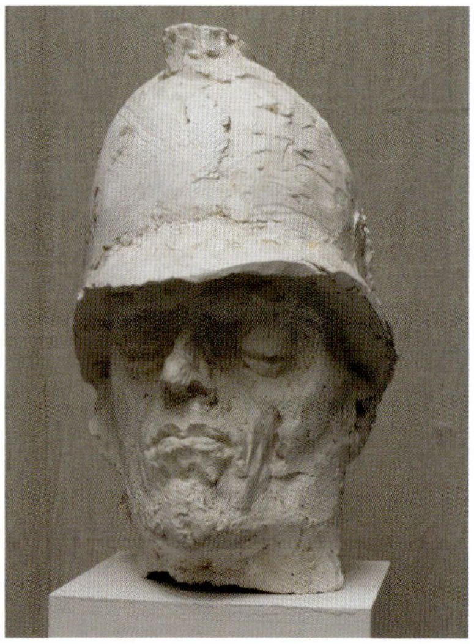

By the time of Ivor's death, in December 1996, he had completed a full-sized plaster model of the memorial's central sculptural element – though the design of the architectural setting was still mired in dispute and endless revision. The model was later found in Ivor's studio by one of his executors, the sculptor (and future president of the Society of Portrait Sculptors) Nigel Boonham. For a number of years, Boonham attempted to find a permanent outdoor home for the sculpture and to have it cast in a more durable material. At one point the work might have gone to the National Memorial Arboretum in Staffordshire – but this plan fell through (Nigel Boonham to Graham Berville, Chairman of the Police Mutual Fund, 6 November 2005, Police Memorial File, Trustees of the Estate of IRJ).

Meanwhile, after Ivor's death, Winner gave the police memorial project to the practice of the eminent architect Sir Norman Foster. It would be Foster's entirely architectural monument, conceived in collaboration with Danish artist Per Arnoldi, that would be unveiled on Cambridge Green, at the junction of Horse Guards Parade and the Mall, by the Queen in April 2005. The memorial commemorates the approximately 1,600 police officers who had been 'unlawfully killed in the line of duty' up to that date (*Independent*, 27 April 2005, p. 5).

Shortly after the unveiling, Boonham secured agreement with Sir Raresby Sitwell for a cast of Ivor's final model for the Police Memorial to be placed in Sitwell's recently created sculpture garden at his home of Renishaw Hall, in Derbyshire. Boonham contacted Winner with the news, and the latter offered to pay £10,000 for the model to be cast in fibreglass resin (Michael Winner to W. R. C. Riley, Executor of the Estate of IRJ, 18 August 2005, Estate of IRJ). This task was performed by Ivor's old foundry, Meridian, and was one of the last works it was to cast before it closed. Supervised by John W. Mills in his capacity as president of the Royal Society of British Sculptors, the plaster cast (which Nigel Boonham had specially strengthened) was cast into resin in the autumn of 2006 and unveiled at Renishaw Hall in March 2007 (W. R. C. Riley to Nigel Boonham, 16 October 2006, Police Memorial File, Estate of Ivor Roberts-Jones).

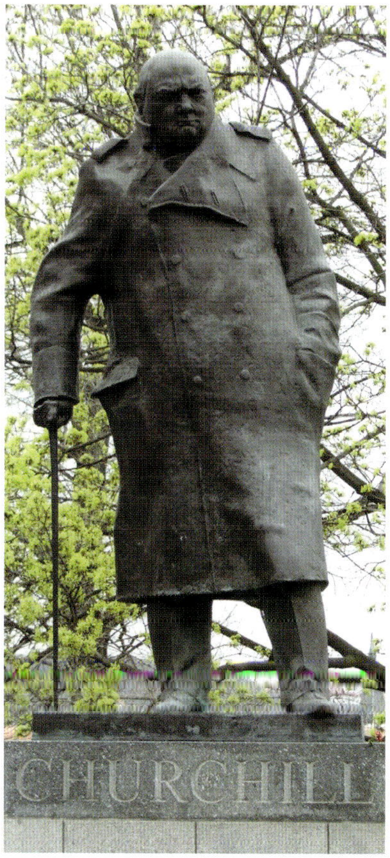

156a

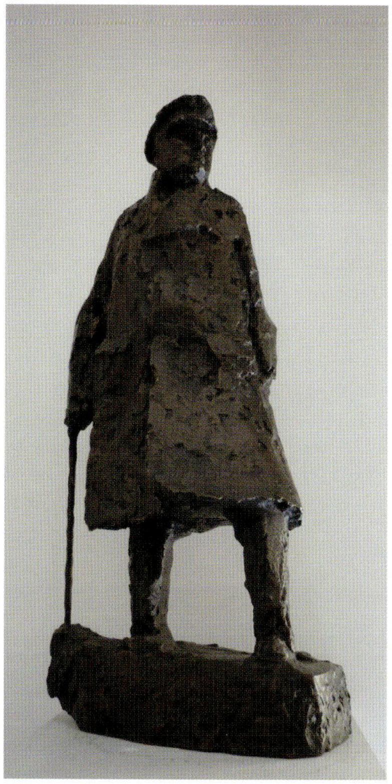

156 *Sir Winston Churchill project for Winston Churchill Square, Prague*

1995–96

Related work: 156a: *Maquette of Sir Winston Churchill for Prague*, 1995–96, bronze, 41.3 x 21.1 x 11.5 cm, private collection x 2
156b: Model for *Monumental Head of Sir Winston Churchill for Prague*, 1996, clay, 53.3 x 84.5 x 57.2 cm, Commerz Bank, Prague; plaster cast, Oswestry School, Shropshire

Comments: In August 1995 Ivor was contacted by Milan Jakobec, press attaché of the Czech embassy in London, with a proposal from a committee headed by Tomáš Mikeska, mayor of Prague's Third 'Zizkov' district. The committee wanted Ivor to make a new cast of his Parliament Square *Churchill*, to stand in a prominent square in the Third District, which had recently been renamed in honour of Churchill. One side of the square was occupied by the city's prestigious Economics University. Intriguingly, Ivor had been recommended to Mikeska and his committee by Ivor's old rival, the London-based Czech-born sculptor Franta Belsky (1921–2000), who had secured the commission early in the 1980s for the Earl Mountbatten memorial in London – much to Ivor's irritation (Milan Jakobec, Czech Embassy, to IRJ, c. mid-August 1995, IRJ Papers, Archives, HMI, Leeds).

Ivor replied that the original mould for his figure of Churchill in Parliament Square had disintegrated, and he doubted very much whether Parliament would allow him to make a cast from the statue itself. However, as he had never been entirely satisfied with any of his previous figures of Churchill, Ivor jumped at this opportunity late in his career to have one more attempt at a statue of Churchill. It would be 'a "variation" on the original theme' of the 3.5-metre-high figure in Parliament Square. He added that he was delighted to be asked: '[I]t would be a great honour to have a sculpture of mine represented in a city so famous for its architecture and its sculpture. The *Jan Hus* Monument by Saloun is pinned up on my studio wall!' For such a 'marvellous site' as Jakobec proposed, 'the sculpture *must* have a commanding presence'. He thought the project would most likely require £100,000, or thereabouts, to be properly realised (IRJ to Milan Jakobec, 21 August 1995, ibid.).

By May 1996 Ivor had entered into a provisional agreement with a recently created Winston Churchill Statue Foundation to produce a figure of Churchill whose body would be closely based on that in Parliament Square, but whose head would be a completely new interpretation (Milan Jakobec to IRJ, 14 May 1996, ibid.).

During the summer of 1996, Ivor worked on a sketch maquette of the Churchill statue, about 35 cm high, as well as what he referred to as 'a large fragment of the most important part of the figure i.e. the upper half'. He evidently anticipated that he might not live to complete the full-sized work, but hoped that the sculptor who came after him to finish the project would be able to 'graft' the new head and shoulders Ivor was hoping to provide onto the remaining portion of the figure based closely upon the *Churchill* in Parliament Square (IRJ to Milan Jakobec, c. July 1996, ibid.).

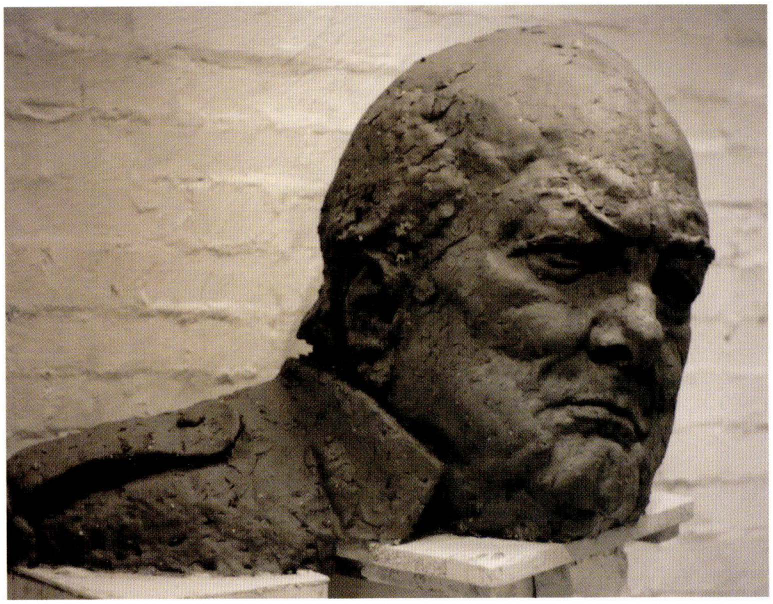

156b (clay)

By early October 1996, Ivor had made a large clay maquette of the new head and shoulders of Churchill for the Prague statue, and sent photographs of it to Jakobec, writing:

> It is still in progress, and in clay, but these [photographs] give a fair idea of it. Of course, to get the full effect it needs to be backed up by the mass of the figure and the thrust of the shoulders leaning on the stick. I believe it to be an improvement on both the Oslo C[hurchill] and the one in Westminster (IRJ to Milan Jakobec, 9 October 1996, ibid.).

Two months after having sent the large head and shoulders to be cast in plaster by the Meridian Foundry, Ivor died on 9 December 1996.

For a few months after his death, the Prague Winston Churchill Statue Foundation discussed with its 'sculpture adviser', Franta Belsky, whether combining Ivor's new head of Churchill with 'a copy of the Winston Churchill Westminster statue body' would be 'technically and legally feasible' (Milan Jakobec to Monica Roberts-Jones, 15 January 1997, IRJ Papers, Archives, HMI, Leeds). By February 1997 it had decided that this was not feasible – a bronze cast would be made from the large head and shoulders Ivor had created in 1996. This would be 'dedicated to the main sponsor of the Winston Churchill statue, [the] Commerce Bank of Prague ... to decorate its premises', and be used as a focal point for activities to raise funds for the full-sized statue. The committee hoped to persuade the Palace of Westminster to allow it to make a latex cast from the statue in Parliament Square, which could then be cast in bronze for the square in Prague (Milan Jakobec to Monica Roberts-Jones, 12 February 1997 and 28 February 1997, ibid.).

Monica Roberts-Jones gave her permission for a copy to be made from the statue in Parliament Square, somewhat swayed by the fact that this proposal had the

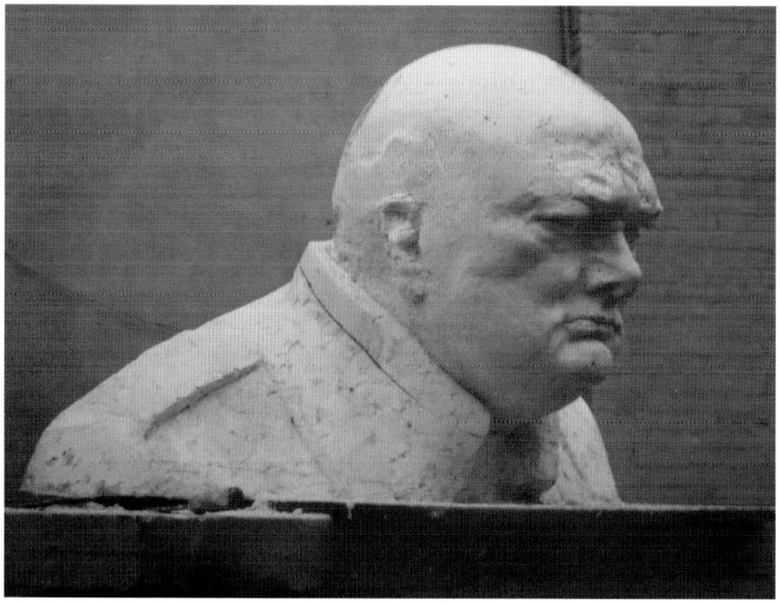

156b (plaster)

support of Lady Thatcher and Czech President Václav Havel. With the British Foreign Office and the Royal Parks Agency also giving the proposal their blessing, permission was granted relatively quickly (David Welch, Chief Executive of the Royal Parks, to Milan Jakobec, 1 August 1997, ibid.). The committee's sculpture adviser, Franta Belsky, urged it to engage an up-and-coming portrait sculptor, Nigel Boonham, to supervise the making of a cast from the *Churchill* in Parliament Square. This would be cast in bronze by a foundry in Prague, and Boonham would supervise the installation of this statue in Winston Churchill Square in the Czech capital (Nigel Boonham to Milan Cesky, Mayor of the Third District, Prague, 5 March 1999, Private Collection, London).

The 3.5-metre-high statue was unveiled in Winston Churchill Square on 17 November 1999. The work occupies a plinth on which once stood the figure of the former Czech Communist president, Antonin Zapotocky (1884–1957) (*Guardian*, 18 November 1999, p. 20).

Unveiling the statue, Lady Thatcher reminded the large audience present that she was also in Prague 'to mark the 10th anniversary of the "velvet" revolution which swept away Communist one-party rule in the former Czechoslovakia'. She added that she was

> very glad you have found a place for this new statue. It will remind you here, as every generation has to be reminded – and amid all this beauty – that the price of freedom can be high, that it may indeed require the sacrifice of 'blood, toil, tears and sweat' ... [T]his statue ... will also remind you, as it reminds me, of something else – that liberty must never be allowed to perish from this earth; it must forever endure (Lady Thatcher speaking in Prague, 17 November 1999, copy: Margaret Thatcher Foundation, London, Document 108384, accessed 24 March 2011).

Notes

Chapter One

Abbreviations Key:
HMI, Leeds: The Henry Moore Institute for the Study of Sculpture, Leeds
IRJ: Ivor Roberts-Jones
LHCMA, KCL: Liddell-Hart Centre for Military Archives, Kings College, London
NMW, Cardiff: National Museum of Wales, Cardiff
RBS: Royal British Society of Sculptors, London
RIBA: Royal Institute of British Architects, London

1 Kyffin Williams, Christies: *Twentieth Century British Art*, exhibition catalogue, 24 November 2005 (London: Christies), p. 31.
2 John W. Mills interview with Dr J. Black, 12 April 2011.
3 Etienne Millner interview with Dr J. Black, 16 January 2012.
4 Terence Mullaly, 'Ivor Roberts-Jones, Obituary', *Guardian*, 24 December 1996, p. 12.
5 John W. Mills interview with Dr J. Black, 12 April 2011; Brian Jarvis interview with Dr J. Black, 5 May 2011; Etienne Millner interview with Dr J. Black, 16 January 2012; and Bridget Heriz-Smith interview with Dr J. Black, 21 February 2013. Mills was a technician at Goldsmiths from 1956 to 1966. Millner studied under Ivor at Goldsmiths from 1972 to 1976, while Jarvis was Ivor's main assistant from around 1984 to 1994.
6 Rosemary Smith interview with Dr S. Ayres, 5 March 2012. Ms Smith studied under Ivor between 1954 and 1958.
7 Peter Cannon-Brookes, *Ivor Roberts-Jones: The Road to Harlech* (London: Trefoil Books, 1983), p. 25; John W. Mills interview with Dr J. Black, 12 April 2011.
8 John W. Mills interview with Dr J. Black, 12 April 2011.
9 Cannon-Brookes, *Ivor Roberts-Jones*, p. 25.
10 Kyffin Williams to Rollo Charles (Keeper of Art, NMW, Cardiff), c. April 1960, IRJ File, Archives, NMW, Cardiff.
11 John W. Mills interview with Dr J. Black, 12 April 2011; Bridget Heriz-Smith interview with Dr J. Black, 21 February 2013.
12 Birth certificate for Ivor Roberts-Jones, IRJ Papers, Archives, HMI, Leeds.
13 Family tree, IRJ Papers, Archives, HMI, Leeds.
14 Sir John Rothenstein, 'Ivor Roberts-Jones I', *The Artist*, September 1978, p. 12; clipping IRJ File, RAA Lib 2 136, Archives, Royal Academy, London.
Sir John Rothenstein (1901–1992): director of the Tate Gallery 1938–64; knighted 1952; published *Modern English Painters* (1952–74).
15 IRJ to Sir John Rothenstein, c. September 1985, Rothenstein Papers, Archives, Tate Britain.
16 Ibid.
17 Notes by Tim Walker, 3 March 2005, IRJ Papers, 2005. 456/C/6/2-11, Archives, HMI, Leeds.
18 Cannon-Brookes, *Ivor Roberts-Jones*, p. 25.
19 G. Gore Browne, Oswestry Grammar School, to Dr J. Black, 29 March 2011.
20 Jane Collard, archivist, Worksop College, to Dr J. Black, 28 September 2011.
21 *The Cuthbertian*, July 1931, p. 8; clipping, Library, Worksop College, Notts.
My thanks to Jane Collard for locating this detail.
22 Rothenstein, 'Ivor Roberts-Jones I', p. 12.
23 Ibid.
24 Ibid.
25 In April 1969, Weight was the first among five painters, along with Bernard Dunstan, William Coldstream, James Fitton and Cosmo Clark, to nominate Ivor for election to the Royal Academy in London as an Associate. Nominations Book for Associates, Royal Academy, London, Archives, Royal Academy, London.
26 'Carel Weight, Obituary', *Independent*, 15 August 1997, p. 17.
27 IRJ to the Reverend James Farmiloe, 30 July 1957, Raymond Erith Papers, RIBA Archives, Victorian and Albert Museum, London.
28 Rothenstein, 'Ivor Roberts-Jones I', p. 12.
29 *The Times*, 3 October 1935, p. 1.
30 IRJ File, RAA Lib 2 136, Archives, Royal Academy, London.
31 Cannon-Brookes, *Ivor Roberts-Jones*, p. 13.
32 In 1947 Hardy left Koestler and married the German émigré graphic designer F. K. H. Henrion. During the 1950s she established herself as a distinguished portrait sculptor, looking to the example of Wilhelm Lehmbruck but also to that of Alberto Giacometti, with whom she became friendly during the decade. Obituaries appeared in the *Independent* (9 December 2003, p. 20) and the *Guardian* (27 November 2003, p. 29).

[33] IRJ to Kyffin Williams, 3 January 1977, A1/9/1, Williams Papers, National Library of Wales, Aberystwyth.

[34] Rothenstein, 'Ivor Roberts-Jones I', p. 12.

[35] *The Times*, 4 July 1938, p. 10.

[36] Marriage certificate, dated 6 May 1940, IRJ Papers, HMI Archives, Leeds.

[37] IRJ to Sir John Rothenstein, c. September 1985, Rothenstein Papers, Archives, Tate Britain.

[38] Brian Morley to Dr J. Black, 14 April 2011. Morley studied at Goldsmiths under Ivor around 1954–56.

[39] IRJ interview with June Shepherd, *Norfolk and Suffolk Express*, 22 May 1987, p. 22, Press Clippings, IRJ Papers, Archives, HMI, Leeds.

[40] IRJ to Jack Crofton, c. September 1979, Meridian Foundry Papers, courtesy of Megan Crofton-Thomas.

[41] Rothenstein, 'Ivor Roberts-Jones I', p. 12.

[42] *The Cuthbertian*, July 1930, p. 24; clipping, Library, Worksop College, Notts.
My thanks to Jane Collard for locating this reference to Ivor's budding interest in military matters.

[43] Anthony Powell, *To Keep the Ball Rolling: The Memoirs of Anthony Powell* (London: Penguin, 1983), pp. 269–71. Like Ivor, Powell was maternally English and paternally Welsh.

[44] Powell, *To Keep the Ball Rolling*, p. 1[illegible]

[45] Mervyn Roberts-Jones, born 4 August 1941, at Downpatrick County Infirmary, Northern Ireland, 2005. 456/A/2/3, IRJ Papers, Archives, HMI, Leeds.

[46] Kyffin Williams, notes for an entry in auction catalogue *Christies: Twentieth Century Art*, c. October 2005, IRJ Papers, Archives, HMI, Leeds.

[47] Rothenstein, 'Ivor Roberts-Jones I', p. 12.

[48] IRJ to Dr Peter Cannon-Brookes, 29 December 1981, IRJ 1983 Exhibition File, Archives, NMW, Cardiff.

[49] Robert Lyman, *Slim, Master of War: Burma and the Birth of Modern Warfare* (London: Constable and Robinson, 2005), p. 253.

[50] Ivor was not alone among British veterans of the war against Japan in feeling this way. Max Hastings, *Nemesis: The Battle for Japan, 1944–45* (London: HarperCollins, 2007), pp. 521–2.

[51] George MacDonald Fraser, *Quartered Safe Out Here: A Recollection of the War in Burma* (London: HarperCollins, 2000 [1993]), pp. xxiv, 338–9.

[52] IRJ to Dr Peter Cannon-Brookes, 29 December 1981, IRJ 1983 Exhibition File, Archives, NMW, Cardiff.

[53] Ibid.

[54] Frank McLynn, *The Burma Campaign: Disaster into Triumph, 1942–45* (London: Vintage, 2011), pp. 444–5.

[55] The committee's chairman, Sir John Tilney, had fought in the Second World War, while committee member Lord Chandos had won the DSO and MC in the First World War.

[56] IRJ to Dr Peter Cannon-Brookes, 7 June 1983, IRJ File, Archives, NMW, Cardiff; IRJ to Field Marshal Lord Carver, 29 May 1993, Alanbrooke Statue File, Alanbrooke Papers, Liddell Hart Centre for Military Archives, King's College, London.

[57] IRJ to Dr Peter Cannon-Brookes, autobiographical notes, c. September 1983, IRJ Archive, NMW, Cardiff. The Gutai Group was formed around 1954 in Japan by Jiro Yoshihara (1905–72) and Shozo Shimamoto (1928–). A Gutai ('Concrete') Manifesto was published in 1956, and expressed fascination with the beauty of decay, damage and destruction – cracks and scars and flaking surfaces. The group dissolved shortly after the death of Yoshihara.

[58] Rosemary Smith interview with Dr S. Ayres, 5 March 2012.

[59] IRJ to Kyffin Williams, 3 January 1977, A1/9/1, Williams Papers, National Library of Wales, Aberystwyth.

[60] IRJ, Autobiographical Notes, to Dr Peter Cannon-Brookes, 15 September 1982, IRJ File, NMW, Cardiff.

[61] James Beechey and Chris Stephens, eds, *Picasso and Modern British Art* (London: Tate Publishing, 2012), p. 30.

[62] Cannon-Brookes, *Ivor Roberts-Jones*, p. 17.

[63] Rothenstein, 'Ivor Roberts-Jones I', p. 12.

[64] Cannon-Brookes, *Ivor Roberts-Jones*, p. 17.
British sculptors had been looking for inspiration and stimulation to work by ancient so-called 'primitive' cultures in the British Museum from at least the early years of the twentieth century, when senior figures within the British art education establishment such as Eduard Lanteri, Professor of Sculpture at the Royal College of Art, had urged his students to closely inspect examples of Ancient Egyptian and Assyrian sculpture in the Museum. See Jonathan Black, 'The Illusion of Permanence: Archaeology, Imperialism and British Public Sculpture Between the Wars', in Paul Bonaventura and Simon Callery, eds, *Sculpture and Archaeology: Debates and Speculations* (London: Ashgate, 2011), pp. 71–[illegible]

[65] *Listener*, 5 June 1935, p. 946, quoted in Alan Wilkinson, ed., *Henry Moore: Writings and Conversations* (Aldershot: Lund Humphries, 2002), pp. 101–2. Moore declared: 'for me, Sumerian sculpture ranks with Early Greek, Etruscan, Ancient Mexican, Fourth and Twelfth Dynasty Egyptian and Romanesque and Early Gothic sculpture, as the great sculpture of the world.'

[66] Eric Newton, *British Sculpture 1944–46* (London: John Tiranti, 1947), pp. viii–ix.

[67] Ibid., p. x. In 1946 legislation was passed authorising the construction of fourteen New Towns, including Hatfield, Stevenage, Harlow, Basildon, Corby, Cwmbran, Peterlee and East Kilbride. Peter Hennessy, *Never Again: Britain 1945–1951* (London: Vintage, 1993), p. 172.

[68] Newton, *British Sculpture 1944–46*, p. ix.

[69] Neil Cox, *The Picasso Book* (London: Tate Publishing, 2010), p. 51.

[70] In the early 1970s, photographs of Moore's shelter drawings cut from magazines were seen pinned to the wall of Ivor's studio in St James's Gardens. See *Illustrated London News*, 27 March 1971, p. 12, Press Clippings, IRJ Papers, Archives, HMI, Leeds.

[71] Cox, *Picasso Book*, pp. 28–33.

[72] Rosemary Smith interview with Dr S. Ayres, 5 March 2012, and Etienne Millner interview with Dr J. Black, 16 January 2012.

[73] Peter Davison, ed., *George Orwell: A Life in Letters* (London: Penguin, 2011), p. 516.

[74] IRJ, Autobiographical Fragment, c. March 1993, IRJ Papers, Archives, HMI, Leeds.

[75] Davison, *George Orwell*, p. 520.

[76] Daphne Hardy-Henrion to IRJ, 19 October 1981, IRJ Papers, Archives, HMI, Leeds.

[77] Cannon-Brookes, *Ivor Roberts-Jones*, p. 33. Moore's *King and Queen* was reproduced on the front cover of John Rothenstein's 1962 study *British Art Since 1900* – which also mentioned Ivor's recent sculpture.

[78] Cannon-Brookes, *Ivor Roberts-Jones*, p. 33.

79 He was doubtless well aware that the carvings at Ajanta had, from before the First World War, been of tremendous interest to a whole generation of sculptors working in Britain, including Epstein, Gill, Gaudier-Brzeska, Kennington and Underwood. See Sarah Victoria Turner, 'Stone, Sex and Empire: Direct Carving and "British" Sculpture', in Penelope Curtis and Keith Wilson, eds, *Modern British Sculpture* (London: Royal Academy of Arts, 2011), pp. 100–4.

80 Sir Charles Wheeler, *High Relief* (London: Country Life Books, 1968), pp. 100–1. Wheeler was the Society's first president.

81 'The Beaux Arts Gallery', *The Times*, 30 July 1954, p. 11.

82 David Kynaston, *Family Britain: 1951–57* (London: Bloomsbury, 2009), p. 438.

83 Marina Lambraki-Plaka and Giuliano Scrafini, *Marino Marini: An Archaic Sculptor of Modern Art* (Athens: National Alexandros Soutzos Museum, 2006), p. 261.

84 John W. Mills, interview with Dr J. Black, 12 April 2011.

85 Stephen Gardiner, *Frink: The Official Biography* (London: Harper Collins, 1999), p. 54.

86 IRJ to Fiona Pearson (Assistant Keeper of Art, NMW, Cardiff), 27 May 1983, IRJ File, Archives, NMW, Cardiff.

87 'Mr. Jones's Sculpture', *The Times*, 29 May 1957, p. 3.

88 Rollo Charles (Keeper of Art, NMW, Cardiff) to IRJ, 22 November 1971, IRJ File, Archives, NMW, Cardiff.

89 'Sculpture at the Beaux Arts Gallery', *Guardian*, 20 May 1957, p. 5.

90 John Lehmann, ed., *Demetrios Capetanakis: A Greek Poet in England* (London: John Lehmann, 1947), frontispiece image.

91 IRJ to Dr Peter Cannon-Brookes, 21 March 1983, IRJ File, Archives, NMW, Cardiff.

92 Gardiner, *Frink*, p. 47.

93 Rothenstein, 'Ivor Roberts-Jones I', p. 12.

94 D. Brynmor Anthony, Secretary, Contemporary Art Society of Wales, to Augustus John, 9 July 1960, MS 22800E 21, John Papers, National Library of Wales, Aberystwyth. As it was, a bronze figure of Lloyd George, by Welshman Glynn Williams (1939–), would not be unveiled in Parliament Square until 2007. Peter Matthews, *London's Statues and Monuments* (Oxford: Shire Publications, 2012), p. 31.

95 Williams later recalled that he had met Ivor some time in the late 1940s. Cannon-Brookes, *Ivor Roberts-Jones*, p. 39. At the time he sat for the portrait head he was part-time senior art master at Highgate School. He occupied the post from 1944 until his retirement in 1973.

96 The Trustees of the Tate Gallery, on the recommendation of Sir John Rothenstein, purchased the head of *Claudel* for ninety guineas in August 1960. IRJ to Miss Bellow (Registrar, Tate Gallery), 11 August 1960, IRJ File, Archives, Tate Britain.

97 Rothenstein, 'Ivor Roberts-Jones I', p. 12.

98 Kyffin Williams to Rollo Charles (Keeper of Art, NMW, Cardiff), April 1960, IRJ Papers, Archives, NMW, Cardiff.

99 Rollo Charles (Keeper of Art, NMW, Cardiff) to IRJ, 4 May 1971, IRJ File, Archives, NMW, Cardiff.

100 Cannon-Brookes, *Ivor Roberts-Jones*, p. 69.

101 In fact Ivor stood at just over 1.62 metres, or 5' 4'.

102 Kyffin Williams, *Christies*, lot 31, 24 November 2005.

103 IRJ to Roger Lamb (Registrar), 8 April 1978, Archives, Beaverbrook Art Gallery, New Brunswick, Canada.

104 Mervyn's death was announced in *The Times*, November 1961, p. 1.

105 IRJ to Sir John Rothenstein, 15 July 1960, IRJ File, Archives, Tate Britain.

106 IRJ to Margaret Wagstaff, 2 May 1984, Archives, Arts Council, London.

107 IRJ to Sir John Rothenstein, 9 November 1960, IRJ File, Archives, Tate Britain. Gaspero de Corso (1911–97) and his wife Irene Brin – real name Maria Vittoria Rossi (1911–69) – opened the gallery L'Obelisco in November 1946. Among the artists they promoted were Morandi, Dalí, Magritte, Tanguy, Calder and Rauschenberg.

108 Lambraki-Plaka and Scrafini, *Marino Marini*, p. 262.

109 The first UK retrospective of Pollock's work was held at the Whitechapel Art Gallery in November 1958. Chris Stephens and Katherine Stout, *Art and the Sixties: This Was Tomorrow* (London: Tate Publishing, 2004), p. 139.

110 Chris Stephens, ed., *Henry Moore* (London: Tate Publishing, 2010), p. 127.

111 It would appear that the first of Marini's bronzes on the theme of the Horseman to be exhibited in the UK was at the second London County Council 'Open Air Sculpture' exhibition, held in Battersea Park, London, May–June 1951. Lambraki-Plaka and Scrafini, *Marino Marini*, p. 261.

112 Frink began exploring the 'horse and rider' theme during the early 1970s. Gardiner, *Frink*, pp. 203–5.

113 Stephens and Stout, *Art and the Sixties*, p. 10.

114 The exhibition was held at the NMW, Cardiff, 15 July–2 September 1961, before touring to Swansea, Aberystwyth and Bangor, where it closed on 26 November 1961.

115 'New Exhibition at the National Museum of Wales', *Western Mail*, 27 June 1961, clipping, Press Clippings Book, Library, NMW, Cardiff.

116 'Modern British Sculpture at the National Museum', *Western Mail*, 20 July 1961, clipping, Press Clippings Book, Library, NMW, Cardiff.

117 Maurice Cooke, 'Sculpture at the National Museum', *Western Mail*, 15 July 1961, Press Clippings Book, Library, NMW, Cardiff.

118 Sir John Rothenstein, *British Art Since 1900* (London: Phaidon, 1962), p. 34.

119 IRJ to Dr A. Westlake (Chairman of Ringwood and Fordingbridge Rural District Council), 2 May 1964, Augustus John Statue File, Archives, Fordingbridge Museum Trust, Hampshire.

120 IRJ to Philippa Duckworth, c. September 1995, Augustus John Statue File, Archives, Fordingbridge Museum Trust, Hampshire.

121 Ivor had first been nominated for the position of ARA in April 1965, but only received three votes and was eliminated in the first round. In April 1969 he received fifteen votes in the first round and then a majority in the second, securing his election as an ARA. IRJ File, RAA Lib 2 136, Archives, Royal Academy, London.

122 Meeting of the Winston Churchill Statue Committee, 8 March 1971, copy, Duncan Sandys Papers, Churchill Archive, Churchill College, Cambridge.

123 'The Churchill Statue', *The Times*, 6 November 1973, p. 21.

124 Minutes of Elections and General Assemblies, Royal Academy, London, 11 December 1973, Archives, Royal Academy, London.

125 IRJ interviewed by Byron Rogers, *Sunday Telegraph*, 27 June 1993, p. 5, Press Clippings File, IRJ Papers, Archives, HMI, Leeds.

126 IRJ interviewed by Ian Collins, *Eastern Daily Press*, 4 January 1994, p. 6, Press Clippings, IRJ Papers, Archives, HMI, Leeds.

[127] Examples of Giacometti's Surrealist 'table-top' sculptures were included in an exhibition of Modern Sculpture held at the Hanover gallery during the summer of 1959. *The Times*, 20 July 1959, p. 8.
[128] IRJ to Sir John Rothenstein, 8 October 1977, Rothenstein Papers, Archives, Tate Britain.
[129] Barry Martin, notes for a catalogue essay in *Contemporary British Sculpture*, Battersea Park, London (June–September 1977), dated March 1977, copy, IRJ File, Archives, NMW, Cardiff.
[130] Brian Jarvis, interview with Dr J. Black, 10 May 2011.
[131] Etienne Millner interview with Dr J. Black, 16 January 2012. Mr Millner studied under Ivor from 1974 to 1976, and recalls he could not accept Craig-Martin's celebrated installation *An Oak Tree* (1973) as 'proper sculpture'. In Ivor's opinion it was, in fact, a 'stunt'.
[132] 'This was the time when it had been declared that there was no such thing as "sculpture". So Bobbie [Jones] used to come in to sign on, have a cup of coffee, chat and go home.' Robert Brazil to Bernard Cheese, c. July 1999, Private Collection. Brazil had started teaching at Goldsmiths shortly after Ivor started there in 1946.
[133] Meeting of the Earl Attlee Statue Committee, 22 February 1978, PWO/2/35, 'Proposals to Commemorate Earl Attlee by Busts and/or Statues', 1975–78, House of Commons Archives, London.
[134] IRJ to Sir Richard Hyde Parker, 26 October 1981, Hyde Parker Papers, Melford Hall, Suffolk. In later life Ivor mused that he would rather like to make a statue of Lady Thatcher, 'fiercely coiffured [*sic*] and with deadly handbag', for the Members' Lobby of the House of Commons. IRJ interview with Ian Collins, *Eastern Daily Press*, 4 January 1994, p. 6, Press Clippings, IRJ Papers, Archives, HMI, Leeds.
[135] IRJ to Yolande Bird (Secretary to the Board of the National Theatre), 12 February 1979, Archives, National Theatre, London.
[136] IRJ to Dr Mark Davis (Registrar, NMW, Cardiff), 19 July 1986, IRJ File, Archives, NMW, Cardiff.
[137] Gerda Roper, *The Western Mail*, 5 August 1978, Press Clippings File, IRJ Papers, Archives, HMI, Leeds.
[138] IRJ, *Ivor Roberts-Jones: Sculpture* (Cardiff: Oriel Art Gallery, 1978), unpaginated.
[139] IRJ to Kyffin Williams, 3 January 1977, A1/9/1, Williams Papers, National Library of Wales, Aberystwyth.
[140] Entry for 2 September 1978, IRJ Diary, IRJ Papers, Archives, HMI, Leeds.
[141] IRJ to Fiona Pearson (Assistant Keeper of Art, NMW, Cardiff), 3 July 1983, IRJ File, Archives, NMW, Cardiff.
[142] Isabel Hitchman (Welsh Arts Council) to Dr Peter Cannon-Brookes, 17 June 1983, IRJ File, Archives, NMW, Cardiff.
[143] *Western Mail*, 20 March 1980, Press Cuttings File, IRJ Papers, Archives, HMI, Leeds.
[144] Cannon-Brookes was also the author of the first book on Ivor, *Ivor Roberts-Jones: The Journey to Harlech*, published in July 1983 to accompany the opening of Ivor's exhibition on Anglesey.
[145] Diary entry, 1 June 1980, IRJ Papers, Archives, HMI, Leeds and Dr Peter Cannon-Brookes interviewed by Dr J. Black, 18 April 2013.
[146] *South Wales Echo*, 1 August 1981, p. 3, Clippings Book, Library, NMW, Cardiff.
[147] Gordon Young, *Sculpture in a Country Park* (Margam: Welsh Sculpture Trust, 1983), p. 6. It would seem Ivor was asked to become a Trustee by Judge Bruce Griffiths QC, who was Chairman of the Trustees; he was also a founder member of the Welsh Portrait Sculpture Trust and had already sat to Ivor for a portrait head (1980). It is worthy of note that the president of the Welsh Sculpture Trust (WST), George Thomas MP, and the chairman of the WST's Executive Council, architect Sir Alex Gordon, had both sat to Ivor for portrait heads during the previous three years.
[148] IRJ to Bridget Heriz, 6 March 1988, Private Collection.
[149] IRJ to Sir Richard Hyde Parker, 16 March 1983, Melford Hall, Suffolk.
[150] Sir John Rothenstein, 'Ivor Roberts-Jones, II', *The Artist*, October 1978, p. 33; clipping, IRJ File, RAA Lib 2 136, Archives, Royal Academy, London.
[151] Isabel Hitchman interviewed by Dr S. Ayres, 17 August 2012.
[152] Diary entry, 24 August 1980, IRJ Papers, Archives, HMI, Leeds.
[153] IRJ to Yolande Bird (Secretary to the Board of the National Theatre, 21 February 1980, Archives, National Theatre, London.
[154] IRJ to Kyffin Williams, 29 June 1981, A1/13/38, Williams Papers, National Library of Wales, Aberystwyth.
[155] IRJ to Bridget Heriz, 6 March 1988, private collection.
[156] 'Sculpture is at centre of Festive Fun', *Oswestry Advertiser*, 9 December 1992, p. 16.
[157] Sue Lary, 'Tribute to Stand the Test of Time', *Rugby Advertiser*, 8 September 1988, p. 17.
[158] 'Programme for the Unveiling of the Statue of Field Marshal Viscount Slim of Yarralumla and Bishopton, KG, GCB, GCMG, GBE, DSO, MC by H.M. The Queen', 28 April 1990, copy, IRJ Papers, Archives, HMI, Leeds.
[159] General Sir Martin Farndale (Master Gunner, St James's Park, 1988–96) to Field Marshal Lord Carver, 22 March 1991, Alanbrooke Memorial File, Alanbrooke Papers, Liddel Hart Centre for Military Archives, King's College, London.
[160] Byron Rogers, 'Public Men, Private Faces: The Last of the Great Icon-Makers: Ivor Roberts-Jones', *Sunday Telegraph*, 27 June 1993, p. 5.
[161] His Hon. Judge Bruce Griffiths OC to IRJ, 3 July 1994, IRJ Papers, Archives, HMI, Leeds. Corrine Roberts-Jones (1946–96) studied at Folkestone School of Art, where she met and married the painter Ken Back (1944–2002) in 1971. They had two children, Caroline and Edmund. However, early in 1994 she fell seriously ill and died a few months before her father in 1996.
[162] Milan Jakobec (Embassy of the Czech Republic, London) to IRJ, August 1995, IRJ Papers, Archives, HMI, Leeds.
[163] 'Ivor Roberts-Jones, Obituary', *Daily Telegraph*, 13 December 1996, p. 29.
[164] Kyffin Williams to Monica Roberts-Jones, 16 December 1996, IRJ Papers, Archives, HMI, Leeds.
[165] Brian Morley to the *Guardian*, 24 December 1996, p. 12.
[166] 'Ivor Roberts-Jones', *The Times*, 14 December 1996, p. 21.
[167] John W. Mills interview with Dr J. Black, 12 April 2011; Brian Jarvis interview with Dr J. Black, 5 May 2011.
[168] Etienne Millner FRBS (current president of the Society of Portrait Sculptors) interview with Dr J. Black, 16 January 2012; John W. Mills FRBS (past president of the Royal British Society of Sculptors) interview with Dr J. Black, 12 April 2011; Martin Jennings FRBS interview with Dr J. Black, 6 December 2012.

Chapter Two

[1] 'Ivor Roberts-Jones', *The Times*, 14 December 1996, p. 21.
[2] Sir John Rothenstein, 'Ivor Roberts-Jones, II', *The Artist*, October 1978, p. 33.
[3] Isabel Hitchman (formerly arts officer, Welsh Arts Council) interview with Dr S. Ayres, 17 August 2012.
[4] IRJ interview with Byron Rogers, *Sunday Telegraph*, 27 June 1993, p. 5; Press Clippings, IRJ Papers, Archives, HMI, Leeds.
[5] IRJ on Rembrandt in the *RA Magazine*, Autumn 1985, p. 25, clipping, IRJ File, Archives, Royal Academy, London.
[6] IRJ interview with Byron Rogers, *Sunday Telegraph*, 27 June 1993, p. 5, Press Clippings, IRJ Papers, Archives, HMI, Leeds.
[7] *Illustrated London News*, 27 March 1971, p. 12, Press Clippings, IRJ Papers, Archives, HMI, Leeds.
[8] IRJ to Judge Bruce Griffiths, c. March 1994, IRJ Papers, Archives, HMI, Leeds.
[9] IRJ interview with Ian Collins in the *Eastern Daily Press*, 4 January 1994, p. 6; Press Clippings, Archives, HMI, Leeds.
[10] Ivor praised the overtly 'caricatural' style of Gillray and Schiele to many of his students while teaching at Goldsmiths College. Brian Morley interview with Dr J. Black, 14 April 2011, and Etienne Millner interview with Dr J. Black, 16 January 2012.
[11] IRJ interview with Byron Rogers, *Sunday Telegraph*, 27 June 1993, p. 5, Press Clippings, IRJ Papers, Archives, HMI, Leeds.
[12] Ivor Roberts-Jones, 'Introduction', *Ivor Roberts-Jones: Sculpture 27 July–2 September 1978* (Cardiff: Oriel Gallery, Welsh Arts Council, 1978), unpaginated.
[13] Sir John Rothentsein, 'Ivor Roberts-Jones, I', *The Artist*, September 1978, p. 14.
[14] Ibid., p. 12.
[15] Peter Cannon-Brookes, *Ivor Roberts-Jones: The Road to Harlech* (London: Trefoil Books, 1983), p. 25.
[16] Brian Morley interview with Dr J. Black, 14 April 2011. Mr Morley studied drawing under Ivor at Goldsmiths, c. 1954–56, and recalls him urging his students to study the portraiture of Klimt, Schiele and Kokoschka.
[17] Ivor had been introduced to Kokoschka in London in the late 1940s by their mutual friend Kyffin Williams. David Meredith and John Smith, *Obsessed: The Biography of Kyffin Williams* (Ceredigion: Gomer Press, 2012), p. 109.
[18] Cannon-Brookes, *Ivor Roberts-Jones*, p. 23.
[19] Ibid.
[20] Ibid.
[21] IRJ to Raymond Erith, 17 October 1956, Raymond Erith Papers, RIBA Archives, Victoria and Albert Museum, London.
[22] Cannon-Brookes, *Ivor Roberts-Jones*, p. 23.
[23] Chris Stephens, ed., *Henry Moore* (London: Tate Publishing, 2010), p. 127.
[24] Belsky, for example, was on the short lists with Ivor in 1970 for the *Winston Churchill* statue in Parliament Square and in 1977 for the figure of *Clement Attlee* in the House of Commons. On the other hand, in 1995 Belsky recommended Ivor to a committee in Prague who wanted to commission a statue of Churchill for a square in the city.
[25] IRJ, Autobiographical Notes, c. March 1990, IRJ Papers, Archives, HMI, Leeds. Ivor recalled that in the 1960s he had admired Marini's bronze head of Moore when it was donated to the National Portrait Gallery in 1969. But he had been even more impressed by Marini's head of one of Ivor's favourite composers, Stravinsky.
[26] The term 'rock and roll' entered the lexicon of the British press shortly after 'Rock Around the Clock', by Bill Haley and the Comets, entered the British charts in November 1955. Dominic Sandbrook, *Never Had It So Good: A History of Britain from Suez to the Beatles* (London: Little Brown, 2005), p. 431.
[27] John Osborne's *Look Back in Anger* opened in May 1956; by July that year the *Daily Express* had taken to referring to Osborne and novelist Kingsley Amis as 'angry young men'. Sandbrook, *Never Had It So Good*, p. 166.
[28] Kyffin Williams to Robert 'Rollo' Charles (Keeper of Art, NMW, Cardiff), c. March 1960, IRJ File, Archives, NMW, Cardiff.
[29] Kyffin Williams to Rollo Charles, c. April 1960, IRJ File, Archives, NMW, Cardiff.
[30] IRJ to Kyffin Williams, c. April 1960, A1/6/98, Williams Papers, National Library of Wales, Aberystwyth.
[31] Kyffin Williams, *Across The Straits: An Autobiography* (Ceredigion: Gomer Press, 2009), pp. 173–4.
[32] IRJ to Dr Peter Cannon-Brookes, 29 December 1981, IRJ 1983 Exhibition File, Archives, NMW, Cardiff.
[33] IRJ to Dr Peter Cannon-Brookes, 7 June 1983, IRJ 1983 Exhibition File, Archives, NMW, Cardiff
[34] Rothenstein, 'Ivor Roberts-Jones, II', p. 14.
[35] John Lehmann, ed., *Demetrios Capetanakis: A Greek Poet in England* (London: John Lehmann, 1947), p. 26.
[36] Ibid., p. 30.
[37] Ibid., p. 181.
[38] Andre Vauchez, *Francis of Assisi: The Life and Afterlife of a Medieval Saint* (New Haven and London: Yale University Press, 2012), p. 129.
[39] IRJ to Dr Peter Cannon-Brookes, 21 March 1983, IRJ File, Archives, NMW, Cardiff.
[40] Rothenstein, 'Ivor Roberts-Jones, II', p. 14.
[41] The work, alongside an announcement of the purchase by the Tate Gallery, was reproduced in *The Times*, 25 July 1960, p. 3.
[42] Max Aitken, First Lord Beaverbrook (1879–1964), ennobled 1917, owner of the *Daily Express* from 1916, and of the *London Evening Standard* from 1921.
[43] IRJ to Robert Lamb, 8 April 1977, Archives, Beaverbrook Art Gallery, Fredericton, New Brunswick, Canada.
[44] There is a distinct possibility that Ivor was also brought to Beaverbrook's attention by Sir John Rothenstein, who had been acting since 1956 as an adviser to the newspaperman for purchases to the new Beaverbrook Art Gallery, which opened in Beaverbrook's native New Brunswick in 1959. Indeed, in September 1961, shortly after Beaverbrook first approached Ivor regarding the Maugham commission, he invited Rothenstein to visit the new art gallery, and ensured that the University of New Brunswick awarded Sir John an honorary degree. John Rothenstein, *Brave Day, Hideous Night: An Autobiography, 1939–1965* (London: Hamish Hamilton, 1966), pp. 369–72.
[45] Anne Chisholm and Michael Davie, *Beaverbrook: A Life* (London: Hutchinson, 1992), p. 499.
[46] Ibid., p. 473.
[47] Ivor to Kyffin Williams, 3 August 1978, A1/10/22, Williams Papers, National Library of Wales, Aberystwyth.

48 Selina Hastings, *The Secret Lives of Somerset Maugham* (London: John Murray, 2010), pp. 519–20.
49 Ibid., p. 521
50 Ibid., pp. 526–7.
51 David Kynaston, *Family Britain: 1951–57* (London: Bloomsbury, 2009), p. 516.
52 Ibid., p. 608. Maugham had denounced Amis and the influence of the 'Angry Young Men' in the *Sunday Times* in December 1955.
53 Cannon-Brookes, *Ivor Roberts-Jones*, p. 47.
54 *Guardian*, 15 August 1978, Press Clippings, Library, NMW, Cardiff.
55 IRJ to Roger Lamb, 8 April 1978, Archives, Beaverbrook Art Gallery, New Brunswick, Canada.
56 IRJ interview with Byron Rogers, *Sunday Telegraph*, 27 June 1993, p. 5.
57 Hastings, *Secret Lives of Somerset Maugham*, p. 509.
58 Ibid., p. 530.
59 IRJ to Margaret Wagstaff, 2 May 1984, Archives, Arts Council, London.
60 Ibid.
61 Frances Morris, *Paris Post-War: Art and Existentialism, 1945–1955* (London: Tate Publications, 1993), pp. 89–100.
62 IRJ to Rollo Charles (Keeper of Art, NMW, Cardiff), c. January 1974, IRJ File, Archives, NMW, Cardiff.
63 *Guardian*, 29 February 2012, p. 24.
64 *Daily Telegraph*, 7 March 2012, p. 18.
65 *Daily Telegraph*, 20 May 1987, p. 26.
66 Humphrey Burton, *Menuhin* (London: Penguin, 2001), p. 369.
67 Ibid., p. 404.
68 Cannon-Brookes, *Ivor Roberts-Jones*, p. 69.
69 *Illustrated London News*, 27 March 1971, p. 12, Press Clippings, IRJ Papers, Archives, HMI, Leeds.
70 IRJ to Rollo Charles (Keeper of Art, NMW, Cardiff), 6 December 1971, IRJ File, Archives, NMW, Cardiff.
71 A/CE/A/13/2, papers related to the Duke of Edinburgh's tenure as Society president, 1966–1981, Archives, Royal College of General Practitioners, London.
72 June Shepherd, *Norfolk and Suffolk Express*, 22 May 1987, p. 22, Press Clippings, IRJ Papers, Archives, HMI, Leeds.
73 IRJ interview with Byron Rogers, *Sunday Telegraph*, 27 June 1993, p. 5, Press Clippings, IRJ Papers, Archives, HMI, Leeds.
74 Dr Peter Cannon-Brookes, interview with Dr J. Black, 3 May 2013.
75 Meredith and Smith, *Obsessed*, p. 147.
76 Gerder Roper, 'Ivor Roberts-Jones at the Oriel Gallery', *Western Mail*, 5 August 1978, Press Clippings, IRJ Papers, Archives, HMI, Leeds.
77 IRJ to Dr Mark Evans (Acting Keeper of Art, NMW, Cardiff), 28 June 1987, IRJ File, Archives, NMW, Cardiff.
78 IRJ to Dr Mark Evans (Acting Keeper of Art, NMW, Cardiff), 22 April 1987, IRJ File, Archives, NMW, Cardiff.
79 Entry for 21 June 1978, IRJ Diary for 1978, IRJ Papers, Archives, HMI, Leeds.
80 Giardelli taught art and art history at University College of Wales, Aberystwyth, sat on the Welsh Arts Council (1965–75), and worked for BBC Wales during the 1960s. For many years he was the chairman of the moderately modernist '1956' Group of Welsh Painters. Meredith and Smith, *Obsessed*, p. 227.
81 Dr Richard Edgcumbe (Registrar, NMW, Cardiff) to IRJ, 16 October 1984, IRJ File, Archives, NMW, Cardiff. The cast of the head of Rees was purchased at the behest of the Keeper of Art, Dr Peter Cannon-Brookes.
82 Entry for 30 December 1980, IRJ Diary for 1980, IRJ Papers, Archives, HMI, Leeds.
83 John Davies, *A History of Wales* (London: Penguin, 2007), pp. 649–52.
84 Yolande Bird (secretary to the board of the National Theatre) to Lord Mishcon, 3 August 1978, Archives, National Theatre, London.
85 Yolande Bird to Lord Mishcon, 18 September 1978, Archives, National Theatre, London.
86 Yolande Bird to Lord Mishcon, 26 October 1978, Archives, National Theatre, London.
87 Entry for 5 March 1979, IRJ Diary for 1979, IRJ Papers, Archives, HMI, Leeds.
88 IRJ to Yolande Bird, 5 April 1979, Archives, National Theatre, London.
89 Second Viscount Chandos to Franta Belsky, 24 October 1979, Archives, National Theatre Archives, London.
90 Second Lord Chandos to Yolande Bird, 26 October 1979, Archives, National Theatre, London.
91 Yolande Bird to the Second Lord Chandos, 1 November 1979, Archives, National Theatre, London.
92 Dr Peter Cannon-Brookes, interview with Dr J. Black, 3 May 2013.
93 Judge Bruce Griffiths QC interview in the *South Wales Echo*, 28 January 1984, p. 5; Press Clippings, Library, NMW, Cardiff.
94 Ivor may have been introduced to Thomas already in November 1979, when the Speaker officiated at the unveiling in the Members' Lobby of the House of Commons of Ivor's full-length 2.74-metre-high bronze figure of *Clement Attlee* (cat. 143).
95 IRJ to Kyffin Williams, 8 February 1980, A1/12/4, Williams Papers, National Library of Wales.
96 IRJ to Yolande Bird, 27 August 1980, Archives, National Theatre, London.
97 'Achnaton' was the radical Pharaoh Akhenaten/Amenhotep IV (1351–34 BCE), who overthrew centuries of precedent to introduce a new state religion to Ancient Egypt.
98 IRJ to Robin Gibson (curator of twentieth-century British art, National Portrait Gallery, London), 27 February 1983, IRJ Acquisition File, Archives, NPG, London.
99 IRJ interview with Ian Collins, *Eastern Daily Press*, 4 January 1994, p. 6, Press Clippings, IRJ Papers, HMI, Leeds.
100 'George Thomas, Lord Tonypandy: Obituary', *Guardian*, 23 September 1997, p. 16, Press Clippings, Library, NMW, Cardiff.
101 The referendum to recommend devolution for Wales took place on 1 March 1979. Barely 12 per cent voted 'yes'. Andy Beckett, *When the Lights Went Out: What Really Happened to Britain in the Seventies* (London: Faber & Faber, 2009), pp. 502–3.
102 IRJ interview with Byron Rogers, *Sunday Telegraph*, 27 June 1993, p. 5, Press Clippings, IRJ Papers, HMI, Leeds.
103 IRJ to Dr Richard Edgecumbe (Registrar, NMW, Cardiff), November 1985, IRJ File, Archives, NMW, Cardiff.
104 Ivor owned a postcard depicting this very work; IRJ Papers, Archives, HMI, Leeds.
105 IRJ to Dr Richard Edgecumbe (Registrar, NMW, Cardiff), 12 January 1985, IRJ File, Archives, NMW, Cardiff.

[106] Bridget Heriz-Smith email to Dr J. Black, 22 February 2013.
[107] Ibid.
[108] Sir Nicholas Proctor Goodison, 'Sitting for a Portrait', notes dated September 2000, private collection.
[109] Ian Jones (arts officer, Oriel Ynys Môn) email to Dr J. Black, 25 February 2013.
[110] Meredith and Smith, *Obsessed*, p. 150.
[111] Entry for 12 December 1978, IRJ Diary, IRJ Papers, Archives, HMI, Leeds.
[112] Judge Bruce Griffiths to IRJ, c. March 1995, IRJ Papers, Archives, HMI, Leeds.
[113] Judge Bruce Griffiths to IRJ, 3 July 1995, IRJ Papers, Archives, HMI, Leeds.
[114] IRJ interview with Ian Collins in the *Eastern Daily Press*, 4 January 1994, p. 6; Press Clippings, IRJ Papers, Archives, HMI, Leeds.
[115] 'Ivor Roberts-Jones', *Daily Telegraph*, 13 December 1996, p. 29; Terence Mullaly, 'Ivor Roberts-Jones', *Guardian*, 24 December 1996, p. 12, Press Clippings, IRJ Papers, HMI, Leeds.
[116] Ivor's portraiture is held in high regard by the current president of the Society of Portrait Sculptors (SPS), Etienne Millner, and also by Society member Martin Jennings. Etienne Millner interview with Dr J. Black, 16 January 2012, and Martin Jennings interview with Dr J. Black, 8 April 2013.
[117] Nigel Doonham (former president of the SPS), 'Ivor Roberts-Jones CBE, RA', *Catalogue to the 43rd Annual Exhibition of the Society of Portrait Sculptors* (London, May 2006), pp. 58–68.

Chapter Three

[1] IRJ interview with *Royal Academy Magazine*, Winter 1985, p. 51; clipping IRJ File, Archives, Royal Academy, London.
[2] *The Times*, 14 December 1996, p. 21.
[3] Rt Hon. George Osborne MP, email to Dr J. Black, 4 June 2013.
[4] IRJ File, Archives, Royal Academy, London.
[5] IRJ interview with Byron Rogers, *Sunday Telegraph*, 27 June 1993, p.5; Press Clippings File, IRJ Papers, Archives, HMI, Leeds.
[6] IRJ interview with Bryon Rogers, *Daily Telegraph*, 12 January 1973, Press Clippings File, IRJ Papers, Archives, HMI, Leeds.
[7] IRJ interview with June Shepherd, *Norfolk and Suffolk Express*, 22 May 1987, p. 22, Press Clippings File, IRJ Papers, Archives, HMI, Leeds.
[8] IRJ interview with Bryon Rogers, *Daily Telegraph*, 12 January 1973, Press Clippings File, IRJ Papers, Archives, HMI, Leeds.
[9] Paul Hubbard interview with Dr S. Ayres, 11 June 2012.
[10] IRJ Autobiographical Notes to Dr Peter Cannon-Brookes, 29 December 1981, IRJ File, Archives, NMW, Cardiff.
[11] Winston S. Churchill, 'Cartoons and Cartoonists', originally published in the *Strand Magazine*, June 1931, reprinted in James W. Miller, ed., *Winston Churchill: Thoughts and Adventures* (Wilmington, DE: ISI Books, 2009 [1932]), pp. 24–7.
[12] Ibid, p. 30. Churchill believed that the visual origin for the cartoonists' preference to depict him wearing hats that were comically too small for him could be traced to a photograph taken of him 'at Southport during the General Election of [February] 1910'.
[13] Ibid., p. 22.
[14] Dennis Wardleworth, *William Reid Dick, Sculptor* (Farnham: Ashgate, 2013), p. 200.
[15] June Rose, *Daemons and Angels: A Life of Jacob Epstein* (London: Constable & Robinson, 2002), pp. 230–1.
[16] John Ramsden, *Man of the Century: Winston Churchill and his Legend since 1945* (London: HarperCollins, 2003), pp. 110–11.
[17] *Hansard*, 3 July 1969, p. 63.
[18] Tilney (1907–1994), educated at Eton and Magdalen College, Oxford, was Conservative MP for Liverpool Wavertree between 1950 and 1974. He was knighted early in 1973.
[19] Rodgers (1906–1993) was Conservative MP for Sevenoaks (1950–79) and was knighted in 1970. He had been, from the early 1920s, a close friend of one of Churchill's closest acolytes former Conservative MP and wartime Minister of Information (1941–45) Brenden Bracken (1901–1958).
[20] Nemon's statue in the Members' Lobby is only accessible to the public when the House of Commons is not sitting; when it is sitting, individuals may view it if they are accompanied by their Member of Parliament. Sir John Tilney to Lady Clementine Spencer-Churchill, 29 March 1968, copy – Papers of Duncan Sandys, Churchill Archive, Churchill College, Cambridge.
[21] Sir John Tilney to Harold Wilson, 18 December 1967, copy, Department of the Environment, PWO 1/105 AD, National Archives, Kew Gardens, London.
[22] *Hansard*, 3 July 1969, p. 638.
[23] Edwin Duncan Sandys (1908–1987): married to Diana Churchill (1935–1960), minister in Conservative government of 1951–64 and Conservative MP for Streatham (1951–74).
[24] Arnold Goodman (1915–1995): Labour Party-supporting lawyer, adviser to Prime Minister Harold Wilson (1964–76), chairman of the Arts Council (1965–72); created a Life Peer in 1965 and made a Companion of Honour in 1972.
[25] Emmanuel 'Manny' Shinwell (1884–1986): Labour MP for Easington in County Durham (1951–86); Minister for Fuel and Power in Attlee's government, then Secretary of State for War, and finally Minister of Defence, 1945–51. Created Baron Shinwell in 1970.
[26] George Strauss (1901–1993): Labour MP for Lambeth North (1934–50) and Vauxhall (1950–79). Minister of Supply in Attlee's government (1947–51); created a Life Peer in 1979.
[27] Meeting of the WCMC, 23 September 1969, copy, Papers of Duncan Sandys, Churchill Archive, Churchill College, Cambridge.
[28] Report to the WCMC by John Tilney, 23 February 1970, copy, Papers of Duncan Sandys, Churchill Archive, Churchill College, Cambridge.
[29] Meeting of the WCMC, 25 February 1970, copy, Papers of Duncan Sandys, Churchill Archive, Churchill College, Cambridge.
[30] Meeting of the WCMC Adjudication Sub-Committee, 19 March 1970, copy, Papers of Duncan Sandys, Churchill Archive, Churchill College, Cambridge.
[31] Patricia Strauss was for many years chairwoman of the London County Council Parks Department and, in 1948, a key proponent of the LCC's 'Sculpture in the Open Air' series of exhibitions.

[32] George Strauss to John Tilney, 23 April 1970, Department of the Environment, PWO1/105 AD, National Archives, Kew Gardens, London.

[33] Entry for 24 April 1953, Lord Moran, *Winston Churchill: The Struggle for Survival* (London: Sphere Books, 1968), pp. 427–8.

[34] Entry for 15 June 1954, Moran, *Winston Churchill*, p. 583.

[35] Meeting of the WCMC Adjudication Sub-Committee, 1 July 1970, copy, Papers of Duncan Sandys, Churchill Archive, Churchill College, Cambridge.

[36] Meeting of the WCMC Adjudication Sub-Committee, 3 November 1970, copy, Papers of Duncan Sandys, Churchill Archive, Churchill College, Cambridge.

[37] IRJ to Kyffin Williams, 3 August 1978, A1/10/22, Williams Papers, National Library of Wales, Aberystwyth.

[38] Entry for 30 November 1954, Moran, *Winston Churchill*, p. 652.

[39] Ibid., p. 653.

[40] Ibid., pp. 653–4.

[41] IRJ interview with Byron Rogers, *Sunday Telegraph*, 27 June 1993, p. 5, Press Clippings File, IRJ Papers, Archives, HMI, Leeds.

[42] IRJ interview with *Royal Academy Magazine*, Autumn 1985, p. 25; clipping, IRJ File, Archives, Royal Academy, London.

[43] Richard Holmes, *In The Footsteps of Churchill* (London: BBC Books, 2006), pp. 55–60.

[44] Ibid., pp. 65–7.

[45] Winston S. Churchill, *My Early Life* (London: Eland, 2002 [1930]), pp. 189–92.

[46] Holmes, *In the Footsteps of Churchill*, pp. 152–4.

[47] IRJ interview with Ian Collins, *Eastern Daily Press*, 4 January 1994, p. 6, Press Clippings File, IRJ Papers, Archives, HMI, Leeds.

[48] IRJ interview with *Illustrated London News*, 27 March 1971, p. 12, Press Clippings File, IRJ Papers, Archives, HMI, Leeds.

[49] Juliet Gardiner, *The Blitz: The British Under Attack* (London: Harper Press, 2010), pp. 344–7.

[50] Entry for 11 May 1941, Jock Colville, *The Fringes of Power: Downing Street Diaries, 1939–1945* (London: Phoenix, 2004 [1985]), pp. 333–4.

[51] Guy Eden, 'Churchill in High Office', in *Churchill by His Contemporaries* (London: Reprint Society, 1955), pp. 62–3.

[52] Ruth Butler, *Rodin: The Shape of Genius* (New Haven/London: Yale University Press, 1993), pp. 302–17. Ivor appears to have been particularly interested in Rodin's full-sized plaster model of Balzac exhibited at the Paris Salon in April 1898.

[53] John Blackwood, *London's Immortals: The Complete Outdoor Commemorative Statues* (London: Savoy Press, 1989), p. 222.

[54] Ibid. In 1978 Ivor had indicated to Sir John Rothenstein: 'It is a personal belief of mine that the magnificent Egyptian hawk owned by Rodin was very much in his mind when he conceived the *Balzac*. The leaning backwards stance, the helmet-like force of the brow as it folds down over the stubby beak of the nose and the ample breast – all are closely paralleled in the small hawk.' However, on this occasion he did not proceed to link the Egyptian hawk and Rodin's *Balzac* explicitly to his Parliament Square *Churchill*. Sir John Rothenstein, 'Ivor Roberts-Jones, II', *The Artist*, October 1978, p. 33.

[55] Ivor was well aware that Churchill had been a huge admirer of the veteran French politician who had taken over as prime minister, aged 76, in November 1917, when the French war effort was experiencing a severe crisis. Clemenceau was the subject of a riveting chapter in Churchill's book of essays, *Great Contemporaries*, published in 1937.

[56] Michael Shelden, *Young Titan: The Making of Winston Churchill* (London: Simon & Schuster, 2013), p. 168.

[57] Meeting of the WCMC Adjudication Sub-Committee, 3 November 1970, Papers of Duncan Sandys, Churchill Archive, Churchill College, Cambridge.

[58] F. Fielden (secretary of the RFAC) to John Tilney, 17 November 1970, copy, Papers of Duncan Sandys, Churchill Archive, Churchill College, Cambridge.

[59] John Tilney to Duncan Sandys, 10 December 1970, Papers of Duncan Sandys, Churchill Archive, Churchill College, Cambridge.

[60] IRJ interview with June Shepherd, *Norfolk and Suffolk Express*, 22 May 1987, p. 22, Press Clippings File, IRJ Papers, Archives, HMI, Leeds.

[61] Meeting of the WCMC, 2 February 1971, copy, Papers of Duncan Sandys, Churchill Archive, Churchill College, Cambridge.

[62] Ibid. Tilney indicated he had received word from Lady Clementine that she 'much preferred Mr Nemon's work'.

[63] Sarah Churchill to Lady Clementine Spencer-Churchill, 8 February 1971, NEMO 2/6, Papers of Oscar Nemon, Churchill Archive, Churchill College, Cambridge.

[64] Oscar Nemon to John Tilney, 15 February 1971, NEMO 2/6, Papers of Oscar Nemon, Churchill Archive, Churchill College, Cambridge.

[65] Meeting of the WCMC, 22 February 1971, copy, Papers of Duncan Sandys, Churchill Archive, Churchill College, Cambridge.

[66] IRJ interview with Ian Collins, *Eastern Daily Press*, 4 January 1994, p. 6, Press Clippings File, IRJ Papers, Archives, HMI, Leeds.

[67] Press Release from the WCMC, 16 March 1971, copy, Papers of Duncan Sandys, Churchill Archive, Churchill College, Cambridge.

[68] Michael Lake, 'Churchill Statue Sculptor Named', *Guardian*, 17 March 1971, p. 7.

[69] IRJ interview with the *Illustrated London News*, 27 March 1971, p. 12, Press Clippings File, IRJ Papers, Archives, HMI, Leeds.

[70] IRJ interview with John Windsor, *Guardian*, 23 February 1973, p. 10, Press Clippings File, IRJ Papers, Archives, HMI, Leeds.

[71] Ibid.

[72] IRJ interview with June Shepherd, *Norfolk and Suffolk Express*, 22 May 1987, p. 22, IRJ Press Clippings File, Archives, HMI, Leeds.

[73] Ibid.

[74] Ivor's student Brian Morley had noted his enthusiasm for German and Austrian Expressionism in the late 1950s. Brian Morley interview with Dr J. Black, 14 April 2011.

[75] Blackwood, *London's Immortals*, p. 225.

[76] Report from Richard Crawfurd-Benson to the WCMC, 5 March 1970, copy, Papers of Duncan Sandys, Churchill Archive, Churchill College, Cambridge.

[77] John Tilney to Duncan Sandys, 23 September 1971, Papers of Duncan Sandys, Churchill Archive, Churchill College, Cambridge.

[78] Ibid.

[79] Richard Crawfurd-Benson to Sir John Tilney, 24 February 1972, copy, Papers of Duncan Sandys, Churchill Archive, Churchill College, Cambridge.

[80] McFall had been one of the four sculptors who, in April 1969, nominated Ivor for election to the Royal Academy as an Associate. The other three were Charles Wheeler, James Woodford and Robert Buhler. Entry for 24 April 1969, Nominations Book for Associates, Archives, Royal Academy, London.

[81] Ramsden, *Man of the Century*, p. 111.
[82] Paul Hubbard interview with Dr S. Ayres, 11 June 2012.
[83] Ibid.
[84] IRJ interview with Byron Rogers, *Daily Telegraph*, 12 January 1973, Press Clippings, Department of the Environment, PWO 1/105 AD II, National Archives, Kew Gardens, London.
[85] IRJ interview with John Windsor, *Guardian*, 23 February 1973, p. 10.
[86] Richard Crawfurd-Benson to Sir John Tilney, 24 February 1972, copy, Papers of Duncan Sandys, Churchill Archive, Churchill College, Cambridge.
[87] Ivor thought Michael Gaskin of Art Bronze had done a 'superb job' regarding the casting of the second version of *Mrs Griffiths.* However, 'He just hasn't the facilities for Winston though, unfortunately.' IRJ to Rollo Charles (Keeper of Art, NMW, Cardiff), c. July 1972, IRJ File, Archives, NMW, Cardiff.
[88] IRJ Testimonial for the Meridian Foundry, 12 July 1993, Meridian Foundry Archives, courtesy of Megan Crofton Thomas.
[89] Richard Crawfurd-Benson to Sir John Tilney, 7 April 1972, copy, Papers of Duncan Sandys, Churchill Archive, Churchill College, Cambridge.
[90] Paul Hubbard interview with Dr S. Ayres.
[91] Kyffin Williams, 'Ivor Roberts-Jones', *Christies: Twentieth Century British Art*, auction catalogue (London: Christies South Kensington, 24 November 2005), p. 31.
[92] Richard Crawfurd-Benson to Sir John Tilney, 7 April 1972, copy, Papers of Duncan Sandys, Churchill Archive, Churchill College, Cambridge.
[93] Entry for 15 October 1951 in Moran, *Winston Churchill*, p. 371.
[94] Entry for 26 September 1939 in Nigel Nicolson, ed., *The Harold Nicolson Diaries: 1907–1964* (London: Phoenix, 2005), p. 228.
[95] Entry for 6 November 1942 in ibid., p. 301.
[96] Richard Crawfurd-Benson to John Tilney, 7 April 1972, copy, Papers of Duncan Sandys, Churchill Archive, Churchill College, Cambridge.
[97] John Tilney to Duncan Sandys, 5 May 1972, Papers of Duncan Sandys, Churchill Archive, Churchill College, Cambridge.
[98] John Tilney, Progress Report to the WCMC, 26 October 1972, copy, Papers of Duncan Sandys, Churchill Archive, Churchill College, Cambridge.
[99] John Tilney, Progress Report to the WCMC, 22 January 1973, copy, Papers of Duncan Sandys, Churchill Archive, Churchill College, Cambridge. In making the plaster cast Ivor was assisted considerably by assistants John Dellow and Paul Hubbard.
[100] Ibid.
[101] Richard Crawfurd-Benson to Winston Churchill MP (Churchill's grandson), 28 February 1973, copy, Papers of Duncan Sandys, Churchill Archive, Churchill College, Cambridge.
[102] John Tilney, Progress Report for the WCMC, 11 June 1973, copy, Papers of Duncan Sandys, Churchill Archive, Churchill College, Cambridge. The Meridian Foundry stood on Consort Road, Peckham.
[103] IRJ interview with Bryon Rogers, *Daily Telegraph*, 12 January 1973, Department of the Environment, PWO 1/105 AD II, National Archives, Kew Gardens, London.
[104] Ibid.
[105] Ibid.
[106] John Tilney, Progress Report for the WCMC, 21 June 1973, copy, Papers of Duncan Sandys, Churchill Archive, Churchill College, Cambridge.
[107] Sir John Tilney quoted in *The Times*, 2 November 1973, p. 2.
[108] Ibid.
[109] *The Times*, 6 November 1973, p. 21. Wheeler, Woodford and McFall had all voted for Ivor to become an ARA in 1969 and, in December 1973, for him to be raised to the status of full Academician. Entry for 9 December 1973, Nominations Book for Academicians, Archives, Royal Academy, London.
[110] IRJ to George Pearce (director of works and principal architect, Department of the Environment), 10 November 1973, WORK 17/801, National Archives, Kew Gardens, London.
[111] George Pearce to IRJ, 15 November 1973, WORK 17/801, National Archives, Kew Gardens, London.
[112] Walker apparently purchased one of the 1,500 bronze casts of Ivor's original maquette of his Churchill statue, which the WCMC marketed from September 1974 to raise funds for the Churchill Foundation. *The Times*, 12 September 1974, p. 11.
[113] Dominic Sandbrook, *Seasons in the Sun: The Battle of Britain, 1974–1979* (London: Penguin, 2012), pp. 134–40.
[114] John Campbell, *Margaret Thatcher, Volume II: The Iron Lady* (London: Pimlico, 2004), p. 515.
[115] Mark Garnett, *From Anger to Apathy: The Story of Politics, Society and Popular Culture in Britain since 1975* (London: Vintage, 2008), p. 330.
[116] From Wilde's novel *The Picture of Dorian Gray* (1890). Churchill was not above appropriating some of Wilde's bons mots for himself, such as, in 1948: 'My tastes are simple, I am easily satisfied with the best', derived from Wilde's 'I have the simplest tastes, I am always satisfied with the very best', uttered early in the 1890s. Peter Clarke, *Mr Churchill's Profession: Statesman, Orator, Writer* (London: Bloomsbury, 2012), pp. 109–10.
[117] Churchill first mentioned the 'Black Dog' in a letter he wrote to his wife Clementine in July 1911, but it is implied that he had referred already to the beast in their previous correspondence. Andrew Norman, *Winston Churchill: Portrait of an Unquiet Mind* (Barnsley: Pen & Sword, 2012), pp. 66–7.
[118] Ironically, Churchill had, from 1941 to 1945, harboured serious doubts about the ethics and military efficacy of the RAF's strategy of 'area bombing'. In February 1945, after the destruction visited upon Dresden, he had tried to place some distance between himself and that policy. Max Hastings, *Finest Years: Churchill as Warlord, 1940–45* (London: Harper Press, 2009), pp. 558–63.
[119] IRJ interview with June Shepherd in the *Norfolk and Suffolk Express*, 22 May 1987, p. 22, Press Clippings File, Archives, HMI, Leeds.
[120] IRJ interviewed by Byron Rogers, *Sunday Telegraph*, 27 June 1993, p. 5, Press Clippings File, IRJ Papers, Archives, HMI, Leeds.
[121] IRJ interview with Ian Collins, *Eastern Daily Press*, 4 January 1994, p. 6, Press Clippings File, IRJ Papers, Archives, HMI, Leeds.

Chapter Four

[1] The Austrian writer Robert Musil famously observed that there is nothing as invisible as a monument. R. Musil, *Prosa Dramen, Späte Briefe*, ed. Adolf Frisé (Hamburg: Rowohlt, 1957).

[2] The concepts of nation, state and nation-state are discussed in E.J. Hobsbawm, *Nations and Nationalism since 1780: Programme, Myth, Reality* (Cambridge: Cambridge University Press, 1990) and in B. Anderson, *Imagined Communities: Reflections on the Origin and Spread of Nationalism* (London/New York: Verso, 1991).

[3] Benedict Anderson argues that the nation is an 'imagined political community', limited and sovereign. Anderson, *Imagined Communities*, pp. 6–7. 'In fact, all communities larger than primordial villages of face-to-face contact (and perhaps even these) are imagined' (p. 6). The community imagined by the Churchill statues is transnational, but guaranteed by the common concept of nation and the rights of limited sovereign nations to their inalienable integrity.

[4] Gunnar Sønsteby was the most highly decorated Norwegian Resistance fighter active during the Second World War. He became SOE Agent 24 after he crossed the border into Sweden and offered his services to the British embassy there. He spent time training in Britain in 1942, and on his return to Oslo in 1943 organised a series of successful and strategic sabotage operations. At the time of writing, plans appeared to be in place to move the statue of Gunnar Sønsteby to the more prominent Karl Johans Gate.

[5] See G. Sørensen, *Fargelegg byen! Oslo kommunes utsmykninger* (Oslo: Kommune Kulturetaten, 2009).

[6] Norway's famously joyful mass celebrations on its national day, 17 May, which commemorate the signing of the Norwegian National Constitution at Eidsvoll on 17 May 1814, also demonstrate the pristine newness of its national identity.

[7] In 1995 Roberts-Jones wrote to a client, offering another perspective on the brief for the Oslo commission: 'I was asked to make a Winston for Oslo – they wanted exactly the same pose but the head was to be more that of a great statesman. Also it was to be slightly smaller ...' IRJ Papers, 2005.456/C/1/8/28, Archives, HMI, Leeds.

[8] '-En anderledes Churchill-statue', in *Aftenposten*, 8 September 1975, p. 4.

[9] 'Jeg tror nordmenn ser anderledes på Churchill enn engelskmenn flest. Vi ser på ham som krigslederen, som en bastion mot farene som truet vårt land direkte. For nordmenn er han mer menneskelig, mannen som kjempet for frihet og rett generelt. Derfor er London-monumentet av mer architektonisk virkning, mer av krigssymbolet. ... Det måtte bli en anderledes Churchill i Oslo enn i London.' *Aftenposten*, 8 September 1975, p. 4.

[10] Winston Churchill, 1941. Copyprint, New York World-Telegram & Sun Collection, Prints and Photographs Division, Library of Congress (118), at www.loc.gov/pictures/item/2004666491.

[11] 'Det var like efter at deler av parliaments-bygningen var bombet og lagt i grus. På bildet så jeg Churchill akkurat slik som jeg fremstiller ham i Oslo. Han sto midt i ruinene, det var ingen krige i vanlig forstang, men et menneske fylt av sorg og fortvilelse over at vi i det hele tatt var nodt til å fore en slik krig.... Derfor er det blitt noe mer trist over hele holdningen enn jeg matte gjøre i London-utgaven.' *Aftenposten*, 8 September 1975, p. 4.

[12] 'Teknisk sett er Oslo-monumentet røffere i utførelsen, grovere i detaljene og med et starkere preg av å vaere håndlaget.' Ibid.

[13] For more information, see C. Mann, *British Policy and Strategy towards Norway, 1941–45* (Basingstoke: Palgrave Macmillan, 2012).

[14] In 2000 Anton Smith-Meyer published *Forsoning I Vår Tid 1945–1980* or *It Was Time for Reconciliation*, on the history of reconciliation between Norway and Germany following the Second World War. See A. Smith-Meyer, *Forsoning i vår tid 1945–1980* (Oslo: Historieforlaget: Distribusjon, Forlagssentralen ANS, 2000).

[15] Letter from Frithjof Jacobsen, London, 14 July 1975, in Oslo Kulturetaten curatorial file.

[16] Michael Stewart, 'Labour's Role in Europe', *Daily Telegraph*, 7 July 1975, p. 28.

[17] National Archives, File No: FCO33/2603: WRY 18/1: Memo from R. G. Britten to C. Hulse on the Proposed Erection of Statue of Sir Winston Churchill in Oslo.

[18] Britten also informed London that 'the Ambassador has pointed out that if it proves possible to go firm on 5 May 1975 as the date for the unveiling, it would be desirable to let Mr Winston Churchill Jnr and Lady Churchill know as it would be very appropriate to ask them to attend the ceremony.' Ibid.

[19] Letter from Hans Høegh to Knut Frydlund, 16 December 1974, Norwegian National Archives, 078Ku.

[20] Memo from Alv Heltne, Finansdepartmentet, Norwegian National Archives, 616Ku75MØ:KV.

[21] 'Sakomslag for proposisjoner og meldinger til Stortinget', 13 June 1975, Norwegian National Archives, 616Ku.

[22] Letter from Alv Heltne to Hans Høegh, 23 June 1975, Norwegian National Archives, 2248Ku75 MØ:MB.

[23] 'Over 60,000 til statue', *Aftenposten*, 29 November 1974, pp. 1, 20.

[24] 'Churchill-monumentet har fått sin sokkel', *Aftenposten*, 3 December 1974, p. 40.

[25] 'Stor forståelse for å hedre Churchill', *Aftenposten*, 5 December 1974, p. 23.

[26] 'Nye bidrag til Churchill-statue', *Aftenposten*, 8 September 1975, p. 4. See also '144,000 kroner til Churchill-monument', *Aftenposten*, 17 December 1974, p. 10.

[27] 'Churchill-statuen til Oslo bestilt', *Aftenposten*, 27 February 1975, p. 42.

[28] Author interview with Odd Grann, 4 October 2012.

[29] A cast of Rodin's *Burghers of Calais* is situated in Victoria Tower Gardens underneath the west end of Westminster Palace. It was purchased by the state in 1911.

[30] Memo from IRJ, Oslo, 6 September 1975, p. 2, in Oslo Kulturetaten curatorial file.

[31] Letter from Christian Eitzen to the Fellessekfetariatet, 5 December 1975, in Oslo Kulturetaten curatorial file. This statement should be seen in the context of Norway's long history but comparatively recent existence as an independent nation with its own culture and constitution.

[32] Letter from John Engh to Hans Høegh, 19 January 1976, in Oslo Kulturetaten curatorial file.

[33] Letter from Dagfinn Austad to Bydelsutvalg 1, 20 January 1976, in Oslo Kulturetaten curatorial file.

[34] Letter from Kjell Lund, Oslo, 1 July 1975, p. 2, in Oslo Kulturetaten curatorial file.

[35] Letter from Skulpturkontoret, Norsk Billedhoggerforening, 21 February 1976, in Oslo Kulturetaten curatorial file.

[36] Letter from Bildende Kunstneres Styre, 26 February 1976, in Oslo Kulturetaten curatorial file.

[37] 'Churchill-monumentet avduket i Oslo', *Aftenposten*, 10 May 1976, p. 52; 'Churchill-statue i Oslo', Stavanger *Aftenblad*, 10 May 1976, p. 8.

[38] Interview with Odd Grann, 4 October 2012.

[39] Ibid.

[40] Ibid.

[41] George Lipsitz, 'New Orleans in the World and the World in New Orleans', *Black Music Research Journal* 31: 2 (Fall 2011), pp. 261–90, at p. 267.

[42] IRJ to Jack Crofton at the Meridian Foundry, 24 August 1976, in the collection of Megan Crofton.

[43] Author interview with James Coleman Jr, 22 October 2012.

[44] Kyffin Williams Papers, National Library of Wales, A1/9/1.

[45] Author interview with James Coleman Jr.

[46] J. Mark Souther, *New Orleans on Parade: Tourism and the Transformation of the Crescent City* (Louisiana: Louisiana State University Press, 2006); K. Fox Gotham, *Authentic New Orleans* (New York: NYU Press, 2007). New Orleans's 'authenticity' in the light of the many urban changes it has witnessed continues to be strongly debated. The development of New Orleans in the 1970s was contested by many different interest groups, not all of whom welcomed the International Rivercenter. J Mark Souther has described the development as 'Houstonization', meaning the development of a town into a large, modern, perhaps generic city: 'Like the Superdome [built in 1975] that anchored one end of Poydras Street, the tree-lined boulevard created to accommodate the city's office building boom, the "Houstonization" of downtown New Orleans also touched the river end of Poydras. There Lester Kabacoff managed to persuade the Dock Board to grant air rights atop its wharves for International Rivercenter, his planned riverfront complex anchored by a 1,200 room Hilton hotel.' Mark Souther, *New Orleans on Parade*, p. 177.

[47] Author interview with James Coleman Jr.

[48] K. Holliday, 'Whose City Hall Is It? Architecture and Identity in New Orleans', *Journal of Urban Design* 14: 3 (2009).

[49] Mark Souther, *New Orleans on Parade*, p. 171. See also TI07641106-TI07641109, 1343. Susan Stuntz – Box F, Tobacco Institute, UCSF Tobacco Archives.

[50] In fact Lester Kabacoff composed the letter. Kabacoff wrote to Mrs Helen Lorio in Landrieu's office enclosing a draft of the letter on 27 May 1976. See the file 'British Circle', New Orleans Public Library, Louisiana Division and the City Archives.

[51] Letter from Mayor Moon Landrieu to the American ambassador to Britain, 14 July 1976, 'British Circle', New Orleans Public Library, Louisiana Division and the City Archives.

[52] See G. Adamson and J. Pavitt, eds, *Postmodernism: Style and Subversion, 1970–1990* (London: V&A, 2011).

[53] M. Ball, 'A Bit of Old England Graces New Orleans', New Orleans *Times-Picayune*, 20 November 1977, p. 1.

[54] Author interview with James Coleman Jr, 22 October 2012.

[55] Ball, 'A Bit of Old England Graces New Orleans', p. 1.

[56] Author interview with James Coleman Jr, 22 October 2012.

[57] Ball, 'A Bit of Old England Graces New Orleans', p. 1.

[58] Author interview with James Coleman Jr, 22 October 2012.

[59] Author interview with Milan Jakobec, by telephone, 11 December 2012. Tomáš Mikeska and Milan Jakobec were interviewed with Kamil Janáček, then the most senior economist in Commerzbanka, 5 March 2013.

[60] The addition of a memorial should not be seen as an attempt to graft a permanent identity onto the square. The statue of a former Communist president that stood in the square until its renaming was taken down and disposed of. The plinth on which it stood was also removed, and the statue of Churchill sited on new coordinates.

[61] This list is given in the memorial booklet accompanying the inauguration, held in Žižkov Town Hall's archives.

[62] IRJ Papers, 2005.456/C/1/8/27, Archives, HMI, Leeds.

[63] Author interview, by telephone, with Milan Jakobec, 11 December 2012.

[64] Author interview with Milan Jakobec and Tomáš Mikeska at Žižkov Town Hall, 5 March 2013.

[65] Milan Jakobec, Czech Embassy, to IRJ, no date [probably mid August 1995], IRJ Papers, 2005.456/C/1/8/28, Archives, HMI, Leeds.

[66] IRJ to Milan Jakobec, 21 August 1995, IRJ Papers, 2005.456/C/1/8/32, Archives, HMI, Leeds.

[67] Author interview, by telephone, with Milan Jakobec, 11 December 2012.

[68] The presence of Antonín Zápotocký has been thoroughly effaced from the space of the square. A further effacement was suggested by one of the committee members during the project's planning stages. Presidium member Tomáš Pštross, the serving Czech ambassador to Oslo, suggested casting the statue from metal melted down from an old Communist monument – presumably that of Antonín Zápotocký's statue. IRJ Papers, 2005.456/C/1/8/26, Archives, HMI, Leeds. Megan Crofton asserts that Meridian would never have consented to cast a bronze from recycled metal, and that only quality ingots were used at the foundry, so this idea is not likely to have been realised.

[69] Author interview with Milan Jakobec and Tomáš Mikeska, 5 March 2013.

[70] Ibid.

[71] IRJ Papers, 2005.456/C/1/8/23, Archives, HMI, Leeds.

[72] The plaster cast for this last portrait of Churchill is now owned by Oswestry School.

[73] IRJ Papers, 2005.456/C/1/8/10, Archives, HMI, Leeds.

[74] IRJ Papers, 2005.456/C/1/8/7, Archives, HMI, Leeds.

[75] Prague File, Nigel Boonham, London.

[76] IRJ Papers, 2005.456/C/1/8/3, Archives, HMI, Leeds.

[77] Author interview with Milan Jakobec and Tomáš Mikeska, 5 March 2013.

[78] Author interview with Professor Kamil Janáček, 14 December 2012.

[79] Author interview with Milan Jakobec and Tomáš Mikeska, 5 March 2013.

[80] Ibid.

[81] L. Ward and K. Connolly, 'Czechs Look Back with Bittersweet Nostalgia', *Guardian*, Thursday, 18 November 1999. The full text of Lady Thatcher's speech can be found on the Margaret Thatcher Foundation website, at www.margaretthatcher.org/document/108384.

[82] Author interview with Milan Jakobec and Tomáš Mikeska, 5 March 2013.

[83] Ibid.

[84] Ibid.

[85] Ibid.

[86] J. L. Meikle and M. Orvell, 'Introduction', in their *Public Space and the Ideology of Place in American Culture* (Amsterdam: Rodopi, 2009), pp. 9–17, at p. 10.

[87] 'Protests Erupt in Violence: "Guerrilla Gardening" Action Turns Ugly with Looted Shops and Battles with Police', *Guardian*, 2 May 2000.

[88] www.channel4.com/info/press/news/channel-4-straitjackets-winston-churchill.

[89] Churchill did claim that he had 'taken more out of alcohol than alcohol had taken out of him'. Perhaps, it would be more accurate to describe him as 'alcohol dependent' rather than as a full-blown alcoholic. A. Norman, *Winston Churchill: Portrait of an Unquiet Mind* (Barnsley: Pen & Sword Military, 2012), p. 190.

[90] In his essay, 'The Work of Art in the Age of its Mechanical Reproducibility' (1936), Walter Benjamin argues that, under the right conditions, the proliferation of the artwork by means of film, photography and print contains the possibility of rendering the artwork newly available to the masses as a political tool. W. Benjamin, *Illuminations: Essays and Reflections*, ed. H. Arendt, trans. H. Zohn (New York: Schocken, 1968). See also A. Benjamin, ed., *Walter Benjamin and Art* (New York: Continuum, 2005).

[91] J. Winter, 'Sites of Memory and the Shadow of War', in A. Erll, A. Nünning and S.B. Young, eds, *Cultural Memory Studies: An International and Interdisciplinary Handbook* (Berlin/New York: Walter de Gruyter, 2008), p. 61.

[92] Ibid., p. 73.

Chapter Five

[1] *The Times*, 'The Monumental in Sculpture', 2 October 1956, p. 3.

[2] IRJ to Dr Peter Cannon-Brookes, 'Autobiographical Notes', 15 September 1982, IRJ File, Archives, NMW, Cardiff.

[3] W. Packer, B. Robertson and B. Martin, *Contemporary British Sculpture in Battersea Park* (London: Arts Council/London County Council, 1977), p. 8.

[4] Ivor was to meet King much later, in the early 1980s, when both sat as trustees for the Welsh Sculpture Trust, established in 1981. Ivor was somewhat surprised that they got on rather well.

[5] Packer et al., *Contemporary British Sculpture*, p. 10.

[6] IRJ to Sir John Rothenstein, 24 August 1977, Rothenstein Papers, Archives, Tate Britain, London.

[7] Butler was some seven months older than Ivor; it rather rankled with him that Butler appeared to have achieved recognition from the art world so much faster than he had. Author interview with Brian Jarvis, 10 May 2011.

[8] Ivor had taken an interest in Frink's work from the mid 1950s onwards, but he does not seem to have met her until the early 1980s, introduced by a collector of Frink's work, the architect and friend of Kyffin Williams, Sir Alex Gordon, who had recently sat to Ivor for a portrait head (1981–82, cat. 54). Thereafter relations between Ivor and Frink were polite but not particularly friendly. From 1982 both were trustees of the Welsh Sculpture Trust. Author interview with John W. Mills, 12 April 2011.

[9] Packer et al., *Contemporary British Sculpture*, p. 15.

[10] T. Hyman, 'Figurative Sculpture Since 1960', in S. Nairne and N. Serota, eds, *British Sculpture in the Twentieth Century* (London: Whitechapel Art Gallery, 1981), p. 185.

[11] R. Oxenaar, 'A Dutch View of British Sculpture', in Gordon Young, ed., *Sculpture in a Country Park: An Outdoor Exhibition in the Grounds of Margam* (Margam: Welsh Sculpture Trust, 1983), p. 17. Ivor was represented in the catalogue, though of course he was a trustee of the WST – see pp. 40–3.

[12] Ivor was aware of Gilbert and George's performance piece *Singing Sculpture* (1970), but did not think much of it. In 1974 he hoped such 'stunts' would prove a 'flash in the pan'. IRJ to Rollo Charles (Keeper of Art, NMW, Cardiff), January 1974, IRJ File, Archives, NMW, Cardiff.

[13] IRJ to Sidney Hutchison (secretary of the Royal Academy, London), February 1979, IRJ File, Archives, Royal Academy, London.

[14] Millner studied under Ivor between 1972 and 1976, before moving on to the RA Schools for a further three years. Thereafter he has essentially championed the type of sculpture Ivor advocated – for example, as a fellow of the Royal British Society of Sculptors and playing a key role in the revival in 1993–94 of the Society of Portrait Sculptors, of which he is currently president. Author interview with Etienne Millner, 16 January 2012.

[15] Ivor never forgave Nemon when he found out that the Croat sculptor had done his best to wrest the commission for the Churchill in Parliament Square from him in 1971 by utilising his strong relationship with Churchill's family. He also came greatly to resent the fact that Nemon in 1979 had been given the commission to make the figure of Field Marshal Montgomery for Whitehall (unveiled in July 1980). As for Belsky, Ivor resented what he regarded as underhand attempts by the Czech sculptor in 1978–79 to secure the commission for a head of the First Lord Chandos for the National Theatre in London, when Belsky was already represented by other portrait heads in the same building.

[16] IRJ interview with Ian Collins in the *Eastern Daily Press*, 4 January 1994, p. 6; Press Clippings, IRJ Papers, Archives, HMI, Leeds.

[17] Milan Jakobec (deputy head of mission, Czech embassy in London) to IRJ, c. August 1995, IRJ Papers, Archives, HMI, Leeds.

[18] L. Archer, ed., Raymond Erith: *Progressive Classicist, 1904–1973* (London: Sir John Soane Museum, 2004), p. 19.

[19] Raymond Erith to IRJ, 12 November 1955, Erith Papers, RIBA Archive, V&A Museum, London.

[20] D. Meredith and J. Smith, *Obsessed: The Biography of Kyffin Williams* (Ceredigion: Gomer Press, 2012), p. 83.

[21] Meeting of St Mary's Ardleigh Parochial Church Council (PCC), 23 April 1956, *Parish Magazine*, June 1956, Essex County Record Office.

[22] IRJ to Raymond Erith, 17 October 1956, Erith Papers, RIBA Archive, V&A Museum, London.

[23] Meeting of St Mary's Ardleigh PCC, 7 November 1956, Committee Minutes Book, Essex County Record Office, Chelmsford.

[24] Rodin's final full-sized plaster model of Balzac was cast in 1897 and exhibited at the Salon of 1898. R. Butler, *Rodin: The Shape of Genius* (New Haven/London: Yale University Press, 1993), pp. 303–5.

[25] *The Burghers of Calais* was unveiled in Calais in June 1895 (ibid., p. 296). The cast destined for London was purchased by a group of British admirers of Rodin in 1911 (ibid., pp. 496–7).
[26] Peter Cannon-Brookes, *Ivor Roberts-Jones: The Journey to Harlech* (London: Trefoil, 1983), p. 45.
[27] D. Farmer, *The Oxford Dictionary of Saints* (Oxford: Oxford University Press, 2011), p. 173.
[28] A. Vauchez, *Francis of Assisi: The Life and Afterlife of a Medieval Saint* (New Haven/London: Yale University Press, 2012), p. 206.
[29] Raymond Erith to IRJ, 12 November 1956, Erith Papers, RIBA Archives, V&A Museum, London.
[30] IRJ to Raymond Erith, 2 December 1956, Erith Papers, RIBA Archives, V&A Museum, London.
[31] Connolly discussed 'intelligent humanism' in several issues of *Horizon* magazine during the latter half of 1946. J. Beechey and C. Stephens, eds, *Picasso and British Art* (London: Tate Publishing, 2010), p. 33. Ivor later recalled that he had enjoyed reading *Horizon* on returning to London after his war service, and had greatly missed the publication when it ceased in 1949. IRJ to Dr Peter Cannon-Brookes, c. September 1982, IRJ File, Archives, NMW, Cardiff.
[32] F. Morris, *Paris Post War: Art and Existentialism, 1945–1955* (London: Tate Publishing, 1993), p. 17.
[33] C. Stephens, ed., *Henry Moore* (London: Tate Publishing, 2010), p. 14.
[34] IRJ to Raymond Erith, 17 October 1956, Erith Papers, RIBA Archives, V&A Museum, London.
[35] J. Rose, *Daemons and Angels: A Life of Jacob Epstein* (London: Constable, 2002), p. 254.
[36] Ibid., p. 266.
[37] Vauchez, *Francis of Assisi*, pp. 128–9.
[38] Meeting of St Mary's Ardleigh PCC, 26 February 1957, *Parish Magazine*, April 1957, Essex County Record Office, Chelmsford.
[39] Chelmsford Diocesan Advisory Board to the Rev. James Farmiloe, 23 July 1957, copy, Erith Papers, RIBA Archive, V&A Museum, London.
[40] Rev. James Farmiloe to Raymond Erith, 8 October 1957, Erith Papers, RIBA Archives, V&A Museum, London.
[41] IRJ to the Rev. James Farmiloe, 30 July 1957, copy, Erith Papers, RIBA Archive, V&A Museum, London.
[42] Ibid.
[43] Raymond Erith to IRJ and the Rev. James Farmiloe, 8 August 1957, Erith Papers, RIBA Archive, V&A Museum, London.
[44] As John painted a number of works of Dorelia, from around 1904 to 1910, she quickly became a feminine embodiment of gypsy or bohemian freedom. M. Holroyd, *Augustus John: The New Biography* (London: Vintage, 1997), pp. 368–9.
[45] IRJ to Raymond Erith, received 19 August 1957, Erith Papers, RIBA Archive, V&A Museum, London.
[46] IRJ to Raymond Erith, 30 October 1957, Erith Papers, RIBA Archive, V&A Museum, London.
[47] Meeting of St Mary's Ardleigh PCC, 9 December 1957, Minutes Book, Essex County Record Office, Chelmsford.
[48] IRJ to Raymond Erith, 30 October 1958, Erith Papers, RIBA Archive, V&A Museum, London.
[49] IRJ to Raymond Erith, 16 October 1958, Erith Papers, RIBA Archive, V&A Museum, London.
[50] Cannon-Brookes, *Ivor Roberts-Jones*, pp. 45–7.
[51] Angela Mathias to the Rev. G. H. A. T. Roe (Rector of Wheathampstead), c. September 1961, Diocese of St Albans Archives, Hertfordshire Local Studies, Hertford.
[52] Angela Mathias to the Rev. G. H. A. T. Roe, c. October 1962, Diocese of St Albans Archives, Hertfordshire Local Studies, Hertford.
[53] S. Wheeler, *Cherry: A Life of Apsley Cherry-Gerrard* (London: Vintage: 2002), p. 170.
[54] Ibid., pp. 5–7.
[55] Ibid., p. 118.
[56] Ibid., p. 33.
[57] Ibid., pp. 92–3.
[58] IRJ to the Rev. G. H. A. T. Roe, 12 December 1961, copy in Diocese of St Albans Archives, Hertfordshire Archives and Local Studies, County Hall, Hertford.
[59] Wheeler, *Cherry*, p. 160.
[60] Ibid., p. 136.
[61] IRJ interview with Byron Rogers, *Sunday Telegraph*, 27 June 1993, p. 5, Press Clippings, IRJ Papers, HMI, Leeds.
[62] R. Huntford, *Scott and Amundsen: Their Race to the South Pole* (London: Abacus, 2012 [1999]), pp. 93–6. Amundsen grasped the superiority of cold-weather clothing made from animal products from spending time with the Inuit of northern Canada.
[63] Wheeler, *Cherry*, pp. 110–11.
[64] Mrs Angela Mathias to the Rev G. H. A. T. Roe, 12 January 1962, copy, Diocese of St Albans Archives, Hertfordshire Archives and Local Studies, County Hall, Hertford.
[65] Wheeler, *Cherry*, p. 242.
[66] Author interview with Etienne Millner, 16 January 2012.
[67] C. Stephens and K. Stout, *Art and the 60s: This Was Tomorrow* (London: Tate Publishing, 2004), p. 140.
[68] *Hertfordshire Advertiser*, 12 October 1962, clipping courtesy of Ruth Jeavons.
[69] N. Stone, *The Atlantic and its Enemies: A History of the Cold War* (London: Penguin, 2011), pp. 204–6.
[70] D. Brynmor Anthony to Augustus John, 9 July 1960, with regard to John's letter concerning Ivor, which had arrived two days previously. John Papers, National Library of Wales, Aberystwyth.
[71] Dorelia (Dorothy) McNeill (1881–July 1969) was born in Camberwell into a lower-middle-class household. She was introduced to Augustus in 1903 by his sister Gwen – she and Gwen were both students at the Westminster School of Art. By the autumn of 1904 Dorelia was living with Augustus and his wife Ida in a ménage a trois – until Ida died in 1907 (Holroyd, *Augustus John*, pp. 127–62).
[72] *Salisbury Journal*, 4 December 1964, p. 21.
[73] Augustus John Archive, Fordingbridge Museum, Hampshire.
[74] *Salisbury Journal*, Friday, 27 November 1964, p. 25.
[75] Holroyd, *Augustus John*, p. 267.
[76] N. Cox, *The Picasso Book* (London: Tate Publishing, 2010), p. 156.
[77] Holroyd, *Augustus John*, pp. 421–2.
[78] Ibid., pp. 498–9.
[79] IRJ to Mrs Dorelia John, 18 January 1964, John Papers, National Library of Wales, Aberystwyth.
[80] Humphrey Brooke (secretary of the Royal Academy) to Dr Aubrey Westlake, 19 February 1964, copy, John Archive, Fordingbridge Museum, Hampshire.
[81] Dorelia John to Mr J. D. Bartlett (clerk to Fordingbridge Parish Council), 21 March 1964, John Archive, Fordingbridge Museum, Hampshire.

82 IRJ to Dr Aubrey Westlake, 2 May 1964, John Archive, Fordingbridge Museum, Hampshire.
83 Lady Cynthia Asquith, c. October 1917, quoted in Holroyd, *Augustus John*, p. 428.
84 *Salisbury Journal*, Friday, 27 November 1964, p. 25.
85 IRJ to Mr J. D. Bartlett (Fordingbridge Parish Council), 10 July 1964, John Archive, Fordingbridge Museum, Hampshire.
86 *The Times*, 24 November 1964, p. 22.
87 *Salisbury Journal*, 27 November 1964, p. 25.
88 *Salisbury Journal*, 4 December 1964, p. 21.
89 Mr Ballard (clerk, Fordingbridge Parish Council) to Simon Beddoe (hon. secretary Augustus John Appeal Committee), 25 March 1965, copy, John Archive, Fordingbridge Museum, Hampshire.
90 C. Wheeler, *A Loan Exhibition of Drawings and Murals by Augustus John in Aid of the AJ Memorial Appeal* (London: Upper Grosvenor Galleries, April 1965), unpaginated, copy, John Archive, Fordingbridge Museum, Hampshire.
91 *Salisbury Journal*, 9 April 1965, p. 17.
92 *The Times*, 25 August 1965, p. 10.
93 IRJ to Simon Beddoe, 8 September 1965, John Archive, Fordingbridge Museum, Hampshire.
94 IRJ to Philippa Duckworth (chairwoman of the Fordingbridge Museum Trust), c. October 1996, John Archive, Fordingbridge Museum, Hampshire.
95 Cecil Beaton in the *Evening Echo*, Bournemouth, 13 September 1965, clipping in the John Archive, Fordingbridge Museum, Hampshire.
96 *The Times*, 16 April 1966, p. 5.
97 Romilly John to IRJ, 1 May 1966, John Archive, Fordingbridge Museum, Hampshire. John pondered that if the Victoria Assembly Rooms site fell through, Ivor's memorial might have to be erected in Chelsea or Tenby. For many years John had a studio on Mallord Street, and then Tite Street in Chelsea, while Tenby was his birthplace.
98 *Guardian*, 8 June 1966, p. 18. Dr Westlake admitted that only £6,000, rather than the required £10,000, had been raised from public donations. Ivor had assured the Memorial Committee that this would be sufficient for a single figure – even if his own fee had to be reduced accordingly.
99 Holroyd, *Augustus John*, p. 446.
100 Ibid., p. 439.
101 Ivor once mentioned to Brian Jarvis, his assistant in the 1980s and early 1990s, that John had been a model draughtsman but not a model to emulate when it came to finishing work. Author interview with Brian Jarvis 5 May 2011.
102 IRJ interview with June Shepherd, *Norfolk and Suffolk Express*, 22 May 1987, p. 22, Press Clippings, IRJ Papers, Archives, HMI, Leeds.
103 IRJ interview with Byron Rogers, *Sunday Telegraph*, 27 June 1993, p. 5, Press Clippings, IRJ Papers, Archives, HMI, Leeds.
104 E. Toynton, *Jackson Pollock* (New Haven/London: Yale University Press, 2012), p. 77.
105 IRJ to Simon Beddoe, c. 12 August 1967, John Archive, Fordingbridge Museum, Hampshire.
106 Ibid.
107 IRJ to Philippa Duckworth (chairwoman, Fordingbridge Museum Trust), c. September 1996, John Archive, Fordingbridge Museum, Hampshire.
108 Lord Louis Mountbatten, speech made at the unveiling of the Augustus John Memorial Statue, 1 October 1967, John Archive, Fordingbridge Museum, Hampshire.
109 *Western Gazette*, 6 October 1967, John Archive, Fordingbridge Museum, Hampshire.
110 Rollo Charles (Keeper of Art, NMW, Cardiff) to IRJ, 24 November 1967, IRJ File, Archives, NMW, Cardiff. Charles had also been present in the audience at the unveiling. He was an old acquaintance of Coldstream's.
111 A. Powell, *To Keep The Ball Rolling: The Memoirs of Anthony Powell* (London: Penguin, 1983), pp. 138–40.
112 IRJ to Philippa Duckworth, c. September 1996, John Archive, Fordingbridge Museum, Hampshire.
113 Author interview with Phillipa Duckworth, 7 September 2011.
114 James J. Coleman interview with Dr S. Ayres, 22 October 2012.
115 IRJ, Autobiographical Notes, to Sir John Rothenstein, 8 October 1977, Rothenstein Papers, Archives, Tate Britain.
116 J. Neils, *Ancient Greece: The British Museum Concise Introduction* (London: British Museum Press, 2008), pp. 96–101.
117 S. Gardiner, *Frink: The Official Biography* (London: Harper Collins, 1999), pp. 203–5.
118 Horse-and-rider sculptures by Marini were included in the May 1951 and May 1954 London County Council 'Sculpture in the Open Air' exhibitions, where Ivor could have seen them at first hand. Marina Lambraki-Plaka and Giuliano Scrafini, *Marino Marini: An Archaic Sculptor of Modern Art* (Athens: National Alexandros Soutzos Museum, 2006), p. 261.
119 A. Causey, *Sculpture since 1945* (Oxford: Oxford University Press, 1998), pp. 29–30.
120 IRJ, autobiographical notes, c. March 1990, IRJ Papers, Archives, HMI, Leeds.
121 From his reading, Ivor was well aware of how much Jagger's depiction of horses on his relief panels for the Royal Artillery Memorial were informed by seventh-century BCE Assyrian relief carvings in the Assyrian Galleries of the British Museum.
122 IRJ to Rollo Charles (Keeper of Art, NMW, Cardiff), 18 December 1972, IRJ File, Archives, NMW, Cardiff.
123 IRJ to Dr Peter Cannon-Brookes, 18 March 1983, IRJ Papers, Archives, NMW, Cardiff.
124 J. Lehmann, *Demetrios Capetanakis: A Greek Poet in England* (London: John Lehmann, 1947), p. 175.
125 Ibid., p. 181.
126 C. Frayling, *The Face of Tutankhamun* (London: Faber & Faber, 1992), pp. 1–4.
127 G. Robins, *The Art of Ancient Egypt* (London: British Museum Press, 2008), pp. 32–3.
128 Sir Richard Hyde Parker interview with Dr S. Ayres, 20 April 2012.
129 Isabel Hitchman interview with Dr S. Ayres, 17 August 2012.
130 Isabel Hitchman (arts officer, Welsh Arts Council) to Dr Peter Cannon-Brookes, 17 June 1983, IRJ File, Archives, NMW, Cardiff).
131 Sir Richard Hyde Parker interview with Dr S. Ayres, 20 April 2012.
132 IRJ to Sir Richard Hyde Parker, c. October 1979, Hyde Parker Papers.
133 IRJ to Sir Richard Hyde Parker, 3 November 1979, Hyde Parker Papers.
134 IRJ to Sir Richard Hyde Parker, 16 September 1980, Hyde Parker Papers.
135 IRJ to Dr Peter Cannon-Brookes, received 21 March 1983, IRJ File, Archives, NMW, Cardiff.

[136] IRJ to Sir Richard Hyde Paker, 16 March 1983, Hyde Parker Papers.
[137] Sir Richard Hyde Parker interview with Dr S. Ayres, 20 April 2012.
[138] IRJ Autobiographical Notes for Dr Peter Cannon-Brookes, 15 September 1982, IRJ File, Archives, NMW, Cardiff.
[139] N. T. Symonds, *Attlee: A Life in Politics* (London: I.B.Tauris, 2010), p. 129.
[140] Entry for 11 April 1978, IRJ Diary for 1978, IRJ Papers, Archives, HMI, Leeds.
[141] K. Harris. *Attlee* (London: Weidenfeld and Nicolson, 1995), pp.34–41.
[142] Michael Rizzello (1926–2004) OBE (1977) was a fellow of the RSBS from 1955, and president of the Society (1977–86). In 1988 he and Ivor would be among the competitors for the statue of Field Marshal Viscount Slim.
[143] Meeting of the Earl Attlee Memorial Committee, 30 October 1977, Proposals to Commemorate Earl Attlee by Busts and or Statues File, 1975–78, Archives, House of Commons.
[144] Meeting of the Earl Attlee Memorial Committee, 20 November 1977, Proposals to Commemorate Earl Attlee by Busts and or Statues File, 1975–78, Archives, House of Commons.
[145] Symonds, *Attlee*, p. 132.
[146] Harris, *Attlee*, p. 240.
[147] Meeting of the Earl Attlee Memorial Committee, 22 February 1978. The sculptor's fee was set at £20,000, the project not to exceed £26,000 overall. Proposals to Commemorate Earl Attlee by Busts and or Statues File, 1975–78, Archives, House of Commons.
[148] Harris, *Attlee*, p. 544.
[149] Meeting of the Earl Attlee Memorial Committee, 9 March 1977, Proposals to Commemorate Earl Attlee by Busts and or Statues File, 1975–78, Archives, House of Commons.
[150] Harris, *Attlee*, p. 244.
[151] Ibid.
[152] Entry for 8 June 1959, in Lord Moran, *Winston Churchill: The Struggle for Survival, 1940–1966* (London: Sphere Books, 1968), p. 790.
[153] Harris, *Attlee*, p. 194.
[154] Symonds, *Attlee*, p. 142.
[155] IRJ to Mrs B. A. Mason (Department of the Environment), 30 June 1978, Proposals to Commemorate Earl Attlee by Busts and or Statues File, 1975–78, Archives, House of Commons.
[156] Emmanuel 'Manny' Shinwell (1884–1986), from a Polish–Jewish–Glaswegian background, was Labour MP for Easington in County Durham (1951–May 1986). He was minister for fuel and power between July 1945 and October 1947. Attlee felt he had lost control of his Ministry, and in 1947 unceremoniously removed Shinwell to become secretary of state for war. Shinwell was later chairman of the Labour Party (1964–67), and was created Baron Shinwell CH in 1970.
[157] Lord Shinwell, 'Address for the Unveiling of the Attlee Statue, 12 November 1979', copy, Proposals to Commemorate Earl Attlee by Busts and or Statues File, 1975–78, Archives, House of Commons.
[158] Harris, *Attlee*, p. 253.
[159] Isabel Hitchman (Welsh Arts Council) to Dr Peter Cannon-Brookes, 17 June 1983, IRJ File, Archives, NMW, Cardiff.
[160] J. Davies, *A History of Wales* (London: Penguin, 2007), pp. 166–7.
[161] IRJ to Fiona Pearson, 27 May 1983, IRJ File, Archives, NMW, Cardiff.
[162] IRJ to Kyffin Williams, 8 February 1980, A1/12/4, Williams Papers, National Library of Wales, Aberystwyth.
[163] IRJ to Kyffin Williams, 24 January 1980, A1/12/3, Williams Papers, National Library of Wales, Aberystwyth.
[164] *Western Mail*, 20 March 1980, press cuttings, IRJ Papers, Archives, HMI, Leeds.
[165] IRJ to Kyffin Williams, 24 January 1980, A1/12/3, Williams Papers, National Library of Wales, Aberystwyth.
[166] The castle was first attacked by Welsh rebels in 1294–95. Davies, *History of Wales*, pp. 162–3.
[167] In April 1404, four years into his rebellion, Glyndŵr actually succeeded in capturing Harlech Castle after a short siege. Ibid., p. 194.
[168] Ibid., p. 272.
[169] Nearly 60 Welsh Guardsmen were killed and over 150 injured in two bombing raids on the Royal Fleet Auxiliaries *Sir Galahad* and *Sir Tristram*, at anchor in Bluff Cove on the east coast of the Falkland Islands, on 8 June 1982. A. W. Turner, *Rejoice! Rejoice! Britain in the 1980s* (London: Aurum, 2010), p. 114.
[170] IRJ to Dr Peter Cannon-Brookes, Autobiographical Notes, 15 September 1982, IRJ File, Archives, NMW, Cardiff.
[171] In August 1979 alone, eighteen British soldiers were killed by an IRA bomb at Warren Point, while on the same day an INLA bomb blew up Lord Louis Mountbatten. Three years later a series of IRA bombs exploded in London's Regent's and Hyde Parks. M. Garnett, *From Anger to Apathy: The Story of Politics, Society and Popular Culture in Britain since 1975* (London: Vintage Books, 2008), p. 78.
[172] IRJ to Fiona Pearson, 3 July 1983, IRJ File, Archives, NMW, Cardiff.
[173] Isabel Hitchman (Welsh Arts Council) to Dr Peter Cannon-Brookes, 17 June 1983, IRJ File, Archives, NMW, Cardiff.
[174] IRJ to Fiona Pearson (deputy keeper of art, NMW, Cardiff), 27 May 1983, IRJ File, Archives, NMW, Cardiff.
[175] Isabel Hitchman (Welsh Arts Council) to Dr Peter Cannon-Brookes, 17 June 1983, IRJ File, Archives, NMW, Cardiff.
[176] Certainly the castle had been commissioned by an English king, Edward I, but was designed and built by a Savoyard with largely Welsh labour.
[177] Author interview with Dr Peter Cannon-Brookes, 3 May 2013.
[178] IRJ to Isobel Johnstone (Arts Council of Great Britain), 7 July 1984, Archives, Arts Council, England, Southbank Centre, London.
[179] IRJ to Dr Peter Cannon-Brookes, received 19 June 1984, IRJ File, Archives, NMW, Cardiff.
[180] IRJ to Jack (Crofton), 21 April 1994, IRJ Papers, Archives, HMI, Leeds.
[181] Davies, *History of Wales*, pp. 63–4.
[182] Ibid., p. 207.
[183] IRJ Autobiographical Notes to Dr Peter Cannon-Brookes, 15 September 1982, IRJ File, Archives, NMW, Cardiff.
[184] *Oswestry Advertiser*, 23 September 1992, p. 3.
[185] IRJ Autobiographical Notes to Dr Peter Cannon-Brookes, c. December 1981, IRJ File, Archives, NMW, Cardiff.
[186] IRJ to Jack Crofton, 19 June 1990, Megan Crofton-Thomas Archive.

[187] J. Beechey and C. Stephens, eds, *Picasso and Modern British Art* (London: Tate Publishing, 2012), p. 214.

[188] A. Wilkinson, *Henry Moore: Writings and Conversations* (Aldershot: Lund Humphries, 2002), pp. 300–2.

[189] IRJ to Bernard Mitchell (Oswestry Borough Council), September 1990, IRJ Papers, Archives, HMI, Leeds.

[190] Gardiner, *Frink*, p. 205.

[191] IRJ interview with Byron Rogers, *Sunday Telegraph*, 27 June 1993, p. 5, Press Clippings, IRJ Papers, Archives, HMI, Leeds.

[192] H. Carpenter, *Benjamin Britten: A Biography* (London: Faber & Faber, 1993), pp. 408–10.

[193] IRJ to Byron Rogers, c. April 1993, Private Collection.

[194] IRJ interview with Ian Collins, *Eastern Daily Press*, 4 January 1994, p. 6, Press Clippings, IRJ Papers, HMI, Leeds.

[195] *Oswestry Advertiser*, 16 December 1992, p. 2.

[196] IRJ to Bernard Mitchell, 3 November 1991, IRJ Papers, Archives, HMI, Leeds.

[197] IRJ to Dr Peter Cannon-Brookes, received 19 June 1984, IRJ File, Archives, NMW, Cardiff.

[198] IRJ to Jack Crofton, c. September 1992, Meridian Foundry Papers, Megan Crofton-Thomas Archive.

[199] J. Elwyn Roberts to the editor, *Oswestry Advertiser*, 16 December 1992, p. 2.

[200] Ibid.

[201] IRJ to Kyffin Williams, c. April 1993, Williams Papers, National Library of Wales, Aberystwyth.

[202] E. Waugh, *Decline and Fall* (London: Penguin, 2001 [1928]), p. 61.

[203] Richard Hooper, 'New Sculpture for Oswestry School', November 2006, Archives, Oswestry School, Shropshire.

[204] IRJ Autobiographical Notes, to Dr Peter Cannon-Brookes, 29 December 1981, IRJ File, Archives, NMW, Cardiff.

[205] IRJ interview with Ian Collins, *Eastern Daily Press*, 4 January 1994, p. 6, Press Clippings, IRJ Papers, Archives, HMI, Leeds.

[206] Lehmann, *Demetrios Capetanakis*, p. 137, and IRJ Autobiographical Notes to Dr Peter Cannon-Brookes, 29 December 1981, IRJ File, Archives, NMW, Cardiff.

[207] D. Todman, *The Great War: Myth and Memory* (London: Hambledon Continuum, 2007), p. 163.

[208] *Rugby Advertiser*, 8 September 1988, p. 17.

[209] *The Times*, 15 May 1986, p. 4.

[210] N. Jones, *Rupert Brooke: Life, Death and Myth* (London: BBC Books, 2003), p. 122.

[211] Turner, *Rejoice! Rejoice!* p. 218.

[212] Ibid. p. 219.

[213] Early in January 1987 the council voted to give the Brooke statue project £3,000, towards the £14,000 which it was estimated was needed to pay for the project. A year later, with public donations not sufficiently forthcoming, Rugby Council felt it had to vote a further £4,000 grant to the Committee to ensure the statue would be finished and erected in 1988. *Rugby Advertiser*, 28 January 1988, p. 1.

[214] *Sunday Times*, 22 February 1987, p. 18.

[215] Jones, *Rupert Brooke*, p. 427.

[216] Ibid., p. 428.

[217] Ibid., p. 316.

[218] IRJ to Dr Mark Evans (Registrar, NMW, Cardiff), 22 April 1987, IRJ File, Archives, NMW, Cardiff.

[219] Jones, *Rupert Brooke*, p. 180.

[220] IRJ quoted in the *Rugby Advertiser*, 11 August 1988, p. 3.

[221] Jones, *Rupert Brooke*, p. 179.

[222] Ibid., p. 179.

[223] Ibid., p. 96.

[224] Ibid., p. 137.

[225] *Rugby Advertiser*, 8 September 1988, p. 17.

[226] Author interview with Dame Mary Archer, 24 August 2012.

[227] Ibid.

[228] Jones, *Rupert Brooke*, p. 428.

[229] IRJ Autobiographical Fragment, c. March 1990, IRJ Papers, Archives, HMI, Leeds.

[230] F. McLynn, *The Burma Campaign: Disaster into Triumph, 1942–45* (London: Vintage, 2011), p. 17.

[231] W. H. P. Clarke (Memorial Project Co-ordinator, Burma Star Association) to IRJ, 9 February 1988, IRJ Papers, Archives, HMI, Leeds.

[232] IRJ Autobiographical Fragment, c. March 1990, IRJ Papers, Archives, HMI, Leeds.

[233] Hugh Casson (1910–1999), president of the Royal Academy (1976–84), acting as 'an expert assessor' to the Clement Attlee Memorial Committee in 1977–78, had recommended Ivor as a gifted public sculptor, and then commended the maquette he submitted. He had been a trustee, along with Ivor, of the Welsh Sculpture Trust since 1982.

[234] In compiling the short-list of sculptors he had submitted to the Memorial Committee, Casson had also taken soundings from the Royal Fine Art Commission, the Royal Society of British Sculptors and Roger de Grey at the Royal Academy. Sir Hugh Casson to Sir David Piper, c. March 1988, Slim Memorial File, Sir David Piper Papers, Archives, HMI, Leeds.

[235] List of Assessors, Viscount Slim Memorial Competition, 17 May 1988, Slim Memorial File, Sir David Piper Papers, Archives, HMI, Leeds.

[236] Slim was very attached to the slouch hat of the Gurkhas, since he had been an officer in the 6th Gurkhas since 1919. McLynn, *Burma Campaign*, p. 17.

[237] W. H. P. Clarke (Burma Star Association) to Sir David Piper, 10 February 1988, Slim Memorial File, Piper Papers, Archives, HMI, Leeds.

[238] McLynn, *Burma Campaign*, pp. 417–31.

[239] IRJ to Dr Mark Evans (Keeper of Art, NMW, Cardiff), 12 April 1988, IRJ File, Archives, Cardiff.

[240] S. Crellin, *The Sculpture of Charles Wheeler* (Farnham: Lund Humphries, 2012), pp. 80–2.

[241] Author interview with John W. Mills, 12 April 2011.

[242] A. Compton, *The Sculpture of Charles Sargeant Jagger* (Aldershot: Lund Humphries, 2004), pp. 46–7.

[243] Author interview with Etienne Millner, 16 January 2012.

[244] G. MacDonald Fraser, *Quartered Safe Out Here: A Recollection of the War in Burma* (London: HarperCollins, 1993), pp. 52–3.

[245] Sir Bernard Chacksfield (chairman, Viscount Slim Memorial Committee) to Sir David Piper, 24 May 1988, Slim Memorial File, Piper Papers, HMI, Leeds.

[246] Jarvis had been head of the Casting Workshop at Goldsmiths College since 1978, succeeding John Dellow, Ivor's previous main studio assistant, who died in March 1978.

[247] Author interview with Brian Jarvis, 5 May 2011.

[248] Ibid.

[249] Ibid.
[250] Ibid.
[251] IRJ to Megan Crofton, 8 June 1990, Megan Crofton Thomas Archive.
[252] Ivor enjoyed meeting the Queen – for one thing, they were about the same height so could look each other directly in the eye. IRJ to Moira Curig (Director's Office, NMW, Cardiff), 26 April 1990, IRJ File, Archives, NMW, Cardiff.
[253] IRJ Autobiographical Notes, c. April 1993, IRJ Papers, Archives, HMI, Leeds.
[254] Field Marshal Lord Carver to General Sir Martin Farndale, 20 March 1990, Alanbrooke Memorial File, Papers of Lord Carver, Liddell Hart Centre for Military Archives (LHCMA), Kings College, London (KCL).
[255] General Sir Martin Farndale to Field Marshal Carver, 11 April 1990, Alanbrooke Memorial File, Papers of Lord Carver, LHCMA, KCL.
[256] W. H. P. Clarke (Field Marshal Lord Alanbrooke Memorial Project organiser and fundraiser) to Lord Carver, 22 April 1991, Alanbrooke Memorial File, Papers of Lord Carver, LHCMA, KCL.
[257] Author interview with Brian Jarvis, 5 May 2011.
[258] W. H. P. Clarke to Lord Carver, 28 May 1991, Alanbrooke Memorial File, Papers of Lord Carver, LHCMA, KCL.
[259] Author interview with Brian Jarvis, 5 May 2011. Ivor was somewhat behind the times in what was considered cutting edge in the contemporary art world; the 'pile of bricks' presumably referred to Carl André's controversial minimalist *Equivalent VIII* (1966), exhibited to a huge furore at the Tate in the spring of 1976. A. Beckett, *When the Lights Went Out: What Really Happened to Britain in the Seventies* (London: Faber & Faber, 2009), p. 286.
[260] A. Powell, *A Dance To The Music of Time* (London: Arrow Books, 2002), pp. 533–4.
[261] General Sir David Fraser's *Alanbrooke* was first published in 1982, to excellent reviews.
[262] Entry for 27 May 1944 quoted in M. Burleigh, *Moral Combat: A History of World War II* (London: Harper Press, 2010), p. 342.
[263] D. Fraser, *Alanbrooke* (London: Hamlyn, 1983), p. 83.
[264] Entry for 23 July 1945, Moran, *Winston Churchill*, p. 305.
[265] Entry for April 1957, ibid., pp. 747–52.
[266] W. H. P. Clarke to Lord Carver, 28 June 1991, Alanbrooke Memorial File, Lord Carver Papers, LHCMA, KCL
[267] Entries for 2–8 October 1941 in A. Danchez and D. Todman, eds, *War Diaries, 1939–1945, Field Marshal Lord Alanbrooke* (London: Phoneix, 2002), pp. 187–8.
[268] IRJ interview with Byron Rogers, *Sunday Telegraph*, 27 June 1993, p. 5, Press Clippings, IRJ Papers, HMI, Leeds.
[269] IRJ to Lord Carver, 29 May 1993, Alanbrooke Memorial File, Papers of Lord Carver, LHCMA, KCL.
[270] IRJ interview with Byron Rogers, *Sunday Telegraph*, 27 June 1993, p. 5, Press Clippings, IRJ Papers, HMI, Leeds.
[271] IRJ, Review of *Rodin's Drawings and Watercolours* by Ernest-Gerhard Güse in the *Royal Academy Magazine*, Autumn 1986, p. 41; clipping, IRJ File, Archives, RA, London.
[272] IRJ to Dr Mark Evans (keeper of art, NMW, Cardiff), 28 June 1987, IRJ File, Archives, NMW, Cardiff.
[273] Lord Carver to W. H. P. Clarke, 29 June 1991, Alanbrooke Statue File, Papers of Lord Carver, LHCMA, KCL.
[274] Ibid.
[275] Sir John Rothenstein, 'Ivor Roberts-Jones', *The Artist*, September 1978, p. 14.
[276] Ivor's copy of a guidebook to the Vigeland Museum in Olso is in the Archives of the HMI, Leeds. He may have purchased it in May 1976, when he visited the Norwegian capital to be present at the unveiling of his Churchill statue in Solli Square.
[277] IRJ interview with Byron Rogers, *Sunday Telegraph*, 27 June 1993, p. 5, Press Clippings, IRJ Papers, HMI, Leeds.
[278] W. H. P. Clarke to Lord Carver, 1 October 1991, Alanbrooke Memorial File, Papers of Lord Carver, LHCMA, KCL.
[279] Author interview with John W. Mills, 12 April 2011.
[280] IRJ interview with Byron Rogers, *Sunday Telegraph*, 27 June 1993, p. 5, Press Clippings, IRJ Papers, HMI, Leeds.
[281] Lord Carver to Tom King MP (minister of defence), 4 June 1991, Alanbrooke Memorial File, Papers of Lord Carver, LHCMA, KCL.
[282] Author interview with Brian Jarvis, 5 May 2011.
[283] Ibid.
[284] Ibid.
[285] W. H. P. Clarke to Lord Carver, 20 January 1992, Alanbrooke Memorial File, papers of Lord Carver, LHCMA, KCL.
[286] W. H. P. Clarke to Lord Carver, 14 October 1992, Alanbrooke Memorial File, Papers of Lord Carver, LHCMA, KCL.
[287] Lord Carver to Sir Robert Fellowes (Private Secretary to the Queen), 29 October 1992, Alanbrooke Memorial File, Papers of Lord Carver, LHCMA, KCL.
[288] General Sir Martin Farndale, address given on the occasion of the unveiling of a statue of Field Marshal Viscount Alanbrooke, 25 May 1993, Alanbrooke Memorial File, Papers of Lord Carver, LHCMA, KCL.
[289] Sir Robert Fellowes to Lord Carver, 26 May 1993, Alanbrooke Memorial File, Papers of Lord Carver, LHCMA, KCL.
[290] Carver was referring to Alfred Hardiman's nearby contentious equestrian statue of Field Marshal Earl Haig, unveiled in November 1937, which stands in the centre of Whitehall opposite the Banqueting House. P. Matthews, *London's Statues and Monuments* (Botley: Shire Publications, 2012), pp. 20–1.
[291] Lord Carver to IRJ, 26 May 1993, IRJ Papers, Archives, HMI, Leeds.
[292] General Sir Martin Farndale to IRJ, 26 May 1993, Papers of Lord Carver, Liddell Hart Military Archives, KCL.
[293] IRJ to Lord Carver, 29 May 1993, Alanbrooke Statue File, Carver Papers, Liddell Hart Military Archive, KCL.
[294] (Ex-Bombardier) Robert Smalls to IRJ, 29 June 1993, IRJ Papers, Archives, HMI, Leeds.
[295] IRJ to Judge Bruce Griffiths, c. March 1994, IRJ Papers, Archives, HMI, Leeds.
[296] Lord Carver, memo for William Clarke, November 1992, Alanbrooke Memorial File, Papers of Lord Carver, Liddell Hart Military Archive, KCL.
[297] Lord Carver to W. H. P. Clarke, 5 November 1992, Alanbrooke Memorial File, Papers of Lord Carver, LHCMA, KCL.
[298] IRJ draft of a letter to Michael Winner, c. April 1996, IRJ Papers, Archives, HMI, Leeds.
[299] *Independent*, 4 April 1993, press clipping, IRJ Papers, Archives, HMI, Leeds.
[300] IRJ to Judge Bruce Griffiths, c. March 1994, IRJ Papers, Archives, HMI, Leeds.
[301] IRJ to Fiona Pearson (deputy keeper of art, NMW, Cardiff), 27 May 1983, IRJ File, Archives, NMW, Cardiff.

[302] Designed in 1920–21, Gropius's cast concrete monument was erected in Weimar's main cemetery in 1922. In February 1936 it was partially demolished and removed at the orders of the Nazi government that had come to power three years previously. The monument was restored in the 1950s by the Communist regime of the DDR. F. Whitford, *Bauhaus* (London: Thames & Hudson, 2000), p. 39.

[303] IRJ interview with Byron Rogers, *Sunday Telegraph*, 27 June 1993, p. 5, Press Clippings, IRJ Papers, HMI, Leeds.

[304] Author interview with John W. Mills, 12 April 2011.

[305] Michael Winner interview with Dr S. Ayres, 2 April 2012.

[306] Author interview with Nigel Boonham, 28 January 2012.

[307] Richard Coleman (chairman of trustees, Care of Police Survivors Group) to Nigel Boonham, 5 February 2006, IRJ National Police Memorial File, Boonham Papers.

[308] John W. Mills to Nigel Boonham, 23 June 2006, IRJ National Police Memorial File, Boonham Papers.

[309] Michael Winner to W. R. C. Riley (Estate of IRJ), 11 October 2006, IRJ National Police Memorial File, Boonham Papers.

[310] Michael Winner interview with Dr S. Ayres, 2 April 2012.

[311] Kyffin Williams to Monica Roberts-Jones, 16 December 1996, IRJ Papers, Archives, HM, Leeds.

[312] IRJ to Kyffin Williams, December 1995, IRJ Papers, Archives, HMI, Leeds.

[313] Author interview with John W. Mills, 12 April 2011.

[314] Author interview with Etienne Millner, 16 January 2012.

[315] For example, Ivor admired Winter's 1992 bronze of *Air Chief Marshal Sir Arthur 'Bomber' Harris* for the RAF Church, St Clement Danes, on the Strand in London. Author interview with Dr Peter Cannon-Brookes, 3 May 2013.

[316] IRJ to David Backhouse, c. July 1994, copy, IRJ Papers, Archives, HMI, Leeds.

[317] Author interview with Etienne Millner, 16 January 2012.

[318] G. Pooke, *Contemporary British Art: An Introduction* (London/New York: Routledge, 2011), pp. 171–2.

[319] See sections on Turk, Mueck and Lane in N. Rosenthal, ed., *Sensation: Young British Artists from the Saatchi Collection* (London: Thames & Hudson, 1997). For Turk and the figure, see also J. Collins and I. Sinclair, *Gavin Turk* (London/New York: Prestel, 2013), pp. 10–11.

[320] IRJ to Judge Bruce Griffiths, c. March 1994, IRJ Papers, Archives HMI, Leeds.

[321] Parker's dramatic installation was first exhibited during September–October 1991 at the Chisenhale Gallery, London. Her later installation *The Maybe*, staged at the Serpentine Gallery in September 1995, included the stub of cigar reputed to have been smoked by Churchill early in May 1945 and set aside by him on hearing of the death of Hitler. I. Blazwick, *Cornelia Parker* (London: Thames & Hudson, 2013), pp. 82–7.

[322] *Away from the Flock* (1994) caused a considerable stir when displayed at the Serpentine Gallery in the March 1994 exhibition *Some Went Mad, Some Ran Away*. J. Cooper, *Growing Up: The Young British Artists At 50* (London/New York: Prestel, 2012), p. 41.

[323] IRJ interview with Ian Collins, *Eastern Daily Press*, 4 January 1994, p. 6, Press Clippings, IRJ Papers, Archives, HMI, Leeds.

Chronology

Jonathan Black

2 November 1913
Ivor Roberts Jones born to William Roberts Jones (born Aberystwyth) and Florence Owles (born Ludlow), Oswestry, Shropshire, United Kingdom

September 1923–December 1931
Secondary education at Oswestry Grammar School and St Cuthbert's College, Worksop, Nottinghamshire (now known as Worksop College)

1932–34
Painting student at Goldsmiths College of Art, London

1934–39
Sculpture student at the Royal Academy Schools, London

December 1936
Awarded a Landseer Scholarship for Sculpture by the Royal Academy

August 1939
Declaration at Chelsea Town Hall that he will henceforth be known as 'Ivor Roberts-Jones'

6 May 1940
Marries Goldsmiths student Monica Booth (1915–2002); shortly before the wedding, buys a house at 31 St James's Gardens, Holland Park, London

1940–1945
Wartime service with the Royal Artillery; saw combat during 18 months service in India and Burma as Captain in the 72nd Brigade, Royal Field Artillery, December 1943–July 45

October 1945
Demobilised from the Army, returns to London in December 1945

October 1946
Starts work as a part-time tutor in sculpture at Goldsmiths College of Art

1947
His terracotta *Winged Figure with Bird* (1946) reproduced in Eric Newton's *British Sculpture 1944–1946* (London)

1953
Founder member of the Society of Portrait Sculptors; exhibits plaster head of *William Pleeth* (1952–53) at the Society's inaugural exhibition, Imperial Institute, London, November 1953

July 1954
His life-sized plaster *Seated Woman with a Cat* and first version of *Mrs Griffiths* exhibited in Beaux Arts Gallery Summer Exhibition

1956
Commission for two 0.6-metre figures in bronze (*St Francis* and *Madonna and Child*) for St Mary's Anglican Church, Ardleigh, Essex (completed 1958)

April 1956
First sculpture accepted for exhibition in that year's Royal Academy Summer Exhibition

May 1957
Holds well-received first solo exhibition, consisting of plaster sculptures, at the Beaux Arts Gallery, London

April 1958
Represented by two works, including life-sized plaster of *Mrs Griffiths*, in the Fifth Annual Open Exhibition of Welsh Painting and Sculpture, Wrexham

March 1960
First purchase by a major public collection – bronze head of *Kyffin Williams* (1959) by the National Museum of Wales, Cardiff

September 1960
Purchase of bronze head of *Paul Claudel* by Tate Gallery, London

July–September 1961
Represented by ten works in plaster (8) and bronze (2) in Arts Council-supported exhibition, *Sculpture in 1961*, held at National Museum of Wales, Cardiff; exhibition then tours to Swansea, Aberystwyth and Bangor; closes November 1961

October–November 1961
Purchase of bronze head of *Sam Rabin* (1960) by the Beaverbrook Foundation, Canada, and the Welsh Committee of the Arts Council, and of a bronze head of *Clive Gardiner* (1955–57) by the Welsh Committee of the Arts Council

November 1961
Death in hospital in London of only son Mervyn, aged 20

1962–63
Commission from Lord Beaverbrook to produce a bronze portrait head of *Somerset Maugham* for the collection of the Beaverbrook Foundation, Canada

1962
Commission from the Welsh Committee of the Arts Council for a bronze portrait bust of the Council's secretary-general, *Sir William Emrys Williams*

1962
Represented in an Open Exhibition of Contemporary Welsh Painting and Sculpture organised by the Welsh Committee of the Arts Council of Great Britain

October 1962
Unveiling of his 1-metre-high bronze figure of polar explorer *Apsley Cherry-Garrard*, St Helen's Anglican Church, Wheathampstead, Hertfordshire

1964
Appointed head of the sculpture department, Goldsmiths College of Art; holds post until July 1978

1964–67
Commission for a bronze 2-metre-high figure of *Augustus John* for Fordingbridge, Hampshire (unveiled October 1967)

1965
Represented in the *The Face of Man* exhibition at the Whitechapel Art Gallery, London

1966–67
Commission from Highgate School for a bronze portrait head of *Yehudi Menuhin*

1966
Moves from 31 St James's Gardens to Woodbridge, Suffolk, but retains ownership of the London house and studio

April 1969
Elected an Associate of the Royal Academy, London

1971–73
Commission for a 3.6-metre-high bronze figure of *Sir Winston Churchill* for Parliament Square, London (unveiled November 1973)

1971
Moves from Woodbridge to larger home and studio at Cratfield, near Halesworth, Suffolk

1972–73
Commission from the Grierson Memorial Trust for a posthumous bronze head of documentary filmmaker *John Grierson*

March 1973
Purchase by the National Museum of Wales, Cardiff, of re-worked bronze version of *Mrs Griffiths* (1966)

December 1973
Elected a Full Academician of the Royal Academy, London

1973–74
Commission from the Welsh Committee of the Arts Council for a bronze portrait head of its chairman, *Colonel Sir William Crawshay*

1974
Awarded Gold Medal by the Royal British Society of Sculptors

1974–75
Commission from the Royal College of General Practitioners, London, for a bronze portrait head of its patron, *Prince Philip, Duke of Edinburgh*

1974–76
Commission for 3.6-metre-high bronze figure of *Sir Winston Churchill* for Solli Plass, Oslo (unveiled May 1976)

1975
Awarded the CBE

1975–79
Produces series of small-scale plaster still lifes entitled *Little Monuments*

1976–77
Commission for 2.4-metre-high bronze figure of *Sir Winston Churchill* for the Riverside, New Orleans, USA (unveiled November 1977)

June–September 1977
Represented by 1.6-metre-high plaster *Girl in a Long Coat* in Silver Jubilee exhibition of *Contemporary British Sculpture*, Battersea Park, London

July–September 1978
Retrospective exhibition supported by the Welsh Arts Council, Oriel Gallery, Cardiff

1978–79
Commission for a 2.7-metre-high bronze figure of Clement Attlee, Members' Lobby, House of Commons, London (unveiled November 1979)

July 1978
Retires from Goldsmiths College of Art

1979–82
Commission from the Board of the National Theatre, London, for a bronze portrait head of its first chairman, *The First Lord Chandos* (unveiled November 1982)

1979–83
Ccommission for large equestrian figure *Lazarus Rider* for Sir Richard Hyde Parker, Suffolk

1979–84
Commission from the Welsh Office and the Welsh Arts Council for 3.6-metre-high bronze figure group, *Two Kings*, for site outside Harlech Castle (installed June 1984)

1980–81
Commissions from the Welsh Portrait Sculpture Trust for bronze heads of *Prince Charles, The Prince of Wales*, for St David's Concert Hall, Cardiff (unveiled 1983) and *George Thomas*, Speaker of the House of Commons, for the National Museum of Wales, Cardiff (presented July 1981)

1982
Commission from the Royal Institute of British Architects for a bronze portrait head of its president, *Sir Alex Gordon PRIBA*

1983
Head of *George Thomas* purchased by the National Portrait Gallery, London – his first work in this collection

1983
Represented in exhibition *Sculpture in the Park*, organised by the Welsh Sculpture Trust, Margam, West Glamorgan

July–August 1983
Retrospective exhibition *Ivor Roberts-Jones: The Road to Harlech* (34 works – 20 bronzes and 14 drawings) organised by the Welsh Arts Council and the National Museum of Wales, Cardiff, held during the Royal National Eisteddfod of Wales, Llangefni, Anglesey

1983–84
Commission from the Welsh Portrait Sculpture Trust of opera singer *Sir Geraint Evans* (presented to the National Museum of Wales January 1984)

1984–85
Bronze statuette of explorer and writer *Dame Freya Stark*

1986–88
Commission for a 1.7-metre bronze figure of *Rupert Brooke*, Jubilee Gardens, Rugby (unveiled September 1988)

1986–92
Commission from Oswestry Borough Council for a 1.7-metre-high bronze *Borderland Farmer and Ram*, Festival Square, Oswestry (unveiled December 1992)

December 1986
Moves from Cratfield, Suffolk, to Shimpling, near Diss, Norfolk

1987–88
Commission from the Welsh Portrait Sculpture Trust for a bronze portrait head of *Lord Callaghan of Cardiff* (presented to the National Museum of Wales, Cardiff, November 1989)

1987–90
Commission from the Burma Star Association for a 2.7-metre-high bronze figure of *Field Marshal Viscount Slim of Burma*, Whitehall, London (unveiled April 1990)

1991–93
Commission from the Royal Artillery for a 3-metre-high bronze figure of *Field Marshal Viscount Alanbrooke*, Whitehall, London (unveiled May 1993)

1991–96
Unrealised commission from film director Michael Winner for a 2.7-metre-high bronze *National Police Memorial*, Horse Guards

Parade, London; posthumous resin cast unveiled at Renishaw Hall Gardens, Derbyshire, 2007

June 1992
Exhibited for the last time at the Royal Academy, London

1995–96
Commission from the Third District of Prague for a new statue of *Sir Winston Churchill*, Winston Churchill Square, Prague; unrealised owing to sculptor's death; bronze cast of Parliament Square *Churchill* installed instead (unveiled November 1999)

9 December 1996
Died aged 83 at home in Norfolk

Sculpture by Ivor Roberts-Jones is represented in the following UK public collections:
National Library of Wales, Aberystwyth; Oriel Ynys Môn Gallery, Anglesey; Fitzwilliam Museum, Cambridge; National Museum of Wales, Cardiff, Wolsey Gallery, Christchurch Mansions, Ipswich; Leeds City Art Gallery; Arts Council Art Collection, Southbank Centre, London; Government Art Collection, London; National Portrait Gallery, London; Tate Britain, London; Victoria and Albert Museum, London; Glynn Vivian Art Gallery, Swansea; The Hepworth, Wakefield.

Posthumous Exhibitions and Displays
'Ivor Roberts-Jones', Royal Academy, London, May–August 1997 (six bronze sculptures)
'Ivor Roberts-Jones', Royal Cambrian Academy, Conwy, February–March 1999
'Ivor Roberts-Jones', Wolsey Gallery, Christchurch Mansions, Ipswich, December 1999–January 2000 (73 sculptures, nine of which were bronzes)
'Ivor Roberts-Jones CBE, RA: Sculptures and Drawings', Chappel Galleries, Colchester, July–August 2000 (40 sculptures, of which the majority were plaster casts).

Sources and Bibliography

Archives

Field Marshal Lord Alanbrooke Statue File, Papers of Field Marshal Lord Alanbrooke, Liddell Hart Centre for Military Archives, Kings College, London (15/1/1990–1994).

Earl Attlee Statue Files, Parliamentary Archives, Houses of Parliament, London (PWO/2/35 and PWO/11/82).

Franta Belsky Papers, Henry Moore Institute for the Study of Sculpture, Leeds (2001/94/D/5/1).

Nigel Boonham FBRS Papers.

Dr Peter Cannon-Brookes FRSA Papers, Private Collection.

Archives of the Diocese of the Bishopric of Chelmsford, Essex, Essex County Record Office, Chelmsford (D/CF 97/25).

Sir Winston Churchill Statue in Parliament Square, London, Files, National Archives, Kew Gardens, London (AIR 8/2765; PREM/15/1551; PWO 1/105 AD II; WORK 17/801 and WORK 59/92).

Sir Winston Churchill Statue in Oslo Files, National Archives, Kew Gardens, London (FCO33/2603 and FCO 371/1947).

James J. Coleman OBE Papers, private collection, USA.

Raymond Erith Papers, Archives, Royal Institute of British Architects, British Architecture Library, Victoria and Albert Museum, London (ErR/38/1-2, Job no. 193).

Archives of Fordingbridge Parish Council, Hampshire Record Office, Winchester (87M76DDC30).

Archives of the Royal College of General Practitioners, London (A/CE/A/13/1 and A/CE/A/13/2).

Sir Nicholas Goodison Papers, private collection, London.

Odd Grann Papers, private collection, Oslo.

Augustus John Papers, National Library of Wales, Aberystwyth (MS 22789D and 22800E/21 21).

Augustus John Statue Archive, Fordingbridge Museum, Hampshire.

Meridian Foundry Papers, Private Collection, Wales.

National Archives of Norway, Oslo (078 KU/75; 616 KU/75; 2248 KU/75 2393 KU/75; 3742 KU/75; 3874 KU/75).

Oscar Nemon Papers, Churchill Archive, Churchill College, Cambridge (NEMO 2/6).

Archives, Oswestry School, Shropshire.

Sir David Piper CBE Papers, Archives, Henry Moore Institute for the Study of Sculpture, Leeds (1996/12).

Press Clippings Book, Library, National Museum of Wales, Cardiff.

Ivor Roberts-Jones File, Archives, Army Personnel Centre (Historical Disclosures Branch), Glasgow.

Ivor Roberts-Jones File, Archives, Arts Council, England, | Southbank Centre, London.

Ivor Roberts-Jones File, Archives, Beaverbrook Art Gallery, Fredericton, New Brunswick, Canada.

Ivor Roberts-Jones Papers, Archives, Henry Moore Institute for the Study of Sculpture, Leeds (2005.456/A-N).

Ivor Roberts-Jones File, Archives, National Museum of Wales, Cardiff.

Ivor Roberts-Jones File, Archives, National Portrait Gallery, London.

Ivor Roberts-Jones File, Archives, National Theatre, London (B/83).

Ivor Roberts-Jones File, Archives, Oriel Ynys Môn (Anglesey).

Ivor Roberts-Jones File, Archives, Royal Academy, London.

Ivor Roberts-Jones File, Archives, Tate Britain, London (TGA 4/2/890/1).

Sir John Rothenstein Papers, Archives, Tate Britain (TGA 8726.2.80).

Duncan Sandys Papers, Churchill Archive, Churchill College, Cambridge (DSND 13/8/1969–1975).

Archives of the Diocese of the Bishopric of St Albans, Hertfordshire Archives and Local Studies, Hertford (DSA2/1/236/90).

Minutes of the Parochial Church Council, St Helen's Parish Church, Wheathampstead, Hertfordshire, Hertfordshire Archives and Local Studies, Hertford (DS2/18/1/1-10).

Minutes of the Parochial Church Council, St Mary's Parish Church, Ardleigh, Essex, County Record Office, Chelmsford (D/P 263/28-29).

Bridget Heriz-Smith Papers.

Lady Thatcher Papers, Thatcher Foundation, London (Document 108384).

Welsh Arts Council Archives, Victoria & Albert Museum, London (ACGB/33/25/1-6).

Sir John Kyffin Williams Papers, Archives, National Library of Wales, Aberystwyth (A1/6-12).

Archives, Worksop College, Nottinghamshire.

Selected Published Works

Ball, Simon, *The Guardsmen: Three Friends and the World They Made* (London: HarperCollins, 2004).
Beckett, Andy, *When The Lights Went Out: What Really Happened to Britain in the Seventies* (London: Faber & Faber, 2009).
Black, Jonathan, and Brenda Martin, Dora Gordine: *Sculptor, Artist, Designer* (London: Philip Wilson Publishers, 2008).
Black, Jonathan, 'The Illusion of Permanence: Archaeology, Imperialism and British Public Sculpture between the World Wars', in Paul Bonaventura and Andrew Jones, *Sculpture and Archaeology* (Farnham: Ashgate, 2011).
Blackwood, John, *London's Immortals: The Complete Outdoor Commemorative Statues* (London: Savoy Press, 1989).
Blazwick, Iwona, *Cornelia Parker* (London: Thames & Hudson, 2013).
Bonnefoy, Yves, *Alberto Giacometti: A Biography of His Work* (Paris: Flammarion, 2012 [1991]).
Boonham, Nigel, 'Ivor Roberts-Jones CBE, RA (1913–1996)', in Nigel Boonham, ed., *The 43rd Annual Exhibition: The Society of Portrait Sculptors* (London: Gallery in Cork Street, May 2006).
Burleigh, Michael, *Moral Combat: A History Of World War II* (London: Harper Press, 2010).
Burton, Humphrey, *Menuhin: A Life* (London: Faber & Faber, 2000).
Butler, Ruth, *Rodin: The Shape of Genius* (New Haven and London: Yale University Press, 1993).
Calvocoressi, Richard, 'Public Sculpture in the 1950s', in Sandy Nairne and Nicholas Serota, eds, *British Sculpture in the Twentieth Century* (London: Whitechapel Art Gallery, 1981).
Campbell, John, *Margaret Thatcher, Volume II: The Iron Lady* (London: Pimlico, 2004).
Cannon-Brookes, Peter, *Ivor Roberts-Jones: The Journey to Harlech* (London: Trefoil Books, 1983).
Causey, Andrew, *Sculpture since 1945* (Oxford: Oxford University Press, 1998).
Chisholm, Anne, and Michael Davie, *Beaverbrook: A Life* (London: Hutchinson, 1992).
Churchill, Winston S., *My Early Life* (London: Eland, 2000 [1930]).
Thoughts and Adventures (Wilmington, DE: ISI Books, 2009 [1932]).
Great Contemporaries (London: Macmillan, 1943 [1937]).
Clarke, Peter, *Mr Churchill's Profession: Statesman, Orator, Writer* (London: Bloomsbury, 2012).
Crellin, Sarah, *The Sculpture of Charles Wheeler* (Farnham: Lund Humphries, 2012).
Cremoncini, Roberta, and Andrea Baldinotti, *Giorgio Morandi: Lines of Poetry* (Milan: Silvana Editoriale and the Estorick Collection of Modern Italian Art, 2012).
Collins, Judith, and Iain Sinclair, *Gavin Turk* (London and New York: Prestel, 2013).
Colville, John, *The Fringes of Power: Downing Street Diaries, 1939–1955* (London: Phoenix, 2005 [1985]).
Cooper, Jeremy, *Growing Up: The Young British Artists at 50* (London and New York: Prestel, 2012).
Cox, Neil, *The Picasso Book* (London: Tate Publishing, 2010).
Curtis, Penelope, and Keith Wilson, eds, *Modern British Sculpture* (London: Royal Academy, 2011).
Danchev, Alex, and Daniel Todman, *War Diaries 1939–1945: Field Marshal Lord Alanbrooke* (London: Phoenix, 2002).
Davies, John, *A History of Wales* (London: Penguin, 2007 [1993]).
Eade, Charles, ed., *Churchill by His Contemporaries* (London: Reprint Society, 1955).
Farmer, David, *The Oxford Dictionary of Saints* (Oxford: Oxford University Press, 2011 [2004]).
Fraser, David, *Alanbrooke* (London: Hamlyn, 1983).
Fraser, George MacDonald, *Quartered Safe Out Here: A Recollection of the War in Burma* (London: HarperCollins, 2000 [1993]).
Gardiner, Juliet, *The Thirties: An Intimate History* (London: Harper Press, 2010).
The Blitz: The British Under Attack (London: Harper Press, 2010).
Gardiner, Stephen, *Frink: The Official Biography of Elisabeth Frink* (London: HarperCollins, 1998).
Garlake, Margaret, *New Art/New World: British Art in Postwar Society* (New Haven and New York: Yale University Press, 1998).
Garnett, Mark, *From Anger to Apathy: The Story of Politics, Society and Popular Culture in Britain since 1975* (London: Vintage Books, 2008).
Cherry-Garrard, Apsley, *The Worst Journey In The World* (London: Vintage, 2010 [1922]).
Harris, Kenneth, *Attlee* (London: Weidenfeld & Nicolson, 1995 [1982]).
Hastings, Max, *Nemesis: The Battle for Japan, 1944–45* (London: Harper Press, 2007).
Finest Years: Churchill as Warlord, 1940–45 (London: Harper Press, 2009).
Hastings, Selina, *The Secret Lives of Somerset Maugham* (London: John Murray, 2010).
Hay, Malcolm, and Jacqueline Riding, *Art in Parliament: The Permanent Collection of the House of Commons* (London: Palace of Westminster, 1996).
Hennessy, Peter, *Never Again: Britain 1945–1951* (London: Vintage, 1993).
Having It So Good: Britain in the Fifties (London: Penguin/Allen Lane, 2006).
Hewison, Robert, *Under Siege: Literary Life in London, 1939–45* (London: Methuen, 1988).
In Anger: Culture in the Cold War, 1945–60 (London: Methuen, 1988).
Culture and Consensus: England, Art and Politics since 1940 (London: Methuen, 1997).
Holmes, Richard, *In The Footsteps of Churchill* (London: BBC Books, 2006).
Holroyd, Michael, *Augustus John: The New Biography* (London: Vintage, 1997).
Huntford, Roland, *Scott and Amundsen: Their Race to The South Pole* (London: Abacus, 2012 [2000]).
Hyman, Timothy, 'Figurative Sculpture Since 1960', in Sandy Nairne and Nicholas Serota, eds, *British Sculpture in the Twentieth Century* (London: Whitechapel Art Gallery, 1981).
Jones, Nigel, *Rupert Brooke: Life, Death and Myth* (London: BBC Books, 2003).
Kynaston, David, *Austerity Britain, 1945–51* (London: Bloomsbury, 2007).
Family Britain, 1951–57 (London: Bloomsbury, 2009).
Lambraki-Plaka, Marina, and Giuliano Serafini, *Marino Marini: An Archaic Sculptor of Modern Art* (Athens: National Gallery – Alexandros Soutzos Museum, 2006).

Lehmann, John, *Demetrios Capetanakis: A Greek Poet in England* (London: John Lehmann, 1947).
Lyman, Robert, *Slim, Master of War: Burma and the Birth of Modern Warfare* (London: Constable & Robinson, 2004).
McLynn, Frank, *The Burma Campaign: Disaster into Triumph, 1942–45* (London: Vintage, 2011).
Matthews, Peter, *London's Statues and Monuments* (Oxford: Shire Publications, 2012).
Meredith, David, and John Smith, *Obsessed: The Biography of Kyffin Williams* (Ceredigion: Gomer Press, 2012).
Moran, Lord, *Winston Churchill: The Struggle for Survival* (London: Sphere Books, 1968).
Morris, Frances, *Paris Post War: Art and Existentialism 1945–55* (London: Tate Gallery, 1993).
Naire, Sandy, and Nicholas Serota, eds, *British Sculpture in the Twentieth Century* (London: Whitechapel Art Gallery, 1981).
Neils, Jenifer, *The British Museum Concise Introduction to Ancient Greece* (London: British Museum Press, 2008).
Newton, Eric, *British Sculpture 1944–46* (London: John Tiranti, 1947).
Nicolson, Nigel, ed., *The Harold Nicolson Diaries, 1907–1964* (London, Phoenix, 2005).
Norman, Andrew, *Winston Churchill: Portrait of an Unquiet Mind* (Barnsley: Pen & Sword Military, 2012).
Pooke, Grant, *Contemporary British Art: An Introduction* (London and New York: Routledge, 2011).
Ragghianti, Carlo, *Giacomo Manzu: Sculpture and Drawings* (London: Tate Gallery, 1960).
Ramsden, John, *Man of the Century: Winston Churchill and his Legend since 1945* (London: HarperCollins, 2003).
Robins, Gay, *The Art of Ancient Egypt* (London: British Museum Press, 2008 [1997]).
Rose, June, *Daemons and Angels: A Life of Jacob Epstein* (London: Constable, 2002).
Rosenthal, Norman, *Sensation: Young British Artists from the Saatchi Collection* (London: Thames & Hudson, 1997).
Rothenstein, John, *British Art since 1900* (London: Phaidon, 1962).
Brave Day, Hideous Night: Autobiography 1939–1965 (London: Hamish Hamilton, 1966).
Time's Thievish Progress: Autobiography III (London: Cassell & Company, 1970).
'Ivor Roberts-Jones', *The Artist*, September 1978, pp. 12–14.
'Ivor Roberts-Jones', *The Artist*, October 1978, pp. 32–4.
Sandbrook, Dominic, *Never Had It So Good: A History of Britain from Suez to the Beatles* (London: Little Brown, 2005).
White Heat: A History of Britain in the Swinging Sixties (London: Little Brown, 2006).
Seasons in the Sun: The Battle for Britain, 1974–1979 (London: Penguin Allen Lane, 2012).
Shelden, Michael, *Young Titan: The Making of Winston Churchill* (London: Simon & Schuster, 2013).
Sladen, Mark, and Ariella Yedgar, *Panic Attack! Art in the Punk Years* (London: Merrell, 2007).
Solomon, Deborah, *Jackson Pollock: A Biography* (New York: Cooper Square Press, 2001 [1987]).
Spurling, Hilary, *Matisse: The Life* (London: Penguin, 2009).
Stallabrass, Julian, *High Art Lite: The Rise and Fall of Young British Art* (London and New York: Verso, 2006).
Stephens, Chris, and Katherine Stout, *Art and the 60s: This Was Tomorrow* (London: Tate Publishing, 2004).
Stone, Norman, *The Atlantic and its Enemies: A History of the Cold War* (London: Penguin, 2011).
Thomas-Symonds, Nicklaus, *Attlee: A Life in Politics* (London: I.B.Tauris, 2010).
Toye, Richard, *Lloyd George and Churchill: Rivals for Greatness* (London: Pan, 2008).
Toynton, Evelyn, *Jackson Pollock* (New Haven and London: Yale University Press, 2012).
Turner, Alwyn W., *Rejoice! Rejoice! Britain In The 1980s* (London: Aurum, 2010).
Turner, Sarah Victoria, 'Stone, Sex and Empire: Direct Carving and "British" Sculpture', in Penelope Curtis and Keith Wilson, eds, *Modern British Sculpture* (London: Royal Academy of Arts, 2011).
Vauchez, André, *Francis of Assisi: The Life and Afterlife of a Medieval Saint* (New Haven and London: Yale University Press, 2012).
Waller, Maureen, *London 1945: Life in the Debris of War* (London: John Murray, 2005).
Wardleworth, Dennis, *William Reid Dick, Sculptor* (Farnham: Ashgate, 2013).
Wheeler, Charles, *High Relief: The Autobiography of Sir Charles Wheeler, Sculptor* (London: Country Life Books, 1968).
Wheeler, Sara, *Cherry: A Life of Apsley Cherry-Garrard* (London: Vintage, 2002).
Whitford, Frank, *Bauhaus* (London: Thames & Hudson, 2000 [1984]).
Wilkinson, Alan, ed., *Henry Moore: Writings and Conversations* (Aldershot: Lund Humphries, 2002).
Williams, Kyffin, *Across the Straits: An Autobiography* (Ceredigion: Gomer Press, 2009).
Wright, Barnaby, *Becoming Picasso: Paris 1901* (London: Courtauld Gallery and Paul Holberton, 2013).
Young, Gordon, *Welsh Sculpture Trust: Sculpture in a Country Park* (Margam: Welsh Sculpture Trust, 1983).

Catalogue Image Credits

S. Ayres: 119a, 119c, 136, 140, 151, 155, 156

Oriel Ynys Môn, Isle of Anglesey County Council Museum Service: 69

J. Black: 9, 48, 52a, 52b, 64, 132, 133, 135, 153, 154

National Museum of Wales, Cardiff: 20, 21 29, 31, 37, 41, 44, 45, 46, 47, 51, 53, 56, 58, 59, 60, 61, 62, 63, 65, 66, 68, 70, 79, 112a

Henry Moore Institute for the Study of Sculpture, Leeds: 1, 2, 3, 4, 5, 6, 9a, 13, 14, 15, 19, 23, 24, 25, 28, 32, 33, 34, 43, 49, 55a, 55b, 55c, 89, 91, 92, 93, 94, 96, 97, 98, 101, 102, 103, 104, 105, 106, 107, 108, 109, 111, 112, 113, 114, 116, 117, 118, 120, 121, 122, 123, 124, 125, 126, 127, 128, 129, 130, 133f, 133g, 137, 140a, 140b, 141a, 142, 142b, 144, 144a, 145, 146, 147, 148b, 150, 152, 152a, 154b, 156b

Government Art Collection, London: 143a

National Portrait Gallery, London: 67

Palace of Westminster Art Collection, London: 143

Estate of Ivor Roberts-Jones, Norwich: 7, 8, 10, 11, 12, 16, 17, 18, 22, 26, 27a, 30, 35, 36, 38, 39, 55, 71, 73, 74, 75, 76, 77, 78, 80, 81, 82, 83, 84, 85, 86, 87, 88, 90, 95, 99, 100, 117a, 119b, 133a, 133b, 135a, 135b, 135d, 135e, 136a, 138, 139, 141b, 141c, 142a, 148, 149, 153a, 154a, 155a, 155b, 156a

John Grierson Trust, Peterborough: 40

Glynn Vivian Art Gallery, Swansea: 54

Index

Page numbers in **bold** refer to catalogue entries, which include illustrations and biographical information about sitters. Other illustrations are indicated by page numbers in *italics*.

Ivor Roberts-Jones in his studio, 31 St James's Gardens, London, c. 1960–61; Image: Courtesy of the HMI, Leeds

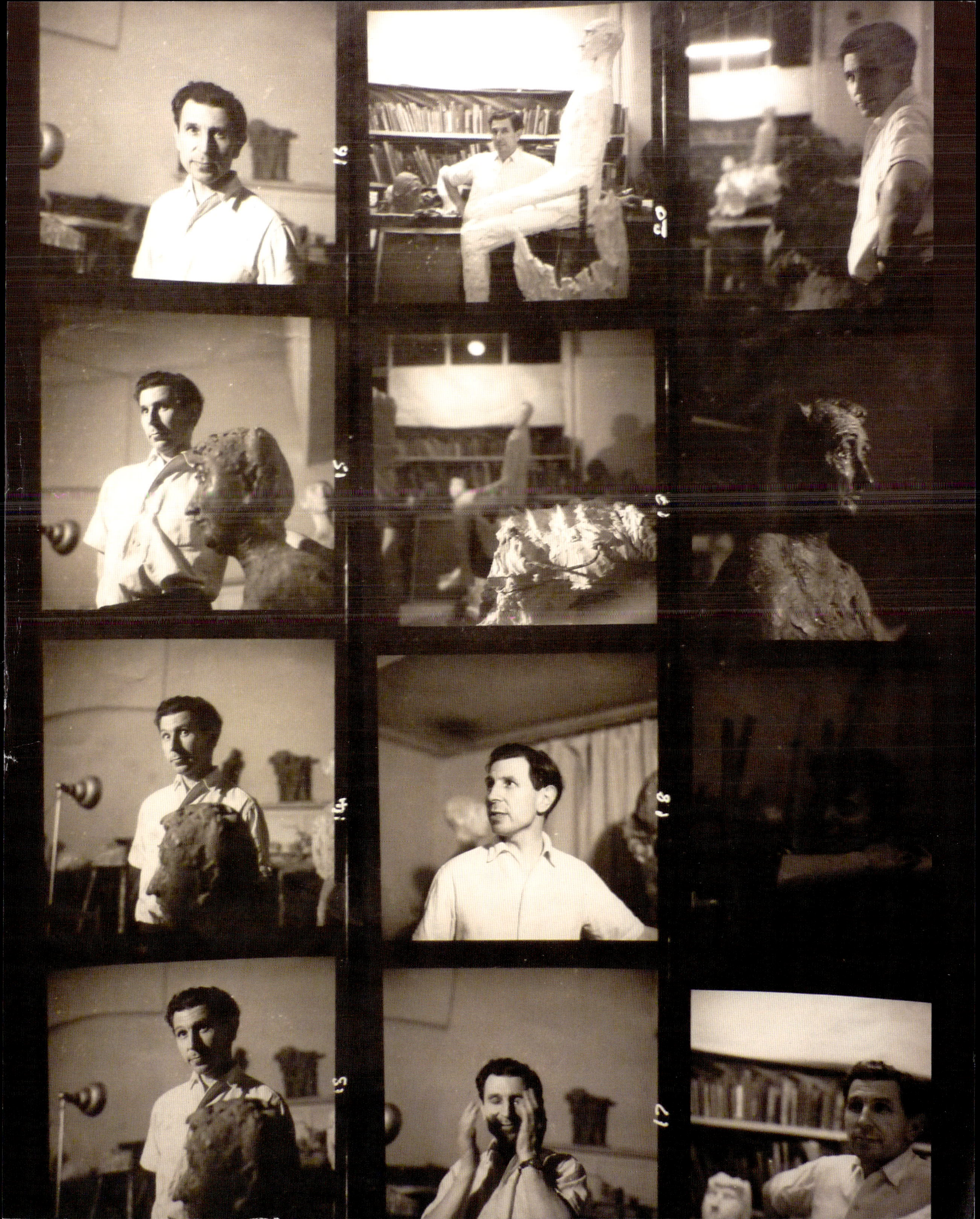

Also published by Jonathan Black

The Graphic Art of Eric Kennington (London: UCL Press, 2001)

The Sculpture of Eric Kennington (Aldershot: Lund Humphries, 2002)

As editor and contributor: *Blasting the Future! Futurism and Vorticism in Britain c. 1910–1920* (London: Philip Wilson Publishers, 2004)

Form, Feeling and Calculation: The Complete Paintings and Drawings of Edward Wadsworth (London: Philip Wilson Publishers, 2006)

With Fran Lloyd and Brenda Martin: Dora Gordine: Sculptor, Artist, Designer (London: Philip Wilson Publishers, 2008)

Essay in London Transport Posters: A Century of Art and Design (London: London Transport Museum and Lund Humphries, 2008)

With Fran Lloyd: *Subtlety and Strength: The Drawings of Dora Gordine* (London: Philip Wilson Publishers, 2009)

Essay in Contested Objects: Material Memories of the Great War (London: Routledge, 2009)

Essay in Lawrence of Arabia: The Birth of a Myth (Mainz: Philipp von Zabern, 2010)

The Face of Courage: Eric Kennington, Portraiture and the Second World War (London: Philip Wilson Publishers, 2011)

Essay in Sculpture and Archaeology: Debates and Speculations (London: Ashgate, 2011)

The Spirit of Faith: The Sculpture of John Bunting (London: John Bunting Foundation, 2012)

With Fran Lloyd; Fiona Fisher, Penny Spark, David Falkner and Rebecca Preston: *The Picker House and Collection: A Late 1960s Home for Art and Design* (London: Philip Wilson Publishers, 2012)

Essay in The View From Above in Twentieth Century European Art (Metz, France: Centre Pompidou-Metz, 2013)